The Significance of the Byzantine Text for Textual Criticism Within the Book of Acts

The Significance of the Byzantine Text for Textual Criticism Within the Book of Acts

HASSAN AZIZ SIDDIQUI

WIPF & STOCK · Eugene, Oregon

THE SIGNIFICANCE OF THE BYZANTINE TEXT FOR TEXTUAL
CRITICISM WITHIN THE BOOK OF ACTS

Copyright © 2025 Hassan Aziz Siddiqui. All rights reserved. Except for brief quotations in critical publications or reviews, no part of this book may be reproduced in any manner without prior written permission from the publisher. Write: Permissions, Wipf and Stock Publishers, 199 W. 8th Ave., Suite 3, Eugene, OR 97401.

Wipf & Stock
An Imprint of Wipf and Stock Publishers
199 W. 8th Ave., Suite 3
Eugene, OR 97401

www.wipfandstock.com

PAPERBACK ISBN: 979-8-3852-4734-9
HARDCOVER ISBN: 979-8-3852-4735-6
EBOOK ISBN: 979-8-3852-4736-3

09/05/25

Unless otherwise noted, Scripture quotations taken from the (NASB®) New American Standard Bible®, Copyright © 1995 by The Lockman Foundation. Used by permission. All rights reserved. lockman.org

Scripture quotations marked (NLT) are taken from the *Holy Bible*, New Living Translation, copyright © 1996, 2004, 2015 by Tyndale House Foundation. Used by permission of Tyndale House Publishers, Inc., Carol Stream, Illinois 60188. All rights reserved.

Scripture quotations marked (KJV) are taken from the KING JAMES VERSION, public domain.

The manuscript (MS) on the cover is better known as MS 2412, according to the Gregory-Aland system. The front cover is of Acts 16:39–17:11 and contains a distinct textual variant (see entry inside for 16:39/2–22). Much of the expanded text is perceptible on lines 1–3 at the top of the page. The back photo is of Acts 15:26–16:1. MS 2412 is closely related to MS 614. Both are core witnesses of a lesser known "Western" tradition. They each point back to an ancient source, called the PWR archetype in this volume.

For Frauke!

Contents

Illustrations | ix

Acknowledgments | xi

Abbreviations | xiii

Introduction | xxi

1 Historic vs. Proposed Use of the Byzantine Text in Textual Criticism | 1
Textual Criticism of the NT: From Erasmus to Bengel | 1
Textual Criticism of the NT: From Griesbach to Tregelles | 6
Textual Criticism of Acts: From WH to Present Day | 9
A Realistic Transmission Theory for the Book of Acts | 17
Interdependence of Transmission Theory and the Text-Critical Canons | 26
Proposed Usage of the Byzantine Text | 27
Key Terminology | 34
Summary | 37

2 Establishing the Antiquity and Quality of the Byzantine Text of Acts | 38
Antiquity of the Byzantine Text of Acts | 38
Quality of the Byzantine Text of Acts | 84
Summary | 103

3 Non-Aligned, Proto-Western Group Readings Are Secondary | 105
Alexandrian and Byzantine Base of the Proto-Western Text | 105
Transmission of the Proto-Western Text: Three Views | 107

Proto-Western Group Revisions | 116
Conclusion | 157
Chapter Summaries Showing PWR Alignment | 159

4 Utilizing an Enhanced Textual Criticism Model | 170
Overview | 170
New Text-Critical "Canon" Proposed | 172
Categories and Ratings | 173
Case Studies | 174
Results | 277

5 Conclusion and Further Research | 280
Noteworthy Text-Critical Findings in Acts | 280
Text-Critical Implications of the Findings | 295
Suggestions for Future Research | 301

Appendix: Three Traditions and PWR Reconstruction | 305
Description for the Reader | 305
Alignments | 306
Calculations | 322

Bibliography | 325

General Index | 339

Scripture Index | 343

Acts Textual Variant Index | 351

Illustrations

2.1. Western Redaction (WR) and Its Witnesses | 41

3.1. PWR Alignment in Acts | 106

3.2. PWR Alignment with BYZ vs. ECM in Acts | 108

3.3. Transmission of 614-Group | 109

3.4. An Example PWR / BYZ Aligned Reading | 115

5.1. Textual History of Acts | 295

Acknowledgments

I WANT TO THANK my Lord Jesus Christ for the wonderful peace he gave me at the age of nineteen when I confessed him as Lord and believed that the Father raised him from the dead! I am so glad God found me when I was not looking for him. I have experienced his great love as being ever present and never changing (see Ps 136:1).

Thank you my beloved Frauke for your unwavering love and gracious support for me and your kindness and patient love for our children: Ilda, John, Sarah, AnneLiya, Amy, Josephine, Gracen, Marleena, and Jerusalem! My dear children, thank you for your love and patience. I am very proud of you all. You bring me much joy and I love you!

I am deeply indebted to my *doktorvater* David Alan Black of Southeastern Baptist Theological Seminary (SEBTS) for his expert language instruction, Christian humility, missionary zeal, insightful scholarship, and for choosing one who is "slow of speech and slow of tongue" (Exod 4:10) to be his student. Dr. Charles L. Quarles is an example of Christian scholarship and leadership. He has provided me steady encouragement along the way and offered helpful feedback. Dr. Stanley Porter graciously reviewed the entire volume and provided many insightful comments. Dr. Maurice Robinson inspired me to the pursuit of excellence in textual criticism by his tremendous scholarship and acts of personal kindness. My dear friend, Dan Hager, shared with me a booklet in 2002 that opened my eyes to my need for understanding textual criticism by showing me that the New Testament (NT) Greek manuscript tradition was not singular. In 2009, another friend, Jesse Gentile, pointed me in the right direction when he urged me to study Dr. Black's Greek grammar. Dr. Stephen Stout was very faithful, reviewing every line, often on short notice. He offered many improvements and words of encouragement. My son, John, gave his expert assistance with Figures 2.1, 3.4, and 5.1. I wish to thank the many Bible scholars past and present upon whose work I have leaned.

Particularly, I want to express my great appreciation to the editors of the 2017 *Editio Critica Maior* of Acts for their outstanding volumes. Lastly, I want to thank the editorial team at Wipf and Stock.

Abbreviations

70	OL 70, Liber Comicus Aemilianus (Lectionary); all versional info is from ECM 3:1:1 and 3:2
72	Liber misticus (Toledo, Bibl. del Cabildo 35-4)
73	Liber misticus (BL MS Add. 30864)
189	Codex Cavensis
( )	Parentheses are used with Greek MSS normally to indicate that it essentially supports that particular wording, but not exactly (e.g., see chapter 3 entry for variant 13:39/13; the PWR and MS 05 have the same wording except MS 05 lacks the article); for translations and fathers, parentheses often indicate that the respective witness could have derived from more than one Greek reading. In such cases, it is commonly listed with multiple readings.
*	Original, i.e., the initial reading before correction, as compared with C
#	Marks a variation unit that is discussed more than once within chapters two through four
3ways	Marks a variation unit where the Alex, Byz, and PWR traditions each preserve their own independent reading
A	Armenian
Ä	Ethiopic
Alex	Marks the best supported reading of the Alexandrian tradition

ABBREVIATIONS

AlMon	Alexander Monachus (VI); all church father info is from ECM 3:2
AmAl	Ammonius Alexandrinus (VI)
Ambr	Ambrose of Milan (IV)
Amph	Amphilochius Iconiensis (IV)
AnastS	Anastasius Sinaita (VII)
ANTF	Arbeiten zur Neutestamentlichen Textforschung
Antioch	Antiochus Monachus (VII)
Apoll	Apollinaris Laodicensis (IV)
ar	OL ar = 61, Codex Ardmachanus
AstA	Asterius Amasenus (V)
AstS	Asterius Sophista (IV)
Ath	Athanasius Alexandrinus (IV)
Ath^T	Athanasius (T = text of edition used vs. apparatus)
Ath^{vid}	Athanasius (ut videtur), apparently
ATO	Alexandrian text is original
Aug	Augustine (V)
Bas	Basilius Caesariensis (IV)
BasSel	Basilius Seleuciensis (V)
BL	Boismard, M.-É., and A. Lamouille. *Le texte occidental des Actes des Apotres: Reconstitution et rehabilitation.* 2 Vols. Éditions recherche sur les civilisations 17. Paris: École Biblique de Jerusalem, 1984
bo	Coptic: Bohairic dialect witnesses
bo^{ms}	Coptic: Bohairic dialect, one witness only
bo^{mss}	Coptic: Bohairic dialect, two or more witnesses
BTO	Byzantine text is original
BW	*BibleWorks*, version 9, © 2013 *BibleWorks*, LLC
Byz	Marks the best supported reading of the Byzantine tradition, per RP05

ByzECM	Denotes the Byz reading according to the ECM editors in those few places when the RP05 Byz reading is different
BZNW	Beihefte zur Zeitschrift für die Neutestamentliche Wissenschaft
C	C-corrector, i.e., a scribe corrected the MS, as compared with *
CBGM	Coherence-Based Genealogical Method; Phase IV data located at: https://ntg.cceh.uni-koeln.de/acts/ph4/
Chrys	Iohannes Chrysostomus (V)
Chrys^{ms}75/^{ms}76	Chrys, MSS 75 and 76 of New College, Oxford
Chrys^{pt}	Iohannes Chrysostomus (V), divided support
ChrysH	Chrysippus Hierosolymitanus (V)
Clem	Clemens Alexandrinus (III)
ConstAp	Constitutiones apostolorum (V)
CosmIn	Cosmas Indicopleustes (VI)
CNTTS	The Center for New Testament Textual Studies NT Critical Apparatus (rev. ed.), version 1.5, © 2014 New Orleans Baptist Theological Seminary
Cyp	Cyprian (III)
Cyr	Cyrillus Alexandrinus (V)
CyrH	Cyrillus Hierosolymitanus (IV)
d	OL d = 5, Codex Bezae
Dam	Iohannes Damascenus (VIII)
Did	Didymus Alexandrinus (IV)
Diod	Diodorus Tarsensis (IV)
e	OL e = 50, Codex Laudianus
ECM	Strutwolf, Holger, et al., eds. *Novum Testamentum Graecum: Editio Critica Maior. 3 Die Apostelgeschichte Teil 1, 1 Text: Kapitel 1–14.* Stuttgart: Deutsche Bibelgesellschaft, 2017
	———. *Novum Testamentum Graecum: Editio Critica*

ABBREVIATIONS

	Maior. 3 Die Apostelgeschichte Teil 1, 2 Text: Kapitel 15–28. Stuttgart: Deutsche Bibelgesellschaft, 2017
EGGNT	Exegetical Guide to the Greek New Testament
Ephr^G	Ephraem Graecus (V)
Ephr^S	Ephraem Syrus (IV)
Epiph	Epiphanius Constantiensis (V)
ETL	*Ephemerides Theologicae Lovanienses*
EulogA	Eulogius Alexandrinus (VII)
Eus	Eusebius Caesariensis (IV)
EustA	Eustathius Antiochenus (V)
Eustr	Eustratius Constantinopolitanus (VI)
Euth	Eutherius Tyanensis (V)
f	f-error (German *Fehler*); indicates the witness has a scribal error
fay	Coptic: Faiyumic dialect witnesses
FlavA	Flavianus Antiochenus (V)
G	Georgian
gig	OL gig, Codex Gigas
GNT	Greek New Testament
GregNy	Gregorius Nyssenus (IV)
GregThaum	Gregorius Thaumaturgus (III)
h	OL h = 55, Codex Floriacensis
HesH	Hesychius Hierosolymitanus (V)
HF1985	Hodges, Zane Clark, and Arthur L. Farstad, eds. *The Greek New Testament According to the Majority Text*. 2nd ed. Nashville: Thomas Nelson, 1985
Hil	Hilary of Potiers (IV)
Hipp	Hippolytus Romanus (III)
Hyp	Hypathius Ephesinus (V)
ICC	International Critical Commentary

ABBREVIATIONS

INS	INS = insignificant and marks a variant reading where the difference is noticeable, but the meaning is nearly the same; this category includes examples such as the interchange of καί, δέ, and οὖν and stands in contrast to both SI and NTR.
IobM	Iobius Monachus (V)
Ir	Irenaeus Lugdunensis (II)
IrLat	Irenaeus Lugdunensis (IV), Latin
Isid	Isodoros Pelusiota (V)
JETS	*Journal of the Evangelical Theological Society*
JSNT	*Journal for the Study of the New Testament*
l	OL l = 67, Palimpsestus Legionensis
Lcf	Lucifer of Cagliari (IV)
LeontB	Leontius Byzantinus (VI)
LeontH	Leontius Hierosolymitanus (VI)
LeontPrCP	Leontinus Presbyter Constantinopolitanus (VII)
LNTS	The Library of New Testament Studies
LXX	Rahlfs, Alfred. *Septuaginta*. Stuttgart: Deutsche Bibelgesellschaft, 1979
MacSym	Ps.-Macarius / Symeon (IV)
mae	Coptic: Middle Egyptian dialect witness (G67)
Marcell	Marcellus Ancyranus (IV)
MarcEr	Marcus Eremita (V)
MaxConf	Maximus Confessor (VII)
MS(S)	Manuscript(s)
MVict	Marius Victorinus (IV)
NA28	Nestle, Eberhard, and Erwin Nestle. *Novum Testamentum Graece*. Edited by Barbara Aland et al. 28th ed. Stuttgart: Deutsche Bibelgesellschaft, 2012
NicC	Nicephorus Constantinopolitanus (IX)

ABBREVIATIONS

NICNT	New International Commentary on the New Testament
NilAnc	Nilus Ancyranus (V)
NovTSup	Supplements to Novum Testamentum
NTR	NTR = not translatable and marks a variant reading so subtle that it cannot or need not be translated into ordinary English. It stands in contrast to both SI and INS.
NTTSD	New Testament Tools, Studies, and Documents
OL	Old Latin
Olymp	Olympiodorus diaconus Alexandrinus (VI)
Or	Origenes (III)
OrLat	Origenes, Latin (V)
OTO	Other text is original
p	OL p = 54, Codex Perpinianus
p/2	OL p corrected
PetAl	Petrus Alexandrinus (IV)
Phot	Photius (IX)
PolycS	Polycarpus Smyrensis (II)
Presb	Sancti presbyteri et martyris Pamphili ex apostolorum synodo Antiochiae celebrata (V)
ProclC	Proclus Constantinopolitanus (V)
Procop	Procopius Gazaneus (VI)
PsCaes	Pseudo-Caesarius (?)
PsClemLat	Clemens Romanus (V)
PsEusA	Pseudo-Eusebius Alexandrinus (V)
PsIgn	Ignatius Antiochenus (V)
PWR	A Proto-Western Reading, as reconstructed
PWR archetype	Refers to the archetype/edition from which the core 614-group MSS arose; the estimated date of origin is AD 125–150

ABBREVIATIONS

Qu	Quodvultdeus (V)
r	OL r = 57, Codex Schlettstadtensis (Lectionary)
RBS	Resources for Biblical Study
RP05	Robinson, Maurice A., and William G. Pierpont, eds. *The New Testament in the Original Greek: Byzantine Textform* 2005. Southborough, MA: Chilton, 2005
RSPT	*Revue des sciences philosophiques et theologiques*
s	OL s = 53, Codex Bobiensis / Vindobonensis
sa	Coptic: Sahidic dialect witnesses
SBL	Society of Biblical Literature
SD	Studies and Documents
SevAnt	Severus Antiochenus (VI)
SevGab	Severianus Gabalensis (V)
SGL	split guiding line; the SGL notation refers to places where the ECM editors have judged two or more variants as having an equal claim to originality (see ECM 3:1:1, intro, 18, 24–25, 31)
SI	SI = significant and marks a variant reading that changes the idea of the passage; whether or not that change is important has to be decided separately and it stands in contrast to both INS and NTR.
sin	OL sin = 74, Sinai, St. Catherine's Monastery
SNTSMS	Society for New Testament Studies Monograph Series
Socr	Socrates Scholasticus (V)
SPCK	Society for Promoting Christian Knowledge
StephH	Stephanus Episcopus Hierapolis Euphratensis (V)
sy^{Aram}	Syriac: Christian Palestinian Aramaic
sy^h	Syriac: Harklensis, AD 616
sy$^{h.txt}$	Syriac: Harklensis text reading (related sy^{hmg})
sy^{h**}	Syriac: Harklensis text with asterisk
sy^{hmg}	Syriac: Harklensis marginal reading (related to sy$^{h.txt}$)

ABBREVIATIONS

sy^p	Syriac: Peshitta
sy$^{p.ms}$	Syriac: Peshitta, one witness only
sy$^{p.mss}$	Syriac: Peshitta, two or more witnesses
sy^{ph}	Syriac: Philoxeniana, Mabbug AD 507/508
SymS	Symeon Stylita Iunior (VI)
t	OL t = 56, Liber Comicus Silensis (Lectionary)
Tert	Tertullian (III)
ThdHer	Theodorus Heracleensis (IV)
ThdMop	Theodorus Mopsuestenus (V)
Thdrt	Theodoretus Episc. Cyri (V)
ThdtAnc	Theodotus Ancyranus (V)
TLG	*Thesaurus Linguae Graecae*®, © 2014, UC Regents, http://stephanus.tlg.uci.edu
UBS5	Aland, Barbara, et al., eds. *The Greek New Testament.* 5th ed. Stuttgart: Deutsche Bibelgesellschaft, 2014
Vg	Vulgate
vid	ut videtur, apparently
w	OL w = 58, Codex Wernigerodensis
WH	Westcott and Hort and their influential work: Westcott, B. F., and F. J. A. Hort. *Introduction to the New Testament in the Original Greek with Notes on Selected Readings*. Peabody, MA: Hendrickson, 1988.
WR	Refers to the Western Redaction from which MSS like Codex D et al. derived; the estimated date of origin is AD 150–175.
WRR	Western Redaction Reading (i.e., a reconstructed reading of the WR)

Introduction

BUILDING UPON THE EDITORS' conclusions in the 2017 ECM for Acts, who identified thirty-six original Byzantine (Byz) readings that stand opposed to NA28, this work proposes eighty-five additional original Byz readings. It also utilizes a reasoned eclecticism textual criticism (TC) approach that is informed by the same Coherence-Based Genealogical Method (CBGM) data for Acts. It is further assisted by a newly proposed text critical "canon." Both the internal and external evidence was carefully weighed in each decision.

Is "Israel" part of the original in Acts 4:8 and/or 13:17? Should "in Egypt" be part of the text in 7:18? Did Stephen say the "Angel" or the "Angel of the Lord" in 7:30? Moreover, did he say "for the house of Jacob" or "for the God of Jacob" in 7:46? Should "fasting" be part of the reading at 10:30? What is the proper location of the words, "and after these things," in 13:20? Did Paul say to the Athenians in 17:23, "What you ignorantly worship, that" or "Whom you ignorantly worship, him"? Should "were afraid" be included in the text at 22:9? Did Paul say "of what you have seen" or "of what you have seen, me" in 26:16? These are a few of the 167 readings discussed in the principal fourth chapter. For every entry, the primary textual support is displayed for the Alex, Byz, and Western readings, the importance to meaning is identified (significant, insignificant, or not translatable), the best reading is justified, and the confidence level of that selection is marked with a notation akin to that used by Bengel three centuries ago.

The quality of these 85 readings seems to imply that the Byz tradition, like the Alex tradition, had its own ancient lineage, one that changed over time but usually without influence from the Alex tradition. In fact, both the present Alex and Byz traditions appear to derive from their respective proto-Alex and proto-Byz archetypes of the approximate date of AD 125 (see figure 5.1). Moreover, a text form very similar to the

INTRODUCTION

proto-Byz archetype of about AD 125 appears to be a primary source for the most primitive "Western" tradition. Although significant, selecting 85 Byz readings (i.e., the ones that display strong justification for being original) is only about 11 percent of the existing differences between the Byz and Alex traditions.[1] The remaining 659 readings demonstrate the usually superior quality of the Alex tradition in Acts.

These judgments were obtained with the assistance of a new text-critical "canon" (see chapter 4), specifically crafted for the book of Acts. Manuscript (MS) 614 and its allies have played a critical role in the analysis. Although MS 614 has typically been considered a secondary "Western" witness for Acts, few scholars have studied it in detail. A thorough study of MS 614 et al. (i.e., the 614-group) suggests that they jointly point back to an archetype predating the famous "Western" Redaction (WR), as roughly preserved by Codex D P38 P48 mae sy^{hmg} et al. (see chapter 2). Although a WR has not been confirmed as a unitary entity by extant documents, ancient witnesses of multiple languages, each upholding distinct expanded readings, seem to imply that it once existed. Using geographically neutral terms, the WR could alternatively be called the Second Century Redaction of Acts (SCROA). The precedence of the 614-group, understood here as having arisen from an ancient Proto-Western Reading (PWR) archetype, is suggested by its textual phenomena. Most importantly, the 614-group / PWR archetype appears to be one of the primary sources used in the creation of the WR / SCROA (see figure 2.1). Given that the SCROA was likely formed before AD 200, perhaps between AD 150 and 175, the PWR archetype is evidently from a generation prior, perhaps between AD 125 and 150. Characteristics such as insertions that are shorter, fewer places of major change, much fewer cases of paraphrase, and identical revisions found only in these two traditions, seem to imply that the PWR archetype was a key ancestor of the SCROA. Here are just six examples. It enables reconstructing the earliest

---

1. The Robinson-Pierpont Byzantine text of 2005 (RP05) differs from NA28 about 1,060 times. However, 181 can be deleted since these are spelling differences or those enclosed by single brackets in NA28. Moreover, the ECM moves a net total of 32 corrections towards RP05, bringing the sum down to 847. See ECM 3:1:1, intro, 34. Finally, these 847 NA28 variants are equivalent to 862 variation units in the ECM apparatus. Moreover, of these 862 variants, there are 118 that fall into the category of being undecided (the ECM editors call them split guiding line (SGL) readings) between competing wordings where the RP05 text is one of the alternatives. Therefore, the total differences between the secure ECM text and RP05 amounts to 744 (862 minus 118). If, in 85 places, the Byzantine is recommended, that means in 659 places the Alexandrian is commended.

INTRODUCTION

"Western" at 5:39—"Neither you nor kings nor tyrants. Therefore, withdraw from these men."[2] It provides the simple addition at 7:43—"says the Lord Almighty"—upon which others added. It presents the purest negative golden rule at 15:29—"And whatever you do not want to happen to you, do not do to another." It seems to be the original gloss at 16:39—"And having arrived at the prison, they exhorted them to go out, saying, 'We did not know the things about you, that you are righteous men' and 'You should depart from this city before those return who cried out against you.'" It has the famous addition that states Paul taught in the school "from the fifth hour until the tenth hour" at 19:9. Finally, at 23:25, it provides the data to reconstruct the most primitive "Western" reading—"For he was afraid, lest having seized [Paul], the Jews might kill [Paul] and he might be blamed as having received a bribe."

More surprising are the numerous indications that the PWR archetype was itself built on a foundation of readings from the Alex and Byz traditions (see chapter 3). Given the general scholarly consensus, beyond WH, that the Byz text is a secondary and nearly fully derived tradition, it is most unexpected that the PWR archetype reflects a composition that is roughly two-thirds Byz, one-third Alex, and otherwise independent (see figure 3.1 and figure 3.2). Contrary to the typical expectations of a thirteenth century minuscule, MS 614 (and MS 2412) has faithfully preserved the text of its inferred, second-century archetype. Eight additional closely related manuscripts (MSS) help to confirm the probable wording of that archetype at each verse of Acts. According to analysis, the PWR tradition also offers five, defensible, original readings of its own. If these conclusions are accepted, the Byz tradition may also provide similar improvements to the standard Greek editions of the Gospels (especially Luke's). In summary, several phenomena help demonstrate that the Byz tradition of Acts is significantly more faithful than both "Western" traditions just described. This conclusion stands against the theory, made popular first by Friedrich Blass and again recently by Boismard and Lamouille, that Luke himself created two *very different* editions of Acts, one Alexandrian and one "Western."[3]

Although this work repeatedly uses the word "text" as in "Alex text" or "Byz text" or "'Western' text," I use it only to indicate that these three

---

2. Unless otherwise noted, all translations are my own.

3. See Metzger, *Textual Commentary*, 223–24; Boismard and Lamouille, *Texte occidental reconstitution*, 1:9.

INTRODUCTION

are separate traditions. The contemporary scholarly debate is highlighted near the end of chapter 1 (see "Key Terminology"). Even as recently as July 2024, at the "Text-Types in New Testament Textual Criticism" colloquium convened at Yarnton Manor in the vicinity of Oxford, most leading textual scholars present argued for the elimination of the term "text type," and its implied concepts, from all future efforts to compare and evaluate the variant units that exist within the field of the Greek NT.

In addition to the above assertions, two other interesting subjects are discussed (see chapter 5). First, ten expanded readings seen in both the Byz and PWR traditions (and in ancient translations), but not in the Alex tradition, each appear to be Lucan. These readings suggest the possibility that the expansions were part of Luke's near-final working edition. The absence of these ten readings may thus reflect Luke's excision of them before his final edition of Acts (but mistakenly reintroduced shortly after). Presumably, Luke removed them to achieve more clarity since they did not add anything essential. Second, despite the outstanding coherence and clarity found in the best supported readings of Acts, there exist two places where a conjectured original reading may best account for the extant evidence. While the wording of NA28 / ECM at Acts 4:25 and 8:7 may be Lucan, the syntax in these editions more likely stems from minor amanuensis errors. The syntax is inconsistent with Luke's typical precision and clarity. The easy-to-make changes may have occurred when Luke's final edition of Acts was copied for Theophilus and then that copy of Acts duplicated for the churches.

These six results—improvements to the standard Greek editions of Acts by the Byz tradition with the help of a new text-critical "canon," the possible identification of the most primitive "Western" tradition known to date, the demonstration that the Byz text of Acts appears more accurate than the oldest "Western" tradition, the justification for why all three core traditions are needed to establish the best edition of Acts, the Lucan but secondary nature of ten variants, and the discussion of two possible conjectures—are demonstrated throughout this volume. They have been presented, especially in chapters 4–5, to be helpful to Greek scholars, expository teachers, and diligent students of the book of Acts.

INTRODUCTION

DESIGN OF THE BOOK

CHAPTER 1 DISCUSSES TEXTUAL criticism from Erasmus until the present day and the impact of Westcott and Hort's (WH's) 1881 revised Greek New Testament (GNT) upon the perceived value of the Antiochian (i.e., the Byz) tradition. After surveying four main approaches to TC since WH, it argues that a reasoned eclecticism using MSS from all traditions is the best approach. Chapter 2 shows the antiquity and quality of the Byz text tradition by looking at its relationship toward two subsets of the "Western" tradition and considering its nearness to the Alex tradition. Having identified the PWR archetype as the earliest "Western" tradition and shown its dependence on both the Alex and Byz traditions for its underlying text, chapter 3 demonstrates that its non-aligned (i.e., isolated) readings are nearly always secondary. Chapter 4 uses a "new" text-critical "canon" to help discern the original text at places of variation within the book of Acts. The canon is based upon the recognition that whenever the PWR archetype aligns with either the Alex or Byz tradition, that reading is nearly always ancient and very often original. The analysis results in ninety-four recommended changes to the ECM text of Acts. Finally, chapter 5 concludes this textual study of Acts by offering six important findings and two critical implications of those findings.

1

Historic vs. Proposed Use of the Byzantine Text in Textual Criticism

DOES THE BYZANTINE (BYZ) text have a significant role to play when applying textual criticism (TC) to the book of Acts to improve the standard editions of the Greek New Testament (GNT)? If evidence indicates that an early form of it was most probably established within the second century, and if many of its characteristic readings are shown to have a mark of originality, such a role would seem to be justified. However, given the widespread contemporary neglect of the Byz text, it may be prudent to commence by briefly considering the historical development of TC since Erasmus.

TEXTUAL CRITICISM OF THE NT: FROM ERASMUS TO BENGEL

When the Complutensian GNT was first printed in 1514 under the oversight of the cardinal primate of Spain, Francisco Ximenes de Cisneros, and the GNT of Dutch humanist Desiderius Erasmus was first published in 1516, neither man could have imagined the impact his work would have upon both Western society and the world at large.[1] From that moment on, the divinely inspired Scriptures could be rapidly reproduced in their original languages.[2] Perhaps even more significantly, translations of

---

1. Metzger and Ehrman, *New Testament*, 137–39.
2. Metzger and Ehrman indicate that the Hebrew Bible was already published in

the Bible could now be produced and disseminated at a pace far exceeding any other period in human history. Multitudes could now read the Bible in their own mother tongue. Martin Luther used Erasmus's second edition of 1519 as the basis for his September 1522 German NT.[3] He continued to revise it and began work on the Hebrew Bible so that by 1534 the entire Christian Bible was available in excellent German.

Meanwhile, William Tyndale utilized both Erasmus's 1519 and 1522 editions to translate into English.[4] The great work of Tyndale in the NT and partly in the OT became a principal foundation for the 1611 King James Version (KJV) that flourished until the English Revised Version (ERV) of 1885 and beyond. Although Erasmus's editions were the basis for these two sixteenth-century European translations, the work of Ximenes was later used by Erasmus to improve his fourth edition of 1527.[5] Similarly, Stephanus built from the work of Erasmus but also utilized the Complutensian NT for his editions, including his most important third edition of 1550. Although the textual basis for these GNT editions was limited by modern standards, the result was a fundamentally accurate text that provided a way to validate and clarify teachings that were previously known in the Western church, for more than a millennium, almost exclusively from Jerome's Latin Vulgate.[6] The 1550 Stephanus GNT is the most important for our purposes because it became the first edition with a critical apparatus.[7] It was the essential basis for the "so-called" Textus Receptus (TR) that dominated biblical studies until its precedence was replaced by the GNT produced by B. F. Westcott and F. J. A. Hort in 1881.[8] By recording the readings from fourteen manuscripts (MSS) and one edition in the margins, Stephanus enabled the scholarly community to compare them against the printed text. However, the more common approach of scholars and theologians apparently was to just use the TR.

1488. See Metzger and Ehrman, *New Testament*, 137.

3. Metzger and Ehrman, *New Testament*, 145.
4. Tyndale, *Tyndale's New Testament*, xvii.
5. Metzger and Ehrman, *New Testament*, 148–50.
6. Metzger and Ehrman, *New Testament*, 140–51. Erasmus used about six manuscripts plus the Complutensian edition, Stephanus about fourteen plus the Complutensian edition, and Ximenes borrowed several ancient manuscripts from the Vatican.
7. Metzger and Ehrman, *New Testament*, 150.
8. Westcott and Hort, *Original Greek*.

The stability of the TR speaks to the widespread appreciation of its general excellence and suitability for teaching the Christian faith.[9] As more ancient MSS were found, the TR came to be evaluated more critically. Working mostly behind the scenes, textual scholars became increasingly convinced of the need to revise the GNT according to the best evidence. The gulf between the scholarly understanding and the common view within the church became manifested when John Mill (1645–1707) published his GNT in 1707 and presented over thirty thousand variant readings against the TR, which he had collated from many Greek MSS, ancient versions, and early fathers. The shock felt by many who loved the Bible is understandable given their perception of the TR as nearly identical to the original text. Daniel Whitby responded by criticizing the work of Mill and condemning it as putting the entire NT wording on shaky ground.[10] The ignorant criticisms by Whitby and others from within the church made the Scriptures vulnerable to an attack from the outside. It was the deist Anthony Collins who raised his voice in 1713. Within his treatise on freethinking, Collins presented seven arguments to explain why freethinking is the duty of every person.[11] Under the last argument, he gave ten examples of priestly conduct to demonstrate that no one should just trust the priests. In his seventh example, he assumes that Whitby was right in accusing Mill for bringing discredit upon the accuracy of the NT with his revised GNT.[12]

In that same year, NT scholar Richard Bentley (1662–1742) took on both Collins and Whitby for their mistaken conclusions. Throughout his response he emphasized the prudence of utilizing all the extant Greek MSS for improving the GNT.[13] Having considered Whitby's severe criticisms against Mill, he categorized Whitby's accusations as being based on fear and not upon the actual facts. According to Bentley, if Mill were still alive, he would have insisted, "The real text of the sacred writers does not now (since the originals have been so long lost) lie in any single MS or edition, but is dispersed in them all. Tis competently exact indeed, even in the worst MS now extant: nor is one article of faith or moral precept either perverted or lost in them."[14] Having skillfully edited the Roman

9. Bentley, *Remarks*, 68.
10. Metzger and Ehrman, *New Testament*, 154–55.
11. Collins, *Discourse of Free-Thinking*, 32–99.
12. Collins, *Discourse of Free-Thinking*, 88–91.
13. Bentley, *Remarks*, 61–62, 68.
14. Bentley, *Remarks*, 69.

playwright Terrance, he knew firsthand that the more copies available, the better one could approximate the original using TC.[15] While it might feel better to have only one MS and thus zero textual variants, he affirmed that such would leave the reader with hundreds of secondary readings and the scholar with no good means to recognize them. On the other hand, if a given GNT MS had one thousand errors it could be compared to another, and the result might be just five hundred common mistakes. The more MSS there are to compare, the more the shared errors can be eliminated. Moreover, he assessed the NT to be much less corrupted than the classics and boasted in the numerical superiority of the GNT MSS. Therefore, he concluded, "Make your 30,000 [variants] as many more, if numbers of copies can ever reach that sum: all the better to a knowing and serious reader, who is thereby more richly furnished to select what he sees genuine."[16] In 1720, Bentley submitted a detailed plan for a revised edition of both the Greek and the Latin NT. He was confident that he could reduce the remaining errors to a maximum of two hundred by means of an appeal to only the oldest Greek and Latin MSS.[17] Unfortunately he never did accomplish the project.

Having reviewed Bentley's papers and being very familiar with the character of the oldest Greek and Latin MSS, Frederick H. A. Scrivener (1813–1893) concluded that Bentley must have given up on his proposal when he learned by research that he had been wrong about the nature of the oldest MSS. They differ too much with each other for his plans to be successful. Moreover, Bentley was a man of determination, and thus it seemed unlikely to Scrivener that antagonists would have stopped him.[18] Tregelles (1813–1875) paints a different picture.[19] He felt that Bentley's 1720 plan for the revision of the GNT were his mature reflections and he saw no reason to think that Bentley's perspective changed before his death in 1742. He agreed with Bentley that the oldest Greek MSS were sufficiently aligned with the oldest versions and fathers, making the modern MSS unnecessary.[20] Tregelles believed that the perpetual opposition to Bentley was the preeminent reason he stopped the work.[21]

15. Bentley, *Remarks*, 63–68.
16. Bentley, *Remarks*, 62–63, 76.
17. Tregelles, *Account*, 61–62.
18. Scrivener, *Contributions Codex Augiensis*, 18–19.
19. Tregelles, *Account*, 60–66.
20. Tregelles, *Account*, 67.
21. Tregelles, *Account*, 65.

However, Tregelles did find some faults with Bentley's plan.[22] First of all, Bentley wrongly assumed that Jerome had used ancient Greek MSS that were close to Origen's. Instead, Jerome relied upon ancient Roman MSS. Secondly, he had an incorrect assumption about the number of Greek archetypes standing behind the Old Latin (OL) MS tradition. Therefore, if his plan had been completed, it would not have portrayed the widespread Greek text at the time of Nicaea (AD 325) but only a snapshot of the Greek within the Western church. Tregelles also praised Bentley's move to eliminate the modern MSS since it would make the project more feasible.[23]

After a long and diligent study regarding Mill's thirty thousand textual variants, Johann Albrecht Bengel (1687–1752) could write in 1721 to a former student,

> I have only to wonder that there is not a much larger number of those readings than there is; and that there are none which in the least affect the foundation of our faith. You may therefore safely and securely have nothing to do with doubts, which at one time so distressingly perplexed myself.[24]

In 1734, he produced his own Greek edition by printing the TR as the main text while placing into the lower margin his recommended changes.[25] Specifically, he rated every significant variant from the TR by marking it on a five-point scale to indicate whether or not it should replace the standard text.[26] In 1742, he published his textual commentary and included his long promised evaluation of Mastricht's forty-three canons that were published in 1713. In their place he offered twenty-seven TC "suggestions" of his own.[27]

---

22. Tregelles, *Account*, 67.
23. Tregelles, *Account*, 67.
24. Burk, *Memoir of John Bengel*, 52.
25. Bengel, *Novum Testamentum Jo. Bengelio.*
26. Metzger and Ehrman, *New Testament*, 159; Bengel, *Novum Testamentum Jo. Bengelio, explicatio signorum.*
27. Burk, *Memoir of John Bengel*, 226, 363; Bengel, *Gnomon*, 1:20, 12–39.

TEXTUAL CRITICISM OF THE NT: FROM GRIESBACH TO TREGELLES

The work of Johann Jakob Griesbach (1745–1812) helped steer the course of TC until the dawning of the work of WH in 1881.[28] However, before some of his contributions can be contextualized, a brief flashback to perspectives of former writers concerning the NT textual history should be considered. First of all, in addition to his 1734 revision of the GNT, Bengel provided a geographic overview of MS interrelationships.[29] In short, he asserted that most MSS have their basis in one of two geographic "nations": the Asiatic and the African. "Asiatic nation" refers to those MSS originating from the vicinity of Constantinople and are the most recent witnesses. On the other hand, the "African nation" contains the oldest MSS and should be divided into two tribes. The first is the presumed origin of Codex Alexandrinus (i.e., Codex A/MS 02) and the second the source from which the OL sprung forth.[30] Salomo Semler (1725–1791) further developed Bengel's ideas and considered these three textual groups as the fruit of separate formal recensions.[31] He renamed the Asiatic nation "Eastern" and attributed it to Lucian of Antioch. He named one tribe of the African nation "Alexandrian" (Alex), associating it with Origen. Finally, he called the OL tribe by the name of "Western." It was upon this basic substructure that Griesbach built.[32] Griesbach then insightfully assigned various MSS, versions, and fathers into each group. He asserted that the Constantinopolitan recension (Bengel's Asiatic and Semler's Eastern) possessed no ancient tradition of its own but was born solely from a critical selection that merged readings from the other groups into a third form.[33] Griesbach skillfully developed his own list of fifteen TC canons. Many of them have been influential ever since. However, it was his assigning of the Constantinopolitan group (i.e., Byz text) to a completely secondary status that would have the greatest impact on TC for the next two centuries.

Though Karl Lachmann (1793–1851) is credited with being the first scholar to fully set aside the TR, Metzger describes how his work suffered

---

28. Metzger and Ehrman, *New Testament*, 165–67.
29. Metzger and Ehrman, *New Testament*, 159.
30. Metzger and Ehrman, *New Testament*, 159.
31. Metzger and Ehrman, *New Testament*, 161–62.
32. Metzger and Ehrman, *New Testament*, 165–67.
33. Metzger and Ehrman, *New Testament*, 166.

from a deficient number of Greek MSS.[34] Based upon Griesbach's theory regarding the origins of the Byz text, Lachmann was able to dismiss the entire bulk of more recent MSS. Following Lachmann, the great MS hunter and collator Tischendorf initially labored under the same perspective. However, according to Scrivener, Tischendorf occasionally avowed an appreciation for their value.[35] In fact, between his 1849 edition and his seventh edition of 1859, he returned to the TR wording about 595 times.[36] However, like WH that followed him, Tischendorf ultimately gave too much credence to a single MS—Codex ℵ—and consequently inserted a grand total of 3,369 changes into his eighth edition.[37]

Tregelles also labored under the vision of Bentley and Griesbach. However, unlike Lachmann, Tregelles traveled widely to acquire more evidence in order to facilitate the production of an excellent edition based upon the oldest data.[38] He investigated Greek MSS, old versions, and citations of the most ancient Greek fathers. Prior to producing his one and only revised edition of the GNT (1857–1872), he previewed his work with a document called *An Account of the Printed Text of the Greek New Testament*.[39] In response, Scrivener gave his reflections on the strengths and weaknesses of Tregelles's critical principles.[40] On the one hand, Scrivener agreed that the ancient Greek MSS are very important for determining the original text. On the other hand, he opposed the conclusion that all the later MSS have no role to play in that endeavor. In particular, he interacted with Tregelles who felt that, because he could prove the authenticity of the most ancient extant reading at Matt 19:16–17 (and provide decisive evidence at seventy-one other places), he had thus validated the principle of ignoring all MSS from the recent period. Tregelles confidently stated,

> But the mass of the MSS, "in the proportion of about ninety to one," oppose what I have proved to be the ancient and widespread reading of this passage:—what does this teach? Why, that the mass of recent documents possess no determining voice, in a question as to what we should receive as genuine readings. We

---

34. Metzger and Ehrman, *New Testament*, 170–71.
35. Scrivener, *Contributions Codex Augiensis*, 5.
36. Scrivener, *Plain Introduction*, 2:282–83.
37. Scrivener, *Plain Introduction*, 2:283.
38. Metzger and Ehrman, *New Testament*, 173–74.
39. Tregelles, *Account*.
40. Scrivener, *Contributions Codex Augiensis*, 7, 11.

are able to take the few documents whose evidence is proved to be trustworthy, and safely discard from the present consideration the eighty-nine ninetieths, or whatever else their numerical proportion may be.[41]

Scrivener counters that for this assertion to be true, one needs to be confident that all the remaining evidence derives from one source. Is there "moral certainty that the evidence of the eighty-nine is drawn exclusively from that of the ninetieth? It has never I think been affirmed by any one . . . that the mass of cursive documents are corrupt copies of the uncials still extant."[42] Moreover, Scrivener felt that the following criteria by Tregelles for dismissing the majority of recent MSS was only occasionally true:[43]

> The testimony of very ancient MSS is proved to be good on grounds of evidence (not mere assertion); and that the distinction is not between the ancient MSS on the one hand, and all other witnesses on the other,—but between the *united evidence* of the *most ancient documents*—MSS, versions, and early citations—together with that of the few more recent copies that accord with them, on the one hand, and the mass of modern MSS on the other.[44]

After assessing the seven readings from Mark within the seventy-two of Tregelles, Scrivener concluded that the witness of the oldest MSS was divided against itself, particularly with respect to Codex A. In addition, the later uncials were usually found opposing the Alex reading as well. Instead, Scrivener believed that the original text "cannot safely be derived from any one set of authorities, whether MSS, versions, or fathers, but ought to be the result of a patient comparison and careful estimate of the evidence given by them all."[45] Moreover, when "real agreement between all the documents prior to the tenth century" exists, "the testimony of later MSS, though not to be rejected unheard, is to be regarded with much suspicion, and unless supported by strong internal evidence, can hardly be adopted."[46] Finally, he argued that in the more

---

41. Tregelles, *Account*, 138; Scrivener, *Contributions Codex Augiensis*, 7.
42. Scrivener, *Contributions Codex Augiensis*, 8.
43. Scrivener, *Contributions Codex Augiensis*, 8–18.
44. Tregelles, *Account*, addenda, 2.
45. Scrivener, *Contributions Codex Augiensis*, 8.
46. Scrivener, *Contributions Codex Augiensis*, 20.

typical situation, "where the most ancient documents are at variance with each other, the later or cursive copies are of great importance, as the surviving representatives of other codices, very probably as early, possibly even earlier, than any now extant."[47] While it is safe to say that Tregelles demonstrated the high value of the oldest Greek MSS, it is also apparent that he did not justify a canon of rejecting all late Byz MSS.[48]

TEXTUAL CRITICISM OF ACTS: FROM WH TO PRESENT DAY

When WH's influential revision of the GNT appeared in 1881, two principal reasons had already been advanced and received by many as justifying the relegation of the Byz text to a secondary status. Principally, Griesbach had suggested that the Byz text type came about solely from the materials of the other text types. In addition, Tregelles had recently made the case that since the oldest Greek MSS basically agree with that of both the ancient versions and the fathers, there is no need to utilize the more recent and numerically superior Byz MSS for text-critical decisions. WH therefore built their transmission theory upon these pillars. In summary, they argued that the Syrian text, i.e., Byz text, is secondary and of limited value because it: (1) has conflated readings; (2) lacks patristic support prior to AD 250; and (3) displays inferior quality.[49] Their proof of conflation was limited both in scope (all examples were taken from the Gospels) and number (only eight), and three cases are far from convincing (Mark 9:49; Luke 12:18; 24:53) since homoeoteleuton may be a factor there.[50] Essentially, they extrapolated from some Byz readings in order to judge the entire tradition as secondary.

As a result, for more than a hundred years the Byz text has played a minor role in the TC of the NT, and for the text of Acts in particular. Ever since WH's GNT was published, this new Alex text-based edition has become and continues to be the GNT of choice. Its text is based primarily upon the fourth-century uncial MSS ℵ and B and has endured with limited changes until the modern editions of NA28/UBS5.[51] In the

---

47. Scrivener, *Contributions Codex Augiensis*, 20.
48. Tregelles, *Account*, 150.
49. Westcott and Hort, *Introduction*, 93–119.
50. Westcott and Hort, *Introduction*, 101, 103–4.
51. Nestle and Nestle, *Novum Testamentum Graece*; Aland et al., *Greek New*

book of Acts alone, NA28 displays about 879 differences from the Byz GNT published by Robinson and Pierpont in 2005 (RP05).[52] Scholars have usually responded to the bold assertions of WH by adopting one of four text-critical approaches.

Byzantine Priority

In some ways the reaction against the new edition of WH was similar to what happened to Mills and Bentley. Defenders of the traditional text such as Dean Burgon (1813–1888) considered the changes to be a great corruption of the original text, accomplished by people having an imperfect understanding of God's providence.[53] The close unity found in the vast majority of MSS was seen as a special work of God by which the genuine text could always be recognized. The alternate approach of depending upon the oldest but discordant MSS was to introduce unnecessary subjectivity into the process. Moreover, the new edition was seen as a threat because it removed or called into question verses that had been sacred to many believers for centuries. It seemed like a great mistake.

Though Burgon believed that the original text was preserved in the Byz majority, others persisted in defending the TR. This latter defense was a lost cause from the start since the TR is by nature an inferior representative of the larger Byz tradition.[54] Edward F. Hills followed Burgon chronologically and attempted to defend the TR priority position.[55] In essence, that viewpoint has resulted from a traditional use of and esteem for the TR and related theological presuppositions about preservation. The Bible declares of itself that it was divinely inspired (2 Tim 3:15–6; 2 Pet 1:21). Additionally, Jesus taught that people are to live by means of every word of God (Matt 4:4), that every part of the law will be fulfilled

---

Testament.

52. Robinson and Pierpont, *Byzantine Textform 2005*. The raw number is about 1,060 per the RP05 apparatus as compared with NA27 (and NA27 = NA28 in Acts). After subtracting 138 places of alternate spelling and 43 cases of single brackets (i.e., the reading is the same if the bracketed words are original) within NA27, the total reduces to 879.

53. Burgon, *Revision Revised*, 24–33, 41.

54. Wallace, "Majority Text Theory," 718. Wallace counted the differences between the TR and the MT and came up with the figure of 1,838. His tally is based upon a comparison with the Byz text of Hodges and Farstad (HF1985) instead of RP05. Nevertheless, these results are representative. See Hodges and Farstad, *Greek New Testament*.

55. Wallace, "Majority Text Theory," 715–17.

(Matt 5:18), and that his words would never cease to exist (Matt 24:36). These latter points all imply the perpetual continuation of God's word. However, the how of preservation is not specified in the Bible.[56] Thus, to demand that since divine inspiration was perfect, divine preservation of a single MS or group of MSS must be nearly perfect as well, is mere speculation. This position undermines unbiased historical research and, according to Sturz, implies that God's providential preservation was effective only for Byz MSS or even just for the TR.[57]

A Byz priority approach to the book of Acts is essentially no different than for any other book of the NT, minus the book of Revelation. In the case of Revelation, the Byz MSS are commonly divided. The Byz text of Acts is slightly longer than the Alex but far shorter than the very expansive Western text, evidenced primarily by Codex D. From the Byz priority perspective, the features of clarity and smoothness that the Byz text shares with the Western are genuine characteristics that remained in the Western text even after it branched away. Similarly, unique Alex readings should be attributed mainly to scribes who made grammatical and stylistic improvements while also deleting words, clauses, or verses that seemed unnecessary or unauthentic.

Thoroughgoing Eclecticism and/or Western Priority

Thoroughgoing eclecticism and Western priority are by no means tied together. They are jointly addressed here only because those scholars who have held the Western text to be the original form of Acts have normally appealed somewhat to the principles of this approach. Since the Western text of Acts is known for its expansions, paraphrases, and particular emphases, it is best understood as a single unified work either created by Luke (which seems unlikely) or by a later reviser. Because the Western textual form is so poorly preserved in the Greek MSS, it must be restored to a great extent by means of ancient translations and fathers. Therefore, there is no pure reasoned eclecticism approach to the problem. Reasoned eclecticism by nature relies upon a balance of external and internal evidence. It looks for the best support of the most ancient witnesses. In this case, the translations are critical and yet they can only provide conclusive evidence when the questions are more obvious. However, in the case of

---

56. See Scrivener, *Plain Introduction*, 1:1–4.
57. Sturz, *Byzantine Text-Type*, 37–49.

fine details (such as choices between nearly synonymous prepositions or Greek word order) the textual critic must rely upon more internal characteristics like authorial style. Josep Rius-Camps and Jenny Read-Heimerdinger have together used aspects of this approach for their textual and theological studies in the book of Acts.[58]

In 1685, Jean Leclerc first proposed that Luke might have published the book of Acts in two separate editions.[59] The hypothesis was intended to explain the comprehensive differences between the Western and Alex forms of the book.[60] In 1896, Friedrich Blass popularized the theory that Luke's first edition was a longer and less polished draft that came to reside at the church in Rome. Subsequently, Luke's shorter revised edition was presented to Theophilus as the finished product. This text form is now present in most of the MSS.[61] M.-É. Boismard and A. Lamouille (BL) submitted a modern form of this approach in 1984.[62] These men utilized extensive stylistic analysis both to demonstrate that Luke had to be the author of each edition and to enable them to make textual decisions. BL concluded that a third edition was then produced utilizing the other two. This consummate edition is best approximated by the Alex MSS of Acts.[63] Similarly, Delebecque used stylistic criteria to associate two editions to Luke. However, he concluded that Luke wrote the first shorter edition when Paul was in prison and then composed the longer one a few years later after Paul's death.[64] In contrast, W. A. Strange asserted that Luke died before publication. Luke's unfinished draft of the book was equipped with extra details throughout the pages. Subsequently, two editors worked independently to finalize two separate editions.[65] Meanwhile, Albert C. Clark perceived different persons at work. The first edition was the original Western text, while the later came from an Alex editor.[66]

F. G. Kenyon perceived that the overreliance of WH on their favored MSS promoted a counter trend among textual critics to minimize

---

58. Elliott, "Thoroughgoing Eclecticism," 756.
59. Metzger, *Textual Commentary*, 223–24.
60. Metzger, *Textual Commentary*, 222–36.
61. Metzger, *Textual Commentary*, 224.
62. Boismard and Lamouille, *Texte occidental reconstitution*.
63. Boismard and Lamouille, *Texte occidental reconstitution*, 1:1–9.
64. Metzger, *Textual Commentary*, 227.
65. Strange, *Problem of the Text*, 182–89.
66. Clark, *Acts of the Apostles*, xxiv-xxxii.

emphasis upon external evidence and to place more reliance upon internal criteria such as context, authorial style, and scribal proclivities.[67] In the early twentieth century, C. H. Turner was a strong proponent of thoroughgoing eclecticism.[68] Following him, both George D. Kilpatrick and J. Keith Elliott have carried the torch for this perspective, producing a tremendous amount of quality works up to the present day. Characteristically, they are willing to choose a reading with sparse external support whenever internal factors suggest its originality.[69]

Reasoned Eclecticism and Alexandrian Priority

Having studied the textual nature of the book of Acts in great detail, James Hardy Ropes was convinced that the Alex text form, and particularly that found in Codex B, was the purest tradition.[70] He concluded his assessment of von Soden's theory by saying that von Soden was mistaken to claim the entire Alex textual tradition was derived from a single second-century archetype. Furthermore, von Soden was incorrect to assume that the Antiochian (i.e., Byz) text arose in the second century from its own local MSS, uninfluenced by von Soden's presumed Alex archetype.[71] Instead, Ropes asserted that the old uncial Alex text is the best basis for reconstruction since neither the I-text (i.e., Jerusalem text) nor the K-text (i.e., Koine or Byz) is pure. He considered the I-text to be a mixture of the Western revision together with the old uncial Alex text. He perceived the K-text to be a combination of the Western revision, the Lucianic revision, and an old uncial MSS from somewhere. He asserted,

> Even if ancient Antiochian [i.e., Byzantine] readings departing from all, or from one sub-group, of the Old Uncials can sometimes be identified, these merely represent a lost second-century or third-century MS. parallel to the (somewhat younger) Old Uncial codices, not necessarily independent of their text, and by no means necessarily better.[72]

---

67. Kenyon, *Greek Bible*, 254–55.
68. Metzger and Ehrman, *New Testament*, 223–25.
69. Metzger and Ehrman, *New Testament*, 224–26.
70. Ropes, *Beginnings of Christianity*, ccv, cclxxiv.
71. Ropes, *Beginnings of Christianity*, ccci–cccii.
72. Ropes, *Beginnings of Christianity*, ccci.

Therefore, Ropes sought after the best readings of the old uncial text and was confident they would come from Alexandria. However, he acknowledged that original readings could come from the Byz old uncial tradition. In fact, he admitted that it is seldom possible to determine whether a particular reading in Lucian's Byz recension arose from an Alex old uncial, a Western revision uncial, or from an old uncial native to Antioch.[73] As a result, he asserted that the Byz text should not be neglected.[74]

Ropes believed that various characteristics of the textual tradition represented by Codex D et al. reveal its secondary nature.[75] In fact, he asserted that the reviser who formed the Western text, approximated by Codex D, was clearly not the author of the "non-Western text."[76] He considered both 614 and 383 to be mixed text MSS that provide further evidence for the Western text.[77] However, he urged for a complete study to be done because these MSS surprisingly offer Western readings overlaid upon a Byz text. Moreover, they also preserve old uncial readings.[78] He had expected these MSS to have features proving they were copied from a Western archetype that became mixed over time from Byz intrusion. Instead, he found them to agree with the Byz text in the finer details. Therefore, the direction of mixture appears to be reversed.

Reasoned Eclecticism Using All Text Traditions

Shortly after WH published their edition, Scrivener, as he had previously done with Tregelles, respectfully challenged their absolute claims against the Byz text. Yet for the most part his voice was drowned out.[79] On the other hand, von Soden thought that the I-text, H-text, and K-text were each a product of separate recensions occurring close to the year AD 300.[80] However, they were all corrupted in some measure by

---

73. Ropes, *Beginnings of Christianity*, ccviii-ccix, cclxxxiv.
74. Ropes, *Beginnings of Christianity*, cclxxxviii.
75. Ropes, *Beginnings of Christianity*, lxxviii–lxxxiv, cvi-cviii; see also T. E. Paige in Metzger, *Textual Commentary*, 225–26.
76. Ropes, *Beginnings of Christianity*, ccxxxi.
77. Ropes, *Beginnings of Christianity*, ccxvi.
78. Ropes, *Beginnings of Christianity*, ccxvii.
79. Scrivener, *Plain Introduction*, 2:287–301.
80. Soden, *Schriften des Neuen Testaments*, 2:xiii.

the antecedent second-century Western recension.[81] In particular, he pointed to Tatian's *Diatesseron* as a primary corrupting influence for the Gospels. More uniquely, he asserted that Tatian could be responsible for the Western recension of Acts. Therefore, the textual critic must first sift out the secondary elements from Tatian's revisions and then reconstruct each of the I, H, and K recensions as purely as possible. Armed with these, one could usually be confident that readings having the agreement of two out of three are the original text.[82] It is interesting to note that even though Ropes disagreed with von Soden's approach, he confessed, "It has led to a result not very different from that produced by what appears to be a sounder process."[83]

Sturz defended the Byz text against the claims of WH. He asserted that conflated readings exist from the earliest times in all text types, and thus they do not make a text type late.[84] In addition, he tried to demonstrate that the Byz text existed in the second century by presenting 150 examples where its readings are supported by papyri older than AD 300.[85] Moreover, he asserted that favorable characteristics of Byz readings do not justify categorically labeling them secondary.[86]

Although these men were criticized for defending the Byz text, recent studies are beginning to confirm both the antiquity and quality of numerous Byz readings. For example, the 2017 *Editio Critica Maior* (ECM) of Acts selected 36 Byz readings as superior to the competing Alex readings currently found in the main text of NA28. In addition, it marked as indecisive 105 more occasions—out of the total of 622 "undivided" Byz readings—where they judged the Byz form as having an equal chance of being original.[87] That raises a question—are all the other 517 variants secondary? Similarly, when the full list of variants between RP05 and NA28 is considered, only 83 or about 10 percent of the 879 differ in length by more than a single word.[88] This figure manifests the nearness of

---

81. Soden, *Schriften des Neuen Testaments*, 1:1833–36.
82. Soden, *Schriften des Neuen Testaments*, 2:xxviii.
83. Ropes, *Beginnings of Christianity*, ccci.
84. Sturz, *Byzantine Text-Type*, 82–89.
85. Sturz, *Byzantine Text-Type*, 82.
86. Sturz, *Byzantine Text-Type*, 55–69.
87. ECM 3:1:1, 30–31, 34–37, and ECM 3:2, 8. See also ECM 3:1:2; and Wachtel, "Text-Critical Commentary," 1–38.
88. The number of differences between RP05 and NA28 is much higher than that between the "Byz" marked ECM apparatus reading and the ECM chosen reading

wording between these two editions. My breakdown of the categories includes 425 substitutions, 325 one-word differences in length (out of 408 total word-length variants), and 128 variations in the word order.[89] The Byz text is the longer one 257 times and the shorter one 151 times. James Royse has shown that scribes of the earliest papyri were more prone to omit words than they were to add them.[90] If most of these differences can be explained as accidental, might the length of the Byz text suggest that its scribes did a better job of correcting the omissions? Conversely, if one prefers the shorter reading with Griesbach and WH, would not the Byz text have priority in many of the 151 occasions? Royse's contribution combined with the textual condition of Acts raises important questions and will be discussed more fully later.

Historically, in such cases, text critics often relied upon the generalization that Alex MSS are superior qualitatively. While it seems reasonable to pass over Byz readings that are opposed by a unified testimony of the oldest Greek MSS, most primitive versions, and earliest fathers, what should be done when their testimony is divided? Unfortunately, Byz readings are commonly rejected merely because the scholarly consensus is that *some* Byz readings are manifestly secondary. However, even Codex B (and much more ℵ) has obvious secondary readings. Should the many excellent readings of these two MSS be rejected because of that? The current mentality ought to change if the Byz text can be shown to be a real entity in the second century. For these reasons, the proposed study is relevant. If the antiquity of the Byz text can be solidly established, and if it can be shown to repeatedly preserve high quality readings, its variants should be considered legitimate contenders for originality.[91] When its readings have superior justification, the GNT should be revised.

---

because the methods for identifying a Byz reading are not equal. Robinson and Pierpont, *Byzantine Textform 2005*, xiv, generally looked for readings with more than 70 percent attestation from all MSS, while ECM 3:2, 8, selected seven nearly pure Byz MSS as the standard. They considered the reading to be Byz only if these stayed relatively undivided. The total is near 1,060 but 181 do not impact meaning (see the appendix).

89. Some variants required classification into more than one category.

90. Royse, "Scribal Tendencies," 470.

91. High quality readings are those that fit the context well and generally avoid the common Byz tendencies to "normalize, clarify, and smooth the wording linguistically or with respect to content" (my translation of "den Wortlaut sprachlich oder inhaltlich normalisieren, verdeutlichen und glätten"). Wachtel, *Byzantinische Text*, 73. They are readings whose overall justification for originality is either strengthened or at least not reduced by the application of text-critical canons.

A REALISTIC TRANSMISSION THEORY FOR THE BOOK OF ACTS

Already in 1854, Tregelles had concluded that Griesbach's system of recensions was to be set aside. After explaining how Griesbach had assumed the Alex recension was a purification of an older Western text, he declared, "The untenable point of Griesbach's system . . . was the impossibility of drawing an actual line of distinction between the Alexandrian and Western recensions."[92] In fact, Griesbach had discovered for himself that he could no longer reasonably link Origen with the Alex recension as he once thought.[93] Similarly, Scrivener wrote in 1859, "The schemes of recension promulgated by Griesbach and his imitators in the last generation . . . were bold, ingenious, imposing, but utterly groundless," and "it were needless to revert to them, for I believe that no one at present day seriously entertains any one of them."[94]

In addressing the meaning of Jerome's comments about Lucian and Hesychius in his letter to Damasus, often found preceding the Latin Vulgate Gospels, Tregelles clarified that Jerome referred to "certain MSS of the Gospels" that were merely called according to those popular names but were apparently "only received and used by a few, and they could not have been revisions of the κοινὴ ἔκδοσις, if (as it seems from Jerome) they contained various additions from parallel places."[95] Tregelles was endeavoring to show that Professor Hug's modification of Griesbach's theory was also false. Hug had asserted that at first there was a common text that was then converted by recension into the three text types. The recensions, per Griesbach, were created solely from the raw material of that common edition (although Griesbach considered the common

---

92. Tregelles, *Account*, 88, 90–91.
93. Tregelles, *Account*, 91.
94. Scrivener, *Contributions Codex Augiensis*, 1.
95. Tregelles, *Account*, 90. Jerome wrote to Pope Damasus, "I pass over those codices that are named after Lucian and Hesychius. Some men allege a perverse controversy. By them it is certainly not permitted to correct the Old Testament subsequent to the seventy translators nor is it profitable to correct the New [Testament], since the Scripture, [having been] previously translated into the language of many nations, shows whatever they have added to be false" (my translation of "Praetermitto eos codices quos a Luciano et Hesychio nuncupatos paucorum hominum adserit perversa contentio, quibus utique nec in Veteri instrumento post septuaginta interpretes emendare quid licuit nec in Novo profuit emendasse, cum multarum gentium linguis Scriptura ante translata doceat falsa esse quae addita sunt," as found in Weber and Gryson, *Biblia sacra*, 1515).

edition as the actual Western text).⁹⁶ According to Hug, Jerome referred to the recensions in the above quotation (see footnote). In response, Tregelles explains that Jerome could not have meant an authentic Lucianic recension (if Griesbach was right about a common first edition) because such a recension should not (according to Griesbach) contain substantial additions.⁹⁷

Similarly, Klaus Wachtel gives several reasons why Jerome's statements regarding Lucian, here and elsewhere, do not in the least demand that a Byz NT revision be attributed to him.⁹⁸ First, Jerome does not speak of Lucian and Hesychius, but rather of those who, with wrong zeal, use Gospels attributed to them. It is not likely that Jerome would censor a NT work by Lucian when in other places he praises him for his expertise in the Scriptures, attributing to him the version of the LXX used from Antioch to Constantinople. Moreover, only the Vulgate Gospels were indisputably produced by Jerome.⁹⁹ Thus, at most, only a Gospel revision could be extracted from the statement.

Considering the lack of historical evidence for a Lucianic Recension, and in view of a careful assessment of Jerome's statement, it is no wonder that scholars for the most part have abandoned Griesbach's theory of three recensions. In its place has entered the idea that the Byz text slowly developed over the centuries. Yet in practice, the process has done little to change the conclusion that Griesbach and others had drawn from that faulty premise. The Byz text is still commonly regarded as completely derived from the other text traditions and thus wholly void of any significance for making original text decisions. In his studies of the Byz text in the Catholic Letters, Wachtel demonstrates that the process view of a developing Byz tradition agrees with the textual characteristics of its MSS and with the known historical circumstances.¹⁰⁰ He asserts that unlike the Byz Gospels, which seem to be relatively fixed already in the fourth century (as validated by the patristic citations of Chrysostom, the Greek text of Codex A, and the Gothic translation), the Catholic letters do not reach a solid form until the ninth century. Wachtel even indicates that they received changes by a twelfth-century recension, signified as K^r.¹⁰¹

---

96. Tregelles, *Account*, 84.
97. Tregelles, *Account*, 90–91.
98. Wachtel, *Byzantinische Text*, 166–68.
99. Wachtel, *Byzantinische Text*, 166–68.
100. Wachtel, *Byzantinische Text*, 197–98.
101. Wachtel, *Byzantinische Text*, 198, 201; see also Fee, "Majority Text," 187.

He attributed the expanded time window largely to the separate canonical history of each group of books. According to C. E. Hill, "At least by the second half of the second-century churches throughout the empire had received the same four Gospels."[102] In contrast, four of the Catholic Letters (i.e., 2 Peter, 2 John, 3 John, and Jude) only received the unanimous support of the Greek and Latin speaking churches in the fourth century and a divided acceptance in the official Syriac church in AD 508.[103] The Syrian delay probably impacted the Byz text tradition the most, as compared to the others, due to its close ties with Antioch of Syria.

Wachtel identifies three layers of variants in the Greek text.[104] Yet importantly, his approach seems to uphold the antiquity of the base layer underneath the Byz tradition.[105] He views the layers as generally evidencing movement away from the original.[106] He dates the first layer to the third/fourth century and sees it as a natural development.[107] All layers are marked by a general scribal preference for selecting the smoother, more standard, or more harmonized reading when faced with variants. Likely that choice was often influenced by how scribes heard it read in church.[108] Fee suggests that many alternate readings came from scribes who were seeking to transmit the meaning accurately.[109]

Wachtel is amazed to find the very same features recur in the oldest MSS whose textual affiliation is far from Byz.[110] The uniqueness of the Byz text form is not in these scribal changes but in their quantity.[111] Their concentration is partly attributable to the long continuous history of the Byz tradition. As a complicating factor, the relatively meager Byz MS evidence prior to the fifth century casts a veil over its more ancient history. In contrast, the period when the Alex tradition flourished is relatively short and its extant MSS provide many windows into its scribal activities before the fourth century. Wachtel concludes that the parallel processes of copying and correction (i.e., διόρθωσις) together with the reading of

---

102. Hill, *Who Chose the Gospels*, 233.
103. Wachtel, *Byzantinische Text*, 5–6, 134; Bruce, *Canon of Scripture*, 199, 208, 215.
104. Wachtel, *Byzantinische Text*, 196–98.
105. Wachtel, *Byzantinische Text*, 148–49.
106. Wachtel, *Byzantinische Text*, 199–202.
107. Wachtel, *Byzantinische Text*, 132, 197.
108. Wachtel, *Byzantinische Text*, 178.
109. Fee, "Majority Text," 195.
110. Wachtel, *Byzantinische Text*, 200.
111. Wachtel, *Byzantinische Text*, 76.

the MSS in church services, promoted the changes.[112] Additionally, he suggests that the increased rate of MS production after AD 300 would have intensified the smoothing. Since MSS that scribes mark as a basis for copying are compared to others, those variants that are more desirable are given preference.[113] He identifies a second layer in the fifth/sixth century and a third layer in the ninth.[114]

He also found numerous insights by reflecting upon the writings of Origen.[115] For example, Origen stated that variant readings commonly result from one of four factors: (1) inattention by scribes; (2) audacity of rascals; (3) negligence of the corrector; or (4) correctors who added or removed according to their own ideas.[116] Jerome likewise made similar statements.[117] Thus, these scholars recognized the corrector as an important figure in the process of textual transmission. Even more instructive is the way Origen dealt with variant readings.[118] He appears to have been adverse toward deleting glosses and sometimes even offered exegesis for variants he considered dubious.[119] What worked for him does not necessarily work for the scribe, since Origen could mention several variants and then allow the reader to choose. In contrast, the scribe was forced to copy only one reading into the text. This difference promoted standardization.[120] Thus, rather than being a good candidate for promoting the shorter Alex text, as seen in many of the earliest papyri, Origen's cautious attitude is more like that of a Byz scribe.[121] In the same vein, Gordon Fee has identified a curious exception in P66.[122] Unlike the scribe of P75, who was very careful about the precise wording, the scribe of P66 displayed a willingness to clarify and simplify the text. Therefore P66 provides a window to observe the kinds of scribal activity that have become characteristic of the Byz tradition.[123]

112. Wachtel, *Byzantinische Text*, 178, 197–98.
113. Wachtel, *Byzantinische Text*, 199.
114. Wachtel, *Byzantinische Text*, 198.
115. Wachtel, *Byzantinische Text*, 171–80.
116. Wachtel, *Byzantinische Text*, 171–72.
117. Wachtel, *Byzantinische Text*, 173–74.
118. Wachtel, *Byzantinische Text*, 174–76.
119. Wachtel, *Byzantinische Text*, 177.
120. Wachtel, *Byzantinische Text*, 178.
121. Fee, "P75, P66, and Origen," 257.
122. Fee, "P75, P66, and Origen," 258.
123. Fee, "P75, P66, and Origen," 258–59, 272.

Wachtel approached his evaluation by first categorizing the variants into three classes: typical, atypical, and other Byz readings.[124] The typical readings are those that appear to smooth, clarify, or simplify the text beyond the original form. The atypical ones appear to be errors, many of them ancient, that have no apparent advantage. Their antiquity can often be recognized by the fact that, were it not for their place in a recognized authoritative standard form, they should have been corrected long ago. Finally, the third class are those readings that are very good by internal considerations and may be original.[125] Wachtel thoroughly reevaluated the 98 variant units chosen by Kurt Aland across the Catholic Letters and found the Byz reading to be original fifteen times.[126] When he expanded the study to incorporate 364 total test locations, the quality of the Byz text was even better. He judged as many as 138 (i.e., 38 percent) to be original in the Byz text (95 were marked as probably original and 43 as possibly).[127] The Byz text here clearly provides a significant contribution towards establishing the original text. In many of the 138 occasions, the Byz text avoids the errors found in the oldest MSS.[128] Given that the Gospels were solidified at least five hundred years earlier, the potential importance of the Byz text in those books is even greater. Likewise, given that the reception history of the book of Acts is closer to that of the Gospels and knowing that the fourth-century Byz text of Acts can be confirmed by Chysostom's quotations (ca. 90 percent Byz), the Byz text has much to offer in Acts as well.[129]

In contrast, decades earlier Zuntz had identified a different scribal mentality in the early period of Alexandria. He found in P46, and likewise in the later Codex B and the much later MS 1739, a very high quality text of the Pauline Epistles as evaluated on both external and internal evidence, even though the actual copyist of P46 performed below average.[130] Having noticed so much corruption in MSS from all textual traditions, he wondered what might have caused the higher purity in the Alex region. He concluded that such excellence implies the diligent work of scribes

---

124. Wachtel, *Byzantinische Text*, 73.
125. Wachtel, *Byzantinische Text*, 75.
126. Wachtel, *Byzantinische Text*, 87.
127. Wachtel, *Byzantinische Text*, 131.
128. Wachtel, *Byzantinische Text*, 92–109.
129. Fee, "Majority Text," 188; Büsch, "'Western' Text of Acts," 189.
130. Zuntz, *Text of the Epistles*, 56–57, 157, 212, 269.

in Alexandria across many decades.[131] In fact, the special character of these scribes versus the average ones indicated a tradition built upon "expert philological criticism."[132] He perceived the process as one where the scribes continually obtained the best MSS and used these "as a norm for the correctors in the provincial Egyptian scriptoria."[133] As an analogy, he referred to the work of philologist Aristarchus ca. 150 BC upon the writings of Homer. The papyri before 150 BC have many words that were added to the original, and yet the standard text following that boundary "substantially agrees with that of the Byzantine manuscripts."[134] Therefore, it was possible through philological skill to produce an excellent edition, and apparently such was also done for the NT. Incidentally, this example provides additional justification for using the late MSS as correctors of the earliest tradition. While the value of unique Byz or isolated Western readings for Zuntz was very low, he insisted that whenever a Byz MS aligns with a Western MS the result is a second-century tradition.[135] Yet he reserved his highest commendation for the Alex group—i.e., P46 B 1739 sahidic (sah) bohairic (boh) Clement of Alexandria (Clem) Origen (Orig)—stating, "Where Western witnesses are joined by a member, or some members, of the Alexandrian group, the authority of the relevant reading is powerfully increased."[136] He asserted that the odds of choosing the right reading increase with each additional "authoritative witness," and that in such "calculations the Byzantine text is by no means *quantité négligeable*."[137]

Zuntz's overall approach was to trace the existing MS evidence back to their archetypes and then by extension to seek the original text.[138] Insightfully, he affirmed that definite progress will only occur if scholars utilize the Western evidence and cease to set aside the entire Byz tradition. He considered the Byz text to be "a most helpful instrument" and believed Griesbach was wrong to suggest that it was born from the other two recensions.[139] He discovered that P46 preserved "a number of Byzantine

---

131. Zuntz, *Text of the Epistles*, 214.
132. Zuntz, *Text of the Epistles*, 251.
133. Zuntz, *Text of the Epistles*, 271, 273, 278–82.
134. Zuntz, *Text of the Epistles*, 281.
135. Zuntz, *Text of the Epistles*, 283.
136. Zuntz, *Text of the Epistles*, 156, 283.
137. Zuntz, *Text of the Epistles*, 283.
138. Zuntz, *Text of the Epistles*, 8.
139. Zuntz, *Text of the Epistles*, 12. Sturz, *Byzantine Text-Type*, 130–36, previously

HISTORIC VS. PROPOSED USE OF THE BYZANTINE TEXT

readings, most of them genuine, which we discarded as late."[140] In light of this fact, he wondered about Byz readings in places for which P46 is not extant, asking, "Are all Byzantine readings ancient?"[141] Commenting on the fidelity of the Byz scribes, he asserted, "Indeed, it seems to me unlikely that the Byzantine editors ever altered the text without manuscript evidence. They left so many hopelessly difficult places unassailed!"[142] Yet he was also quick to add that Burgon was misguided in his defense of Byz priority since it has the most "corruptions," especially in its tendency "to adopt the smoothest of the readings."[143] In quantifying his assessment of Byz text quality, he stated that when the tradition stands alone or nearly alone it rarely preserves the original text.[144] Having found various Western readings within Alex witness P46, he asserted that "Western readings in non-Western witnesses [e.g., P46] are, generally, ancient survivals" and that Western readings found also in the Byz text predate P46 and go far back into the second century.[145] As an example of the potential value of cursives and the antiquity of the Western tradition, he demonstrated that tenth-century MS 1739 had preserved second-century Western elements that were later removed from the Alex tradition.[146]

While assessing the value of Alex MSS, Fee concluded that since P75 and B have a high coherence and since they share scribal tendencies, they must independently go back to the same archetype.[147] Although assessing these as upholding the highest quality of text, he noticed a propensity in both documents to omit prepositions in certain contexts, read a simple instead of a compound word, drop the possessive, lose the article, and show common word order uniquely (or nearly so). Since these phenomena occurred in both documents and often in different places, he attributed such features to the scribe of their archetype.[148] These secondary features caution the textual critic against placing too much confidence in

---

identified Zuntz's insightful conclusions.

140. Zuntz, *Text of the Epistles*, 55.
141. Zuntz, *Text of the Epistles*, 55.
142. Zuntz, *Text of the Epistles*, 55.
143. Zuntz, *Text of the Epistles*, 55–56.
144. Zuntz, *Text of the Epistles*, 60.
145. Zuntz, *Text of the Epistles*, 142, 150–51. He defined Western readings as those found uniquely in MSS related to the Western part of the Roman Empire (p. 85).
146. Zuntz, *Text of the Epistles*, 155–56.
147. Fee, "P75, P66, and Origen," 261.
148. Fee, "P75, P66, and Origen," 261.

the readings of any one MS or group of MSS and highlight what kinds of readings are most likely secondary in these particular documents.

B. H. Streeter provided important insights as to how patterns of variants may have arisen in various church centers within the Roman Empire.[149] Although his theory of five major local texts in Alexandria, Antioch, Caesarea, Italy-Gaul, and Carthage may remain unprovable, it has a lot of explanatory power. Moreover, it is not necessary to agree with him concerning the existence of formal recensions to accept the thrust of the argument.[150] He wanted to know the cause of local texts and the reason why the Byz form became the standard of correction. Counterintuitively he argued that it is the agreement in the minor variants rather than in the obvious ones that provides the best indicator for local text identification.[151] In any given region where churches exist, MSS became copied, and mistakes naturally entered the transmission stream.[152] He explained that initially the pattern of mistakes in one MS would usually be quite different from those in other MSS. However, as those churches grew in their sense of the Gospels being inspired, the leaders would tend to seek improved accuracy. Such feelings would promote the establishment of exemplars for use in correcting their MSS. He seems to imply that the exemplars would be formed by comparing the local MSS among themselves and selecting the best variants. The impact would tend to create MSS in one region that agree more with each other than those of more distant regions. According to Streeter, such practices continued until a push for standardization across the regions occurred after AD 200, which created mixture. Therefore, the textual critic should attempt to obtain the earliest form of each local text prior to mixture in order to assist in the determination of the original readings.[153]

Streeter observed that witnesses assignable to a fixed location were typically most closely aligned with those of their adjacent regions.[154] He illustrated the problem of mixing by considering Codex B's reading at Luke 22:43–44.[155] Streeter indicates that this codex is the purest Alex MS and that it lacks these verses. However, Western mixture came in and

---

149. Streeter, *Four Gospels*, 32, 108.
150. Streeter, *Four Gospels*, 39, 125.
151. Streeter, *Four Gospels*, 36.
152. Streeter, *Four Gospels*, 37–38.
153. Streeter, *Four Gospels*, 61.
154. Streeter, *Four Gospels*, 65–89.
155. Streeter, *Four Gospels*, 61.

HISTORIC VS. PROPOSED USE OF THE BYZANTINE TEXT

caused the archetype of ℵ to add them. He concludes that although ℵ has experienced "corruption" from the Western tradition, it appears that this mixing of traditions has restored the original reading to ℵ.[156] While he favors a pure Alex text for the Gospels over that of the Byz because of harmonization, he says that he would probably not do so for the book of Acts.[157]

When discussing his view of the Lucianic recension, Streeter keenly asserts that Lucian's initial "bias" would be to use the ancient text of Antioch. Yet perhaps under Griesbach's influence, he hypothesizes that Lucian may have borrowed the best MSS he could find from "Alexandria, Ephesus, and, perhaps, even Rome," and then selected the Alex MSS to be his foundation.[158] Nevertheless, he declares, "The majority of the readings in which the earliest form of the Lucianic text differs from that of ℵ B L is likely to represent a text traditional at Antioch."[159] He then accounts also for the Western element in the Byz text as having sprung from the Greek archetype undergirding sy^s, since it was established before Lucian's edition. Lastly, he presumes additional Western mixture may have come from MSS of Rome or Ephesus.[160] If Streeter is right about the ancient Antiochian local text, the foundation of the Byz text in the Gospels is old indeed.

Scrivener provides a concise overview of the scribal characteristics of each of the main text traditions, saying,

> The tendency to licentious paraphrase and unwarranted additions distinguished one set of our witnesses from the second century downwards; a bias toward grammatical and critical purism and needless omission appertained to another; while a third was only too apt to soften what might seem harsh, to smooth over difficulties, and to bring passages, especially of the Synoptic Gospels, into unnatural harmony with each other.[161]

As a result, such proclivities need to be considered when evaluating MS evidence for or against a reading. Moreover, the testimony of

---

156. Streeter, *Four Gospels*, 61.
157. Streeter, *Four Gospels*, 146.
158. Streeter, *Four Gospels*, 117.
159. Streeter, *Four Gospels*, 117.
160. Streeter, *Four Gospels*, 116–18.
161. Scrivener, *Plain Introduction*, 2:297–98.

any textual tradition or even of a solitary MS may provide the necessary clue(s) for a correct decision.

INTERDEPENDENCE OF TRANSMISSION THEORY AND THE TEXT-CRITICAL CANONS

Some argue that the oldest MS are best because they are closer to the source. Such is the viewpoint commonly held by those who are reasoned eclectics. Yet the advantage of antiquity is somewhat mitigated by the commonly held viewpoint that the "great majority" of textual variants were already created by AD 200, as famously asserted by Kilpatrick.[162] Others say that the great store of newer MSS are best because they are normally faithful representatives of much older uncial archetypes whose text is as old or older than that found in the famed ℵ and B.[163] In contrast, Timothy Ralston has urged Byz-priority proponents to subtract MSS derived from the twelfth-century K^r recension from their Majority Text calculations because their testimony is equal to just one MS.[164]

In truth, both old and young MSS must be utilized together. The bulk of newer MSS can never be excluded without consideration because of the nature of how variant readings were transmitted (see "realistic transmission theory" above). Oldest MSS are superior to later ones, all things being equal. However, their authoritative advantage is quickly reduced or relinquished whenever the minuscule Greek MSS, supporting a competing reading, show more geographic diversity among themselves, when they are joined by at least one ancient Greek MS, or when they manifest support from the earliest versions and/or fathers.

According to Epp, the very common "prefer the shorter reading" canon has received the most scrutiny in recent decades.[165] Although Royse has shown it to be suspect in some ways and particularly in Griesbach's axiom that scribes were more prone to add than to delete, the rule continues to be widely used.[166] Other recent studies appear to confirm Royse's results and suggest that either the rule should be discarded or

---

162. Metzger and Ehrman, *New Testament*, 225.
163. Scrivener, *Contributions Codex Augiensis*, 20.
164. Ralston, "Majority Text and Byzantine," 233, 286. Robinson, "Case for Byzantine Priority," 556–57, agrees.
165. Epp, "Traditional 'Canons,'" 107.
166. Royse, "Scribal Tendencies," 465–75.

redefined. For example, Epp offers that there should be a canon that favors either the longer or shorter reading as required.[167] Building upon the work of those before him, Wilson completed a comprehensive investigation.[168] He expanded the test range beyond Royse's analysis of the most ancient papyri to an inspection of ancient papyri, old uncials, and recent uncials across selected chapters of the Gospels, Acts, Pauline Letters, Catholic Letters, and the book of Revelation.[169] Surprisingly, his analysis of singular readings continued to bring consistent results when traversing many centuries of scribal activities. Overall, scribes tended to omit about 60 percent of the time and to add about 40 percent of the time.[170] Equally important are his conclusions about the harder and simpler readings. When assessing the impact of 2,279 singular readings, Wilson discovered that about 37 percent of these errors led to more difficult readings, and only about 9 percent became easier.[171] Due to their surprising results, these studies call for further verification and application to the field of NT TC.

The reading that can best explain the derivation of the rest is preferred. Most textual critics agree with this guideline, and many consider it to be the most important.[172] The Coherence-Based Genealogical Method (CBGM) utilizes this canon heavily for constructing local stemmata.[173] It seeks to determine which reading is genealogically prior to the other(s).[174] But what if the internal quality of two readings is essentially equal? Should the Alex reading still be preferred over the Byz reading? What if either the Western group or proto-Western group joins the Byz? The latter question will be discussed next.

PROPOSED USAGE OF THE BYZANTINE TEXT

The approach of the ECM editors regarding the utilization of the Byz text for assisting in the determination of the original text can most likely be

---

167. Epp, "Traditional 'Canons,'" 106.
168. Wilson, "Scribal Habits," 95–126.
169. Wilson, "Scribal Habits," 96.
170. Wilson, "Scribal Habits," 98–105.
171. Wilson, "Scribal Habits," 105–10.
172. Epp, "Traditional 'Canons,'" 93–96.
173. Wachtel, "Notes on Acts," 28–30; Wasserman and Gurry, *New Approach*, 4–5.
174. Wachtel, "Conclusions," 223–24.

enhanced by the adoption of a new canon of TC that looks for alignments between ancient layers of the Western tradition and the Byz tradition.

Sturz claimed that the antiquity of the Byz text should no longer be in question since he could show about 150 examples (13 within Acts) where a Byz reading was supported by papyri, all dated no later than the end of the third century and therefore closely linked to archetypes from the second century.[175] Fee responded that isolated readings do not prove the primitive existence of the Byz text. There must be a particular pattern of readings.[176] Those isolated readings could simply be remnants of an ancient text that were later infused into what became the Byz text. Though Sturz had successfully disproved WH's claim for no Byz support prior to AD 250, he had not thereby established the Byz text as a characteristic entity prior to that year.

This study will address the antiquity of the Byz text by utilizing an approach related to another aspect of Sturz's research. In his "List 2," he indicated about 170 places (13 in Acts) where the old papyri support the reading jointly testified by the Byz and Western text traditions but standing against the Alex.[177] Sturz found such combined evidence as even more convincing since they involve two independent traditions.[178] In a similar way, the method envisioned here will also focus upon alignment. However, instead of comparing ancient papyri with the two traditions, it will counter-intuitively compare a thirteenth-century minuscule MS against both the Byz text and the Alex text. Specifically, it will utilize the textual characteristics of MS 614, as the leader of a "proto-Western" group of minuscule MSS, to demonstrate the existence of a second-century Byz text of Acts. Minus its poorly supported variants, MS 614 appears to preserve faithfully the readings of an ancient second-century archetype. This MS 614 archetype displays the surprising phenomenon of being a text with proto-Western revisions built upon a mixed Byz and Alex base. In fact, its foundation is significantly more Byz. In contrast to Sturz's study of fragmented papyri, the approximated archetype standing behind MS 614 provides not just 13 examples of Western-Byz alignment against the Alex, but over 500 *proto*-Western-Byz alignments against the Alex.

175. Sturz, *Byzantine Text-Type*, 62, 145, 159.
176. Fee, "Majority Text," 184.
177. Sturz, *Byzantine Text-Type*, 74, 160–74.
178. Sturz, *Byzantine Text-Type*, 75.

The 614-group of MSS (383 614 1292 1505 1611 1890 2138 2147 2412 2495)[179] is not merely an anomaly of late Byz MSS adopting ancient Western readings just before or during the time of their production.[180] Rather, as Barbara Aland discussed, the Western textual character of the 614-group is best explained if its sources were generally more ancient than those of the Western Redaction.[181] My research even suggests that this group is the most ancient and reliable layer (as compared to Codices D and E, Old Latin (OL) MSS, sy^{hmg}, sy^{h**}, mae, and others) of the MS tradition historically called the Western text. Von Soden seems to be the first person to delineate I-text MSS into three subgroups and then use them to assist with recovering the original I-text recension. This study will instead put priority on the above MSS as the key, not for identifying the I-text recension but rather for discerning the archetypical text of the 614-group, a group that seems to have preceded all formal text recensions. Also, unlike the I-text recension of von Soden, the 614-group archetype is evidently dependent on both the Alex and Byz traditions.

Barbara Aland found it indefensible to maintain that the archetype for Codex D could explain the origin of MSS like 614.[182] If a D-text (or interchangeably "Western") Redaction was the genealogical basis for the

---

179. This list was created based upon the suggestions of the following sources and from personal observation: Wachtel, "A Plea Against the Text-Type Concept," 138–42; Epp, "Isolating a Distinctive D-Text," 242; Boismard and Lamouille, *Texte occidental reconstitution*, 1:25–27; Gäbel, "P127 and Codex Bezae," 142–43. All these lists are closely related to von Soden's I-text group C (Soden, *Schriften des Neuen Testaments*, 1:1688).

180. That was the conclusion of Geer, "Investigation of Western Cursives," 109–10.

181. Aland, "Entstehung, Charakter und Herkunft," 26–28, 65. In the places where MS 614 stands alone or nearly alone or another member of the group is isolated, those readings should normally be considered later deviations from the proto-Western archetype. An exception occurs when Codex D or sy^{hmg} or sy^{h**} or mae joins such an isolated reading. In such cases, the reading may indeed still be that of the proto-Western archetype. Barbara Aland uses the term *Redaktion* and here redaction has been used to indicate the same thing. The idea I intend to convey is that a comprehensive revision was made to the book of Acts and its subsequent popularity implies that it was made and valued within a prominent church center.

182. Aland, "Entstehung, Charakter und Herkunft," 26–28. The original German reads, "Mir scheint, wie immer man sich den Weg, auf dem die 614 (und Verwandte) zu ihren 'westlichen' Lesarten gekommen ist, im einzelnen vorstellt, er bleibt unverständlich, wenn man den Typ einer Handschrift wie 614 nach der 'westlichen' Hauptredaktion ansetzt" (p. 27). In contrast, Boismard and Lamouille, *Texte occidental reconstitution*, 1:8–10, sought to find the purer form of the D-text that later became a much-corrupted Codex D. Moreover, they did not see the Western tradition as fundamentally secondary. Instead, they thought the Western text was Luke's first edition of the book and proto-Alex was his revised edition. In addition, they judged that the editions were merged together to create the original of Acts.

MS 614-group, a scribe would have needed to partially purge the Western Redaction of many characteristic modifications small and large (still extant in MSS like Codex D, mae, and the Harclean Syriac apparatus) by an apparently random pattern, and then to have subsequently inserted new additions on the way to creating the MS 614-group archetype. Instead, she concluded that a MS similar to 614 was the foundation upon which the D-text Redaction was applied.[183] For this reason, the readings of 614 et al. will be named proto-Western to distinguish them from those denoted as Western and usually found within or related to those of Codex D.

Given that thirty-six of the forty-five agreements between D and Irenaeus (Ir) against the Alex reading (represented by the ECM) have limited to no additional support, one might think that the Western Redaction was utilized by Ir.[184] However, while some of these readings display striking agreements, many of them are insignificant. Moreover, as both Barbara Aland and Holger Strutwolf suggest, the numerous differences between D and Ir as well as the closer relationship between the Alex text and Ir indicate that Ir's Greek text did not derive genealogically from the D-text.[185] Rather, Ir used a Greek MS of the same character as the archetype upon which the D-text redaction was accomplished, one similar to MS 614. Therefore, the citations of Ir are inconclusive for deciding whether the Western Redaction had been completed before Ir wrote ca. AD 180. In any case, the archetype for the 614-group likely arose before AD 150, given that its proto-Western form is less developed than any reconstructed form of the Western Redaction.[186] Therefore, the

183. Aland, "Entstehung, Charakter und Herkunft," 26–28, 65.

184. Strutwolf, "Text Apostelgeschichte bei Irenäus," 181. The nine exceptions in Acts are found at: 1:16/13; 2:37/32; 3:26/6–10; 4:8/27; 7:7/18–22; 15:11/14; 15:25/10; 15:28/8–12; 17:24/32–34. However, about sixteen more cases should be added to the thirty-six. I noticed them when reviewing Tuckett, "How Early," 78–82. These agreements are listed according to how they are annotated in the ECM: 2:30/30; 3:13/8, 12 b-c; 3:13/42–44 b-c; 3:13/59 b-c; 3:17/17 b-c; 4:9/9 b-c; 4:12/2–40 (see b-c-d); 4:22/22–26 b-d; 4:31/49; 8:37/32–44 (Codex D is missing but E et al. have it); 9:20/13 (D missing but h and mae have it); 15:15/4–6; 15:20/37; 15:29/17 b; 17:26/2–8; 17:28/22–30.

185. Aland, "Entstehung, Charakter und Herkunft," 55–56. However, Barbara Aland acknowledges that these facts do not prove the D-text Redaction had not already occurred in a distant location such as Syria, but only that it was unknown to Ir (p. 64). Strutwolf has shown that Ir and D disagree with each other about 122 times. Of these, Ir agrees with NA28 73 times, D agrees with NA28 38 times, and all three disagree 11 times (Strutwolf, "Text Apostelgeschichte bei Irenäus," 184–85).

186. Soden, *Schriften des Neuen Testaments*, 1:1836, also could not account for "Western" readings across such a wide geographic region represented by Codex D, the

HISTORIC VS. PROPOSED USE OF THE BYZANTINE TEXT

archetype for the 614-group is the earliest. The Greek text used by Ir may be contemporary or later than the 614-group archetype. Finally, the D-text redaction likely occurred sometime between when this archetypical MS was created and the time of Ir's own writings. If these conclusions are valid, utilizing the ancient readings of the 614-group will partially fulfill the desire of Ropes for a purer Western text.[187]

Next, it will be shown that assuming the group's archetype was originally predominantly Alex in nature is not viable for explaining the numerous agreements between the 614-group and the Alex text. Naturally, that would be expected if MS 614 is representative of a second-century archetype and if the Alex text is closest to the original. Instead, Geer statistically found MS 614 to be associated with the Byz text.[188] Moreover, his theory that MS 614 infused its Western readings no earlier than the ninth century is unrealistic.[189] Beyond the second century, the popular D-text redaction was the more likely source. In addition, this later period was a time of great Byz textual stability. It is doubtful that many minority Western readings would then be inserted into Greek MSS.

Barbara Aland, on the other hand, saw the order of corruption reversed.[190] Based upon her text-critical perspective, its transmission would likely proceed from a pure Alex MS, to an early mixture due to infusion from a proto-Western element, and finally advance to a greater mixture as a result of a prolonged assimilation to the Byz standard text.[191] However, such an assertion fails for the similar reason as Aland identified above. How could an Alex MS with a strong Western element be revised according to the Byz standard and yet be edited so incompletely?

OL, and the Old Syriac (and now by the Middle Egyptian [mae]) unless he assumed that a second-century text "recension" occurred.

187. Ropes, *Beginnings of Christianity*, ccxl. MS 614 is normally one of the best representatives of this text. However, its singular and sub-singular (being defined here as having two or less Greek MSS that support it) readings can generally be assigned to a later date in its transmission (i.e., after AD 200), and removed from original text decisions.

188. Geer, "Investigation of Western Cursives," 106–7, 109–10.

189. Geer, "Investigation of Western Cursives," 9–14. The fact that an ancient text can be found in a recent MS is implied if one holds to the high value of Codex B. According to CBGM Phase IV results for the ECM of Acts, eleventh-century MS 81 stands third in the overall ranking of MSS closest to the initial text of Acts. The top three are Codex B at 96.51 percent, P74 at 95.70 percent, and MS 81 at 95.45 percent. The comparison data is derived using the CBGM website.

190. Aland, "Entstehung, Charakter und Herkunft," 65.

191. Aland and Aland, *Text*, 49–71.

MS 614 contains a great number of Western expansions, unique or nearly unique readings, and a large Alex element.[192] Instead, the nature of MS 614 suggests that its archetype was created from a Byz-Alex mixed text by overlaying proto-Western readings. It is often more primitive and contains fewer modifications than Codex D et al. These factors imply it was created some time prior to the Western Redaction. Therefore, I estimate the origin of the 614-group to the period of AD 125–150. The conclusion that the Byz text stands underneath the 614-group is consistent with the recent groundbreaking work of the ECM editors who incorporated Byz readings into their 2017 edition of Acts as described above. The implications of what has thus far been stated are yet to be appreciated. Either *both* a proto-Alex *and* proto-Byz text tradition existed already by the middle of the second century, or else the "mixed readings" of the Proto-Western Reading (PWR) archetype (the ancestor of the 614-group) actually preserve *a purer form* of Acts that existed prior to the polarization and fuller development of the Alex and Byz texts.[193] In both scenarios, all three traditions are extremely early and important for TC.

This PWR archetype appears to be tied genealogically to Codex D and the Western group. First, an editor started with an ancient authoritative MS and revised it according to additional information, possibly from the margins of Greek MSS and popular oral tradition. He also made numerous stylistic adjustments. The result of this work was the PWR archetype, i.e., the ancestor of the 614-group.[194] Not long after, this proto-Western form was further modified, at an important Christian community, probably in Syria, possibly in Antioch,[195] or perhaps at Rome,[196] into the Western Redaction and published within or before the period of AD 150–175. That text is the archetype standing several generations

---

192. Here is a list of some Acts verses in MS 614 that have Western expansions: 2:1; 5:39: 6:8; 7:37; 12:25; 13:33, 39; 15:29; 16:39; 19:9; 23:15, 25, 29; 26:14–15; 27:15, 35; 28:16, 19, 30.

193. Colwell, "Origin of Texttypes," 138. Robinson, "Textual Interrelationships," 124–26, cites C. C. Tarelli regarding papyri studies, and discusses the possibility that the original text might be best preserved in what are today classified as mixed MSS. Text types would then be seen as a development away from the "mixed" text. Such mixed texts differ from MSS that are assigned to a text type since they tend to have few characteristic group readings.

194. See Klijn, *Survey of Researches*, 66–68; Strange, *Problem of the Text*, 173.

195. Klijn, *Survey of Researches*, 68. Aland, "Entstehung, Charakter und Herkunft," 63, said Antioch was possible but found it hard to understand how that city would have such an extravagant text.

196. Streeter, *Four Gospels*, 57, 67.

away from Codex D. According to Metzger, an expressive Western text was popular and became a template from which Greek copies were made and disseminated into various parts of the Roman Empire.[197] It quickly found its way into North Africa, Europe, and deep into Egypt where it was then translated into local languages. In North Africa, copies of the Greek Western text became the basis for possibly the earliest translations into OL. Cyprian (Cyp) utilized a Western OL text.[198] The OL NT likely spread from there into Europe in a short time.[199] In Egypt, the Middle Egyptian (mae) translation was based upon a closely related Greek MS.[200] Moreover, due to its many minor agreements with the Western text, Metzger considers the ancient Sahidic to have been Western first and then later thoroughly revised by Alex Greek MSS.[201] In Syria, possibly not far from the hypothesized location of the Western Redaction, Polycarp, under the direction of Monophysite Bishop Philoxenius, utilized a Greek MS or MSS to create a translation that would be closely aligned with the Greek. Later, Thomas of Harkel selected the Philoxenian NT as his base text for the NT. He then revised it so that it would conform accurately with Greek MSS (for Acts he used only one) that he described as "accurate and reliable."[202] In the revision, he utilized Origen-style textual annotations to show what to change in the text.[203] For example, within the Syrian text, he used asterisks and obeli primarily to show words that did not exist in the Greek and that should therefore be removed (marked as S:H^A in the ECM; as sy^{h**} in NA28). In the margins (marked as S:H^M in the ECM; as sy^{hmg} in NA28), he showed words, clauses, or sentences that formerly existed in the Philoxenian edition but do not exist in the Greek

---

197. Metzger, *Early Versions of NT*, 133, 286–90, 325. Although the origin of Metzger's Western text is undefined and different from the Western Redaction of Acts detailed above, he provides a realistic outline for how the Western tradition may have spread through the empire.

198. Metzger, *Early Versions*, 315–16.

199. Metzger, *Early Versions*, 286–90, says Rome and North Africa both have strong arguments for being the origin of the OL.

200. Richter, "Mittelägyptischen," 221–27.

201. Metzger, *Early Versions*, 133.

202. Juckel, "'Harklensische Apparat,'" 230.

203. Though a Syrian, Thomas was exiled to Enaton near Alexandria. Nearly simultaneously with his work on the NT, his coworker Paul of Tella translated the OT utilizing a Syriac form of Origen's hexapla and tetrapla (Juckel, "'Harklensische Apparat,'" 129–30; Metzger, *Early Versions of NT*, 67–70).

and should also be removed.²⁰⁴ Ephraem (Ephr^S) is a fourth-century Syrian father that often preserves Western readings in Acts.²⁰⁵

Finally, each form of the Western Redaction was subsequently corrupted in various amounts.²⁰⁶ The most prominent witnesses are codex D, P38, P48, P127, various OL MSS, the apparatus of sy^h, the text of mae, and fathers such as Cyp and Augustine (Aug). These witnesses, especially Codex D, have their share of post-redaction modifications that can usually be detected by their sparse textual support. Therefore, the proto-Western form is the most important stage.²⁰⁷ The proto-Western archetype is best confirmed when the 614-group is nearly unified or when at least one prominent member of the 614-group aligns with at least one Western stage derived MS listed above.

KEY TERMINOLOGY

Partly due to the invalidation of longstanding theories that attributed the existence of the Alex and Byz textual traditions to early formal recensions, the suitability of perpetuating the term "text type" has been heavily debated in recent years.²⁰⁸ For many, the speaking of a text type is equivalent to affirming a formal recension. Therefore, the traditional phrase has been avoided except as necessary to describe a historical viewpoint or a text critic's position. Instead, the terms Alex text, Byz text, and "Western" text will be used to refer to three competing textual traditions (not text types) that arose very early and stood the test of time. Alex text broadly describes MSS like Codex B (03), P74, and their relatives, whose archetypes were apparently copied and corrected with the assistance of the text-critical expertise of Alexandria, Egypt (see Zuntz above). Byz text refers to MSS like 025, 35, and what is typically found in the mainstream MSS. Finally, "Western" text includes MSS like 614, Codex D (05), and all

---

204. Scholars have not all agreed on the preceding explanation regarding Thomas's approach or his use of symbols. However, this understanding does seem to rest on solid footing.

205. Ropes, *Beginnings of Christianity*, cxlviii.

206. Boismard and Lamouille, *Texte occidental reconstitution*, 1:111–18, present detailed analysis of textual mixture especially in Codex D. Their solution was not to rely on the 614-group, but rather to use all Western witnesses to reconstruct the original Lucan Western text edition (p. 10).

207. In contrast, Epp, "Distinctive D-Text," 235–44, considers Codex D et al. as the primary Western witnesses and the 614-group MSS as secondary.

208. Epp, "Textual Clusters," 556–57; Gäbel, "Western Text," 86–92.

that show a distinct relationship with the Proto-Western Reading (PWR) archetype and/or the "Western" Redaction (WR) archetype, both detailed above. Although Epp has recently promoted the phrase "textual clusters" in lieu of text types, his term has a particular weakness. He defines a cluster as "a group of NT MSS whose texts are more closely related to one another than the cluster—as a group, or as individual members—is related to other groups or to other MSS."[209] As a result, "Western" MSS identified by him as primary witnesses of the "D-text cluster," namely P38, P48, P127, and 05, should agree more with each other than with representative MSS of the other traditions.[210] Yet, as Wachtel shows from CBGM data, 05 agrees statistically with Alexandrian text MSS about as much as it agrees with the majority text MSS (i.e., Byz MSS).[211] In fact, the online tool shows 05 agrees at 68.9 percent with Alexandrian MS P74, 68.2 percent with Byzantine MS 35, and just 50.1 percent with "D-text cluster" MS P127.[212] Similarly, P38 agrees with Alexandrian MS 03 at 69.4 percent but only 59.7 percent with "D-text cluster" MS 05. Epp's cluster definition does not work for the "Western" textual tradition.

Alternatively, Gäbel has instructively advocated for the term "Bezan trajectory" to describe the phenomena of "Western" variants arising from a certain editorial freedom practiced in various places across many decades during early church history.[213] The concept is accurate but perhaps not sufficient by itself. In his first study on the subject, he concluded (as did Barbara Aland) that there must have been a "Western" redaction to account for the large number of distinctive agreements found across various combinations of witnesses, to include a select few Greek MSS, ancient versions, and patristic citations.[214] By redaction, Gäbel evidently opposed the idea of a first-century recension of Acts by Luke or some other editor. Instead, he pointed to a later revision of Acts that is secondary in quality. In his later study, he described four competing models scholars have used to explain the data.[215] Having reviewed about fifty-two other places of variation, this time he concluded that no redaction

209. Epp, "Textual Clusters," 571.
210. Wachtel, "Plea Against the Text-Type," 138, 142–43, 146–47.
211. Wachtel, "Plea Against the Text-Type," 142.
212. Wachtel, "Plea Against the Text-Type," 142; Gäbel, "Western Text," 88.
213. Gäbel, "Western Text," 83–84, 91.
214. Gäbel, "P127 and Codex Bezae," 150–52; Aland, "Entstehung, Charakter und Herkunft," 26–28.
215. Gäbel, "Western Text," 89–92.

is required to account for the data.[216] However, not much should have been expected in the first four chapters of Acts since "Western" redactional activity there produced little of semantic significance (as will be shown). In the end, he appears to doubt whether an early redaction of Acts ever occurred. Nevertheless, he presents his conclusions as preliminary and encourages a "new wave of research."[217] The results that follow align most closely with his "Trajectory/Redaction" model.[218] Meanwhile, Wachtel, whose CBGM-based analysis and editorial work for ECM 3 is noteworthy, is more certain. Not only does he argue that both "text type" and "text cluster" terminology should be dispensed with immediately, but he also declares that the search for a once-popular, second-century "Western text," as envisioned by Hort, "should be abandoned once and for all."[219] On the one hand, like Wachtel, the present study *has not found* evidence to suggest that Luke or a first-century editor/council created a thoroughly revised edition of Acts. On the other hand, it *has found* strong inferential evidence that a second-century "Western" redaction of Acts did in fact occur.

Moreover, von Soden, Ropes, Haenchen, Barbara Aland, Delobel, Epp, and Gäbel have all affirmed that the "Western" text once had a solitary form in the second (or early third) century.[220] This author considers its cause to be a textual redaction that quickly spread to several countries and their associated languages. The wording of that redaction must be reconstructed from Codex D and its relatives. Alongside the "Western" Redaction (WR) witnesses, this study has also evaluated Proto-Western Reading (PWR) witnesses. The 614-group clearly points back to a common PWR archetype that became a primary source for the WR. Even though the present evidence will not allow the wording of the WR to be precisely defined, its existence is implied by the many characteristic readings found isolated in the tradition, especially those of significant length. If one follows Epp in the effort to use "geographically neutral"

---

216. Gäbel, "Western Text," 109–34. He assessed thirty-six variation units in Acts 3:2—4:18 and sixteen in 11:1–2; 14:18–20.

217. Gäbel, "Western Text," 134.

218. Gäbel, "Western Text," 91.

219. Wachtel, "Plea Against the Text-Type," 147.

220. Soden, *Schriften des Neuen Testaments*, 1:1833–36; Ropes, *Beginnings of Christianity*, ccxxii–iii; Haenchen, *Acts of the Apostles*, 50–56; Aland, "Entstehung, Charakter und Herkunft," 26–28, 65; Delobel, "Nature of 'Western Readings,'" 69–70; Epp, "Anti-Judaic Tendencies," 126–27; Epp, "Textual Clusters," 556; Gäbel, "P127 and Codex Bezae," 145–52.

terms, the WR could instead be called the Second-Century Redaction of Acts (SCROA).[221] This study will focus on four subjects: the Alex text, the Byz text, the PWR archetype, and the WR.

SUMMARY

The following pages provide objective data that challenge the common opinion annunciated by Fee, who declared that the Byz "text-form is completely unknown by any of the evidence up to AD 350."[222] Moreover, these phenomena lead to a surprising conclusion. Although MS 614 (copied in the thirteenth century) is far from preserving a pure Byz text, its quality as a MS that accurately represents the text of a second-century archetype, seems to meet Fee's request for objective proof of Byz pattern readings in the second century. In concrete terms, whenever MS 614 aligns with one of the two more defined textual traditions, it agrees more often with the Byz than with the Alex.[223] Given that all three traditions are represented in the second century, the fundamental idea of von Soden is now feasible. He thought that readings having the concurrence of two of the three text types are most likely original because of their independent witness.[224] Although I see only two independent text traditions (and no text types) and a third tradition that is built on the other two, it appears that all three text forms are necessary for best discerning the original text within the book of Acts.

221. Epp, "Textual Clusters," 554–56.

222. Fee, "Majority Text," 184.

223. Although Geer, "Investigation of Western Cursives," 20, 93, compared MS 614 against a different Byz tradition, HF1985 (vs. RP05), and compared MS 614 against Codex B (vs. NA28), his results should be similar. He discovered that MS 614 aligned with the "Majority Text" at a rate of 68.5 percent and with Codex B at 50.9 percent. In addition, as chief representative of the group, MS 614 is also quite independent of these two traditions. Very often it stands against the united Byz-Alex reading.

224. Soden, *Schriften des Neuen Testaments*, 2:xxviii, where he states, "If the readings of the recensions are firm, the reading represented in the two recensions is usually included in the text" (my translation of "Stehen die Lesarten der Rezensionen fest, so ist in der Regel die von zwei Rezensionen vertretene Lesart in den Text aufgenommen"). Less specific than von Soden, who utilized the idea of two out of three in his Greek edition, Sturz, *Byzantine Text-Type*, 10, simply asserted that all text-type readings are before AD 200 and therefore the Byz text (like the others) should be included "in the weighing of external evidence for various readings to the Greek text of the New Testament" (p. 10). He argued that the Byz text "should be given equal weight, along with the Alexandrian and 'Western' texts, in evaluating external evidence for readings" (p. 130).

2

Establishing the Antiquity and Quality of the Byzantine Text of Acts

ANTIQUITY OF THE BYZANTINE TEXT OF ACTS

Is THE BYZANTINE TEXT very old? This section will seek to demonstrate the antiquity of the Byzantine text by successive reverse chronological movements from Codex D et al. to the approximated proto-Western text archetype. It will then look at its foundation.

Although most textual critics acknowledge the existence of a very ancient "Western" text, there is no consensus regarding what criteria should be used to identify it. Questions remain as to how accurately Codex D (05) reflects that "Western text," whether there ever existed a single "Western" archetype, and many others. Numerous text-critical experts have offered their own assessments of the value of a reconstructed "Western" text.[1] Any evaluation must consider the merits of Codex D itself. On the one hand, it is the best "Western" Greek representative covering large portions of text. On the other, it is a very mixed text with many obvious secondary changes. As a rule, Codex D must be purged of readings that lack confirmation from at least one of the following: Greek MSS beyond just 08 (and/or 1884), "Western" versions (e.g., OL, Syriac Harklensis, Coptic Middle Egyptian), or "Western" fathers (e.g., Irenaeus, Tertullian,

---

1. Metzger, *Textual Commentary*, 222–36, provides a concise summary of various viewpoints, covering the last hundred years and more.

Cyprian, Marius Victorinus, Hilary of Potiers, Ephraem of Syria, Ambrose of Milan, Quodvultdeus, Lucifer of Cagliari, or Augustine).² Moreover, the mere alignment of Codex D with a citation of Augustine does not prove that a reading dates from the second century. Since both witnesses are from the fifth century, the variant could have been created after the second century. On the other hand, due to their distinctiveness, the approximate agreement of various "Western" witnesses is usually enough to confirm that a reading came from the same ancient source. Codex D is extant except for lacunae at 8:29—10:14, 21:2–10, 21:16–18, 22:10-20, and 22:29—28:31.

A Coptic translation of the Middle Egyptian dialect (mae) is another very important source for "Western" readings. It is extant from 1:1—15:3. Like Codex D, it has many readings that were added at a later stage, corrected to the mainstream, or revised by the editor's preference.³ The third critical Western representative comes in the Syriac language and is known at the Syriac Harklensis. Its apparatus provides numerous ancient "Western" readings. Unlike the first two, it survives for the entire book of Acts.⁴ The fourth prominent witness is OL Codex Floriacensis (h) but it has only been preserved in about one fourth of Acts.⁵ When key witnesses align, there is high probability that one is looking at a genuine relic of the "Western" text. Here the "Western" text is understood as that formal textual redaction that took place within or before the period of AD 150–175, and then became the basis for what is now seen in the surviving mixed-text "Western" witnesses. While a formal text redaction has not been confirmed historically, it seems to be the cause of the "Western" text enigma. The Western Redaction can be partially reconstructed by using

---

2. While Irenaeus (Ir) is tremendously important, his testimony is mainly able to confirm that such and such a reading is very old. As was mentioned in chapter 1, his Greek text was much closer to the Alexandrian tradition than to the Western. As a result, his quotations alone are not able to prove independently that any reading was certainly within the popular "Western" text. Moreover, Irenaeus's citations from Acts lack many of the obvious secondary changes currently seen in Codex D. Unfortunately, his intermittent citations from Acts were mostly from places that do not have the long Western variants seen in 05, sy^{h**}/sy^{hmg}, mae, h, and others. Thus, it is difficult to know how expansive his text was. On a similar note, the ECM also considers Tertullian to be a good witness for the ancient Greek text. Though a Latin father, his citations seem to come directly from the Greek. See ECM 3:2, 139. The Latin fathers mentioned above were taken from the same volume (pp. 136–40).

3. Richter, "Mittelägyptischen," 221–27.

4. Juckel, "'Harklensische Apparat," 228–45.

5. Ropes, *Beginnings of Christianity*, cvi.

available evidence to identify distinctive readings. These characteristic variants will be denoted here as Western Redaction Readings (WRRs).

The Western Text of Acts

In this section, many WRRs will be identified and some others mentioned that need to be disregarded as being merely secondary corruptions. Those prefixed by the # sign will be further reviewed later in this chapter or subsequent chapters. NA28 can be assumed to agree with the 2017 ECM for Acts unless stated otherwise. Byz can be assumed to agree with RP05 unless noted. Figure 2.1 should be very helpful in seeing visually what is explained about how the major Western witnesses possibly developed to their present state. The following list considers about ninety possible "Western" readings from Acts.

1. (1:2/2–24) 05 moves ἀνελήμφθη from the end to the more natural fourth word of the verse and more significantly has + καὶ ἐκέλευσεν κηρύσσειν τὸ εὐαγγέλιον. It is supported by sy[hmg] (sa mae) (ar) (gig t 70 72). It is a WR gloss that, according to BL, was designed to be an inclusio with 28:31.[6] Some Western fathers like Tert and Aug and other witnesses have διδάσκων in place of λέγων in 1:3/38 and thus read, διδάσκων τὰ περὶ τῆς βασιλείας τοῦ θεοῦ. The result:

    (1:2) κηρύσσειν τὸ εὐαγγέλιον
    (1:3) διδάσκων τὰ περὶ τῆς βασιλείας τοῦ θεοῦ
    (28:31) κηρύσσων τὴν βασιλείαν τοῦ θεοῦ
    (28:31) διδάσκων τὰ περὶ τοῦ κυρίου Ιησοῦ

2. (1:5/23) 05f reads + ὃ καὶ μέλλετε λαμβάνειν and is joined by Aug Hil d gig t 70 72 73 189. Since mae and sy[h] equal the standard text and since the support is purely Latin, this reading probably entered the Greek after the WR (see figure 2.1).

3. (1:5/33) 05* shows + ἕως τῆς πεντηκοστῆς and is joined by d sa mae. The fact that 05* was corrected gives reason to think that the AD 507 sy[ph] (shown as sy[hmg] whenever Thomas of Harkel relegated its reading to the margin of his AD 616 sy[h] edition) was also corrected. Thus, Thomas possibly revised sy[ph] in sy[h] without noting it in his apparatus (see 12:20/14–22). Therefore, 05 is probably the WRR.

---

6. Boismard and Lamouille, *Texte occidental reconstitution*, 2:2–3.

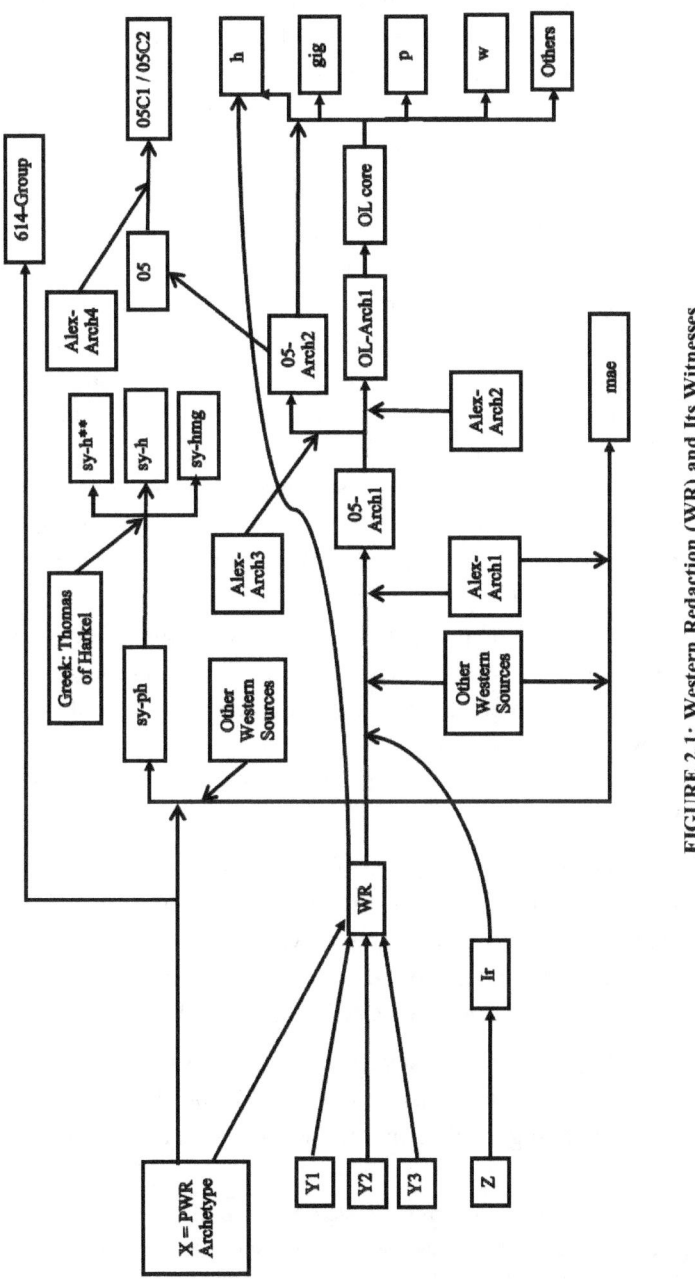

FIGURE 2.1: Western Redaction (WR) and Its Witnesses

4. (1:14/19) 05 has + καὶ τέκνοις and is joined by just d. Its lack of support indicates that it was generated subsequent to the WR.

5. (1:26/30) 05 reads δώδεκα instead of the standard ἕνδεκα but is joined by only Eus OrLat^ms d. Although the difference could be theological as suggested by J. Rius-Camps and J. Read-Heimerdinger who think Matthias was hastily and incorrectly chosen to complete the apostolic group, its minimal support shows it to be subsequent to the WR.[7]

6. (2:1/2–22) 05 paraphrases the passage and is joined by d mae. Apparently sy^ph was corrected back to the standard in sy^h, but Thomas did not supply a sy^hmg notation (see 1:5/33 above). 05 is the WRR. Given the lack of OL support in cases like this one, it appears that after the WR there were at least two Greek ancestors that preceded the production of 05 and most OL translations (see figure 2.1).[8] Specifically, at least one Western MS and at least one Alex MS (often returning parts to the Alex standard) were sporadically used to modify the WR text. As a result, it became 05 Archetype One (05-Arch1).[9] The transmission then divided. In the first branch, 05-Arch1 was potentially revised by Alex-Arch3 in order to become 05-Arch2. It was then copied to create 05. In the other branch, 05-Arch1 was potentially revised by Alex-Arch2 and became OL-Arch1. The intermediate generations explain the intermittent support by "Western" witnesses for "Western" readings. Naturally, if no changes occurred in a given variation unit, the WRR = 05 = OL = sy^h**/sy^hmg = mae.

7. (2:12/17) 05 has + ἐπὶ τῷ γεγονότι καὶ and is joined by Aug d sy^hmg. The gloss is probably a WRR that was removed from mae by reference to an Alex MS and likewise was removed from OL-Arch1 before it was translated into the OL. OL d can be explained as a later translation from a Greek MS very similar to 05.[10]

8. (2:14/14) 05* reads δέκα instead of the standard ἕνδεκα and is joined only by 1243 d. Was the mention of only ten apostles standing with Peter meant to suggest that Matthias was not truly an apostle? When

---

7. Rius-Camps and Read-Heimerdinger, *Message of Acts*, 1:133–39.

8. Figure 2.1 was created by analyzing every distinctive reading in WR witnesses within the ECM apparatus of Acts.

9. Ropes, *Beginnings of Christianity*, lxxx-lxxxii, discusses the corrections of Codex D by an Alexandrian text. Boismard and Lamouille, *Texte occidental reconstitution*, 1:115–18, also elaborate on this very problem at length.

10. Ropes, *Beginnings of Christianity*, lxxviii–lxxx.

9. (2:14/18-22) 05* adds the superlative πρῶτος as a nominative after επῆρεν and is joined by d p/2^vid. Similarly, 08 adds πρότερον after αὐτοῦ and is joined by 1884 e. The Coptic mae supports both readings. They emphasize that Peter was either the primary or first apostle to speak out on the day of Pentecost. It is probably the WRR and sy^h was apparently corrected to standard.

10. (2:16/18) 05 omits Ἰωήλ and is joined by IrLat d r. The change indicates a shared tradition that probably does not come from the WR but entered 05's lineage perhaps at 05-Arch1 or 05-Arch2 (see figure 2.1).

11. (2:17/16-18) 05 reads κύριος instead of ὁ θεός and is joined by 08 254 467 617 629 (1884) plus GregNy Phot SevGab IrLat Vg 11/11 OL MSS sa^mss bo^mss sy^p.ms. Given the diversity that includes partial Egyptian support and the complete OL evidence, it appears κύριος was the WRR. The reviser apparently noticed that יהוה, in the Hebrew Bible (HB), and κύριος, in the Septuagint (LXX), was more prominent in the citation of Joel 2:28-32 (3:1-5 LXX) and conformed the text. The immediate archetypes of mae and sy^h were presumably corrected to standard.

12. (2:18/42-44) 05 omits καὶ προφητεύσουσιν perhaps by an eye skip that overlooked the entire line and is joined by p* Tert. While there is apparently some shared tradition with Tertullian, the mistake was probably never part of the WR.

13. (2:19/28-38) 05 omits αἷμα καὶ πῦρ καὶ ἀτμίδα καπνοῦ and is joined by d gig p* r. Again, an archetype of 05 probably lost the words by an eye skip. This mistake is not shared by sy^h or mae and thus indicates the error occurred somewhere downstream from the WRR. Most OL MSS also avoid the error. 05-Arch2 apparently influenced the OL MSS with the mistake (see figure 2.1).

14. (2:24/18) 05 reads ᾅδου instead of the standard θανάτου and is joined by Cyr^ms Epiph^vid IrLat PolycS Vg e gig p t r w 70 189 bo mae sy^p. The WRR harmonized to the neighboring verses while Thomas probably corrected sy^ph in his sy^h.

15. (2:32/4) 05*f has + οὖν and is joined by 08 1243 1884 d e gig p r mae. Though an insignificant variant, its focused Western support suggests that it was the WRR from which sy^h must have corrected itself at some point.

16. (2:33/38–42) 08 reads τοῦτο <u>τὸ δῶρον</u> ὃ <u>νῦν</u> ὑμεῖς (vs. τοῦτο ὃ <u>νῦν</u> ὑμεῖς, Byz/614, vs. τοῦτο ὃ ὑμεῖς, NA28, vs. ὑμῖν ὃ, 05*) and it is built upon the Byz and 614-group reading. It is joined by 1884 IrLat e sa mae sy^p sy^h and is probably the WRR. Subsequent to the WR, 05* first deviated by simplification perhaps from Alex-Arch3. Similarly, the WRR never entered the OL MSS. Apparently, Alex-Arch2 restored the text to NA28 before it could reach OL-Arch1. 05* was corrected later presumably by Alex-Arch4 into 05C2/NA28 (see figure 2.1).

17. (2:34/16–22) 05 reads εἴρηκεν γὰρ αὐτός λέγει instead of the standard λέγει δὲ αὐτός εἶπεν and is joined by d gig r mae. 05 is probably the WRR with sy^h revising to the standard.

18. (2:37/37) 05 has + ὑποδείξατε ἡμῖν and is joined by 08 1884 d e gig p t r w ar 70 mae sy^hmg. Here the WRR is easy to validate by its key Western witnesses.

19. (2:45/2–12) 05 reads καὶ ὅσοι κτήματα εἶχον ἢ ὑπάρξεις (vs. καὶ τὰ κτήματα καὶ τὰς ὑπάρξεις, NA28/Byz) and is joined by d sy^p mae. 05 is probably the WRR that was corrected to the standard in sy^h.

20. (2:45/22–46/26) 05C2 has <u>καθ' ἡμέραν</u> πᾶσιν καθότι ἄν τις χρείαν εἶχεν καθ' ἡμέραν <u>πάντες</u> τε προσε<u>καρτεροῦν</u> ἐν τῷ ἱερῷ <u>καὶ</u> κατ' <u>οἴκους ἐπὶ τὸ αὐτὸ</u> κλῶντές τε ἄρτον (vs. πᾶσιν καθότι ἄν τις χρείαν εἶχεν καθ' ἡμέραν τε προσ<u>καρτεροῦντες ὁμοθυμαδὸν</u> ἐν τῷ ἱερῷ κλῶντές τε κατ' <u>οἶκον</u> ἄρτον, NA28/Byz) and is joined by (05*) (gig p r mae). The witnesses paraphrase the standard reading and change the activities from two (i.e., meeting in the temple and breaking bread in the house) to three (i.e., meeting in the temple, meeting in the homes, and breaking bread). Rius-Camps and Read-Heimerdinger think the structure indicates that they valued meeting in homes as much as meeting in the temple.[11] 05C2 preserves the WRR though the exact wording is uncertain due to several variations.

---

11. Rius-Camps and Read-Heimerdinger, *Message of Acts*, 1:198.

21. (3:3/2) 05 reads about the lame man that οὗτος ἀτενίσας τοῖς ὀφθαλμοῖς αυτοῦ καὶ in place of just ὅς. This gloss parallels similar wording in 3:4. MS 05 is joined by mae h and is probably the WRR.

22. (3:8/2–32) 05 d (h) (mae) all add some form of χαίρω but they each drop the subsequent phrase περιπατῶν καὶ ἁλλόμενος καὶ. Moreover, (h) also drops ἔστη. The Coptic mae drops both ἔστη and καὶ περιεπάτει. 08 deviates the least from the standard reading by only adding χαίρων and is joined by 1884 e. Somewhere in this mess is the WRR and it most likely is nearer to 05 than the others. The mainstream MSS avoid these variations.

23. (3:11/2–28) The ECM retroverts the mae as τοῦ δὲ Πέτρου καὶ Ιωάννου ἐκπορευομένων συνεξεπορεύετο κρατῶν αὐτοὺς τότε συνέδραμεν πᾶς ὁ λαός πρὸς αυτοὺς <u>καὶ θαμβηθέντες ἔστησαν</u> instead of the standard. It is joined by (05) (d) (h) and is closest to the original WRR. OL (h) offers the same reading but with a different and probably original WR word order at the first six words. It also deletes the ending <u>καὶ θαμβηθέντες ἔστησαν</u> probably considering it a double reading. Meanwhile 05 revises the plural participle into ἐκπορευομένου perhaps to tie it to Peter rather than to Peter and John. In contrast to h, MS 05 removes the standard ending of συνέδραμεν . . . αὐτοὺς, probably also thinking it was a double reading. It would appear that the WRR entered the 05-Arch1 with little or no changes. When it branched to 05-Arch2, the changes were made that created 05. When it branched to OL-Arch1, the reading was apparently revised to the standard since the changes are absent from all OL MSS except d and h (see figure 2.1). It would appear that h has its own lineage going back to the WR independent of 05's ancestry (cf. 4:18/2; 18:12/26–36). This example points to the WR and also demonstrates how the underlying Greek continued to change after the WR.

24. (3:13/42–44) 05 reads + εἰς κρίσιν and 08 has + εἰς κριτήριον and these synonymous terms are supported by 1884 IrLat d e p h mae sy[hmg]. Such is a great example of a WRR and one already known by Ir. The unity with Ir should probably be understood as showing a common background between Ir's reference Greek MS and that of one of the MSS used to create the WR (see figure 2.1).

25. (3:14/14) 05 reads ἐβαρύνατε instead of the standard ἠρνήσασθε and is supported by just IrLat d mae. 05 is probably the WRR even though the support is sparse. Alternatively, this reading known by Ir may have independently entered the ancestral lines of both 05 and mae. However, given the many distinct agreements between these witnesses, that cause is less likely. The alignment of IrLat gives another example where at least one of the MSS used to create the WR was similar to that of Ir. The change may have been prompted by the Hebrew text of Isa 53:7.

26. (3:17/5) 05 has + ἄνδρες and is joined by 08 1884 d e p h w 73 mae and is probably the WRR with sy^h having corrected to the standard.

27. (3:17/17) 05*/05C1 have + (τὸ) πόνηρον and are joined by IrLat d h sy^{hmg} (Aug gig p w ar 73 mae). They supply a direct object where it was left unwritten. 05 is the only Greek MS within the ECM apparatus with this reading and yet it is widely dispersed. This paradoxical phenomenon of solitary or extremely limited Greek support combined with widespread influence is a common characteristic of WRRs that points back to the presumed WR Greek text. In contrast, the PWRs in the next section are distinguished by a coherent group of Greek MSS that often have limited diversity in translation support (see also chapter 3). The alignment of 05 with a corresponding word in each of principle languages (Latin, Syriac, and Egyptian) into which the WR was translated makes it almost certain that πόνηρον (or a synonym) was found in the WR.

28. (3:19/16–20) 05 has τὰς ἁμαρτίας ὑμῶν instead of the standard ὑμῶν τὰς ἁμαρτίας and is joined by IrLat Tert d gig p h^{vid} ar 72 73 189. The Latin witness is strong. Due to translation ambiguity, the ECM apparatus implies that neither the mae nor sy^h can reveal the word order of their *Vorlagen*. 05 is possibly the WRR.

29. (4:10/67) 08 has + καὶ ἐν ἄλλῳ οὐδενί and is joined by (1884) e h (Cyp mae sy^{hmg}). 08 preserves the WRR while an ancestor of 05, perhaps 05-Arch1, was corrected to the standard (see figure 2.1). The plus is assimilated from 4:12/8–12.

30. (4:12/2–40) 05*/05C1 reads καὶ οὐκ ἔστιν ἐν ἄλλῳ οὐδενί οὐ γάρ ἐστιν ἕτερον ὄνομα ὑπὸ τὸν οὐρανὸν [τ]ὸ δεδομένον ἀνθρώποις and manifests a rewording of the original reading as found in NA28/ ECM. It also lost of ἡ σωτηρία. Its unique order demonstrates that

05*/05C1 has likely preserved the identical reading lying behind the text of several ancient church fathers and two translations. The association is possible since these witnesses (i.e., IrLat Aug Ambr Cyp Qu^vid G (h)) have a deficient text resulting from a homoeoteleuton whose cause is easily explained from the unique 05*/05C1 Greek word order.¹² Since IrLat did not use the WR (as discussed already) but instead a Greek MS similar to one of those underlying the WR, this variant is illuminating. The section preserved in IrLat includes Peter's entire quote from 4:8b–12 except for the portion missing between ἐστίν and ἐστίν, each underlined above. Thus, the Greek text of Ir, estimated to date from AD 150 or earlier, did not have the missing portion. Thus, since it derived from an archetype of 05, the reading preserved in 05*/05C1 must be even more early. Such data proves that 05 has ancient readings. The other fathers presumably used Greek MSS akin to that of Ir.

31. (4:17/19) 08 has + τὰ ῥήματα ταῦτα and is joined by 1884 e gig sa^ms mae sy^p sy^hmg and upholds the WRR that was apparently expunged by 05.

32. (4:18/2) 05 has συνκατατιθεμένων δὲ αὐτῶν τῇ γνώμῃ (vs. καὶ, NA28/Byz) and is joined by d h^vid mae sy^hmg. It is the WRR and it appears to be a gloss based upon Luke 23:51. Its presence in 05 but not in most OL MSS suggests that subsequent to the WR, it came into 05-Arch1 without change. When it branched to 05-Arch2 and was copied into 05, there was also no change. However, when it branched to OL-Arch1 the addition was removed by editorial work that corrected toward the Alex tradition (see figure 2.1). Since OL h^vid retains it, once again it seems to have a relatively direct connection back to the WR (cf. 3:11/2–28; 18:12/26–36).

33. (4:24/7) 05 reads + καὶ ἐπιγνόντες τὴν τοῦ θεοῦ ἐνέργειαν and is joined by just d mae. It is possibly the WRR. If so, it was corrected by sy^h and not part of the OL.

34. (4:31/49) 05 has + παντὶ τῷ θέλοντι πιστεύειν and is joined by 08 1884 Ir d e r w ar mae. The variant is the WRR and was anticipated by Irenaeus.

35. (4:32/23) 08 has + οὐκ ἦν χωρισμὸς ἐν αὐτοῖς τις and is joined by (05) 1884 e r mae (d). 08 is probably the WRR. (05) has the synonym

---

12. Strutwolf, "Text Apostelgeschichte bei Irenäus," 158.

διάκρισις. There was no separation or class distinction among them in contrast to ordinary society.

36. (5:12/37) 05 has + ἐν τῷ ἱερῷ and is joined by (08 1884 sy^p) sa mae. Those in parentheses likely derived from the 05 and contain ἐν τῷ ναῷ συνηγμένοι. Its existence also in sa suggests the reading was common in ancient Egypt. Its presence in sy^p is consistent with the assumption that it was once in the sy^h tradition as a result of the WR but was removed later. 05 is probably the WRR.

37. (5:15/47) 05 reads + ἀπηλλάσσοντο γὰρ ἀπὸ πάσης ἀσθενείας ὡς εἶχεν ἕκαστος αὐτῶν and is joined by p mae. The idea is of being set free and ἀπηλλάσσοντο is a Lucan word used in the same way at 19:12/30. Its conjunction with mae makes it likely the source WRR that caused the others. 08 1884 e read καὶ ῥυσθῶσιν ἀπὸ πάσης ἀσθενείας ἧς εἶχον and has the idea of being rescued. The use of ῥυσθῶσιν may be a simplification for ἀπαλλάσσω. 629 gig w ar seem to revise 05 by replacing the unusual ἀπαλλάσσω with a form of θεραπεύω as seen at 5:36 and they read, καὶ ἐθεραπεύοντο ἀπὸ τῶν ἀσθενείων αὐτῶν.

38. (5:18/27) 05 has + καὶ ἐπορεύθη εἷς ἕκαστος εἰς τὰ ἴδια and is joined by d mae. It is possibly the WRR and appears to be a gloss from John 7:53 (Byz). Cf. 14:18/23.

39. (5:21/40) 05 has ἐγερθέντες τὸ πρωὶ καὶ συνκαλεσάμενοι (vs. συνεκάλεσαν, NA28/Byz) and is joined by d mae. 05 is a gloss and possibly the WRR also.

40. (5:31/18) 05* reads δόξῃ instead of the standard δεξιᾷ and arose apparently by an unconscious substitution of a contextually appropriate word with a similar sound. It is joined by gig p sa IrLat. The reading found in the Greek of Ir made its way into the lineage of 05 sometime after the WR and perhaps at 05-Arch1 (see figure 2.1). All the Greek MSS that once had δόξῃ corrected it including 05C1.

41. (5:35/8) 05 has τοὺς ἄρχοντας καὶ τοὺς συνέδριους instead of the standard αὐτούς and is joined by d (h) sa mae. It is probably the WRR and it influenced the sa.

42. (5:37/40) 05 omits πάντες and is joined P45 d gig p h. The variant was probably not the WRR but rather a change made after the WR in its descendant 05-Arch2 that led to the production of 05. The

word may have been removed by reference to an ancient authority akin to P45 (see figure 2.1).

43. (5:38/27) 05 reads + μὴ μιάναντες τὰς χεῖρας (vs. μὴ μολύνοντες τὰς χεῖρας ὑμῶν, 08, vs. omits, NA28/Byz) with the support of e (mae). 08 is nearly the same. It is joined by 1884 e h (mae) and is probably the WRR. Is it an eyewitness detail?

44. (5:42/30–34) While the Alex tradition, MS 614, and many Westerns have τὸν χριστὸν Ἰησοῦν, the Byz differs in word order and reads Ἰησοῦν τὸν χριστόν. In contrast, 05 reads the gloss τὸν κύριον Ἰησοῦν Χριστόν and is joined by 1875 d gig p h^{vid} 189 sa sy^p. Apparently mae lost Χριστον by an eye skip but otherwise once agreed with 05. The agreement of the sa and sy^p with 05 seems to be a result of a time when these two translations were distinctively Western.[13] Most likely Thomas corrected sy^{ph} by his model Greek MS in sy^h. 05 is probably the WRR.

45. (6:5/9) 05 has + οὗτος and is joined by d gig h t 70 sa mae sy^p Ä. 05 is probably the WRR. While sy^h seems to have corrected, sy^p confirms its presence in Syria.

46. (6:10/10–22) 05 expands to τῇ σοφίᾳ <u>τῇ οὔσῃ ἐν αὐτῷ</u> καὶ τῷ πνεύματι <u>τῷ ἁγίῳ</u> ᾧ ἐλάλει instead of the standard τῇ σοφίᾳ καὶ τῷ πνεύματι ᾧ ἐλάλει. 05 08 are joined by 1884 d e h^{vid} mae. 05 is probably the WRR.

47. (6:10/23) 05 reads + διὰ τὸ ἐλέγχεσθαι αὐτοὺς ὑπ' αὐτοῦ μετὰ πάσης παρρησίας μὴ δυνάμενοι οὖν ἀντοφθαλμεῖν τῇ αληθείᾳ and 08 has the similar διότι ἠλέγχοντο ὑπ' αὐτοῦ μετὰ πάσης παρρησίας ἐπειδὴ οὐκ ἠδύναντο ἀντιλέγειν τῇ αληθείᾳ. 05(*f) is joined by sy^{hmg}. 08 is joined by 1884f mae. Either are supported by d e h^{vid} t w 70. 05 brings in a NT hapax legomenon from 27:15/16. Here is a clear WRR.

48. (6:13/9) 05*/05C1 has + κατ[ὰ] αὐτοῦ and is joined by d h mae Ä. It is probably the WRR.

49. (6:15/35) 05 presents + ἑστῶτος ἐν μέσῳ αὐτῶν and is joined by d h t 70 mae. It is probably the WRR.

50. (7:1/9) 05 has + τῷ Στεφάνῳ and is joined by 08 1884 d e gig p h w ar 70 189 mae. It is the WRR.

---

13. Metzger, *Early Versions*, 133; McConaughy, "Early History," 335; Ropes, *Beginnings of Christianity*, ccxxi.

51. (7:4/53) 876 reads καὶ οἱ πατέρες ὑμῶν πρὸ ὑμῶν (vs. καὶ οἱ πατέρες ὑμῶν, 08, vs. καὶ οἱ πατέρες ἡμῶν οἱ πρὸ ἡμων, 05, vs. omits, NA28/Byz/614) and is joined by 1611 2138 sy^{h**}. 08 is joined by 1884 e mae and appears to have shortened the 876 wording by an eye skip but it does confirm the second person pronoun. 05 is joined by just d and seems to have revised 876 by changing the pronouns to first person so as to include the speaker and then inserts a second οἱ for balance. The double pronouns in 05 seem to confirm the longer reading. The similarity and diversity of the readings make it highly probable that 876/sy^{h**} maintain the original WRR from which both mae and 05 deviated.

52. (7:24/9) 08 reads + ἐκ τοῦ γένους αὐτοῦ and is joined by (05) 1884 d e gig sy^p sy^{h**} (mae). This is the WRR and 05 derived from it by dropping αὐτοῦ.

53. (7:24/22–26) 05 has + καὶ ἔκρυψεν αυτὸν ἐν τῇ ἄμμῳ and is joined by (629* 629C) d (w) fay Ä. Given its support, it appears that this gloss entered certain MSS following the WR and was based upon Exod 2:12.

54. (7:55/26–38) 05 reads καὶ Ἰησοῦν τὸν κύριον ἐκ δεξιῶν τοῦ θεοῦ ἑστῶτα (vs. καὶ Ἰησοῦν ἑστῶτα ἐκ δεξιῶν τοῦ θεοῦ, NA28/Byz) and is joined by d h sa^{mss} mae. It is probably the WRR and was cut from OL-Arch1. OL h has a purer line to the WR.

55. (#8:37/2–44) Alex, Byz, and the 614-group MSS avoid adding the verse. Its presence is supported by 08 945 1739 and 34 others including 10 Westerns plus mae sy^{h**} 10/11 OL MSS and Ir. It is clearly the WRR. As stated earlier, the agreement with Ir shows that his Greek *Vorlage* and at least one of the MSS used to create the WR are closely related (see figure 2.1). The caution shown by all three primary traditions is remarkable.

56. (8:39/14–16) 1739 expands to πνεῦμα ἅγιον ἐπέπεσεν ἐπὶ τὸν εὐνοῦχον ἄγγελος δὲ κυρίου (vs. πνεῦμα κυρίου, NA28/Byz) and is joined by Western leaning Alex MSS 467 876 945 1891 2298 and 14 others plus p w ar (l) mae sy^{hmg}. 05 is not extant but its archetype almost certainly had it. 1739 retains the WRR. The gloss inserted between the underlined words makes the ἄγγελος κυρίου the agent who is leading at both 8:26 and 8:39. The editor may have felt the need to show that the eunuch also received the Holy Spirit (see 2:4;

8:18; 10:44; 19:6). Conversely, M. Black argues that the longer variant should be considered the original and gives Ephr^S as another witness for it.[14]

57. (9:4/29 and 9:6/2-4) 08 reads + σκληρόν σοι πρὸς κέντρα λακτίζειν in 9:4 and is joined by 431 1292C (1884) L1188 AstA + sy^p sy^{h**} G (e mae). The wording is borrowed from the original text at 26:14/42-50. 05 is lacuna. 08 clearly preserves the WRR. Other Western witnesses have the same plus in 9:6, i.e., 629 gig r 72. There is a longer addition at 9:6 where 69C 808Cf (h) p t w ar l 189 mae have + σκληρόν σοι πρὸς κέντρα λακτίζειν τρέμων τε καὶ θαμβῶν εἶπεν κύριε τί με θέλεις ποιῆσαι καὶ ὁ κύριος πρὸς αὐτόν ἀνάστηθι instead of the standard ἀλλ' ἀνάστηθι. Here the words κύριε τί με θέλεις ποιῆσαι were apparently a paraphrase of the genuine text τί ποιήσω κύριε found at 22:10/6-10. Once the duplicated reading at the start is removed, i.e., σκληρόν . . . λακτίζειν, these witnesses preserve the WRR at 9:6. Similarly, while sy^{h**} Hil avoid the doublet, they add the clarification in 9:6, ἐπὶ τῷ γεγονότι αὐτῷ after θαμβῶν. In summary, sy^{h**} best preserves the WRR at 9:4 and 9:6 except for the four-word insertion.

58. (9:5/20) 08 has + ὁ Ναζωραῖος and is well supported by 02 04 467 1838 1884 and 7 others plus Chrys HesH Phot e gig h t w bo^{mss} sy$^{p.mss}$ sy^{h**} Ä. 05 is lacuna. 08 is the WRR and most likely mae corrected to the standard. Note that 614 and its nearest relatives avoided the gloss that came from the original text at 22:8/28-30. It appears that this WRR was popular in Egypt and Syria.

59. (10:25/2-32) 05C1 (05*) reads προσεγγίζοντος δὲ τοῦ Πέτρου εἰς τὴν Καισάρειαν προδραμών εἷς τῶν δούλων διεσάφησεν παραγεγονέναι αυτόν ὁ δὲ Κορνήλιος ἐκπηδήσας καὶ συναντήσας αὐτῷ πεσὼν πρὸς τοὺς πόδας προσεκύνησεν αὐτῷ (vs. standard text of NA28/Byz) and is joined by d gig mae sy^{hmg}. 05C1 gives the WRR and it has 27 words versus the standard of 16 words. The main difference is that one of Cornelius's servants ran ahead to tell his master that Peter had come.

60. (10:33/40-46) 05 has τὰ προστεταγμένα σοι (vs. πάντα τὰ προστεταγμένα σοι, NA28/Byz) and thus drops πάντα perhaps by

---

14. Black, "Holy Spirit," 166-67.

accident. 05 represents the WRR and is joined by P127 1127 1251 d sa mae. For the WRR to shorten is unusual.

61. (10:33/48) 05 reads ἀπό instead of the standard reading ὑπό and is joined by P45 P74 P127 01C2 02 04 1595 1642. Similarly, 08 and 1884 changed the reading to παρά. 05 is probably the WRR and it impacted some key Alexandrians. The difference is too subtle for distinguishing in the translations.

62. (10:34/2-10) 05 has ἀνοίξας δὲ τὸ στόμα Πέτρος (vs. ἀνοίξας δὲ Πέτρος τὸ στόμα, NA28/Byz/614) and is joined by P45^vid d gig G. The following translations support either reading: (sa bo mae sy^p Ä). 05 is possibly the WRR.

63. (10:38/28) 05 reads οὗτος instead of the standard ὅς and is joined by IrLat and 9/11 OL MSS + sy^p. The reading is possibly the WRR from which the archetype of mae deviated to ὡς. Perhaps Thomas corrected sy^ph in sy^h but without notation.

64. (11:2/2-12) 05 has ὁ μὲν οὖν Πέτρος διὰ ἱκανοῦ χρόνου ἠθέλησεν πορευθῆναι εἰς Ἱεροσόλυμα καὶ προσφωνήσας τοὺς ἀδελφοὺς καὶ ἐπιστηρίξας αὐτοὺς πολὺν λόγον ποιούμενος διὰ τῶν χωρῶν διδάσκων αὐτοὺς ὅς καὶ κατήντησεν αὐτοῖς καὶ ἀπήγγειλεν αὐτοῖς τὴν χάριν τοῦ θεοῦ (vs. ὅτε δὲ ἀνέβη Πέτρος εἰς Ἱερουσαλήμ, NA28/Byz) and is joined by d P127^vid mae sy^h**. 05 seems to have changed the more explicit εἰς Ἱεροσόλυμα after κατήντησεν found in mae and P127^vid into αὐτοῖς. The reading of mae lacks the μὲν, lacks the καὶ before προσφωνήσας, rewords πολὺν λόγον ποιούμενος . . . διδάσκων αὐτούς ὅς καὶ instead to καὶ ἐξῆλθεν πορευόμενος . . . διδάσκων αὐτοὺς τῷ λόγῳ, and adds the standard reading to the end. Finally, sy^h** is quite near to both 05 and mae for the first half but is corrupt following ἐπιστηρίξας showing only ἐξῆλθεν διδάσκων αὐτούς and then like mae, it adds the standard reading to the end. Therefore, 05 and P127 (only extant from 05's ποιούμενος onward) best preserve the WRR here. BL provide a detailed assessment with very similar results. They suggest that the first αὐτούς in 05 was incorrectly added and in its place should be ἐξῆλθεν (see mae sy^h**) because it was lost by accident. In addition, they assert that the first αὐτοῖς in 05 should be replaced by the adverb αὐτοῦ because it was a transmission error (see 04 05* d at 15:34).[15] In summary, to recover the WRR, one

---

15. Boismard and Lamouille, *Texte occidental reconstitution*, 1:161, 2:77.

probably needs to start with the 05 reading, retain the first αὐτούς, add ἐξῆλθεν, insert εἰς Ἱεροσόλυμα (see mae P127^vid) for αὐτοῖς even though 05's *Vorlage* likely had the gloss αὐτοῦ.[16]

65. (11:2/14–24) 05 reads οἱ δὲ ἐκ περιτομῆς ἀδελφοὶ διεκρίνοντο πρὸς αὐτὸν (vs. διεκρίνοντο πρὸς αὐτὸν οἱ ἐκ περιτομῆς, NA28/Byz) and is joined by (P127) (d gig l sa mae) Ä. 05 preserves the WRR that reorders the standard text and adds δέ and also ἀδελφοί. The reordering helps to complete the large expansion at 11:2/2–12.

66. (11:26/2–54) 05C2 is joined by (05*) (05C1) d p* mae (sy^hmg). This portion is a lengthy paraphrase of the standard reading. The WRR seems best preserved by mae. 05*/05C1 give evidence of an eye skip from the ending of συναχθῆναι to the end of διδάξαι and then reworded it to συνεχύθησαν ὄχλον ἱκανόν. However, 05C2 corrected this error while retaining other mistakes. The resultant meaning is nearly the same.

67. (13:14/2–4) 08 joined by 1884 e mae in reading Παῦλος δὲ καὶ Βαρναβᾶς (vs. αὐτοὶ δὲ, NA28/Byz). It is possibly the WRR from which 05 and sy^h corrected.

68. (13:28/12–29/16) The WRR appears to be closest to mae. It does not change the standard text but adds ἠτοῦντο τὸν Πιλᾶτον αὐτὸν σταυρῶσαι πάλιν ἐπιτυχόντες (αὐτοῦ) καὶ after it and prior to 13:29/18–30. 05 in several variations proceeded to change the WRR by paraphrasing 13:28/12–18 into κρίναντες δὲ αὐτὸν παρέδωκαν Πιλάτῳ ἵνα εἰς ἀναίρεσιν. 05*f was corrected first to 05C1 and then to 05C2b. The advance in thought here is that the Jews had judged Jesus before bringing him to Pilate. It then goes with the standard text at 13:29/2–16 as does mae. Also, like mae, it proceeds by portraying the Jews as pleading with Pilate for permission to crucify Jesus and indicate that he agrees. The addition stops there. As a result, the fulfillment in 13:29/2–16 refers not to the climactic death of Christ but rather to the trial of Jesus prior to crucifixion. OL 70 and sy^hmg match very closely and seem to build upon the WRR. Just as mae, they present the standard text from 13:28/12–29/16. However, they make the text say that *after* Jesus was crucified the rulers asked Pilate to take Jesus down from the tree. Pilate assents. By changing

---

16. Boismard, "Problem of Literary Criticism," 148–53, identifies the long reading as Lucan because of its style.

the time to after, these editors include the death of Jesus as part of what had been fulfilled. The result is a text more in line with the standard. Here is a good example of how the WR Greek text was often further revised before being translated into various languages. In summary, the original revision denoted as the WRR did nothing but confuse the text. The corrections to it were not much better.

69. (13:33/28–36) 05 is joined by just Or[vid] d gig in reading τῷ πρώτῳ ψαλμῷ γέγραπται. This reading apparently entered the transmission lineage of 05 d gig some time after the WR.

70. (14:2/29) 05 reads + ὁ δὲ κύριος ἔδωκεν ταχὺ εἰρήνην (vs. ὁ κύριος δὲ τάχει δέδωκεν εἰρήνην, 619, vs. ὁ δὲ θεός εἰρήνην ἐποίησεν, 08) and is joined by d sy[hmg] (mae). 619 is joined by gig p w (mae). 08 is joined by 1884 e. Given that the three main translations align with the 05 reading, it is the WRR.

71. (14:7/7) 05 has + καὶ ἐκινήθη ὅλον τὸ πλῆθος ἐπὶ τῇ διδαχῇ ὁ δὲ Παῦλος καὶ Βαρνάβας διέτριβον ἐν Λύστροις (vs. τὸν λόγον τοῦ θεοῦ καὶ ἐξεπλήσσετο πᾶσα ἡ πολυπληθία ἐπὶ τῇ διδαχῇ αὐτῶν ὁ δὲ Παῦλος καὶ Βαρνάβας διέτριβον ἐν Λύστροις, 08) and is joined by d h[vid] w[vid] mae. 08 and 1884f e start with 05 and then add τὸν λόγον τοῦ θεοῦ in front of it, replace ἐκινήθη with the more positive ἐξεπλήσσετο, ὅλον with πᾶσα, πλῆθος with πολυπληθία (not used in the NT), and place αὐτῶν after διδαχῇ. The expansions emphasize the impact from the preaching of Paul and Barnabas and confirm that they stayed a while in Lystra. 05 is the WRR and Thomas probably revised sy[ph] to the standard in sy[h] (without giving a sy[hmg] note).

72. (14:15/28–38) 05 includes ὑμῖν τὸν θεὸν following the word εὐαγγελιζόμενοι meaning "proclaim God to you" and is joined by just IrLat[vid] d mae. However, given its pre-redaction support in IrLat[vid] and its post-redaction agreement with mae, this variant is possibly the WRR.

73. (#14:19/2–4) 08 reads + διατριβόντων δὲ αὐτῶν καὶ διδασκόντων and is joined by many others including 05C1 (h mae sy[hmg] G) and is the WRR.

74. (#14:19/16–22) The sy[hmg] shows καὶ διαλεγομένων αὐτῶν παρρησίᾳ (ἀν)έπεισαν τοὺς ὄχλους ἀποστῆναι (ἀπ)' αὐτῶν λέγοντες ὅτι οὐδὲν ἀληθὲς λέγουσιν ἀλλὰ πάντα ψεύδονται ἐπισείσαντες τοὺς ὄχλους (vs. [καὶ] ἐπισείσαντες τοὺς ὄχλους, 05*/05C1, vs. καὶ πείσαντες τοὺς

ὄχλους, NA28/Byz/614-group) and is closely joined by some key Alex MSS 04 81 181 1175 1739(Cf3) and many others plus mae A G. There are twenty alternatives in the ECM. 05* and 05C1 are joined by d^vid e gig sy^p and indirectly reflect the WRR after their purging since they retain ἐπισείσαντες instead of the standard πείσαντες. The WRR is well preserved by sy^hmg mae and some key Alex MSS. The Byz, most core Alex MSS, and the 614-group stay pure.

75. (15:2/30–48) sy^hmg has ἐλέγον γὰρ ὁ Παῦλος μένειν οὕτως καθώς τις ἐπίστευσεν διισχυριζόμενος οἱ δὲ ἐληλυθότες ἀπὸ Ἰερουσαλὴμ παρήγγειλαν τότε τῷ Παύλῳ καὶ Βαρναβᾷ καί τισιν ἄλλοις ἀναβαίνειν (vs. ἔταξαν ἀναβαίνειν Παῦλον καὶ Βαρναβᾶν καί τινας ἄλλους ἐξ αὐτῶν, NA28/Byz) and is joined by (05) (d) mae. Since sy^hmg and mae agree, they are probably the WRR. 05 tweaks it by changing τις ἐπίστευσεν to επιστευσαν and replacing τότε with αὐτοῖς. The gloss adds the idea that Paul insisted that gentiles should not conform to Jewish customs. It then portrays the men from Jerusalem as ordering Paul and Barnabas to go up to the leaders in Jerusalem. In the standard text, it is presumably the church and not the visitors that made the plan. Moreover, they appoint them to go rather than command. None of the OL MSS except d have the WRR. It appears 05-Arch1 was corrected by Alex-Arch2 before it became OL-Arch1 from which most OL MSS sprouted (see figure 2.1).

76. (15:20/37) 1739 reads + καὶ ὅσα ἂν μὴ θέλωσιν αὐτοῖς γίνεσθαι ἑτέροις μὴ ποιεῖν and is joined precisely by twelve other MSS and is similar to four more. It also has the support of (IrLat ar sa Ä). 05 d has four apparently derived changes. It lacks ἄν, has ἑαυτοῖς, θέλουσιν, and ποιεῖτε. The overall gloss came from the PWR/WRR in 15:29. Note that 614 does *not* have the plus here. It shows more faithfulness than 05 or IrLat. MS 1739 is probably the WRR. The mae is not extant beyond 15:3 and sy^h probably was conformed to the standard.

77. (16:35/8–12) 05 reads <u>συνῆλθον</u> οἱ στρατηγοὶ <u>ἐπὶ τὸ αὐτὸ εἰς τὴν ἀγορὰν καὶ ἀναμνησθέντες τὸν σεισμὸν τὸν γεγονότα ἐφοβήθησαν καὶ</u> ἀπέστειλαν (vs. ἀπέστειλαν οἱ στρατηγοί, NA28/Byz) and is joined by d sy^hmg (P127^vid). MS 05 is the WRR.

78. (18:4/18–20) 629 reads <u>ἐντιθέμενος τὸ ὄνομα τοῦ κυρίου Ἰησοῦ ἔπειθέν τε</u> (vs. <u>καὶ ἐντιθεὶς τὸ ὄνομα τοῦ κυρίου Ἰησοῦ ἔπειθεν δὲ</u>,

05(*f), vs. ἔπειθέν τε, NA28/Byz) and is joined by gig w (h ar sy^hmg). 05(*f) is joined by d. MS 629 is the WRR. It appears that when 05 copied the text of 05-Arch2, it replaced the middle voice ἐντιθέμενος with καὶ ἐντιθεὶς and changed the τε to δὲ.

79. (18:6/1) 05 has + πολλοῦ δὲ λόγου γινομένου καὶ γραφῶν διερμηνευομένων and is joined by d h sy^hmg. 05 is probably the WRR (cf. 05 wording at 11:2/2–12).

80. (18:12/26–36) sy^h** reads *καὶ ἐπε(τί)θεντο τὰς χεῖρας ἐπ᾽ αὐτὸν† καὶ ἤγαγον αὐτὸν *πρὸς τὸν ἀνθύπατον† ἐπὶ τὸ βῆμα (vs. καὶ ἐπιθέντες τὰς χεῖρας ἤγαγον αὐτὸν ἐπὶ τὸ βῆμα, 05, vs. επε(τί)[θεντο αὐτῷ τὰς χεῖρας καὶ ἤγαγον πρὸς τὸν ἀνθύπατον, h, vs. καὶ ἤγαγον αὐτὸν ἐπὶ τὸ βῆμα, NA28/Byz) and is joined by (05) (d) (h) (sa). Thomas of Harkel corrected sy^ph as noted in sy^h** by retaining the six underlined words that match the standard. It appears that sy^h** was the original WRR. Downstream, 05-Arch1 paraphrased the first seven words of sy^h** into καὶ ἐπιθέντες τὰς χεῖρας and also dropped πρὸς τὸν ἀνθύπατον. The revised form became distributed to 05 d sa. OL h possibly started with the WRR but with καί already lost from the start. It then shortened ἐπ᾽ αὐτὸν to αὐτῷ. Next it removed αὐτὸν before πρὸς, and ἐπὶ τὸ βῆμα from the end perhaps because they were judged as mixture from the NA28 reading. OL h appears to have its own lineage back to the WR separate from that of 05 (cf. 3:11/2–28; 4:18/2).

81. (18:27/2–30) 05 tells the reader why Apollos took interest in Corinth. It is joined by d sy^hmg. The gloss states that some visiting Corinthians heard him speak and therefore urged him to go to Corinth. When he consented, the brethren wrote to the disciples in Corinth so that they might receive him. The gloss could be part of genuine tradition. BL add the testimony from Vg(R^mg), i.e., a marginal reading in *la bible de Rosas*. They consider this expansion to be from Luke's first longer edition.[17] 05 is probably the WRR.

82. (19:1/2–30) P38^vid reads θέλοντος δὲ τοῦ Παύλου κατὰ τὴν ἰδίαν βουλὴν πορεύεσθαι εἰς Ἱεροσόλυμα εἶπεν αὐτῷ τὸ πνεῦμα ὑποστρέφειν εἰς τὴν Ἀσίαν διελθὼν δὲ τὰ ἀνωτερικὰ μέρη ἔρχεται (vs. ἐγένετο δὲ ἐν τῷ τὸν Ἀπολλὼ εἶναι ἐν Κορίνθῳ Παῦλον διελθόντα τὰ ἀνωτερικὰ μέρη [κατ]ελθεῖν/ἐλθεῖν, NA28/Byz) and is joined by 05 d sy^hmg. The

---

17. Boismard and Lamouille, *Texte occidental reconstitution*, 2:131.

ECM shows a split guiding line (SGL) between κατελθεῖν and ἐλθεῖν. The addition shows the Spirit correcting Paul and is based upon the 614/Byz reading at 18:21/9 combined with an incorrect interpretation of 18:22. The longer 614/Byz reading at 18:21/9 explains why Paul could not stay at Ephesus. Acts 18:22 then implies that Paul went up to Jerusalem at that time. However, it is vague enough that someone might think he only went up to the church at Caesarea. To remove the apparent contradiction, the WRR editor justified why Paul never went. P38[vid] is the WRR.

83. (19:2/34–40) P38[vid] reads πνεῦμα ἅγιον <u>λαμβάνουσίν τινες</u> ἠκούσαμεν (vs. πνεῦμα ἅγιον <u>ἔστιν</u> ἠκούσαμεν, NA28/Byz/05C2) and is joined by 05* d sy[hmg] (P41) (sa). It is an attempt to make these disciples seem less ignorant.[18] P38[vid] is the WRR.

84. (19:14/2–20, 21) 05(*f) rewords and expands the entire section as ἐν οἷς καὶ υἱοὶ Σκευᾶ τινος ἱερέως ἠθέλησαν τὸ αὐτὸ ποιῆσαι ἔθος εἶχαν <u>τοὺς τοιούτους</u> ἐξορκίζειν καὶ εἰσελθόντες πρὸς τὸν δαιμονιζόμενον ἤρξαντο ἐπικαλεῖσθαι τὸ ὄνομα λέγοντες παραγγέλλομέν σοι ἐν Ἰησοῦ ὃν Παῦλος <u>ἐξελθεῖν κηρύσσει</u>. It is joined by (P38 d h sy[hmg]). 05 appears to give the WRR with the exception of the word order. The first underlined section disagrees with P38 and sy[hmg], which place the words after ἐξορκίζειν. The ECM considers the second a simple mistake. The next closest witness is sy[hmg]. Its only weakness is that it adds ἑπτά in front of υἱοί as an intrusion from the standard reading. P38 shows the least stability. Its edits were to add Ἰουδαίου after Σκευᾶ, add ἀρχ- before ἱερέως, write ἔχοντες instead of εἶχαν, drop τόν, and add ὁ ἀπόστολος after Παῦλος. The first two changes were insertions from the standard text. Although longer, the WRR more generally identifies the exorcists as sons of a priest rather than sons of a Jewish chief priest. Moreover, their practice was to call upon the Name, i.e., upon Jesus. Thus, it recalls the understanding of the primitive disciples seen in the standard text at 5:40/22–28. They considered suffering for the name of Yahweh (implied) and for the name of Jesus to be equivalent. In short, their words imply that Jesus is fully God (see Exod 3:14; John 8:58).

85. (21:1/45) 05 reads Πάταρα <u>καὶ Μύρα</u> (vs. Πάταρα <u>ἔπειτα Μύρα</u>, gig/sa, vs. Πάταρα, NA28/Byz) and is joined by P41 plus (gig w sa). BL

---

18. Barrett, *Commentary on Acts*, 2:894.

believe the longer text should be taken more seriously because it seems to be the one that avoided a homoeoteleuton. They complain that if key Alex witnesses had the longer text, the members of the GNT committee would have said that the shorter one came by an eye skip.[19] 05 is possibly the WRR. However, it may have entered the 05 lineage at 05-Arch1 after the WR. In either case, it appears to be a gloss.

86. (22:7/31) 08 has σκληρόν σοι πρὸς κέντρα λακτίζειν (vs. omits, NA28/Byz) and is joined by 228 996^vid 1884 Ath Marcell e gig ar sy^hmg. 08 is probably the WRR and was likely assimilated from the standard text at 26:14/42–50.

87. (25:24/58–68) Instead of βοῶντες μὴ δεῖν αὐτὸν ζῆν μηκέτι, sy^hmg/ar have a long expansion where Festus discusses how the Jews wanted Paul delivered to torture without trial contrary to the Roman law established by Caesar. Though poorly supported, its clarifying and expansive nature makes it possibly the WRR.

88. (25:25/2–32) Instead of the standard verse, sy^hmg has ἀκούσας δὲ καὶ τουτὸ κατὰ μέρος κατελαβόμην ἐν μηδενὶ αὐτὸν ἔνοχον εἶναι θανάτου (ὡς δὲ εἶπον/εἰπόντος δέ μου) θέλεις κριθῆναι μετ᾽ αὐτῶν ἐν Ἱεροσολύμοις Καίσαρα ἐπεκαλέσατο. It could be translated, "Now when I heard this also, I partly understood that there was not a single deed that made him liable to death. Then after I said, 'Do you want to be judged among them in Jerusalem,' he appealed to Caesar." It is possibly the WRR. However, its absence from all other witnesses makes that unlikely.

The Proto-Western Text of Acts

Readings of the reconstructed proto-Western text will be called Proto-Western Readings (PWRs) or Primary Western Readings. The proto-Western text (X) is presented here as the archetypical MS that both preceded and contributed to the original form of the WR (see figure 2.1). Many PWRs entered the WR but a greater portion did not. For this reason, the proto-Western archetype (or a copy from it) is thought to be one of several Greek MSS that contributed to the WR archetype. This

---

19. Boismard and Lamouille, *Texte occidental reconstitution*, 1:6, are referring to Metzger, *Textual Commentary*, 427.

section will demonstrate that the proto-Western text is very ancient since it can be repeatedly shown to be more primitive than the ancient WR. The following ten MSS are reliable bearers of the PWR in the book of Acts: 383 614 1292 1505 1611 1890 2138 2147 2412 2495. Overall, the most faithful representatives are 614 and its sister 2412, which were both copied from the same *Vorlage*.[20] The ten will often be referred to as the "core PWR MSS." The following list provides about one hundred variant units. Most of them describe a PWR. Some examples are also given to show readings that were set aside because of secondary features. Many of them discuss the apparent relationship between the PWR and the WRR.

1. (1:21/37) 1611 reads κύριος Ἰησοῦς <u>Χριστός</u> (vs. κύριος Ἰησοῦς, NA28/Byz) and is joined by 05 876 1718 1838 plus d mae sy[h]. The leaders of the core PWR MSS mentioned above are 614 and 2412. Yet both have the standard reading here. As BL have observed, these MSS have been clearly revised with a Byz standard MS across 1:1–5:32.[21] As a matter of fact, none of the core PWR MSS have a significant amount of characteristic readings in this portion. Thus, 614/2412 provide only partial evidence for the PWR archetype in the early chapters. Given the characteristic "Western" nature of this variant, its three "Western" related MSS of 876 1611 and 1838 and sy[h] may uphold the PWR (though only 1611 is within the core group).[22] Moreover, the alignment of 05 with mae suggests that it is possibly the WRR also. Because across Acts the PWR manifests itself as the foundation of the WRR, the places where they are equal also imply that the PWR archetype (or a copy from it) was one of the sources for the WR that is presumed to have occurred within or just before the AD 150–175 period (see figure 2.1).

2. (#2:1/22) 614 has <u>οἱ ἀπόστολοι</u> ὁμοθυμαδὸν (vs. ὁμοθυμαδὸν, Byz, vs. ὁμοῦ, NA28) and is joined by core MSS 1505 2412 2495 and 40 others. Byz is joined by 04C3 08 18 35 etc. plus Ath[mss] Chrys Eus[vid] LeontPrCP SevGab (sy[p] sy[h]). NA28 is joined by 01 02 03 04* 81 94

---

20. MS 614 is a sibling rather than a descendent of MS 2412 because, while they repeatedly preserve the common errors of their *Vorlage*, they also disagree when their own scribe has produced the mistake.

21. Boismard and Lamouille, *Texte occidental reconstitution*, 1:25.

22. However, in this case, the limited support from the core PWR MSS suggests that this expansion might rather be a WRR that was later placed into a few "Western" related MSS. Stanley Porter provided this observation during his review.

323 945 1704 Ath^T Cyr Vg d e gig r 189 Ä (sy^p sy^h). 614 probably retains the PWR.

3. (2:30/16–18) *1611* reads αὐτῷ ὤμοσεν (vs. ὤμοσεν αὐτῷ, NA28/Byz) and is joined by *876 1718 2138* IrLat. Although the support is minimal, the italicized ones are common allies of MS 614. *1611* is possibly the PWR.

4. (2:38/28–30) 614 has <u>τοῦ κυρίου</u> Ἰησοῦ Χριστοῦ (vs. <u>τοῦ κυρίου ἡμῶν</u> Ἰησοῦ Χριστοῦ, 876, vs. Ἰησοῦ Χριστοῦ, NA28/Byz) and is joined by 05 08 2412 and 15 others plus Bas^T Chrys^pt d e r sa. It is probably the PWR. 876 is joined by 1611 1718 2138 p mae sy^h plus Bas^mss Cyr CyrH^vid Epiph^vid Hyp MarcEr^T Thdrt Lcf. It is the WRR and was apparently formed by adding ἡμῶν to the PWR. Both 05 and 08 apparently reversed the process and thus equal the PWR here.

5. (2:40/28–32) 614 reads ταύτης τῆς σκολιᾶς (vs. τῆς σκολιᾶς ταύτης, NA28/Byz) and is joined by Western leaning 05 1838f2 2298 2412 2495 and 9 others. Translations usually cannot distinguish between such subtle changes. 614 is probably the PWR that became the WRR.

6. (2:43/22–28) There are ten alternatives. 614 has + τῶν χειρῶν and is joined by relatives (08) (181) 431 876 1127 (1501) (1884) and core PWR MSS 1292 1611 2138 2412 and a few others plus (e sy^h). 614 is the PWR.

7. (3:23/31) 614 has + αὐτῆς and 467 has + αὐτοῦ. 614 is joined by relatives 1501 2412 2652 and Chrys^pt ConstAp^T Eus bo sy^p Ä. 467 seems to be a gloss upon 614 and is joined by AnastS ConstAp^mss Or. Moreover, PsClemLat Tert and the OL p support either of them. The mass of early fathers shows that this reading is ancient. 614 has preserved the PWR. The addition of αὐτῆς is unusual because its antecedent ἡ ψυχή is located twelve words earlier and because the feminine noun makes it appear to say that anyone disobedient to Christ would be cut off from "her people" but the reference is generic, causing some to revise to "his people."

8. (3:26/20) *1611* omits (vs. αὐτὸν, NA28/Byz) and is joined by relatives 05 876 945 1890* 2138 and 5 others plus IrLat d gig p* sy^h. It maintains the PWR when most Westerns including 614 were corrected to the standard.

9. (4:1/13) 1611 has + τὰ ῥήματα ταῦτα and is joined by relatives 05 (08) 876 (1884) 1890 2138 and 3 others plus d (e) (gig) h (p) w. Those in parentheses only change the word order. Both readings can be supported by sy^p sy^{hmg}. 1611 is probably the PWR that became the WRR. Meanwhile, 614 and mae were corrected to standard.

10. (4:9/9) 1611 has the gloss + ὑφ' ὑμῶν and is joined by relatives (05) (08) (876) 915 (1884) 1611 2138 and 2 others. Those with a parenthesis have ἀφ' in the place of ὑφ'. Either may be joined by: IrLat d e gig p* h sa^{ms} mae sy^p sy^h. 1611 is probably both the PWR and the WRR. Most of the 614-group was corrected.

11. (5:22/10-20) 05f has <u>καὶ ἀνοίξαντες τὴν φυλακὴν</u> οὐκ εὗρον αὐτοὺς <u>ἔσω</u> (vs. <u>καὶ ἀνοίξαντες τὴν φυλακὴν</u> οὐχ εὗρον αὐτούς, 629, vs. <u>ἀνοίξαντες τὴν φυλακὴν</u> οὐκ εὗρον αὐτοὺς ἐν τῇ φυλακῇ, 1611, vs. οὐκ εὗρον αὐτοὺς ἐν τῇ φυλακῇ, NA28/Byz/614) and is joined by d mae. 05f is the WRR. 629 is joined by Vg w 72 189. MS 1611 is joined by relatives 876 2138 plus p/2^{vid} sy^{h**} and is probably the PWR. The WRR may have started with the PWR, added a conjunction at the beginning, and replaced ἐν τῇ φυλακῇ with ἔσω at the end to avoid repetition. The added participle comes from 5:23. An ancestor of MS 629 responded to the WRR by removing ἔσω from the end. Apparently the WRR made it to 05-Arch1 unchanged. However, when it branched to OL-Arch1, it was changed by a MS like 629 and flowed downstream to the OL w 72 189 and the Vg (see figure 2.1). All the core PWR MSS (except for 1611 2138) were revised to the standard. Significantly, take notice that after 5:32 both 614 and 2412 demonstrate remarkable independence, showing little evidence of conformity to any standard.

12. (5:33/7) 614 has + τὰ ῥήματα ταῦτα and is joined by 431^{vid} 876 1127 1292 1563C 1611 2138 2412 and p bo^{mss} mae sy^p sy^{h**}. Every MS is Western related except 1563C. The constellation of witnesses indicates that 614 is both the PWR and the reading that became the WRR. An ancestor of 05 such as 05-Arch1 presumably was revised according to the standard. Notice that 614 became joined by a solid group of MSS as soon as the 5:32 threshold was crossed.

13. (5:36/16-22) 614 offers + μέγαν (vs. omits, NA28/Byz) and is joined by 02C (05) 08 1127 1292 1884 2147 2412 (2495) and many others plus (d e gig w ar 189) mae sy^p. 614 is therefore the PWR that also

became the WRR. 05/d is unique, having adjusted the placement of μέγαν. NA28/Byz preserves the original.

14. (5:39/19) 876 reads οὔτε ὑμεῖς οὔτε βασιλεῖς οὔτε τύραννοι <u>ἀπόσχεσθε</u> οὖν ἀπὸ τῶν ἀνδρῶν τούτων and is joined by 1611 2138 sy^h** (mae). It seems to be the PWR that became the identical WRR. 614 reads + <u>ἀπόσχεσθε</u> οὖν ἀπὸ τῶν ἀνδρῶν τούτων and is joined by relatives 431 1127 1292 2412. These MSS lack the first half of the gloss. 08 has + οὔτε ὑμεῖς οὔτε οἱ ἄρχοντες ὑμῶν and is joined by 1884 e gig ar. It dropped the second part of the gloss perhaps thinking it was a doublet from 5:38/12–20. Moreover, it may have sanitized the potentially seditious reference to Roman leaders and replaced it with one referring to Jewish leaders only. It seems unrealistic as it is. Gamaliel was already speaking to the rulers of Israel and it is doubtful that he would recognize the Romans as their rulers. 05 reads οὔτε ὑμεῖς οὔτε βασιλεῖς οὔτε τύραννοι <u>ἀπέχεσθε</u> οὖν ἀπὸ τῶν <u>ἀνθρώπων</u> τούτων and is supported by 913 d h. It seems to derive from 876 by harmonizing ἀνδρῶν to ἀνθρώπων in 5:38 and by adjusting the imperative to the present tense. Though on the surface the longer readings could be a conflation of the shorter ones (see 08 and 614), the development seems to be reversed. NA28/Byz is original. BL also regard the longer version as the Western text but prefer the wording of 08 for the first half of the reading.[23]

15. (5:41/7) 614 has + ἀποστόλους and is joined by Westerns 05 431 876 1292 1611 2138 2412 plus d p mae sy^h. Such is the PWR and likely the WRR.

16. (#5:41/22–28) 614 has ὑπὲρ τοῦ ὀνόματος <u>τοῦ κυρίου Ἰησοῦ</u> κατηξιώθησαν and is found in 6/10 core PWR MSS and in its relatives 08 431 1884 and just four others plus e. 614 is the PWR and a gloss that inserts three words.

17. (6:7/10) 614 reads κυρίου (vs. θεοῦ, NA28/Byz) and is joined by 05 08 044 431 1292 1611 1884 2138 2412 plus Chrys OrLat d e p h t w 70 sy^h. Of the Greek MSS, only 044 is not Western leaning. 614 preserves the PWR and the WRR.

18. (6:8/29) 614 has διὰ τοῦ ὀνόματος <u>τοῦ</u> κυρίου Ἰησοῦ Χριστοῦ (vs. διὰ τοῦ ὀνόματος κυρίου Ἰησοῦ Χριστοῦ, 05, vs. <u>ἐν τῷ</u> ὀνόματι <u>τοῦ</u> κυρίου Ἰησοῦ Χριστοῦ, 08, vs. omits, NA28/Byz) and is joined by

---

23. Boismard and Lamouille, *Texte occidental reconstitution*, 1:141, 2:40–41.

its relatives 431 876 915 1292 1611 1838 2138 2412 and thirteen others. In addition, it has the support of the translations (d p 70 sa mae sy^(h**)). 614 is the PWR. The fact that 05 08 1884 are very similar but poorly supported confirms that the 614 reading also became the WRR.

19. (#7:20/39) 614 has + αὐτοῦ and is joined by 05 08 383 1292 1611 including many Westerns and many others plus Vg d e gig p w 189 sy^p sy^h. The pronoun polishes the sentence where the article τοῦ is being used as a pronoun in τοῦ πατρός. Here it appears that the PWR became the WRR as seen in 05 and some OL MSS.

20. (#7:37/40) 614 reads + αὐτοῦ ἀκούσεσθε and is joined by 04 (05*) 05C1 08 1292 1611 1890 and many others plus d e gig p w ar bo mae sy^p sy^h A G. 614 offers the PWR. Its tremendous influence probably arose because it became part of the WR and was tied to an important Messianic text. It was added from the LXX of Deut 18:15. Here is another great example of the purity within the core Alex and Byz.

21. (#7:43/49) 614 has Βαβυλῶνος λέγει κύριος παντοκράτωρ (vs. Βαβυλῶνος λέγει κύριος ὁ θεὸς ὁ παντοκράτωρ ὄνομα αὐτῷ, 1611, vs. Βαβυλῶνος, NA28/Byz) and is joined by 431 1292 2412 sy^h and is probably the PWR. 1611 is joined by 876 1832 1890 mae sy^(h**) and is four words longer. Since sy^(h**) indicates places where Thomas of Harkel marked for deletion words absent from his Greek exemplar (i.e., those underlined above), it is evident that Thomas perceived the 614/sy^h reading as more primitive and authentic than that of 1611.[24] Moreover, the fact that 1611 precisely matches the wording of the LXX (see Amos 5:27b) suggests it was harmonized. Finally, if the primitive reading was the fuller one why should it be curtailed in the manner seen here? Therefore, 1611 is probably the WRR. The WRR was removed somewhere in 05's lineage and thus never became part of MS 05. The change may have occurred in 05-Arch1. Once removed, the gloss never reached OL-Arch1 and the OL (see figure 2.1). The fate of 08 would seem to be parallel. NA28/Byz is joined by 05 08 etc. plus Vg d e gig p h w 189 sy^p Ä A G.

22. (9:30/18) 614 offers + νυκτός and is joined by (08) 431 876 1292 1501 1611 1832 (1884) 1890 2138 2412 L1825 sy^p sy^(h**) (e gig p w r 189 sa mae). 614 preserves both the PWR and the WRR.

---

24. See Juckel, "Harklensische Apparat," 231–43.

23. (9:34/18–20) 614 reads ὁ Χριστός (vs. ὁ κύριος Ἰησοῦς (ὁ) Χριστός, 02, vs. Ἰησοῦς ὁ Χριστός, Byz, vs. Ἰησοῦς Χριστός, NA28) and is supported by 1292 1505 1611* 1890 2138 2495 and 9 others plus Cyr. It is the PWR. ECM shows a SGL between the Byz and Alex. The SGL marks places where the ECM editors found two or more variants with an equal claim to originality.[25] 02 is joined by 14 others plus gig p t w 67 70 sa bo^{ms} mae. Given the expansive nature and support for its reading, 02 probably represents the now lost 05 reading and the WRR.

24. (11:28/28–30) 614 omits μέλλειν and is joined by P45 P74 35* 2147 2412 and 36 others including numerous Westerns plus Epiph. P45 confirms that the reading was ancient. It was also found in the Byz 35*. 614 preserves the PWR but most of its core group were corrected to the standard.

25. (12:1/35) 614 has + ἐν τῇ Ἰουδαίᾳ and is joined by P127^{vid} 05 1595 2412 d p w mae sy^{h**}. 614 is the PWR and the WRR. The others returned to the standard.

26. (12:14/23) 614 reads + αὐτῷ and is joined by 08 876 1127 1611 1832 1884 1890 2138 2412 e sy^p sy^{h**}. 614 is the PWR.

27. (12:20/14–22) 614 reads ὁμοθυμαδὸν δὲ <u>ἐξ ἀμφοτέρων τῶν μερῶν παρῆσαν πρὸς αὐτὸν</u> (vs. <u>οἱ</u> δὲ ὁμοθυμαδὸν <u>ἐξ ἀμφοτέρων τῶν πόλεων</u> παρῆσαν πρὸς <u>τὸν βασιλέα</u>, 05/sy^{hmg}, vs. ὁμοθυμαδὸν δὲ παρῆσαν *ἐξ αμφοτέρων τῶν πόλεων† πρὸς αὐτόν, sy^{h**}, vs. ὁμοθυμαδὸν δὲ παρῆσαν πρὸς αὐτὸν, NA28/Byz/sy^h) and is joined by (808 1127) 2412. ECM offers eleven alternatives. 05 is joined by d mae sy^{hmg}. The reading of sy^{h**} is unique. The 614 reading was apparently modified into 05's (changes underlined) by specifying Tyre and Sidon as cities instead of regions and referring to Herod explicitly as τὸν βασιλέα. The reading of sy^{h**} represents changes in a Greek MS that began with the reading of 05 and partially returned to the standard by removing οἱ and replacing τὸν βασιλέα with αὐτον. It also moved παρῆσαν earlier in order to smooth out the reading. 614 is the PWR and 05 the WRR. The ancestry of this variant in Syria prior to reaching the form in the Syriac Harklensis (sy^h) can be traced and is instructive. First, the variant seen in 614 was an ancient one current in Syria. It was then revised according to the popular WR. Next, the Greek text

---

25. ECM 3:1:1, intro, 18, 24–25, 31.

was translated into Syriac ca. AD 507 as part of the Philoxeniana NT (sy^{ph}), whose reading is now shown in sy^{hmg}. Finally, Thomas revised the sy^{ph} in AD 616 by his Greek exemplar to the precise wording of sy^{h**}, first without the markings. However, he was not done. Knowing also the standard reading, he preferred it and thus marked the portion of text to be removed (as shown above) with an asterisk and an obelisk (†) in order to form sy^{h}.

28. (12:25/8) 614 has Σαῦλος <u>ὅς ἐπεκλήθη Παῦλος</u> (vs. Σαῦλος, NA28/Byz) and is joined by 1127(*f) 2412 p mae sy^{h**}. 614 gives the PWR and also the WRR. 05 and all the remaining Westerns were presumably corrected to the standard. 614 makes an associated change in 13:7/24–28 so that it already reads Παῦλον.

29. (#13:5/38) 614 reads ὑπηρετ<u>οῦντα</u> <u>αὐτοῖς</u> (vs. ὑπηρέτην, NA28/Byz) and is joined by 05 1292 2412 d p sa mae sy^{p} sy^{hmg}. This PWR became the WRR. Most of the Westerns removed it by correcting to the standard over time.

30. (#13:7/24–28) 614 has Βαρναβᾶν καὶ <u>Π</u>αῦλον (vs. Βαρναβᾶν καὶ <u>Σ</u>αῦλον, NA28/Byz) and is joined by 1127 1243 1611 2138 2412 w 189 sa^{mss} bo^{mss} mae. 614 is the PWR even though most Westerns corrected it. The PWR is probably also the WRR with both 05 and sy^{h} having been returned to the standard.

31. (#13:28/11) 614 has + ἐν αὐτῷ and is joined by 05 629 1127 1292 1611 2412 Vg d gig p t w 70 sin 189 sa bo mae sy^{h**} Ä. 614 is both the PWR and the WRR.

32. (#13:31/29) 614 reads + ἄχρι and is joined by 05 876 1127 1292 1611 1832 1890 2138 2243 2412 Vg d p t w 70 73 189 sy^{h}. 614 is the PWR and possibly also the WRR, given its OL support. The ECM apparatus should add 05 to its attestation.

33. (#13:33/20) 614 has <u>τὸν κύριον ἡμῶν</u> Ἰησοῦν (vs. <u>τὸν κύριον</u> Ἰησοῦν <u>Χριστόν</u>, 05, vs. Ἰησοῦν, NA28/Byz) and is joined by 1292 2412 sy^{h**}. 614 could be the PWR that was adjusted to become the WRR or it might be that no PWR exists in this passage. If the latter is true, MSS 614, 1292, and 2412 would have revised the WRR. By their agreement in error, these MSS do sometimes manifest later changes (e.g., 17:24/32–34; 18:2/60). However, normally such mistakes were not influenced by the WRR. Because 05 equals mae, one can confidently call it the WRR. Given the normal chronological priority of

the PWR and its support from sy^(h**), MS 614 most likely preserves the PWR.

34. (#13:39/13) 614 shows + παρὰ τῷ θεῷ and is joined by (05) 383 1127 1292 1501 (1611) 2147 2412 2652 sy^(hmg). 614 is the PWR and probably the WRR too.

35. (#13:41/10) 614 has <u>ἐπιβλέψατε καὶ</u> θαυμάσατε instead of the standard θαυμάσατε and is found in 35* and 7/10 core PWR MSS and 21 others plus sy^h. MS 044 and 19 others reverse the order of the 614 reading. Although 05 now agrees with the standard, its close relative 08 approximates the 614 reading. 614 retains the PWR that was created by assimilation from the LXX.

36. (#13:41/49) 614 reads + καὶ ἐσίγησεν and is joined by (05) (1127) 2412 d mae sy^(h**). 614 is the PWR that also became the WRR. Most Westerns dropped it.

37. (#13:43/35) 614 shows + ἀξιοῦντες βαπτισθῆναι and is joined by 383 1127 1501 2147 2412 2652 sy^(h**). 614 seems to imply that those who believed Paul's message were baptized at that time. 614 is the PWR.

38. (#13:47/33) 614 reads + ἐν τοῖς ἔθνεσιν and is joined by 1127 1501 2412 sy^(h**). The gloss is not from the LXX. 614 is the PWR but most Westerns eliminated it.

39. (#13:48/10–26) 614 has ἔχαιρον καὶ ἐδόξαζον <u>τὸν θεὸν</u> καὶ ἐπίστευσαν <u>τῷ λογῷ τοῦ κυρίου</u> (vs. ἔχαιρεν/ἔχαιρο<u>ν</u> καὶ ἐδόξαζον <u>τὸν λόγον τοῦ κυρίου</u> καὶ ἐπίστευσαν, RP05^(txt)/NA28-RP05^(mg), vs. same as NA28 except <u>τοῦ θεοῦ</u>, 03, vs. ἔχαιρον καὶ <u>ἐδέξαντο</u> τὸν λόγον <u>τοῦ θεοῦ</u> καὶ ἐπίστευσαν, 05) and is found in 7/10 core PWR MSS and its relatives 876 1127 1501 2652 and three others plus sy^p sy^h. RP05^(txt) includes Westerns 1505 2495 and (sa). NA28/RP05^(mg) is semantically equal to RP05^(txt) but it has the plural ἔχαιρον and is joined by P74 01 02 04 etc., including many Westerns plus Chrys Vg e p w 189 (sa). 05 revises the 03 reading by putting ἐδέξαντο in the place of ἐδόξαζον and is joined by d gig mae. 05 is probably the WRR. The solid grouping of 614 with its core MSS in a place of eighteen alternatives is a strong testimony to its unity. This distinctive PWR presents the gentiles as giving glory directly to God rather than glory to the Lord's word. It also inserts a prepositional phrase after ἐπίστευσαν to serve as its object.

ESTABLISHING THE ANTIQUITY AND QUALITY

40. (14:13/24–26) 614 reads + αὐτοῖς and is joined by (05) 08 621 1501 1611 1842 1884 1890 2138 2412 2805 L1825 e (sy^h). 614 is the PWR.

41. (14:18/6) 614 has εἰπόντες (vs. λέγοντες, NA28/Byz) and is joined by 1501 1611 1890 2138 2412 L1825 sy^hmg. 614 is the PWR.

42. (14:18/23) 614 reads + ἀλλὰ πορεύεσθαι ἕκαστον εἰς τὰ ἰδία and is joined by 04 81 431 383 1292f 2147 2412 and many others plus sy^hmg. It is the PWR and was popular over a wide region. Cf. John 7:53 (Byz) and Acts 5:18/27 (WRR).

43. (14:25/19) 614f has + εὐαγγελιζόμενοι αὐτοῖς and is joined by 05f 383 1292f 1501f 2147 2412f 2652 L1825f d mae sy^h**. 614 is both the PWR and the WRR.

44. (#15:1/13) 614 reads + τῶν πεπιστευκότων ἀπὸ τῆς αἱρέσεως τῶν Φαρισαίων and is joined by 044 383 467 1127 1292f 1501 2147 2412 2652 L1825 sy^hmg. This is the PWR and was possibly also the WRR.

45. (#15:2/64–70) 614 includes + ὅπως κριθῶσιν ἐπ' αὐτῶν right after περὶ τοῦ ζητήματος τούτου and is joined by (05* 05C1) (383) (1127) 1292 (1501 2147) 2412 (2652^vid L1825) sy^h**. 05* and 05C1 are the only ones to place the words before περὶ ... τούτου and thereby prove to be secondary to 614. Some MSS read αὐτοῖς instead of αὐτῶν. 614 is the both the PWR and WRR.

46. (#15:4/11) 614 has + μεγάλως and is joined by 04 05(*f) 383 1292 1501 1611 2147 2412 2652 L1825 sa sy^h**. 614 is the PWR and probably also the WRR.

47. (#15:7/10–12) 614 has + ἐν πνεύματι ἁγίῳ and is joined by (05*) 1292 1501 2412 L1825 sy^hmg (d l). 614 is both the PWR and the WRR. Most Westerns corrected.

48. (#15:10/32–40) 614 reads ἡμεῖς οὔτε οἱ πατέρες ἡμῶν (vs. οἱ πατέρες ἡμῶν οὔτε ἡμεῖς, NA28/Byz) and is joined by 1292 1297 1611 1735 1890 2138 2412 ConstAp Cyr Did OrLat Tert sy^h. 614 is the PWR and clearly an old reading.

49. (#15:26/27) 614 has + εἰς πάντα πειρασμόν and is joined by 05 (08) 383 1127 1292 1501 1884 2147 2412 d e l sy^hmg. 614 is both the PWR and WRR. The editor has apparently assimilated the idea from Luke 22:28.

50. (#15:29/17) 614 reads + καὶ ὅσα μὴ θέλετε αὐτοῖς γενέσθαι ἑτέρῳ μὴ ποιεῖτε (vs. καὶ ὅσα μὴ θέλετε ἑαυτοῖς γίνεσθαι ἑτέροις μὴ ποιεῖν, 206)

and is joined by (05* 05C2 206 323 429 522 630 636 945 *1003 1127*) *1292 1501* (1509 1609 1704 1739 1891 2200) *2412* (L1178) plus (sa Ä IrLat d p ar l sy^(h**)). *614* (reading g.) is the PWR. It seems to be the source for the reading of the MSS inside the parentheses. *614* lacks four "improvements" found in 206 and 11 other MSS (reading c.). It has the contracted αὐτοῖς instead of full form of the reflexive ἑαυτοῖς, an aorist infinitive instead of the continuous present γίνεσθαι, the finite ποιεῖτε instead of the infinitive ποιεῖν that parallels the first infinitive, and the singular ἑτέρῳ instead of the plural ἑτέροις that matches the plural ἑαυτοῖς/αὐτοῖς. MS 206 and others also share these last features at 15:20/37. Since 206 agrees with sy^(h**) and matches 05* except for the minor detail of ἑτέρῳ in 05*, it is the WRR. Moreover, 206 is one of just 16 ECM MSS (together with MS 05 and IrLat sa) that repeat the negative golden rule at 15:20/37. Only the italicized MSS above refrained from the doublet. Once again, the PWR represented by *614* shows itself as more primitive than the WRR. Here it may be shown to also precede Ir and the Sahidic version.

51. (16:9/27) 614 shows + κατὰ πρόσωπον αὐτοῦ and is joined by 05 383 1127 1292 1501 2147 2412 2652 d sa sy^(h**). 614 is both the PWR and WRR.

52. (16:11/2–4) 614 has τῇ δὲ <u>ἐπαύριον</u> ἀναχθέντες (vs. ἀναχθέντες δὲ, NA28, vs. ἀναχθέντες <u>οὖν</u>, Byz/ECM) and is joined by 05C2 383 1127 1292 1501 2147 2412 2652 sy^(hmg). 614 is both the PWR and the WRR. It provides a temporal gloss.

53. (16:35/26) 614 has + οὓς χθές παρέλαβες and is joined by (P127) (05) 383 1292 1501 2147 2412 2652 d (sy^h). 614 is both the PWR and the WRR.

54. (16:39/2–22) 614 is longer by about twenty words and reads καὶ ἐλθόντες εἰς τὴν φυλακὴν παρεκάλεσαν αὐτοὺς ἐξελθεῖν εἰπόντες ἠγνοήσαμεν τὰ καθ' ὑμᾶς ὅτι ἐστὲ ἄνδρες δίκαιοι καὶ ἐκ ταύτης τῆς πόλεως ἐξέλθετε μὴ πῶς ἐπιστραφῶσιν πάλιν οἱ ἐπικράξαντες καθ' ὑμῶν (vs. καὶ ἐλθόντες παρεκάλεσαν αὐτοὺς καὶ ἐξαγαγόντες ἠρώτων ἀπελθεῖν ἀπὸ τῆς πόλεως, NA28/Byz) and is joined by (383) 1292 (1501) (1751) 2147 2412 2652 sy^(h**). 614 is the PWR. (05 d P127) build upon it mainly by replacing καὶ ἐλθόντες with more details. For example, 05 reads καὶ παραγενόμενοι μετὰ φίλων πολλῶν. 05

is the WRR. Both versions show the magistrates to be God fearing people and could be historical or just intended to show the gentiles/ Romans in the best light. Cf. the WRR above at 16:35/8–12.

55. (#17:4/10) 614 has ἐπίστευσαν (vs. ἐπείσθησαν, NA28/Byz) and is found in 08 33 1127 and 9/10 core PWR MSS and 13 others plus Vg e gig p w l 189 sa^mss bo sy^p sy^h. 614 is the PWR and has substituted, using a common synonym.

56. (#17:11/47) 614 reads + καθώς Παῦλος ἀπαγγέλλει and is joined by 383 1127 1292 1501 (2147) 2412 2652 (gig ar sy^h**). It is a PWR and possibly the WRR also. BL consider the phrase to be Lucan.[26]

57. (#17:12/13) 614 shows ἐπίστευσάν τινες δὲ ἠπίστησαν (vs. ἐπίστευσαν, NA28/Byz) and is joined by 05 383 1292 1501 2147 2412 2652 d. It is a PWR gloss.

58. (#17:17/24–36) 614 has καὶ τοῖς ἐν τῇ ἀγορᾷ κατὰ πᾶσαν ἡμέραν (vs. καὶ ἐν τῇ ἀγορᾷ κατὰ πᾶσαν ἡμέραν, NA28/Byz). It added τοῖς for stylistic reasons. It is joined by 05 383 1292 1501 2147 2412 2652 sa sy^p sy^hmg. 614 is the PWR/WRR.

59. (17:24/32–34) 614f reads ὑπάρχων (vs. ὑπάρχων κύριος, NA28, vs. κύριος ὑπάρχων, Byz) and is joined by 1292f 1718f 2412f. A scribe overlooked κύριος probably in an ancient archetype where it was written ΚΣ with a line over it. This agreement in error seen in MSS 614, 1292, and 2412 helps confirm their especially close relationship (see 13:33/20; 18:2/60). The isolated support for the reading suggests that it occurred downstream from the PWR archetype.

60. (#17:26/10–14) 614 reads πᾶν γένος ἀνθρώπων (vs. πᾶν ἔθνος ἀνθρώπων, NA28/Byz) and is joined by 383 1292 1505 1890 2147 2412 2495 and 16 others plus Chrys^ms76 Clem (sy^hmg). 614 is the PWR and was created by assimilation from 17:28/40. It is possibly the WRR too.

61. (18:2/60) 614f has προσῆλθον (vs. προσῆλθεν, NA28/Byz) and is joined by 1292f 2412f. These 3 MSS share an itacism, generating a nonsense reading that reveals their very close relationship. Therefore, if *only* these three support a Western reading, it is doubtful that they represent the PWR. Instead, they came about from later copying or editing (cf. 17:24/32–34).

---

26. Boismard and Lamouille, *Texte occidental reconstitution*, 1:185.

62. (18:8/38–40) 614 reads + διὰ τοῦ ὀνόματος τοῦ κυρίου Ἰησοῦ Χριστοῦ καὶ ἐβαπτίζοντο (vs. καὶ ἐβαπτίζοντο, NA28/Byz, vs. καὶ ἐβαπτίζοντο πιστεύοντες τῷ θεῷ διὰ τοῦ ὀνόματος τοῦ κυρίου ἡμῶν Ἰησοῦ Χριστοῦ, 05) and is joined by 383 1292 1501 (2147) 2412 2652 sy^h**. It is the PWR. 05 is joined by d h^vid and apparently built on 614. Perhaps it utilized 16:34/24–28, πεπιστευκὼς τῷ θεῷ. In contrast, BL suggests a different solution where the genuine Western reading is close to that of 05.[27] Since 05 repeatedly changes and/or expands other readings, it is probably also secondary here (cf. 16:39/2–22; 18:19/10–14), especially since 05 is nearly alone. It is possibly the WRR. More likely it entered 05's ancestry as part of 05-Arch1 and came into both 05 and h^vid.

63. (18:19/10–14) 383 has τῷ ἐπιόντι σαββάτῳ κἀκείνους κατέλιπεν αὐτοῦ (vs. κἀκείνους κατέλιπεν αὐτοῦ, NA28, vs. καὶ ἐκείνους κατέλιπεν αὐτοῦ, Byz) and is joined by (05) (614f) 1292 1501 (2147) 2412f 2652 plus (d sy^h**). 383 is slightly purer than 614f and nearest to the PWR. 05 is joined by d and revised the PWR by breaking out κἀκείνους into καί and ἐκείνους, changing the word order, and adding ἐκεῖ. However, Ropes and Zahn are probably right that these readings represent a corrupted Western text.[28] Most likely κἀκείνους κατέλιπεν αὐτοῦ was clumsily added later from the standard reading (see sy^p sa). The original PWR/WRR had dropped it so that Paul's decision to leave Aquilla and Priscilla there could be mentioned later at 18:22/1. The PWR/WRR should only be τῷ ἐπιόντι σαββάτῳ. NA28 and the Byz offer equivalents.

64. (18:22/1) 614(*f1) has + τὸν δὲ Ἀκύλαν εἴασεν ἐν Ἐφέσῳ αὐτὸς δὲ ἀνενεχθείς ἦλθεν εἰς Καισάρειαν (vs. same as 614 except ἀναχθείς, sy^p/sy^hmg, vs. τὸν δὲ Ἀκύλαν εἴασεν ἐν Ἐφέσῳ/Ἐφεσον, 383, vs. omits, NA28/Byz) and is joined by 2412f2 L809f1 (sy^p sy^hmg). 383 is joined by (1127) 1501 2147 2652 and dropped the later part of the 614 reading when they saw that it was a doublet with 18:22/2–8. Ropes is probably right that the 614 reading was intended to replace the standard at 18:21/24–18:22/8.[29] Unfortunately, 614 also has the standard reading, creating confusion. The wording of 614(*f1) nearly represents the PWR/WRR as long as the standard wording

---

27. Boismard and Lamouille, *Texte occidental reconstitution*, 2:127.
28. Ropes, *Beginnings of Christianity*, 176.
29. Ropes, *Beginnings of Christianity*, 176.

is removed. However, BL is probably right that sy^p/sy^{hmg} are the best option with their verb coming from the root of ἀνάγω versus ἀναφέρω.[30]

65. (18:27/35) 614 reads + εἰς τὴν Ἀχαΐαν and is joined by (P38) 05 383 1292 1501 2147 2412 2652 L1825 Chrys^{vid} (d gig sy^{h**}). The agreement of P38 (c. AD 300) provides confirmation of the reading's antiquity. 614 is the PWR and WRR.

66. (18:27/44–48) 614 lacks διὰ τῆς χάριτος and is found in P38 05 629 and 7/10 core PWR MSS plus Chrys Vg d gig p sy^h. The identical phrase occurs in 15:11/4–8. Note the support from P38 and 05. 614 is the PWR and WRR.

67. (18:28/13) 614 shows + διαλεγόμενος καὶ and is joined by (P38) 05 383 1292 1501 2147 2412 2652 L1825 plus d. 614 is the PWR and probably the WRR.

68. (#19:5/19) 614 reads + Χριστοῦ εἰς ἄφεσιν ἁμαρτιῶν (vs. omits, NA28/Byz) and is joined by P38^{vid} 05 383 1127 1501 2147 2412 2652 d sy^{h**}. It inserts the words from 2:38. MS 614 is both the PWR and the WRR.

69. (#19:9/8–24) 614 has τινες <u>τῶν ἐθνῶν τότε</u> ἐσκληρύνοντο καὶ ἠπείθουν κακολογοῦντες τὴν ὁδὸν ἐνώπιον τοῦ πλήθους (vs. τινες ἐσκληρύνοντο καὶ ηπείθουν κακολογοῦντες τὴν ὁδὸν ἐνώπιον <u>παντὸς</u> τοῦ πλήθους <u>τῶν ἐθνῶν</u>, 876/sy^{h**}) and differs from the standard in the added underlined words. 614 is joined by (383) 1501 (2147) 2412 (2652) but the purer form is found in 103 876 1832 sy^{h**}. Yet 876 mistakenly added παντός. 08 1884f e sy^p confirm the purer form but uniquely added τοῦ κυρίου after ὁδόν. 05 d are alone but agree with the placement of τῶν ἐθνῶν at the end. The *Vorlage* of 614 and 2412 displays errors subsequent to the PWR archetype. The mistakes were to move τῶν ἐθνῶν to the start of the clause and to add τότε. It is highly unlikely that gentiles who were humbly learning under Jewish authority would have behaved this way in the synagogue. It is equally unlikely that the ancient PWR editor would have thought any differently. Thus, 876 minus παντός is both the PWR and the WRR.

70. (#19:9/51) 614 shows + ἀπὸ ὥρας πέμπτης ἕως ὥρας δεκάτης and is joined by (05) 383 1127 1409 1501 2147 2412 2652(*f) (d) gig w ar

---

30. Boismard and Lamouille, *Texte occidental reconstitution*, 2:129–30.

sy^(h**). This interesting gloss could be an authentic detail. 614 is both the PWR and WRR.

71. (#19:13/46) 614 reads ἐξορκίζομεν (vs. ὁρκίζομεν, Byz, ὁρκίζω, NA28) and is found in relatives P38 206 431 522 945 1501 1739 1891 2298 2652 and 6/10 core PWR MSS. It is the PWR. Byz is joined by 014 020 025 35 etc. plus Chrys. NA28 is joined by P74 01 02 03 05 08 etc. plus Vg d e gig p r w 189 sa^(ms) bo. Note that P38 aligns with 614-group rather than with 05. Either 614 or the Byz is supported by (ar sa bo^(ms) sy^p sy^h). This combination of translations is usually very ancient since the sa preceded the bo and the Syriac is united. Did the Byz improve the text by creating plural harmony with the preceding word λέγοντες, or did the Alex change the word to a 1S, perceiving it as a direct quotation spoken in the singular (see chapter 3)? The PWR may have added the ἐξ- prefix to the Byz in order to harmonize with ἐξορκιστῶν earlier in the sentence.

72. (#19:28/13) 614(*f2, Cf1) has + καὶ δραμόντες εἰς τὸ ἄμφοδον and is joined by (05) 383 (1127) 1292 1501 2147 2412 2652 sy^(hmg). It is the PWR. Most spell the noun as ἄμφοδον and its entry in *TLG* defines it as either a "block of houses surrounded by streets" or a certain "quarter of a town".

73. (#19:35/2) 614 reads κατασείσας (vs. καταστείλας, NA28/Byz) and is a prominent word to describe the waving at a crowd to get their attention (see 21:40). It occurs four times in the NT. The other word means to let down or pacify and occurs only twice. 614 is found in relatives 05 08 1884C and 8/10 core PWR MSS and four others plus Ä. It has harmonized. 614 is the PWR and probably also the WRR.

74. (#19:37/11) 614 has + ἐνθάδε and is joined by 05 383 1127 1292 2147 2412 2652 d sa bo sy^(Aram) sy^(hmg) A. 614 is both the PWR and the WRR.

75. (20:23/35) 614 has ἐν Ἱεροσολύμοις (vs. ἐν Ἱερουσαλήμ, P41, vs. omits, NA28/Byz) and is joined by (P41) 05 1127 2412 d gig w (OrLat sa sy^(h**)). 614 and P41 differ only in orthography. MS 614 is probably the PWR and WRR.

76. (20:24/36) 614 reads παρέλαβον (vs. ἔλαβον, NA28/Byz) and is found P41 P74 05 0142 876 2652 and 10/10 core PWR MSS and 7 others. NA28/Byz is joined by 01 02 03 04 08 014 020 35 etc., including numerous Westerns plus Bas Chrys. High quality evidence

ESTABLISHING THE ANTIQUITY AND QUALITY

exists on both sides, including a mix of Alex, Byz, and Western MSS. Since the παρ- prefix yields a more precise word for the occasion, it is probably a gloss. NA28/Byz is original.

77. (21:21/48) 614f has ἔθνεσιν (vs. ἔθεσιν, NA28/Byz) and is clearly a mistake and found in relatives 05 522 1838 1891 and 5/10 core PWR MSS and twenty others. Some have been corrected. Since the error was so pervasive among the Westerns, it points back to a common source. 614 is both the PWR and WRR.

78. (22:6/30) 614f reads περιήστραψεν (vs. περιαστράψαι, NA28/Byz) and is found in 05C2 08f 044 1175 1884 and 7/10 core PWR MSS and 6 others plus Ath Marcell. This PWR changed the infinitive to the aorist apparently to help the reader. The infinitive fits with the following accusative neuter subject φῶς. However, if it is read as a nominative, the infinitive would be awkward.

79. (22:20/12–18) 614 shows Στεφάνου τοῦ πρωτομάρτυρός σου (vs. Στεφάνου τοῦ μάρτυρός σου, NA28/Byz) and is found in 10/10 core PWR MSS and 020 1739C and 22 others plus Chrys[ms] sy[h]. 614 is the PWR and offers a gloss.

80. (22:25/24–42) 614 has εἰ ἄνθρωπον Ῥωμαῖον καὶ ἀκατάκριτον ἔξεστιν ὑμῖν μαστίζειν (vs. same except ἔξεστιν ὑμῖν placed after εἰ, 05, vs. same except + ὁ Παῦλος before εἰ, NA28/Byz) and is found in 9/10 core PWR MSS and 2652 plus Chrys gig sy[h]. 05 equals 614 except it uniquely reorders and once again shows by its variations a secondary character to the PWR. NA28/Byz is original.

81. (23:15/6–18) 614 reads + ὑμεῖς ἐμφανίσατε τῷ χιλιάρχῳ σὺν ὅλῳ τῷ συνεδρίῳ (vs. same except omits ὅλῳ, NA28/Byz, vs. παρακ[α]λοῦμ[εν ὑμᾶς] ποιήσατε ἡμῖν [του]τὸ συνα[γα]γόντ[ες το συνέ]δριον ἐμφα[νίσατε τῷ χιλιάρ]χῳ, P48) and is found in 7/10 core PWR MSS and 876 1448 1832 2243 2652 sy[h.txt]. P48 (III) is joined by (sy[hmg] h sa). However, sy[hmg] revises it by adding ἵνα twice, reads with the subjunctive ἐμφανίσητε, and makes a word order change. 614 is the PWR and P48 preserves the paraphrastic WRR.

82. (23:25/2–12) 614*/614C has γράψας ἐπιστολὴν ἔχουσαν τὸν τύπον τοῦτον ἐφοβήθη γὰρ μήποτε ἁρπάσαντες αὐτὸν οἱ Ἰουδαῖοι ἀποκτένωσι καὶ αὐτὸς μεταξὺ ἔγκλη[σιν] σχῇ ὡς ἀργύριον εἰληφὼς ἔγραψε δὲ ἐπιστολὴν περιέχουσαν τάδε (vs. ἐφοβή]θη γὰρ μήποτε ἐξαρπάσαντες αὐτὸν [οἱ Ἰουδαῖοι] ἀποκτείνωσιν καὶ αὐτὸς μεταξὺ

ἔγκλημ[α] ἔχῃ ὡς εἰληφὼς ἀργύρια γράψας δὲ αὐτοῖς ἐπιστολὴν ἐν ᾗ ἐγέγραπτο, P48, vs. ἐφοβήθη γὰρ μήποτε (ἐξ)αρπάσαντες αὐτὸν οἱ Ἰουδαῖοι ἀποκτείνωσιν αὐτὸν καὶ αὐτὸς μεταξὺ ἔγκλημα ἔχῃ/σχῇ ὡς ἀργύριον εἰληφώς, syʰ⁎⁎, vs. ἔγραψεν δὲ ἐπιστολὴν περιέχουσαν τάδε, syʰᵐᵍ, vs. γράψας ἐπιστολὴν ἔχουσαν τὸν τύπον τοῦτον, NA28, vs. γράψας ἐπιστολὴν περιέχουσαν τὸν τύπον τοῦτον, Byz) and is joined by (P48) (2147f1) 2412 (2652f2) syʰ⁎⁎/syʰᵐᵍ. MS 614*/614C has a doublet because it acquired the NA28 reading at the front. 614* has ἔγκλη- by accident but 614C revised it to ἔκλησιν, apparently correcting it from his own mind. Although the scribe of 2147f1 evidently had the same problem, he fixed the error by reference to ἔγκλημα in 23:29. Seeing that P48 and 2652f2 have ἔγκλημα in the first hand, they confirm that this word was in the PWR edition. Ironically, P48, the oldest "Western" MS (ca. AD 250), manifests the most deviation away from the reconstructed PWR. If one removes the NA28 reading from the start of 614C, changes ἔγκλησιν to the synonym ἔγκλημα (see P48/2652f2), and supplies the missing iota to ἀποκτένωσιν, it best preserves the PWR in the Greek. The editorial work on the Syriac provides a distinct confirmation. The six words of NA28 at the start of 614C are kept by syʰ, the five words of 614C at the end are marginalized by syʰᵐᵍ in favor of the NA28, and the PWR words in between are marked for deletion by syʰ⁎⁎. Overall, 2147f1 and 2652f2 are secondary to 614C since they add a καί and merge the PWR ending with the standard one in order to create ἔγραψε δὲ καὶ ἐπιστολὴν περιέχουσαν τὸν τύπον τοῦτον. The Byz differs from NA28 only in giving περιέχουσαν instead of ἔχουσαν. This subtle detail suggests that the PWR was built upon a Byz base. NA28 is joined by P74 01 03 08 etc. Byz is joined by 02 014 020 35 etc. plus Chrys. The following translations support either NA28 or the Byz: (Vg e p* 189 sa bo syʰ·ᵗˣᵗ syᵖ Ä). The PWR is accurately preserved by syʰ⁎⁎ combined with syʰᵐᵍ. It is probably also the WRR. Make a SGL reading between NA28 and Byz.

83. (23:29/12–16) 614 reads τοῦ νόμου αὐτῶν Μωϋσέος καὶ Ἰησοῦ τινος (vs. τοῦ νόμου αὐτῶν, NA28/Byz) and is joined by 1292 2147 2412 2652 gig syʰᵐᵍ. Though the witnesses are few, 614 is the PWR and probably also the WRR.

84. (23:29/33) 614 has ἐξήγαγον αὐτὸν μόλις τῇ βίᾳ (vs. omits, NA28/Byz) and is joined by 1127 1292 2147 2412 2652 gig sy[h**]. Once again the few preserve the PWR. It is probably also the WRR.

85. (23:34/5) 614 has τὴν ἐπιστολὴν (vs. ὁ ἡγεμὼν, Byz, vs. τὴν ἐπιστολὴν ὁ ἡγεμὼν, 2147/2652, vs. ὁ ἡγεμὼν τὴν ἐπιστολὴν, 1292, vs. omits, NA28) and is joined by 2412 gig bo sy[p] sy[hmg]. Byz is joined by 014 020 35 etc. plus sa. NA28 is joined by P74 01 02 03 08 33 81 etc. plus Chrys Vg e p w 189 sy[h.txt] Ä. The nature of + τὴν ἐπιστολὴν and its support from sy[hmg] and gig suggests it was part of the WR. If so, the independence of 614 and 2412 here might suggest they were conformed to the WRR rather than the source. However, other core PWR MSS (see 1292 2147 2652) give indirect support by conflating τὴν ἐπιστολὴν with the Byz ὁ ἡγεμὼν. Their variation in word order suggests that the scribes were unsure where to add ὁ ἡγεμὼν. Essentially, two separate two-word attempts were made to smooth the transition to Felix. Once again, 614 is at the root of both the PWR and the WRR. Both 614 and the Byz appear to be glosses. NA28 is probably original.

86. (23:34/6–26) 614 reads ἐπηρώτησεν τὸν Παῦλον ἐκ ποίας ἐπαρχίας εἶ ἔφη Κίλιξ καὶ πυθόμενος (vs. καὶ ἐπερωτήσας ἐκ ποίας ἐπαρχείας ἐστίν καὶ πυθόμενος ὅτι ἀπὸ Κιλικίας, NA28/Byz) and is joined by (2147) 2412 2652[vid] (sy[hmg]). The paraphrase occurs because the editor preferred direct speech. Though the support is limited, 614 preserves the PWR and probably also the WRR.

87. (23:35/2–6) 614 has ἔφη ἀκούσομαί σου (vs. διακούσομαί σου ἔφη, NA28/Byz) and is joined by 2147 2412 2652 sy[p] sy[hmg]. The paraphrase completes the revision from indirect to direct speech that was accomplished by the same MSS at 23:34/6–26. MS 614 is the PWR and probably also the WRR.

88. (24:27/19) 614 has + τὸν δὲ Παῦλον εἴασεν ἐν τηρήσει διὰ Δρούσιλλαν and is joined by 1292 2147 2412 2652 sy[hmg]. Though most Westerns removed the plus, 614 retains the PWR. Given its sy[hmg] support, it is possibly also the WRR.

89. (25:10/32) 614 reads οὐχ ἠδίκησα (vs. οὐδὲν ἠδίκησα, NA28/Byz, vs. οὐδὲν ἠδίκηκα, 01/03) and is found in 9/10 PWR MSS and 2652 plus Vg e gig p w 189 bo[ms] sy[h]. NA28/Byz is joined by 02 04 08 014 etc.

plus Chrys sa bo sy^p sy^(h**). The PWR provides a simplifying gloss. NA28/Byz is original. BL considers the 614 reading to be Lucan.³¹

90. (#26:14/10–14) 614 has + διὰ τὸν φόβον ἐγὼ μόνος and assimilates ideas of fear and about Paul exclusively hearing the voice, taken probably from 22:9/19 (Byz and Western text only). It is joined by (1292) 1611 2147 2412 2652 (gig sy^hmg sa bo^mss). 614 is the PWR and probably the WRR as well.

91. (#26:15/26) 614 reads Ἰησοῦς <u>ὁ Ναζωραῖος</u> (vs. Ἰησοῦς, NA28/Byz) and is joined by 1292 (1611) 2412 and 19 others plus gig p/2 sy^(h**) (sy^p). It has been harmonized with 22:8 and represents the PWR. It is probably the WRR also.

92. (#27:5/21) 614 has διαπλεύσαντες <u>δι' ἡμερῶν δεκαπέντε</u> (vs. διαπλεύσαντες, NA28/Byz) and may be eyewitness testimony (cf. 12:10, + κατέβησαν τοῦ ζ βάθους καί, per 05 mae). It is found in 7/10 core PWR MSS and 1127 2652 h^vid ar sy^(h**). 614 is the PWR and probably also the WRR, given its character and its alignment with h^vid and sy^(h**). BL consider this detail Lucan.³²

93. (#27:15/23) 614 has ἐπιδόντες <u>τῷ πλέοντι καὶ συστείλαντες τὰ ἱστία</u> ἐφερόμεθα (vs. ἐπιδόντες ἐφερόμεθα, NA28/Byz) and is found in 7/10 core PWR MSS and 876 (1127) 1832 2243 (*^vid, C2) 2652f sy^(h**). It is the PWR and is possibly the WRR also. It could be translated as "having given up on sailing and lowered the sails, we were driven." It should be considered a clarifying gloss.

94. (#27:35/31) 614 has + ἐπιδιδοὺς καὶ ἡμῖν and is joined by (1127) 1292 1409 1611 2147 2412 2652 (sa sy^(h**)). Was it an eyewitness that introduced this later change into the book of Acts? This variant offers a good example of where the sa still retains a distinctly Western reading. 614 is the PWR and possibly the WRR also. Only a few of the Western MSS sustained the reading over the centuries.

95. (28:16/20–22) 614 reads + ἔξω τῆς παρεμβολῆς and clarifies. It is joined by 1127 1292 1611 2147(*f) 2412 2652 w (sy^(h**)) and should be considered the PWR. It is possibly the WRR also. Other than its limited support, it does not seem to be original since the assertion

---

31. Boismard and Lamouille, *Texte occidental reconstitution*, 1:214.
32. Boismard and Lamouille, *Texte occidental reconstitution*, 1:219.

is already evident by inference. BL considers the addition to be Lucan.[33]

96. (28:18/3) 614 has οἵτινες <u>πολλὰ</u> (vs. οἵτινες, NA28/Byz) and is found in 7/10 core PWR MSS and 2652 plus sy[h**]. 614 is the PWR and possibly the WRR.

97. (28:19/9) 614 reads + καὶ ἐπικράζοντων αἶρε τὸν ἐχθρὸν ἡμῶν and is found in 7/10 core PWR MSS and 876 1832 2652 sy[h**]. 614 is the PWR and probably the WRR also. It could be an eyewitness detail that was added.

98. (28:30/29) 614 has + Ἰουδαίους τε καὶ Ἕλληνας and is apparently an interpolation from 19:10. It is found in 7/10 core PWR MSS and 876 1127 1832 2243 2652 plus gig p 189 sy[h**]. It is the PWR and probably the WRR too. The addition might be from the editor's zeal to show that the evangelization of the Jews never ceases. Conversely, it could be eyewitness testimony.

99. (28:31/35) 614 reads ἀκωλύτως <u>ἀμήν</u> (vs. ἀκωλύτως, NA28/Byz, vs. ἀκωλύτως <u>εἰπὼν ὅτι οὗτος ἐστιν (ὁ) Χριστὸς Ἰησοῦς ὁ υἱός (τοῦ) θεοῦ δι' οὗ μέλλει πᾶς/ὅλος ὁ κόσμος κρίνεσθαι ἀμήν</u>, sy[h]) and is joined by 9/10 core PWR MSS and thirty-two others plus Chrys p/2. It is the PWR. NA28/Byz is joined by P74 01 02 03 08 etc. plus Chrys Vg e gig s sa bo sy[p] Ä A G. The long ending of sy[h] is joined by just p w 189 and seems to recall 17:31. It is possibly the WRR that was once a part of 05, mae, and others. It was refused in the PWR MSS except for the ending ἀμήν. BL also considers the long ending to be a reading of secondary nature.[34] The Alex and Byz traditions resisted even the minor gloss ἀμήν.

The Proto-Western Group Built Upon a Mixed Foundation

The previous two sections have endeavored to show that the PWR archetype is more primitive than the ancient WR. This one will begin to look at the underlying base text of the PWR archetype. As above, the agreement of core proto-Western Group MSS will be used as a key criterion for identifying genuine readings going back to the PWR archetype.

---

33. Boismard and Lamouille, *Texte occidental reconstitution*, 1:224.
34. Boismard and Lamouille, *Texte occidental reconstitution*, 2:194.

The fact that the PWR archetype builds upon readings from both the Byz and Alex traditions will be brought to light here. It will be assumed that such readings were part of those two traditions from the earliest of times unless there is clear evidence to the contrary. The following list will demonstrate that the Byz tradition features more prominently as a probable base of the individual PWRs. The overall dependence of the PWR archetype upon the Byz and Alex traditions will be covered in chapter 3.

Cases Where the PWR Is Built Upon a Byzantine Base

1. (#2:1/22) 614 has οἱ ἀπόστολοι ὁμοθυμαδὸν (vs. ὁμοθυμαδὸν, Byz, vs. ὁμοῦ, NA28) The PWR has inserted οἱ ἀπόστολοι into the base Byzantine reading.

2. (9:28/10–14) 614 and the Byz read εἰσπορευόμενος (vs. εἰσπορευόμενος καὶ ἐκπορευόμενος, NA28). Their agreement in a primitive error of homoeoteleuton is found in P74 014 020 025 etc. and includes 6/10 core PWR MSS plus Ä. 614 is the PWR. NA28 is joined by 01 02 03 04 08 18 35 181 1175 etc., 4/10 core PWR MSS, and many Westerns plus Chrys Vg e gig p w l 189 sa bo mae sy^p sy^h. Thus, four of the PWR MSS were corrected to the original reading in NA28.

3. (9:38/44–50) 614 has ὀκνῆσαι ἕως αὐτῶν διελθεῖν (vs. ὀκνῆσαι διελθεῖν ἕως αὐτῶν, Byz, vs. ὀκνήσῃς διελθεῖν ἕως ἡμῶν, NA28) and is found in 6/10 core PWR MSS and 431. Byz is joined by P45 04* 04C3 014 020 35 etc. and includes core PWR MSS 383 2147 (1505 2495) plus Bas Chrys sy^h. NA28 is strongly supported in the translations and matches the Byz word order. It appears that the Byz derived from the Alex by switching to the third person. Next, the PWR archetype changed the Byz word order. Later four core PWR MSS revised to the Byz.

4. (11:3/6–18) 614 reads πρὸς ἄνδρας ἀκροβυστίαν ἔχοντας εἰσῆλθεν καὶ συνέφαγεν (vs. πρὸς ἄνδρας ἀκροβυστίαν ἔχοντας εἰσῆλθες καὶ συνέφαγες, Byz, vs. εἰσῆλθες πρὸς ἄνδρας ἀκροβυστίαν ἔχοντας καὶ συνέφαγες, NA28/ECM, vs. εἰσῆλθεν πρὸς ἄνδρας ἀκροβυστίαν ἔχοντας καὶ συνέφαγεν, P45^vid/03) and is found 5/10 core PWR MSS and eight others plus sy^h.txt. 614 is the PWR and is only supported by a single Byz MS (see 1448), suggesting that the Byz did not come from it. The PWR does possess one key Alex witness in MS 33. The

Byz is joined by 08 014 025 etc., 5/10 core PWR MSS, several more Westerns, and Chrys e sy^hmg. Thus five members of the 614-group were revised to the Byz. NA28 is joined by P74^vid 01 02 05 18 35 1739 etc., including some Westerns plus Epiph^ms.vid Vg gig w l 189 Ä. P45^vid/03 is joined by 81 1175 and ten others plus Epiph^T.vid. The minimal support for the P45^vid/03 and 614/PWR readings seems to exclude them. Beyond 81 and 1175, the allies of P45^vid/03 are weak. P45^vid/03 and 614/PWR may have influenced each other in the move to the third person. Perhaps these editors assumed that the Jews would have been more respectful and thus mentioned their concerns to the group indirectly. Still, it appears that direct discourse fits more naturally. Therefore, the question should rather be whether the Byz reordered to emphasize the "unlawful" interaction with the gentiles or did NA28 place a verb at the start for easy reading? NA28 has the most translations. While all four readings are very early, NA28 seems to be original. ECM made it a SGL between NA28 and P45^vid/03.[35] Significantly, the PWR word order came from the Byz.

5. (11:12/4–12) 614 has δέ μοι καὶ τὸ πνεῦμα συνελθεῖν (vs. δέ μοι τὸ πνεῦμα συνελθεῖν, Byz, vs. δὲ τὸ πνεῦμά μοι συνελθεῖν, NA28) and is joined by 1127 1292 1611 2138 2412 plus sy^h. 614 is the PWR. Byz is joined by 08 014 020 35 etc., including core PWR MSS 383 1505 1890 2147 2495 plus Chrys e l. The PWR added καί to the Byz. Later, 5/10 its core MSS were corrected back to the Byz.

6. (#13:40/10–18) 614 reads τὸ εἰρημένον ἐν τοῖς προφήταις εἰς ὑμᾶς (vs. εφ' ὑμᾶς τὸ εἰρημένον ἐν τοῖς προφήταις, Byz, vs. τὸ εἰρημένον ἐν τοῖς προφήταις, NA28) and is joined by 1292 1611 1890 2138 2412. It is the PWR. The similarity links the PWR with the Byz reading. Given the isolated support for the PWR, it is far more likely that it derived from the Byz. In addition, the Byz is joined by key Alex MSS 81 1175 and all four of the church fathers who offer testimony.

7. (14:2/6–10) 614 reads ἀπειθοῦντες Ἰουδαῖοι ἐπήγειραν διωγμὸν (vs. ἀπειθοῦντες Ἰουδαῖοι ἐπήγειραν, Byz, vs. ἀπειθήσαντες Ἰουδαῖοι ἐπήγειραν, NA28, vs. ἀρχισυνάγωγοι καὶ οἱ ἄρχοντες ἐπήγειραν διωγμὸν, sy^hmg, vs. ἀρχισυνάγωγοι τῶν Ἰουδαίων καὶ οἱ ἄρχοντες τῆς συναγωγῆς ἐπήγαγον αὐτοῖς διωγμὸν κατὰ τῶν δικαίων, 05) and is

---

35. Wachtel, "Text-Critical Commentary," 17.

ESTABLISHING THE ANTIQUITY AND QUALITY

joined by 08 1127 1501 1884f 2652 and 8/10 core PWR MSS plus e w ar sy^h.txt. It is the PWR. It starts with the Byz with its present participle and adds διωγμόν. The WRR is best represented by sy^hmg and it builds on the 614 reading with διωγμόν by specifying the disobedient ones. Next, 05 and d expand the WRR by acquiring τῶν Ἰουδαίων from the standard Ἰουδαῖοι, and by indicating that the targets of the persecution are the righteous ones. The mae translation was probably corrected back to the standard (see figure 2.1). This sequence of successive emendations apparently began with the Byz.

8. (16:9/12–16) 614 has ἐφάνη τῷ Παύλῳ (vs. τῷ Παύλῳ ὤφθη, NA28, vs. ὤφθη τῷ Παύλῳ, Byz) and is found in 8/10 core PWR MSS and 1501 1563. It is the PWR and adjusts the Byz reading, using a synonym. The other direction would be feasible if the PWR had substantial Byz support. However, only the little known thirteenth-century Byz MS 1563 agrees with it.

9. (16:12/12–16) 614 reads πρώτη τῆς (vs. πρώτη τῆς μερίδος τῆς, Byz, vs. πρώτη τῆς μερίδος, P74/ECM, πρώτη[ς] μερίδος τῆς, NA28) and is found in 8/10 core PWR MSS, 35* 1127 1241 1739 2298, and 4 others plus Chrys bo^ms sy^h (sy^p) Ä. It is the PWR. Byz is joined by 014 020 18 etc. P74/ECM is joined by 01 02 04 33 81 181 1175 etc. Both the Byz and ECM could be joined by (sa bo Vg e gig p*vid w l 189). NA28 is supported by a conjecture. 03 and 35Cf have made a clear error and have πρώτη μερίδος τῆς. 614 means "a leading city of Macedonia" and that is saying too much.[36] Similarly, 05 d reads κεφαλὴ τῆς, could be translated "a chief city of Macedonia," and likely derives from 614. 614/PWR evidently resulted from a homoeoteleuton of the Byz text with an eye skip from τῆς to τῆς. Wachtel recognizes this natural conclusion but since 1739 is closer to the purest Alex MSS, decides that "more likely" 614 came from the ECM reading.[37] Barrett explains that the τῆς before μερίδος should be taken as a demonstrative.[38] Semantically the Byz equals the ECM in saying "a leading city of that district of Macedonia." The NLT seems to get it correct with "a major city of that district of Macedonia." Since the Byz text is of high quality and has nearly

---

36. Barrett, *Commentary on Acts*, 2:778–80.
37. Wachtel, "Text-Critical Commentary," 23–24.
38. Barrett, *Commentary on Acts*, 2:778.

the equivalent support as the ECM reading, these two should form a SGL reading.

10. (#19:13/46) 614 reads ἐξορκίζομεν (vs. ὁρκίζομεν, Byz, ὁρκίζω, NA28) and is joined by P38 and many other Westerns. Probably the PWR added the ἐξ- prefix to the Byz in order to harmonize with the related noun earlier in the sentence.

11. (23:7/14–20) 614 has τῶν Σαδδουκαίων καὶ τῶν Φαρισαίων (vs. τῶν Φαρισαίων καὶ τῶν Σαδδουκαίων, RP05^{mg}, vs. τῶν Φαρισαίων καὶ Σαδδουκαίων, NA28, vs. τῶν Φαρισαίων, RP05^{txt}, vs. τῶν Σαδδουκαίων καὶ Φαρισαίων, 01, vs. τῶν Σαδδουκαίων, P74) and is found in 9/10 core PWR MSS and six others. It is the PWR. It seems to begin with the RP05^{mg} and then reverse the order of the groups to align with the sequence in 23:8. RP05^{mg} (=ByzECM) is joined by 014 020 049 35 etc. and has a second τῶν in contrast to NA28. RP05^{txt} is an eye skip most likely upon RP05^{mg}. NA28 is joined by 02 03 04 etc. and best explains the readings of 01 and P74. 01 probably comes directly from NA28 by swapping the order of the nouns just as 614. P74 likely comes as an eye skip from 01. Both RP05^{mg} and NA28 show (sy^p sy^h) as possible support. Did RP05^{mg} add the τῶν to distinguish the two groups or did NA28 remove it to show them as one Sanhedrin that was ironically being pulled apart? It seems that these two should be a SGL reading. The PWR has reordered based upon the better Byz (i.e., RP05^{mg}) reading.

12. (24:21/32–38) 614 has σήμερον κρίνομαι ὑφ᾽ ἡμῶν (σήμερον κρίνομαι ὑφ᾽ ὑμῶν, 1292, vs. κρίνομαι σήμερον ὑφ᾽ ὑμῶν, Byz vs. κρίνομαι σήμερον ἐφ᾽ ὑμῶν, NA28) and is joined by 2412. Their reading ἡμῶν should be considered an itacism (not noticed in the ECM) that occurred subsequent to the PWR. The reading of 1292 is found in 7/8 of the remaining core PWR MSS and thirteen others plus gig. 1292 differs in word order from NA28/Byz but it agrees with the Byz preposition ὑφ᾽. Therefore the PWR is based on the Byz text.

13. (24:22/2–10) 614 displays ἀκούσας δὲ ταῦτα ὁ Φῆλιξ ἀνεβάλλετο αὐτοὺς (vs. ἀκούσας δὲ ταῦτα ὁ Φῆλιξ ἀνεβάλετο αὐτοὺς, Byz, vs. ἀνεβάλλετο δὲ ὁ Φῆλιξ αὐτοὺς, 1505, vs. ἀνεβάλετο δὲ αὐτοὺς ὁ Φῆλιξ, NA28) and is found in 4/10 core PWR MSS and nine others plus (sa). 614 is the PWR. Byz is joined by 014 020 35 etc. plus (sa). 1505 is found in 4/10 core PWR MSS plus (bo sy^p). NA28 is

found in P74 01 02^vid 03 04 08 etc. plus (Vg e gig s p w 189 bo sy^h sy^p). ECM lists sixteen alternatives. NA28 is clearly the original as shown by the translations. The PWR and Byz were known early in Egypt as seen in the Sahidic. 1505 arose from the PWR by a partial correction toward NA28. When it removed ἀκούσας ταῦτα, it also fronted the verb. The others derive from NA28 or the Byz. The Byz is the slightly earlier form that became the PWR merely by adding a lambda to the verb.

14. (#26:1/30–36) 614 reads ἀπελογεῖτο ἐκτείνας τὰς χεῖρας (vs. ἀπελογεῖτο ἐκτείνας τὴν χεῖρα, Byz, vs. ἐκτείνας τὴν χεῖρα ἀπελογεῖτο, NA28) and is found in 7/10 core PWR MSS and no others. It is the PWR. The ECM lists eight alternatives. Byz is joined by 014 020 025 35 etc. plus Chrys. NA28 is joined by P74 01 02 03 04 08 etc. plus A G (sa bo sy^p) (Vg e p w 189). The PWR apparently revised the Byz reading by uniquely choosing the plural τὰς χεῖρας.

15. (28:14/10–14) 614 has ἐπ' αὐτοῖς ἐπιμείναντες (vs. ἐπ' αὐτοῖς επιμεῖναι, Byz, vs. παρ' αὐτοῖς ἐπιμεῖναι, NA28) and is found in 8/10 core PWR MSS and sixteen others plus sy^p sy^h** (sy^h, μείναντες). It is the PWR. Byz is joined by 020 025 1 35 etc. plus Chrys. NA28 joined by P74^vid 01 03 33 81 etc. plus A (Vg p w 189 G). Either the Byz or NA28 are supported by (sa bo). The bo would normally support NA28 but the sa sometimes joins the Byz and/or the PWR. The ECM lists thirteen readings: three with παρ', eight with ἐπ,' and two with neither. The main difference is offered by the PWR. By giving the participle, it suggests that Paul's group was the recipient of encouragement and ended up staying seven days. The syntax of the Byz and NA28 readings suggests that παρεκλήθημεν refers to their being urged to stay with the church seven days. Perhaps the PWR archetype's editor found a request to stay seven days to be odd. Given that παρεκλήθησαν is used in 20:12 in the sense of "they were encouraged," and noting that Paul receives courage also in 28:15, the participle made more sense to him. A primitive substitution occurred between παρ' and ἐπ' but it is unclear which direction the change went. NA28 and Byz should be a SGL reading. The PWR is from the Byz.

16. (28:19/31) 614 has κατηγορῆσαι ἀλλ' ἵνα λυτρώσομαι τὴν ψυχήν μου ἐκ θανάτου (vs. κατηγορῆσαι, Byz, vs. κατηγορεῖν, NA28) and is

found in 7/10 core PWR MSS and 1127 2652 plus gig p sy^(h**). It is the PWR and builds on the Byz.

Cases Where the PWR Is Built Upon an Alexandrian Base

1. (#11:8/12–18; cf. 10:14/20–26) 614 has οὐδέποτε κοινὸν ἢ ἀκάθαρτον (vs. κοινὸν ἢ ἀκάθαρτον οὐδέποτε, NA28, vs. πᾶν κοινὸν ἢ ἀκάθαρτον οὐδέποτε, Byz) and is found in 6/10 core PWR MSS and 424C plus Epiph sy^h. It is the PWR. It has simply reworded NA28.

2. (#13:6/6–10) 614 has τὴν νῆσον ὅλην (vs. ὅλην τὴν νῆσον, NA28, vs. τὴν νῆσον, Byz) and is joined by 1292 1611 2138 2412 plus 2 others and Chrys and is the PWR. NA28 has solid support, including Vg d e gig p w 189. Byz is joined by sa^ms. The other translations (sa bo mae sy^p sy^h Ä) could support either NA28 or the PWR. The NA28 reading is original with the PWR reordering it.

3. (#13:23/18–26) 614 reads ἤγειρεν τῷ Ἰσραὴλ σωτῆρα Ἰησοῦν (vs. ἤγαγεν τῷ Ἰσραὴλ σωτῆρα Ἰησοῦν, NA28, vs. ἤγαγεν τῷ Ἰσραὴλ σωτηρίαν, Byz, vs. ἤγειρεν τῷ Ἰσραὴλ σωτηρίαν, 1) and is joined by 04 (05) and many Westerns, including a total of forty-two MSS. It is also found in Thdrt A G (d sy^p sy^h sa mae). There are fifteen alternatives. NA28 is joined by 01 02 03 08 025 and eight others plus Ath Vg e p w (bo). Byz is joined by P74 014 020 35C etc. plus AnastS Chrys^mss CosmIn Ä. MS 1 is joined by seventeen others. 614 has the very best versional support. However, it is instructive to realize that it is very likely secondary. It probably spun off from NA28 by assimilating ἤγειρεν from the near context (see 13:22, 30, 37). Since 614 is supported by (05 mae sy^h), it is the WRR also. The Byz derives from the Alexandrian as a primitive error. The scribe seems to have misread the uncial ΣPAIN (with a line over each nomina sacra) as ΣPIAN (with just one line over it).[39] The error made sense, agreed with 13:26, and persevered. NA28 preserves the original text and the Western MSS tweaked it.

4. (24:13/6–14) 614 has παραστῆσαι δύνανται περὶ ὧν νυνὶ (vs. παραστῆσαί με δύνανται περὶ ὧν νῦν, RP05, vs. παραστῆσαί με νῦν δύνανται περὶ ὧν νῦν, ByzECM, παραστῆσαι δύνανταί σοι περὶ ὧν

---

39. Metzger, *Textual Commentary*, 359.

νυνὶ, NA28) and is found in 7/10 core PWR MSS, 1509 1832, and fourteen others (same except they have νῦν) plus sa sy^h. It seems to understand παραστῆσαι as "to prove" and probably dropped σοι from NA28 to simplify. RP05 lacks many of its typical core MSS and has no translations. ByzECM is joined by 014 025 049 1 330 1241 etc. and has no translations. NA28 is joined by 01 02(*f2) 03 33 81 etc. plus (bo Vg e p w 189). The Byz may have taken παραστῆσαι as "convict" and hence the use of με. Similarly, the *TLG* does list "prove" as a possible gloss. NA28 achieves the idea of "prove to you" by the words παραστῆσαι . . . σοι. In terms of popularity, νυνί is more unusual (NT: 20x; Acts: 1x, at 22:1) than νῦν (NT: 147x; Acts: 25x).[40] It is interesting that the only other occasion where νυνί appears in Acts is also in the mouth of Paul. 614 is the PWR built on the Alex one. NA28 is original.

5. (28:30/2) 614 reads ἐπέμεινεν (vs. ἐνέμεινεν, NA28, vs. ἔμεινεν, Byz) and is found in 8/10 core PWR MSS and eight others. NA28 joined by 01(*f) 03 33 81 1175 and eleven others. Byz is joined by 01C2 02 (08) 020 025 35 etc., including many Western leaning MSS plus Chrys. The Byz probably accidentally dropped the ἐν- prefix. The PWR most likely came from the original word in NA28.

QUALITY OF THE BYZANTINE TEXT OF ACTS

This second part of chapter 2 will present evidence for the quality of the Byz text of Acts. The first section will consider proof for its faithful transmission while at the same time acknowledge some of its worst mistakes. The second section will briefly look at the big picture relationship between the Byz and Alex traditions. It will assert that the two traditions are very similar semantically. The total number of variations that produce a significant change to the meaning is extremely limited.

---

40. Data was calculated using *BibleWorks* (*BW*).

ESTABLISHING THE ANTIQUITY AND QUALITY

A Tradition of Faithful Copying

Limited Intrusion of Western and Other Secondary Readings

1. (#8:37/2–44) Alex, Byz, and 614-group MSS all avoid the strongly supported WRR. In addition to it being found in many Western leaning Greek MSS, it is preserved by the following: Ir 10/11 OL MSS sy^{h**} mae.

2. (#15:34/2–12) 614 contains ἔδοξεν δὲ τῷ Σιλᾷ ἐπιμεῖναι αὐτοῦ (vs. omits, NA28/Byz) and is joined by many MSS, including most Westerns plus d gig w ar l 189 Ä A G. This very popular reading became both the PWR and the WRR. Both the Alex and Byz traditions show their excellence by resisting the addition.

3. (20:15/28–30) 614/Byz has <u>καὶ μείναντες ἐν Τρωγυλ[λ]ίῳ</u> τῇ (vs. τῇ δὲ, NA28) and is joined by 014 020 025 etc., including most Westerns plus Chrys d gig sa^{ms} (sa^{mss}) sy^p sy^h. It is the PWR. It is probable that this reading stands at the base of both the Western and Byz traditions. NA28 is joined by P41 P74 01 02 03 04 08 33 1175 etc. plus (Vg p w 189 A G)(e bo)(sa^{ms}). The longer reading appears to be a gloss perhaps from an eyewitness. Its absence is not readily explainable as an eye skip. However, it should be noted that the oldest Coptic translation (see sa^{mss}) evidently included the gloss. However, it had been inserted into its Greek archetype somewhat clumsily without dropping δέ. NA28 is probably original.

4. (22:20/31) 614/Byz reads συνευδοκῶν <u>τῇ ἀναιρέσει αὐτοῦ</u> (vs. συνευδοκῶν, NA28) and is joined by 10/10 core PWR MSS, 014 020 025 35, and most of the Western leaning MSS plus Chrys sy^p sy^h. NA28 is joined by P74 01 02 03 05 08 181 629* 1409 1875 1884 L1188 Vg d e gig p w 189 sa bo Ä. Was the phrase deleted or was it assimilated from 8:1? It appears that Paul has said in a different way what Luke described at Acts 7:58 and 8:1. The editor did not notice that fact. Therefore, the words were most likely a primitive Syrian gloss that became both the Byz text and the PWR. NA28 is original.

5. (#27:19/19) 614 has εἰς τὴν θάλασσαν (vs. omits, NA28/Byz) and brings in a phrase from 27:30, 38, and 40. It is found in 7/10 core PWR MSS and five others plus (gig s w 189 sa sy^{Aram} sy^{h**} Ä). It is

ESTABLISHING THE ANTIQUITY AND QUALITY

both the PWR and the WRR. In comparison, the standard reading is joined by Chrys Vg p bo sy^p sy^h. Both the Alex and Byz scribes resisted the gloss. NA28/Byz is original.

Limited Harmonization

1. (#2:31/22–24) 614/Byz has + ἡ ψυχὴ αὐτοῦ and seems to assimilate the idea from 2:27 or from Ps 16:10. It is the PWR. The NA28/Alex reading has minimal Greek MSS but it dominates in the translations. NA28 is original.

2. (7:35/25) 08 reads δικαστὴν ἐφ' ἡμᾶς (vs. δικαστὴν ἐφ' ἡμῶν, 01, vs. δικαστήν, NA28/Byz/614) and is joined by 0142 33 1739 2200, 3/10 core PWR MSS, and forty-two others plus Chrys. 01 is supported by 04 05 81 180 307 1175 and fifteen others and matches the LXX exactly. The readings of 08 and 01 may be joined by (d e gig p w 189 sa bo mae sy^p sy^h** Ä A G). NA28/Byz/614 is found in P45 P74 02 03 181 etc., including 7/10 core PWR MSS, plus Vg sy^h. 08 is the WRR. Its influence was dramatic. Core Alex MSS 01 04 81 1175 have begun with the WRR and conformed it to the LXX. The nearly unanimous translation support for the incorrect reading shows the WR's tremendous impact and should caution every textual critic from making overly confident decisions based solely on translation evidence. Only the Byz tradition, 30 percent of the best ECM MSS (i.e., P74 02 03), and 70 percent of the core PWR MSS maintain the original.

3. (#7:37/40) 614 has + ἐμὲ αὐτοῦ ἀκούσεσθε (vs. ἐμέ, NA28/Byz) and is found in 6/10 core PWR MSS, 04 (05*) 05C1 08 33 424C 1241 (1175) 1739 2200, and A G (d e gig p w ar bo mae sy^p sy^h.txt/sy^hmg). 614 is the PWR that also became the WRR. NA28/Byz is joined by 4/10 core PWR MSS and P45 P74^vid 01 02 03 81 etc. plus Chrys Vg sa Ä. 614 has introduced the words directly from the LXX at Deut 18:15. Once again, nearly all the translations have gone astray to include the bo. Some of the core PWR MSS have been revised to the standard. Beyond that, only the Byz, 5/10 core Alex MSS, and three translations kept the original.

4. (#10:12/8-28) 614/Byz has πάντα τὰ τετράποδα <u>τῆς γῆς καὶ τὰ θηρία</u> καὶ <u>τὰ</u> ἑρπετὰ καὶ <u>τὰ</u> πετεινὰ τοῦ οὐρανοῦ (vs. πάντα τὰ τετράποδα καὶ ἑρπετὰ <u>τῆς γῆς</u> καὶ πετεινὰ τοῦ οὐρανοῦ, NA28) and is found in 10/10 core PWR MSS and 020 025 35 etc. plus Chrys. There are twenty alternatives in the ECM. NA28 has limited Greek support but together with related readings b-c, it has all the translation support. NA28 is the original, especially since the PWR/Byz is a harmonization with 11:6/14–42. The shared error between the Byz and the PWR among twenty readings shows their tight coherence. Either could be the source of the error or they may have the same foundational archetype.

5. (#11:8/12–18; cf. 10:14/20–26) 614 has οὐδέποτε κοινὸν ἢ ἀκάθαρτον (vs. κοινὸν ἢ ἀκάθαρτον οὐδέποτε, NA28, vs. <u>πᾶν</u> κοινὸν ἢ ἀκάθαρτον οὐδέποτε, Byz) and is found in 6/10 core PWR MSS and 424C plus Epiph sy^h. It is the PWR. NA28 is joined by P45 P74^{vid} 01(*f) 02 03 05 08 33 81 etc. plus Chrys Vg e w l 189. Byz is joined by 014 020 35 etc. The Coptic translations (sa bo mae) further strengthen either NA28 or 614. The Byz πᾶν probably came by harmonization from 10:14/20–26 and the PWR has reordered NA28. Similarly, the Alex text πᾶν κοινὸν καὶ ἀκάθαρτον is firm at 10:14, having the support of P45 P74 01 02 03 etc. plus Vg d p sy^p A G S (sa) Clem ConstAp Did Or. The following witnesses also retain καὶ and thus indirectly support NA28: Ambr Aug gig 189 sy^h. In contrast, 614 and the Byz (including 9/10 core PWR MSS and 04 05 08 plus Bas Chrys^{pt} Cyr^{pt} Or^{ms} sa^{ms} bo mae) both harmonize at 10:14 by acquiring ἢ from 11:8. The Byz harmonization is complete.

6. (15:38/34–38) 614/NA28 reads συμπαραλαμβάνειν (vs. συμπαραλαβεῖν, Byz) and is joined by P74 (01 02 3* 04) 03C2 81 and many Westerns. The Byz text probably harmonized with 15:37. 614/NA28 is the original.

7. (19:35/47) 614/N28 omits θεᾶς and is joined by P74 01 02 03 05 08 etc., including many Westerns plus Isid Vg d e gig p w 189 sa bo sy^p sy^h. Byz is joined by 014 020 35 etc. and Chrys Isid^T. Byz harmonized with 19:27. 614/NA28 is original.

8. (21:8/10) 614/NA28/RP05^{mg} has ἤλθομεν (vs. <u>οἱ περὶ τὸν Παῦλον ἦλθον</u>, RP05^{txt}, vs. <u>οἱ περὶ τὸν Παῦλον</u> ἤλθομεν, 0142) and is found in 10/10 core PWR MSS and P74 01 02 04 08 18 35* etc. plus Chrys

Eus sa bo sy^Aram sy^p sy^h Ä. 614 is the PWR. RP05^txt is joined by 014 020 025 etc. and appears to be a harmonization with 13:13. MS 0142 is joined by twenty-nine MSS and was probably a merger of the two main readings. NA28 is original as confirmed by the PWR and the translations.

9. (21:40/38) 614/NA28 reads προσεφώνησεν (vs. προσεφώνει, Byz) and is joined by P74 01 02 03 05 08 014 020 025 049 056 etc., including all Westerns plus Chrys ByzECM. RP05 is joined by 18 35C etc. The Byz has harmonized with 22:2/14 as confirmed by the Westerns. 614/NA28 is original.

10. (22:2/14) 614 reads προσεφώνησεν (vs. προσεφώνει, NA28/Byz) and is joined by P74 020 etc., including most Westerns. It is the PWR. NA28/Byz is joined by 01 02 03 025 18 35 etc. This time the PWR has harmonized with 21:40/38.

11. (25:8/2–6) 614/NA28 reads τοῦ Παύλου ἀπολογουμένου (vs. ἀπολογουμένου αὐτοῦ, Byz) and is joined by P74 01 02 03 04 etc., including 9/10 PWR MSS, and thirty-three total MSS plus ar sy^Aram (sa bo sy^h) (Vg e gig p w^vid 189 sy^p). It is the PWR. The ECM lists eight alternatives. Byz is joined by 014 025 35 etc. Core Byz MS 020 uniquely conflates the two. Personal names, being swapped with pronouns, were normally corrupted in the direction toward more specificity. However, in this case, Paul is mentioned repeatedly (see 25:2, 4, 6, 9–10). There is no apparent "need" for another mention. Given the absence of translation support for the Byz, it is much more likely the secondary reading. The editor replaced τοῦ παύλου with αὐτοῦ and then moved it after ἀπολογουμένου, in order to harmonize the grammatical structure with the start of 25:7. Notice that here the "clarifying" variant is not secondary. 614/NA28 is original as confirmed by the translations.

12. (25:26/54) 614/NA28 has γράψω (vs. γράψαι, Byz) and is joined by P74 01 02 03 04 etc., including 7/10 core PWR MSS, and the Vg e gig s p w 189 sa bo sy^h. The wording is a bit more awkward than the alternative. Byz is joined by 08 014 020 35 etc., including many Westerns, plus Chrys. It appears to harmonize with γράψαι earlier in the verse. The divided Westerns show that both readings are old. The translations show that 614/NA28 is original.

13. (28:23/43) 614/NA28 reads αὐτούς (vs. αὐτοὺς τὰ, Byz) and is found in 9/10 core PWR MSS and 01 02 03 33 81 1175 etc. plus AlMon. Byz is joined by 020 049 0142 35 etc. The Byz has "improved" the style by harmonizing with 28:31/16. NA28 is original as confirmed by the PWR.

Limited Conflated Readings or Glosses

1. (13:42/7) 614/NA28 shows αὐτῶν (vs. ἐκ τῆς συναγωγῆς τῶν Ἰουδαίων, RP05^{txt}) and is found in P74 01 02 03 04 05 08 33 35* 1890* etc., including 5/10 core PWR MSS, plus Chrys Vg d e gig p w 189 sa bo mae sy^p sy^h. 614 is the PWR. RP05^{txt} is joined by (020) 025 35C 1890C etc. and has no versional support. Notice how the relatively pure Byz 35* and the core PWR MS 1890* both began with the best reading. RP05^{txt} has added words possibly to emphasize the conflict with the Jews (see 13:42/8–16). NA28 and the PWR preserve the original.

2. (13:42/8–16) Byz reads + τὰ ἔθνη and has no translation support. Once again Byz MS 35* originally agreed with the NA28/614 reading but was then revised to the Byz. NA28/614 retains most of the same witnesses as in 13:42/7. NA28 and the PWR uphold the original.

3. (20:28/40) 614/NA28 reads τοῦ θεοῦ (vs. τοῦ κυρίου, P41, vs. τοῦ κυρίου καὶ θεοῦ, Byz) and is found in 10/10 core PWR MSS and 01 03 0142 35* etc. plus Antioch Ath Bas Chrys ConstAp Cyr Dam Epiph PetrAl ThdMop Vg w 189 bo^{ms} sy^p sy$^{h.txt}$. 614 is the PWR. P41 is joined by P74 02 04* 05 08 etc. plus AmAl Chrys ConstAp^{mss} Dam Did IrLat Thdrt d e gig p sa bo sy^{hmg}. P41 is the WRR and became a popular Alex reading. It may result from an attempt to distinguish textually between the Father and the Son by utilizing κυρίου here for Jesus as compared to the typical θεοῦ for the Father.[41] Since Jesus redeemed the church, the WRR favored the reading κυρίου. Byz is joined by 014 020 025 35C etc. The Byz conflates the two other readings into a third longer one. NA28/614 preserve the original reading as best confirmed by the core PWR MSS and the

---

41. Hurtado, *Texts and Artefacts*, 70.

ESTABLISHING THE ANTIQUITY AND QUALITY

4. (#23:30/10–18) 614/NA28 reads εἰς τὸν ἄνδρα ἔσεσθαι ἐξαυτῆς (vs. εἰς τὸν ἄνδρα ἔσεσθαι ἐξ αὐτῶν, 01, vs. εἰς τὸν ἄνδρα μέλλειν ἔσεσθαι ὑπὸ τῶν Ἰουδαίων ἐξαυτῆς, Byz). The Byz apparently resulted from a conflation of these two readings, an expansion of ἐξ αὐτῶν into ὑπὸ τῶν Ἰουδαίων (see 23:27), and the addition of μέλλειν (see 23:15, 20, 27).

Difficult Readings

1. (#2:37/32) Byz reads ποιήσομεν (vs. ποιήσωμεν, NA28/614) and is joined by 05 18 35 etc., including 5/10 core PWR MSS, plus Bas Chrys^pt CyrH^T Dam^vid EulogA IrLat Phot Thdrt. NA28/614 is found in P74 P91 01 02 03 04 08 025 049 0142 1 81 1175 etc., including 5/10 core PWR MSS, plus Chrys^pt CyrH^mss Epiph Hipp Ä. The Byz reads the more difficult FAI-1P form against the common syntax of AAS-1P. The Byz is not only harder but has greater paternal support. The Byz text is probably original.

2. (#4:16/6) 614/Byz has ποιήσομεν (vs. ποιήσωμεν, NA28) and is found in 6/10 core PWR MSS and 05 025 18 35 etc. plus BasSel Chrys. 614 is the PWR. NA28 is found in 4/10 core PWR MSS and 01 02 03 08 1 33 1175 etc. ECM records it as a SGL reading. As above, the Byz has more paternal support and is more difficult. The Byz text as confirmed by the PWR is probably original (cf. 2:37/32).

3. (#4:21/20) 614/Byz reads κολάσονται (vs. κολάσωνται, NA28) and is found in 9/10 core PWR MSS and 025 049 0142 18 35 180 1175* etc. plus Chrys. 614 is the PWR. NA28 is joined by 01 02 03C2 05 08 1175C and eighteen others. The ECM records it as a SGL reading. The Byz scribes were apparently more comfortable with the use of the unusual FAI-3P form with the subjunctive sense (cf. 2:37/32; 4:16/6). Byz is probably original as confirmed by the PWR.

4. (12:25/10–14) 614/RP05^mg has ἀπὸ Ἰερουσαλήμ (vs. εἰς Ἰερουσαλήμ, NA28/RP05^txt, vs. ἐξ Ἰερουσαλήμ, P74, vs. ἀπὸ/ἐξ Ἰερουσαλὴμ εἰς Ἀντιόχ[ε]ιαν, 08) and is found in 6/10 core PWR MSS, (05*) 05C2, and twenty-seven others plus Chrys^ms (d gig 189 sy^h.txt bo mae).

614 is the PWR. NA28/RP05[txt] is joined by 01 03 014 020 025 81 etc., including core Westerns 383 1505 2147 2495, and sy[hmg]. P74 is joined by 02 33 459 547 2344 Chrys[T] (d gig 189 sy[h.txt] bo mae). 08 is joined by thirty-two others plus (e p w sa sy[p]). None of the translations except sy[hmg] withstood the attempts to "correct" the text. Yet the primary Byz tradition and a few core Alex MSS 01 03 81 remained steady. It is hard to explain their agreement for the hard reading if it were not original. Since Paul and Barnabas are found in Antioch in 13:1, many scribes assumed that the verse must refer to their return journey there. The solution might be found in 11:29–30. Paul and Barnabas were to assist the brethren in Judea by sending relief money to the elders. The text does not specify which elders. They may have gone to the elders of each individual church in Judea rather than to put a burden on the Jerusalem church to distribute the gifts. Therefore, if they started their ministry in Jerusalem by touching base with the apostles/elders, departed for the scattered churches, and then returned to Jerusalem, bringing John Mark back, the hardest reading makes sense. Their actual return to Antioch need not be stated (cf. 15:34, 40).[42]

5. (#14:17/40) 614/NA28 reads ὑμῶν (vs. ἡμῶν, Byz) and is found in 01* 03 04 05 08 1 81 1175 etc., including 5/10 core PWR MSS, plus IrLat Thdrt[T] Vg d e p h w 72 189 bo mae sy[h]. Byz is joined by P74 01C2 02 014 020 etc., including 5/10 core PWR MSS, plus Ath Chrys ConstAp Thdrt[mss] gig sy[p] Ä. 614/NA28 has greater translation support. It is possible the difference came from an itacism. However, given that ὑμῖν is found earlier in the verse (14:17/16), a harmonizing change is the most likely cause. The ECM provides 135 Greek MSS at this variant and only 26 avoid the harmony (9 delete the first pronoun, 5 have ἡμῖν then ὑμῶν: *614 1611 1827 2412 L809*, and 12 go from ὑμῖν to ἡμῶν: Byz plus *945 996 1505 1704 1739 1751 1838 1891 2200 2298 2495 2805* + gig). Since 10 (italicized above) of the 17 are Western leaning MSS, it appears the Western editors had some appreciation for the disharmony. All translations and fathers harmonize except for gig. Only the Byz witnesses

---

42. See Wachtel, "Text-Critical Commentary," 18–19, where he gives a well received explanation of the NA28/Byz reading. He says that εἰς Ἰηρουσαλὴμ, despite its awkward placement, refers to the place of their completed ministry and ὑπέστρεψαν refers to their return to Antioch.

consistently maintained the diversity. The Byz is probably the original. See 26:26/28–40 below for a clear case of Byz faithfulness.

6. (19:14/6–20) 614f3/Byz preserves τινες υἱοὶ Σκευᾶ 'Ιουδαίου ἀρχιερέως ἑπτὰ οἱ τοῦτο ποιοῦντες (vs. τινες Σκευᾶ 'Ιουδαίου ἀρχιερέως ἑπτα υἱοὶ τοῦτο ποιοῦντες, ECM, vs. τινος Σκευᾶ 'Ιουδαίου ἀρχιερέως ἑπτὰ υἱοὶ τοῦτο ποιοῦντες, NA28) and is joined by 08 014 020 35C etc., including 10/10 core PWR MSS, plus Chrys sy^h. 614 is the PWR. ECM is joined by P74 01 02f1 33 1175* and nine others. Either may be supported by (sa). NA28 is joined by P41 03 431 1175C 1739 1891 2200 plus (sa bo sy^p). There are ten alternatives. NA28 probably smoothed the ECM reading by changing τινες to τινος. The ECM reading appears to simplify the Byz syntax. The Byz is possibly original as confirmed by the PWR.

7. (#26:26/28–40) 614 has αὐτὸν τούτων πείθομαι οὐθέν οὐ (vs. αὐτόν τι τούτων οὐ πείθομαι οὐθέν/οὐδέν οὐ, NA28/Byz, vs. αὐτόν τι τούτων οὐ πείθομαι οὐ, P74, vs. αὐτὸν τούτων οὐ πείθομαι οὐθέν οὐ, 03). The phrase is part of an extremely complex sentence. In fact, the ECM lists twenty alternatives. 614 simplifies the construction by dropping both τι and the first οὐ and is found in 8/10 core PWR MSS and four others plus sy^h. It is the PWR. NA28/Byz have only an orthographic difference but NA28 is not Alex. Of the thirty-seven MSS listed in the apparatus in support of NA28/Byz, only 01* and 048 are Alex.[43] Instead, P74 best preserves the Alex reading and is joined by 01C2 02 33 93 etc. 03 is joined by just 1243 and has merely dropped the τι. The resistance to change by the Byz text here is remarkable given the complex syntax that includes a double negative immediately followed by a negative that starts the next clause. Both NA28 and the ECM recognize the quality of the Byz text at this variant.

High Quality Readings (Equal or Better Quality Than Alex Tradition)

1. (2:41/6–8, 6–14) The key to this example is to look at two related variant units together. 614/Byz reads οὖν ἀσμένως ἀποδεξάμενοι τὸν λόγον αὐτοῦ (vs. οὖν ἀποδεξάμενοι τὸν λόγον αὐτοῦ, NA28,

---

43. CBGM.

οὖν <u>ἀσμένως</u> ἀποδεξάμενοι τὸν λόγον <u>καὶ ἐπίστευσαν καὶ</u>, sy^hmg, οὖν <u>πιστεύσαντες</u> τὸν λόγον αὐτοῦ, 05) and is joined by 08 025 18 35 etc., including 7/10 core PWR MSS. It is the PWR. NA28 is joined by P74 01 02 03 04 81 1175 and five others plus Clem Eus^vid Vg gig p t r w 70 189 Ä. Since 614/Byz lacks versional support it appears that it could be excluded despite its dominant Greek evidence. However, NA28 is limited to the Latin and the Ä. The situation changes significantly when the other two readings above are examined. The text of sy^hmg is joined by Aug mae sy^p. The alignment of sy^hmg and mae shows that it is probably the WRR. Though they replace the standard αὐτοῦ with καὶ ἐπίστευσαν καὶ, they confirm the antiquity of the 614/Byz reading by preserving ἀσμένως. 05/d can be considered indirect support for the WRR. By having πιστεύσαντες instead of αποδεξάμενοι, 05 reveals that its lineage goes back to the WRR even though it has been revised. In summary, both 614/Byz and NA28 are equally strong and should probably be a SGL reading.

2. (2:43/29, 22–29) 614/NA28/Byz reads ἐγίνετο (vs. ἐγίνετο <u>ἐν Ἰερουσαλὴμ φόβος τε ἦν μέγας ἐπὶ πάντας</u>, 01) and is found in 7/10 core PWR MSS, 03 05 025 049 18 35 81 1739 2200 etc., and Chrys d gig p* r sa sy^h Ä. It is the PWR. The ECM shows nine alternatives. MS 01 is joined by 02 04 1175 and six others plus Vg p/2^vid t w 70 73 189. The core Alex MSS are divided. In fact, CBGM Phase IV data indicates that just four (see 03 81 1739 2200) of the top ten ECM MSS display the NA28 reading.[44] The division is further confirmed by the variant at 2:43/22–29. There, MS 629 reads <u>διὰ τῶν ἀποστόλων ἐν Ἰερουσαλήμ</u> ἐγίνοντο καὶ φόβος ἦν μέγας ἐπὶ πάντας <u>τοὺς ανθρώπους</u> and is joined by bo mae. In contrast, the sa stays with the short reading. While some Alex MSS like 03 weathered the storm, the Byz and most core PWR MSS avoided it altogether. Given the expansive nature of the variant, the WRR probably caused the confusion.

3. (#3:6/46–48) This example exists to show that an Alex reading, standing against a Byz reading, should not be overly favored just because it has 01 and 03 on its side. Here 01 is joined by only 03 05 Dam d sa in omitting the words ἔγειρε καὶ or their equivalent ἔγειραι καὶ. NA28 put the words in brackets, suggesting the editors were not confident. ECM allows this lightly supported reading to be

44. CBGM.

part of a SGL. Rather than a time for indecision, the situation shows an agreement in error and should caution any editor from giving too much weight to these MSS, especially when they are joined by just 05. The Sahidic also shows a tendency to retain the more subtle Western readings. Not only does the standard reading include all remaining translation support but it is also confirmed by eighteen fathers against just one. There is no need for a SGL here.

4. (#4:8/27) 614/Byz has + τοῦ Ἰσραήλ and is found in all Western MSS available at this passage, including 05 08. It is also joined by Chrys IrLat^vid d e gig p* h mae sy^p sy^h A G. The NA28/ECM reading is supported by just P74 01 02 03 0165 629 1175 1409* Cyr Procop Vg 189 sa bo Ä. All its witnesses appear to be tied to Egypt. Wachtel cites other authors and concludes that τοῦ Ἰσραήλ is more likely to be an addition.[45] Note that τοῦ Ἰσραήλ only occurs eleven times in the NT and just once in Acts at 28:20 (three times in Luke: 1:68; 2:25; 22:30). Of those eleven, not once does it refer to Jewish leaders. Metzger argues that it was added to create balance with the former phrase ἄρχοντες τοῦ λαοῦ.[46] Given the difficulty of + τοῦ Ἰσραήλ because of its unique NT usage, the setting of recorded speech (i.e., the words need not be Lucan style), the variety of the translations supporting it, the domination of the Western MSS aligned with the Byz, the original text apparently was balanced in a very fine manner.

5. (#4:17/20) The Byz and the 614-group have + ἀπειλῇ. Neither the translations nor the fathers provide a deciding voice. The Semitic nature of the Byz/614 reading appears original.

6. (#4:24/28–30) 614/Byz has + ὁ θεός before ὁ ποιήσας and is joined by 9/10 core PWR MSS and 05 08 etc. plus AstS Ath^mss Chrys HesH gig p 189 A G (Ä) (sa mae). 614 is the PWR. NA28 is joined by just P74 01 02 03 69 1409 2774 Ath^T Did Vg w bo A^ms. In addition, MS 522 and others plus IrLat d sy^p sy^h add εἶ in front of the PWR/Byz reading to make the meaning more explicit and thus derive from it. The short reading is easily explainable from a homoeoteleuton. The mass of the translations and the Western testimony point to 614/Byz being original.

---

45. Wachtel, "Text-Critical Commentary," 9.
46. Metzger, *Textual Commentary*, 276.

7. (5:15/4–10) Byz reads <u>κατὰ</u> τὰς πλατείας, "along the streets," and is joined by its typical support plus several Westerns. NA28 has <u>καὶ εἰς</u> τὰς πλατείας, "also into the streets," and is joined by P74 01 02 03 05C2 etc., including several Westerns, and a total of 40 MSS. 08 has <u>καὶ ἐν ταῖς</u> πλατείαις and may be a gloss of NA28. 1611 appears to drop καὶ from NA28 and is joined by just 3 others. 05* should be seen as secondary to the Byz, having dropped τὰς. It was then corrected to agree with NA28. The translations undergird either 05*, 1611, or the Byz, but not NA28. Therefore, it is most likely that Vg d e gig t w 70 73 189 sa bo mae sy^p sy^h demonstrate the originality of the Byz.

8. (7:32/3) 08 has + εἰμὶ and is joined by only 049 1241 1884 Ath d e gig p w ar Ä. It reads, ἐγώ <u>εἰμι</u> ὁ θεὸς <u>τῶν πατέρων</u> σου. NA28, the Byz, and the PWR each lack the addition. If scribes were so prone to change the text, how is it that only a few supplied the "missing" verb of "being"? This scribal conservatism is even more noteworthy here since the LXX reads, ἐγώ <u>εἰμι</u> ὁ θεὸς <u>τοῦ πατρός</u> σου (Exod 3:6). Note also that the LXX refers to a solitary father, while all the ECM MSS have the plural. This unchanged disharmony should be considered when discussing which variant is correct later in the same verse (see chapter 4, 7:32/21, 25).

9. (#7:46/22–24) 614/Byz has τῷ <u>θεῷ</u> (vs. τῷ <u>οἴκῳ</u>, NA28) and has more diversity and makes more sense. The Alex reading could be explained by an accidental assimilation to οἶκον in the nearby context at 7:47/10 (see chapter 4).

10. (7:56/26–30) NA28/Byz/614 reads ἐκ δεξιῶν ἑστῶτα (vs. ἑστῶτα ἐκ δεξιῶν, P45) and is found in P74 01C2 03 05 81 etc., including 9/10 core PWR MSS, plus AstA Ath Chrys ConstAp^mss Dam Epiph GregNy^mss IrLat^T Marcell NicC Vg d h^vid 189. P45 is joined by 01* 02 04 08 etc. plus Antioch Ath^mss ConstAp^T CyrH Epiph GregNy^T HesH IrLat^mss MacSym Phot SevGab Thdrt e gig p t w 70. Both readings have a great amount of paternal support. However, the standard one provides the best mixture of all three textual traditions and is the more awkward reading. Byz/614 stands with NA28 and avoids the popular ancient gloss.

11. (#7:60/22–28) 614/Byz displays αὐτοῖς τὴν ἁμαρτίαν ταύτην (vs. αὐτοῖς ταύτην τὴν ἁμαρτίαν, NA28) and is joined by 9/9 core PWR

MSS (MS 1890 is lacking) and P74 01 08 014 025 35 etc. plus AnastS AstA^mss Bas Chrys CosmIn Cyr Ephr^G Eus GregNy HesH IrLat^T Olymp Or PetrAl^mss Phot Thdrt d e G. NA28 is joined by 02 03 04 05 IrLat^mss PetrAl^T Vg p h w 70 Ä A. The following translations may support either one: (sy^h sy^p sa bo mae). 614/Byz clearly maintains an ancient reading. It would be hard to find a place in Acts that has more united paternal testimony. Neither alternative appears to be a result of smoothing (see chapter 4).

12. (#8:18/31) 614/Byz has τὸ πνεῦμα τὸ ἅγιον (vs. τὸ πνεῦμα, NA28) and is found in 9/9 core PWR MSS (MS 1890 is lacking) and includes all Western MSS. In fact, these are joined by P45 P74 02 04 05 08 014 020 35 81 1175 etc. plus Amph Ath Bas Chrys Dam Phot 9/9 OL bo sy^p sy^h. NA28 is joined by 01 03 ConstAp sa mae. The only thing the short variant shows is that the sa has a close relationship with 01 03. Yet Metzger et al. state, "After πνεῦμα the addition of τὸ ἅγιον was as natural for Christian scribes to make as its deletion would be inexplicable."[47] If the scribal tendency was that great, why does τὸ πνεῦμα stand alone in every ECM MS except 431 and 1292 at 8:29/6–8? It is puzzling why 01 03 should have so much authority in Acts. For example, P74 and 81 stand against them and are as likely to be correct. According to CBGM Phase IV, these four MSS match the reconstructed original in the following percentages: 01 (94.6), 03 (96.5), P74 (95.7), and 81 (95.5).[48] In fact, eight of the top ten CBGM MSS depart from 01/03 here. The Coptic dialects are also divided. If one adds to this evidence the complete unity of the Western and Byz traditions, the variety of translation support, and the strength of the fathers, it is hard to conclude otherwise. 01/03 lost the words by accident. Byz/614 should be regarded as original.

13. (8:22/16–22) 614/NA28 reads καὶ δεήθητι τοῦ <u>κυρίου</u> (vs. καὶ δεήθητι τοῦ <u>θεοῦ</u>, Byz), is joined by 01 02 03 04 05 08 etc., including many Westerns, plus Ath Bas Chrys e gig t r sa bo sy^h, and is probably the PWR. Byz is joined by 014 020 etc., including many Westerns, plus ConstAp Phot Vg p w 70 189 mae sy^p. The translations are divided evenly. At first, it appears that the Byz avoids a harmonization with 8:24/16–24 where the NA28/Byz reading includes δεήθητε ὑμεῖς ὑπὲρ ἐμοῦ πρὸς τὸν <u>κύριον</u>. In contrast, the PWR includes δεήθητε

---

47. Metzger, *Textual Commentary*, 314.
48. CBGM.

ὑμεῖς ὑπὲρ ἐμοῦ πρὸς τὸν θεὸν and seems to have avoided the harmony in an opposite manner. However, it is more likely that the Byz harmonized to the nearer τοῦ θεοῦ of 8:21/32–40 and that the PWR "improved" the wording at 8:24/16–24 (see chapter 3). NA28/PWR is probably original.

14. (#13:26/26) 614/NA28 reads ἡμῖν ὁ λόγος (vs. ὑμῖν ὁ λόγος, Byz) and is found in 6/10 core PWR MSS, P74 01 02 03 05 33 81, and seven others plus CosmIn d 74 sa mae sy^hmg. 614 is both the PWR and the WRR, as seen by the unity of 05 mae sy^hmg. Byz is joined by P45 04 08 014 020 35 etc. plus AnastS Chrys Or Phot Vg e gig p t w 70 73 189 bo sy^p sy^h.txt Ä. The ECM marks it as a SGL reading. At first sight, the 614/NA28 could be original because its ἡμῖν avoids harmonizing with ὑμῖν earlier in the verse. However, the alignment of 614 and friends suggests a different cause. Since the PWR became the WRR here, it would have been widespread and a natural source of corruption. In contrast, the Byz has great variety. It is upheld by Alex witnesses (i.e., P45 04 1175 bo), the remaining Western-leaning Greek MSS, slightly more translations, including the Vg, and has more fathers, including Or. Byz is probably the original (see chapter 4).

15. (#13:33/16) 614/NA28/Byz has αὐτῶν ἡμῖν (vs. ἡμῖν, ECM conjecture, vs. ἡμῶν, 03, vs. αὐτῶν, 1175) and is joined by 04C3 08 014 020 35 81 etc. plus AnastS AstS Chrys e sa sy^p sy^h A G. ECM conjecture is joined by (mae). 03 is joined by P74 01 02 04* 05 1409 CosmIn Vg d t w 73 (mae) Ä. 1175 is joined by 629 2147 gig bo. Wachtel defends the ECM choice by pointing to the small chance that 03 would arise from a mental contraction of the Byz reading. On the other hand, if ἡμῖν is original, it could have been easily corrupted to ἡμῶν.[49] True, but consider the alternative. How "easy" would it be for many scribes to independently corrupt τοῖς τέκνοις ἡμῖν ἀναστήσας Ἰησοῦν by inserting αὐτῶν before ἡμῖν? It still seems a bit awkward. Would it not be more natural to insert αὐτῶν in place of ἡμῖν as seen in 629 1175 2147? While the cause of the Alex reading is mysterious, errors are often of that nature. The presence of both 05 and mae may provide a clue. If ἡμῶν came from the WR as a simplifying gloss, it may have been adopted in a primitive Alex archetype. Nevertheless, the Sahidic demonstrates that it was not

---

49. Wachtel, "Text-Critical Commentary," 20.

the only reading common in Egypt. Moreover, the Bohairic dialect provides indirect support for the Byz as well. Byz is probably the original (see chapter 4).

16. (#13:40/10–18) 614 reads τὸ εἰρημένον ἐν τοῖς προφήταις εἰς ὑμᾶς (vs. ἐφ' ὑμᾶς τὸ εἰρημένον ἐν τοῖς προφήταις, Byz, vs. τὸ εἰρημένον ἐν τοῖς προφήταις, NA28) and is found in 6/10 core PWR MSS (sa bo mae). Byz is joined by 02 04 08 020 025 81 1175 etc., including many Westerns plus AnastS^{vid} Bas^{mss} Chrys CosmIn d gig p w 61 (sa bo mae). NA28 is joined by just (P74) 01 03 05 33^{vid} and eleven others plus Vg d 189 Ä. Since sy^p and sy^h could support either the Byz or Alex, their testimony provides no assistance. The Byz has the most variety with Alex MSS 02 04 81 1175, many Western MSS, most of the OL, and a unified Coptic. The Byz is probably original (see chapter 4).

17. (#14:8/8–18) Byz has ἐν Λύστροις ἀδύνατος τοῖς ποσὶν ἐκάθητο (vs. ἀδύνατος ἐν Λύστροις τοῖς ποσὶν ἐκάθητο, NA28, vs. ἐν Λύστροις ἐκάθητο ἀδύνατος τοῖς ποσίν, 383) and is joined by P74 01C2 02 04 044 5 33 etc., including many Westerns, and Chrys A G (Vg p w 72 189). The ECM lists nine alternatives. The following could support any of the above readings: (sa bo sy^p sy^h Ä). NA28 is joined by just 01* 03 1175. MS 383 is joined by other core PWR MSS: (614) 1292 (1611) (1890) (2138) 2147 (2412) and seems to smooth out the Byz by moving ἐκάθητο forward in the clause. While the Byz is smoother than NA28, the latter appears to be a clumsy mistake. NA28 may derive from an archetype that did not have ἐν Λύστροις in the first hand. The corrector then fixed it by placing the words directly over ἀδύνατος. The next copyist of the archetype reintroduced the phrase into the main text but carelessly placed it after ἀδύνατος. Alternatively, the NA28 reading may have occurred when a scribe overlooked ἐν Λύστροις. He realized it after writing ἀδύνατος and decided not to erase his minor error. Impressively, seven of the ten best CBGM Phase IV MSS support the Byz.[50] Byz is original.

18. (14:10/9) 383 has + σοι λέγω ἐν τῷ ὀνόματι τοῦ κυρίου Ἰησοῦ Χριστοῦ (vs. omits, NA28/Byz) and is joined by 04 05 (614) 2147 (2412) plus numerous other Westerns, including a total of thirty-six MSS, plus (d sy^p sy^{hmg} IrLat^T). NA28/Byz is joined by the translations: Vg gig

---

50. CBGM.

bo^mss sy^Aram sy^h.txt Ä. MS 08 reads similarly to MS 383 and is joined by (e sa^mss mae A G). Byz MS 35* removes κυρίου and is joined by (OL 189 sa^mss bo^mss). 614 and 2412 are in parentheses because they dropped τοῦ. The ECM lists eleven expansive readings in competition to the standard. 383 is the PWR that became the WRR. Interestingly, 6/10 core PWR MSS corrected to the standard. The plus was probably encouraged by 3:6/32–40 and 6:8/29 (see reading of MS 614). The versions indicate the popularity of the gloss. Despite that, the Byz and Alex traditions remained faithful.

19. (#14:19/2–4) 08 reads διατριβόντων δὲ αὐτῶν καὶ διδασκόντων ἐπῆλθον (vs. ἐπῆλθ[α/ο]ν, NA28/Byz/614) and is joined by (04) (05*) 05C1 33 35* 81 1175 1739 2200 and many Westerns, including 60 total MSS, plus (h mae sy^hmg). 08 is the WRR. The only ECM MSS outside the Byz that preserve the original include the Alex (P45) (P74) 01 02 03, 8/10 core PWR MSS (the other two have + καί), the Western leaning 1501 1838 (2652), and the unassigned 044 629. The Byz tradition, PWR tradition, and five key Alex MSS demonstrate great quality here.

20. (#14:19/16–22) 1739(Cf3) (reading e.) has καὶ <u>διαλεγομένων αὐτῶν παρρησίᾳ ἀνέπεισαν τοὺς ὄχλους <u>ἀποστῆναι ἀπ' αὐτῶν λέγοντες ὅτι οὐδὲν ἀληθὲς λέγουσιν ἀλλὰ πάντα ψεύδονται</u> (vs. καὶ πείσαντες τοὺς ὄχλους, NA28/Byz/614) and is joined by 81 945 1175 1891 etc. plus (mae) A G. The ECM lists twenty alternatives. Some MSS like 467 (reading k.) preserve a form of the expansion with the standard wording appended. Uniquely, sy^hmg (reading t.) has the long addition of 1739(Cf3) with the standard text revised to ἐπισείσαντες τοὺς ὄχλους at the end. These final words are the only ones found in 05C1 gig (05* d^vid e sy^p), reading c. Their agreement with sy^hmg in a unique synonym suggests that 05*/05C1 once equaled sy^hmg. These clues indicate that sy^hmg is the original WRR. Therefore, 467 (k.) replaced the concluding words of the WRR with the standard. On the other hand, 1739(Cf3) dropped the final words as being a doublet. The original text has limited Greek support outside the Byz. That testimony includes Alex P45^vid P74 01 02 03 33, 10/10 core PWR MSS, Western leaning 08 1501 1838 1884 2652, and nonaligned 044 441C 629 1409 2344 L1188. It is further confirmed by Chrys Vg p w 189 sa bo sy^h.txt Ä. The purity of the Byzantine tradition, the core Alex MSS, and the PWR tradition is impressive.

21. (14:25/13) 614 has λόγον <u>τοῦ κυρίου</u> (vs. λόγον <u>τοῦ θεοῦ</u>, P74, vs. λόγον, NA28/Byz,) and is found in 01 02 04 81 etc., including 5/10 core PWR MSS, plus A. 614 is the PWR. P74 is joined by 08 1884 e gig bo^ms G and has probably derived from the PWR. Both longer readings may be joined by (Vg p w l 189 sy^p sy^h**). NA28/Byz is joined by 03 05 014 20 35 1175 1739 2200 etc., including 5/10 core PWR MSS, plus Chrys d sa bo mae sy^h Ä. Several core Alex MSS (P74 01 02 04) were drawn to the PWR or a variation of it while others (see 03 1175 1739 2200) did not waver. With the Alex and PWR core groups divided, the best witness here for the original is the Byz tradition.

22. (#18:21/4–6) 614/Byz reads ἀπετάξατο αὐτοῖς (vs. ἀποταξάμενος καὶ, NA28, vs. ἀποταξάμενος αὐτοῖς καὶ, 08) and is found in 014 020 044 35 etc., including 10/10 core PWR MSS, plus gig 189 sy^h. It is the PWR. NA28 is joined by P74 01 02 03 05 33 1409 L1188 plus Vg e p. 08 is joined by 181 1175 etc. plus d w. Either 614/Byz or NA28 may receive the support of (sa bo sy^p). 614/Byz seems to have clearer grammar than NA28. 08 is possibly an attempt to fix the awkwardness of NA28 and does so by conflating the other two. Both 614/Byz and NA28 have solid support, and either could be original (see chapter 4).

23. (#18:21/9) 614/Byz reads εἰπών <u>δεῖ με πάντως τὴν ἑορτὴν τὴν ἐρχομένην ποιῆσαι εἰς Ἱεροσόλυμα</u> (vs. εἰπών, NA28) and is joined by 05(C2f) 014 020 35 1175 etc., including 10/10 core PWR MSS, plus Chrys (sy^p.mss sy^h d gig w ar). It is the PWR and BL consider it to be written by Luke.[51] NA28 is joined by P74 01 02 03 08 33 1739 2200 and seventeen others plus Vg e p 189 sa bo Ä A G. There are thirteen alternatives but twelve of them support a long reading. While NA28 displays support from Ä A G, it is also true that these translations unite to preserve the gloss of 15:34. Coptic translation alignment with Alex MSS is a common occurrence, and the agreement with the Vg may be due to Or. Contextually, the longer reading fits the context in an excellent manner and agrees with Lucan style. What would be the reason to add it if it were not original?[52] The sentence

---

51. Boismard and Lamouille, *Texte occidental reconstitution*, 1:190.

52. Barrett, *Commentary on Acts*, 2:879, suggests that an editor added it to explain why Paul was in such a hurry to depart. Moreover, he calls the long reading Western even though it is as much Byz as it is Western. Wachtel, "Against the Text-Type Concept," 146, agrees, and shows that calling it Western is presuppositional and based upon

as read in the Alex seems to lack something. It has, "But after saying goodbye and speaking, 'God willing I will come again to you,' he sailed away from Ephesus." Since there is ancient evidence that some scribes struggled with the idea of Paul planning to go to Jerusalem but never going, the same concern may have motivated an early scribe to delete the clause. As an example, a Western editor interpreted καὶ κατελθὼν εἰς Καισάρειαν ἀναβὰς καὶ ἀσπασάμενος τὴν ἐκκλησίαν κατέβη εἰς Ἀντιόχειαν, in 18:22, as Paul going up to the church at Caesarea rather than up to Jerusalem. Therefore, the editor inserted a reason at 19:1 to explain why Paul never made it there (see 19:1/2–30). Was the short Alex reading another way to deal with that difficulty? Sometimes the argument is made that the presence of numerous long readings in contrast to a single short one proves that the short one is original. However, this guideline is of limited application since variants exist where every reading is long (cf. 17:32/26–33/8; 18:17/24–32). Would it not be reasonable for an ancient scribe, facing the same problem, to instead delete the words? This variant in combination with three others will be fully addressed in chapter 4.

A Tradition Essentially Near to the Alexandrian Text

For the purposes of comparing the Byz and Alex traditions, the modern edition of RP05 was compared with that of NA28. To quantify and qualify the differences between them, three categories will be utilized: significant (SI), insignificant (INS), and not translatable (NTR). Significant indicates a variant that changes the idea of the passage. The impact it makes upon the reader is yet another consideration. It is sometimes the case that significant differences have only minor impacts upon the reader. For example, "word of God" versus "word of the Lord" is significant but does not provide a substantial difference to the meaning. Insignificant means the difference is noticeable but the meaning is nearly the same. In this category are included differences such as the interchange of καί, δέ, and οὖν. Not translatable refers to a difference that is so subtle that it cannot or need not be translated into ordinary English.

Overall, there are approximately 1,060 variant units between RP05 and NA28. After removing the instances of single brackets in NA28 and

---

longstanding popular views about text types.

the alternate spellings of the same word, that number comes down to 879.[53] Using the categories above, the approximate numbers in each category are as follows: 98 SI, 364 INS, and 598 NTR. Since a mere 98 SI variants separate the two traditions, they are very near in their message. To put that number in context, it should be remembered that there are over 7,400 differences recorded in the ECM apparatus, acquired from 183 Greek witnesses.[54] Therefore, RP05 and NA28 are about 98.7 percent alike in terms of essential meaning.

There is perhaps another useful way to compare. The number of potential differences in a document is easily much greater than the number of words, since almost every word could be substituted or lost, and there could be innumerable word order variations, not to mention the potential additions. On the other hand, in a location where a single variant is the addition of twelve words (see 28:29), counting it as one difference might seem to overstate the agreement. Given these conflicting factors, it seems appropriate to also utilize the number of words in a book as another measure of coherence. There are about 18,453 words in the text of Acts as contained in NA28.[55] If this total is used instead, the fundamental agreement between RP05 and NA28 ends up being about 99.5 percent.

Since there are eighty-three occasions (RP05 = sixty-eight; NA28 = fifteen) where one edition is two or more words longer, I decided to start by comparing these variant units. It turns out that forty-five of the variants fell into the SI category. The remaining thirty-eight cases are either INS or NTR. The SI variants differing in length by two or more words are listed (forty-five cases):

> 1:14/15; 2:30/34; 2:47/38—3:1/4; 3:13/8–12; 3:22/4–6; 4:8/27; 4:12/22–40; 4:24/28–30; 4:25/2–24; 4:27/6–26; 5:24/14–28; 5:41/22–28; 7:37/26–28; 9:28/10–14; 9:38/30–34; 10:11/14–30; 10:12/8–28; 10:30/25; 10:32/37; 13:42/8–16; 14:15/42–44; 15:18/2–6; 15:23/16–20; 15:24/30–34; 17:13/50–56; 18:17/6; 18:21/9; 20:4/7; 20:15/28–30; 20:24/27; 20:25/39; 20:28/40; 21:8/10; 21:22/10–14; 21:25/16–20; 22:9/19; 23:7/14–20;

---

53. See the appendix for a listing of the 181. From the RP05 apparatus, only 3:19–20 was ignored because 3:20 merely starts at a different word as compared to NA28. These 1,060 variant units are equal to 1,075 in the ECM. The +15 are from ECM editors selecting different lengths for the variant units.

54. ECM 3:1:1, intro, 19; Wachtel, "Notes on Acts," intro, 28.

55. The number was estimated using *BW*. RP05 has about 221 more words than NA28.

ESTABLISHING THE ANTIQUITY AND QUALITY

23:9/59; 23:30/10–18; 24:23/30–32; 24:26/21; 25:6/6–20; 25:16/23; 28:16/12–16; and 28:29/2–24.

The INS/NTR variants differing in length by two or more words are listed (thirty-eight cases):

2:7/8–10; 2:20/24–28; 2:31/22–24; 2:38/36–40; 3:11/6; 4:5/22–34; 4:32/12–20; 7:18/12–14; 7:31/24–28; 7:32/21–25; 8:18/31; 9:5/15; 9:19/14–22; 9:26/4–8; 11:25/6–8; 12:20/5; 13:24/20–26; 13:40/10–18; 13:42/7; 13:45/29; 15:17/48–52; 18:1/2–6; 18:20/14; 19:3/5; 19:12/50; 20:24/6–8; 21:20/30–34; 22:20/31; 22:30/31; 23:34/5; 24:14/46–56; 24:20/14–18; 24:22/2–10; 25:7/30; 25:22/23; 26:14/18–24; 26:30/2–4; and 28:30/6–14.

To make sure that every important difference was recorded, I proceeded to review the comprehensive listing of differences between RP05 and NA28 that is recorded in the lower apparatus of RP05. These were then correlated with the numbering system of the variants per the ECM volumes. As a result, fifty-three more SI variants were found. These differ by zero or one word in length:

1:15/22; 1:25/4–12; 2:41/6–8; 3:26/17; 4:36/2; 6:13/22–24; 7:17/18; 7:30/27; 7:38/54; 7:46/22–24; 8:10/30–32; 8:13/30–38; 8:16/32–34; 8:22/16–22; 9:17/40–44; 9:20/16; 9:25/6–22; 9:28/28–30; 9:38/44–50; 10:33/52; 10:48/8–18; 13:20/2–16; 13:23/18–26; 13:44/22–28; 14:14/24–30; 15:40/20; 16:7/34; 16:10/30–36; 16:31/17; 17:3/34–40; 17:5/2–22; 17:23/32–40; 17:26/2–8; 17:27/4–6; 17:30/26–30; 18:5/28–30; 18:7/16–20; 18:25/36–38; 19:4/44; 19:10/35; 19:27/54–58; 20:1/24–26; 20:5/6 (RP05 = ECM ≠ NA28); 21:20/12–18; 22:16/30; 22:26/19; 23:20/38; 24:2/30; 24:24/44–52; 26:16/44; 27:2/10; 28:13/4; and 28:26/2.

A careful study of the above ninety-eight SI differences will enable the reader to see that the two traditions present a very harmonious message.

SUMMARY

The preceding five sections have sought to demonstrate that the Alex, Byz, and PWR traditions each preserve a text that is exceptionally ancient and of high quality. First, many readings characteristic of the WR were identified. Next, many significant readings of the PWR archetype were considered in terms of their relationship with the WRRs. Numerous examples were offered to show that the PWRs are predominantly more primitive and more excellent than those of the WR. Next, some examples were given to display how the PWR archetype seems to have started with a mixed-text archetype that combined readings that are essential parts of the Byz and Alex traditions. The PWR archetype seems to be a result of taking this foundation and making many adjustments to it. Most significantly, it has been asserted that this process occurred in the early decades of the NT era. As discussed in chapter 1, the WR appears to have been created within or just prior to the period of AD 150–175. The PWR archetype is estimated to originate from a generation before, in the window of AD 125–150. The preceding approach has identified many genuine PWRs so that they could be compared with the oldest forms of the Alex and Byz traditions. With the best of each tradition, it is possible to better approximate the wording of the original text. After briefly considering the foundation of the PWR archetype, the Byz text of Acts was shown to have a tradition of faithful copying up to the present day. In fact, some examples were provided that suggest the Byz text may have numerous readings with equal or even better quality than competing ones from the Alex text. The last section compared the Byz and Alex traditions and concluded that they are very near with respect to essential meaning. If the Alex text of Acts is of great value for the textual critic, the Byz must be also since they are closely related. Now that the antiquity and quality of all three traditions has been observed, it will be helpful to consider how often MS 614—the best representative of the PWR archetype—aligns with one of the other two textual traditions or if it instead goes its own way.

3

Non-Aligned, Proto-Western Group Readings Are Secondary

ALEXANDRIAN AND BYZANTINE BASE OF THE PROTO-WESTERN TEXT

IT IS INDISPUTABLE THAT the proto-Western text aligns with the Byzantine (Byz) text more often than it does with the Alexandrian (Alex) text. However, few would agree upon the cause of that alignment. It is also verifiable that the proto-Western text deviates abundantly from both other traditions. This chapter will begin by looking at a mathematical comparison of how the three traditions agree and disagree with each other. As stated previously, the term proto-Western text refers to that reconstructed archetype from which the 614-group derives and refers to a MS created by an editor sometime between AD 125 and 150. This text is the sum of all the Proto-Western Readings (PWRs) whether they agree with the other traditions or stand alone. Although it was never considered a formal redaction, it became a principal contributor to that which became the first redaction of Acts, i.e., the Western Redaction (WR). The WR was probably finalized in the period of AD 150–175. It then led to the production of Codex D (05), the Coptic mae translation, a Syriac translation (whose characteristic readings are represented by sy^{h**} and sy^{hmg}), P38, and possibly P48. It also impacted many OL MSS.

In the book of Acts, the PWR agrees with the Byz 507 times, with the *Editio Critica Maior* (ECM) 242 times, stands against a united ECM/Byz 411 times, and is part of a three-way division a total of 105 times (see figure 3.1 below).

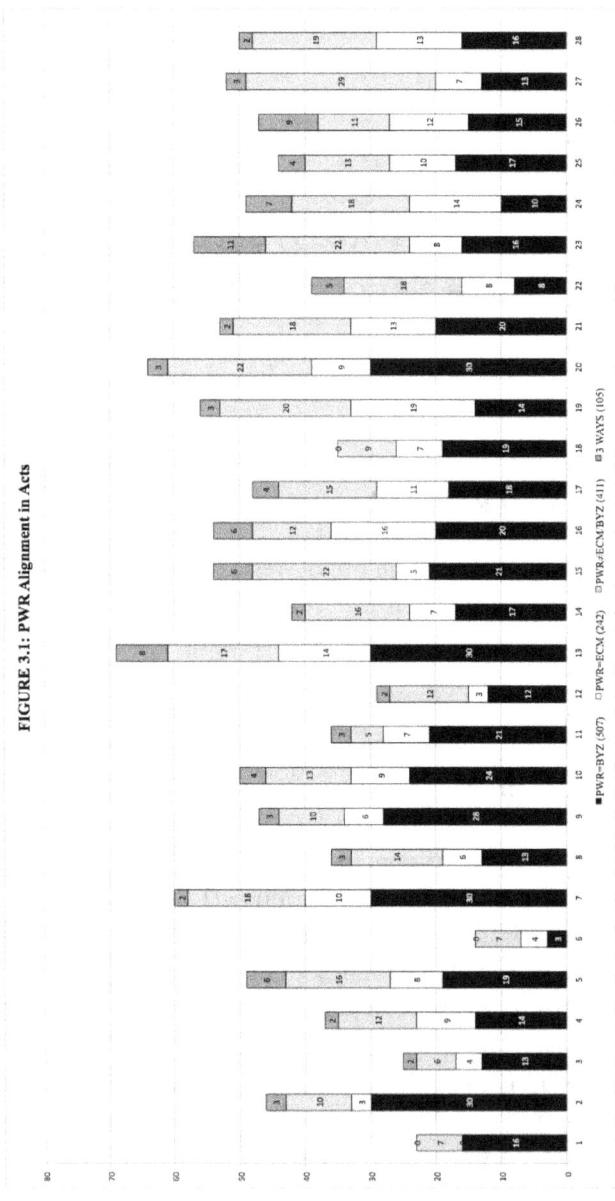

FIGURE 3.1: PWR Alignment in Acts

If it could be established that the PWR has essentially built upon the other two traditions, the numbers suggest that its archetype was twice as much Byz as it was Alex (see figure 3.2 below). The Byz has a majority of support in every chapter except chapters 6, 19, 22, and 24. The fact that the PWR deviates from a unified ECM/Byz reading 411 times is consistent with the theory that these formed the basis of departure. In particular, the PWR deviates from the unified tradition at least 18 times in the following chapters: 7, 15, 19–24, and 27–28. The fact that chapters 7 and 22 include substantial dialogue demonstrates that widespread variation was not limited to the narrative portions. The greatest variation occurs in chapter 27 where the PWR stands against the other two traditions 29 times and is part of a three-way division 3 times. The most intense concentration of triple readings occurs in chapters 23 (11 times) and 26 (9 times). In terms of overall disagreement, the ECM differs from the PWR 1,023 times, the ECM from the Byz 854 times, and Byz from the PWR 758 times. A detailed breakdown has been placed in the final section of this chapter: "Chapter Summaries Showing PWR Alignment." The following section will now attempt to interpret the significance of the above data.

TRANSMISSION OF THE PROTO-WESTERN TEXT: THREE VIEWS

As discussed in chapter 1, Barbara Aland came to the remarkable conclusion that the 614-group could not have derived from the inferred WR.[1] The more sober characteristics of the 614-group, combined with its many agreements with a reconstructed WR, indicate that the archetype underlying the 614-group (or a similar MS) was a primary source document for the WR itself. Chapter 2 of this study has provided abundant data in support of Aland's thesis. Judging by her comments in the above article and the remarks jointly made with her husband in their indispensable manual on textual criticism, she views the Alex tradition to be closest to the original, the mixed-text MSS to be next in importance, and both the "Western" and Byz traditions to be of a tertiary value.[2] Taking her views and applying them to the present discussion suggests a transmission for the 614-group according to that depicted in figure 3.3.

---

1. Aland, "Entstehung, Charakter und Herkunft," 26–28.
2. Aland and Aland, *New Testament*, 332–37.

NON-ALIGNED, PROTO-WESTERN GROUP READINGS

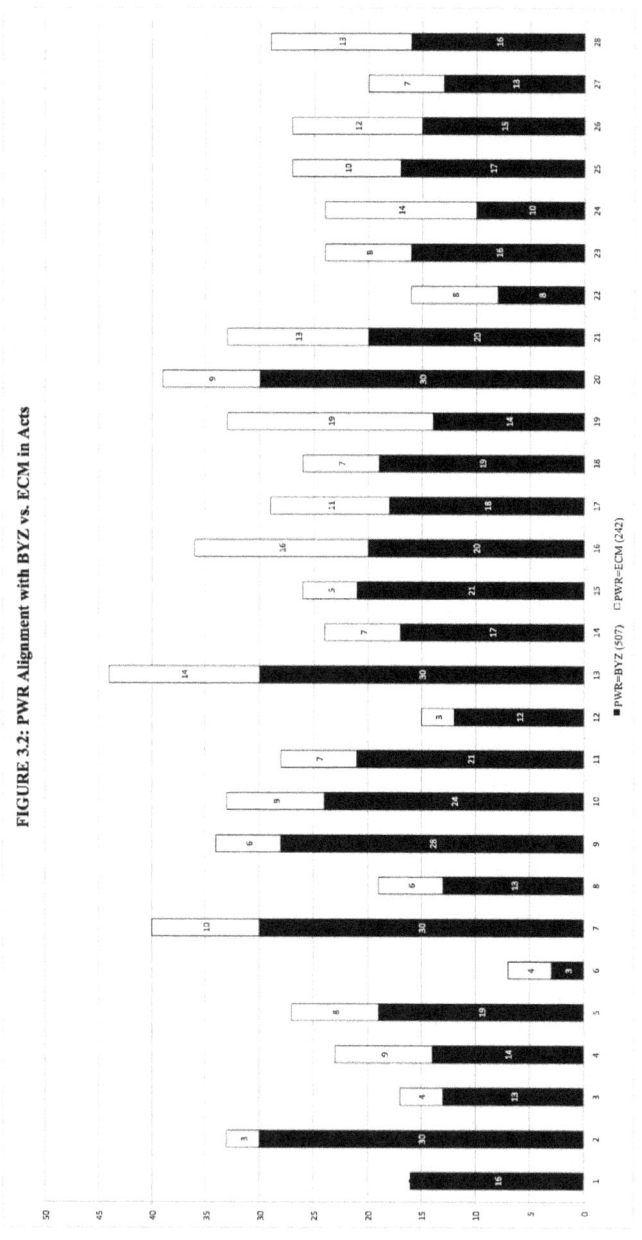

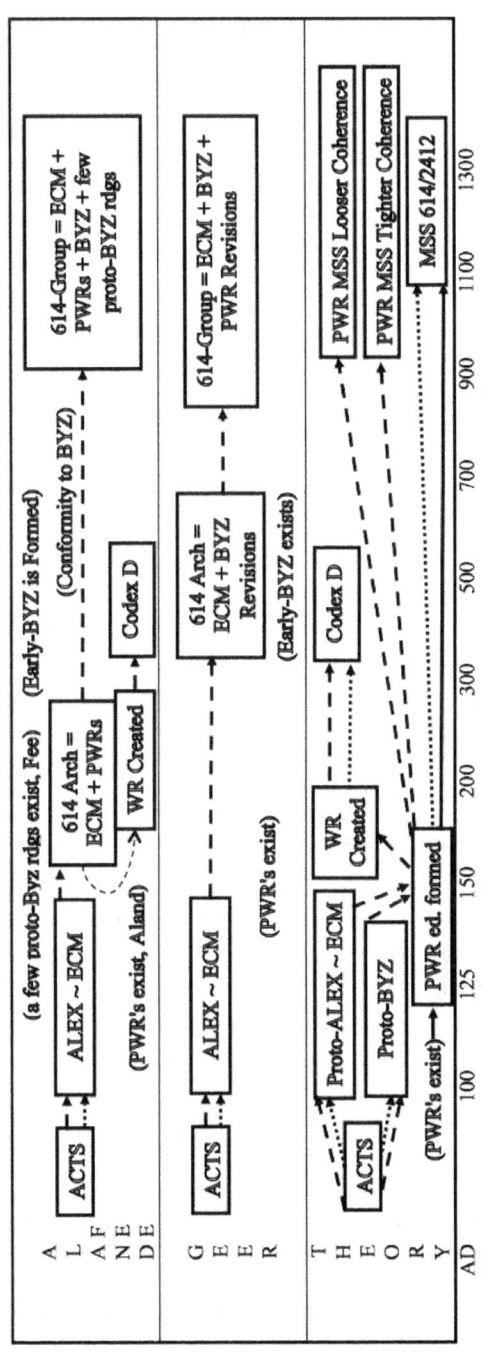

FIGURE 3.3: Transmission of 614-Group

Essentially a relatively pure Alex MS would have been modified by Western influence in the second century to create the archetype for the 614-group. Then across the centuries the offspring MSS of that archetype would have been progressively adjusted to the Byz standard text. The rich mixture of Alex, Western, and Byz readings in the 614-group are a natural outcome.[3] How does it match up with the characteristics of the group? It order to make an accurate evaluation, several preparatory steps were prudent. A number of MSS needed to be selected as being representative of the group in order to increase the accuracy of the results. Also, the 614-group needed to be purged of its various mistakes that often surfaced in a minority of its MSS. Such readings were never part of the archetype, standing behind the 614-group. With these and other preliminary steps, it was then possible to compare the PWR against the Byz and Alex traditions. As can be seen in figure 3.2 above, the PWR-Byz aligned readings outnumber PWR-ECM readings by 2:1.

For Barbara Aland's theory to hold, the 614-group would have required a very comprehensive correction process. At first, evidence appears to be readily available because the 614-group has extensive agreements with the Byz text, including many fine details. This study has identified about 240 subtle and insignificant agreements. However, the purposeful conformity to the Byz text required to achieve those agreements is the Achilles's heel of the theory.[4] A lengthy standardization process would certainly have purged the 614-group of most of its readings that are clearly different than the recognized text. However, the opposite is the case. This study has found about 201 obvious differences from the Byz text that were never purged away from the whole 614-group.[5] These readings almost always have between 3/10 and 10/10 core PWR MSS in support. In those places where it has only 2 core MSS, it is reliably joined by 1 or more other "Western" friendly Greek MSS (e.g., 05 08 431 876 1127; 1718 in Acts 1–4) and/or by one or more ancient translations such

---

3. The top band of figure 3.3 includes the phrase "a few proto-Byz readings," and recalls Fee's criticism of Sturz. Sturz had demonstrated that second-century Byz readings exist in the papyri. From this evidence, Sturz also concluded that a second-century Byz text type existed (Sturz, *Byzantine Text-Type*, 62, 145, 159). Yet Fee responded that scattered readings do not prove the antiquity of the Byz text type since a text type is defined by distinguishable pattern of readings (Fee, "Majority Text," 184).

4. Fee, "Majority Text," 184, used this term against the conclusions of Sturz.

5. For a full chapter-by-chapter listing of these 201 obvious differences from the Byz text and the 240 subtle and insignificant agreements with the Byz text, refer to the last section of this chapter titled, "Chapter Summaries Showing PWR Alignment."

as the Coptic mae, the Syriac Harklensis apparatus, various OL MSS, sy^p, and the Coptic sa. Since these obvious differences were still not removed after more than one thousand years (e.g., 614 is a thirteenth-century MS), the implication is strong (with some exceptions) that neither the 240 insignificant agreements nor the overall total of 507 were a product of an extended process. Instead, they appear to be a native part of the original archetype from which the MSS of the 614-group sprouted.

Similarly to Barbara Aland, Thomas Geer investigated the nature of MS 614. His study, completed one year before Aland's article, was much more comprehensive. He considered MS 614 at every reading within the book of Acts that differed from the standard edition. That excellent study was also much broader because it compared every variant from thirty-five well preserved MSS and fourteen fragmentary ones.[6] His particular attention was upon ten "Western cursives" (i.e., MSS 181 383 614 913 945 1175 1518 1611 1739 1891) with the goal to: "1) determine precisely their relationship to each other and to the three textual traditions of Acts; 2) reveal their connection especially with the 'Western' tradition; and 3) bring to light what they might reveal about the history of the text of Acts."[7] He concluded that five of them were associated with the Alex text (i.e., 181 945 1175 1739 1891) and the others (i.e., 383 614 913 1518 1611) were related to the Byz text.[8] These MSS are dated between the tenth and the fourteenth centuries. He believed that the Western readings were added to these MSS at the time of their origination. In terms of sources, he confessed that was still a mystery. Though he assumed these Western readings entered late, he also admitted that Western readings were already inserted into the sixth-century Byz MS 08. For example, he called 08 a "Majority text with 'Western' alterations."[9] Realizing the enigma 08 creates with its Byz foundation, he acknowledged that the question remains unanswered whether MSS like 08 acquired their Byz nature by corruption from a contemporary Byz MS or rather by reference to "one of the ancient bases on which the Majority text rests."[10] Despite the unanswered questions about Western sources and Byz readings in

---

6. Geer, "Investigation of Western Cursives," 19–20.
7. Geer, "Investigation of Western Cursives," v.
8. Geer, "Investigation of Western Cursives," 109–10.
9. Geer, "Investigation of Western Cursives," 12.
10. Geer, "Investigation of Western Cursives," 12.

mixed-text MSS, he still affirmed, "Nowhere is there evidence for the use of the Majority Text in Acts before the fourth century."[11]

There are several difficulties with Geer's theory of the late entry of Western readings into otherwise Byz or Alex MSS. First, as shown in chapter 2, there are numerous places where the readings of the 614-group show the character of having started with a Byz reading and then having made changes.[12] If these readings are much older than the Byz, why do they appear to have utilized the Byz tradition when they were created? Second, the willingness of the scribal culture to introduce Western readings at a late time period has been suggested without being demonstrated. Since no feasible sources have been suggested, the alternate hypothesis that the Western readings are instead remnants of a distant past is far more likely. The probability is further increased because the dominant practice of that period was to correct MSS according to the Byz tradition.[13] Third, the behavior of the core PWR MSS runs counter to Geer's theory. If Western readings were placed into MSS in the late period, why do the MSS display the kinds of agreements and disagreements that they do? Specifically, why did many scribes happen to adopt the very same insignificant variants while simultaneously and repeatedly rejecting the most important ones? Consider three examples of the former. At 22:2/14, 9/10 core MSS read the aorist προσεφώνησεν instead of the imperfect προσεφώνει as a harmonization with the same word at 21:40/38. At 22:15/8, 10/10 core have ὅτι ἔσῃ μάρτυς αὐτοῦ instead of ὅτι ἔσῃ μάρτυς αὐτῷ. Thirdly, 9/10 core at 22:25/8–12 read the word order τοῖς ἱμᾶσιν αὐτόν instead of αὐτὸν τοῖς ἱμᾶσιν. For the latter, at 19:9/51 only 4/10 PWR MSS contain the gloss, ἀπὸ ὥρας πέμπτης ἕως ὥρας δεκάτης. Secondly at 19:28/13, only 5/10 core contain the addition, καὶ δραμόντες εἰς τὸ ἄμφοδον. Finally, at 22:29/47, only 4/10 of the MSS have the addition, καὶ παραχρῆμα ἔλυσεν αὐτόν. The behavior of the core MSS is far better explained as all having undergone different amounts of standardization across many centuries. For example, beyond Acts 5:32, both 614 and 2412 display great resistance to correction.[14] Similarly, both

11. Geer, "Investigation of Western Cursives," 12. See Fee, "Majority Text," 184.

12. There are sixteen examples in chapter 2.

13. Aland and Aland, *New Testament*, 70–71.

14. Boismard and Lamouille, *Texte occidental reconstitution*, 1:25. In contrast, in the first four chapters of Acts, MS 614 upholds the PWR just fifteen out of thirty-two times (see the "Chapter Summaries Showing PWR Alignment" section at the end of the chapter). Interestingly, MS 1292 offers even fewer PWRs from 1:1—5:32, but after that stays close to MSS 614 and 2412.

NON-ALIGNED, PROTO-WESTERN GROUP READINGS

1292 and 1611 usually retain the PWR. On the other hand, the other six core PWR MSS generally demonstrate more inconsistency.

In contrast to Aland and Geer, this study proposes that the testimony of the Byz cannot be ignored. In the early days of the church, the text of Acts was copied repeatedly both in and around Antioch (Byz) and Alexandria (Alex). The nature of textual variants suggests that the earliest copying was done with limited controls. However, Günther Zuntz has noticed that the Alex school evidently had a head start in the knowledge of how to faithfully preserve literature.[15] As a result of the early process, the most popular exemplars of each region independently moved away from the original text.[16] Because the mistakes and polishing would normally be at different places in the text, the differences between those two MSS if compared would quickly become nearly doubled. Due to their ancient history of textual labors, these two regional texts would be the most likely sources for the PWR editor to use as the basis for his work. As depicted in figure 3.2, the PWR archetype is significantly closer to the Byz tradition and yet also has a very substantial Alex proportion. The mixed basis of the PWR edition has a number of possible explanations. A contemporary editor may have recently produced a copy of Acts by merging the readings of a MS from each region. Perhaps more likely, the PWR editor may have begun with a proto-Byz MS and then, as part of his textual labors, compared it with a proto-Alex MS, introducing changes periodically. It is also feasible that he began with a proto-Byz MS that was significantly more Alex than the modern Byz text. Under this hypothesis, many of the agreements the 614-group now sustains with the Alex text were in actuality places where the proto-Byz text was later revised on its way to becoming the standard Byz text.

The PWR editor was also armed with significant additional historical information covering the period and events included in the book of Acts. Possessing a solid textual basis, what he perceived as trustworthy historical details, an eye for style, and a skill for clarifying meaning, he proceeded to revise the text of Acts into the PWR archetype. His endeavor was linguistically a success and his edition or a copy of it became an important source for the WR that was produced a short time later. The PWR edition received a different fate in the various members of the 614-group. The least amount of changes apparently happened in the

---

15. Zuntz, *Text of the Epistles*, 251–52.
16. Streeter, *Four Gospels*, 35–39.

genealogy that led to MSS 614 and 2412. As a result of the foregoing process, whenever the Byz disagrees with the Alex, ascertaining which tradition diverged is not possible without the careful evaluation of each case.[17] The reconstructed PWR archetype is very important in this process. Its alignment with either tradition greatly strengthens each in its claim to antiquity and often to authenticity. The fruitful results of such comparing of the traditions will be a major focus of chapter four.

Before moving on, it will be helpful to look at an example taken from Acts 15:18/2–6. The overall impression is that the proto-Byz text added to the original reading and the PWR editor inherited that revision. Figure 3.4 illustrates a proposed sequence of transmission. 614/Byz (reading g.) has γνωστὰ ἀπ αἰῶνος ἐστιν <u>τῷ θεῷ πάντα τὰ ἔργα</u> αὐτοῦ (vs. γνωστὸν ἀπ' αἰῶνος ἐστιν <u>τῷ κυρίῳ τὸ ἔργον</u> αὐτοῦ, 05 (reading e.), vs. γνωστὰ ἀπ' αἰῶνος, NA28). The ECM lists twenty-three alternatives. The reading of 614/Byz is found in 08 014 020 025 35 etc., including 7/10 core PWR MSS, plus sy[h.txt]. 614 is the PWR (g.). 05 (e.) is joined by Vg p/2 w l 189 sy[hmg] A[mss]. 05 is probably the Western Redaction reading (WRR). NA28 (a.) is joined by 01 03 04 81 1175 and some others, including core PWR MSS 1505 2495, plus Eus A (sa bo Ä). Except for the unique readings of MSS 459 (b.) and L1188 (c.), the others diverge far from NA28. The fact that 614 and the Byz are aligned with so much divergence highlights their similar ancestry. The generation of the other twenty readings can be understood as follows: first, NA28 was expanded to form the PWR represented by 614/Byz (g.); next, it was adjusted stylistically to become the WRR (e.) by changing the plural πάντα τὰ ἔργα to the singular τὸ ἔργον. In addition, the WRR changed τῷ θεῷ into τῷ κυρίῳ, possibly by harmonization with 15:17. From it derived readings d/o/v/w. In fact, the move from 614 (g.) to 05 (e.) is also what Thomas of Harkel perceived.

---

17. Often variant units are linked and must be considered in concert (see analysis of 7:21/2–10 and 7:21/22 below for an example).

NON-ALIGNED, PROTO-WESTERN GROUP READINGS

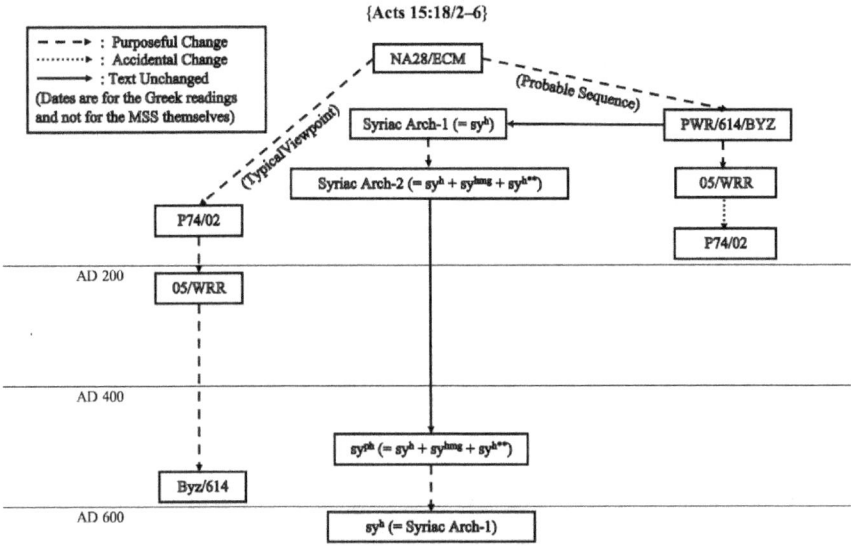

FIGURE 3.4: An Example PWR/BYZ Aligned Reading

Notice how he reversed the process of corruption by adjusting the sy^{hmg} reading (e.) in order to form the sy$^{h.txt}$ reading (g.), by reference to his trusted Greek source. Although Wachtel suggests reading d. (γνωστὸν ἀπ' αἰῶνος τῷ κυρίῳ τὸ ἔργον αὐτοῦ, P74 02) came from NA28 and was the source of 05 (e.), that derivation seems unlikely given that P74 and 02 are not known for expansions.[18] Moreover, if an editor added for clarity, why would he do so awkwardly, leaving out the expected ἐστίν? Rather, it is probable that P74 and 02 simply preserve a corrupt form of the WRR, one that lacks ἐστίν. The textual evidence for an expansion without ἐστίν is weak, being found in just 2/20 long readings and represented by merely four MSS. It appears that at least 16/20 long readings have their source in 614/Byz. The shortness of readings s/t/u suggests that they may come directly from NA28. However, reading t. is conceivably a simplified paraphrase of the 614/Byz and the other two are related to it. In conclusion, NA28 is original but 614/Byz diverged not far from the source.

---

18. Wachtel, "Against the Text-Type Concept," 145.

PROTO-WESTERN GROUP REVISIONS

When evaluating the PWRs across the book of Acts, it becomes evident, with some exceptions, that these readings are secondary unless they align with the Alex or Byz text. This section will present evidence to demonstrate this phenomenon by means of two sample chapters selected from each of the four quarters of the book (i.e., 1–7, 8–14, 15–21, 22–28). The actual chapters chosen (i.e., 7/8, 13/15, 17/19, 26/27) were offset a little for practical reasons. For example, the best representatives of the PWR edition (i.e., MSS 614 and 2412), show repeated evidence of conformity to the Byz text in Acts 1:1—5:32. Therefore, the determination of the PWR in this portion is less certain. Secondly, the brevity of Acts 6 provides a limited basis for evaluation. Finally, the composition of Acts offers a providential opportunity to evaluate variant units in chapters that are both discourse heavy and those that are mainly narrative. In order to increase the variety in the sampling and the accuracy of the results, it was decided to select one chapter with discourse and one chapter marked by narrative within each major section of Acts.

As discussed above, the PWR editor has apparently built his revision upon an Alex and Byz base text. The discussion of chapter 7 will also consider the possibility that he overlaid his changes directly upon a proto-Byz archetype, rather than on a mixed text. The reconstructed PWR archetype of Acts 7 has a total of thirty agreements with the Byz text as compared to just ten with the ECM. In addition, two places manifest a three-way division. When these twelve readings are considered, it will be shown how each one could be explained as a departure from a presumed common proto-Byz archetype. The changes made to the Byz could have accumulated over time and the revisions to the PWR would generally be those of the earliest period. Such an approach to account for PWR/ECM alignments over against the Byz can be duplicated for most chapters of Acts with similar results. Even those chapters (i.e., 6, 19, 24) where the PWR archetype aligns closer to ECM text can be explained in this fashion. The preliminary results suggest that this idea is worthy of more investigation.

PWR Revisions: Acts 7 (Dialogue)

In the book of Acts, chapter 7 uniquely offers almost pure discourse from start to finish. It opens a window to the personality of Stephen and beams forth with the intelligence and graciousness of Christianity's first martyr. As it could be expected, it has a large number of textual variants. Some of them pertain to quotations from the Greek Old Testament, i.e., the LXX. The revisions that the PWR editor made to the chapter will be reviewed first. Not all the PWR variations need be revisions. One must evaluate them carefully and always watch out for places where the PWR may have retained the original wording. Next, an excursus will consider the places where the PWR agrees with the ECM against the Byz for the reasons mentioned above.

PWR Revisions

There are eighteen places in Acts 7 where the PWR stands against the aligned ECM/Byz reading. These aligned readings are listed as "NA28/Byz" or "ECM/Byz." In addition, there are two occasions where all three traditions are divided. They are annotated as "3ways" next to the verse reference.

1. (7:4/32–34) 614/PWR has μετῴκησεν αυτὸν (vs. μετῴκισεν αυτὸν, NA28/Byz) and is found in 8/10 core PWR MSS (i.e., 383^{vid} 614 1505 1292 1611^{vid} 1890 2147 2412) and others. This variant is not listed in the ECM. The standard reading is based upon μετοικίζω, while this reading has the synonym based on μετοικέω. The PWR probably arose due to an itacism, mistaking the ι as an η.

2. (7:5/28–34) 614/PWR displays δοῦναι αὐτῷ εἰς κατάσχεσιν (vs. δοῦναι αὐτῷ εἰς κατάσχεσιν <u>αὐτὴν</u>, NA28/Byz, vs. δοῦναι <u>αὐτὴν</u> εἰς κατάσχεσιν αὐτῷ, P74) and is joined by 1890* 2138 2412. It lost αὐτήν by accident. Editors of other core PWR MSS detected and fixed the error. For example, two were corrected to match NA28/Byz and four were corrected to P74. It is uncommon for a group of PWR MSS to be corrected to readings other than the Byz. Therefore, the P74 reading was very popular. In fact, it is found in 7/9 best ECM MSS and in the strong majority of Westerns. It offers a smoother word order than the original. Though such changes found in MS 614 are subtle, they may reveal a lot about the PWR archetype.[19]

---

19. From his work on the Gospels, Streeter, *Four Gospels*, 36, explained that the types of variants that best reveal a local text of the earliest period is a plurality of insignificant readings that are found either solely or at least predominantly in just one group of MSS.

3. (7:9/15) 614/PWR reads ἀπέδοντο <u>αὐτὸν</u> (vs. ἀπέδοντο, NA28/Byz) and is found in 7/10 core PWR MSS, related MSS 431 876 1127, and MS 996 plus sy^p sy^h. It has added αὐτόν in order to smooth the sentence.

4. (7:10/32) 614/PWR omits (vs. Φαραώ, NA28/Byz/sy^{h**}) and is joined by just 431 1292 2412 plus sy^h. Even though the support is minimal, the agreement of sy^h affirms the reading's antiquity. Moreover, the fact that sy^{h**} had Φαραώ indicates that Thomas of Harkel considered it an ancient gloss and removed it according to his model Greek MS. The PWR seems to have lost "Pharaoh" by accident.

5. (7:14/26–32) 614/PWR has ἐν ἑβδομήκοντα <u>καὶ</u> πέντε ψυχαῖς (vs. ἐν ψυχαῖς ἑβδομήκοντα πέντε, NA28/Byz, vs. ἐν ἑβδομήκοντα πέντε ψυχαῖς, 014) and is joined by 05 044 431 1292 1611 1642C 1890 2138 2412* plus Chrys. The change to the word order does not appear to smooth the verse. It may instead be a purposeful harmonization to the OT. In Deut 10:22 (LXX), seventy souls are mentioned and written as ἐν ἑβδομήκοντα ψυχαῖς. The editor could not just match the LXX since the NT speaks of seventy-five souls. Whenever that number is given in Exod 1:5, it included a conjunction, i.e., πέντε καὶ ἑβδομήκοντα. The PWR approximates the LXX but in doing so makes the flow more difficult (cf. 7:41/16 below).

6. (#7:20/39) 614/PWR has + αὐτοῦ and is found in 7/10 core PWR MSS and 05 08 etc., including eighteen Westerns, plus Vg d e gig p w 189 sy^p sy^h. The pronoun polishes the sentence where the article τοῦ is being used as a pronoun in τοῦ πατρός.

7. (7:21/2–10) (3ways) 614/PWR displays ἐκτεθέντα δὲ αὐτὸν ἀνείλ[ε/α]το <u>αὐτὸν</u> (vs. ἐκτεθέντα δὲ αὐτὸν ἀνείλ[ε/α]το, Byz, vs. ἐκτεθέντος δὲ <u>αὐτοῦ</u> ἀνείλ[ε/α]το αὐτόν, NA28, vs. ἐκτεθέντος δὲ <u>αὐτοῦ παρὰ τὸν ποταμόν</u> ἀνείλατο αὐτόν, 05, vs. ἐκτεθέντα δὲ αὐτὸν <u>εἰς τὸν ποταμόν</u> ἀνείλατο αὐτόν, 08) and is found in 7/10 core PWR MSS. There are ten alternative readings. NA28 is probably original. It uses a genitive absolute and includes αὐτόν both here and in the following variant (see 7:21/22). Barrett asserts that only one αὐτόν was needed in the verse.[20] At some point, the Byz and PWR readings revised to an accusative participle and both traditions then

---

20. Barrett, *Commentary on Acts*, 1:354.

found αὐτὸν twice in the first clause and once in the second clause to be excessive. The Byz editor balanced the verse by removing the second αὐτόν from the first clause. The PWR editor created an isolated reading by removing αὐτόν from the second.

8. (7:21/22) 614/PWR reads ἀνεθρέψατο (vs. ἀνεθρέψατο <u>αὐτὸν</u>, NA28/Byz) and is found in 6/10 core PWR MSS and 05* 044 431 1251 1718. All these MSS except 044 and 1890 have the αὐτόν in the first clause and thus found it unnecessary here (see 7:21/2–10 above). Both the Byz and PWR traditions have made a stylistic change at 7:21.

9. (7:22/22–26) 614 has ἔργοις (vs. <u>λόγοις καὶ</u> ἔργοις, NA28/Byz, vs. λόγοις καὶ <u>ἐν</u> ἔργοις, 08, vs. ἔργοις καὶ <u>λόγοις</u>, 2412) and is joined by only L1188. The text of MS 614 does not preserve the PWR here because it has made an eye skip. In contrast, its sister MS 2412, which is based on the same *Vorlage*, has preserved the PWR.[21] It is joined by core MSS 1292 1611 1890 2138 and twelve others, plus Thdrt. The change seems to portray Moses's works as an Egyptian prince more prominently than his words. Notice also that the PWR avoided the smoothing seen in the 08 reading.

10. (7:28/8–10) 614/PWR displays θέλεις (vs. <u>σὺ</u> θέλεις, NA28/Byz) and is joined by just two core PWR MSS 2147 2412, Byz uncial 0142, core Alex 81, secondary Western 1891, and five others. Despite its limited support, its variety and nature suggests that it is the PWR. The editor deleted σύ in order to "fix" the awkward sentence. Ironically, by doing so, he has deharmonized the text from the LXX (see Exod 2:14).

11. (7:28/18–22) 614/PWR reads τὸν Αἰγύπτιον ἐχθὲς (vs. ἐχθὲς τὸν Αἰγύπτιον, NA28/Byz) and is joined by core PWR MSS 1611 2138 2412, core Alex 02, and 2243. It has smoothed the word order.

12. (7:36/18–20) 614/PWR has γῇ Αἰγύπτου (vs. γῇ Αἰγύπτῳ, NA28/Byz, vs. <u>τῇ</u> Αἰγύπτῳ, 03) and is joined by core PWR MSS 1292 1611 1890 2138 2412, best ECM MSS P74[vid] 1739 2200, and 05 etc. plus Vg e/2 gig p 189 sy[p] sy[h]. The editor has simplified the dative of apposition. The reading was popular. Two more of the best ECM MSS (i.e., 03 04) and others have made a mistake. Thus, of the ten best ECM MSS, only 01 02 33 81 1175 preserve the original. In contrast,

---

21. See Boismard and Lamouille, *Texte occidental reconstitution*, 1:25.

all seven of ECM's representative Byz MSS and the overall Byz tradition stay the course.

13. (7:37/6) 614/PWR reads Μωϋσῆς (vs. ὁ Μωϋσῆς/Μωσῆς, NA28/Byz) and is found in 9/10 core PWR MSS, P74 05 014 049 1 35C 1175 1739, and many others. The editor may have dropped the article as detracting from the emphatic οὗτος at the beginning of the verse. The article seems to be original since it continues the emphasis: "This is <u>that</u> Moses who" (KJV). However, there is a chance the PWR could be original, given its simplicity and broad support.

14. (7:37/26–28) (3ways) 614/PWR displays κύριος (vs. ὁ θεὸς, NA28, vs. κύριος ὁ θεὸς, Byz) and is found in 6/10 core PWR MSS, 431 522 1891 2200, and six others plus Chrys bo^mss sy^p.mss sy^h. NA28 does not harmonize with either 3:22/22 or the OT and NA28/PWR jointly reject the addition of ἡμῶν found in RP05 at the following ECM variant (see 7:37/30–36 below). The PWR most likely revised ὁ θεὸς in preference for the OT personal name for God translated in the LXX as κύριος (cf. 7:41/16 below). RP05 apparently made a complete assimilation to the RP05 reading at 3:22/16–22.[22]

15. (#7:37/40) 614/PWR has + αὐτοῦ ἀκούσεσθε. It is found in 6/10 core PWR MSS, 5/10 best ECM MSS (i.e., 04 33 1739 2200 and ~1175), (05*) 05C1 08, and many others, including most Westerns plus d e gig p w ar bo mae and sy^p sy^h A G. NA28/Byz is joined by 5/10 best ECM MSS (i.e., P74^vid *01 02 03 81*), 4/10 core PWR MSS (i.e., 383 1505 2147 2495 returned to the Byz), and P45 044 etc., including Chrys Vg sa Ä. The PWR and much of the overall tradition added these two words to Stephen's quotation by a direct reference to the text of Deut 18:15 (LXX). It is significant that while 50 percent of the best ECM MSS and 60 percent of the PWR MSS have the addition, 6/7 core Byz MSS (per the ECM's classification) do not. Similarly, the Byz tradition at large also rejected the gloss. Thus, the Byz text best preserves the original wording here. It is also noteworthy that a similar phenomenon occurs above at 7:36/18–20. The 5/10 ECM MSS that keep the more difficult original reading there are *01 02 33 81 1175*. In a short range of text, two occasions occur where the core Alex MSS cannot give a majority voice for the text. The only

---

22. According to HF1985, the Byz tradition is divided, with the other part reading κύριος ὁ θεὸς ὑμῶν, which happens to be the ByzECM reading. In contrast, RP05 lists no alternate reading in the margin.

core Alex MSS supporting the standard at both places are 01 02 81 (italicized above). Thus, 30 percent of the best ECM MSS give the original in contrast to 85.7 percent (6/7) of the core Byz MSS. The simple lesson is that the consensus of one tradition is not sufficient as a basis for textual decisions. Lastly, this passage also shows that the bulk of the translations are sometimes wrong. The only faithful ones here are Vg sa Ä.

16. (7:41/16) 614/PWR reads ἀνή<u>νεγκαν</u> (vs. ἀνή<u>γαγον</u>, NA28/Byz) and is found in 6/10 core PWR MSS, 431 424C 996, and 3 others. The editor chooses a synonym related to προσηνέγκατε at 7:42/46 (see Amos 5:25 LXX) and better suited to the subject of sacrifice. Both words are common in the LXX in the context of sacrifice. For example, the root of the PWR reading is ἀναφέρω, and it occurs 169 times in the LXX and 26 times in the Leviticus.[23] It is repeatedly used to describe the placing of an offering upon the altar so that it might be burned (e.g., Lev 2:16; 3:5, 11). The word used in Acts 7:42 is based on the root προσφέρω, and it occurs 165 times in the LXX and 69 times in Leviticus. It occurs consistently in the context of offering sacrifices (e.g., Lev 1:1, 3, 5, 13, 14). In contrast, the NA28/Byz word has the root ἀνάγω and it can be found 114 times in the LXX but only 7 times in Leviticus. It is used in a different situation to distinguish some animals that regurgitate their food (see Lev 11:3, 4 (twice), 5, 6, 7) and once for God's bringing up Israel from Egypt (Lev 11:45). This precise revision might show that the PWR editor was a LXX expert.

17. (#7:43/49) 614/PWR has Βαβυλῶνος λέγει κύριος παντοκράτωρ (vs. Βαβυλῶνος λέγει κύριος <u>ὁ θεὸς ὁ</u> παντοκράτωρ <u>ὄνομα αὐτῷ</u>, 1611, vs. Βαβυλῶνος, NA28/Byz) and is joined by 431 1292 2412 sy[h]. As discussed in chapter 2, MS 614 more likely represents the PWR gloss upon which 1611 et al. expanded into the WRR that has created a full harmony with the LXX (see Amos 5:27b). The changes were apparently inserted to magnify the majesty of the Lord.

18. (7:44/10) 614/PWR displays <u>ἐν</u> τοῖς πατράσιν (vs. τοῖς πατράσιν, NA28/Byz) and is found in the core MSS 1292 1611 2138 2412, 05* 08 etc., including many Westerns, plus d p/2 w. The addition of ἐν makes the implicit "with" explicit.

---

23. These numbers were calculated using *BW*.

19. (7:52/28–34) 614/PWR reads τῆς ἐλεύσεως τοῦ δικαίου <u>τούτου</u> (vs. τῆς ἐλεύσεως τοῦ δικαίου, NA28/Byz) and is joined by <u>431</u> <u>1127</u> <u>1292</u> <u>2412</u> and 4 others. Though limited in support, 614 is possibly the PWR since it has the same four key supporters as at the following characteristic Western variant (see 7:55/2–4). It adds emphasis.

20. (7:55/2–4) 614/PWR has <u>Στέφανος</u> δὲ ὑπάρχων (vs. ὑπάρχων δὲ, NA28/Byz) and is joined by <u>431</u> <u>1292</u> 1501 <u>2412</u> and ten others, plus Dam (GregNy bo). It is also joined in a different word order by 044 33 <u>1127</u> and seven others, plus ProclC w. Because Stephen was last mentioned by name way back at 6:9, the PWR clarifies the referent. Though limited in support, 614 is probably the PWR (cf. 7:52/28–34).

Excursus: The Proto-Byz Text of Acts 7

This excursus will consider the possibility that the PWR editor began his work from a proto-Byz text rather than from a mixed MS that a scholar had made by merging the readings of a proto-Alex MS with a proto-Byz MS. The reconstructed PWR archetype agrees a total of thirty times with the Byz tradition in Acts 7. The pressing question is how could the ten places where the PWR edition agrees with the Alex tradition (see ECM) be explained? Also, what scenario might explain the two places of three-way division?

1. (7:16/20–22) 614[vid]/ECM has ᾧ ὠνήσατο (vs. ὅ ὠνήσατο, Byz). 614 is the PWR and is joined by six of its core and many others. The Byz has little support outside its tradition. It appears that 614 retains the genuine proto-Byz reading from which the later Byz tradition deviated. If taken literally, the phrase appears to say, "Placed in a tomb in which Abraham purchased." The revised edition reads, "Placed in a tomb which Abraham purchased."

2. (#7:32/21, 25) 614/ECM reads Ἰσαὰκ καὶ Ἰακώβ (vs. <u>ὁ θεὸς</u> Ἰσαὰκ καὶ <u>ὁ θεὸς</u> Ἰακώβ, Byz, vs. <u>θεὸς</u> Ἰσαὰκ καὶ <u>θεὸς</u> Ἰακώβ, 05). Cf. 3:13/8, 12. The tradition is mainly split between the first two readings. 614 is the PWR and is joined by its core 1611 1890* 2138 2412. Both readings are well supported. Most of the MSS lacking ὁ θεός here include it in 3:13. The Byz is just the opposite. On the other hand, some like 05 Vg bo mae have (ὁ) θεός in both passages. Others like

NON-ALIGNED, PROTO-WESTERN GROUP READINGS

03 and 614 (=PWR) lack ὁ θεός in both locations. Is seems highly unlikely that harmony between 3:13 and 7:32 is authentic. Therefore, the Byz is potentially original in both locations (see chapter 4). The PWR/ECM agreement may arise from the independent efforts of both the PWR and Alex editors to harmonize with the mainstream reading at 3:13/8, 12.

3. (7:34/46) 614/ECM displays ἀποστείλω (vs. ἀποστελῶ, Byz). 614 is the PWR and is joined by its core of 1611 1890 2138 2412. It presents the verb as AAS-1S, matching the LXX of Exod 3:10. The Byz has the future tense. The PWR has possibly departed from the proto-Byz reading by harmonizing with the LXX. The ECM reading may be the result of an independent harmonization by Alex scribes.

4. (7:35/32) 614/ECM has θεὸς καὶ (vs. θεὸς, Byz). 614 is the PWR as evidenced by its core of 1611 1890 2138 2412 and 01C1 03 05 08 81 etc. plus sy^h. Both readings are well supported, and the ECM has marked it as a SGL. The PWR may be responsible for the addition and its partial infusion into the Alex tradition. In contrast, most of the best ECM MSS lack the conjunction (i.e., P74 01* 02 04 33 1739 2200) as well as the primitive P45. The presence of καί provides a greater contrast between the human rejection and the divine selection of Moses: "God sent to be both a ruler and a deliverer." Yet since contrast already exists between the rejected judge and the appointed redeemer, the additional emphasis might be secondary.

5. (7:35/40) 614/ECM reads ἀπέσταλκεν (vs. ἀπέστειλεν, Byz). 614 is the PWR as evidenced by its core 1292 1611 1890 2138 2412, and it reads with the perfect. The perfect is more unusual, and the Byz may reflect smoothing. However, the Byz shows no reticence in using the perfect (see 7:52/48 below). More importantly, the problem is that the perfect appears to mimic the LXX, which uses the same form three times at Exod 3:13–15. Thus, the PWR may very well be a harmonization to the LXX in both the Western and Alex texts. The PWR editor seems to be closely acquainted with the LXX (see 7:41/16). Such harmony could have occurred independently. Alternatively, the PWR editor may have used a proto-Alex MS as part of his labors and selected the perfect as superior once he knew it was in the Alex tradition. Thus, it is very possible that the PWR began with the aorist that is preserved in the Byz.

NON-ALIGNED, PROTO-WESTERN GROUP READINGS

6. (7:35/42–44) 614/ECM displays σὺν χειρὶ (vs. ἐν χειρί, Byz). 614 is the PWR and is joined by the core 1292 1611 1890 2138 2412 plus sy^h. On the surface, the Alex reading seems less refined. The phrase σὺν χειρί occurs only here in the NT and does not even occur in the LXX. In contrast, ἐν χειρί occurs once at Gal 3:19 and 249 times in the LXX (BW). The similar phrase, ἐν τῇ χειρί, occurs 9 times in the NT (e.g., Matt 3:12) and 90 times in the LXX (e.g., Exod 4:2, 4, 17, 20). Byz editors evidently polished the proto-Byz reading.

7. (7:37/30–36) 614/ECM has ἐκ τῶν ἀδελφῶν ὑμῶν (vs. ἡμῶν ἐκ τῶν ἀδελφῶν ὑμῶν, RP05, vs. ὑμῶν ἐκ τῶν ἀδελφῶν ὑμῶν, ByzECM). 614 is the PWR as found in its core MSS 1292 1611 1890 2138 2412 and is very well supported. RP05 is joined by 08 014 35C etc. plus OL e. ByzECM includes a mix of non-Byz MSS. Both forms of the Byz were harmonized to variants in 3:22/22. Moreover, RP05 completely lacks versional support. If the PWR began with a proto-Byz MS, it most likely lacked the first pronoun. The addition probably came from Byz scribes.

8. (7:38/54) 614/ECM/RP05^mg displays λόγια (vs. λόγον, RP05^txt) and is found in 9/10 core PWR MSS, 10/10 best ECM MSS, 7/7 ECM core Byz MSS (i.e., 1 18 35 330 398 424 1241), several core Byz uncials (i.e., 014 025 049 056), and essentially all ECM MSS except the twelve standing with RP05^txt. Of those, the only important one is PWR MS 2147. The best MSS of all three traditions are united. The Byz reading reflects a corruption away from the proto-Byz reading.

9. (7:52/48) 614/ECM reads ἐγένεσθε (vs. γεγένησθε, Byz) and is found in just 4/10 core PWR MSS (i.e., 614 1611 2138 2412). Despite that, most Western MSS side with it and help confirm it as the PWR. Moreover, 10/10 best ECM MSS also preserve the aorist. The other five extant PWR MSS were revised by the Byz text. If the proto-Byz text displayed the aorist, a move to the perfect was a natural improvement. The later Byz editors apparently "fixed" the text.

10. (7:58/26) 614/ECM has ἱμάτια αὐτῶν (vs. ἱμάτια, Byz) and is found in 5/8 core PWR MSS, 8/8 best ECM MSS, 05 08 etc., including almost all Westerns, and Chrys sy^p sy^h Vg d e p h t w 70 189. 614 is the PWR. Byz has little support outside its tradition. The Byz is harder because it uses the article τά as a pronoun. However, its poor attestation suggests that αὐτῶν was more likely lost by accident or

NON-ALIGNED, PROTO-WESTERN GROUP READINGS

dropped as unnecessary. Once again, it would be easy for the proto-Byz to have had the pronoun and then for later Byz scribes to have removed it.

11. (7:21/2–10, see above) (3ways) If the proto-Byz text contained the same reading as RP05, it is easy to explain how the PWR may have simply smoothed it by choosing to remove the unnecessary pronoun from second clause instead of the first.

12. (7:37/26–28, see above) (3ways) The proto-Byz reading may have equaled the PWR as a simple substitution for the Alex reading. Later, Byz editors possibly replaced κύριος with the fuller title κύριος ὁ θεὸς ἡμῶν by harmonizing with 3:22/16–22. The foregoing twelve examples demonstrate that in Acts 7 there is little to oppose the hypothesis that the PWR editor started with a proto-Byz MS. Subsequently, both it and the Byz tradition deviated from it in different ways.

PWR Revisions: Acts 8 (Narrative)

There are fourteen places in Acts 8 where the PWR stands against the aligned ECM/Byz reading and three occasions where all three traditions are divided, i.e., "3ways."

1. (8:7/2–20) (3ways) 614* reads πολλῶν γὰρ τῶν συνεχόντων πνεύματα ἀκάθαρτα βοῶντα φωνῇ μεγάλῃ ἐξήρχοντο (vs. πολλοὶ γὰρ τῶν ἐχόντων πνεύματα ... ἐξήρχοντο, NA28, vs. πολλῶν γὰρ τῶν ἐχόντων πνεύματα ... ἐξήρχετο, Byz, vs. πολλῶν γὰρ τῶν ἐχόντων ... ἐξήρχοντο, 614C/2412, vs. ἀπὸ πολλῶν γὰρ [omit] πνεύματα ἀκάθαρτα βοῶντα φωνῇ μεγάλῃ ἐξήρχοντο, BL) and stands alone. The ECM has eleven readings at this difficult sentence. BL find all readings unintelligible and provide their own reading based upon combining 05* d, Byz, and the omission of τῶν ἐχόντων by conjecture.[24] Haenchen is right that the verse as it stands in the Alex (and Byz too) is an anacoluthon and seems to confuse the people with the spirits. He translates it, "For many of those who had unclean spirits—crying with a loud voice they came out."[25] Did Luke write

---

24. Boismard and Lamouille, *Texte occidental reconstitution*, 1:149, 2:56.
25. Haenchen, *Acts of the Apostles*, 302.

it that way? The πολλῶν of the Byz and 614C lead to similar problems. Barrett concludes that the NA edition preserves the original text that has a mistaken structure.[26] Metzger cites Torrey who called it a "suspended construction" that came by translation from the Aramaic.[27] However, Metzger concludes that Luke himself was the creator and never had a chance to revise this wording.[28] Ironically, although 614* is the only extant reading that utilized ordinary grammar, its corrector changed it to agree with a common one. If συνέχω is taken as "to oppress," 614* could be translated, "For the unclean spirits of many that were oppressed, came out as they shouted with a loud voice." Was 614* simply a clever conjecture by the copyist? Given that both 614 and 2412 were apparently copied from the same archetype and that συνεχόντων makes sense, it is feasible that the *Vorlage* preserved the unusual reading. When the scribe of MS 2412 copied his model MS, he decided to correct his copy at this verse, using a common Byz reading. That "correction" may have already existed as a marginal reading in the *Vorlage* itself. In contrast, the scribe of 614* maintained the continuous text. Yet the word συνέχω is Lucan enough, occurring nine of its twelve times in Luke-Acts (Luke 4:38; 8:37, 45; 12:50; 19:43; 22:63; Acts 7:57; 18:5; 28:8). Moreover, it occurs in proximity at 7:57, and in a similar context in 28:8. Therefore, the idea that 614* is the original is even more likely than BL's thoughtful approach. It avoids conjecture and requires no mix of readings. Though anacoluthon may be the answer, the brilliant skill of Luke militates against it. 614* is therefore a theoretical contender for the original reading. In support of the quality of 614, one can observe that the unusual SGL reading of 03 at 26:16/44 has its best support not in Alexandria but in 614 and its relatives. The main weakness with συνεχόντων is its transmissional improbability.[29] If correct, should there not be other MSS with the reading? If it was a correct conjecture, what could have caused its loss from all remaining Greek MSS? By analogy, the practice of ancient letter writing may provide a clue. Various scholars have explained that it would have been consistent with contemporary practice if Paul had made

---

26. Barrett, *Commentary on Acts*, 1:403–4.
27. Metzger, *Textual Commentary*, 312–13.
28. Metzger, *Textual Commentary*, 313.
29. Robinson, "Case for Byzantine Priority," 544–45, refers to the concept of transmissional probability as a key criterion for evaluating variant readings.

a copy of his letters before sending them to the churches.³⁰ If Luke decided to use a similar procedure, he may have kept his original edition and produced a copy for Theophilus. It is conceivable that his amanuensis may have miscopied συνεχόντων as εχόντων. If the formal edition was the copied MS, and Luke's original edition was kept privately until it wore out or was destroyed by persecution, the missing syllable would lack verification. The mystery is yet unsolved. As a practical note, if 614* was merely a conjecture, the PWR should be assigned to the reading found in MSS 614C 1292 1611 2138 2412 etc. The MS 614C reading is semantically identical to the Byz text.

2. (8:7/24) 614/PWR displays δὲ <u>καὶ</u> (vs. δὲ, NA28/Byz) and is joined by core 1292 1611 2138 2412 and some others plus Chrys e sy^h. It smooths the narrative.

3. (8:9/36–40) 614/PWR reads τινα ἑαυτὸν εἶναί (vs. εἶναί τινα ἑαυτὸν, NA28/Byz) and is joined by 431 1292 1611 2138 2412. The PWR adjusts the style.

4. (8:10/15) 614/PWR has μεγάλου <u>αὐτῶν</u> (vs. μεγάλου, NA28/Byz) and is joined by 383 1292 2138 2412 and some others plus sy^h. It adds αὐτῶν to improve the style.

5. (8:10/30–32) (3ways) 614/PWR reads ἡ <u>λεγομένη</u> μεγάλη (vs. ἡ <u>καλουμένη</u> μεγάλη, NA28, vs. ἡ μεγάλη, Byz) and is joined by 431 1292 1611 2138 2412 plus sy^h. It replaces the NA28 reading with a more common synonym. The editor may have polished the reading by making it agree with λέγοντες earlier in the verse or simply preferred to reserve the καλέω root for proper nouns and not titles. The Byz appears to have lost NA28's καλουμένη by an eye skip.

6. (8:14/18) 614 displays δέδεκται <u>καὶ</u> (vs. δέδεκται ἡ, NA28/Byz, vs. δέδεκται καὶ ἡ, 1611) and is joined by only 467 547 1251 1297 1595. It probably dropped ἡ from the PWR by accident. 1611 is probably the PWR and is joined by 431 1127 1292 2138 plus gig r bo sy^h. It appears καί was added to tie the narrative with 1:8.

7. (8:19/26) 614/PWR has λαμβάν<u>ει</u> (vs. λαμβάνῃ, NA28/Byz) and is joined by core 383 1505 2147 2412 and some others, including 08 33. The present indicative may be result of the PWR editor making an itacism. This variant is not recorded in the ECM.

---

30. Köstenberger et al., *Cradle, the Cross*, 21.

8. (8:20/18–22) 614/PWR reads σὺν σοὶ εἰς (vs. σὺν σοὶ <u>εἴη</u> εἰς, NA28/Byz) and is joined by core 1505 2147 2412 2495 and some others, plus some fathers such as third-century Hipp. The cause was likely an eye skip with εἴη being overlooked because it stood next to εἰς. Once it occurred, the verbless clause made good sense, and thus the new reading became relatively popular.

9. (#8:21/32–40) (3ways) 614/PWR displays ἐνάντι<u>ον</u> (vs. ἔναντι, NA28, vs. ἐνώπιον, Byz) and is found in 6/10 core PWR MSS, 6/9 best ECM MSS (i.e., 04 33 81 1175 1739 2200), core Byz MSS 18 35 etc., including forty-four total MSS, and Bas Chrys[pt] Dam. NA28 is joined by just 3/9 best ECM MSS (i.e., 01 02 03), MS 05, eight others, and no fathers. Byz is joined by 4/10 core PWR MSS (i.e., 383 1505 2147 2495), 08 014 020 025 etc., and Ath Chrys[pt] ConstAp Phot. P45 can support either NA28 or 614. MS 614 is the PWR and the hardest reading because its word can mean either opposite or in the presence of. The other two, ἔναντι and ἐνώπιον, have the common gloss "in the presence of" (*TLG*) and may be improvements. The PWR has the best variety. ECM shows a SGL reading between 614 and NA28. 614/PWR is probably original. In contrast to its readings that stand against a united NA28/Byz, the PWR demonstrates a higher potential for originality in places of triple division.

10. (8:24/11) 614/PWR has εἶπεν <u>παρακαλῶ</u> (vs. εἶπεν, NA28/Byz, vs. εἶπεν <u>πρὸς αὐτοὺς παρακαλῶ</u>, 05, vs. εἶπεν <u>παρακαλῶ οὖν ὑμας</u>, 1501) and is joined by core 1292 1611 2138 2412, Western friendly (05) 431 876 1127 (1501), and ConstAp[T] gig r sy[h**] (mae). The editor enhances the emphasis.

11. (8:24/16–24) 614/PWR reads ὑπὲρ ἐμοῦ πρὸς τὸν <u>θεόν</u> (vs. ὑπὲρ ἐμοῦ πρὸς τὸν <u>κύριον</u>, NA28/Byz) and is joined by core 1505 1611 2147 2412 2495, (05) 05C (33), and many others plus Chrys p sy[h.txt] (mae sy[p]). It seems possible that the editor considered it more appropriate to have the more generic θεόν into the mouth of Simon, given that Simon evidently did not truly know the κύριον Jesus Christ. In contrast, the PWR/NA28 at 8:22/16–22 records that Peter commanded Simon to δεήθητι τοῦ κυρίου. It is probable that Peter was referring to the Lord Jesus. It is very difficult at these two verses to understand the cause of the divided testimony.

12. (8:25/18–20) 614/PWR displays κυρίου (vs. τοῦ κυρίου, NA28/Byz) and is joined by 431 1292 1611 2138 2412. The editor may have dropped τοῦ on purpose as he does at other places (see 3:20/16; 9:31/40; PWR=Byz at 13:10/38). Moreover, the dropping of the article is consistent with LXX style. However, it may have been accidental.

13. (8:26/22) 614/PWR has πρὸς μεσημβρίαν (vs. κατὰ μεσημβρίαν, NA28/Byz) and is joined by core 1292 1611 1890 2138 2412 and 08 044 431 1884 plus Chrys. Most likely the editor changed the preposition to disambiguate the meaning as "to the South." The κατά preposition allows the idea of either "to the South" or "at noon."

14. (8:29/16–24) 614/PWR reads αὐτοῦ (vs. τούτῳ, NA28/Byz) and is joined by 044 1243 1611 2138 2412. It translates as "his chariot" instead of "this chariot." The change probably came from assimilation to 8:28/18.

15. (8:35/28) 614/PWR displays εὐηγγελίζετο (vs. εὐηγγελίσατο, NA28/Byz) and is joined by 636 1175 1611 2412 L60. The PWR harmonized to the imperfect at 8:40/16. It seems that most core PWR MSS restored the primary reading.

16. (8:38/16–22) 614/PWR has εἰς τὸ ὕδωρ ἀμφότεροι (vs. ἀμφότεροι εἰς τὸ ὕδωρ, NA28/Byz) and is found in 6/10 core PWR MSS and twenty-three others plus Chrys e bo sy^h. There seems to be no advantage in changing the word order. The change may be accidental.

17. (8:39/8) 614/PWR reads ἀπὸ τοῦ ὕδατος (vs. ἐκ τοῦ ὕδατος, NA28/Byz) and is found in 6/10 core PWR MSS, 08 044, and twenty-six others, including about half the Westerns. The PWR presents a synonym.

PWR Revisions: Acts 13 (Dialogue)

There are seventeen places in Acts 13 where the PWR stands against the aligned ECM/Byz reading and eight occasions where all three traditions are divided, i.e., "3ways."

1. (13:4/24–26) (3ways) 614/PWR has κἀκεῖθεν (vs. ἐκεῖθέν τε, NA28, ἐκεῖθεν δὲ, RP05^txt) and is joined by 1292 1611 1890 2138 2412. The editor has polished NA28 by using just one word.

2. (#13:5/38) 614/PWR reads ὑπηρετοῦντα αὐτοῖς (vs. ὑπηρέτην, NA28/Byz). The PWR has smoothed by expanding.

3. (#13:6/6–10) (3ways) 614/PWR displays τὴν νῆσον ὅλην (vs. ὅλην τὴν νῆσον, NA28, vs. τὴν νῆσον, Byz) and is joined by 1292 1611 2138 2412 and 2 others plus Chrys. The PWR has reordered the NA28 reading. It may be that the PWR editor inherited the Byz eye skip and then restored the missing ὅλην in the position that seemed best.

4. (#13:7/24–28) 614/PWR has Βαρναβᾶν καὶ Παῦλον (vs. Βαρναβᾶν καὶ Σαῦλον, NA28/Byz). Saul is introduced as Paul earlier in the PWR archetype. This variant is apparently the result of another one at 12:25/8 where the PWR (supported by 614 1127 (*f) 2412 p mae sy[h**]) displays, "Barnabas and Saul, who is called Paul."

5. (13:8/28–32) 614/PWR reads τὸν ἀνθύπατον διαστρέψαι (vs. διαστρέψαι τὸν ἀνθύπατον, NA28/Byz) and is joined by 1611 1890 2138 2412. Though the word order is different, it does not seem to be smoother.

6. (13:10/30) 614/PWR displays παύῃ (vs. παύσῃ, NA28/Byz) and is joined by 9/10 core and many others. The editor uses the present subjunctive rather than the aorist possibly to agree with present participle διαστρέφων immediately following.

7. (13:17/22–26) 614/PWR has διὰ τὸν λαὸν καὶ (vs. καὶ τὸν λαὸν, NA28/Byz) and is joined by 1292 1611 2138*[vid] 2412 Chrys[ms76] gig[vid] sy[h]. The meaning of διὰ in the verse is not clear. Perhaps the editor thought that Paul's mention of fathers included men like Moses, Aaron, and Joshua. Therefore, he attempted to bring out the idea that God chose men like Moses for the benefit of the whole nation and used them to help bring the people out of Egypt (see Stephen's speech in Acts 7). Regardless, the secondary nature of the variant is evident.

8. (#13:20/2–16) (3ways) 614 reads ἔτεσιν τετρακοσίοις καὶ πεντήκοντα καὶ (vs. ὡς ἔτεσιν τετρακοσίοις καὶ πεντήκοντα καὶ, 1611, vs. ὡς ἔτεσιν τετρακοσίοις καὶ πενήκοντα καὶ μετὰ ταῦτα, NA28, vs. καὶ μετὰ ταῦτα ὡς ἔτεσιν τετρακοσίοις καὶ πεντήκοντα, Byz). Either 614 or 1611 represents the PWR with the difference being the presence or absence of ὡς at the start. Given the presence of ὡς in nearly every MS, 1611 is apparently more primitive and should be considered the PWR. It is joined directly by 1890* 2138 sa[mss] sy[h]. It also gains the indirect support of 614 629* 1292 2412 sa[ms] sy[p]. This difficult

variant will be covered in detail in chapter 4. The leading two readings are NA28 and the Byz, and the key difference is the placement of καὶ μετὰ ταῦτα. Wachtel is right to call the PWR deficient.[31]

9. (#13:23/18–26) (3ways) 614/PWR reads ἤγειρεν τῷ Ἰσραὴλ σωτῆρα Ἰησοῦν (vs. ἤγαγεν τῷ Ἰσραὴλ σωτῆρα Ἰησοῦν, NA28, vs. ἤγαγεν τῷ Ἰσραὴλ σωτηρίαν, Byz, vs. ἤγειρεν τῷ Ἰσραὴλ σωτηρίαν, 1). The editor "improved" NA28 by replacing ἤγαγεν with ἤγειρεν in order to better parallel God's raising up for Israel Jesus as Savior with God's raising up for Israel David as king (see 13:22/8). The Byz was corrupted by accident but otherwise would agree with NA28 (see chapter 2).

10. (13:27/8) 614/PWR has Ἰερουσαλὴμ (vs. ἐν Ἰερουσαλὴμ, NA28/RP-05^txt) and is found in 10/10 core PWR MSS, 3/10 best ECM MSS (i.e., 04 33 81), and P45 08 18 35 etc. The PWR receives the ancient support of P45 and offers a more difficult shorter form. However, such a structure already occurs in a similar context at 2:14/36–40 where only L156S sought to fix it. The editor was aware of the terse syntax in Acts 2 and thought it should be repeated here.

11. (#13:28/11) 614/PWR displays εὑρόντες ἐν αὐτῷ (vs. εὑρόντες, NA28/Byz) and is joined by 05 629 1127 1292 1611 2412 Vg d gig p t w 70 sin 189 sa bo mae sy^h** Ä. This clarifying gloss probably entered the NT tradition through the PWR edition and then became popular in the WR. The gloss was so natural that it was received by most translations. However, e 73 sy^h sy^p A G were not corrupted by it.

12. (#13:31/29, 30–32) (3ways) 614/PWR reads ἄχρι νῦν εἰσιν (vs. νῦν εἰσιν, NA28, vs. εἰσιν, Byz) and is joined by 876 1127 1292 1611 1832 1890 2138 2243 2412 Vg d p t w 70 73 189 sy^h. It seems that both the PWR and Byz editors adjusted the text found in NA28. The PWR added emphasis by inserting ἄχρι. The Byz smoothed the passage by dropping the νῦν.

13. (#13:33/20) 614/PWR displays τὸν κύριον ἡμῶν Ἰησοῦν (vs. τὸν κύριον Ἰησοῦν Χριστόν, 05, vs. Ἰησοῦν, NA28/Byz/sy^h) and is joined by 1292 2412 sy^h**. The PWR editor has inserted an edifying gloss. 05 has done the same thing. Its agreement with mae suggests that 05/mae preserves the WRR.

14. (13:34/2) 614/PWR has ὅτε (vs. ὅτι, NA28/Byz/sy^h) and is joined by 05 1175 1292 1751 2412 d gig ar. The PWR appears to be an itacism

---

31. Wachtel, "Against the Text-Type Concept," 145.

that became retained. Though ὅτε has the more common meaning of "when," *TLG* mentions a causal usage such as "seeing that." Ropes considered ὅτε to be a mistake.³² This agreement in error seems to be another indicator of a related ancestry between 614 and 05 despite their vast number of differences.

15. (13:39/5) 614/PWR reads <u>οὖν</u> πᾶς (vs. πᾶς, NA28/Byz) and is joined by 05 1292 1611 2412 d sy^hmg. The PWR added a conjunction as if 13:38 ended with a period. However, the editor seems to change the original stream of thought.

16. (#13:39/13) 614/PWR displays δικαιοῦται <u>παρὰ τῷ θεῷ</u> (vs. δικαιοῦται, NA28/Byz) and is joined by (05) 383 1127 1292 1501 (1611) 2147 2412 2652. The editor clarifies that Paul is talking about being justified before God and not just before man.

17. (#13:40/10–18) (3ways) 614/PWR has τὸ εἰρημένον ἐν τοῖς προφήταις <u>εἰς ὑμάς</u> (vs. <u>ἐφ' ὑμᾶς</u> τὸ εἰρημένον ἐν τοῖς προφήταις, Byz, vs. τὸ εἰρημένον ἐν τοῖς προφήταις, NA28) and is found in 6/10 core PWR MSS. Either the PWR or the Byz may be joined by sa bo mae. The PWR may have begun with the Byz and considered ἐφ' ὑμᾶς after ἐπέλθῃ to be superfluous where it stood and determined it must have a different function. Moving it to the end and changing the preposition could be rendered as, "So that what was spoken by the prophets <u>to you</u> may not fall upon [you]" (also see chapter 4).

18. (#13:41/10) 614/PWR reads <u>ἐπιβλέψατε καὶ</u> θαυμάσατε (vs. θαυμάσατε, NA28/Byz) and is joined by (08) (044) 35C 104 (323) 383 440 (927) (945) 1270 1611 (1739) 1890 (1891) 2138 2147 2412 and others plus sy^h. The added words bring Stephen's citation more in line with the LXX of Hab 1:5.

19. (13:41/34) 614/PWR displays ᾧ (vs. ὅ, NA28/Byz) and is joined by 383 1611 1890 2138 2147 2412. This variant is not listed in the ECM. The editor has made a stylistic gloss by changing to the dative.

20. (#13:41/49) 614/PWR has ὑμῖν <u>καὶ ἐσίγησεν</u> (vs. ὑμῖν, NA28/Byz) and is joined by (05) (1127) 2412 d mae sy^h**. The PWR added the phrase possibly to punctuate the end of Paul's sermon. Luke uses the word in a similar context (see Acts 15:12–13).

---

32. Ropes, *Beginnings of Christianity*, 125.

21. (#13:43/35) 614/PWR reads Βαρναβᾷ <u>ἀξιοῦντες βαπτισθῆναι</u> (vs. Βαρναβᾷ, NA28/Byz) and is joined by 383 1127 1501 2147 2412 2652 sy^(h**). It seems the editor believed he had accurate information that should be included. Perhaps he wanted show that the message spoken by Paul had yielded a harvest that day, as implied by the baptism of the converts.

22. (13:47/6-8) 614/PWR displays <u>ἡμῖν</u> ἐντέταλται ὁ κύριος (vs. ἐντέταλται <u>ἡμῖν</u> ὁ κύριος, NA28/Byz) and is joined by 8/10 core PWR MSS and ten others plus Cyr. The PWR adjusted the word order apparently out of a stylistic preference. By moving the pronoun, he placed the verb and subject next to each other.

23. (#13:47/33) 614/PWR has εἰς σωτηρίαν <u>ἐν τοῖς ἔθνεσιν</u> (vs. εἰς σωτηρίαν, NA28/Byz) and is joined by 1127 1501 2412 sy^(h**). The editor adds the phrase possibly to emphasize that the gospel is not merely a light, removing the ignorance of the gentiles, but rather it is the saving message for gentiles everywhere. The phrase is not part of the original quote from the LXX (see Isa 49:6). It seems to come from parallels in Acts (see 15:12; 21:19; 26:20, 23; 28:28).

24. (#13:48/10-26) (3ways) 614/PWR reads ἔχαιρον καὶ ἐδόξαζον <u>τὸν θεὸν</u> καὶ ἐπίστευσαν <u>τῷ λόγῳ τοῦ κυρίου</u> (vs. ἔχαιρεν/ἔχαιρον καὶ ἐδόξαζον <u>τὸν λόγον τοῦ κυρίου</u> καὶ ἐπίστευσαν, RP05^(txt)/NA28-RP-05^(mg), vs. same as NA28 except τοῦ θεοῦ, 03, vs. ἔχαιρον καὶ ἐδέξαντο τὸν λόγον τοῦ θεοῦ καὶ ἐπίστευσαν, 05) and is found in 7/10 core PWR MSS, its relatives 876 1127 1501 2652, and 3 others plus sy^p sy^h. The editor thought the text should put the emphasis on glorifying God himself. He also wanted to clarify that their belief was not vague but in the word of the Lord.

25. (13:51/12-14) (3ways) 614/PWR has <u>ἀπὸ</u> τῶν ποδῶν <u>αὐτῶν</u> (vs. τῶν ποδῶν <u>αὐτῶν</u>, Byz, vs. τῶν ποδῶν, NA28) and is found in 8/10 core PWR MSS and 08 049 etc. plus Chrys d e gig. The PWR added two words apparently by reference to Luke 9:5. The Byz added just one word possibly from Matt 10:14. The original seems to be NA28.

PWR Revisions: Acts 15 (Narrative)

There are twenty-two places in Acts 15 where the PWR stands against the aligned ECM/Byz reading and six occasions where all three traditions are divided, i.e., "3ways."

1. (#15:1/13) 614/PWR has + τῶν πεπιστευκότων ἀπὸ τῆς αἱρέσεως τῶν Φαρισαίων and is joined by 044 383 467 1127 1292f 1501 2147 2412 2652 L1825 sy^{hmg}. The addition comes from 15:5 and was apparently inserted to link the people. The PWR editor has terribly confused the text. The men mentioned in the standard text of 15:1 are most likely unsaved Jews who taught circumcision as a necessary means to salvation. They were the same kind of people that Paul referred to in Gal 2:4–5. On the other hand, those Jews in 15:5 were believers and probably taught that in order to be good disciples and walk with God, the gentiles also needed to keep the law. The former were divisive, and the latter were expressing their convictions respectfully.

2. (#15:2/64–70) 614/PWR displays + ὅπως κριθῶσιν ἐπ᾽ αὐτῶν right after περὶ τοῦ ζητήματος τούτου and is joined by (05* 05C1) (383) (1127) 1292 (1501 2147) 2412 (2652^{vid} L1825) sy^{h**}. The editor attempted to clarify the reason for the delegation. As in 15:1/13 above, he has once again changed the tone of the narrative. The standard text has Paul and the others go to Jerusalem to get help with the question of circumcision. The editor puts Paul and the others under a critical eye, saying that they were to be personally judged by the apostles and elders.[33] Perhaps he has sought to bring out the rudeness and prideful behavior of the Jews who stirred up trouble in Antioch. However, it does not follow that the church at Antioch or even Paul himself would have allowed themselves to be subdued by brethren from another church.

3. (#15:4/11) 614/PWR reads + μεγάλως and is joined by 04 05(*f) 383 1292 1501 1611 2147 2412 2652 L1825 sa sy^{h**}. In contrast to the negative vibes above, the PWR editor inserts an adverb to emphasize how respectfully and honorably the church of Jerusalem received Paul and Barnabas.[34]

---

33. Barrett, *Commentary on Acts*, 2:701.
34. Barrett, *Commentary on Acts*, 2:703.

4. (15:4/30–32) 614/PWR has δὲ (vs. τε, NA28/Byz) and is joined by 1292 1611* 1838 2344 2412 e. The editor made a minor change to the linkage.

5. (15:4/36–44) 614/PWR displays ἐποίησεν ὁ θεὸς μετ' αὐτῶν (vs. ὁ θεὸς ἐποίησεν μετ' αὐτῶν, NA28/Byz) and is 614 joined by P45 05 383 1718 2147 2412 2652 and eight others. The editor may have preferred the more common verb-subject-object (VSO) order.[35] The original text fronted the subject.

6. (15:4/45) 614/PWR reads + καὶ ὅτι ἤνοιξεν τοῖς ἔθνεσιν θύραν πίστεως and is joined by 04C3 014 020 1292 1505 2147 2412 2495, including a total of forty-eight Greek MSS, plus G^{ms}. The editor has enhanced the narrative, using words from 14:27.

7. (15:6/15) 614/PWR has οἱ πρεσβύτεροι σὺν τῷ πλήθει (vs. οἱ πρεσβύτεροι, NA28/Byz) and is joined by 383 1127 1292 1501 2147 2412 2652 L1825 sy^h Ephr^S. It appears that the editor used the insight gleaned from 15:22/16–22 to make explicit for the reader that all the church was present to hear this important dialogue.

8. (15:6/20–24) 614/PWR displays τοῦ ζητήματος τούτου (vs. τοῦ λόγου τούτου, NA28/Byz) and is joined by 08 1127 1292 1501 1611 1890 2138 2412 L1825 plus e gig sy^h. The PWR has likely harmonized to agree with 15:2/68.

9. (#15:7/10–12) 614/PWR reads + ἐν πνεύματι ἁγίῳ and is joined by (05*) 1292 1501 2412 L1825 sy^{hmg} (d l) Ephr^S. The editor wants to make it clear that Peter was not offering his opinion but instead expressing divine revelation. Barrett agrees.[36]

10. (15:7/36–44) (3ways) 614 has ἡμῖν ὁ θεὸς ἐξελέξατο (vs. ἐν ἡμῖν ὁ θεὸς ἐξελέξατο, 05C1/1611, vs. ὁ θεὸς ἐν ἡμῖν ἐξελέξατο, Byz, vs. ἐν ἡμῖν ἐξελέξατο ὁ θεός, 044, vs. ἐν ὑμῖν ἐξελέξατο ὁ θεός, NA28, vs. ὁ θεὸς ἐν ὑμῖν ἐξελέξατο, 18, vs. ὁ θεὸς ἐξελέξατο, 69) and has dropped ἐν by accident and is joined by 05* 2412. Therefore, 1611 preserves the PWR. It is joined by core MSS 383 1292 1890 2138 2147 and 05C1 323 1501 2652^{vid} L1825 plus d gig. NA28 has the support of 10/10 best ECM MSS and should be given the benefit of the doubt, especially since ὑμῖν seems less natural. A proto-Byz editor is perhaps responsible for the rewording of NA28 as seen in the Byz. The

---

35. Runge, *Discourse Grammar*, 182–84.
36. See Barrett, *Commentary on Acts*, 2:713.

PWR may have inherited the Byz but then moved the noun next to the verb for stylistic reasons. It receives indirect support from 69 sa sy^p Ä, which evidently simplified the PWR by dropping ἐν ἡμῖν from the start. MS 18 et al. begin with the Byz and then restore the ὑμῖν of the original, without touching the word order.

11. (#15:10/32–40) 614/PWR displays ἡμεῖς οὔτε οἱ πατέρες ἡμῶν (vs. οἱ πατέρες ἡμῶν οὔτε ἡμεῖς, NA28/Byz) and is joined by 1292 1297 1611 1735 1890 2138 2412 ConstAp Cyr Did OrLat Tert sy^h. The editor places the Messianic community first for emphasis while the original mentions the fathers first, according to natural and spiritual ancestry.

12. (15:11/2) 614/PWR reads ἀλλ᾽ ἤ (vs. ἀλλά, NA28/Byz) and is joined by 383 1292 1611 1890 2138 2147 2412 and some others plus ConstAp^mss Thdrt. The PWR editor may have inserted the conjunction next to ἀλλά in order to mean "rather" as found in Luke 12:51. The above PWR MSS accent it accordingly. However, perhaps Ropes is right that the accent originally was for the adverb ἦ that means "truly."[37] The PWR increases the contrast with the previous verse.

13. (15:14/8–14) 614/PWR displays πρῶτος ὁ θεὸς ἐξελέξατο (vs. πρῶτον ὁ θεὸς ἐπεσκέψατο, NA28/Byz) and is joined by (08) (459) 1292 1611 (1884 1890*) 2138 (2147) 2412 (sy^p sy^h). It harmonizes the verb to match that of 15:7.

14. (15:19/22) 614/PWR has πρὸς τὸν θεόν (vs. ἐπὶ τὸν θεόν, NA28/Byz) and is joined by 383 1292 1501 1611 1751 1890 2138 2147 2412 Chrys ConstAp^mss. The PWR preferred a different preposition.

15. (15:22/24) 614/PWR reads ἐκλεξαμένοις (vs. ἐκλεξαμένους, NA28/Byz) and is joined by core 383C 1292 1611 2138 2412, 4/10 best ECM MSS (i.e., P74 33 1739 2200), and 206 323 429 522 636 808 945 1501 1704 1751f 1842 1891 2298 L1188 sy^p. Thus, various important MSS give the dative and seem to assimilate with the previous seven datives in the verse. Barrett asserts that the Greek will permit either case in such a context.[38] Wachtel points out that the use of the dative here is probably by harmonization with 15:25/10.[39]

---

37. Ropes, *Beginnings of Christianity*, 142.
38. Barrett, *Commentary on Acts*, 2:739.
39. Wachtel, "Text-Critical Commentary," 22–23.

16. (15:22/40–46) (3ways) 614/PWR displays τῷ Παύλῳ καὶ τῷ Βαρνάβᾳ (vs. τῷ Παύλῳ καὶ Βαρνάβᾳ, NA28, vs. Παύλῳ καὶ Βαρνάβᾳ, Byz) and is joined by 383 522f 945 1292 1611 1890* 2138 2147 2412 and about eighteen others. The editor balances the syntax of NA28 by adding a second article. In contrast, the Byz editor balances it by removing the existing one.

17. (#15:23/4–8) (3ways) 614/PWR has διὰ χειρὸς αὐτῶν ἐπιστολὴν καὶ πέμψαντες περιέχουσαν τάδε (vs. διὰ χειρὸς αὐτῶν, NA28, vs. διὰ χειρὸς αὐτῶν τάδε, Byz, διὰ χειρὸς αὐτῶν ἐπιστολὴν περιέχουσαν τάδε, 04(*f)) and is joined by 383 1292 1501 2147 2412 sy[hmg]. The ECM lists nine alternatives. Barrett wonders why there were so many expansions.[40] The PWR builds upon the Byz and is possibly the cause of most variations. The open question is whether NA28 or the Byz is original (see chapter 4).

18. (15:23/24–28) 614/PWR reads κατὰ Ἀντιόχειαν (vs. κατὰ τὴν Ἀντιόχειαν, NA28/Byz) and is joined by 18 35 1127 1243 1292 1501 1609 1611 1837 1890* 2138 2147 2243C 2344 2412 Chrys ConstAp[ms]. The editor dropped the article so that none of the three named places would have an article.

19. (15:25/29) 614/PWR displays τε καὶ (vs. καὶ, NA28/Byz) and is joined by 044 5 383 619 623 1162 1292 1501 1611 1827 1890 2138 2147 2412 2805 Socr e. The PWR editor probably added τε in preference for common Lucan style. In Acts alone, Luke uses this construction twenty-seven times (*BW*).

20. (#15:26/27) 614/PWR has εἰς πάντα πειρασμόν and is joined by 05 (08) 383 1127 1292 1501 1884 2147 2412 d e l sy[hmg]. The editor has assimilated the words and idea from Luke 22:28. He saw a parallel between the sacrificial life of Paul and Barnabas with the life of Christ (see 1 Cor 11:1) and wanted to share it with the reader.

21. (15:27/16–24) 614 reads διὰ λόγου καταγγέλλοντας ταῦτα (vs. διὰ λόγου ἀπαγγέλλοντας τὰ αὐτά, NA28/Byz, διὰ λόγου ἀπαγγέλλοντας ταῦτα, 1611) and is joined by just 2412. ECM lists fourteen alternatives. These two witnesses and others have reduced two words into one probably by the accidental loss of an alpha from ΤΑΑΥΤΑ to form ΤΑΥΤΑ. The cause may be a primitive error, dating from when the script was all uppercase and without spaces. In addition,

---

40. Barrett, *Commentary on Acts*, 2:739.

only 614 and 2412 have changed the prefix from ἀπ- to κατ- before the participle, manifesting their later deviation from the PWR. Instead, 1611 preserves the PWR and is joined by 044 181 467 915f 1175 1292 1501 1890* 2138 and nine others plus Amph ConstAp[mss] Socr[mss] (d sa). Once the error occurred it would seem like an improvement to the reader.

22. (#15:29/17) 614/PWR has + καὶ ὅσα μὴ θέλετε αὐτοῖς γενέσθαι ἑτέρῳ μὴ ποιεῖτε (vs. καὶ ὅσα μὴ θέλετε ἑαυτοῖς γίνεσθαι ἑτεροῖς μὴ ποιεῖν, 206) and is joined by core 1292 2412 and others with similar readings plus (sa Ä IrLat d p ar l sy[h**]). The gloss appears to have been a common saying. It may have been added here to give gentile readers a broader guideline for holy living rather than just a list of prohibitions. Yet it was still framed with a negative delivery in contrast to the Golden Rule.

23. (#15:34/2-12) 614/PWR contains ἔδοξεν δὲ τῷ Σιλᾷ ἐπιμεῖναι αὐτοῦ (vs. omits, NA28/Byz) and is found in 6/10 core PWR MSS and by many others, including most Westerns, plus d gig w ar l 189 Ä A G. Four of its core MSS were corrected to the standard text. The gloss apparently was created to anticipate the question of how Silas could depart with Paul in 15:40 if he was no longer in Antioch.

24. (15:36/27) (3ways) 614/PWR reads τοὺς ἀδελφοὺς τοὺς (vs. τοὺς ἀδελφοὺς, NA28, vs. τοὺς ἀδελφοὺς ἡμῶν, Byz) and is found in 8/10 core PWR MSS, 05, and 9 others plus sy[h**]. The Byz attempts to smooth by adding a pronoun. The PWR editor adds the article apparently to make explicit that what follows describes the specific brothers and sisters Paul had in mind.

25. (15:37/6-8) (3ways) 614/PWR displays ἠβούλετο λαβεῖν (vs. ἐβούλετο συμπαραλαβεῖν, NA28, vs. ἐβουλεύσατο συμπαραλαβεῖν, Byz) and is joined by 1292 1501 1611 (1890 2138) 2412 L1825. The PWR has limited support and has probably accidentally dropped the double prefix to the infinitive. The Byz presents Barnabas as more intentional. However, the PWR helps confirm βούλομαι was the original root.

26. (15:37/10) (3ways) 614/PWR has καὶ τὸν Ἰωάννην (vs. τὸν Ἰωάννην, Byz, vs. καὶ Ἰωάννην, ECM) and is found in 5/10 core PWR MSS (i.e., 614 1292 1611 2138 2412), 3/9 best ECM MSS (i.e., 01 03 81), and some others. The above text is followed by an attributive participle,

either τὸν καλούμενον or τὸν ἐπικαλούμενον (PWR). The PWR and Byz apparently added the article in order to match the adjectival participle. The Byz may have dropped the conjunction later.[41]

27. (15:37/16) 614/PWR reads ἐπικαλούμενον (vs. καλούμενον, NA28/Byz) and is likely harmonized with 12:12/26. MS 614 is joined by 6/10 best ECM MSS (i.e., 04 33 81 1175 1739 2200), 10/10 core PWR MSS, and 01C2a 05 044 etc., including nearly all Westerns. Nearly all Byz MSS and the core Alex MSS P74 01* 01C2b 02 03 resisted the strong attraction to equalize.

28. (15:39/10) 614/PWR has ἀποχωρῆσαι (vs. ἀποχωρισθῆναι, NA28/Byz) and is joined by 08 1292 1501 1611 1884 2138 2412 L1825. The PWR utilizes a synonym based upon the root ἀποχωρέω and has harmonized with 13:13/32.

PWR Revisions: Acts 17 (Dialogue)

There are fifteen places in Acts 17 where the PWR stands against the aligned ECM/Byz reading and four occasions where all three traditions are divided, i.e., "3ways."

1. (17:2/28–30) 614f1/PWR has διελέχθη (vs. διελέξατο, NA28/Byz). 614f1 (614, διηλέχθη) is joined by 383f1 1292f2 1505f2 1611f2 1890 2138f2 2412f1 2495f2, 05 08 044 1501f1 2652f1, and fourteen others plus Chrys^pt. It parses as an API-3S and seems to be a deponent. The editor used a synonym and evidently misspelled it as well.

2. (17:3/34–40) (3ways) 614/PWR reads Ἰησοῦς Χριστὸς (vs. ὁ χριστὸς Ἰησοῦς, Byz, vs. ὁ χριστὸς ὁ Ἰησοῦς, NA28/03, vs. χριστὸς Ἰησοῦς, P74, vs. Ἰησοῦς ὁ χριστὸς, 08) and is found in 8/10 core PWR MSS and 01 1501 2652 L1825 plus (e ar l/2 bo sy^p). ECM shows it as a SGL reading between 03, Byz, and P74. The NA28 reading is unique in the NT and for that reason could be original but it is only supported by 03 33 441 621. The Byz reading is so normal that it would not have caused the others if it were original. Reading 08 is even easier than the Byz. It appears that P74 is unusual enough to cause the variation.[42] It is also joined by 02 05 81 and 5 others. Either the Byz or NA28 or

---

41. See Wachtel, "Text-Critical Commentary," 23.
42. Barrett, *Commentary on Acts*, 2:811, also sees quality in the P74 reading.

P74 may have the support of (Vg d gig p w l* sa sy^h). P74 could be translated as, "This is Messiah Jesus," which seems to be original.

3. (#17:4/10) 614/PWR displays ἐπίστευσαν (vs. ἐπείσθησαν, NA28/Byz) and is found in 08 33 1127, 9/10 core PWR MSS, and thirteen others plus Vg e gig p w l 189 sa^mss bo sy^p sy^h. The editor's motive seems to be doctrinal clarity. He has replaced ἐπείσθησαν with the more common word to describe life-transforming faith in the Gospel.

4. (17:5/2–22) (3ways) 614/PWR has ζηλώσαντες δὲ οἱ Ἰουδαῖοι καὶ προσλαβόμενοι οἱ ἀπειθοῦντες τῶν ἀγοραίων τινὰς ἄνδρας πονηροὺς (f.) (vs. ζηλώσαντες δὲ οἱ Ἰουδαῖοι οἱ ἀπειθοῦντες καὶ προσλαβόμενοι τῶν ἀγοραίων ἄνδρας τινὰς πονηρούς, 206 (k.), vs. ζηλώσαντες δὲ οἱ Ἰουδαῖοι καὶ προσλαβόμενοι τῶν ἀγοραίων ἄνδρας τινὰς πονηρούς, ECM (a.), vs. προσλαβόμενοι δὲ οἱ Ἰουδαῖοι οἱ ἀπειθοῦντες τῶν ἀγοραίων τινὰς ἄνδρας πονηρούς, Byz (s.)) and is joined by 383 1292 1501 1611 1890 2138 (2147) 2412 2652 L1825 (sy^h). ECM lists twenty-four alternatives. ECM is the original reading. 206 expanded it by inserting οἱ ἀπειθοῦντες immediately after οἱ Ἰουδαῖοι to contrast these Jews with those of 17:4/10. When the word order of ἄνδρας τινὰς was swapped, reading k. became l. as found in MS 1241. Later, reading l. accidentally lost ζηλώσαντες. Without it, the Byz editors were forced to reorder and ended up with reading s. On the other hand, the PWR is closely related to reading k. Unfortunately, when it inserted the words οἱ ἀπειθοῦντες, it incorrectly added them before τῶν ἀγοραίων, confusing the sense. Probably at the same time, the PWR also smoothed the sequence by placing τινάς in front of ἄνδρας.

5. (17:6/30) 614/PWR omits (vs. οἱ, NA28/Byz) and is found in 8/10 core PWR MSS. The editor most likely removed the article to simplify the sentence.

6. (#17:11/47) 614/PWR reads οὕτως καθὼς Παῦλος ἀπαγγέλλει (vs. οὕτως, NA28/Byz) and is joined 383 1127 1292 1501 (2147) 2412 2652 (gig ar sy^h**). The editor provides an explanatory gloss.

7. (17:12/4–6) 614* omits (vs. μὲν οὖν, NA28/Byz/614C, vs. οὖν, 383) and is joined by 2412. They have deviated from the PWR. Instead, 383 preserves the PWR and is found in 8/10 core MSS and 2652 plus sa bo^mss sy^h. The μέν was probably removed in order to smooth the sentence.

8. (#17:12/13) 614/PWR displays ἐπίστευσάν <u>τινες δὲ ἠπίστησαν</u> (vs. ἐπίστευσαν, NA28/Byz) and is joined by 05 383 1292 1501 2147 2412 2652 d. The gloss informs the reader that the exceptionally positive Jewish response was not absolute.[43]

9. (17:13/12) 614/PWR has Θεσσαλονίκης (vs. <u>τῆς</u> Θεσσαλονίκης, NA28/Byz) and is found in 8/10 core MSS and P74 05 08 945 1359 1704 1718 1884 2374 Thdrt[vid]. The editor probably deleted τῆς because of a stylistic preference.

10. (17:14/2-8) 614/PWR reads εὐθέως δὲ τὸν (vs. εὐθέως δὲ <u>τότε</u> τὸν, NA28/Byz) and is found in 10/10 core PWR MSS and 180 181 996 1501 1838 1875 2652 plus Chrys sy[h]. The editor probably deleted τότε because it was not necessary with εὐθέως.

11. (17:14/28) (3ways) 614/PWR displays ὑπέμειν<u>εν</u> (vs. ὑπέμειν<u>αν</u>, NA28, vs. ὑπέμενον, Byz) and is found in 10/10 core PWR MSS and 02 05 1501 2652 L156 (d sa bo[mss] sy[p.mss]). It apparently was changed from 3P to 3S by itacism. The singular of the PWR seems to clash here. However, its aorist supports NA28 indirectly. The Byz has limited support and apparently dropped a iota, causing the imperfect tense. If it gained the iota back it would read ὑπέμεινον and be equivalent with NA28.

12. (#17:17/24-36) 614/PWR has καὶ <u>τοῖς</u> ἐν τῇ ἀγορᾷ κατὰ πᾶσαν ἡμέραν (vs. καὶ ἐν τῇ ἀγορᾷ κατὰ πᾶσαν ἡμέραν, NA28/Byz) and is joined by 05 383 1292 1501 2147 2412 2652 sa sy[p] sy[hmg]. The editor added τοῖς to smooth the grammar of the sentence.

13. (17:18/6) 614/PWR reads δὲ (vs. δὲ <u>καί</u>, NA28/Byz) and is found in 10/10 core PWR MSS and many others plus Chrys[pt] Vg e gig p w l 189. The PWR made the sentence smoother by deleting καί.

14. (17:18/18) 614/PWR displays συνέβαλον (vs. συνέβαλλον, NA28/Byz) and is found in 8/10 core PWR MSS. The editor apparently simplified the imperfect to the aorist.

15. (17:18/68) 614/PWR has εὐηγγελίζετο <u>αὐτοῖς</u> (vs. εὐηγγελίζετο, NA28/Byz, <u>αὐτοῦ</u> εὐηγγελίζετο <u>αὐτοῖς</u>, 1739) and is found in 9/10 core PWR MSS, P74 01C2 02 08 014 etc., and Vg e p w l/2 189 (l* sy[p]). It added αὐτοῖς for clarity and was popular.

---

43. See Barrett, *Commentary on Acts*, 2:818.

16. (17:19/2-4) 614f/PWR reads <u>μετὰ δὲ ἡμέρας τινὰς</u> ἐπιλαβόμενοι τε (vs. ἐπιλαβόμενοι τε, NA28/Byz) and is joined by (05) (383C) 383f* 1292f (2147) 2412f d (sy^h**). The editors of the ECM apparently gave the f symbol because they think 614 offers a reading that combined that of 05 with the standard.[44] However, given that 614 is usually more primitive than 05 and that it would be unlikely to add the τε if it were not there already, the 614 reading probably preceded that of 05. Later 383C shows a correction to drop τε and that correction is found in 05 sy^h**. The PWR editor inserted a temporal reference to transition the narrative or because he knew that Paul was there for a while before the philosophers brought him to the Areopagus.

17. (17:20/24-30) (3ways) 614 has τίνι ταῦτα θέλ<u>οι</u> εἶναι (vs. <u>τίνα</u> ταῦτα θέλ<u>οι</u> εἶναι, 1292, vs. <u>τὶ ἂν</u> θέλ<u>οι</u> ταῦτα εἶναι, Byz, vs. <u>τίνα</u> θέλ<u>ει</u> ταῦτα εἶναι, NA28) and is joined by 2412 and has corrupted the PWR from τίνα to τίνι. The ECM mistakenly lists 614 1292 1501 1505 1611 2138 2412 as having θέλει. All have θέλοι instead. 1292 preserves the PWR and is joined by 1501 1505 1611 2138 2495. The PWR may actually be a merger of the Byz with NA28. The Byz seems more complex, but it is a result of harmonization with 17:18/28-32. NA28 preserves the original and is joined by 9/9 best ECM MSS.

18. (17:25/20-26) 614/PWR has πνοὴν καὶ ζωὴν (vs. ζωὴν καὶ πνοὴν, NA28/Byz) and is found in 10/10 core PWR MSS, 044 876 1501 2652, and about fifteen others plus Chrys^pt Clem^pt. The editor possibly adjusted the word order to better match the LXX (see Gen 2:7), which reads πνοὴν ζωῆς.

19. (#17:26/10-14) 614/PWR reads πᾶν <u>γένος</u> ἀνθρώπων (vs. πᾶν <u>ἔθνος</u> ἀνθρώπων, NA28/Byz) and is found in 8/10 core MSS and sixteen others plus Chrys^ms76 Clem (sy^hmg). The editor assimilated γένος from 17:28-29. Perhaps he made a word play between γένος as meaning God's offspring and γένος as referring to the various subgroups within mankind. Their common denominator is that God created them all.

---

44. ECM 3:1:2, 649.

PWR Revisions: Acts 19 (Narrative)

Acts 19 includes the witness of P38, a very important Western MS dated to ca. AD 300. P38 preserves early evidence for both WRRs and PWRs. It is extant for much of 18:27–19:6, 12–16. It is more closely aligned with the WR/05 than it is to the PWR archetype and MS 614. P48 is also a noteworthy Western witness because it is dated even earlier, being assigned to the third century. It is preserved at 23:11–17, 25–29. Moreover, because Acts 23 is not one of the eight chapters selected for sampling, P48 is addressed briefly here. P48 is likewise more closely aligned with the WR than the PWR edition. It was these two papyri that gave Barbara Aland important insight as she fine-tuned her understanding of the relationship of the WR to the archetype underneath the 614-group.[45] As mentioned previously, she concluded that the 614-group archetype stands chronologically before the WR and that its text (or one similar to it) was used as a source document for the WR.[46] In summary, P38 and P48 have three primary alignments in terms of their characteristic Western readings. First, they agree with both the PWR and WRR at the following places: 18:27/35 (P38), 18:27/44-48 (P38), 18:28/13 (P38), 19:5/19 (P38), 23:15/65 (P48), and 23:25/2-12 (P48). Second, they agree with just the WRR in these passages: 19:1/2-30 (P38), 19:2/34-40 (P38), 19:14/2-20, 21 (P38), 23:15/6-18 (P48), and 23:16/19 (P48). Finally, they have limited support at these locations: 18:27/36-42 (P38 + 05 d), 23:27/36-42 (P48 + gig), and 23:29/2 (P48 + gig). The third category probably indicates readings that were formed after the WR. Uniquely, P38 joins the PWR alone at 19:13/46.

There are twenty places in Acts 19 where the PWR stands against the aligned ECM/Byz reading and three occasions where all three traditions are divided, i.e., "3ways."

1. (19:3/2-4, 6-10) 614* has εἶπέν οὖν (vs. εἶπέν οὖν εἰς τί οὖν, 1611, vs. εἶπέν τε εἰς τί οὖν, NA28/Byz/614C) and is joined by only 2412. The *Vorlage* of these two MSS by implication had a text maligned by an eye skip from the first οὖν to the second one as found in the PWR. The PWR itself is maintained by 1611 and joined by 1292 1501 1505 1890 2138 2412 2495 (sy^h). The editor replaced the original τε with a second οὖν. It may have been an accidental replacement caused

---

45. Aland, "Entstehung, Charakter und Herkunft," 9–10.
46. Aland, "Entstehung, Charakter und Herkunft," 26–28.

by dittography from looking ahead to the οὖν that follows in the standard text. Here is a rare case where 614 was corrected by the standard text. However, its correction only happened in the thirteenth century or later. Its sister MS 2412 was never fixed.

2. (#19:5/19) 614/PWR reads + Χριστοῦ εἰς ἄφεσιν ἁμαρτιῶν (vs. omits, NA28/Byz) and is joined by P38^{vid} 05 383 1127 1501 2147 2412 2652 d sy^{h**}. The editor has inserted the words from 2:38. It seems to be a gloss intended to remind the reader of that day when the church began and to emphasize that belief in the gospel always brings the individual the forgiveness of sins.

3. (#19:9/8–24) 614 displays τινες <u>τῶν ἐθνῶν τότε</u> ἐσκληρύνοντο καὶ ἠπείθουν κακολογοῦντες τὴν ὁδὸν ἐνώπιον τοῦ πλήθους (vs. τινες ἐσκληρύνοντο καὶ ἠπείθουν κακολογοῦντες τὴν ὁδὸν ἐνώπιον <u>παντὸς</u> τοῦ πλήθους <u>τῶν ἐθνῶν</u>, 876/sy^{h**}) and differs from the NA28/Byz in the added underlined words. By looking at all the ECM variants it is possible to recognize the PWR. It is best preserved in 876 except that παντός must be dropped. The editor wanted the reader to understand that the reference to the multitude was not to the common mixture of Jews and God-fearing gentiles regularly found at the synagogues. Instead, he perceived the event as a particular effort on the part of the unbelieving Jews to defame the message in front of the gentiles who were attending the synagogue.

4. (19:9/37) 614/PWR has <u>τὸ</u> καθ' ἡμέραν (vs. καθ' ἡμέραν, NA28/Byz) and is found in 10/10 core PWR MSS, 05 044, and fourteen others. *TLG* offers that τό may be used to mean "wherefore" (see entry under A/VIII. Abs. uses of single cases/3). It seems to be a gloss inserted to enhance the causal sense. Since Paul could no longer teach in the synagogue of Ephesus, he found a new place to teach at the school of Tyrannus.

5. (#19:9/51) (3ways) 614/PWR states + τινὸς ἀπὸ ὥρας πέμπτης ἕως ὥρας δεκάτης (vs. τινός, Byz, vs. omits, NA28) and is joined by (05) 383 1127 1409 1501 2147 2412 2652(*f) (d) gig w ar sy^{h**}. Most PWR MSS corrected to the Byz. The editor inserted what he understood to be an authentic explanatory detail. The PWR apparently began with the Byz reading.

6. (#19:13/46) (3ways) 614/PWR reads <u>ἐξ</u>ορκί<u>ζομεν</u> (vs. ὁρκί<u>ζομεν</u>, Byz, ὁρκίζω, NA28) and is found in relatives P38 206 431 522 945 1501

1739 1891 2298 2652 and 6/10 core PWR MSS. It is interesting that P38 aligns here with the PWR but not with 05 and the OL. Since both NA28 and the Byz lack the prefix, it is likely that the original did not have one. The PWR is closest to the Byz and probably derived from it. The plural apparently came from a Byz editor who sought agreement with the preceding plural participle. NA28 is probably original.

7. (19:15/6-8) 614/PWR displays ἀποκριθὲν δὲ ποτὲ (vs. ἀποκριθὲν δὲ, NA28/Byz) and is joined by 1505 1611 2138 2412 2495 2718 sy^h. The editor apparently wanted to explain that the exorcists were casting out demons in Jesus's name for a while before they were opposed by the demons. Yet that time period is not given.

8. (19:15/19) 614/PWR/NA28 reads τὸν μὲν (vs. τὸν, Byz/ECM) and is found in 10/10 core MSS and P41 01C2 03 08 etc. plus Chrys^pt IobM Phot sy^h. The editor added μέν in order to create emphasis.

9. (19:17/24) 614/PWR has Ἔφεσον (vs. τὴν Ἔφεσον, NA28/Byz) and is found in 10/10 core PWR MSS and 02* 08 044 1501 1884 2652 2718. The PWR dropped the article probably from a stylistic preference.

10. (19:18/8) 614/PWR displays τῶν πιστευόντων (vs. τῶν πεπιστευκότων, NA28/Byz) and is found in 8/10 core MSS and 05 044 1501. The editor simplified the perfect participle by harmonizing it with the two following present participles. The original wording has a pluperfect sense.[47]

11. (19:19/4) 614/PWR reads τε (vs. δὲ, NA28/Byz) and is found in 9/10 core PWR MSS, 08 2652, and eleven others plus Bas Chrys sy^h. The PWR editor changed the conjunction to make the verses more connective than contrastive. However, Runge explains that δέ marks a development that can be either contrastive or connective.[48] The editor apparently wanted to make the meaning explicit.

12. (19:21/48) 614/PWR has γενέσθαι (vs. γενέσθαι με, NA28/Byz) and is joined by 044 619* 1292 1505 1611 1642 1890* 2138 2412 2495. The PWR has apparently dropped the first με by accident and has reduced the clarity.

13. (19:25/2) 614/PWR displays οὗτος (vs. οὓς, NA28/Byz) and is joined by 05 1292 1501 1505 1611 1890 2138 2412 2495 sa sy^p sy^h. The

---

47. Barrett, *Commentary on Acts*, 2:912.
48. Runge, *Discourse Grammar*, 25-36, 42.

editor may have accidentally changed the relative to the demonstrative when he saw the nominative singular participle that followed. Conversely, he may have read οὕς as a scribal error and thus made a correction. He did not realize that οὕς was Luke's precise way of connecting the previous group of craftsmen, τοῖς τεχνίταις (see 19:24/22–24), with the latter group of common workers, τὰ τοιαῦτα ἐργάτας (see 19:25/12–16), to show that Demetrius gathered them both together.[49] It is not clear whether the editor perceived two groups or just one. As a result of this one change, various Western, related witnesses noticed just one group. For example, the archetype for 05 proceeded to delete the καί from the sequence οὗτος συναθροίσας καὶ τοὺς περὶ τὰ τοιαῦτα ἐργάτας εἶπεν and thereby explicity refers to one group. That error trickled into the OL MSS d gig ar 189. In a similar way, the editor of sy[h**] saw only one group though it retained the καί. His understanding can be seen at 19:25/21 where Demetrius addresses the crowd as συντεχνῖται rather than simply as ἄνδρες in the original. Moreover sy[h**] (with 05 d) is also joined by sa in this latter change. In summary, the small change in the PWR led to further changes in the WRR.

14. (19:26/57) 614/PWR reads χειρῶν ἀνθρώπων (vs. χειρῶν, NA28/Byz) and is found in 10/10 core PWR MSS and others plus Chrys[pt] bo[mss] sy[p] Ä. The editor clarified by adding a word.

15. (19:27/8–16) 614/PWR has τοῦτο τὸ μέρος κινδυνεύει ἡμῖν (vs. τοῦτο κινδυνεύει ἡμῖν τὸ μέρος, NA28/Byz) and is found in 10/10 core PWR MSS and 02 1501 2652 sy[h]. The editor has reordered in order to smooth the reading.

16. (19:27/46–52) (3ways) 614/PWR displays μέλλειν τε καθαιρεῖσθαι (vs. μέλλειν δὲ καὶ καθαιρεῖσθαι, Byz, vs. μέλλειν τε καὶ καθαιρεῖσθαι, NA28) and is found in 7/10 core PWR MSS, 08 1501 1884 2652, and three others. While the PWR could be original, it seems unlikely that the other two traditions would both preserve two conjunctions if that form were not original. The ECM lists eighteen alternatives. The preservation of τε in the PWR provides indirect support for NA28. Despite the centuries of transmission, the 70 percent coherence of the PWR amid manifold splintering indicates a solid ancient text form with a tenacious stability up to the present day.

---

49. Barrett, *Commentary on Acts*, 2:924.

17. (#19:28/13) 614(*f2, Cf1)/PWR reads θυμοῦ <u>καὶ δραμόντες εἰς τὸ ἄμφοδον</u> (vs. θυμοῦ, NA28/Byz) and is joined by (05) 383 (1127) 1292 1501 2147 2412 2652 sy^hmg. The editor seems to introduce some additional knowledge he had about the event. He says that the public ran out into the "street" first and only later into the theater (see *TLG*).[50] Was his explanation an eyewitness account or simply a reasonable inference based upon his general knowledge?

18. (19:33/14) 614 displays προβαλλόντων (vs. προβαλόντων, NA28/Byz) and is joined by 383 2147 2412 plus many others. 614 is probably the PWR because its friends are those that support other key PWR readings nearby (see 19:5/19; 19:9/8–24; 19:9/51). Both readings have a lot of support. The PWR appears to smooth the passage by adjusting the verb to the present tense.

19. (19:34/16) 614/PWR has ἐγένετο (vs. ἐγένετο μία, NA28/Byz) and is found in 9/10 core PWR MSS and 044 2652 plus sy^h. The word was dropped either to simplify or by accident.

20. (#19:35/2) 614/PWR displays κατα<u>σείσ</u>ας (vs. κατα<u>στείλ</u>ας, NA28/Byz) and is found in 8/10 core PWR MSS and 05 08 044 1 228 996 1884C Ä. The editor has most likely assimilated his word from 19:33/28 (cf. 12:17; 13:16; 21:40) perhaps because he considered it more appropriate. The standard reading means to let down or pacify, and it occurs elsewhere only at 19:36. The editor may have considered "having pacified" to be a mistaken intrusion from 19:36.

21. (#19:37/11) 614/PWR reads + ἐνθάδε and is joined by 05 383 1127 1292 2147 2412 2652 d sa bo sy^Aram sy^hmg A. The editor inserted a word to smooth the sentence.

22. (19:37/20–22) 614/PWR has τὴν θεὰν (vs. τὴν θεὸν, NA28/Byz) and is found in 8/10 core PWR MSS and 05* 08C 025 1241 etc., including thirteen Westerns. The editor removed the nonstandard spelling for goddess. It is remarkable that the vast majority of MSS resisted the changes.

23. (19:38/2–6) 614/PWR displays εἰ μὲν οὖν <u>ὁ</u> (vs. εἰ μὲν οὖν, NA28/Byz) and is joined by 1292 1505 1611 1890 2138 2412 2495 2652. The editor added an article before Demetrius to be consistent with the article before craftsmen.

---

50. Metzger, *Textual Commentary*, 419; Wilson, *Acts Translated*, 88.

PWR Revisions: Acts 26 (Dialogue)

There are eleven places in Acts 26 where the PWR stands against the aligned ECM/Byz reading and nine occasions where all three traditions are divided, i.e., "3ways."

1. (26:1/14) 614/PWR has ἐπιτέτραπται (vs. ἐπιτρέπεταί, NA28/Byz) and is found in 8/10 core PWR MSS and 020f 81 424C etc. The editor has changed to the perfect passive since it seemed to fit the context better. Barrett says that the standard reading is original, should be classified as an "aoristic present," and means, "It is hereby permitted you to speak."[51]

2. (26:1/18–22) (3ways) 614/PWR displays λαλεῖν περὶ σεαυτοῦ (vs. περὶ σεαυτοῦ λέγειν, NA28, vs. ὑπὲρ σεαυτοῦ λέγειν, Byz, λέγειν περὶ σεαυτοῦ, 014) and is found in 8/10 core PWR MSS and 876 1448 1832 2243. NA28 and Byz agree in word order and verb choice. The PWR appears to start with NA28 and then smooths the word order and substitutes another verb meaning "to speak" probably out of preference. The Byz starts with NA28 and "improves" the preposition. The 014 reading appears to start with the PWR and then partially corrects it by replacing the verb.

3. (#26:1/30–36) (3ways) 614/PWR reads ἀπελογεῖτο ἐκτείνας τὰς χεῖρας (vs. ἀπελογεῖτο ἐκτείνας τὴν χεῖρα, Byz, vs. ἐκτείνας τὴν χεῖρα ἀπελογεῖτο, NA28) and is found in 7/10 core PWR MSS and no others. The Byz appears to reorder NA28 in order to smooth the verse. The PWR begins with the Byz and for some reason preferred to speak of "hands" in the plural.

4. (26:3/4–24) (3ways) 614f/PWR has γνώστην ὄντα σε πάντων τῶν κατὰ Ἰουδαίους ἐθῶν τε καὶ ζητημάτων ἐπιστάμενος (vs. minus the last word, NA28/RP05[mg], minus the last word and reads ἠθῶν, RP-05[txt]) and is joined by 01C2 33C 1611 1891 (2147) 2298 2412 and six others. The ECM lists twenty-two readings here. The fact that NA28, Byz, and 614 represent the best-supported variants, argues for their precedence. They also agree in word order. Moreover, 614 is very near to 4/10 best ECM MSS (i.e., P74 02(*f2, Cf1) 04 33*). Notice that 01C2 and 33C even correct to the PWR. Most translations support NA28 and either form of the Byz. RP05[txt] was

---

51. Barrett, *Commentary on Acts*, 2:1, 148.

apparently improved by use of the synonym ἠθῶν (found in only 5/22 readings) that only occurs at 1 Cor 15:33. The Byz word has the prominent meaning of moral standards (see *TLG*). The PWR editor inserted ἐπιστάμενος to clarify the meaning.

5. (26:5/4) 614/PWR omits (vs. με, NA28/Byz) and is joined by 330* 1292 1505 1611 1890 2138 2147 2412 2495 2652 OL 189. Editor dropped με to smooth the text.

6. (26:6/20–22) 614/PWR displays γενομένης ἐπαγγελίας (vs. ἐπαγγελίας γενομένης, NA28/Byz) and is found in 9/10 core MSS and 044 1127 1409 2652 plus Chrys ThdHer. The editor has probably changed the word order accidentally since the revised order is less clear.

7. (26:10/44) 614/PWR reads ἀναιρουμένων δὲ (vs. ἀναιρουμένων τε, NA28/Byz) and is found in 9/10 core MSS, P74 014, and secondary Alex MSS 945 1501 1739 1884 1891 2298 2652 etc. plus Did e. The editor may have changed the conjunction so that Paul's direct actions of throwing the saints into prison and his indirect actions of giving assent to their execution might be contrasted, but that seems unlikely for a motive. On the other hand, δέ may have the meaning of a continued development.[52] Since that fits the context and since the support from Alex MSS is strong, the PWR may preserve the original wording.

8. (#26:14/10–14) 614/PWR has + διὰ τὸν φόβον ἐγὼ μόνος and assimilates ideas of fear and about Paul exclusively hearing the voice. The source is probably 22:9/19 (Byz/PWR only). MS 614 is joined by (1292) 1611 2147 2412 2652 (gig sy[hmg] sa bo[mss]). The editor has enriched the narrative by use of a cross-reference.

9. (#26:15/26) 614/PWR displays Ἰησοῦς ὁ Ναζωραῖος (vs. Ἰησοῦς, NA28/Byz) and is joined by 1292 (1611) 2412 and nineteen others plus gig p/2 sy[h**] (sy[p]). It has been harmonized with 22:8 to present more completely the words Jesus spoke.

10. (26:17/26–28) (3ways) 614/PWR reads ἀποστέλω σε (vs. σε ἀποστέλλω, Byz, vs. ἀποστέλλω σε, NA28, vs. ἐξαποστέλω σε, 81) and is found in 8/10 core PWR MSS and thirty-seven others. The PWR and many others have partly harmonized to the more natural future tense as found in 22:21/22. However, they did not add the prefixed

---

52. Runge, *Discourse Grammar*, 36.

preposition ἐξ-. The PWR retains the word order of NA28. The Byz has little support beyond its tradition and thus may have placed σε first for emphasis. There is a small chance that its word order preserves the original. Several of the best ECM MSS (i.e., 81 1175 1739 2200) et al. witness to reading f., a complete harmonization to 22:21. The ECM actually has a mistake here. While the apparatus identifies reading f. as part of the SGL by means of the diamond symbol, the main text line displays reading e. in its place (i.e., ἐξαποστέλλω σε).[53]

11. (26:18/10) (3ways) 614/PWR has ἀποστρέψαι (vs. ἐπιστρέψαι, NA28/RP05[mg], vs. ὑποστρέψαι, RP05[txt]). The words are synonymous, and the most fitting is the PWR, "to turn away" (*TLG*). All three readings have significant support, including key Byz MSS. 614 is found in 9/10 core PWR MSS and 02 014 044 0142 etc., including about half the Westerns, plus Chrys. NA28/RP05[mg] is joined by P74 01 03 04 08 020 048 096 18 35 etc., the other half of the Westerns, and Clem. RP05[txt] has core Byz MSS 025 049 1 etc. but only one Western. The PWR utilizes a word found nine times in the NT; contextually, it normally means "to turn away from" (e.g., Acts 3:26; Rom 11:26). In contrast, the word of NA28 occurs thirty-five other times in the NT and ten in Acts. In the context of repentance, every time it means to turn toward God (see Acts 3:19; 9:35; 11:21; 14:15; 15:19; 26:20; 28:27). Therefore, NA28 has likely harmonized with 26:20/42. The Byz contains a word very common to Luke (32/35 are in Luke-Acts) but found in a different context. It usually describes returning from a place (see Luke 10:17; 24:33; Acts 8:25; 22:17). The PWR is probably original.

12. (26:18/20) 614/PWR displays ἀπὸ τῆς ἐξουσίας (vs. τῆς ἐξουσίας, NA28/Byz) and is found in 9/10 core PWR MSS and 04 08 020 044 etc., including nearly all Westerns, plus Chrys Vg e p w 189. It has smoothed the grammar by adding ἀπό in order to balance with ἀπὸ σκότους earlier in the verse. This PWR was very influential.

13. (26:20/15) 614/PWR reads τοῖς ἐν Ἱεροσολύμοις (vs. Ἱεροσολύμοις, NA28/Byz) and harmonizes the wording to the previous clause. It is found in 9/10 core PWR MSS and four others plus e.

14. (26:21/6–10) (3ways) 614/PWR has Ἰουδαῖοι συλλαβόμενοί με (vs. οἱ Ἰουδαῖοι συλλαβόμενοί με, 876, vs. με Ἰουδαῖοι συλλαβόμενοι, NA28, vs. οἱ Ἰουδαῖοι με συλλαβόμενοι, RP05[txt], vs. με οἱ Ἰουδαῖοι

---

53. ECM 3:1:2, 987.

συλλαβόμενοι, RP05^mg/ByzECM). ECM lists fifteen readings here. 614 is joined by just 436 2412 CosmIn^txt and has dropped οἱ by accident. 876 maintains the PWR and is joined by 02 1292 1505 1611 1890 2138 2495 and four others. NA28 is joined by P74 01*f1 03 33 and fifteen others and appears original. RP05^txt has no variety and has evidently smoothed the word order of RP05^mg. RP05^mg/ByzECM has some uncial support (i.e., 01C2f 014 044 048^vid 049) and includes some Westerns. It has merely added οἱ to NA28 in order to smooth it. The PWR and its corruption in 614 have reordered the text into its smoothest form. They are the only readings with με at the end.

15. (26:22/10) (3ways) 614/PWR reads ὑπὸ τοῦ θεοῦ (vs. ἀπὸ τοῦ θεοῦ, NA28, vs. παρὰ τοῦ θεοῦ, Byz) and is joined by 180 1292 1505 1611 1890 2138 2412 2495. Both the PWR and Byz apparently change the preposition in order to emphasize that Paul is recalling the assistance that belongs to God alone and descends from him.[54]

16. (26:22/50) 614/PWR displays προελάλησαν (vs. ἐλάλησαν, NA28/Byz) and is apparently a gloss, emphasizing the predictive ability of the prophets, and is found in 8/10 core PWR MSS and MS 180.

17. (26:24/14-20) (3ways) 614/PWR has εἶπεν (vs. ἔφη, Byz, vs. φησίν, NA28) and has smoothed by substituting a common verb and is found in 8/10 PWR MSS and 1718. The Byz word choice also occurs at 26:1, 32. NA28's choice is found at 26:25. NA28 is probably correct because that would show literary design by Luke with φησίν, being used in successive verses, and with ἔφη used at the start and end of the chapter as a literary device to mark the boundaries.

18. (26:25/28) 614/PWR displays φθέγγομαι (vs. ἀποφθέγγομαι, NA28/Byz) and is found in 8/10 core PWR MSS and eight others plus SevGab. The PWR is a semantic gloss rather than an accidental loss. It uses an apt technical term (see *TLG*).

19. (#26:26/28-40) 614/PWR reads αὐτὸν τούτων πείθομαι οὐθέν οὐ (vs. αὐτόν τι τούτων οὐ πείθομαι οὐθέν/οὐδέν οὐ, NA28/Byz, vs. αὐτόν τι τούτων οὐ πείθομαι οὐ, P74, vs. αὐτὸν τούτων οὐ πείθομαι οὐθέν οὐ, 03). The PWR simplifies by dropping both τι and the first οὐ and is found in 8/10 core PWR MSS and four others plus sy^h.

---

54. See Barrett, *Commentary on Acts*, 2:1164-65.

20. (26:31/18–28) (3ways) 614/PWR has ἄξιον θανάτου ἢ δεσμῶν πράσσει (vs. θανάτου ἄξιον ἢ δεσμῶν πράσσει, Byz, vs. θανάτου ἢ δεσμῶν ἄξιόν τι πράσσει, NA28) and is found in 9/10 core MSS and thirteen others. ECM lists eleven alternatives. Wachtel seems correct that the NA28 reading is the source of all the rest since the presence of τι makes it more difficult.[55] Barrett states that the removal of τι would make the Greek better.[56] Perhaps it was the Byz that simplified NA28, and then the PWR merely swapped the order of θανάτου ἄξιον to achieve the smoothest reading of all.

PWR Revisions: Acts 27 (Narrative)

There are twenty-nine places in Acts 27 where the PWR stands against the aligned ECM/Byz reading and three occasions where all three traditions are divided, i.e., "3ways."

1. (27:1/30–34) 614/PWR has τινας δεσμώτας (vs. τινας ἑτέρους δεσμώτας, NA28/Byz) and is joined by 8/10 core MSS and 81* 1852 2374 plus Eustr sy[h.txt]. It seems that the editor removed ἑτέρους because even the Romans agreed that Paul was innocent.

2. (27:2/5) 614(*f)/PWR displays ἐν πλοίῳ (vs. πλοίῳ, NA28/Byz) and is found in 8/10 core MSS and 441 1448. The added preposition smooths the text.

3. (27:2/14) (3ways) 614/PWR reads ἐπὶ τοὺς (vs. εἰς τοὺς, NA28, vs. τοὺς, Byz) and is joined by 9/10 core PWR MSS and twenty others plus sy[h]. NA28 is joined by 9/9 best ECM MSS etc. and includes nine secondary PWR MSS. Byz has limited support. Though it is the most difficult, it has become so by dropping the preposition by mistake. The different preposition seen in the PWR may be a result of the PWR inheriting the error in its proto-Byz base and then unilaterally correcting it by supplying a suitable preposition. NA28 has good support and is probably original.

4. (27:2/34–38) 614f (PWR) after correction has Ἀριστάρχου Μακεδόνος Θεσσαλονικέων δὲ Ἀριστάρχου καὶ Σεκούνδου (vs. Ἀριστάρχου Μακεδόνος Θεσσαλονικέως, NA28/Byz) and is joined by 876f 1292f

---

55. Wachtel, "Text-Critical Commentary," 36.
56. Barrett, *Commentary on Acts*, 2:1173.

1448*f 1505f 1611f 1832*f^vid 1890f 2138f 2147 2412f 2495f 2652 sy^h. Most of these mistakenly copied down Ἀρίσταρχος καὶ Σεκοῦνδος in the nominative pulled directly from 20:4/14-22. The MS 614 reading is found in 9/10 core PWR MSS. The editor apparently perceived the listing of Aristarchus by both region and city to be odd and sought to restore what was deleted. He found Θεσσαλονικέων . . . Σεκοῦνδος in 20:4 and inserted the "missing" text as is. He understood Luke as listing two separate men named Aristarchus.

5. (#27:5/21) 614/PWR displays διαπλεύσαντες <u>δι' ἡμερῶν δεκαπέντε</u> (vs. διαπλεύσαντες, NA28/Byz) and may be eyewitness testimony (cf. 12:10, + κατέβησαν τοῦ ζ βάθους καὶ, per 05 mae).

6. (27:6/22) 614/PWR reads <u>ἀν</u>εβίβασεν (vs. <u>ἐν</u>εβίβασεν, NA28/Byz) and is found in 8/10 core PWR MSS and 049 1 33 330 1241 1739 etc., including most Westerns and many others, plus Chrys. NA28/Byz is joined by 6/10 best ECM MSS (i.e., 01 02 03 81 1175 2200) and 020 025 35 383 etc. NA28/Byz uses the more explicit word for embarking. Most likely the variation in the PWR was caused by a sensible itacism.

7. (27:7/40-42) 614/PWR has Κρήτην (vs. Κρήτη<u>ν</u> κατὰ Σαλμώνη<u>ν</u>, NA28/Byz) and is found in 6/10 core MSS and 876 1832* plus sy^h. It probably lost two words by an eye skip from -ην to -ην. If it was removed on purpose, the reason is not evident.

8. (27:9/12-20) 614/PWR displays τοῦ πλοὸς ἐπισφαλοῦς (vs. ἐπισφαλοῦς τοῦ πλοὸς, NA28/Byz) and is joined by 9/10 core PWR MSS and nine others plus Chrys. Perhaps the PWR editor wanted the subject τοῦ πλοός to stand before the adjective.

9. (#27:15/23) 614/PWR has ἐπιδόντες <u>τῷ πλέοντι καὶ συστείλαντες τὰ ἱστία</u> ἐφερόμεθα (vs. ἐπιδόντες ἐφερόμεθα, NA28/Byz) and is found in 7/10 core PWR MSS, 876 (1127), and three others plus sy^h**. The editor inserted a clarifying gloss.

10. (27:17/21) 614/PWR reads μή<u>πως</u> (vs. μὴ, NA28/Byz) and is found in 7/10 core PWR MSS and sixteen others. It is a smoothing gloss since it did not seem right to say that the sailors were afraid *not* to run aground on the Syrtis sands. The original construction, φοβούμενοί τε μή + subjunctive is idiomatic. According to *TLG*, μή used in a context of a warning and with either a present or aorist subjunctive has the idea of "take care that you do not become." In this context, it would

mean, "They lowered the gear so that they would not run aground at the Syrtis sands." In other words, one should not read μή as "not" but instead as "so that not." The same problem occurs again at 27:29/6–8, 10–12. Commenting on the latter passage, Barrett explains that μή has the contextual meaning of "lest perhaps."[57] The Alex and Byz scribes were familiar with the usage and made no changes.

11. (#27:19/19) 614/PWR has εἰς τὴν θάλασσαν (vs. omits, NA28/Byz) and inserts a phrase from nearby (see 27:30, 38, 40). It is found in 7/10 core PWR MSS and five others plus (gig s w 189 sa sy[Aram] sy[h**] Ä). The gloss adds more color to the narrative.

12. (27:20/12–18) 614/PWR displays ἐπιφαινομένων (vs. ἐπιφαινόντων, NA28/Byz) and is found in 9/10 core PWR MSS and three others plus Chrys. The editor "improves" the sense to "neither the sun nor the stars were seen" instead of the active "neither the sun nor the stars were shining." His "correction" removed the figure of speech.

13. (27:21/22) 614/PWR reads ἡμῶν (vs. αὐτῶν, NA28/Byz) and offers a personal touch (cf. PWR at 27:35/31). It is found in 8/10 core PWR MSS and no others.

14. (27:21/40) 614/PWR has ἀναγαγέσθαι (vs. ἀνάγεσθαι, NA28/Byz) and is joined by 8/10 core PWR MSS and two others. The editor has changed to the aorist infinitive most likely to agree with the following aorist infinitive κερδῆσαι.

15. (27:27/36) 614/PWR displays προσεγγίζειν (vs. προσάγειν, NA28/Byz) and is joined by 9/10 core PWR MSS and 2652. The editor has kept the prefix but replaced the verb with the infinite of ἐγγίζω. It has the common meaning "to draw near" and is found twenty-four times in Luke-Acts. The original word has a larger range of meaning. The gloss clarifies the meaning.

16. (27:29/4) 614/PWR reads δέ (vs. τε, NA28/Byz) and is found in 9/10 core PWR MSS, 5/10 best ECM MSS (i.e., P74 01 33 81 1175), Western friendly 467 876 915 2652, and ten others plus Vg gig s p w 189 sy[h]. The standard is joined by 5/10 best ECM MSS (i.e., 02 03 04[vid] 1739 2200) and 020 025 35 383 etc. The evidence is divided, and the PWR is potentially original.

---

57. Barrett, *Commentary on Acts*, 2:1204.

17. (27:29/6-8, 10-12) (3ways) 614f/Byz has μή πως/μήπως εἰς τραχεῖς τόπους (vs. μή που κατὰ τραχεῖς τόπους, NA28, μή που εἰς τραχεῖς τόπους, 2412). Is the ECM right to take 614's μή πος and correct it to μή πως? In fact, 614f should read μή που because the scribe of 2412 utilized the same *Vorlage* and it preserves μή που. This judgment is confirmed in that 7/10 core PWR MSS agree. Therefore, 2412 is the PWR instead. While this variant is listed as two in the ECM, it should be treated as one because ~28/39 of those with μή πως also have εἰς τραχεῖς τόπους and ~28/39 of those with μή που also have κατὰ τραχεῖς τόπους. The variation here is almost certainly connected to the difficult construction in the NA28 reading. At first, μή που appears nonsensical. If που means "somewhere," why would the sailors be afraid not to fall somewhere against the rocks? It would seem that either μή needs to be dropped or μή πως needs to be adopted. However, as discussed above at 27:17/21, μή in this context means "so that not" or "lest perhaps." Here the axiom that the difficult reading should be preferred rings true. The lack of πως following μή is not unusual for Luke since he does not use that sequence. The scribal inclination to "correct" μή που is not surprising because this phrase is only here in the NT. Overall, the PWR is a mess when both variants are considered as one. It is represented purely only by 1611, 2412, and Chrys. In contrast, NA28 is joined here by 8/10 best ECM MSS, and it preserves the original. Finally, the Byz error of μή πως suggests that its linked reading of εἰς τραχεῖς is also incorrect.

18. (27:30/10) 614/PWR displays ἐκφυγεῖν ἐκ (vs. φυγεῖν ἐκ, NA28/Byz) and is found in 9/10 core PWR MSS, 02, and eighteen MSS in all. The editor probably compounded the verb because "to escape" fit the context better. Although the expansion could be from dittography, a purposeful revision is consistent with the style of the editor.

19. (27:30/26-38) 614/PWR reads ὡς (vs. προφάσει ὡς, NA28/Byz) and is found in 7/10 core PWR MSS. 614 is the PWR. The ECM presents nine alternatives. Most likely, the PWR is a result of some kind of oversight. The PWR lacks clarity, for why would the sailors go down to cast out more anchors if they wanted to escape?

20. (27:31/22-30) 614/PWR has οὗτοι ἐν τῷ πλοίῳ μείνωσιν (vs. οὗτοι μείνωσιν ἐν τῷ πλοίῳ, NA28/Byz) and is joined by 29 total MSS. The word order change is found in the Alex 01*, Byz 18 and 35, and 9/10 core PWR MSS. It resulted either out of preference or by accident.

21. (27:33/16–22) 614/PWR reads ὁ Παῦλος πάντας μεταλαβεῖν (vs. ὁ Παῦλος ἅπαντας μεταλαβεῖν, NA28/Byz) and is found in 8/10 core PWR MSS and 1241. Because the editor has shown no apparent preference for πᾶς, the change was likely accidental.

22. (27:34/9) 614/PWR displays τινος τροφῆς (vs. τροφῆς, NA28/Byz) and is found in 8/10 core PWR MSS and seven others plus sy^h. The editor has smoothed the text.

23. (27:34/18–22) 614/PWR has ἡμετέρας (vs. ὑμετέρας, NA28/Byz) and is found in 6/10 core PWR MSS and 02 020 025 18 35 and thirty others. For the PWR editor, changes to the first person are attested (see 27:21/22; 27:35/31). The change was most likely purposeful. It made Paul's statement inclusive.

24. (27:34/30–38) (3ways) 614/PWR displays ὑμων θρὶξ τῆς κεφαλῆς (vs. ὑμων θρὶξ ἀπὸ τῆς κεφαλῆς, NA28, vs. ὑμῶν θρὶξ ἐκ τῆς κεφαλῆς, Byz) and is found in 7/10 core PWR MSS and 1874 plus Chrys. NA28 is joined by 9/10 best ECM MSS and 181 915 etc. Byz is joined by 01 020 025 044 049 35 etc. The PWR lost the preposition by accident, or else its proto-Byz base had lost the preposition. If the latter, the Byz reading is a result of a scribal correction. If it was restored initially by conjecture, that would explain the variation.

25. (#27:35/31) 614/PWR reads + ἐπιδιδοὺς καὶ ἡμῖν and is joined by (1127) 1292 1409 1611 2147 2412 2652 (sa sy^{h**}). It is interesting to speculate where the editor might have obtained his information.

26. (27:36/14) 614/PWR has μετελάμβανον τροφῆς (vs. προσελάβοντο τροφῆς, NA28/Byz) and is joined by 1292 1611 2147 2412 2652. The editor probably revised the phrase so that the same verb would appear each time with τροφῆς (see 27:33/22–24; 27:34/8). He also changed the tense.

27. (27:39/16) 614/PWR displays ἐγίνωσκον (vs. ἐπεγίνωσκον, NA28/Byz) and is found in 03 330, 8/10 core PWR MSS, and nine others. The editor apparently dropped the ἐπ- prefix either by accident or to simplify the style.

28. (27:40/38) 614/PWR reads τῇ γῇ πνεούσῃ (vs. τῇ πνεούσῃ, NA28/Byz) and is found in 9/10 core MSS and 1832 2652. The ECM considers γῇ to be an error but it might be a nautical term, i.e., "and after raising the foresail into the land breeze, they held a straight

course for the shore." A sea breeze, more common in the daytime, would blow them to shore. A land breeze, common in the night or early morning would have made sailing to shore more difficult. It is a detail that probably only a sailor would remember. In order to use an opposing land breeze for advantage, the desired landing site must have been diagonal to them.

29. (27:41/28–30) 614/PWR displays ἔμενεν (vs. ἔμεινεν, NA28/Byz) and is found in 02 18 35 307, 9/10 core PWR MSS, and ten others. The editor apparently harmonized to match the imperfect later in the verse, i.e., "the prow was remaining immovable and the stern was being destroyed."

30. (27:41/38) 614/PWR reads διελύετο (vs. ἐλύετο, NA28/Byz) and offers a word that speaks more explicitly to the idea of destruction (*TLG*). It is joined by 020 330 1175, 8/10 core PWR MSS, and fifteen others.

31. (27:43/26) 614/PWR has δὲ (vs. τε, NA28/Byz) and is joined by 04 33 81 181 1739, 8/10 core PWR MSS, and fifteen others. The PWR editor may have changed the conjunction to help contrast the centurion's negative command with that of his positive command.

32. (27:44/8) 614/PWR reads τοὺς (vs. οὓς, NA28/Byz) and is found in 8/10 core PWR MSS and 044. ECM considers it a mistake. The editor wrote the article instead of the relative pronoun because of an accidental glance two words prior.

CONCLUSION

The foregoing analysis of PWR revisions demonstrates two important characteristics of the PWR archetype. First, even though the PWR edition has been assessed to be very ancient (i.e., this study assigns it to the window AD 125–150), nearly every one of its non-aligned readings has secondary characteristics. When considered from the perspective of internal evidence, there are few cases where it has good justification for being original. In terms of external evidence, the probability of its limited attested readings being authentic is already severely degraded. Even in those places where all three traditions divide, though it generally performs better, most of its variations are manifestly secondary. Secondly, since its remaining text is aligned with one or both of the other traditions, its foundation seems to be self-evident. Therefore, the probability is high that Byz readings that agree with the reconstructed PWR archetype did not result from centuries of conformity to the Byz text. Instead, they are an essential part of its underlying base. The creative and skillful PWR archetype editor revised his base layer of Byz and Alex readings in order to improve the grammar and syntax, clarify meaning, and enrich the text with interesting details.

CHAPTER SUMMARIES SHOWING PWR ALIGNMENT

The chapter-by-chapter results are provided below. In the process of evaluation, numerous MS 614 readings were found to be simple errors and never part of the PWR. They have been excluded from the comparisons. Variant spellings that the ECM considers equivalent do not figure into variant alignments. The results from comparing against the ECM of Acts do not differ much from comparing against NA28. These two editions agree in all but fifty-two locations.[58] The ECM also incorporates the SGL annotation to mark variants where the editors considered one or more alternate readings as equal competitors for the original text.[59] In such cases, reading a. is still that of NA28. Therefore, in all places of a SGL, this study compares against reading a. Finally, the specific variant units that undergird all alignment summaries will be listed in the appendix by their ECM chapter, verse, and word numbers (e.g., PWR = Byz (30): 7:1/12, 7:3/36, etc.). The appendix will also list every place where MS 614 does *not* preserve the PWR. In those cases, the leading core MS that retains the PWR will be listed within parentheses. With this information, it will be possible to reproduce the wording of a reconstructed PWR archetype for the entire book of Acts. Such an edition could be useful for research.

Acts 1: PWR = Byz (16); PWR = ECM (0); PWR ≠ ECM/Byz (7); 3Ways (0)

  a. (1) Obvious differences from Byz never corrected: 1:21/37 (MS 1611)

  b. (10) Subtle/Insignificant agreements with the Byz that stand against the ECM: WO at 1:5/16–22; ἐπηρώτων vs. ἠρώτων at 1:6/10; μοι vs. μου at 1:8/24; WO at 1:13/8–14; καὶ σὺν vs. καὶ at 1:14/33; ὡς vs. ὡσεὶ at 1:15/40; + τὸν at 1:16/45; ἐν ᾧ vs. ᾧ at 1:21/20; WO at 1:22/34–38; ἐξ vs. ἀφ' at 1:25/18

  c. Comments: MS 614 corrected the only obvious difference from the Byz

---

58. ECM 3:1:1, intro, 34–35.
59. ECM 3:1:1, intro, 31, 35–37.

NON-ALIGNED, PROTO-WESTERN GROUP READINGS

Acts 2: PWR = Byz (30); PWR = ECM (3); PWR ≠ ECM/Byz (10); 3Ways (3)

a. (3) Obvious differences from Byz never corrected: 2:1/22; 2:38/28-30; 2:43/22-28

b. (14) Subtle/Insignificant agreements with the Byz that stand against the ECM: ἅπαντες vs. πάντες at 2:4/6-10; WO at 2:4/30-32; πάντες οὗτοί vs. ἅπαντες οὗτοί at 2:7/16-26; χλευάζοντες vs. διαχλευάζοντες at 2:13/6-8; ἅπαντες vs. πάντες at 2:14/42; WO at 2:22/22-28; καὶ αὐτοὶ vs. αὐτοὶ at 2:22/63; ᾅδου vs. ᾅδην at 2:27/16; τοῦ θρόνου vs. τὸν θρόνον at 2:30/38-40; οὐδὲ ἡ vs. οὔτε ἡ at 2:31/26; ἁγίου πνεύματος vs. πνεύματος τοῦ ἁγίου at 2:33/20-26; νῦν ὑμεῖς vs. ὑμεῖς at 2:33/38-40; τῇ vs. ἐν τῇ at 2:41/18-28; ἐγένετο vs. ἐγίνετο at 2:43/2

c. Comments: of the 10 PWRs ≠ ECM/Byz, MS 614 has seven, 1611 has five, and 2138 has five

Acts 3: PWR = Byz (13); PWR = ECM (4); PWR ≠ ECM/Byz (6); 3Ways (2)

a. (4) Obvious differences from Byz never corrected: 3:11/6; 3:18/22-28; 3:20/30-32; 3:23/31

b. (8) Subtle/Insignificant agreements with the Byz that stand against the ECM: WO at 3:7/24-28; τε vs. δὲ at 3:10/2-4; οὗτος vs. αὐτὸς at 3:10/10; Ἰωάννην vs. τὸν Ἰωάννην at 3:11/14; WO at 3:11/20-28; Πέτρος vs. ὁ Πέτρος at 3:12/6; υἱοὶ vs. οἱ υἱοὶ at 3:25/6-8; WO at 3:26/6-10

c. Comments: of the six PWRs ≠ ECM/Byz, MS 614 has three and MS 1611 has three.

Acts 4: PWR = Byz (14); PWR = ECM (9); PWR ≠ ECM/Byz (12); 3Ways (2)

a. (7) Obvious differences from Byz never corrected: 4:1/13; 4:5/22-34; 4:9/9; 4:11/14-16; 4:12/22-40; 4:22/4-14 (awkward WO); 4:27/6-26

b. (7) Subtle/Insignificant agreements with the Byz that stand against the ECM: ἐν μέσῳ vs. ἐν τῷ μέσῳ at 4:7/8-12; οὔτε vs. οὐδὲ at 4:12/18; ποιήσομεν vs. ποιήσωμεν at 4:16/6; κολάσονται vs. κολάσωνται at 4:21/20; ἅπαντες πνεύματος ἁγίου vs. ἅπαντες τοῦ ἁγίου πνεύματος at 4:31/26-32; ὑπῆρχεν vs. ἦν at 4:34/6-12; παρὰ vs. πρὸς at 4:37/18-20

NON-ALIGNED, PROTO-WESTERN GROUP READINGS

c. Comments: of the twelve PWRs ≠ ECM/Byz, MS 1611 has nine and MS 614 has just four

Acts 5: PWR = Byz (19); PWR = ECM (8); PWR ≠ ECM/Byz (16); 3Ways (6)

a. (11) Obvious differences from Byz never corrected: (led by 1611) 5:3/6–10; (led by 1611) 5:10/14; 5:33/7; 5:36/16–22; 5:36/26; 5:36/50; 5:37/28; 5:39/18; 5:39/19; 5:41/7; 5:41/22–28

b. (7) Subtle/Insignificant agreements with the Byz that stand against the ECM: παρὰ vs. πρὸς at 5:10/8; WO at 5:12/18–28; + αὐτῶν at 5:18/9; WO at 5:22/2–8; πρὸ vs. ἐπὶ at 5:23/28; + δὲ at 5:32/21; WO at 5:36/28–30

c. Comments: the PWR is much more formed after 5:32; of the twenty-two PWRs without Byz or ECM support, MS 614 maintained 16/22 (i.e., 5/10 in 5:1–32 and 11/12 in 5:33–42); similarly, MS 1611 preserved 18/22 overall

Acts 6: PWR = Byz (3); PWR = ECM (4); PWR ≠ ECM/Byz (7); 3Ways (0)

a. (4) Obvious differences from Byz never corrected: 6:3/21; 6:7/10; 6:8/8–12; 6:8/29

b. (2) Subtle/Insignificant agreements with the Byz that stand against the ECM: οὖν vs. δὲ at 6:3/4; Μωσῆν vs. Μωϋσῆν at 6:11/24–30 (orthographic only)

c. Comments: the four PWRs that are clearly different from the Byz were corrected every time by the Byz text in the following core PWR MSS—383 1505 2147

Acts 7: PWR = Byz (30); PWR = ECM (10); PWR ≠ ECM/Byz (18); 3Ways (2)

a. (8) Obvious differences from Byz never corrected: 7:10/32; 7:22/22–26; 7:32/21–25; 7:37/26–28; 7:37/40; 7:38/54; 7:43/49; 7:55/2–4

b. (9) Subtle/Insignificant agreements with the Byz that stand against the ECM: WO at 7:7/18–22; ὁ Ἰσαὰκ vs. Ἰσαὰκ at 7:8/37; + ὁ Ἰακὼβ vs. Ἰακὼβ at 7:8/45; WO at 7:14/10–16; WO at 7:19/24–30; WO at 7:25/28–30; ἡμᾶς vs. ἡμῶν at 7:27/32; ἐν᾽ ᾧ vs. ἐφ᾽ ᾧ at 7:33/30–32; WO at 7:60/22–28

NON-ALIGNED, PROTO-WESTERN GROUP READINGS

c. Comments: there are many cases where 9/9 or 10/10 core PWR MSS agree with the Byz—7:1/12; 7:3/36; 7:7/18–22; 7:12/12–14; 7:14/10–16; 7:17/18; 7:19/24–30; 7:22/28; 7:25/28–30; 7:26/18; 7:27/32; 7:30/27; 7:31/24–28; 7:33/30–32; 7:39/26–36; 7:46/22–24; 7:56/14; 7:60/22–28; thus, 18/30 alignments with the Byz are perfectly coherent; in contrast, 0/10 alignments with the ECM are fully coherent

Acts 8: PWR = Byz (13); PWR = ECM (6); PWR ≠ ECM/Byz (14); 3Ways (3)

a. (5) Obvious differences from Byz never corrected: 8:16/32–34; 8:22/16–22; 8:24/11; 8:24/16–24

b. (6) Subtle/Insignificant agreements with the Byz that stand against the ECM: ἐποιήσαντο vs. ἐποίησαν at 8:2/16; τε vs. δὲ at 8:6/2–8; τὸν Πέτρον vs. Πέτρον at 8:14/34; τῆς βασιλίσσης vs. βασιλίσσης at 8:27/22; WO at 8:30/16–20; τὴν δὲ vs. τὴν at 8:33/19

c. Comments: there is a significant addition at 8:39/8 that is upheld by many of the secondary core PWR MSS, including MS 1739; the PWR edition did not receive it

Acts 9: PWR = Byz (28); PWR = ECM (6); PWR ≠ ECM/Byz (10); 3Ways (4)

a. (6) Obvious differences from Byz never corrected: 9:17/2–6; 9:17/40–44 (but 5 core PWR MSS correct to the Byz); 9:19/14–22; 9:20/16; 9:34/18–20; 9:38/30–34

b. (10) Subtle/Insignificant agreements with the Byz that stand against the ECM: ὁ Σαῦλος vs. Σαῦλος at 9:8/4; WO at 9:10/26–32; WO at 9:13/28–38; WO at 9:29/22–24; WO at 9:33/12–14; κραββάτω vs. κραββάττου at 9:33/26; WO at 9:36/32–34; WO at 9:37/24–26; θεὶς vs. καὶ θεὶς at 9:40/14; WO at 9:42/18–20

c. Comments: MSS 383 1505 2147 offer very few PWRs in Acts 5–9

Acts 10: PWR = Byz (24); PWR = ECM (9); PWR ≠ ECM/Byz (13); 3Ways (4)

a. (3) Obvious differences from Byz never corrected: 10:31/24; 10:33/52; 10:48/8–18

b. (7) Subtle/Insignificant agreements with the Byz that stand against the ECM: ἐνώπιον vs. ἔμπροσθεν at 10:4/50; WO at 10:5/8–12; WO at 10:8/6–8; διότι vs. ὅτι at 10:20/20–22; ἀρξάμενον vs. ἀρξάμενος at 10:37/20; ὁ Πέτρος vs. Πέτρος at 10:46/23; WO at 10:47/8–12

c. Comments: the common ancestry of the PWR and the Byz text is highlighted at 10:11/14–30 where they agree on one of eighteen readings and again at 10:12/8–28 where they align on one of twenty readings

Acts 11: PWR = Byz (21); PWR = ECM (7); PWR ≠ ECM/Byz (5); 3Ways (3)

a. (4) Obvious differences from Byz never corrected: 11:3/6–18; 11:25/12; 11:26/16–24; 11:28/28–30

b. (13) Subtle/Insignificant agreements with the Byz that stand against the ECM: Καὶ ὅτε ἀνέβη vs. Ὅτε δὲ ἀνέβη at 11:2/2–6; ὁ Πέτρος vs. Πέτρος at 11:4/4; ἤκουσα δὲ vs. ἤκουσα δὲ καὶ at 11:7/2–6; WO at 11:10/14–18; μηδὲν διακρινόμενον vs. μηδὲν διακρίναντα at 11:12/16–18; ἐγὼ δὲ τίς ἤμην vs. ἐγὼ τίς ἤμην at 11:17/38–42; Ἄρα γε vs. Ἄρα at 11:18/21; εἰσελθόντες vs. ἐλθόντες at 11:20/22; ἐλάλουν vs. ἐλάλουν καὶ at 11:20/28–30; πιστεύσας vs. ὁ πιστεύσας at 11:21/20; χάριν vs. χάριν τὴν at 11:23/12–14; πρῶτον vs. πρώτως at 11:26/44; μέγαν . . . ὅστις καὶ vs. μεγάλην . . . ἥτις at 11:28/26–40

c. Comments: none.

Acts 12: PWR = Byz (12); PWR = ECM (3); PWR ≠ ECM/Byz (12); 3Ways (2)

a. (5) Obvious differences from Byz never corrected: 12:1/35; 12:12/36; 12:20/14–22; 12:25/8; 12:25/10–14

b. (9) Subtle/Insignificant agreements with the Byz that stand against the ECM: Καί ἰδὼν vs. Ἰδὼν δὲ at 12:3/2–4; ὑπὲρ vs. περὶ at 12:5/28–42; Περίζωσαι vs. Ζῶσαι at 12:8/14; Μαρίας vs. τῆς Μαρίας at 12:12/14; WO at 12:15/34–36; Εἶπεν δὲ vs. Εἶπεν τε at 12:17/34–36; τὴν Καισάρειαν vs. Καισάρειαν at 12:19/37; δόξαν vs. τὴν δόξαν at 12:23/22–24; καὶ Ἰωάννην vs. Ἰωάννην at 12:25/23

c. Comments: none.

Acts 13: PWR = Byz (30); PWR = ECM (14); PWR ≠ ECM/Byz (17); 3Ways (8)

a. (14) Obvious differences from Byz never corrected: 13:5/38 (the only core are 614 1292 2412); 13:7/24–28; 13:23/18–26; 13:24/20–26;

13:28/11; 13:33/20; 13:39/13; 13:41/10; 13:41/49 (only core are 614 2412 but others confirm); 13:42/7; 13:42/8-16; 13:43/35 (only core are 383 614 2147 2412); 13:47/33 (only core are 614 2412 but others confirm); 13:48/10-26

b. (12) Subtle/Insignificant agreements with the Byz that stand against the ECM: Οὗτοι vs. Αὐτοὶ at 13:4/2; τοῦ πνεύματος τοῦ ἁγίου vs. τοῦ ἁγίου πνεύματος at 13:4/12-16; τὴν Σελεύκεισαν vs. Σελεύκεισαν at 13:4/21; τὴν Κύπρον vs. Κύπρον at 13:4/31; ἐστιν vs. τίς ἐστιν at 13:15/38-40; WO at 13:22/10-14; WO at 13:33/28-36; διὸ vs. διότι at 13:35/2; WO at 13:41/18-22; ὅ vs. ἔργον ὅ at 13:41/32; λεγομένοις vs. λαλουμένοις at 13:45/28; δὲ vs. τε at 13:52/4

c. Comments: it should be noted as many as seventeen of the thirty alignments with the Byz text do so with a perfect coherence of 10/10 PWR MSS; the locations are as follows—13:1/5; 13:4/2; 13:4/12-16; 13:4/31; 13:15/38-40; 13:19/18-22; 13:22/10-14; 13:25/16-18; 13:35/2; 13:38/41; 13:41/18-22; 13:43/40; 13:44/22-28; 13:45/28; 13:46/4-6; 13:46/36; 13:50/15; in contrast, only at two of the fourteen alignments with the ECM manifest perfect coherence (see 13:42/20-26; 13:43/44-46)

Acts 14: PWR = Byz (17); PWR = ECM (7); PWR ≠ ECM/Byz (16); 3Ways (2)

a. (6) Obvious differences from Byz never corrected: 14:2/6-10; 14:10/9; 14:14/24-30; 14:18/23; 14:25/13; 14:25/19

b. (13) Subtle/Insignificant agreements with the Byz that stand against the ECM: περιπεπατήκει vs. περιεπάτησεν at 14:8/34; WO at 14:9/24-26; ἥλλετο vs. ἥλατο at 14:10/24; δὲ vs. τε at 14:11/2-4; δὲ vs. τε at 14:13/2-4; Καίτοιγε vs. Καίτοι at 14:17/2; 14:17/8-10 (orthographic only); ἀγαθοποιῶν vs. ἀγαθουργῶν at 14:17/12; νομίσαντες αὐτὸν τεθνάναι vs. νομίζοντες αὐτὸν τεθνηκέναι at 14:19/40 and 14:19/42-44 (both verbs are RAI); Ἰκόνιον vs. εἰς Ἰκόνιον at 14:21/28; Ἀντιόχειαν vs. εἰς Ἀντιόχειαν at 14:21/34-36; WO at 14:23/8-12; Παμφυλίαν vs. τὴν Παμφυλίαν at 14:24/14

c. Comments: there are two long variants in this chapter that are refused by the PWR (see 14:19/2-4; 14:19/16-22), showing its high quality alongside the Alex and Byz traditions

Acts 15: PWR = Byz (21); PWR = ECM (5); PWR ≠ ECM/Byz (22); 3Ways (6)

a. (10) Obvious differences from Byz never corrected: 15:1/13; 15:2/64–70; 15:4/11; 15:4/45; 15:6/15; *15:7/10–12; 15:23/4–8; 15:26/27; *15:29/17; 15:34/2–12; however, observe that 5/10 core PWR MSS (i.e., 1505 1611 1890 2138 2495) have been expunged of most long Western readings in the chapter; as a result, there are two occasions (marked with the *) where only 3/10 core MSS preserve the group's native reading

b. (10) Subtle/Insignificant agreements with the Byz that stand against the ECM: περιτέμνησθε vs. περιτμηθῆτε at 15:1/26; Μωϋσέως vs. τῷ Μωϋσέως at 15:1/32–34; οὖν vs. δὲ at 15:2/4; τὴν Φοινίκην vs. τήν τε Φοινίκην at 15:3/18–20; δὲ vs. τε at 15:6/4; ἀπὸ τῶν vs. τῶν at 15:20/11; ἁγίῳ πνεύματι vs. πνεύματι τῷ ἁγίῳ at 15:28/8–12; WO at 15:36/12–16; WO at 15:36/30–32; οὖν vs. δὲ at 15:39/4–6

c. Comments: the alignment of the PWR with the best ECM MSS at 15:29/8–12 is a sign of its antiquity

Acts 16: PWR = Byz (20); PWR = ECM (16); PWR ≠ ECM/Byz (12); 3Ways (6)

a. (7) Obvious differences from Byz never corrected: 16:7/34; 16:9/27; 16:11/2–4; 16:21/6–20 (distinctive word order); 16:27/12–14; 16:35/26; 16:39/2–22

b. (11) Subtle/Insignificant agreements with the Byz that stand against the ECM: καὶ τῶν vs. καὶ at 16:4/33; τὴν Γαλατικὴν vs. Γαλατικὴν at 16:6/11; πορεύεσθαι vs. πορευθῆναι at 16:7/20; WO at 16:9/20–26; προσευχήν vs. τὴν προσευχήν at 16:16/10–12; Πύθωνος vs. Πύθωνα at 16:16/24; ἀπαντῆσαι ἡμῖν vs. ὑπαντῆσαι ἡμῖν at 16:16/26–28; ὁ Παῦλος vs. Παῦλος at 16:18/16; WO at 16:24/28–30; καὶ ἐφοβήθησαν vs. ἐφοβήθησαν δὲ at 16:38/20–30; ἐκ vs. ἀπὸ at 16:40/6–10

c. Comments; none

Acts 17: PWR = Byz (18); PWR = ECM (11); PWR ≠ ECM/Byz (15); 3Ways (4)

a. (9) Obvious differences from Byz never corrected: 17:3/34–40; 17:4/10; 17:5/2–22; 17:11/47; 17:12/13; 17:13/50–56; 17:19/2–4; 17:25/20–26; 17:26/10–14

b. (8) Subtle/Insignificant agreements with the Byz that stand against the ECM: Ἀπολλωνίαν vs. τὴν Ἀπολλωνίαν at 17:1/6-16; ἡ συναγωγὴ τῶν vs. συναγωγὴ τῶν at 17:1/26-28; WO at 17:5/18-20; ἐπιστάντες τε vs. καὶ ἐπιστάντες at 17:5/34-36; Τιμόθεον vs. τὸν Τιμόθεον at 17:15/32; τῶν Στοϊκῶν vs. Στοϊκῶν at 17:18/13; ἀνθρώπων vs. ἀνθρωπίνων at 17:25/6-8; πάλιν περὶ τούτου vs. περὶ τούτου καὶ πάλιν at 17:32/26-17:33/8

c. Comments: the PWR equals the Byz at 17:32/26-33/8 as one of the 15 readings

Acts 18: PWR = Byz (19); PWR = ECM (7); PWR ≠ ECM/Byz (9); 3Ways (0)

a. (9) Obvious differences from Byz never corrected: 18:5/28-30; 18:7/6; 18:8/38-40; 18:19/10-14; 18:22/1; 18:25/36-38; 18:27/35; 18:27/44-48; 18:28/13

b. (9) Subtle/Insignificant agreements with the Byz that stand against the ECM: δὲ vs. omits at 18:1/2-6; ἐκ vs. ἀπὸ at 18:2/54; ἦλθεν vs. εἰσῆλθεν at 18:7/8; WO at 18:9/10-20; ἀνθυπατεύοντος vs. ἀνθυπάτου ὄντος at 18:12/6-8; WO at 18:13/12-14; γὰρ ἐγὼ τούτων vs. ἐγὼ τούτων at 18:15/34-36; WO at 18:18/44-50; WO at 18:26/22-26

c. Comments: the 18:21/9 variant is very interesting (see chapter 4)

Acts 19: PWR = Byz (14); PWR = ECM (19); PWR ≠ ECM/Byz (20); 3Ways (3)

a. (10) Obvious differences from Byz never corrected: 19:3/5; 19:4/44; 19:5/19; 19:9/8-24; 19:9/51; 19:10/35; 19:12/50; 19:16/28-30; 19:28/13; 19:35/2

b. (7) Subtle/Insignificant agreements with the Byz that stand against the ECM: εἶπον vs. εἶπαν at 19:3/18 (equivalent); προεφήτευον vs. ἐπροφήτευον at 19:6/38 (equivalent); WO at 19:11/12-24; WO at 19:20/8-20; WO at 19:24/26-30; Τοῦ δὲ Παύλου vs. Παύλου δὲ at 19:30/2-6; ἕνεκεν vs. ἕνεκα at 19:32/36 (equivalent)

c. Comments: none.

Acts 20: PWR = Byz (30); PWR = ECM (9); PWR ≠ ECM/Byz (22); 3Ways (3)

NON-ALIGNED, PROTO-WESTERN GROUP READINGS

a. (7) Obvious differences from Byz never corrected: 20:1/24–26; 20:7/16; 20:19/7; 20:23/35; 20:26/18–20; 20:28/40; 20:32/49

b. (10) Subtle/Insignificant agreements with the Byz that stand against the ECM: WO at 20:3/12–14; γνώμη vs. γνώμης at 20:3/34; Καθήμενος vs. Καθεζόμενος at 20:9/2; εἰς τὴν vs. ἐπὶ τὴν at 20:13/16; WO at 20:13/36–38; ἦν vs. εἴη at 20:16/36–42; τὸν θεὸν vs. θεὸν at 20:21/15; πίστιν τὴν vs. πίστιν at 20:21/23; WO at 20:22/8–10; ἐποικοδομῆσαι vs. οἰκοδομῆσαι at 20:32/32 (all of these have 10/10 core PWR MSS in support except 20:3/34 which has 9/9 and 20:21/15 which has 9/10)

c. Comments: on twenty-one occasions either 9/9 or 10/10 core PWR MSS align with the Byz—20:1/14; 20:3/12–14; 20:3/34 (9/9); 20:4/7; 20:4/10; 20:9/2; 20:13/16; 20:13/36–38; 20:16/2; 20:16/36–42; 20:19/16; 20:21/23; 20:22/8–10; 20:23/20; 20:24/6–8; 20:24/27; 20:27/14–24; 20:29/2; 20:29/5; 20:32/32; 20:32/38; complete coherence with the ECM only occurs two times at 20:1/24–26 and 20:28/40; complete coherence against Byz/ECM occurs two times at 20:6/43 and 20:23/6–12; the PWR is deeply related to the Byz

Acts 21: PWR = Byz (20); PWR = ECM (13); PWR ≠ ECM/Byz (18); 3Ways (2)

a. (8) Obvious differences from Byz never corrected: 21:8/10; 21:11/26–34; 21:21/48; 21:22/10–14; 21:27/42; 21:33/2–4; 21:36/10–12; 21:36/19

b. (9) Subtle/Insignificant agreements with the Byz that stand against the ECM: κατήχθημεν vs. κατήλθομεν at 21:3/26; μαθητάς vs. τοὺς μαθητάς at 21:4/6; WO at 21:9/8–12; εἰπόντες vs. εἶπόν τε at 21:20/14–18; γνῶσιν vs. γνώσονται at 21:24/30; καὶ τὸ vs. καὶ at 21:25/30–38; δὲ vs. τε at 21:31/2–4; τίς ἂν εἴη vs. τίς εἴη at 21:33/28–30; κρᾶζον vs. κράζοντες at 21:36/14

c. Comments: it is remarkable that there are at least twenty-eight places where the PWR MSS are completely agreed; they join the Byz fifteen times (B), the ECM five times (E), and stand independent on eight occasions (P); the list, in order, includes—21:3/26 (B); 21:4/6 (B); 21:4/34 (B); 21:5/56–21:6/6 (B); 21:8/10 (E); 21:11/22–24 (E); 21:11/26–34 (P); 21:13/2–8 (P); 21:14/14–22 (B); 21:17/14 (B); 21:20/12 (B); 21:20/14–18 (B); 21:20/30–34 (B); 21:24/30 (B); 21:24/54–60 (E); 21:27/14 (P); 21:27/16–34 (P); 21:27/42 (P); 21:27/48–54 (E); 21:31/2–4 (B); 21:31/24–26 (B); 21:33/28–30 (B);

21:34/18–24 (B); 21:36/10–12 (P); 21:36/14 (B); 21:37/2–4 (P); 21:39/4 (P); 21:40/38 (E); the PWR is extremely cohesive here and simultaneously shows ties with the other traditions.

Acts 22: PWR = Byz (8); PWR = ECM (8); PWR ≠ ECM/Byz (18); 3Ways (5)

   a. (8) Obvious differences from Byz never corrected: 22:3/56–58; 22:12/26–28; 22:16/30; 22:20/12–18; 22:25/2–6; 22:25/24–42; 22:26/19; 22:29/47

   b. (2) Subtle/Insignificant agreements with the Byz that stand against the ECM: δὲ vs. τε at 22:23/4; WO at 22:29/42–46

   c. Comments: none.

Acts 23: PWR = Byz (16); PWR = ECM (8); PWR ≠ ECM/Byz (22); 3Ways (11)

   a. (12) Obvious differences from Byz never corrected: 23:7/14–20; 23:11/21; 23:15/65; 23:20/38; 23:23/34; 23:24/17; 23:25/2–12; 23:29/12–16; 23:29/33; 23:30/10–18; 23:34/5; 23:34/6–26

   b. (7) Subtle/Insignificant agreements with the Byz that stand against the ECM: πρὸς vs. εἰς at 23:15/26; WO at 23:17/36–40; WO at 23:21/52–56; νεανίαν vs. νεανίσκον at 23:22/14; δὲ vs. τε at 23:28/4; WO at 23:29/30–32; ἐπαρχίας vs. ἐπαρχείας at 23:34/14 (orthographic only)

   c. Comments: there are thirteen cases where 9/9 or 10/10 core PWR MSS support a reading—23:1/36–40 (P); 23:6/48–50 (B); 23:10/6–8 (B); 23:13/12–18 (B); 23:15/26 (B); 23:17/36–40 (B); 23:21/52–56 (B); 23:22/14 (B); 23:27/36–42 (B); 23:28/4 (B); 23:30/45 (B); 23:32/14–18 (B); 23:35/8–10 (P); in total, eleven align with the Byz and two are unique; the three traditions are also diverse here with eleven examples of triple division.

Acts 24: PWR = Byz (10); PWR = ECM (14); PWR ≠ ECM/Byz (18); 3Ways (7)

   a. (7) Obvious differences from Byz never corrected: 24:2/30; 24:6/20–24:8/14; 24:9/2–6; 24:10/31; 24:18/4; 24:23/10; 24:27/19

   b. (3) Subtle/Insignificant agreements with the Byz that stand against the ECM: στάσιν vs. στάσεις at 24:5/16–20; Οὔτε vs. Οὐδὲ at 24:13/2;

NON-ALIGNED, PROTO-WESTERN GROUP READINGS

ἔχων vs. ἔχειν at 24:16/14–16; in this chapter, the details of the PWR seem to agree more often with NA28 than with the Byz

c. Comments: none.

Acts 25: PWR = Byz (17); PWR = ECM (10); PWR ≠ ECM/Byz (13); 3Ways (4)

a. (6) Obvious differences from Byz never corrected: 25:2/8–10; 25:5/22–28; 25:6/6–20; 25:18/20–24; 25:19/34; 25:24/32

b. (8) Subtle/Insignificant agreements with the Byz that stand against the ECM: δὲ vs. τε at 25:2/4; ἐν Καισαρείᾳ vs. εἰς Καισάρειαν at 25:4/18–20; WO at 25:5/6–12; κρίνεσθαι vs. κριθῆναι at 25:9/40; γὰρ vs. οὖν at 25:11/6; δίκην vs. καταδίκην at 25:15/36; ἐπιβοῶντες vs. βοῶντες at 25:24/58; WO at 25:24/64–66

c. Comments: 10/10 core PWR MSS agree in joining the Byz in sixteen locations—25:2/4 (B); 25:4/18–20 (B); 25:5/6–12 (B); 25:7/10–14 (B); 25:7/30 (B); 25:9/40 (B); 25:11/6 (B); 25:15/36 (B); 25:22/11 (B); 25:22/23 (B); 25:23/52–54 (B); 25:24/58 (B); 25:24/64–66 (B); 25:25/6 (B); 25:25/18–20 (B); 25:25/33 (B); PWR is related closely to the Byz.

Acts 26: PWR = Byz (15); PWR = ECM (12); PWR ≠ ECM/Byz (11); 3Ways (9)

a. (7) Obvious differences from Byz never corrected: 26:1/18–22; 26:1/30–36; 26:3/4–24; 26:14/10–14; 26:15/26; 26:16/44; 26:22/50

b. (4) Subtle/Insignificant agreements with the Byz that stand against the ECM: WO at 26:2/30–32; πρὸς vs. εἰς at 26:6/10–12; πολλοὺς vs. πολλοὺς τε at 26:10/12–16; τῶν vs. ἐκ τῶν at 26:17/12–14

c. Comments. All three traditions divide nine times in the chapter.

Acts 27: PWR = Byz (13); PWR = ECM (7); PWR ≠ ECM/Byz (29); 3Ways (3)

a. (10) Obvious differences from Byz never corrected: 27:2/34–38; 27:5/21; 27:7/40–42; 27:15/23; 27:19/19; 27:21/22; 27:23/14–28; 27:30/26–38; 27:35/31; 27:40/38

b. (17) Subtle/Insignificant agreements with the Byz that stand against the ECM: πορευθέντα vs. πορευθέντι at 27:3/36; WO at 27:11/10–20; τοῦ Παύλου vs. Παύλου at 27:11/27; WO at 27:16/14–16; WO at 27:20/34–36; WO at 27:30/40–44; WO at 27:33/8–10; Ἥμεν vs.

Ἤμεθα at 27:37/2; WO at 27:37/6–16; the last eight address agreements in orthography when there were alternate ways to spell a particular word; these occasions are marked with (B) combined with italics below.

c. Comments: the PWR is very coherent in chapter 27; there are at least twenty-seven places where 9/10 or 10/10 core PWR MSS agree against one or both other traditions (italicized if orthographic only); see 27:2/10 (9/10, E); 27:2/14 (9/10, P); 27:2/34–38 (9/10, P); 27:3/36 (10/10, B); *27:6/8 (10/10, B)*; 27:9/12–20 (9/10, P); 27:11/10–20 (10/10, B); 27:11/27 (10/10, B); *27:12/18 (10/10, B)*; *27:14/20–15/2 (10/10, B)*; 27:16/14–16 (10/10, B); 27:19/18 (10/10, B); 27:20/12–18 (9/10, P); 27:27/36 (9/10, P); 27:29/4 (9/10, P); 27:30/40–44 (10/10, B); 27:33/8–10 (10/10, B); *27:33/36–42 (10/10, B)*; 27:34/40 (10/10, B); *27:35/2 (10/10, B)*; *27:37/2 (10/10, B)*; 27:37/6–16 (10/10, B); 27:39/34 (10/10, B); 27:40/36 (9/10, E); *27:41/12 (10/10, B)*; *27:43/6 (10/10, B)*; *27:43/34 (10/10, P)*; in these places of 90 to 100 percent coherence, the PWR agrees with the Byz (B) eighteen times, stands independently (P) seven times, and matches the ECM (E) two times.

Acts 28: PWR = Byz (16); PWR = ECM (13); PWR ≠ ECM/Byz (19); 3Ways (2)

a. (10) Obvious differences from Byz never corrected: 28:1/6–8; 28:14/10–14; 28:16/20–22; 28:17/14; 28:19/9; 28:19/31; 28:30/6–14; 28:30/29; 28:31/26; 28:31/35

b. (8) Subtle/Insignificant agreements with the Byz that stand against the ECM: πλῆθος vs. τι πλῆθος at 28:3/12; διεξελθοῦσα vs. ἐξελθοῦσα at 28:3/34; μεταβαλλόμενοι vs. μεταβαλόμενοι at 28:6/46; WO at 28:6/50–54; WO at 28:9/16–24; ἤλθομεν εἰς vs. εἰσήλθομεν εἰς at 28:16/6; κατηγορῆσαι vs. κατηγορεῖν at 28:19/30; WO at 28:22/28–32

c. Comments: none.

4

Utilizing an Enhanced Textual Criticism Model

OVERVIEW

THE PRECEDING CHAPTERS HAVE brought to light several important conclusions that are going to be utilized concurrently with the goal of improving the printed text of the ECM of Acts and follow-on editions of NA28. The excellent readings of both the Byz and PWR editions need to be fully utilized. Comparing the Alex, Byz, and PWR traditions should yield carefully reasoned, recommended revisions to the standard text. In addition, the results should strengthen confidence in the standard text of today. Chapter 2 has shown that reconstructed readings of the proto/primary-Western reading (PWR) archetype are usually more ancient than those of the Western Redaction (WR), i.e., the formal revision of Acts that can be approximated by looking at WR textual witnesses, i.e., Codex D (05), the mae, the Syriac Harklensis apparatus, and others. The WR is here perceived as the first formal redaction of the NT that was evidently published within or before the time period of AD 150–175. Having served as a critical building block for the WR, the PWR archetype was likely both produced and copied within the window of AD 125–150. Moreover, chapter 2 has argued that the PWR edition displays qualities that reveal its dependence upon both the proto-Byz and proto-Alex traditions. As a result, the readings of the proto-Byz tradition are either as old or older than those of the PWR archetype. Unfortunately, while many times it is possible to discern the proto-Byz reading, often it is not. In addition, while the established Byz text includes readings that are clearly secondary, it also possesses readings that are clearly primary. The number of accidental changes that resulted from scribes having to choose between competing readings seems to be greatest in the Byz tradition. The Byz text was the most liable for this kind of error because of its unbroken chain of scribal activity, with respect to the Greek NT (GNT), since the earliest of times. In contrast, the recognized Alex tradition is based more upon the GNT as it stood in Alexandria somewhere in the second to the fourth-century period. Its readings can often be confirmed by old MSS, ancient translations, and/or primitive fathers. Preservation of the ancient Alex text is providential because this form has escaped many of the accidental changes. However, it is still true that there are numerous places where the Alex reading is opposed by another of equal or superior quality. Therefore, all relevant external and internal evidence must be considered.

Similar to the Alex tradition and even to a greater extent, the PWR edition experienced a break in its transmission (i.e., periods when it was not used much), helping to protect it against further development. Yet unlike the Alex text, the PWR tradition did not prevail across any significant geographic area.[1] As a result, the readings of its witnesses tend to be either unrevised from the earliest period or else changed to match the standard Byz. In addition, some of its witnesses (see MSS 614 and 2412) show little subsequent revision. Therefore, the reconstructed PWR edition offers a portal into the past. Like the Alex text and often to a greater extent, many of its readings can be assessed as being current in the early second century (i.e., it is old but not necessarily original). As a result, the reconstructed PWR at any given passage repeatedly helps reveal what the proto-Byz and/or proto-Alex archetype actually read. By comparing the three traditions in this manner, certain necessary corrections can be made to the modern standard GNT with a high degree of accuracy. Though chapter 3 has provided abundant evidence that isolated PWRs are nearly always secondary, chapter 4 will demonstrate that aligned PWRs are nearly always ancient and very often original. In order to best utilize the proto-Western text as preserved by the PWR archetype, it will be helpful to employ a new text-critical canon. That guideline will now be proposed.

1. In contrast, the WR disseminated widely and rapidly after spinning off from the PWR edition.

NEW TEXT-CRITICAL "CANON" PROPOSED

My proposed Proto-Western Text Canon states, when principal members of the MS 614-group (i.e., MSS 383 614 1292 1505 1611 1890 2138 2147 2412 2495) unite, such readings should be considered as reflecting the PWR archetype that was established between AD 125 to 150.[2] Whenever a PWR is isolated, it normally manifests a secondary revision. When the PWR stands with either the Alex or Byz text, it is part of binary aligned tradition that often preserves the original wording (key exception: if the PWR agrees with one text over against the other text that is united with nearly all translations and fathers, the binary aligned tradition is apparently still secondary). Still binary aligned tradition retains other possibilities. Did two of the three preserve the original or did one of the three pull the other away and thus leave the original in only one tradition? Here the testimony of a group of seventeen mixed text MSS (i.e., 08 181 206 431 467 522 876 915 945 1127 *1501* 1739 1838 *1884* 1891 2298 *2652*) and Codex D (05) becomes important.[3] These are all related to the MS 614-group. Most retain a mixed Alex and Byz text, while all have an affinity for PWRs. As a result, their testimony is more unpredictable than MSS from just one text tradition. MS 05 is also included in the group of eighteen because it preserves readings from both the WR and PWR archetypes. When both sets of MSS (the MS 614-group and the mixed-text group) are considered, they often confirm the original in one of the other two traditions. For example, whenever they polarize toward one reading, they offer a strong vote for authenticity. Even when the whole group of 'Westerns' is split between the Alex and Byz readings, it still tends to confirm their antiquity.

After briefly discussing some categories of variant readings and their ratings, the next section will apply both the new text-critical canon and all the time-tested, existing text-critical canons to variant units across the book of Acts.

2. The approach used for selecting these ten MSS is discussed in chapter 1.

3. This group was primarily pulled from the Western affiliated MSS listed by Boismard and Lamouille, *Texte occidental reconstitution*, 1:25–27, who selected them from von Soden's I-text groups B and C and added others. All except the italicized ones are from von Soden's I-text groups.

CATEGORIES AND RATINGS

The results from the application of historic text-critical rules and the proposed new canon to the book of Acts can be viewed from a grid of six different categories: Alex text is original (ATO), Byz text is original (BTO), PWR archetype is original (PAO), Other text is original (OTO), SGL is recommended (SGLR), and Alex-Byz readings of insight (ABI). Each recommended change to the ECM is also accompanied by a α, β, or γ rating showing my confidence in the assessment. In honor of J. A. Bengel's important contributions to the field of textual criticism, my evaluation approach is patterned after his GNT apparatus where he judged leading alternate readings to his printed text on a five-point scale.[4] His five grades include:

> α *innuit marginis lectionem, salvo etiam atque etiam judicio meliore, plane pro genuina habendam:*
> β *eam, quae per codices firmior sit lectione textus, nec tamen plane certa:*
> γ *aequalem lectioni textus; interdum etiam talem, de qua decisio tota lectori relinquatur:*
> δ *minus firmam.*
> ε *non probandam, quamvis a nonnullis probatam.*[5]

In the following pages, α refers to readings that are almost certainly original; β to those that seem better than the ECM but some uncertainty remains; and γ to those where each has an equal claim to originality. The last is intended to be identical with SGL notation as found in the ECM of Acts.[6] Each variant where the Byz disagrees with the ECM will also be described according to its impact on the meaning of the passage (see discussion at the end of chapter 2). The variations will be classified as significant (SI), insignificant (INS), or not translatable (NTR). Also, as mentioned previously, any variant preceded by # indicates that it was already partly discussed at least once in chapters 2 or 3. In addition, readings with the designation "3ways" are those where the Alex, Byz, and

---

4. Bengel, *Novum Testamentum.*

5. "α marks a marginal reading, both secure and also indeed superior, certainly to be held as the original; β that, which according to the MSS is better attested than the reading of the text, yet not completely certain; γ [is] equal to the reading of the text; and [is] also sometimes excellent, but whose entire decision is left for the reader; δ less attested; ε not to be approved, although it is approved by some" (my translation).

6. ECM 3:1:1, intro, 24–25, 35–37.

PWR traditions are divided in three ways. Finally, any reading marked as NA28 is equal to the text of the ECM unless otherwise noted.

CASE STUDIES

1. (BTO) (α-NTR) (1:5/16–22) Byz/614 reads βαπτισθήσεσθε ἐν πνεύματι ἁγίῳ (vs. ἐν πνεύματι βαπτισθήσεσθε ἁγίῳ, NA28, vs. ἐν πνεύματι ἁγίῳ βαπτισθήσεσθε, 05) and is found in 6/9 best ECM MSS (i.e., P74^{vid} 02 04 33 1175 2200), 9/9 core PWR MSS (1890 lacuna until 3:8), and 08 307 etc., including 21/22 Westerns[7] plus Vg e p/2 w 189. In addition, it has the support of 14 fathers. 614 is the PWR. NA28 is joined by only 01* 03 81 1642 with no fathers or versions. It evidently arose in a proto-Alex archetype or the *Vorlage* of 03 when the copyist skipped over the first word of the Byz/PWR and wrote ἐν πνεύματι. He immediately recognized the error but instead of erasing, continued by inserting the first word, βαπτισθήσεσθε, and then wrote the fourth word ἁγίῳ after that. The reading is awkward, and the support is sparse. There are only four times in the NT when any of the forms of ἅγιος and πνεῦμα are separated by anything other than an article (see Matt 1:20; Luke 2:25; Eph 1:13; 1 Thess 4:8). The last two have a genitive modifier. Only the first two appear odd and a form of εἰμί separates both.[8] MS 05 with its secondary reading has as much ancient attestation as NA28, being joined by Did d gig p*^{vid} t 70 72 73 sy^{Aram}. MS 05 is possibly the WRR and either smoothed NA28 or stylistically reordered the Byz. Byz/PWR is original as confirmed by the Westerns and fathers.

2. (BTO) (β-NTR) (1:6/10) Byz/614 has ἐπηρώτων (vs. ἠρώτων, NA28) and is found in 9/9 core PWR MSS (MS 2412 has the prefix but is lacuna at the end), 3/8 best ECM MSS (i.e., 33 81 2200), and 04C3f 05 08 35 etc., including 22/23 Westerns plus Asts^{mss} Bas Chrys Hipp SevGab. 614 is the PWR. NA28 is joined by 5/8 best ECM MSS (i.e., 01 02 03 04* 1175) and just 88 180 915 1409 2774. NA28 looks to be a local Alex reading led by four uncials (cf. 1:8/24–26; 1:13/8–14; 1:16/45; 8:33/19). Fee has shown that MS 03, the top ranked ECM MS, has a proclivity in the Gospels for dropping the prefix from

---

7. MS 383 is still counted even when it is subsumed under the ECM's "Byz" symbol.
8. Quarles, *Matthew*, 20, explains the significance of the construction at Matt 1:20.

3. (BTO) (α-INS) (1:8/24–26) Byz/614 reads μοι μάρτυρες (vs. μου μάρτυρες, NA28) and is found in 7/9 core PWR MSS (1890 is lacuna), 3/8 best ECM MSS (i.e., 33 81 2200), and P56 08 35 etc., including 19 Westerns plus AstS^mss Ath^vid Chrys Cyr Epiph Hipp Or^pt OrLat Procop SevGab^pt StephH ThdMop Vg e gig p t w 70 72 73 189 sa bo mae sy^p sy^h. 614 is the PWR. NA28 is joined by 5/8 best ECM MSS (i.e., 01 02 03 04 1175) and just 05 996 1127 1609 2138 2298 plus Or^pt SevGab^pt d Ä. As in 1:6/10, NA28 preserves a local Alex reading (see also 1:13/8–14; 1:16/45; 8:33/19). It managed to impact some Western friendly MSS (i.e., 05 1127 2138 2298). NA28 would appear to have changed the Byz/PWR accidentally.[10] The genitive appears easier. The dative is consistent with a similar context at 22:15/8. The translations, Westerns, and the fathers together confirm that the Byz/PWR is original.

4. (BTO) (α-NTR) (1:13/8–14) Byz/PWR has ἀνέβησαν εἰς τὸ ὑπερῷον (vs. εἰς τὸ ὑπερῷον ἀνέβησαν, NA28) and is found in 9/9 core PWR MSS (1890 is lacuna), 2/8 best ECM MSS (i.e., 33 2200),[11] and 01C2 05(*f1) 08 35 etc., including 23/23 Westerns plus Chrys^pt SevGab. 614 is the PWR. NA28 is joined by 5/8 best ECM MSS (i.e., 02 03 04 81 1175) and no others plus Chrys^pt. Although the NA28 is a bit less smooth, there is no compelling reason that would cause *all* the rest of the MS tradition to revise NA28 to the Byz word order. Most likely, the NA28 sequence occurred when an ancient Alex scribe accidentally skipped past ἀνέβησαν with his eyes having just looked at εἰσῆλθον. He was not expecting another finite verb, and his *Vorlage* probably lacked punctuation. He immediately noticed his mistake and inserted the verb after the prepositional phrase. Though Hermann von Soden chooses the NA28 reading, he comments that the

---

9. Fee, "P75, P66, and Origen," 261, describes how both 03 and P75 have a trend of sometimes omitting the preposition in partitive phrases, curtailing compound words to a simple form, dropping the possessive, losing the article, and changing the word order.

10. Wachtel, "Text-Critical Commentary," 5, considers the genitive to be "slightly unusual" and settles on a SGL reading.

11. See Geer, "Investigation of Western Cursives," 108–9, who says that MS 33 is a "Majority text" witness in the first ten chapters of Acts rather than an Alex one. CBGM Phase IV data confirms his assessment. In fact, it shows that MS 33 is more Byz than Alex in the first eleven chapters.

construction of ἀναβαίνω followed by εἰς is common with Luke.[12] In fact, Luke's broader style of placing locative prepositions after ἀναβαίνω has only one exception (see Acts 25:9). The other examples all match the Byz wording here (see Luke 2:4; 5:19; 9:28; 18:10, 31; 19:4, 28; 24:38; Acts 2:34; 3:1; 7:23; 8:39; 10:4, 9; 11:2; 15:2; 21:6, 12, 15; 24:11; 25:1). There are only four other exceptions in the entire NT (see John 12:20; 1 Cor 2:9; Rev 13:1; 14:11). Moreover, all traditions preserve the nonstandard sequence of Acts 25:9, manifesting indifference to word order harmony. In summary, the agreement in error by Alex MSS 02 03 04 81 1175 shows their close coherence (cf. 1:6/10; 1:8/24–26; 1:16/45; 8:33/19). Byz/PWR is original.

5. (ATO) (α-SI) (1:14/15) Byz/614 reads + καὶ τῇ δεήσει (vs. omits, NA28) and is found in 9/10 core PWR MSS and 04C3 33 2200 etc., including 19/23 Westerns plus AstS Chrys Dam Or[vid]. 614 is the PWR. NA28 is joined by 7/9 best ECM MSS and 05 08 044 35* 467 1409 1642 1884 2774 plus Eus Vg d e gig p w 189 sa bo mae sy[Aram] sy[p] sy[h] Ä A G. Though NA28 has limited MS support, its solid core is confirmed by the united ancient translations. Byz/PWR has apparently acquired the phrase from Phil 4:6.[13] The verse's wording is not conducive for attributing the short reading to an eye skip. NA28 is original.

6. (ATO) (β-SI) (1:15/22) Byz/614 has μαθητῶν (vs. ἀδελφῶν, NA28) and is found in 9/9 core PWR MSS and 04C3 05 08 etc., including seventeen Westerns plus Chrys d e gig p t 70 73 mae sy[p] sy[h]. 614 is the PWR and probably also the WRR. NA28 is supported by 01 02 03 04* 33 and 21 others, including six Westerns plus Vg w 189 sa bo Ä. Luke commonly uses both words to describe believers but does not use μαθητῶν until 6:1. Since "brethren" occurs in the verse before and after, ἀδελφῶν could have resulted from accidental harmonization. Also, Byz/PWR has more variety. On the other hand, "disciples" may have been inserted from 6:1 in order to disambiguate "brethren" in 1:14, as a reference to the Lord's half brothers, from "brethren" in 1:15, as a reference to the family of all believers.[14] On the whole, it seems more likely that Luke used the

---

12. Soden, *Schriften des Neuen Testaments*, 2:491.

13. See Metzger, *Textual Commentary*, 246; Soden, *Schriften des Neuen Testaments*, 2:492, also cites parallels at Eph 6:18; 1 Tim 2:1; and 1 Tim 5:5.

14. See Metzger, *Textual Commentary*, 247.

same word in 1:14–16, and that the Byz/PWR smoothed the verse. NA28 is probably original.

7. (BTO) (β-INS) (1:16/13) Byz/614 reads τὴν γραφὴν <u>ταύτην</u> ἣν (vs. τὴν γραφὴν ἣν, NA28) and is found in 8/8 core PWR MSS and 04C3 05 08 049 18 33 35C etc., including 16 Westerns plus Chrys IrLat d e gig p t ar 70 73 sa^{ms} sy^h. 614 is the PWR. NA28 is joined by 7/8 best ECM MSS (i.e., 01 02 03 04* 81 1175 2200) and 35* 467 and 18 others, including 6 Westerns plus Ath Did Eus Hipp Or SevGab Vg w 189 sy^p Ä. The important Coptic translations, sa bo mae, cannot help since they may support either reading. While NA28 has the stronger paternal support, 614/Byz has the oldest paternal reading with IrLat. More importantly, there are two factors that could have led to the shorter reading. First, ταύτην could have been easily skipped over by an early copyist, given that the longer reading has the -ην ending in four straight words.[15] Second, ταύτην may have been removed because the following narrative describes two prophecies from Psalms about Judas (see 1:20). Without it, the reference to τὴν γραφὴν could be taken to refer to the Scripture as a whole and thus make two prophecies less of an apparent problem.[16] If ταύτην were lost from factor number one, factor two would also make its restoration unlikely. In actuality, ταύτην does not clash because 1:16 may refer only to the first prophecy about Judas's resting place (see 1:20; Ps 69:25). The second prophecy is concerned not so much about the person of Judas but more with the office he forfeited (see 1:20; Ps 109:8). In fact, Barrett seems to be correct that 1:16 refers to neither of the above prophecies but instead to Ps 41:9, which refers to a friend betraying his friend as Judas had done.[17] If so, a specific verse is emphasized by using ταύτην but it is only cited by allusion. Such is clearly the harder reading. Though ταύτην might have been added for emphasis, that reason is unlikely because of the difficulties it creates. In conclusion, an eye skip is the most likely cause of variation. Byz/PWR is probably original.

8. (BTO) (α-NTR) (1:16/45) Byz/614 reads <u>τὸν</u> Ἰησοῦν (vs. Ἰησοῦν, NA28) and is found in 8/8 core PWR MSS and 4/8 best ECM MSS (i.e., 33 81 1175 2200) and 04C3 05 08 18 35 etc., including 22/22

---

15. See Wachtel, "Text-Critical Commentary," 6.
16. See Barrett, *Commentary on Acts*, 1:96.
17. Barrett, *Commentary on Acts*, 1:96–97.

Westerns plus Chrys. 614 is the PWR. NA28 is joined by 4/8 best ECM MSS (i.e., 01 02 03 04*) and no others, plus Did Eus Hipp. The translations cannot help. The only apparent advantage for adding the article is to make the reference to Jesus anaphoric and point to Acts 1:11. However, its absence would hardly cause scribes everywhere to "correct" it. There are so many examples where it would seem likely for a scribe to "fix" the text, and yet either no scribe or only a small number of scribes ever changed it. Most likely the article was lost by accident. The isolated Alex support exposes its mistake. The unity in error of 01 02 03 04* shows the tight coherence of these MSS (cf. 1:6/10; 1:8/24–26; 1:13/8–14; 8:33/19). Byz/PWR is original.[18]

9. (BTO) (β-SI) (1:25/4–12) Byz/614 has τὸν κλῆρον τῆς διακονίας ταύτης (vs. τὸν τόπον τῆς διακονίας ταύτης, NA28) and is found in 8/8 core PWR MSS and 5/9 best ECM MSS (i.e., 01 33 81 1175 2200) and 08 18 35 etc., including 20/21 Westerns plus Bas Chrys e sy[p] sy[h.txt]. 614 is the PWR. NA28 is joined by 4/9 best ECM MSS (i.e., P74[vid] 02 03 04*) and just (05) 044 plus Did Procop Vg d gig p t w 70 73 189 sa bo mae sy[hmg] Ä. Since 614/Byz agrees precisely with the previous 1:17/16–24, one might assume that it was harmonized to it.[19] However, τόπον appears instead to be an accidental or purposeful assimilation to the τόπον at 1:25/32. It makes perfect sense in the context. One would expect some MSS to harmonize with 1:17 but not almost the entire Greek tradition. On the other hand, since it has creatively used τόπον in both a positive and negative sense, it could be the original. It has great translation support. However, notice that its supporters include mae, 8/9 OL MSS, and sy[hmg], witnesses commonly part of the WR. In addition, sa shows periodic dependence upon the WR. The fact that (05) is one of the six MSS with the reading increases the chances. The change may have been a stylistic desire not to overuse κλῆρος since it is found at 1:17 and twice nearby at 1:26. In fact, Barrett attributes the word choice to

---

18. Soden, *Schriften des Neuen Testaments*, 2:492, agrees. Even though he places the word in brackets, unlike the case with NA28, the brackets evidently do not indicate uncertainty. Instead, it signifies that the word(s), absent in some MSS, should indeed be part of the original text (Soden, *Schriften des Neuen Testaments*, 2:xxiv).

19. Wachtel, "Against the Text-Type Concept," 143; Metzger, *Textual Commentary*, 249.

Luke for that reason.[20] Most likely, the change to τόπον occurred because of its suitability and was inspired by its presence later in the verse. The apostles needed someone to fill the empty "position." If the sa embraced the WRR from its inception, τόπον would easily enter the bo Vg and Ä. Given the unity of the Greek tradition and the likelihood τόπον came from the WRR, Byz/PWR is probably original.

10. (BTO) (β-INS) (2:7/5) NA28/614 reads δὲ (vs. δὲ πάντες, Byz) and is found in 5/8 core PWR MSS, just 1/9 best ECM MSS (i.e., 03), 05 0142 18 35, and thirty-three others, including nine Westerns plus Eus d gig r mae Ä. 614 is the PWR and has some core Byz MSS in support. Byz is found in 8/9 best ECM MSS (i.e., 01C2 02 04 33 81 1175 1739 2200) and (01*) 08 049 1 etc., including sixteen Westerns plus Vg e gig t w 70 72 73 189 sa bo sy^p sy^h. The PWR evidently became the WRR as led by 05 and mae.[21] It seems that the PWR/WRR dropped πάντες to magnify the later use of ἅπαντες/πάντες (see 2:7/16). Under this argument, the main point was not that they were all amazed but that <u>all</u> the Galileans were speaking in a miraculous manner. Alternatively, the word may have been dropped to avoid an apparent conflict with 2:12-13. In 2:12, they were all shocked and at a loss. However, in 2:13 some were mocking. If "all" is retained at 2:7/5, the same ones mocking in 2:13 would have been amazed here. That combination seems incongruent. However, with "all" removed, it could be summarized that all were shocked and confused (see 2:12), though most were shocked and amazed (2:7), but some were shocked and mocked (2:12-13). In contrast, Wachtel favors the idea that πάντες was added to agree with 2:12/6 but marks it as SGL because of "weak attestation."[22] If the NA28 reading were joined by a few more core Alex MSS and by either the sa or bo, it would be strong (cf. 2:7/8-10 and 2:31/22-24). In conclusion, the best ECM MSS, most translations, and most Westerns demonstrate that the Byz is probably original. The SGL can be removed.

20. Barrett, *Commentary on Acts*, 1:103.

21. Metzger, *Textual Commentary*, 252, agrees that the reading without πάντες is part of the Western text. Surprisingly, he considers 03 as preserving the original even though it is the only core Alex witness. The more natural conclusion is that 03 adopted the smoother Western reading. Ropes, *Beginnings of Christianity*, 13, also calls it Western.

22. Wachtel, "Text-Critical Commentary," 6; see Barrett, *Commentary on Acts*, 1:120.

11. (ATO) (β-INS) (2:7/8–10) Byz/614 has + πρὸς ἀλλήλους and is found in 7/8 core PWR MSS and 04C3 05 08 096 etc., including twenty Westerns plus d e sy^h A G. 614 is the PWR. Moreover, with only word order difference, it is also joined by 044 88 467 915 plus gig p* t 70 72 73. Either of the readings are supported by sy^Aram and sy^p. NA28 is joined by 7/10 best ECM MSS and 321 383 1490 plus CyrH^vid Eus and Vg p/2 r w 189 sa bo mae Ä. In contrast to the variant above at 2:7/5, NA28 has little Western influence, has a strong Alex core, and is joined by the sa bo. As a result, NA28 has avoided the clarifying gloss. NA28 is probably original.

12. (ATO) (β-SI) (2:30/34) Byz/614 reads τὸ κατὰ σάρκα ἀναστήσειν τὸν χριστόν καθίσαι (vs. ἀναστήσειν τὸν χριστόν καθίσαι, 1739, vs. καθίσαι, NA28) and is found in 7/9 core PWR MSS and (05*) 025 049 0142 1 18 (33) 35 2200 etc., including 20/24 Westerns (divided into five readings) plus Chrys Eus Or Thdrt A^mss (d) (sy^h mae). 614 is the PWR and probably the WRR. ECM lists seventeen alternatives. MS 1739 is joined by (08) (323) (1884) 1891 (Thdrt^vid) (e) (G). Four of these are Westerns. It has evidently simplified the Byz/PWR. NA28 is joined by 6/9 best ECM MSS (i.e., 01 02 03 04 81 1175) and no others plus Cyr Eus IrLat Or Vg gig p t r w 70 189 sy^Aram sy^p A (sa bo Ä). The question is whether to trust the Alex core and the translations or the near consensus Greek MS tradition. Of the seventeen readings, the Byz/PWR is arguably the hardest of all with its complex construction with τό at the beginning and its use of the rare FAN of ἀναστήσειν that is unique in the NT.[23] Though Metzger and Barrett consider NA28 to be the most difficult reading, it is the one nearest the probable source text of Ps 132:11 (Ps 131:11, LXX).[24] Although the original promise was given to David in 2 Sam 7:12, the wording suggests that Peter was referring to this Psalm. As will be discussed later, it appears that the Byz/PWR reading of 2:30/34 is one of about ten important Lucan readings that were removed by Luke himself before his edition of Acts became final (see 10:32/37; 15:24/30–34; 18:21/9; 20:24/27; 21:25/16–20; 23:30/45; 24:6/20–8/14; 28:16/12–16; 28:29/2–24). Someone from the Lucan circle, who evidently had access to the

---

23. See Wachtel, "Against the Text-Type Concept," 143–44, who discusses the construction and meaning of the Byz/PWR wording.

24. Metzger, *Textual Commentary*, 259; Barrett, *Commentary on Acts*, 1:147–48.

Luke's preliminary working edition, reintroduced the excised words. NA28 is probably original.[25]

13. (ATO) (α-INS) (#2:31/22–24) Byz/PWR has + ἡ ψηχὴ αὐτοῦ and is joined by 7/9 core PWR MSS (though divided three ways) and 04C3 08 044 1739 2200 etc., including 22/23 Westerns plus Ath[ms.vid] Cyr[ms] GregThaum[T.vid] LeontPrCP[pt] SevAnt[vid] ThdMop[pt] (GregNy[vid] LeontB[pt.vid] LeontPrCP[pt] Ath[T.vid] Chrys[vid] GregThaum[ms.vid] ThdMop[pt] Thdrt) (e sy[h]). 614 is the PWR. NA28 is joined by (P74) 01 (02) 03 (04*) (05) 33 81 1175 plus Eus Or (LeontB[pt]) (IrLat) Vg gig p t r w 70 189 sa bo mae sy[p]. Although its paternal support is very strong, and its Greek MS support nearly unanimous, the PWR/Byz reading likely adapts the words from either Acts 2:27 or Ps 16:10 (Ps 15:10, LXX), to provide clarification. The Alex reading shows its fidelity because it has 8/10 best ECM MSS plus 05, dominates in the translations, and is joined by (IrLat) and Or, the oldest fathers extant here. The unity of the Byz/PWR points to an extremely ancient variant at the base of both traditions. Here is a great example of a reading that is nearly universal in the Greek, and yet can be shown as inferior due to its absence from most of the ancient translations and also from most of the best ECM MSS. NA28 is original.[26]

14. (BTO) (β-NTR) (#2:37/32) Byz/PWR reads ποιήσομεν (vs. ποιήσωμεν, NA28/614). The Byz/PWR preserves the more difficult FAI-1P form against the common syntax of AAS-1P.[27] It also has greater paternal support (see chapter 2). The Byz/PWR is probably original (cf. 4:16/6; 4:21/20; 5:15/42; 21:24/22).

15. (ATO) (α-SI) (2:38/36–40) Byz/614 has ἁμαρτιῶν (vs. τῶν ἁμαρτιῶν ὑμῶν, NA28) and is found in 9/9 core PWR MSS, 3/10 best ECM MSS (i.e., 33 1739 2200), and 05 08 025 etc., including 21/22 Westerns plus IrLat d e gig p* r sy[p] sy[h]. 614 is the PWR. NA28 is joined by 7/10 best ECM MSS (i.e., P74 01 02 03 04 81 1175; though 1175 lost ὑμῶν) and 181 467 1409C 1642C 2774 Cyr G (Vg p/2 t w 70 189 sa bo mae). The translations are divided very closely. Have the Byz/Western MSS avoided an expansion? Metzger insightfully explains how the Byz was conformed to the shorter form found in the

---

25. Soden, *Schriften des Neuen Testaments*, 2:496, disagrees and prints the Byz/PWR wording as original.

26. Soden, *Schriften des Neuen Testaments*, 2:497, came to the same conclusion.

27. See Wallace, *Greek Grammar*, 570–71, 465–68.

Gospels.²⁸ Von Soden previously concluded the same thing and also cites Acts 5:31.²⁹ But why? Were the scribes constantly looking for parallels? It seems rather that the two words were dropped to remove the grammatical difficulty of the shift from 2P to 3S back to 2P, μετανοήσατε, φησίν, καὶ βαπτισθήτω ἕκαστος ὑμῶν ἐπὶ τῷ ὀνόματι Ἰησοῦ Χριστοῦ εἰς ἄφεσιν τῶν ἁμαρτιῶν ὑμῶν. Harmonization to parallels provided an easy solution. The Byz could be paraphrased as, "You all need to repent and each of you should be baptized in the name of Jesus Christ with a concern for the forgiveness of sins." NA28 could be paraphrased, "You all need to repent with a concern for the forgiveness of the sins of you all, and each of you should be baptized in the name of Jesus Christ." The NA28 wording subtly distinguishes the main point of conversion from the supporting one of baptism by switching between 2P and 3S.³⁰ On that occasion Peter clarified the meaning with many more words and urged them to "be saved" (see 2:40). Luke specifies that only those who received the word (i.e., were saved) were then baptized (see 2:41). Therefore, Peter's teaching in Acts 2 could be summarized that it is repentance to God and faith in Jesus Christ that brings a person the forgiveness of sins.³¹ New converts are to be baptized to confess their conversion. The PWR/Byz reading is very old but NA28 preserves the original in only a few MSS.

16. (BTO) (β-NTR) (2:41/18–28) (3ways) 1611 reads τῇ ἡμέρᾳ ἐκείνῃ καὶ προσετέθησαν (vs. καὶ προσετέθησαν ἐν τῇ ἡμέρᾳ ἐκείνῃ, NA28, vs. καὶ προσετέθησαν τῇ ἡμέρᾳ ἐκείνῃ, Byz/614) and it rewords the Byz so that the text emphasizes the baptism of the converts on that day. Therefore, it supports the Byz indirectly. 1611 is joined by 876 1718 2138 and is possibly the PWR. NA28 is joined by 7/10 best ECM MSS and sixteen others, including just two Westerns plus Cyr[vid] Eus. Byz/614 is found in 6/9 core PWR MSS, 3/10 best ECM MSS (i.e., 33 1739 2200), and 08[vid] 025 049 0142 18 35 etc., including seventeen Westerns plus Chrys. Although ἐν might have been lost

---

28. Metzger, *Textual Commentary*, 261–62; see Barrett, *Commentary on Acts*, 1:153–54.

29. Soden, *Schriften des Neuen Testaments*, 2:497.

30. Charles L. Quarles suggested the idea to me during his fall 2018 NT textual criticism class.

31. See Bruce, *Book of the Acts*, 70.

by accident, most likely it was a smoothing gloss. The Byz also has better MS variety. Byz is probably original.

17. (OTO) (α-SI) (#3:6/46–48) Byz/614 reads ἔγειρε καὶ (vs. ἔγειρε καὶ in brackets, NA28) and is found in all MSS and translations except for 01 03 05 Dam d sa. 614 is the PWR. ECM marks it as a SGL. The unity of 01 03 05 and the sa points to a primitive error. The textual support for its presence is remarkable, including eighteen fathers and the following translations: Vg e gig p h r w 72 189 bo mae sy^p sy^h Ä A G. Although the words theoretically could have been assimilated from the Gospels (see Matt 9:5; Mark 2:9; Luke 5:23; John 5:8) as mentioned by von Soden and Metzger, both decided to print them.[32] However, Metzger and NA28 have them in brackets to denote uncertainty. Pervo suggests the omission arose because some scribes saw it as contradictory to Peter lifting up the lame man in 3:7.[33] Moreover, he asserts that a command simply to walk is foreign to the NT. Wachtel acknowledges the possibility of an intentional deletion but remains neutral.[34] It would be natural for Peter to follow the example of his Lord when performing his first miracle after Pentecost. If the shorter reading were original, it is almost impossible to explain the dominance of the long one. It is found in 7/9 best ECM MSS, the Coptic bo mae, and almost every father. MSS 01 and 03 cannot justify the omission, and 05 is an unreliable witness for isolated readings. The mainstream is original, and the SGL should be removed.

18. (BTO) (β-NTR) (3:7/14–16) NA28 has ἤγειρεν αὐτόν (vs. ἤγειρεν, Byz/614) and is joined by 7/10 best ECM MSS and 095 307 etc., including 4 Westerns plus Bas BasSel HesH Vg gig h^vid r w 72 189 sy^p sy^h A G. Byz/614 is found in 7/9 core PWR MSS and 05 08 025 049 0142 etc., including 19 Westerns plus Chrys d e ar. 614 is the PWR. Either reading may be supported by: sa bo mae Ä. ECM assigns the variant a SGL. Byz/614 is harder because it lacks the clarifying pronoun at the end and thus must be supplied by the context. It could have been dropped by an eye skip but that is doubtful because αὐτόν would have been expected in the context. While the translations

---

32. Soden, *Schriften des Neuen Testaments*, 2:599; Metzger, *Textual Commentary*, 267; see Barrett, *Commentary on Acts*, 1:183.

33. Pervo, *Acts*, 100.

34. Wachtel, "Text-Critical Commentary," 7.

favor NA28, translation technique might have caused the insertion. Given the alignment of the Byz, PWR, and the overall Western tradition with the less polished reading, Byz/PWR is probably original. The SGL can be removed.[35]

19. (ATO) (β-NTR) (3:21/34–42) 08 reads τῶν ἁγίων τῶν ἀπ' αἰῶνος αὐτοῦ προφητῶν (vs. τῶν ἁγίων αὐτοῦ προφητῶν ἀπ' αἰῶνος, Byz, vs. τῶν ἁγίων αὐτοῦ προφητῶν τῶν ἀπ' αἰῶνος, 1611, vs. τῶν ἁγίων απ' αἰῶνος αὐτοῦ προφητῶν, NA28, vs. τῶν προφητῶν ἁγίων αὐτοῦ ἀπ' αἰῶνος, 614, vs. τῶν ἁγίων αὐτοῦ τῶν προφητῶν, 05*) and is joined by 01C2 03C2 and 8 others. MS 08 has added a second τῶν to NA28. The ECM lists ten alternatives. Byz includes six Westerns plus Chrys[T]. MS 1611 is found in 5/10 core PWR MSS (i.e., 1505 1611 1890 2138 2147) and 044 876 1831S 2718 plus Chrys sy[h]. 1611 is the PWR and has added τῶν to the Byz for clarity. NA28 is found in 9/10 best ECM MSS and twelve others plus CosmIn[T] (OL e). MS 614 is joined by 431, 1292, and 2412, and appears to have accidentally reordered the Byz. Its revised order lacks the necessary article before ἁγίων. Interestingly, 614, 1292, and 2412 sometimes unite with little or no support (see 5:39/11; 5:39/19; 7:10/32; 7:43/49; 13:5/38; 13:33/20; 13:43/38; 17:17/4–6; 17:24/32–34; 18:2/60; 23:28/20–28; 23:30/10–18; 24:14/28–36; 26:30/2–4). These MSS tenuously retain the PWR at the italicized variants. In the other cases, they depart from it. Although NA28 and the Byz differ only in word order, the smoother Byz syntax suggests that NA28 is probably original.[36] 05* and G purposely drop ἀπ' αἰῶνος and are joined by (05C1 467 629 886 Chrys[ms75] IrLat d gig p h A). In summary, this fascinating variant shows NA28 being adjusted in word order to create the Byz, NA28 receiving another τῶν to form 08, the Byz obtaining another τῶν to form 1611, and either NA28 or the Byz trimmed to make the 05* (05C1) reading. All alternatives except the last are possibly supported by: sa bo mae sy[p] Ä. Clearly the complex original promoted efforts to clarify the sense.

20. (ATO) (α-SI) (3:22/4–6) There are sixteen alternatives. The NA28 reading (a.) simply reads μὲν εἶπεν and is joined by 6/9 best ECM MSS and eight others plus Vg w 189 bo sy[p] G. It has limited MS support, but several versions. 1611 (reading c.) has built upon the Alex

---

35. See Wachtel, "Text-Critical Commentary," 7; Barrett, *Commentary on Acts*, 1:183.
36. See Metzger, *Textual Commentary*, 273.

by adding the gloss πρὸς τοὺς πατέρας from the nearby parallel at 3:25 (see also 13:32, 36; 28:25). MS 1611 seems to be the PWR and is joined by key relatives 467 876 945 1739 2138 and sy^h (sa mae). 05 and 08 each reproduced the PWR but also added the pronoun ἡμῶν and ὑμῶν respectively. MS 05 is joined by six others plus IrLat d gig p (sa mae). MS 08 is joined by just 1704(C1f) e. Both 05 and 08 seem to have imported their own reading from 3:25/28–34 to this location. Byz MS 35* and twelve others added γάρ to the PWR as seen in reading g. Finally, at the end of the process, 35* was changed by moving εἶπεν to the end thereby producing the Byz reading (m.) led by 35C. Subsequently, 6/10 core PWR MSS, including 614, were corrected to the Byz standard (note: 614 and 2412 rarely correct to the Byz after 5:32). The Byz provides a stereotypical example of successive development. However, it is remarkable that such examples are rare in the book of Acts. NA28 and the PWR provide the best substantiated readings in terms of translations. NA28 is original. It has avoided the popular expansions and is preserved in a solid core.[37]

21. (BTO) (β-NTR) (3:26/6–10) Byz/614 has ὁ θεὸς <u>ἀναστήσας</u> (vs. <u>ἀναστήσας</u> ὁ θεὸς, NA28) and is found in 9/10 core PWR MSS, 6/10 best ECM MSS (i.e., P74 02 33 81 1739 2200), and 05 08 025 18 35 etc., including nineteen Westerns plus Chrys^pt CosmIn IrLat Vg d e gig p h w 72 189 sy^h. 614 is the PWR and it reads a bit smoother. NA28 is joined by 4/10 best ECM MSS (i.e., 01 03 04 1175) and seventeen others, including three Westerns. Either Byz or NA28 may be joined by: sa bo mae sy^p. Perhaps a common archetype of 01 03 04 had a scribe that accidentally jumped over ὁ θεὸς and caught himself after writing ἀναστήσας. Bengel agreed with Maestricht that this type of error was common and that scribes would often not fix it in order to preserve the beauty of their copies.[38] The external evidence suggests the Byz/PWR is probably original.

22. (ATO) (α-SI) (3:26/17) NA28 reads αὐτοῦ (vs. αὐτοῦ <u>Ἰησοῦν</u>, Byz/614) and is found in 6/9 best ECM MSS, 05 08, and five others plus Chrys CosmIn IrLat Vg d e gig p h w 72 189 sa bo mae sy^p sy^h Ä A. Byz/614 is found in 10/10 core PWR MSS, 3/9 best ECM MSS (i.e., 02 1739 2200), and 181 431 etc., including 21/24 Westerns

---

37. Metzger, *Textual Commentary*, 273.
38. Bengel, *Gnomon of the New Testament*, 1:23.

plus G. 614 is the PWR. Although, the Byz, PWR, and the Westerns agree, the translations reveal that NA28 is original. Byz/PWR is a gloss.

23. (BTO) (β-NTR) (4:5/22–34) (3ways) NA28/35* has τοὺς πρεσβυτέρους καὶ τοὺς γραμματεῖς ἐν Ἰερουσαλήμ (vs. τοὺς πρεσβυτέρους καὶ τοὺς γραμματεῖς εἰς Ἰερουσαλήμ, 1611, vs. πρεσβυτέρους καὶ γραμματεῖς ἐν Ἰερουσαλήμ, 08, vs. πρεσβυτέρους καὶ γραμματεῖς εἰς Ἰερουσαλήμ, Byz/614) and is found in 7/10 best ECM MSS and 307 2147 etc., including seven Westerns. 1611 is joined by 01 876 945 1704 1718 1890 2138, including five Westerns. 1611 is possibly the PWR. 08 is joined by 044 18 33 35C and nine others plus Chrys. Byz/614 is found in 6/10 core PWR MSS and 025 049 1 181 etc., including nine Westerns. 05 is a paraphrase and has the greatest smoothing. Like NA28, it reflects the inclusion of the articles, but shows them in the nominative instead. Byz/614 gives the hardest reading by lacking the articles and maintaining the non-standard use of εἰς to mean "in."[39] The articles appear to be added to clarify the grammar by making it explicit that all three groups should be modified by the preceding αὐτῶν. Moreover, the Alex scribes likely converted εἰς to ἐν at the same time. Luke may have used a single article for stylistic reasons or to imply some unity between the groups.[40] Because 1611/PWR has εἰς, it likely started with the Byz and then inserted the articles to "improve" the text. 08 started with the Byz and then replaced εἰς with ἐν. The Byz seems the most primitive and is probably original.

24. (BTO) (β-SI) (#4:8/27) Byz/614 has + τοῦ Ἰσραήλ and is found in 10/10 core PWR MSS, 3/8 best ECM MSS (i.e., 33 1739 2200), and 05 08 etc., including 25/25 Westerns plus Chrys IrLat[vid] d e gig p* h mae sy[p] sy[h] A G. 614 is the PWR. The NA28 reading is supported by 5/8 best ECM MSS (i.e., P74 01 02 03 1175) and just 0165 629 1409* plus Cyr Procop Vg 189 sa bo Ä. It seems to be a local reading from Egypt. While Metzger says τοῦ Ἰσραήλ is a gloss, when NA28 has + Ἰσραήλ at 13:17/12 against the Byz/PWR, he makes no comment about the variant.[41] Barrett recognizes the quality of the longer

---

39. Barrett, *Commentary on Acts*, 1:224.
40. See Wallace, *Greek Grammar*, 279.
41. Metzger, *Textual Commentary*, 276, 357. Likewise, Barrett, *Commentary on Acts*, 1:631, does not discuss the latter passage.

reading but judges it to be an "elegance" that "is almost certainly secondary."[42] It may have been removed at this place as superfluous since the context already makes it clear that the elders were "of Israel" (see 4:10). If so, the primitive "elegance" would have been lost in some Alex MSS. But why should elegance be dismissed so quickly? In fact, Pervo states, "Verses 9–12 abound with alliteration and assonance."[43] In terms of scribal additions, it would be more natural to clarify by adding "Israel" at 13:17 where Paul is speaking to a mixed crowd in a synagogue far away in Turkey. Moreover, if including Ἰσραήλ is solid at 13:17, where the Alex reading has a solid core and text tradition variety, its authenticity appears at least as firm here where it is supported by a divided Alex core and most extant evidence. The Byz/PWR is probably original.[44]

25. (BTO) (β-NTR) (#4:16/6) Byz/PWR has ποιήσομεν (vs. ποιήσωμεν, NA28). The Byz has more paternal support and is more difficult. The Byz text as confirmed by the PWR is probably original (see 2:37/32; 4:21/20; 5:15/42; 21:24/22). The ECM marks the variant as a SGL.[45]

26. (BTO) (β-INS) (#4:17/20) NA28 reads ἀπειλησώμεθα (vs. ἀπειλῇ ἀπειλησόμεθα, RP05ᵗˣᵗ/614, vs. ἀπειλῇ ἀπειλησώμεθα, RP05ᵐᵍ/HF1985/ByzECM/1611) and is found 6/7 best ECM MSS and 12 others, including 5 Westerns plus BasSel Ä. The longer reading is found in 10/10 core PWR MSS and 08 025 049 0142 35 etc., including 20/26 Westerns plus Chrys. 614 is the PWR. However, the Byz and the PWR MSS are divided between the AMS-1P and FMI-1P form of the verb. It is more likely that the aorist subjunctive of NA28 and RP05ᵐᵍ is original. The future should be attributed to an itacism. The word ἀπειλῇ could be easily lost from an eye skip. A dittography is possible but not very likely if scribal habits in MS 614 are somewhat representative. The discussion in Metzger and Ehrman's manual on textual criticism mentions a sampling of eight examples of "haplography" but lists just two of dittography.[46]

---

42. Barrett, *Commentary on Acts*, 1:227.
43. Pervo, *Acts*, 116.
44. Soden, *Schriften des Neuen Testaments*, 2:502, agrees. However, Wachtel, "Text-Critical Commentary," 9, says the words were more likely added than deleted.
45. Wachtel, "Text-Critical Commentary," 9.
46. Metzger and Ehrman, *New Testament*, 254.

Moreover, the chances of dittography accidentally forming a perfect Aramaic idiom at just the right location must be considered as approximating zero. By analogy, the infinite absolute placed alongside a finite verb is commonly used in the HB to create emphasis.[47] For example, פָּקֹד פָּקַדְתִּי at Exod 3:16 is translated by the LXX as ἐπισκοπῇ ἐπέσκεμμαι and mean, "with a visit I have visited" or "I have truly visited." The Byz could be translated as, "Let us <u>harshly</u> threaten them." In contrast, if the word was lost during copying, its absence would hardly be noticed. Semitic Greek of this nature is rare in Acts. Nevertheless, Luke translates a dialogue using an equivalent form at 23:14/18–20, and he narrates one himself at 28:10/8–10. Outside of 4:17, neither the Byz tradition nor the PWR edition demonstrate a greater tendency for Semitic Greek than the Alex tradition. In summary, NA28 lost the word by accident. RP05^{mg}/1611 is probably original.[48]

27. (BTO) (β-NTR) (#4:21/20) 614/Byz has κολάσονται (vs. κολάσωνται, NA28). The ECM marks it as a SGL reading.[49] The Byz scribes were apparently more comfortable with the unusual FAI-3P form used with the subjunctive sense (see 2:37/32; 4:16/6; 21:24/22). Byz is most likely original as confirmed by the PWR and 3/6 best ECM MSS (i.e., 1175* 1739 2200). The SGL can be removed.

28. (BTO) (α-SI) (#4:24/28–30) PWR/Byz has <u>ὁ θεὸς ὁ ποιήσας</u> (vs. ὁ ποιήσας, NA28). As discussed in chapter 2, both the Byz and the Western traditions preserve the original.[50] They are essentially supported by all translations except Vg w bo A^{ms}. In terms of the best ECM MSS, 4/8 also join the PWR/Byz (i.e., 33 1175 1739 2200). The ECM marks it with a SGL and Wachtel notes the possibility of an eye skip.[51] The Greek MSS joining NA28 are just P74 01 02 03 69 1409 2495 2774 and have evidently resulted from an eye skip.[52]

---

47. Ross, *Introducing Biblical Hebrew*, 167–68.

48. Bruce, *Book of the Acts*, 94, accepts the Byz as original. Barrett, *Commentary on Acts*, 1:236, disagrees and asserts that it came from the "Western reviser."

49. Wachtel, "Text-Critical Commentary," 9.

50. Soden, *Schriften des Neuen Testaments*, 2:504, agrees.

51. Wachtel, "Text-Critical Commentary," 9.

52. Metzger, *Textual Commentary*, 279, judges the longer readings at this variant to be glosses and asserts, "No scribe would have abbreviated" the longer readings if they were original. However, accidents periodically happen in every textual tradition.

29. (OTO) (β-SI) (4:25/2-24) NA28 reads ὁ <u>τοῦ πατρὸς ἡμῶν</u> διὰ πνεύματος ἁγίου στόματος Δαυὶδ παιδός σου εἰπών (vs. ὁ διὰ στόματος Δαυὶδ παιδός σου εἰπών, Byz/614, vs. ὁ διὰ πνεύματος ἁγίου στόματος <u>τοῦ πατρὸς ἡμῶν</u> Δαυὶδ, παιδός σου, εἰπών, Conjecture, vs. ὁ πνεύματι ἁγίω διὰ στόματος τοῦ πατρὸς ἡμῶν Δαυὶδ τοῦ παιδός σου εἰπών, 629, ὃς διὰ πνεύματος ἁγίου διὰ τοῦ στόματος λαλήσας Δαυὶδ παιδός σου, 05) and is joined by 7/8 best ECM MSS and nineteen others. Although it is very complex, it retains the support of AstS Ath^T Chrys^ms75 HesH e (Ä G Vg gig w 189) (sa bo mae sy^h) (IrLat). Byz/614 is found in 6/10 core PWR MSS and the core Byz MSS 025 049 0142 1 18* 35 398 424 1241 etc. plus Chrys^T. 614 is the PWR. The Byz/PWR has greatly simplified by selectively deleting five words. The reading of 18C has spun off from it by adding τοῦ in front of παιδός and is joined by the remaining four core PWR MSS and twenty-five others, including ten Westerns plus Chrys^T. MS 69 is joined by the Vg gig w 189. MS 05 is joined by just d (sy^p) (bo^mss) and has facilitated NA28 by dropping τοῦ πατρὸς ἡμῶν and made a few other adjustments. By preserving the complexity and awkwardness seen in NA28, the Alex scribes have demonstrated extreme faithfulness.[53] Metzger and Barrett both favorably mention Moule's idea that the long text might be a combination of three alternate ways to introduce the second Psalm.[54] Moule inferred that Luke had marked the text with corrections that were misunderstood by the copyist. Wachtel suggests that "the author himself may be liable for the complexities of this reading" because it has strong ancient testimony, and all previous conjectures merely remove or change the hard portions.[55] Metzger and the committee are probably right to say that NA28 offers the form closest to the original of any extant reading.[56] Thankfully there may be a solution simpler than Moule's. It is a conjecture that only requires a change to the word order. NA28 appears to have misplaced the phrase <u>τοῦ πατρὸς ἡμῶν</u> (see MS 69/ Vg reading). If these words are moved to a position before Δαυὶδ, the resulting text makes good sense (see conjecture above). It could

---

53. See Metzger, *Textual Commentary*, 279-81; Barrett, *Commentary on Acts*, 1:244-45.

54. Metzger, *Textual Commentary*, 280; Barrett, *Commentary on Acts*, 1:245.

55. Wachtel, "Text-Critical Commentary," 10; Wachtel, "Against the Text-Type Concept," 144.

56. Metzger, *Textual Commentary*, 281.

be translated as, "Who by the Holy Spirit from the mouth of our father David, your servant, spoke."[57] Surprisingly, NASB previously translated it almost the same way: "Who by the Holy Spirit, through the mouth of our father David Your servant, said." Similarly, Wachtel kept the NA28 text but translated, "Who said by the Holy Spirit through your servant David, our forefather."[58] The primitive NA28 reading would easily generate the fifteen other ECM variant readings due to its complexity and difficulty. The conjecture brings the most clarity with the least adjustment. The corruption that created NA28 would have been possible by a scribe that made a single oversight in a most primitive archetype. Alternatively, the change might have been purposeful. The scribe may have moved the words forward to achieve the normal idea of God guiding a prophet to speak by the Holy Spirit rather than here where God speaks through the Holy Spirit from the prophet's mouth. If that was the scribe's purpose, he did not achieve it. The conjecture is possibly original.

30. (BTO) (β-NTR) (4:32/12–20) NA28 has ἦν καρδία καὶ ψυχὴ μία (vs. ἦν ἡ καρδία καὶ ἡ ψυχὴ μία, Byz/614, vs. ἦν ἡ καρδία καὶ ψυχὴ μία, 05C1) and is joined by 4/7 best ECM MSS (i.e., 01 02 03 1175) and just P8 05* 886K 1642 Bas Cyr^pt MaxConf^vid Or^pt. Byz/614 is joined by 10/10 core PWR MSS, 3/7 best ECM MSS (i.e., 33 1739 2200), and 08 025 044 049 0142 18 35 etc., including 20/25 Westerns plus Bas^T Chrys Cyr^pt Dam LeontH MaxConf^vid Or^vid.pt Procop^vid (Or^pt OrLat). 614 is the PWR. ECM marks it a SGL reading. The inclusion of the articles is a little more smooth but not likely to have been adopted so widely since the meaning is the same. The minimal support for NA28 suggests that it reflects a local Alexandrian stylistic preference. Wachtel observes that the longer reading might have been considered awkward and changed. However, he decides for NA28 because of its "diverse and early A-related *a* attestation."[59] Yet, the agreement of some core Alex, all the Byz, most Westerns,

---

57. Boismard and Lamouille, *Texte occidental reconstitution*, 1:136, 2:31, came up with a different solution for the reconstructed Western text based upon a Dutch version (ndl.1), a writing by Augustine (Augc), Hilary of Potiers, and a Pseudo-Augustine document called "Solutions" (Solut), and they show, ὁ διὰ στόματος τοῦ πατρὸς ἡμῶν Δαυὶδ παιδός σου εἰπών. Notice how they also place τοῦ πατρὸς ἡμῶν in front of David. They choose to drop πνεύματος ἁγίου.

58. Wachtel, "Text-Critical Commentary," 10.

59. Wachtel, "Text-Critical Commentary," 10.

and most of the fathers provides the greatest diversity. The overall evidence indicates that Byz/PWR is probably original.[60]

31. (BTO) (α-NTR) (4:37/18–20) NA28 reads ἔθηκεν πρὸς (vs. ἔθηκεν παρὰ, Byz/614) and is joined by 1/8 best ECM MSS (i.e., 01), P8 08, and just 12 minuscules. Only 2 are Westerns. Byz/614 is found in 7/8 best ECM MSS, 10/10 core PWR MSS, and (P57) 05 044 181 etc., including 22/24 Westerns plus AlMon[vid] Chrys Or. 614 is the PWR. Although πρός appears less natural, the counter evidence is overwhelming from all three traditions. P8/01 is an early reading but seems to be harmonized with the Alex reading at 5:10/8. Byz/614 is typical of Luke as can be seen in Acts 4:35 and 5:2. Byz/PWR is original here.[61] However, πρός is possibly original at 5:10/8 where it has 5/8 best ECM MSS and Or. The ECM marks the latter reading as a SGL.

32. (BTO) (β-INS) (5:16/18) Byz/614 reads εἰς Ἰερουσαλὴμ (vs. Ἰερουσαλὴμ, NA28) and is found in 9/9 core PWR MSS, 4/8 best ECM MSS (i.e., 33 1175 1739 2200), 05 08 181 (467) etc., including 24/24 Westerns plus Chrys CyrH[vid]. 614 is the PWR. NA28 is joined by 4/8 core PWR MSS (i.e., P74 01 02C 03) and just 0189 1162 plus sy[p] sy[h]. There was no need to mention Jerusalem unless the author wanted to state explicitly where they gathered. From the context, it was already evident that any surrounding cities would be those around Jerusalem. Metzger suggests that the preposition was added to smooth the verse because in the preceding τὸ πλῆθος τῶν πέριξ πόλεων, πέριξ was mistakenly thought to modify πόλεων when it actually modifies Ἰερουσαλήμ.[62] Yet the support for NA28 appears too sparse. Moreover, many of the twenty-four Westerns supporting the longer reading are also secondary Alex witnesses and yet they uniformly include εἰς. Why should they all "improve" the text? Based upon a study of singular readings, Wilson has shown that the percentage of mistakes that lead to a more difficult style is significant.[63] After evaluating 2,279 readings, he found that 606 of the errors (i.e., 27 percent) increased the complexity of the style. Therefore, a more

---

60. Soden, *Schriften des Neuen Testaments*, 2:505, agrees.
61. Soden, *Schriften des Neuen Testaments*, 2:506, agrees.
62. Metzger, *Textual Commentary*, 288; Barrett, *Commentary on Acts*, 1:277–78; Ropes, *Beginnings of Christianity*, 48.
63. Wilson, "Scribal Habits," 106.

difficult reading is often caused by a deviation from the original. Moreover, why should Luke decide to separate the preposition from its noun here? The four core Alex MSS supporting it probably derive from a common Alexandrian archetype, where the preposition was lost by accident (cf. 1:5/16–22). In the uncial continuous script, the text would have looked something like this, ΕΙΣΙΕΡΟΥΣΑΛΗΜ. If the eye moved from the EI to the IE, the word would have been lost. It is surprising that sy^p and sy^h join NA28 against the Westerns. Nevertheless, the Byz/PWR is probably original based upon its quality and variety of evidence.

33. (BTO) (α-NTR) (5:19/12) Byz/614 has ἤνοιξεν (vs. ἀνοίξας, NA28) and is found in 9/9 core PWR MSS, 4/8 best ECM MSS (i.e., 03 33 1739 2200), 08 431 etc., including 22/23 Westerns plus Bas Chrys. 614 is the PWR. The ECM makes it a SGL. NA28 is joined by 4/8 best ECM MSS (i.e., P74 01 02 1175) and just eleven others. Its variety consists of one Byz MS (i.e., 2774) and one Western (i.e., 181). Not only do half the best Alex MSS read with the finite verb but also the remaining Byz and Western MSS do as well. In addition, BL judge the participle as a secondary Alexandrian development.[64] Byz/PWR is original.

34. (BTO) (β-INS) (5:32/6–8) NA28/614 reads καὶ ἡμεῖς ἐσμεν μάρτυρες (vs. καὶ ἡμεῖς ἐσμεν αὐτοῦ μάρτυρες, Byz, vs. καὶ ἡμεῖς ἐν αὐτῷ μάρτυρες, 03/IrLat, vs. καὶ ἡμεῖς ἐν αὐτῷ ἐσμεν μάρτυρες, 1739) and is found in 3/9 core PWR MSS (i.e., 614 2147 2412), 4/8 best ECM MSS (i.e., P74 01 02 1175; but 02 reverses two words), and 05* 181 and 17 others, including seven Westerns plus Chrys^{pt} Did Vg w 72 189 (sa bo mae). MS 614 is probably the PWR with 6/9 extant core having revised to the Byz. 614 is possibly also the WRR judging from its agreement with 05* sa mae (gig) (h) w 72 189. Western corruption of the Coptic sa and mae is already seen at 5:31/35 where 05* d p h sa mae Ä add ἐν αὐτῷ.[65] Byz is found in 6/9 core PWR MSS and 05C2 08 014 025 049 33 35 etc., including twelve Westerns plus Chrys^{pt} e. The ECM has a SGL between NA28 and the Byz. 03 is ancient being joined by IrLat but these stand-alone. Ropes is probably right that 03 resulted partly from the Western insertion (herein called the WRR) of ἐν αὐτῷ at 5:31/35,

---

64. Boismard and Lamouille, *Texte occidental reconstitution*, 1:139, 2:36.
65. See Wachtel, "Text-Critical Commentary," 11.

immediately before the subject text. He surmised that this Western insertion was incorrectly placed into MS 03 after ἡμεῖς. In order to fix it, 03 removed ἐσμεν.⁶⁶ If he is right, the changes he suggests were more likely done in series and both were likely completed by AD 150 in order for it to be in the *Vorlage* of Ir (see IrLat). Alternatively, the two changes may have occurred in parallel if they resulted from a rewording of the full WRR, with ἐν αὐτῷ being construed not as the end of 5:31 but as the beginning of 5:32, i.e., ἐν αὐτῷ καὶ ἡμεῖς ἐσμεν μάρτυρες ("For him also we are witnesses"). That reading was simplified to καὶ ἡμεῖς ἐν αὐτῷ μάρτυρες, "And we for him [are] witnesses." Later the ἐσμεν was restored with reference to the broader tradition. Some Alex related MSS (i.e., 1891 2298) inserted the verb before ἐν αὐτῷ (i.e., 1891 2298) while others (i.e., 1739 2200 and ten more) placed it after. The question now turns as to whether NA28 or the Byz is correct. Wachtel considers + αὐτοῦ as more complex because it creates a "double attributive."⁶⁷ He also asserts that many of the MSS siding with NA28 are descendants of earlier Byz MSS, and thus probably had + αὐτοῦ in their ancestry. For example, MSS 104 321 468 607 886 1874 and L587 are classified as Byz in the ECM. Moreover, the three core PWR MSS (i.e., 614 2147 2412) and Westerns 915 and 2652 are all closer to the Byz. Thus, 12/26 MSS joining NA28 imply it may be secondary. Yet Wachtel hesitated to embrace the Byz because it might have been assimilated to 1:8.⁶⁸ The latter reservation is not strong because the Byz reading at 1:8/24 is not conducive to harmonization. The Byz does not read ἔσεσθέ μου μάρτυρες with the Alex text, but rather ἔσεσθέ μοι μάρτυρες. Therefore, NA28 likely derives from the PWR that smoothed the text by removing the pronoun. MSS 03 1739 and 2200 were evidently forged from the WRR. The Byz is unedited and probably original. The SGL can be removed.

35. (PAO) (β-INS) (5:34/30–40) (3ways) 614 has ἐκέλευσεν ἔξω βραχὺ τοὺς ἀποστόλους ποιῆσαι (vs. ἐκέλευσεν ἔξω βραχὺ τοὺς ἀνθρώπους ποιῆσαι, NA28, vs. ἐκέλευσεν ἔξω βραχύ τι τοὺς ἀποστόλους ποιῆσαι, Byz, vs. ἐκέλευσεν ἔξω τοὺς ἀποστόλους βραχύ τι ποιῆσαι, MS 014)

---

66. Ropes, *Beginnings of Christianity*, 52–53.
67. Wachtel, "Text-Critical Commentary," 11.
68. Wachtel, "Text-Critical Commentary," 11; see Metzger, *Textual Commentary*, 290.

and is joined by 3/8 best ECM MSS (i.e., 1175 1739 2200), 5/9 core PWR MSS (i.e., 614 1292 1611 2138 2412), and (05) 08 35* etc., including seventeen Westerns plus d sy^p sy^h (sa mae Ä). 614 is the PWR. NA28 is joined by 4/8 best ECM MSS (i.e., P74f 01 02 03) and just (P45) (629*) plus Chrys^{pt} (bo) (Chrys^{pt} Vg p w). Byz is joined by 025 1 18 33 35C 2147 etc. MS 014 is joined by 049 0142 1505 etc. plus (sa mae). The PWR has better translation support than the Byz. Internally, the PWR is also favored over the Byz since τι was added later as confirmed by its absence from 7/8 best ECM MSS and the key Byz MS 35*. It was likely harmonized with NT usage (see John 6:7; Heb 2:7, 9). Lucan style favors its absence (see Luke 22:58; Acts 27:28). Internally, the PWR is also stronger than NA28. If ἀνθρώπους was original, why change it to ἀποστόλους?[69] Conversely, if ἀποστόλους was original, scribes might be inclined to "correct" it because Gamaliel would not have referred to them in this manner as seems to be implied. However, Luke did not say that Gamaliel called them apostles. On the other hand, NA28 could be attributed to a harmony with Gamiliel's own words (see 5:35, 38). There are ten alternatives in the ECM, and ἀνθρώπους occurs in only six ECM MSS. In summary, the PWR is probably original and the Byz later added τι.

36. (BTO) (β-INS) (5:37/28) (3ways) 614 reads ἱκανὸν λαὸν (vs. λαὸν ἱκανὸν, Byz, vs. λαὸν, NA28, vs. λαὸν πολὺν, 05) and is found in 5/10 core PWR MSS (i.e., 614 1292 1611 2138 2412) and 08 33 etc., including nine Westerns plus Chrys Eus^{mss} e h^v w. MS 614 is the PWR and it has smoothed the Byz word order. NA28 is joined by 5/9 best ECM MSS (i.e., P74 01 02* 03 1175) and 88 915 1241 1642 plus Cyr Eus^T Vg d 189 sa^{mss} bo. It has a solid Alex core and a respectable group of translations. Yet its reading is best explained as an accidental eye skip. The Byz is joined by 2/9 best ECM MSS (i.e., 1739 2200) and indirectly by 3/9 best ECM MSS (i.e., MS 33 listed above, 04* listed below, and 02 corrected). It is also found in 014 025 049 383 1505 2147 etc., including eleven Westerns plus (sy^p sy^h gig p). 05 is joined by (04*) 04C3 Apoll Eus^{ms} G (sa^{mss} mae Ä) and matches the

---

69. See Metzger, *Textual Commentary*, 291, who suggests that scribes wanted to give the twelve apostles more honor. More likely, Luke wrote it thus because of his preference as can be noted in the same chapter at 5:2, 12, 18, 29, and 40. In fact, Boismard and Lamouille, *Texte occidental reconstitution*, 2:39, 271, state that ἀποστόλους is Lucan style.

Byz word order but has replaced ἱκανόν with a synonym. In total, 23/24 Westerns and most translations (i.e., e gig p h^vid w sy^p sy^h sa^mss mae Ä G) agree with the Byz in retaining a modifier for λαόν. While scribes may have added ἱκανόν to fill a perceived void, it is more likely that Luke met the need himself as he did in 5:36. It is also more consistent with his style as noted below. Wachtel considers the word order changes as a sign the text was expanded while observing that λαός stands in Acts without a modifying article/adjective only 3/48 times.[70] But the PWR editor often makes word order changes where there is no addition. BL indicate that using ἱκανόν as a number is strongly Lucan with 21/24 NT examples found in Luke-Acts.[71] Metzger considers ἱκανόν to be a scribal gloss.[72] The overall external evidence combined with the Lucan style point to the probable originality of the Byz.

37. (ATO) (α-INS) (5:38/42) NA28/614 has ἡ βουλὴ αὕτη (vs. ἡ βουλή, Byz) and is found in 7/9 core PWR MSS, 9/9 best ECM MSS, and 05 08 056 etc., including 24/26 Westerns plus Chrys Or Vg d e gig p w 189 sy^p sy^h Ä. 614 is the PWR. Byz is joined by 014 025 035 383 1505 etc. By including αὕτη, NA28 provides more balance with the following ἢ τὸ ἔργον τοῦτο and is the easier reading. The Byz might be a result of an eye skip. The core Alex MSS, Westerns, and translations confirm that NA28 is original even though it is smoother (cf. 5:37/28; 5:40/31).

38. (BTO) (α-NTR) (5:40/31) Byz/614 reads ἀπέλυσαν αὐτούς (vs. ἀπέλυσαν, NA28) and is found in 9/9 core PWR MSS, 3/9 best ECM MSS (i.e., 33 1739 2200), and 05 08 181 etc., including 24/24 Westerns plus Bas Chrys Vg d e p w 189 sy^p sy^h. 614 is the PWR. NA28 is joined by 6/9 best ECM MSS (i.e., P74 01 02 03 04 1175) and 228 996 1409* 1729 plus *no* translations. The Byz/PWR has a pronoun where it is expected, making it easier. Its absence is very awkward and most likely arose when it was dropped accidentally in a key proto-Alex archetype and the error persisted. Perhaps its scribe read ἀπέλυσαν as if it were the passive ἀπελύθησαν (see 15:33). The addition of αὐτούς earlier in the verse, in several witnesses (e.g., 02 08 d e 189 sy^p sy^h), was evidently from attempts to correct NA28. In the

---

70. Wachtel, "Text-Critical Commentary," 12.
71. Boismard and Lamouille, *Texte occidental reconstitution*, 2:40, 238.
72. Metzger, *Textual Commentary*, 292.

NT, ἀπολύω occurs sixty-six times with fourteen of those in Luke and 15 in Acts. According to *TLG*, ἀπολύω can be used intransitively (i.e., "they departed"). Luke does so once in the active voice in the command to forgive at Luke 6:37. When he does so in the middle voice at Acts 28:25, the antecedent is obvious. Here the grammatical antecedent could be either the members of the Sanhedrin or the apostles. Otherwise, Luke aligns the intransitive with the passive voice (see Luke 13:12; Acts 4:23; 15:30, 33; 16:36; 26:32). Moreover, he sometimes has a form of ἀπολύω without a following pronoun. But in every case there exists an antecedent pronoun as its referent (see Luke 14:4; 23:16, 22; Acts 13:3; 28:18). Thus, given Luke's precision and style, the active ἀπέλυσαν should have a pronoun following it or an antecedent pronoun, i.e., "they released them." NA28 has neither. The abundant attestation for the Byz/PWR confirms that it is original even though easier (cf. 5:37/28; 5:38/42).[73]

39. (ATO) (a-SI) (#5:41/22–28) (3ways) 614 has ὑπὲρ τοῦ ὀνόματος <u>τοῦ κυρίου Ἰησοῦ</u> κατηξιώθησαν (vs. κατηξιώθησαν ὑπὲρ τοῦ ὀνόματος, NA28, vs. ὑπὲρ τοῦ ὀνόματος <u>τοῦ Ἰησοῦ</u> κατηξιώθησαν, RP05[txt], vs. ὑπὲρ τοῦ ὀνόματος κατηξιώθησαν, 05) and is found in 6/9 core PWR MSS, the Western relatives 08 431 1884, and five others plus e. MS 614 is the PWR. There are fifteen alternatives but two different word orders depending upon whether κατηξιώθησαν is placed at the start or at the end (MSS italicized below) of the phrase. NA28 is joined by P74 01 02 03 04 *05 014 025 049** etc. plus *d* AmAl[vid] Chrys[pt] *Chrys*[T] Did Or[T] Ä and the translations (sa bo mae). Several of the oldest Byz MSS (e.g., *014 025 049**) also preserve the words of the NA28 reading. It is the most difficult alternative and presents the most profound meaning. Furthermore, it best explains the creation of the others by scribes who sought to clarify. The disciples were rejoicing "because they were counted worthy to suffer for the Name." Luke provides the testimony of the disciples, and it reveals their conviction about the full deity of the Jesus Christ by equating the name of Jesus (5:40) with the OT name for God, namely Yahweh (see Exod 3:13–16; 6:2–3; Isa 45:20–23; John 8:58; Phil 2:10–11). Five key Alex MSS, three key Byz MSS, one key Western, and the Coptic translations manifest great fidelity in retaining the hardest reading (though not all have the same word order). NA28 has the better

---

73. Von Soden, *Schriften des Neuen Testaments*, 2:510, agrees.

evidence for the word order and is the original text. This variant is instructive. It shows how splintered the NT MS tradition can be and yet how key MSS, early translations, and ancient fathers can confirm the original.

40. (BTO) (α-INS) (6:3/4) Byz/614 reads ἐπισκέψασθε <u>οὖν</u> ἀδελφοί (vs. ἐπισκέψασθε <u>δέ</u> ἀδελφοί, NA28, vs. <u>τί οὖν ἐστιν</u> ἀδελφοί ἐπισκέψασθε, 05) and is joined by 9/9 core PWR MSS and 4/9 best ECM MSS (i.e., 04 33 1739 2200) etc., including 22/23 Westerns plus Chrys^pt Dam MarcEr OrLat Phot sy^p sy^h (Vg d e gig p h t 70 189). 614 is the PWR. NA28 is joined by 2/9 best ECM MSS (i.e., 01 03) and only 1642 w. As to the remaining 3/9 best ECM MSS, P74 omits the conjunction, 02 has δή, and 1175 conflates to form δὲ οὖν. Barrett favors P74.[74] Metzger asserts that the scribes revised from δέ.[75] Yet the confusion is mainly in Alexandria. Perhaps the corruption to δέ caused most of the readings. MS 05 is joined by d p h^vid mae and is probably the WRR. Its adjustment to a question seems influenced by 1 Cor 14:26. It supports the Byz/PWR indirectly by including οὖν. The Byz/PWR fits the context very well. NA28 lacks variety and plurality and evidently assimilated δέ by accident because of the common pattern at the start of the surrounding verses (see 6:1, 2, 4). Dominant external evidence confirms that the Byz/PWR is original.

41. (BTO) (α-NTR) (7:7/18–22) Byz/614 reads <u>εἶπεν</u> ὁ θεός (vs. ὁ θεὸς <u>εἶπεν</u>, NA28) and is found in 10/10 core PWR MSS, 3/9 best ECM MSS (i.e., 33 1739 2200), and 05 08 044 181 etc., including 24/24 Westerns plus Chrys IrLat sy^p sy^h. 614 is the PWR. NA28 is joined by 6/9 best ECM MSS (i.e., P74 01 02 03 04 1175) and only P33^vid. While the Byz/PWR is more natural, there is nothing problematic about it that should have inspired the remaining ECM MSS to reorder it. It is much more likely that a primitive Alex MS accidentally moved εἶπεν to the end or else purposeful fronted ὁ θεός for emphasis. The NA28 word order is unique. In the NT, the Byz order occurs at Acts 22:14 (though the syntax is different) and 2 Cor 6:16. The latter use shows Paul's familiarity with this word order. The phrase seems to come from Stephen's fluency with the LXX. The Byz order occurs thirty-four times in the LXX and twenty-four are in Genesis/Exodus. Notice how Stephen quotes here from Gen 15:13–14 and

---

74. Barrett, *Commentary on Acts*, 1:312.
75. Metzger, *Textual Commentary*, 295.

alludes to Exod 3:12. The subject phrase itself occurs nearby in the famous verses of Exod 3:14–15 where God describes his name. In contrast, the NA28 wording occurs only at 1 Chr 28:3 and 2 Chr 35:21. Therefore, the Byz wording is almost certainly right. The isolated agreement of most core Alex MSS on such a minor detail points to a common archetype. Byz/PWR is original as confirmed by perfect Western coherence, LXX style, and IrLat.

42. (BTO) (β-INS) (7:18/12–14) Byz/614 omits (vs. ἐπ' Αἴγυπτον, NA28, vs. ἐν Αἰγύπτῳ, 180) and is found in 9/10 core PWR MSS, 3/10 best ECM MSS (i.e., 33 81 2200), and 05 08 431 etc., including fourteen Westerns plus Chrys d e gig p sy[h.txt]. 614 is the PWR. NA28 is joined by 7/10 best ECMS MSS and forty-one others, including ten Westerns plus A G (sa bo mae fay sy[p] Ä). It is clearly a popular reading. MS 180 is joined by 1751 Vg w 189 sy[hmg] (Ä). ECM marks it as a SGL.[76] NA28 is joined by a solid list of translations especially when the indirect support is added from MS 180. Yet longer readings commonly need to justify themselves against the possibility of being a gloss. Here the task is very difficult given that the citation is from Exod 1:8 (LXX) and ἐπ' Αἴγυπτον fills out Stephen's quotation of it.[77] Moreover, there is no easy reason for an eye skip. Metzger acknowledges the problem but considers scribal deletion of superfluous words as equally probable.[78] While possible, the odds are strongly against it. The Byz text rarely shows a purposeful removal of words unless that curtailment contributes to clarity (see 4:25). Yet NA28 is perfectly clear as it is. Moreover, although the PWR archetype is more prolific at stylistic and clarifying glosses, its omissions are usually subtle. It is true that the PWR lacks Φαραώ in 7:10/32, but this omission was probably an oversight given that it is joined by only three core PWR MSS and 431 sy[h]. More to the point, when the NT cites the LXX, the PWR tends to add the "missing" words from the LXX (see 7:37/40; 7:43/49). The gloss at 7:37 helps to clarify the situation here. The allure of harmony was great. Notice how many translations expanded 7:37 from the LXX: d e gig p *w* 61

---

76. See Wachtel, "Text-Critical Commentary," 12.

77. Barrett, *Commentary on Acts*, 1:352, states that the "Western text" may be original here because it avoids harmony.

78. Metzger, *Textual Commentary*, 302–3.

*bo mae sy*ᵖ syʰ·ᵗˣᵗ *sy*ʰᵐᵍ. The italicized ones also include the addition here. The Byz/PWR is probably original.

43. (BTO) (β-NTR) (7:19/24–30) Byz/614 reads ἔκθεντα <u>τὰ βρέφη αὐτῶν</u> (vs. <u>τὰ βρέφη</u> ἔκθεντα αὐτῶν, NA28, <u>τὰ βρέφη</u> αὐτῶν ἔκθεντα, 81) and is found in 10/10 core PWR MSS and (P45) 05 08 044 181 etc., including 24/26 Westerns (the other 2/26 still support the word order) etc. plus Chrys. 614 is the PWR. NA28 is joined by 5/10 best ECM MSS (i.e., P74 01 02 03 04) and no others. The NA28 reading is awkward. Two more of the best ECM MSS provide indirect support to NA28 (i.e., MSS 81 1175) since they also start with τὰ βρέφη. Theirs is the smoothest reading. Apparently, like the mainstream, they insisted on not separating βρέφη from its pronoun. P45 provides an early witness for the Byz/PWR. NA28 is isolated and may have resulted from an ancient Alex scribe who overlooked the first word of the Byz/PWR and wrote words two and three. When he noticed his error, he did not erase but instead wrote word one, then four, and continued. Byz/PWR is probably original.[79]

44. (BTO) (α-SI) (7:30/27) Byz/614 has ἄγγελος <u>κυρίου</u> (vs. ἄγγελος, NA28) and is found in 10/10 core PWR MSS, 3/10 best ECM MSS (i.e., 33 1739 2200), and 05 08 181 etc., including 25/25 Westerns plus Ath Chrys d e p w boᵐˢ mae syᵖ syʰ Ä. 614 is the PWR. NA28 is joined by 7/10 best ECM MSS (i.e., P74 01 02 03 04 81 1175) and no others plus Vg gig 189 sa bo. Did the Byz/PWR add κυρίου to cohere with LXX or did the Alex drop κυρίου to align with 7:35 and 7:38?[80] In chapter 7, the Byz has shown little willingness to conform to the LXX (see 7:32/21, 25 below). Given the isolation of these seven MSS, it is almost certain that NA28 reflects a local Alexandrian reading that partly spread into the Latin. For the Byz scribes to be responsible, they would have needed to harmonize their text with Exod 3:2 while overlooking the fact that doing so would create disharmony with the near context (see 7:35, 38). That scenario is unlikely especially given that 7:35 alludes to the same appearance of God at the burning bush. The Alex reading predictably became part of the sa and bo traditions. Most likely, it also spread from Egypt into early Latin MSS (see Vg gig 189). Perhaps a proto-Alex editor

---

79. Von Soden, *Schriften des Neuen Testaments*, 2:515, also selected the Byz.

80. Metzger, *Textual Commentary*, 304, says that the Byz added. See Barrett, *Commentary on Acts*, 1:332.

removed κυρίου in order to clarify that all three verses speak of the same person, the "messenger" who is also God, and the one upon whom Moses was afraid to gaze (Exod 3:1–6). The Byz/PWR has the best translation variety appearing in the ancient Latin, Coptic, Syriac, and Ethiopic. It also has the best Greek MS variety. If it will be allowed that these seven best ECM MSS are secondary here (or if not here, at least in other places where they stand with little or no other Greek support), they should not be judged as fully independent witnesses. When their reading is not original, they point to a single archetype just as the ten core PWR MSS often reflect the PWR archetype. Similarly, the alignment of core Byz MSS (e.g., 014 020 025 049 etc.) regularly points to a common source. Byz/PWR is original.[81]

45. (BTO) (α-INS) (#7:32/21, 25) NA28/ECM/614 reads Ἰσαὰκ καὶ Ἰακώβ (vs. ὁ θεὸς Ἰσαὰκ καὶ ὁ θεὸς Ἰακώβ, Byz, vs. θεὸς Ἰσαὰκ καὶ θεὸς Ἰακώβ, 05). Cf. 3:13/8, 12. The tradition is split between the first two readings. 614 is found in 5/10 core PWR MSS (i.e. *614 1611 1890* 2138 2412*), 7/10 best ECM MSS (i.e., P74 01 02 03 04 81 1175), and fifteen others plus w sa sy^p sy^h. MS 614 is the PWR. Byz is joined by 3/10 best ECM MSS (i.e., 33 1739 2200) and 08 431 467 etc., including seventeen Westerns plus Ath Chrys^{pt} (Vg d e gig p 189 sa^{ms} bo mae). Most of the MSS that support NA28/ECM by lacking ὁ θεός here include it at 3:13. The Byz is just the opposite. On the other hand, some like 05 Vg (bo mae) have (ὁ) θεός in both passages. Others like 03/PWR lack ὁ θεός in both locations. If internal Acts harmony was original, the distribution of support is very hard to explain. If both passages had (ὁ) θεός from the start, who would take it away? If neither NT passage had (ὁ) θεός, why would scribes who were zealous to match the LXX change just one location? Moreover, who would harmonize with the LXX and simultaneously insert the definite article contrary to the LXX? In fact, conformity to the LXX is only seen in MS 05. If the ECM is correct in following 03 in both occasions, it is upheld by just 03 044 81 181 321 468 *614 1611 1890 2138 2412* 2718 sa^{mss} sy^p sy^h. MSS 321 and 468 are Byz, 044 and 2718 are predominantly Byz, and 03 81 181 are Alex.[82] Therefore, the italicized PWR MSS tell the story. The PWR evidently found its

---

81. Soden, *Schriften des Neuen Testaments*, 2:516, chose the Byz/PWR.
82. See CBGM.

way into the archetype of 03 and from there into 03 and its relatives: P74 01 02 04 81 1175. The Byz avoids the harmony, preserves ὁ θεός in Stephen's quote where it fits best (contra Peter's allusion in Acts 3:13), and shows Luke's accurate reporting. Notice also how Luke has the plural τῶν πατέρων here vs. τοῦ πατρός of the LXX. It also manifests Luke's stylistic freedom because he included an article before both Isaac and Jacob contra the LXX (see Exod 3:6, 15–16; 4:5). The bulk of the Westerns appear unedited at both places. Here 17/23 Western MSS (exceptions are italicized but not MS 181) join the Byz, and at 3:13 a total of 23/27 MSS (all except: 05 915 1501 2147*) do so. In summary, disharmony between 3:13 and 7:32 is authentic. The Byz is original at both locations.[83]

46. (BTO) (α-SI) (#7:46/22–24) Byz/614 reads τῷ <u>θεῷ</u> (vs. τῷ <u>οἴκῳ</u>, NA28) and has more diversity. It also fits the context better both here and at 2 Sam 7:1–5. Just as most ancient witnesses retain the superior λόγια at 7:38/54, so also most old witnesses preserve τῷ θεῷ here. The minority Alex reading probably arose by an accidental assimilation to οἶκον in the following verse.[84] The Byz/PWR is found in 10/10 core PWR MSS, 7/10 best ECM MSS (i.e., 02 04 33 81 1175 1739 2200), and MSS 01C2 08 etc., including 24/25 Westerns plus AnastS Chrys Vg e gig p h w 189 sy^p sy^h (sa bo mae) Ä A G. NA28 is joined by just P74 01* 03 05 014 049 1595 2344 d sy^ms. Of these eight, only P74 01* 03 2344 are Alex.[85] MS 05 is the sole Western and therefore likely conformed to the Alex.[86] WH reject θεῷ

---

83. In a similar manner at 15:25/10, Wachtel, "Text-Critical Commentary," 22–23, defends the ECM reading by citing the MSS that avoid harmonization with 15:22/24.

84. Contra Metzger, *Textual Commentary*, 518, who cannot imagine a probable cause for scribes to create οἴκῳ if it were not original. He cites Ps 132:5 in the MT (131:5, LXX) as a reason for scribal harmonization. But it is hard to conceive how Stephen would have been anything but crystal clear when recalling a popular fact about David's desire to build a temple for God. Wachtel, "Text-Critical Commentary," 13, suggests that "house" might have been inserted by accident because of its presence as a "leitmotif" of Stephen's discourse. As a minimum, he is confident οἴκῳ entered a few Byz MSS, italicized above, in this manner (i.e., *014 049 1595*).

85. See CBGM.

86. Contra Metzger, *Textual Commentary Greek New Testament*, 308–9, who says MS 05 is the Western reading. He summarizes numerous attempts to either explain τῷ οἴκῳ as original or to offer a conjecture. Yet none are convincing. Barrett, *Commentary on Acts*, 1:372, favors the NA28 reading but cites Preuschen who called οἴκῳ *Unsinn*. Although it could make sense in general, it clearly does not fit in David's original setting or here.

because they thought it would be unlikely for τοῦ θεοῦ and τῷ θεῷ to be found in such close proximity and because scribes would be inclined to change the corrupt οἴκῳ to θεῷ.[87] The first reason seems speculative. The second is worth considering if θεῷ was weakly attested but that is not the case. Therefore, the corruption flowed in the opposite direction. Von Soden favors the Byz and cites Luke 1:33 as a possible source for NA28.[88] Haenchen also favors θεῷ and suggests it was corrupted when an ancient scribe could not read his MS and supplied οἴκῳ "on the analogy of the recurrent οἶκος Ἰακώβ."[89] He apparently refers to its usage in the LXX where it occurs six times in the nominative (see Isa 8:14; 48:1; Jer 2:4; Obad 17, 18; Mic 2:7), six times in the genitive (see Gen 46:27; Ps 113:1; Mic 3:1, 9; Isa 8:17; Ezek 20:5), four times in the dative (see Exod 19:3; 20:22; Amos 3:13; Isa 58:1), and six times in the accusative (Gen 31:33; Amos 7:16; 9:8; Isa 14:1; 29:22; Jer 5:20; data per *BW*). Byz/PWR has overwhelming support. Byz/PWR is original and the SGL should be removed.

47. (BTO) (β-INS) (7:51/8) Byz/614 has τῇ καρδίᾳ (vs. καρδίαις, NA28, vs. καρδίας, 03, vs. ταῖς καρδίαις, 01) and is found in 7/10 core PWR MSS and 08 014 025 35C 81 etc., including fifteen Westerns plus sixteen fathers e gig h p ar 70 189 sy^p. 614 is the PWR. NA28 is joined by 3/9 best ECM MSS (P74 02 04) and just 05 1874 Cyr^T. MS 01 is found in 4/9 best ECM MSS (i.e., 01 1175 1739 2200), 044 35* 181 876, and fifteen others, including nine Westerns plus Chrys^pt Cyr^ms. Either NA28 or 01 may be joined by: Vg d p w sy^h. MS 03 equals NA28 except that it accidentally dropped an iota. MS 01 may have added ταῖς to bring the Alex reading (i.e., NA28) into grammatical balance. In terms of Greek testimony, the Byz/PWR is strongest overall. It includes the unified Byz's, most Westerns, and core Alex MS 81. The fathers, including OrLat, are overwhelmingly in support of Byz/PWR. With respect to internal considerations, if καρδίαις were assumed to be original, could the Byz/PWR clause arise from assimilation to a parallel in either the NT or LXX? Not for the NT because ἀπερίτμητος is a hapax legomenon. In the LXX, it occurs four times alongside a form of καρδία (see Lev 26:41; Jer

---

87. Westcott and Hort, *Introduction*, 92–93.
88. Soden, *Schriften des Neuen Testaments*, 2:518.
89. Haenchen, *Acts a Commentary*, 283.

9:25; Ezek 44:7, 9). Both words are used in the singular at Lev 26:41 and Ezek 44:9. As the Byz does here, it occurs in the plural with the singular of καρδία at Ezek 44:7. However, the Ezekiel passage refers rather to gentiles. As is the case with NA28 here, both words occur in the plural in the LXX of Jer 9:25 (9:26, MT) as part of an exhortation to Israel. Therefore, if an assimilation to a parallel occurred, it would most likely be to Jer 9:25 (LXX) and point to Alex corruption.[90] More realistically, καρδίαις resulted from a proto-Alex editor. By making τῇ καρδίᾳ plural, the four substantives in the first seven words of 7:51 obtain plural agreement. Perhaps the editor's ancient move to the plural did not include the article because of space constraints, i.e., the editor could erase τῇ καρδίᾳ and write in καρδίαις at the same place. Alternatively, ταῖς καρδίαις of 01 might be the primary Alex reading. That would make καρδίαις a stylistic gloss possibly inspired by the WRR, here represented by 05. Among the twenty-three MSS with 01's reading, key support exists for all three traditions (i.e., Alex: 01 1175 1739 etc.; Byz: 35* 103 424C etc.; Western: 876 945 1611 etc.). Therefore, it is quite conceivable that NA28/P74 has shortened 01. This scenario better explains how the Byz/PWR text could lead to the Alexandrian variant readings. The near complete alignment of the fathers with the Byz is perhaps its strongest evidence. It would be reasonable to conclude that 16/18 ancient fathers aligned with a secondary reading if the original was καρδίαις and the fathers preserved the easier ταῖς καρδίαις. As it stands, it is exceedingly difficult to explain the popularity of the singular among the fathers given its mixed characteristics. As compared to NA28, it is equally hard semantically and more difficult grammatically. Byz/PWR is probably original.

48. (BTO) (a-INS) (7:56/14) Byz/614 reads ἀνεῳγμένους (vs. διηνοιγμένους, NA28) and is found in 9/9 core PWR MSS and P74 (05*) 05C1 08 014 025 33 35 etc., including nineteen Westerns plus fifteen fathers. 614 is the PWR. NA28 is joined by 8/10 best ECM MSS and 88 323 424C 630 915 945 1704 1751 1891 L1178, including four Westerns plus Ath^T CyrH^mss. A reading probably arising in the region of Alexandria has apparently strengthened the idea from "were opened" to "were laid open" (*TLG*) or to "were thoroughly

---

90. Ropes, *Beginnings of Christianity*, 72, also cites Jer 9:25 but still prefers NA28.

opened."[91] The compound word might have come from the LXX where it is used thirty-six times (*BW*). There is a similar context of opening the eyes with revelation at Gen 3:5 (see Gen 3:7; 2 Kgs 6:17 (twice); 2 Kgs 6:20). More likely, it was assimilated from the NT where Luke utilizes it six of its seven times (Mark 7:34; Luke 2:23; 24:31, 32, 45; Acts 16:14; 17:3). Both Barrett and BL refer to the compound word as Lucan.[92] In Luke 24:31, the two had their eyes opened to recognize the risen Christ. In Luke 24:32 and 24:45, the disciples had their hearts opened to understand the Scripture. In Acts 16:14, Lydia's heart was opened to hear the gospel. The Byz retains the compound at all the other seven locations. If the original had the διά prefix, why should this descriptive word be changed to the common root ἀνοίγω (NT, seventy-seven times) at this climactic moment in Acts? Moreover, given the differences in orthography, it is unlikely that the NA28 reading that starts with διηνοιγ- accidentally became the Byz/PWR reading that starts with ἀνεῳγ-. The nearly united testimony of the fathers confirms that the Byz/PWR is the unimproved original (cf. 2:36/18–30 where the best two of nine readings have thirteen fathers and ten fathers respectively, 4:25 where the hardest/best reading has the most fathers, 4:27/6–26 where the original reading has seven fathers as compared to the Byz with three, and 20:28/40 where the two best readings have ten fathers and seven fathers respectively).

49. (BTO) (α-NTR) (#7:60/22–28) Byz/614 has αὐτοῖς τὴν ἁμαρτίαν ταύτην (vs. αὐτοῖς ταύτην τὴν ἁμαρτίαν, NA28) and is found in 9/9 core PWR MSS and 7/10 best ECM MSS etc., including 22/24 Westerns plus sixteen fathers and d e G. The fathers include the primitive IrLat[T] and Or. 614 is the PWR. NA28 is joined by just 02 03 04 05 IrLat[mss] PetrAl[T] Vg p h w 70 Ä A. Either Byz/PWR or NA28 may be joined by: sa bo mae sy[h] sy[p]. NA28 is probably an intrusion from the WR, given its isolation and its support from 05 and some Latin. In Lucan style, the NA28 word order might be marked for emphasis as it occurs just 24 out of about 105 places within Acts.[93]

---

91. Gloss was taken from an electronic edition of Thayer's 1885 *Greek-English Lexicon* in *BW*.

92. Barrett, *Commentary on Acts*, 1:384; Boismard and Lamouille, *Texte occidental reconstitution*, 2:53.

93. The NA28 word order at 7:60 occurs at these locations: 1:11; 2:32, 36; 5:31, 36; 7:35; 10:30; 11:27; 14:15; 15:28; 16:12, 17, 20; 19:25, 27; 21:38; 22:4, 22; 23:1, 13, 18;

Of those 24 occasions, the Byz equals NA28 at 21 places and lacks the demonstrative in 2 (see 16:12; 28:28; likely scribal errors). There is only 1 case where the Byz opposes the ECM word order, and that variation also appears accidental (see 15:28). The ECM reading is probably original at 15:28 since it is joined by six core Alex MSS (i.e., 03 04 81 1175 1739 2200) plus fifty-two others, and is equal to the PWR. There is no reason to suspect that the Byz smoothed the word order at 7:60. Byz/PWR is confirmed as original by most of the core Alex's, nearly all Westerns, and almost all fathers.[94]

50. (BTO) (α-INS) (8:5/10) Byz/614 reads πόλιν (vs. τὴν πόλιν, NA28) and is found in 9/9 core PWR MSS and 5/10 best ECM MSS (i.e., 04 33 81 1739 2200) and 05 08 etc., including twenty-three Westerns plus Chrys sa bo mae. 614 is the PWR. NA28 is joined by 5/10 best ECM (i.e., P74 01 02 03 1175) and just 69 181 996 1251 1875 2243 2344 plus Eus. The harder reading is the one not assimilated with the definite article in 8:14/18–20. Thus, the original seems to be "after Philip came down to a city of Samaria." Whether or not the city was called "Samaria" is not stated, nor does 8:14 clarify.[95] Luke records in 8:14 that the apostles heard that ἡ Σαμάρεια had received God's word, a term used to describe the region in 1:8. The Byz/PWR is harder, is supported by nearly all MSS (even half of the best ECM MSS), and is joined by all three Coptic translations. Byz/PWR is original.[96]

51. (ATO) (β-INS) (8:8/2–8) Byz/614(*f) has καὶ ἐγένετο χαρὰ μεγάλη (vs. ἐγένετο δὲ πολλὴ χαρά, NA28, χαρὰ τε μεγάλη ἐγένετο, 05, ἐγένετο δὲ χαρὰ μεγάλη, 1739) and is found in 9/9 core PWR MSS (though 2412f lost a word) and (05) 08 014 025 33 35 431 etc., including sixteen Westerns plus AlMon[vid] Chrys PsEusA (d) e (gig) p sy[h]. 614 is the PWR. NA28 is joined by 7/10 best ECM MSS (i.e., P74 01 02 03 04 81 1175 and just MS 1642 plus no translations or fathers. MS 05 essentially supports the Byz and is joined by d gig.

27:23; 28:20, 28. Stanley Porter kindly brought to my attention that the Byz word order is more common in Acts.

94. Soden, *Schriften des Neuen Testaments*, 2:519, agrees.

95. See Barrett, *Commentary on Acts*, 1:402–3, who agrees that Luke has left it nonspecific. He explains that ancient Samaria, per Josephus, was named Sebaste in NT times. Still, he allows that some may have still referred to it as Samaria. He finds plausible Justin's assertion that the actual city was Gitta, home of Simon Magus.

96. Wachtel, "Text-Critical Commentary," 13–14.

MS 1739 is found in 2/10 best ECM MSS (i.e., 1739 2200) and in twenty-five others, including seven Westerns plus Vg w 189. The reading of 1739 apparently began with NA28 and then replaced πολλὴ χαρὰ with χαρὰ μεγάλη because it better fit Lucan style as seen in Luke 2:10, Luke 24:52, and Acts 15:3. It also appears to magnify the quantity of the joy for emphasis. The Byz/PWR probably started with 1739's wording and then replaced δέ with καί in order to link explicitly the miracles of 8:7 with the joy in 8:8. By doing so, the Byz/PWR broke with Luke's style here where he used δέ as the second word of the clause on twelve occasions from 8:1–12. The word combination of πολύς with χαρά is the harder reading since it never occurs otherwise in Luke. Luke may have chosen to use πολλή in order to avoid overusing μέγας in the immediate context (see 8:1, 2, 7, 9, 10 (twice), 13). Alternatively, he may have decided to link the πολλοί people that were healed with the πολλή joy in the city. The Byz has more Greek MS variety, more translations, and more fathers. Nevertheless, NA28 has avoided the smoothing glosses and is probably original.

52. (BTO) (α-INS) (#8:18/31) Byz/614 reads τὸ πνεῦμα τὸ ἅγιον (vs. τὸ πνεῦμα, NA28) and is found in 9/9 core PWR MSS, 23/23 Westerns, 8/10 best ECM MSS, P45 05 08 etc., and Amph Ath Bas Chrys Dam Phot 9/9 OL bo sy^p sy^h. 614 is the PWR. NA28 is joined by 01 03 ConstAp sa mae. An ancient editor in Alexandria lost τὸ ἅγιον by accident (see chapter 2 discussion). Metzger's suggestion that such domination of support could be explained by a tendency of scribes to add what seems to be lacking is misleading.[97] Moreover, his statement that scribes would not for any reason delete τὸ ἅγιον is not helpful. The simple fact is that scribes made mistakes even at important passages. For example, at 8:15/18 the scribe for MS 1127 accidentally dropped ἅγιον from πνεῦμα ἅγιον. Moreover, scribes did not add words in the vast majority of situations where they would have had opportunity. At 8:29/6–12, the context implies that the Holy Spirit is the referent but the only MSS of the entire ECM to add τὸ ἅγιον to τὸ πνεῦμα are 431 and 1292. At 10:19/23 the Holy Spirit is again in view but the only one to add τὸ ἅγιον is 2147. Finally, at 11:12/4–12 the only ones adding τὸ ἅγιον were MSS 467 and 468. Notice also that the erring MSS were never the same. As

---

97. Metzger, *Textual Commentary*, 314.

53. (PAO) (β-NTR) (#8:21/32–40) (3ways) 614 has ἐνάντιον (vs. ἔναντι, NA28, vs. ἐνώπιον, Byz) and is found in 6/10 core PWR MSS, 6/9 best ECM MSS (i.e., 04 33 81 1175 1739 2200), core Byz MSS 18 35, and thirty others, including thirteen Westerns plus Bas Chrys[pt] Dam. MS 614 is the PWR. It retains the hardest reading and has strong support. Moreover, given that the word is Lucan and rare, it is more likely genuine. Its rarity caused some to replace it with a synonym. It only occurs at five locations (see Luke 1:6; 20:26; 24:19; Acts 7:10; 8:32). 614/PWR is probably original (see chapter 3 discussion).

54. (ATO) (β-INS) (8:32/38–40) NA28/614 reads τοῦ κείραντος (vs. τοῦ κείροντος, Byz) and is found in 10/10 core PWR MSS, 5/10 best ECM MSS (i.e., P74 01 02 04 1175), and P50C* 08 014 020 049 330 etc., including 17 Westerns. 614 is the PWR. ECM shows the variant as a SGL. Byz is joined by 5/10 best ECM MSS (i.e., 03 33 81 1739 2200) and 025 35 522 915 etc., including seven Westerns. The Byz agrees with the LXX at Isa 53:7. MSS 01C and 02 have actually revised their Isa 53:7 LXX reading to match their text in Acts.[99] Both options have nearly the same paternal support. Perhaps Luke did not want to impress the reader with the process, i.e., while a sheep is sheared it remains silent, but rather with the result, i.e., a sheep that has been sheared stands silent. Even after being tortured, Jesus continued silent before his enemies. NA28 does not harmonize and it has variety, being joined by the PWR, most Westerns, and several core Byz MSS. Therefore, NA28 is probably original.[100]

55. (BTO) (α-INS) (8:33/19) Byz/614 has τὴν δὲ γενεὰν (vs. τὴν γενεὰν, NA28) and is found in 10/10 core PWR MSS and 6/10 best ECM MSS etc., including 24/24 Westerns plus Chrys IrLat[T] e gig p t r w l 70 72 (bo). It essentially includes all MSS minus the few behind NA28. 614 is the PWR. NA28 is joined by 01 02 03 04 plus Did Eus GregThaum IrLat[ms] Vg 73 189 sa mae. Evidently, these four closely related Alex MSS harmonized to the LXX. Alternatively, Wachtel

---

98. Soden, *Schriften des Neuen Testaments*, 2:521, came to the same decision.
99. Rahlfs, *Septuaginta*, 639.
100. See Barrett, *Commentary on Acts*, 1:430; Wachtel, "Text-Critical Commentary," 14; Soden, *Schriften des Neuen Testaments*, 2:523.

states that δέ might have been lost by an eye skip due to the following γε-.¹⁰¹ Although the Byz/PWR better matches the HB, a harmonistic change by GNT MSS to the Hebrew would be a rare event indeed. Luke evidently made a slight stylistic improvement to his LXX quotation. Luke's change might conceivably derive from the HB if an expert like Paul suggested it to him. Byz/PWR is original. The unity of the Alex MSS 01 02 03 04 in a primitive error shows their dependence upon at least one common archetype (see 1:6/10; 1:8/24–26; 1:13/8–14; 1:16/45).

56. (ATO) (α-INS) (9:19/14–22) NA28/614 reads μετὰ τῶν ἐν Δαμασκῷ μαθητῶν (vs. ὁ Σαῦλος μετὰ τῶν ἐν Δαμασκῷ μαθητῶν, RP05/M^pt in HF1985, vs. μετὰ τῶν μαθητῶν ὄντων ἐν Δαμασκῷ, 629, vs. ὁ Σαῦλος μετὰ τῶν ὄντων ἐν Δαμασκῷ μαθητῶν, 014/M^pt in HF1985) and is found in 5/10 core PWR MSS (i.e., 614 1292 1611 1890 2412) and (P45) P74 01 02 03 04 08 33 35* 81f1 181 1175^vid etc. plus sa^ms bo^ms Ä (e). 614 is the PWR. There are seventeen readings in the ECM. RP05 is joined by 5 18 35C 2147 etc. MS 629 is joined by (619) (1162) (Chrys) Vg gig p t r w l 72 189 (sa bo mae). 014/M^pt is joined by 020 025 049 0142 1 69 93* 330 424 1241 etc. RP05 does not include any of the core Byz uncials that align with the 014 reading. This cluster around 014 points to a common archetype behind it and thus to a branch within the Byz tradition. RP05 first added ὁ Σαῦλος to the NA28/PWR and later 014 added ὄντων to RP05 under the influence from 629's reading. 629 seems to be the WRR (though 05 is lacuna) as shown by its support from the OL mae and sa. The sa/WRR was then inherited by the bo in contrast to the normal situation where the bo equals the Alex. NA28 has avoided the smoothing and is original. The alignment of the PWR edition with NA28 among seventeen alternatives demonstrates its high quality. When the PWR aligns with either the Alex or Byz traditions, it is very often original. This variant also highlights the sharing of readings that can occur between the Greek archetypes of the Latin translations and the Greek archetypes of the Coptic translations. Therefore, if a competing reading has the support of the bo with the Vg or the sa with the OL, e.g., the agreement of these translations might not be independent testimony. In this case, the unity of the Vg OL sa bo mae probably all arose from the WRR.

---

101. Wachtel, "Text-Critical Commentary," 14.

57. (OTO) (β-SI) (9:25/6–22) MS 69 has οἱ μαθηταὶ <u>αὐτὸν</u> νυκτὸς διὰ τοῦ τείχους καθῆκαν (vs. οἱ μαθηταὶ <u>αὐτὸν</u> νυκτὸς καθῆκαν διὰ τοῦ τείχους, 468, vs. <u>αὐτὸν</u> οἱ μαθηταὶ νυκτὸς καθῆκαν διὰ τοῦ τείχους, RP05/614, vs. <u>αὐτὸν</u> οἱ μαθηταὶ νυκτὸς καθῆκαν <u>αὐτὸν</u> διὰ τοῦ τείχους, 33, vs. οἱ μαθηταὶ <u>αὐτοῦ</u> νυκτὸς διὰ τοῦ τείχους καθῆκαν <u>αὐτὸν</u>, NA28, vs. <u>αὐτὸν</u> οἱ μαθηταὶ νυκτὸς διὰ τοῦ τείχους καθῆκαν <u>αὐτὸν</u>, 1739, vs. <u>αὐτὸν</u> οἱ μαθηταὶ νυκτὸς διὰ τοῦ τείχους καθῆκαν, 08). The ECM lists fifteen alternatives. The complexity of the textual phenomena suggests both a primitive error and primitive editorial work. The error occurred in NA28, and early editing happened in both traditions. Most likely the text as found in RP05/614 and that of NA28 represent the proto-Byzantine and proto-Alexandrian archetypes respectively, as they stood near AD 125 (see figure 3.3 above). In such places of abundant variation, one should suspect unusual textual features in the original that prompted change. Because RP05/614 provide a clear text, it is hard to imagine how they could have caused all the variation. Of all the readings, Byzantine MS 69 appears most likely to be the original. It has complexity and clarity. On the Alexandrian side, it appears that MS 69's reading was corrupted when αὐτόν was miscopied as αὐτοῦ. Though MS 69 is dated to the fifteenth century, MS 614 is also late (i.e., the thirteenth century) and yet preserves exceptionally early readings and sometimes even original ones with limited other support. Similarly, MS 2200 is from the fourteenth century and still is rated tenth out of all ECM MSS. Because MS 69 is Byz, its word order agreements with the Alex MSS would not likely come from them. Those same features make it less smooth than RP05/PWR and unlikely to come from them. The scribes of Alexandria inherited the error of αὐτοῦ but did not judge that to be the problem. Instead, they "fixed" the text by adding αὐτόν as the object for καθῆκαν and the implied object for λαβόντες. NA28 is joined by 6/10 best ECM MSS (i.e., P74 01 02 03 04 81) and just L60 Or[vid] Vg 189. It refers to the followers as Paul's disciples. Metzger and Haenchen consider this meaning an error because it is discordant with the spirit of the NT where all believers are disciples of Jesus Christ alone.[102] While rejecting the Byz, Ropes said regarding Alex reading, "The soundness of our text must remain doubtful unless it can be made to appear natural to describe any Christians

---

102. Metzger, *Textual Commentary*, 321–22; Haenchen, *Acts of the Apostles*, 332.

at Damascus as 'Paul's disciples.'"[103] Barrett has not found any explanation "wholly convincing" and asserts that NA28 could describe "Christians who owed their faith to Paul and stood particularly close to him."[104] The ECM prints the NA28 reading without comment and evidently found it acceptable.[105] From the NA28 reading spun off others. Having found αὐτοῦ problematic, MS 1739, joined by five others, removed and replaced it with αὐτόν at the start. MS 1175, joined by p l, began with NA28 and merely added αὐτόν at the first. MS 2200, joined by nine others plus w, began with NA28 and simply removed αὐτοῦ. The typical textual faithfulness of the best ECM MSS suggests the original word order is probably not far from that of the core Alex MSS (cf. 27:23/14–28). Thus, 3/10 best ECM MSS (i.e., 1739 1175 2200) each used different strategies to "fix" NA28. On the other hand, the ancient Byz tradition proceeded on a different path. One proto-Byz scribe of the earliest period sought to "improve" MS 69's word order by moving καθῆκαν forward in order to follow νυκτός. According to *TLG*, the genitive νυκτός often means "by night" yielding the sensible meaning, "by night through the wall." However, the collocation of νυκτὸς and διὰ τοῦ τείχους in MS 69 may have seemed abrupt because it effectively offers adjacent prepositional phrases. This reading is preserved by just Byz MS 468 and three others. Another proto-Byz scribe made the same change as preserved in MS 468 but also moved αὐτόν from its third position in MS 69 to the initial position of the entire reading. It was natural to move αὐτόν forward to bring it closer to its antecedent λαβόντες. These two simultaneous changes became the RP05/614 reading. It is found in 10/10 core PWR MSS and 044 431 etc., including twelve Westerns plus Chrys gig. 614 is the PWR. A third scribe began with MS 69 and only moved αὐτόν from the third position to the first position (see MS 08 and four others). In a second generation of changes, MS 33, with nineteen others and sy[h], started with RP05/PWR and then added another αὐτόν for clarity. In conclusion, due to primitive error in the Alex tradition and a nonstandard word order, all ECM MSS deviated except one. In the end, the Byz/PWR differs from MS 69 only in word order. Though Metzger asserts that NA28 preserves the "oldest reading extant in the manuscripts,"

103. Ropes, *Beginnings of Christianity*, 89.
104. Barrett, *Commentary on Acts*, 1:466–67.
105. The same goes for Soden, *Schriften des Neuen Testaments*, 2:526.

MS 69 appears to be older. It best explains the other readings and is possibly original.[106] The primitive error in 6/10 best ECM MSS shows their dependence on a common archetype subsequent to the original text (see 1:16/45).

58. (ATO) (α-SI) (9:38/30–34) NA28/614 reads ἀπέστειλαν <u>δύο ἄνδρας</u> (vs. ἀπέστειλαν, Byz) and is found in 6/10 core PWR MSS, 9/9 best ECM MSS, third-century P45 and P53[vid], and many others, including 19/24 Westerns plus Bas Chrys Did[vid] Vg e gig p t r w l 70 189 (sa bo mae fay). 614 is the PWR. Byz is joined by 014 020 35 etc., including 4/10 core PWR MSS plus 0 translations. NA28 is clearly original. It has a perfect core, is dominant in the translations, and is joined by both the PWR and the Westerns overall. Metzger prefers the inclusion of "two men" because it is consistent with customs of that time and location and because the number might have been deleted due to textual questions at the 10:19.[107] Neither argument is strong. The ECM is a great advance for such variants because it lays out the evidence. Moreover, the Western alignment with NA28 provides it with even more confirmation.[108]

59. (OTO) (β-SI) (10:11/14–30) MS 1739 reads καταβαῖνον σκεῦός τι ὡς ὀθόνην μεγάλην τέσσαρσιν ἀρχαῖς <u>δεδεμένον καὶ</u> καθιέμενον (vs. καταβαῖνον σκεῦός τι ὡς ὀθόνην μεγάλην τέσσαρσιν ἀρχαῖς καθιέμενον, NA28, vs. καταβαῖνον <u>ἐπ' αὐτὸν</u> σκεῦός τι ὡς ὀθόνην μεγάλην τέσσαρσιν ἀρχαῖς <u>δεδεμένον καὶ</u> καθιέμενον, Byz/614, vs. τέσσαρσιν ἀρχαῖς <u>δεδεμένον</u> σκεῦός τι ὡς ὀθόνην μεγάλην καταβαῖνον <u>καὶ</u> καθιέμενον, 33) and is joined by 4/10 best ECM MSS (i.e., 04*[vid] 81 1739 2200) and twenty-three others, including six Westerns plus (sa mae sy[p]). ECM lists eighteen alternatives. NA28 is joined by 5/10 best ECM MSS (i.e., P74 01 02 03 1175) and 88f1 181f1 1875(*f2, Cf3) Or bo G (Vg e w 189 sy[p]). Byz/614 is found in 6/10 core PWR MSS, including eight Westerns plus Chrys. 614 is the PWR. MS 33 is joined by core PWR MSS 1890 2138 and ten others, including two Westerns plus sy[h.txt] sy[hmg]. NA28 matches the wording of 11:5/24–40 except the change of gender for καθίημι used as a participle. Why

---

106. Metzger, *Textual Commentary*, 321; Bengel, *Gnomon*, 1:16; Epp, "Traditional 'Canons,'" 93–95.

107. Metzger, *Textual Commentary*, 324.

108. See Barrett, *Commentary on Acts*, 1:484, who cannot explain why the Byz has dropped the words but still judges the Byz as secondary because of the ancient MSS that display δύο ἄνδρας.

would there be eighteen different readings if the wording matches 11:5? There are no significant variations at the latter passage. Notice that each of the four readings listed above even agree with showing the accusative neuter καθιέμενον. The textual variation occurred because there was something else different about the original wording in the two passages. The reading that best explains the others is that of 1739. It is the same as NA28 except it has + δεδεμένον καὶ. Byz/PWR and 33 have it also. These words are not a natural gloss. In all, 10/10 core PWR MSS and 20/25 Westerns include them. In addition, twelve of eighteen readings include δεδεμένον. Thus, the words from 1739 were probably lost by harmonization to 11:5. However, they may have been lost by an eye skip from δεδεμένον to καθιέμενον. Byz/PWR is secondary because it has + ἐπ' αὐτὸν that was evidently added by analogy to ἄχρι ἐμοῦ at 11:5. The Byz/PWR agreement in a place with so much variation shows their related ancestry. MS 33 gives 1739 indirect support, differing only in word order. Though it has a gloss, the Byz/PWR combined with the overall Western tradition provided assistance. 1739 is probably the original wording.[109]

60. (ATO) (a-SI) (#10:12/8–28) NA28 reads πάντα τὰ τετράποδα καὶ ἑρπετὰ τῆς γῆς καὶ πετεινὰ τοῦ οὐρανοῦ and is joined by 6/10 best ECM MSS (i.e., P74 01 02 03 81 1175) and just P45[vid] 04C2 2344 Or. Still the fact that it is joined by nearly all translations shows its quality and originality. The agreement of the Byz with 10/10 core PWR MSS in a variant with twenty alternatives powerfully illustrates their common ancestry. Yet the Byz/PWR has harmonized to the parallel at 11:6/14–42. That mistake caused most of the textual problems. The differences retained in the two accounts demonstrate Luke's precise reporting of eyewitness testimony.

61. (ATO) (a-INS) (10:16/14–16) Byz/614 has πάλιν ανελήφθη (vs. εὐθὺς ἀνελήμφθην, NA28, ἀνελήμφθη, P45) and is found in 10/10 core PWR MSS, 3/10 best ECM MSS (i.e., 33[vid] 1739 2200), and (05) 467 etc., including nineteen Westerns plus e (gig p) sy[h.txt] (sa mae). 614 is the PWR. NA28 is joined by 6/10 best ECM MSS (i.e., P74 01 02 03* 04 81) and 03C2 08 1884 2805 plus Vg p/2[vid] w 189 (bo sy[hmg]). P45 is joined by 1175 ConstAp d sa[ms] bo[ms] sy[p] Ä. P45's limited Greek witness and its spelling of the verb with the μ suggest that it has dropped εὐθύς from NA28. It may reflect a scribal omission

---

109. Soden, *Schriften des Neuen Testaments*, 2:529, agrees.

designed to avoid disharmony with 11:10. ECM lists seven alternatives. Although NA28 has limited MSS, they are important ones. It is also joined by important translations. Most likely, the Byz/PWR replaced εὐθύς with πάλιν to agree with 11:10.[110] As is often the case, NA28 is original despite limited Greek support.

62. (BTO) (α-NTR) (10:19/30) Byz/614 reads ζητοῦσίν (vs. ζητοῦντές, NA28) and is found in 10/10 core PWR MSS, 6/10 best ECM MSS, and P45 05 08C etc., including 25/25 Westerns plus Chrys ConstAp CyrH Did Vg d e gig p w l 189. 614 is the PWR. NA28 is joined by the other four best ECM MSS (i.e., P74 01 03 81) and just 1409 1831. The participle may have been a local gloss made to emphasize imperfective aspect, i.e., "Behold, three men <u>are seeking</u> you." If Luke intended this sense, he could have used better Greek such as a present periphrastic, i.e., εἰσιν ζητοῦντές.[111] Alternatively, he could have used the indicative and left it to the reader to discern between the sense of "three men seek you" vs. "three men are seeking you."[112] Metzger favors the participle because he cannot explain why scribes would have changed the finite verb to a participle.[113] Meanwhile, Barrett asserts that the "better Greek" of the Byz makes it "probably secondary."[114] An evaluation of Luke's usage of ἰδού will be helpful. In his writings, Luke writes ἰδού eighty times (Luke: fifty-seven times; Acts: twenty-three times). On just three occasions does Luke use syntax akin to what is seen here (see Luke 5:18; 13:11; 19:2). At each place, the clause begins with the particle ἰδού with the meaning of "behold there was/were," is followed by a present participle that modifies the subject, and it lacks a finite verb. Here the participle explains that the three men are the three men who are seeking Peter. Yet in contrast to here, the Greek MS tradition at the three other locations has steadfastly retained the construction. Therefore, it is unlikely the Byz would have changed it here. Instead, the better question is why did one primitive editor in Alexandria introduce the participle? The answer might be that he was a skilled Hebraist and thus accidentally or intentionally made the alteration. The fact

---

110. See Metzger, *Textual Commentary*, 327.
111. See Wallace, *Greek Grammar*, 648.
112. Black, *Learn to Read*, 15.
113. Metzger, *Textual Commentary*, 328.
114. Barrett, *Commentary on Acts*, 1:511.

that the Holy Spirit probably spoke the original words to Peter in Aramaic might have inspired the editor to make a Semitic gloss. According to Wallace, independent verbal participles "can stand alone in a declarative sentence as the only verb in a clause or sentence" and such usage "is quite rare."[115] Moreover Wallace adds, "This usage is apparently due to a Semitic influence, for such occurs in Hebrew and Aramaic."[116] Similarly, the participle might have occurred by imitation to the other three passages by a scribe very familiar with Lucan style. Byz/PWR is original.[117]

63. (BTO) (α-SI) (10:30/25, 26–38) Byz/614 has μέχρι ταύτης τῆς ὥρας ἤμην <u>νηστεύων καὶ</u> τὴν ἐνάτην <u>ὥραν</u> προσευχόμενος ἐν τῷ οἴκῳ μου (vs. μέχρι ταύτης τῆς ὅρας ἤμην τὴν ἐνάτην προσευχόμενος ἐν τῷ οἴκῳ μου, NA28, μέχρι ταύτης τῆς ὥρας ἤμην <u>νηστεύων καὶ</u> τὴν ἐνάτην προσευχόμενος ἐν τῷ οἴκῳ μου, P50C*). There are two variants covered here. The support for the two readings is nearly the same in both places. At the first one, NA28 is joined by 8/10 best ECM MSS (i.e., P74 01 02*vid 03 04 81 1739 2200*) and 323 630 945 1642* 1704 1891 plus Vg p w 189 bo Ä A G. At the second variant, the witnesses are the same except P50 05C1 (05*) 103 2298 d now joins them. These four MSS support the Byz/614 reading at 10:30/25 (05* and 05C are not exact), i.e., + νηστεύων καὶ. The Byz/614 reading is found in 10/10 core PWR MSS and P50C* 02C (05) 08 2200C etc. plus Chrys d e gig t r ar l 70 73 mae sy^p sy^h (sa). 614 is the PWR. In the first reading, NA28 has evidently dropped νηστεύων καὶ by accident. This judgment is probable because the verse appears to be missing something and that something was lost by an eye skip. The scribe of an important proto-Alex archetype wrote ἤμην and may have jumped over the next two words because words three and four, i.e., τὴν ἐνάτην, had similar endings that attracted his eyes. A scribe of ca AD 400 can be seen in the midst of the same mistake by considering P50C*. The ECM symbol C* indicates that the original scribe of P50 noticed his own error and corrected it. In this case, the scribe actually wrote ἤμην <u>τ</u> as if he was about to write ἤμην τὴν (NA28). He then changed the <u>τ</u> to a <u>ν</u> and wrote <u>νηστεύων καὶ</u>. Arguably the same situation caused NA28 reading. The later corrector

---

115. Wallace, *Greek Grammar*, 650, 653.
116. Wallace, *Greek Grammar*, 653.
117. Soden, *Schriften des Neuen Testaments*, 2:530, agrees.

of 02*vid recognized the short reading as an error and fixed it. In the second variant, Byz/614 has inserted the gloss ὥραν to make ἐνάτην explicit, i.e., ἐνάτην ὥραν, and thus balance the earlier ταύτης τῆς ὥρας. Byz/614 is found in 10/10 core PWR MSS and 33^vid 1175 etc. Therefore, the proto-Alex tradition made an oversight in the first variant and the proto-Byz tradition smoothed the second one. In summary, Byz/PWR is original at 10:30/25.[118] According to BL, fasting and prayer are found together only in Luke-Acts.[119] This fact increases the odds of its originality here. Barrett identifies many problems with making sense out of NA28.[120] Restoring the omission appears to resolve the issues. Metzger discusses difficulties with the variant but simply discounts the Byz as the product of scribes who perceived that fasting ought to occur before baptism.[121] Metzger admits that νηστεύων καὶ might have been excised because there is no previous statement about Cornelius fasting.

64. (ATO) (β-SI) (10:32/37) Byz/614 reads + ὃς παραγενόμενος λαλήσει σοι and is found in 10/10 core PWR MSS, 5/10 best ECM MSS (i.e., 04 33^vid 1175 1739 2200), and P127^vid 05 08 etc., including 24/26 Westerns plus Chrys d e gig p* t l 70 73 sa mae sy^Aram sy^p sy^h. 614 is the PWR. NA28 is joined by 5/10 best ECM MSS (i.e., P74 01 02 03 81) and P45 94 307 431 453 610 629 1678 2718 2818 plus Vg p/2 w 189 bo. P45 is very ancient. Byz/PWR might appear to have assimilated the words from a parallel. However, they do not occur earlier or later. But a similar idea is found in 10:22 and 11:14. Metzger argues that the addition is awkward and based on 11:14.[122] Yet even half of the best ECM MSS approved the wording. BL shows that the style ὃς/ὅστις παραγενόμενος + verb is uniquely Lucan. It occurs four times in Acts (see 9:39; 11:23; 17:10; 18:27).[123] Was the longer reading purged as superfluous?[124] Barrett says that the "Western text (with some followers) unnecessarily fills out the

---

118. Bengel, *Novum Testamentum*, 188, agrees and rates NA28 as δ.

119. Boismard and Lamouille, *Texte occidental reconstitution*, 2:74, 226, cite four places (see Luke 2:37; 5:33; Acts 13:3; 14:23).

120. Barrett, *Commentary on Acts*, 1:516–17.

121. Metzger, *Textual Commentary*, 330–31.

122. Metzger, *Textual Commentary*, 331–32.

123. Boismard and Lamouille, *Texte occidental reconstitution*, 2:205, 213.

124. See Metzger, *Textual Commentary*, 13.

narrative."¹²⁵ The words seem to flow very smoothly in their position. Notice how earlier in the verse Luke uses another relative clause introduced by ὅς that also says something about Peter. While it is conceivable that an editor copied Luke's style by taking the words ὃς λαλήσει ῥήματα πρὸς σὲ from 11:14 and παραγενόμενος from 10:33, and distilled them into the Byz/PWR's ὃς παραγενόμενος λαλήσει σοι, the odds are stacked against it. The words appear to be from Luke. But why would several excellent MSS and a few important translations reject them? Here is the second of at least ten strongly supported longer readings where the Byz and PWR traditions (plus sy^h or sy^h** and usually gig) stand against the Alex. As Wachtel has observed (see 15:24/30–34; 18:21/9; 24:6/20–8/14; 28:29/2–24), such readings have too much Byz support to be classified simply as Western.¹²⁶ To these five should be added 2:30/34, 20:24/27, 21:25/16–20, 23:30/45, and 28:16/12–16. These are readings at the base of the Byz and PWR traditions. If this study is right to place the proto-Byz text before the PWR archetype, these readings should be titled proto-Byzantine. All ten are strongly supported by "Western" MSS and numerous ancient translations. Moreover, none conflict with Lucan perspective. If there was ever a good time to speak of two editions by Luke, these readings make a case for it. However, the limited number of readings and their consistent clarifying nature indicate that Luke probably did not publish two editions. The most likely explanation is that Luke had penned the longer portions himself but later excised them before his edition became final. They provided nothing essential to the narrative. Their presence today may be the result of a devout friend or successor of Luke who had access to Luke's editorial copy and later decided to reintroduce these readings. Their high quality could not but gain preference among many scribes. However, the persistent original reading was never completely overturned. In summary, Byz/PWR appears to be Lucan but secondary to the final text of Luke. NA28 is probably original. The quality of these ten readings makes it possible that any one of them might be original after all, and NA28 the revised and trimmed text.¹²⁷

---

125. Barrett, *Commentary on Acts*, 1:518.
126. Wachtel, "Against the Text-Type Concept," 143, 146–47.
127. See Boismard and Lamouille, *Texte occidental reconstitution*, 1:8–10.

65. (BTO) (α-INS) (11:11/24) Byz/614 has ἤμην (vs. ἦμεν, NA28) and is found in 10/10 core PWR MSS, 5/9 best ECM MSS (i.e., 33 81 1175 1739 2200), and P45 08 307 etc., including 22/25 Westerns plus Chrys Vg e gig p w l 189 sa bo mae sy^p sy^h Ä. 614 is the PWR. NA28 is joined by 4/9 best ECM MSS (i.e., P74 01 02 03) and 05 025 *1* 61 181 *468 607 876 996* 1003 1162 1490 *1563* 1842 1875 2243 2374 2652 ar. Only an itacism separates the two. Both the singular and plural fit fine but the singular is more natural. Peter reports first what happened to him and then, starting from 11:12, he incorporates his Jewish co-witnesses. The fact that 9/22 MSS (italicized) that join NA28 are Byz, points to itacism as the cause of NA28.[128] In summary, most of the best ECM MSS, the ancient P45, all Coptic translations, and most Westerns favor the Byz. Even the Vg and Ä that commonly agree with P74 01 02 03, depart them here. Byz/PWR is original.[129]

66. (BTO) (α-INS) (11:23/12–14) NA28 reads χάριν <u>τὴν</u> (vs. χάριν, Byz/PWR) and is joined by just 01 02 03 665. All others equal the Byz/PWR except 1874 that reads δόξαν. The article creates the unique NT wording of τὴν χάριν τὴν τοῦ θεοῦ. The Byz wording is found six other times in the NT (see 1 Cor 3:10; 2 Cor 6:1; 8:1, Gal 2:21; Col 1:6; 2 Thess 1:12). The unity of 01 02 03 very often speaks to a common archetype and probably does so here. Wachtel asserts, "It is more likely that the article was dropped than added after a similar sounding ending."[130] That is true as far as accidents go, but the article might have another cause. For example, an editor might have wanted to describe grace as the grace that comes from God alone.[131] On the other hand, the article might have been removed as superfluous.[132] If NA28 is original, it is hard to imagine what could have motivated most ancient scribes to reject τήν. Bengel gives advice to refuse readings that "allure by too great facility" and to receive those with a "native dignity of truth."[133] In conclusion, the

---

128. ECM 3:2, 8.
129. See Metzger, *Textual Commentary*, 339, who says the Byz harmonized with 11:5.
130. Wachtel, "Text-Critical Commentary," 18.
131. See Metzger, *Textual Commentary*, 343.
132. See Metzger, *Textual Commentary*, 343.
133. Bengel, *Gnomon*, 1:16.

Byz/PWR is probably original as evidenced by its dominant support and unedited nature.

67. (BTO) (β-INS) (11:26/16–24) N28/614 reads ἐγένετο δὲ <u>αὐτοῖς</u> <u>καὶ</u> ἐνιαυτὸν ὅλον συναχθῆναι <u>ἐν</u> τῇ ἐκκλησίᾳ (vs. same as NA28 minus <u>καὶ</u>, MS 81, vs. ἐγένετο δὲ <u>αὐτοὺς</u> ἐνιαυτὸν ὅλον συναχθῆναι τῇ ἐκκλησίᾳ, Byz) and is found in 5/10 core PWR MSS (i.e., 614 1611 1890 2138 2412), 5/9 best ECM MSS (i.e., P74f 01 02 03 33^{vid}), and 61 876 1642* 2344 sy^h. 614 is the PWR. MS 81 is found in 3/9 best ECM MSS (i.e., 81, 1175 1739) and 30 others, including nine Westerns plus d. Byz is found in 4/10 core PWR MSS (i.e., 383 1505 2147 2495) and 945 2200 etc., including seven Westerns plus Chrys. The WRR (not shown above) is approximated by (05) (05C1) 05C2 d p* mae sy^{hmg} and is terribly confused at 11:26. The problems in the passage evidently began when the proto-Byz text with αὐτοὺς was changed by itacism to αὐτοῖς, probably in the earliest period, and became part of the Alex tradition (see MS 81). Next, either the proto-Alex or the PWR tradition was responsible for inserting καί to smooth the now awkward text. The revised reading became established in both traditions. Perhaps they read it as, "Now <u>he</u> <u>was</u> with them <u>and</u> <u>he</u> assembled a whole year with the church." By reading ἐγένετο as "he was" instead of "it happened," the reference to Paul might have served as the subject for the following commentary. However, Luke's style suggests that the accusative pronoun has been lost from NA28/PWR. As BL have shown, whenever Luke has ἐγένετο plus an infinitive, he always displays an accusative subject.[134] Barrett is justly doubtful about the NA28 wording and states, "It can hardly be maintained that the Western text is original, but it may stand at least as near the original as the Old Uncial does."[135] By Western text, he means 05 et al. and by Old Uncial he means NA28. Barrett translates, "It now happened that they met in the church for as much as a whole year."[136] He reads NA28's αὐτοῖς as if it were the Byz αὐτούς. In contrast to the above changes, the Byz remained steady. It reads, "Now it happened that they assembled a whole year

---

134. Boismard and Lamouille, *Texte occidental reconstitution*, 2:235, lists twenty-two examples with twenty-one being in Luke-Acts: Luke 6:1, 6, 12; 16:22; Acts 4:5; 9:3, 32, 37, 43; 10:25; 11:26; 14:1; 16:16; 19:1; 21:1, 5; 22:6, 17; 27:44; 28:8, 17 (see Mark 2:23).

135. Barrett, *Commentary on Acts*, 1:555.

136. Barrett, *Commentary on Acts*, 1:544.

with the church." The WRR evidently started with the NA28 reading and set out to correct it. Its witnesses all removed αὐτοῖς and replaced it with a subject, e.g., οἵτινες παραγενόμενοι. Then recognizing the nominative subject does not properly fit with the infinitive, some WRR witnesses (i.e., 05* 05C1 sy^hmg) changed συναχθῆναι into a 3P finite verb. In summary, the Byz avoids the primitive corruptions at 11:26/16–24 and is probably original.[137]

68. (BTO) (α-NTR) (12:15/34–36) Byz/614 has αὐτοῦ ἐστιν (vs. ἐστιν αὐτοῦ, NA28) and is found in 10/10 core PWR MSS, 5/9 best ECM MSS (i.e., 33 81 1175 1739 2200), 26/26 Westerns, and 01C2 014 020 35 etc. plus Chrys CosmIn Did Eus Or SevGab ThdMop Thdrt. 614 is the PWR. NA28 is joined by P45^vid P74 01* 02 03. Even one of its mere five witnesses corrected itself. NA28 might be a touch harder because the pronoun is separated from the noun. However, the interchange was an easy mistake to do, and the isolation of a few Alex witnesses suggests that is exactly what happened. Byz/PWR is original.

69. (BTO) (α-NTR) (13:10/38) Byz/614 reads κυρίου (vs. τοῦ κυρίου, NA28) and is found in 9/10 core PWR MSS and includes all ECM MSS minus 01* 03 383 2652 Chrys. 614 is the PWR. The ECM lists the variant as a SGL.[138] Evidently, the famous pair 01* 03 and two Western friendly MSS inserted the article for stylistic purposes. Perhaps because the surrounding syntax had an arthrous noun on either side, i.e., τὰς ὁδοὺς τοῦ κυρίου τὰς εὐθείας, some scribes thought κυρίου should have an article also. The Byz/PWR records the Lord without the article in accordance with common LXX usage (e.g., only 269/2,566 examples of κυρίου are articular in the LXX; BW data). For example, in Genesis, κυρίου is used fifty-five times. Of those, twenty-one have the article but all refer to human authority. The other thirty-four refer to God without the article. Interestingly, in 13:11, all three traditions align in showing κυρίου without an article. Then, in 13:12, they agree in preserving κυρίου with an article. This fact strongly suggests that nearly all scribes simply copied the text before them. Byz/PWR is original.

---

137. There is also a second variant here (see 11:26/26–30). NA28/PWR includes ἐν and is the original. The Byz has accidentally dropped the preposition.

138. Wachtel, "Text-Critical Commentary," 19.

70. (BTO) (β-SI) (#13:20/2–16) (3ways) 614 reads ἔτεσιν τετρακοσίοις καὶ πεντήκοντα <u>καὶ</u> (vs. ὡς ἔτεσιν τετρακοσίοις καὶ πεντήκοντα <u>καὶ</u>, 1611, vs. ὡς ἔτεσιν τετρακοσίοις καὶ πεντήκοντα <u>καὶ μετὰ ταῦτα</u>, NA28, vs. <u>καὶ μετὰ ταῦτα</u> ὡς ἔτεσιν τετρακοσίοις καὶ πεντήκοντα, Byz). As discussed in chapter 3, MS 614 has a later mistake and thus 1611 should be considered the PWR. The best two readings are NA28 and the Byz, with the only difference being the placement of καὶ μετὰ ταῦτα. NA28 is joined by 8/10 best ECM MSS and eighteen others plus CosmIn Vg p w 189 A G (bo mae). Its translation evidence is strong but not necessarily independent since the Vg A G may have derived from Alexandria. Byz is joined by 05C2 08 044 etc. and AnastS Chrys e A[mss]. Though its direct translation attestation is sparse, it gains significant indirect support as shown below. Other than <u>αὐτοῖς</u>, preserved only in the Byz/PWR, and <u>τοῦ</u>, marked as a SGL in the ECM, the three traditions have the same preceding words, καὶ καθελὼν ἔθνη ἑπτὰ ἐν γῇ Χανάαν κατεκληρονόμησεν <u>αὐτοῖς</u> τὴν γῆν αὐτῶν, and the same following words, ἔδωκεν κριτὰς ἕως Σαμουὴλ <u>τοῦ</u> προφήτου. TLG offers the gloss to "assign as a possession" for κατακληρονομέω. Altogether, NA28 reads, "And having destroyed seven nations in the land of Canaan, he assigned their land as a possession for about 450 years. Then after this he gave judges until Samuel the prophet." Because of its ambiguity, it has been smoothed as, "When He had destroyed seven nations in the land of Canaan, He distributed their land as an inheritance—*all of which took* about four hundred and fifty years. After these things He gave *them* judges until Samuel the prophet."[139] Barrett admits that if the NA28 wording "is taken (following the most obvious sense of the Old Uncial reading) to refer to the time between the Exodus and the settlement in Canaan," the resultant meaning "is manifestly absurd."[140] Yet he does not favor the Byz reading. Instead, he prefers NA28, and the meaning manifested by the NASB. He agrees with Metzger who believed that the 450 years should be rendered from God's promise to Abraham until the division of the land.[141] On the other hand, the Byz has, "And having destroyed 7 nations in the land of Canaan, he assigned their land

---

139. Translation from the New American Standard Bible (NASB); emphasis added.

140. Barrett, *Commentary on Acts*, 1:634.

141. Barrett, *Commentary on Acts*, 1:633–34; see Metzger, *Textual Commentary*, 358–59.

as a possession. And after this he gave them judges for about 450 years until Samuel the prophet." The meaning is clear and unambiguous. Does its clarity require it to be secondary? Barrett believes that scholars like Lake and Cadbury have shown that the time of the Judges to include Eli was indeed 450 years.[142] However, he partly discounts it, saying that it would not be valid for the LXX because it shows Eli as judging only twenty years. Given that the speaker is Paul, the once renowned rabbi, this LXX variant does not seem applicable. In contrast to the Byz, the PWR is less than clear because its lacks μετὰ ταῦτα. Based on a modified NASB, it could be translated, "He distributed their land as an inheritance—*all of which took* about 450 years. And He gave *them* judges until Samuel the prophet." Conversely, it could say, "He distributed their land as an inheritance. For about 450 years, He also gave *them* judges until Samuel the prophet." By understanding καί at the end as "also," it contrasts the 450 years with the 40 years of the Exodus (see 13:18). Interestingly, the testimony of 05* seems to derive directly from the PWR. Wachtel did not think that the 614-group (i.e., the PWR MSS) could be the source for the reading of 05* (here called the WRR).[143] For him, the isolated καί at the end proved the PWR editor and the WR editor had different motivations. But if the latter translation shown above was intended, the WR editor may have simply clarified the wording of the PWR archetype. Even if Wachtel is right about different goals, that does not rule out a close connection between them. Since they were two different editions, the editors could have different goals. The WR editor evidently relocated the awkward καί of the PWR from the clause to the front and then changed ὡς to ἕως (shown as an error in the ECM) to mean something like "as long as" (*TLG*). Therefore, 05* has, "And as long as 450 years he gave them judges until Samuel the prophet." The revisions of 05* are matched by gig. Similarly, d merely moved the καί to the front. According to the ECM notes, sy^p also embraced the Byz interpretation. The ECM editors translate the sy^p, "And for 450 years he gave them judges, until Samuel the prophet."[144] A portion of the ancient Sahidic translation (i.e., sa^mss) agrees and the editors translate it, "And he gave

---

142. Barrett, *Commentary on Acts*, 1:634.
143. Wachtel, "Against the Text-Type Concept," 145.
144. ECM 3:2, 248.

them judges for about 450 years."¹⁴⁵ In summary, although NA28 has better translation support, the Byz has a clear ring of originality. It is joined by the indirect witness of the WR edition, sy^p, and the sa. While the Byz is easier in terms of grammar, it is harder in respect to the accounting of the 450 years. Although Ropes chose the "Western" text as found in 05 as the original, his explanation also works for the Byz. He perceived NA28/03 to be the gloss of an ancient editor who felt the 450 years must include the exodus. Therefore, that scholar adjusted the wording so that the exodus of 13:18 and the land distribution of 13:19 mark the end of the period.¹⁴⁶ Bengel's defense of the Alex reading brings to light a plausible reason for why the Byz might have been revised to form the Alex. He argues that embracing the Alex reading removes the need to do mental gymnastics to make the 450 years of judges fit within the 480 years of 1 Kgs 6:1. The years in the book of Kings start with the exodus from Egypt and end with the foundation of the first temple.¹⁴⁷ He could not cleanly reconcile the 450 years of the judges with the era of 1 Kgs 6:1. Some 200 years later Sir Robert Anderson clarified the 480-year period by showing that it intentionally ignored those years during which Israel as a nation was the servant of a foreign power.¹⁴⁸ Those five periods add up to 93 years and produce a total window of 573 years. That period agrees with the Byz text, i.e., 40 years of the exodus, about 450 years of judges, 40 years of Saul, 40 years of David, and 3 years into Solomon's reign. The WR witnesses like 05 and sy^hmg offer repeated evidence in Acts of how attempted fixes can bring more confusion than clarity. Ancient Alex scribes have done so here. The Byz has resisted scholarly revision despite its historical difficulties and is probably original.

71. (ATO) (α-INS) (13:24/20–26) NA28/614 has παντὶ τῷ λαῷ 'Ισραήλ (vs. τῷ 'Ισραήλ, Byz) and is joined by 6/10 core PWR MSS, 8/10 best ECM MSS, and 01C1 05 08 35*^vid etc., including twenty Westerns plus Chrys^pt CosmIn Vg d e gig p w 189 bo mae sy^p sy^h Ä. Byz is joined by 014 020 35C and 4/10 core PWR MSS etc., including eight Westerns plus AnastS Chrys^pt. The Byz has a shorter unadorned text

---

145. ECM 3:2, 248.
146. Ropes, *Beginnings of Christianity*, 121.
147. Bengel, *Gnomon*, 2:625–27.
148. Anderson, *Coming Prince*, 81–83.

(see 4:25/2–24). However, NA28 is original as confirmed by dominant translation evidence, the PWR, and most Westerns. It has the richer meaning.

72. (BTO) (β-INS) (13:25/16–18) Byz/614 reads τίνα με (vs. τί ἐμὲ, NA28) and is found in 10/10 core PWR MSS, 3/10 best ECM MSS (i.e., 04 1739 2200), and P45 05 08 etc., including 26/26 Westerns plus AnastS Chrys Vg d e gig p w 189 sy^p sy^h. 614 is the PWR. NA28 is joined by 7/10 best ECM MSS (i.e., P74 01 02 03 33 81 1175) and no others plus CosmIn Ä. MSS 33 and 81 show the less emphatic τί με. Metzger agrees with Torrey that NA28 follows Aramaic style and considers the Byz to be a "linguistic improvement."[149] Yet, given Luke's excellent Greek style, it seems that Aramaic features would be secondary unless widely attested (cf. 4:17/20; 10:19/30). Barrett asserts that it would be unnatural for scribes to adjust the very suitable masculine τίνα to the neuter τί, implying that the neuter is superior.[150] His statement is right in terms of normal scribal practices. However, given that the reading occurs in only seven tightly related Alex MSS, it is better explained as the work of a solitary scribe upon a trusted archetype. Moreover, for NA28 to be correct one must assume a change very near the original Acts. That change must then have prevailed almost everywhere except Alexandria. Alternatively, one would need to assume that scribes everywhere except the Alexandrian region had a problem with the neuter. Neither option is likely. NA28's construction τί ἐμὲ is a NT hapax legomenon and is found just ten times in the entire *TLG* database. Even the less emphatic sequence τί με occurs only once in the LXX. However, it does occur thirteen times in the NT and five times in Luke's writings (see Matt 19:17; 22:18; Mark 10:18; 12:15; Luke 18:19; John 7:19; 18:21, 23; Acts 9:4; 16:30; 22:7; 26:14; Rom 9:20). Every time the meaning is "why" instead of "what" with one exception (see Acts 16:30). Thus, Luke would be expected to join the neuter with με and to have written τί με. It is questionable whether he would have used the neuter at all, given its typical NT usage. In contrast, each use of τίνα με in the NT refers to the identity of Jesus. Although found just once in the LXX (see Jer 15:10), it is used six times in the NT (see Matt 16:13, 15; Mark 8:27, 29; Luke 9:18, 20). Luke and Paul were

---

149. Metzger, *Textual Commentary*, 360.
150. Barrett, *Commentary on Acts*, 1:638.

very familiar with this event in the Lord's ministry when Jesus asked his disciples "who" he was. Luke recalls how John the Baptist was careful to say "who" he was and "who" he was not (Luke 3:15–16). When Paul speaks at Ephesus to followers of John, he reminds them that John had taught that they should believe in the Coming One. It is contrary to Lucan style and Pauline clarity for them to use the neuter in the present context. The Alex reading exposes itself as a "grammatical gloss" by its emphatic ἐμέ. Apparently, the neuter was intended to place the emphasis on the messianic office rather than on the person of Christ.[151] The neuter was valued in Alexandria. The unity of seven core Alex's points to a common archetype. Byz/PWR is probably original.

73. (BTO) (β-INS) (#13:26/26) NA28/614 reads ἡμῖν ὁ λόγος (vs. ὑμῖν ὁ λόγος, Byz) and is found in 6/10 core PWR MSS, 6/10 best ECM MSS (i.e., P74 01 02 03 33 81), and eight others, including MS 05 plus CosmIn d 74 sa mae sy[hmg]. 614 is the PWR. It is also the WRR, as seen by the unity of 05 mae sy[hmg]. Byz is joined by P45 04 014 020 35 etc., including nineteen Westerns plus AnastS Chrys Or Phot Vg e gig p t w 70 73 189 bo sy[p] sy[h.txt] Ä. The ECM marks it with a SGL.[152] NA28's support beyond its core is mainly that of the two Western editions, the PWR archetype and the WR. Several important witnesses, that normally uphold the Alex, align with the Byz here (i.e., P45 Or Vg bo Ä). Apparently the PWR made an itacism and is the source of the error. The WR then inherited ἡμῖν and made it popular enough to influence the Alex tradition (see chapter 2). It may be instructive to notice that two of the best ECM MSS listed above (i.e., 02 and 81) deviated to join WR witnesses 05 d gig at 13:26/18. These offer ἡμῖν at 13:26/18 in harmony to their reading here. Byz is probably original.

74. (BTO) (β-INS) (#13:33/16) Byz/NA28/614 has αὐτῶν ἡμῖν (vs. ἡμῖν, ECM conjecture, vs. ἡμῶν, 03, vs. αὐτῶν, 1175) and is found in 9/10 core PWR MSS, 4/10 best ECM MSS (i.e., 33 81 1739 2200), and 04C3 08 etc., including 23/25 Westerns plus AnastS AstS Chrys e sa sy[p] sy[h] A G (see chapter 2). 614 is the PWR, and NA28 has brackets around αὐτῶν. Because many of the Westerns are by nature

---

151. Barrett, *Commentary on Acts*, 1:638.

152. Wachtel, "Text-Critical Commentary," 19–20, mentions that NA28/PWR word choice fits better in the context.

secondary Alex witnesses, they offer to the Byz reading Alex support. The ECM conjecture is possibly joined by (mae) but probably mae is from 03. MS 03 is joined by P74 01 02 04* 05 1409 CosmIn Vg d t w 73 (mae) Ä. 1175 is joined by 629 2147 gig bo. Wachtel explains that the best way to account for the 03 reading is a conjectured ἡμῖν.[153] He may be right. However, the overall textual evidence suggests that ἡμῖν, standing alone, was not the original but instead arose from an eye skip that lost αὐτῶν from the Byz. Alex scribes then "fixed" it by tweaking ἡμῖν to ἡμῶν. Alternatively, ἡμῶν of 03 might be part of grammatical smoothing found in the WR, going across 13:32-33. At 13:32, MS 05 adds ἡμῶν and reads τοὺς πατέρας ἡμῶν with the support of 08 629 1884 Vg d e gig p t w 70 73 189 sa mae sy^p. It is clearly the WRR. Here 05 Vg d t w 73 Ä appear to uphold the WRR again and match 03 in reading ἡμῶν. As a result, their τοῖς τέκνοις ἡμῶν balances with 13:32. Most of the Greek textual tradition avoided these corruptions. Byz/NA28/PWR is probably original.[154]

75. (BTO) (β-INS) (#13:40/10-18) (3ways) 614 reads ἐπέλθῃ τὸ εἰρημένον ἐν τοῖς προφήταις εἰς ὑμᾶς (vs. ἐπέλθῃ ἐφ᾽ ὑμᾶς τὸ εἰρημένον ἐν τοῖς προφήταις, Byz, vs. ἐπέλθῃ τὸ εἰρημένον ἐν τοῖς προφήταις, NA28). 614 is the PWR and it derived from the Byz. The Byz has the best variety in Greek MSS, the most translations, and 4/4 fathers (see chapter 3). Its support includes 6/10 best ECM MSS (i.e., 02 04 81 1175 1739 2200), seventeen Westerns, and d gig p w 61 (sa bo mae). NA28 is joined by just 01 03 05 33^vid and eleven others plus Vg d 189 (Ä). NA28 probably lost ἐφ ὑμᾶς accidentally after ἐπέλθῃ because the idea is implied by the verb.[155] In contrast, Metzger asserts ἐφ᾽ ὑμᾶς would not be lost if genuine.[156] Yet the phrase could have even been removed on purpose to adjust the focus so that ἐπέλθῃ might not refer to the items of 13:41 as "falling" on them, but rather to

---

153. Wachtel, "Text-Critical Commentary," 20.

154. Soden, *Schriften des Neuen Testaments*, 2:544, agrees. In contrast, Westcott and Hort, *Introduction*, 6, 95, argue that because τοὺς πατέρας is absolute in 13:32, and τοῖς τέκνοις is absolute in 13:33, ἡμῶν has arisen from an original ἡμῖν. However, they have not provided an explanation for why τοῖς τέκνοις needs to be absolute. They have assumed what needed to be proved given that they argue for a conjecture. In fact, these words occur absolutely at 2 Cor 12:14 but not the other four times: Matt 7:11, Luke 11:13, Acts 2:39, 2 John 1:1.

155. See Barrett, *Commentary on Acts*, 1:652, who mentions the implication.

156. Metzger, *Textual Commentary*, 366; see Pervo, *Acts*, 341.

the items as "occurring" to them. Both readings warn them of utter destruction in unbelief (see 13:41).[157] Von Soden upholds the Byz and cites parallels where ἐπί also follows ἐπέρχομαι (see Luke 21:35; Acts 1:8; 8:24).[158] The verb occurs only nine times in the NT. Byz is probably original as confirmed by most of the ancient witnesses from Egypt.

76. (SGLR) (γ-INS) (13:46/36) Byz/614 reads ἐπειδὴ δὲ (vs. ἐπειδὴ, NA28, vs. ἐπεὶ δὲ, P45) and is joined by 10/10 core PWR MSS and 4/9 best ECM MSS (i.e., 02 1175 1739 2200) and 01C2 05C1 08 044 etc., including 23/25 Westerns plus Apoll Ath Bas BasSel Chrys[pt] Cyr HesH Or[pt] Procop PsCaes Thdrt. 614 is the PWR. NA28 is joined by 01* 03 05* *254* *617** and seven others plus sy[h.ms] (sy[p]). Notice how 01* 05* and 617* all corrected to the Byz and that NA28 has no paternal support. NA28 seems to give indirect support for the Byz/PWR. P45 is joined by 3/9 best ECM MSS (i.e., P74 04 81) and 61 *326* *1837* *1874* 2344 *2374* 2805 L1188 plus Chrys[pt] Eus Or[pt]. Either Byz/PWR or P45 may be supported by: OrLat Tert Vg d e gig p w 189 sy[h.ms]. Therefore, the translations and fathers point to either Byz/PWR or P45. NA28 likely dropped δέ or changed δέ to -δη by mistake. In uncial script, the three readings are: ΕΠΕΙΔΗ, ΕΠΕΙΔΕ, and ΕΠΕΙΔΗΔΕ. Wachtel asserts that the shorter readings might come from an eye skip or the longer one from "dittography or conflation."[159] He noticed that several Byz MSS (italicized above) support NA28 and P45. Because they probably were shortened by accident, both NA28 and P45 may have likewise erred in the same way. The ECM chose a SGL between NA28 and P45. Given the evidence, the SGL should instead be between the Byz/PWR and P45.[160]

77. (BTO) (β-NTR) (#14:8/8–18) (3ways) Byz has ἐν Λύστροις ἀδύνατος τοῖς ποσὶν ἐκάθητο (vs. ἀδύνατος ἐν Λύστροις τοῖς ποσὶν ἐκάθητο, NA28, vs. ἀδύνατος τοῖς ποσὶν ἐκάθητο, 08, vs. ἐν Λύστροις ἐκάθητο ἀδύνατος τοῖς ποσίν, 1292) and is joined by 7/10 best ECM MSS (i.e., P74 02 04 33 81 1739 2200) and 01C2 206 etc., including thirteen Westerns plus Chrys A G (Vg p w 72 189). ECM lists nine alternatives. The following could support either the Byz or NA28: sa bo

---

157. See Bruce, *Book of the Acts*, 261, 263.
158. Soden, *Schriften des Neuen Testaments*, 2:545.
159. See Wachtel, "Text-Critical Commentary," 20–21.
160. Soden, *Schriften des Neuen Testaments*, 2:546, prints the Byz/PWR.

sy^p sy^h Ä. NA28 is joined by just 01* 03 1175. MS 08 simplifies by dropping the location. It is joined by (05) 1884 Dam (d) e sa^ms mae and is probably the WRR. MS 1292 is supported by other core PWR MSS: 383 (614) (1611) (1890) (2138) 2147 (2412). It is the PWR and evidently smoothed the Byz by moving forward ἐκάθητο in the clause. NA28 appears clumsy and 01* was corrected to the Byz.[161] Most likely, NA28 came from an archetype that lost ἐν Λύστροις by accident. Next its corrector restored it but in the wrong place. The WRR demonstrates that a primitive ancient short reading did indeed exist in Egypt. Alternatively, NA28 might be from an eye skip over ἐν Λύστροις that was corrected on the spot. The copyist recognized the error after writing ἀδύνατος and then inserted the words without fixing the word order. Byz is probably original as confirmed by 70 percent of the best ECM MSS.[162]

78. (BTO) (β-INS) (#14:17/40) NA28/614 reads ὑμῶν (vs. ἡμῶν, Byz) and is found in 5/9 best ECM MSS (i.e., 01* 03 04 81 1175), 5/10 core PWR MSS (i.e., 614 1611 1890 2138 2412), and 05 08 1 424 etc. plus IrLat Thdrt^T Vg d e p h w 72 189 bo mae sy^h. 614 is the PWR. Byz is joined by 4/9 best ECM MSS (i.e., P74 02 1739 2200), 5/10 core PWR MSS, and 01C2 014 020 35 etc. plus Ath Chrys ConstAp Thdrt^mss gig (sy^p) Ä. As discussed in chapter 2, the accidental or purposeful swapping of the 2P and 1P pronoun either here or at 14:17/16 created harmony. Only 26/135 ECM Greek MSS avoid the harmony. Only the Byz witnesses consistently maintain the diversity. Although most translations align with NA28/PWR, the pull to harmony can be very strong. At 7:37/40, only Chrys Vg sa and Ä managed to resist adding "Listen to Him" from to Deut 18:15. Therefore, the Byz is probably the original.[163]

79. (BTO) (β-NTR) (15:20/11, 12–14) 614f1 has ἀπὸ τῶν ἀλιγισμητων (vs. ἀπὸ τῶν ἀλισγημάτων, Byz/1611, vs. τῶν ἀλισγημάτων, NA28) and is joined by 69f1 2412f1. Byz/1611 is found in 8/10 core PWR MSS, 6/10 best ECM MSS (i.e., P74 02 04 33 1739 2200, and 08 014

---

161. Metzger, *Textual Commentary*, 372–73, and the committee felt that the reading of MS 03 "seems to cry out for rearrangement." Still, they chose it because they could not conceive how 03 could derive from the Byz. See Barrett, *Commentary on Acts*, 1:674.

162. Soden, *Schriften des Neuen Testaments*, 2:547, agrees.

163. See Wachtel, "Text-Critical Commentary," 22–23, who uses the same logic to determine the original reading at 15:25/10.

020 35 etc., including 22/26 Westerns plus Chrys ConstAp. 1611 is the PWR. NA28 is joined by 4/10 best ECM MSS (i.e., 01 03 81 1175), P45 05, and ten others, including three Westerns. Was ἀπό a scribal gloss or was it dropped as superfluous since the preceding word ἀπέχεσθαι in the middle voice is commonly translated either as "to keep away" or "to keep away from" (*TLG*)? The fact that the same form is used again at 15:29/2 but without ἀπό provides strong evidence that ἀπό was originally present here. The Byz has avoided the harmony. A proto-Alex archetype lost ἀπό because it seemed superfluous, by an oversight, or by assimilation to the parallel (see 15:29). Byz/PWR is probably original as confirmed by 60 percent of the best ECM MSS and most Westerns.

80. (BTO) (β-INS) (#15:23/4–8) (3ways) 614/PWR reads διὰ χειρὸς αὐτῶν <u>ἐπιστολὴν καὶ πέμψαντες περιέχουσαν</u> τάδε (vs. διὰ χειρὸς αὐτῶν, NA28, vs. διὰ χειρὸς αὐτῶν τάδε, Byz, vs. διὰ χειρὸς αὐτῶν <u>ἐπιστολὴν περιέχουσαν</u> τάδε, 04(*f)) and is found in 5/10 core PWR MSS (i.e., 383 614 1292 2147 2412) and 1501 sy[hmg]. 614 is the PWR. The ECM lists nine alternatives. The PWR builds upon the Byz and may have caused most readings. NA28 is joined by 4/10 best ECM MSS (i.e., P74 01* 02 03) and P33[vid] P45[vid] 629 plus Vg p l 189 bo Ä. Byz is joined by 4/10 best ECM MSS (i.e., 81 1175 1739 2200) and 01C2 08 etc., including fourteen Westerns plus Chrys ConstAp A G (e sy[h.txt]). 04(*f) is joined by (05 d) gig w ar (sa sy[p]). The PWR editor has probably expanded the Byz by imitating the PWR (see MS 614) of 23:25/2–12, the standard text of 15:22 (see πέμψαι), and the standard text of 15:30 (see ἐπιστολήν). When this popular expansion was recognized as secondary, 04(*f), the sa (i.e., the oldest Coptic), and others shortened it by removing καὶ πέμψαντες. 05 approved of 04's content but reordered it. Later, Thomas of Harkel corrected sy[hmg] back to the primitive Byz reading in sy[h.txt]. The presence of τάδε gives the Byz indirect support from: d gig w ar sa sy[p] sy[hmg]. Alex scribes seem to have lost τάδε in efforts to avoid expansion. The corrector of 01 recognized the mistake. The best ECM MSS are split. Nearly all MSS include τάδε or some equivalent. Moreover, the use of γράφω with an object matches Luke's style in the letter of Lysias (see 23:25/2–12). Byz is probably original.[164]

---

164. Soden, *Schriften des Neuen Testaments*, 2:553, agrees, but Wachtel, "Against the Text-Type Concept," 145, selects NA28 instead.

81. (ATO) (α-SI) (15:24/30–34) Byz/614 has + λέγοντες περιτέμνεσθαι καὶ τηρεῖν τὸν νόμον οἷς οὐ διεστειλάμεθα (vs. οἷς οὐ διεστειλάμεθα, NA28, vs. 614 reading + δεῖ, 08, vs. 614 reading with word order changes, 629 IrLat gig) and is found in 7/10 core PWR MSS and 04 014 020 35 etc., including 17/23 Westerns (22/23 are nearly equal) plus Socr (IrLat gig sy^p sy^h) A. 614 is the PWR. NA28 is joined by 6/10 best ECM MSS (i.e., P74 01 02 03 33 81f1), P33^{vid} P45^{vid} (05*) 05C1, and six others plus Amph ConstAp OrLat Vg d p w l 189 sa bo Ä. NA28 has a solid core and better translation support. Byz/PWR repeats the thoughts of 15:5.[165] The nature of this variant is similar to the Byz/PWR long reading at 21:25 because many of the witnesses align the same way. Neither addition is necessary in the context. The dominant Greek evidence in favor of the longer reading, in contrast to fifteen MSS for NA28, suggests that it may be from Luke himself. Perhaps Luke had marked the words for deletion in his working copy, making them absent in the final edition. This passage is one of about ten expanded readings in Acts that appear Lucan (see 2:30/34; 10:32/37; 18:21/9; 20:24/27; 21:25/16–20; 23:30/45; 24:6/20–8/14; 28:16/12–16; 28:29/2–24). Later, a scholar of Luke's circle, with access to Luke's working edition, noticed the clarifying words and restored them in a popular edition of Acts. NA28 preserves the original.[166]

82. (BTO) (β-NTR) (15:28/8–12) Byz/614 reads τῷ ἁγίῳ πνεύματι (vs. τῷ πνεύματι τῷ ἁγίῳ, NA28) and is found in 4/10 best ECM MSS (04 1175 1739 2200) and 10/10 core PWR MSS etc., including 24/24 Westerns plus seventeen ancient fathers (e.g., IrLat^T Or). MS 614 is the PWR. NA28 is found in 6/10 best ECM MSS (i.e., P74 01 02 03 33 81), nineteen others, six ancient fathers (e.g., Clem Tert), and Vg p w 189. The NA28 wording is more emphatic, having the adjective in the "restrictive attributive position" instead of the "ascriptive attributive position" seen in Byz/PWR.[167] Von Soden favors NA28 and cites 10:45 and 16:6 as places from which the Byz/PWR may have harmonized.[168] However, all traditions agree in preserving

---

165. See Boismard and Lamouille, *Texte occidental reconstitution*, 2:107; Metzger, *Textual Commentary*, 385.

166. See Bengel, *Novum Testamentum*, 197, who considered the Byz original and rated the NA28 reading as δ.

167. Black, *Learn to Read*, 44; see Wallace, *Greek Grammar*, 306.

168. Soden, *Schriften des Neuen Testaments*, 2:553.

the restrictive construction in 7:51. In fact, fourteen fathers there keep the emphatic wording vs. only one that has τῷ ἁγίῳ πνεύματι. Therefore, neither the Byz and PWR traditions nor the fathers seem to be against the emphatic form. In contrast, MS 03 (joined by 05C1 1175, core PWR MSS 1292 1611 1890 2412, and 6 others) revises the original τοῦ ἁγίου πνεύματος into the emphatic τοῦ πνεύματος τοῦ ἁγίου at 10:45. Therefore, the emphatic probably entered here from a MS like 03. Here the ratio of seventeen fathers to six and the perfect coherence of the Westerns offer strong evidence for the Byz/PWR. If the emphatic form were original, there is no obvious reason for a widespread departure from it. Therefore, NA28 evidently reflects a primitive change to the emphatic form either by preference or by accident. The Byz/PWR is probably original.

83. (ATO) (a-INS) (15:29/8–12) NA28/614 has αἵματος καὶ πνικτῶν (vs. αἵματος καὶ πνικτοῦ, Byz, vs. αἵματος, 05) is found in 7/10 core PWR MSS, 6/10 best ECM MSS (i.e., 01* 02*vid 03 04 81 1175), and 467 1501 plus Amph[ms] Clem ConstAp[ms] CyrH[mss] Dam OrLat Socr A[mss]. 614 is the PWR. Byz is joined by 4/10 best ECM MSS (i.e., P74 33 1739 2200) and 01C2 02C 08 etc., including thirteen Westerns plus Amph ConstAp[T] CyrH Did Diod Epiph Presb Procop SevGab Vg e gig p w ar 189 sy[h] A. The Byz has more fathers and translations. MS 05 does not have either form of πνικτός and is joined by IrLat Tert d l. The same omission occurs at 15:20 by 05 IrLat d gig and then again at 21:25 by 05 d gig G. The core Alex MSS (though 01* and 02* were revised) and the PWR avoided harmonizing πνικτῶν to the singular πνικτοῦ (see 15:20; 21:25). Both Clem and OrLat provide their ancient confirmation. The ECM editors mark the passage with a SGL because the NA28 reading has non-Alex MSS that support it. Wachtel explains, "There probably was a tendency to use the plural here, although it is not obvious why."[169] Yet it seems most likely that some MSS maintained the plural because of its antiquity. Perhaps the noun sequence of plural-singular-plural-singular helped the two traditions recognize the native structure. NA28/PWR is original and the SGL is not necessary.

84. (BTO) (a-NTR) (15:36/30–32) Byz/614 reads κατὰ πᾶσαν πόλιν (vs. κατὰ πόλιν πᾶσαν, NA28) and is joined by 10/10 core PWR MSS, 3/9 best ECM MSS (i.e., 81 1739 2200), and 05 08 206 307 etc.,

---

169. Wachtel, "Text-Critical Commentary," 23.

including 24/27 Westerns plus Bas Chrys. 614 is the PWR. NA28 is joined by 6/9 best ECM MSS (i.e., P74 01 02 03 04 1175) and P127 with fourteen others. NA28 is awkward and not typical Lucan. The root πᾶς is used 171 times in Acts and normally it precedes the word that it modifies except for genitive uses (*BW*). When it follows and is not part of a prepositional phrase, it normally stands after the noun that it modifies (see 8:40; 16:26; 17:7, 21; 20:25; 21:24; 27:20, 36). On one occasion it follows the participle that it modifies (see 20:32). There are other places where the accusative of πᾶς follows the preposition κατά (see 3:22; 13:27; 15:21; 17:17; 18:4; 26:11). In every case, it precedes the substantive it modifies. For example, at 26:11 the wording is, κατὰ πάσας τὰς συναγωγάς. In addition, 3/21 MSS (i.e., 6 69 1735) supporting NA28 are Byz and thus probably arose from an independent error rather than from NA28. Likewise, NA28 might come from a local error. The similarity of πᾶσαν to πόλιν made it easier for transposition to occur. In summary, NA28 is awkward because of a mistake. Byz/PWR is original as confirmed by Lucan style and the Westerns.

85. (ATO) (α-SI) (16:7/34) NA28/2412 has Ἰησοῦ (vs. omits, Byz, vs. κυρίου, 04*) and is found in 5/10 core PWR MSS (i.e., 1505 1611 2138 2412 2495), 8/10 best ECM MSS (i.e., P74 01 02 03 33 81* 1175 1739), and 04C2 05 08 etc., including thirteen Westerns plus Ath Cyr Did OrLat Vg d e p w l 189 bo fay sy^p.mss sy^h Ä. 2412 is the PWR and 614 is not available here because of an eye skip. Byz is joined by 014 020 35 81C 383 1292 2147 etc., including seven Westerns plus Chrys Epiph sa. The sa helps demonstrate the antiquity of the Byz reading. 04* is joined by 88 915 gig bo^mss sy^p.ms and has replaced Ἰησοῦ to form biblical vernacular. NA28 has the harder reading and the best variety. It is unique in its expression and similar in nature to Matt 10:20 where "the Spirit of your Father" reading is found. NA28 is original as confirmed by the translations and the PWR.

86. (ATO) (β-SI) (16:10/30–36) Byz/614 has ὁ κύριος εὐαγγελίσασθαι αὐτούς (vs. ὁ θεὸς εὐαγγελίσασθαι αὐτούς, NA28, ὁ κύριος εὐαγγελίσασθαι τοὺς ἐν τῇ Μακεδονίᾳ, 05) is found in 10/10 core PWR MSS and 014 020 35 etc., including fourteen Westerns plus Chrys IrLat^ms (IrLat^T gig sa sy^p sy^h). 614 is the PWR. NA28 is joined by 7/10 best ECM MSS (the other 3/10 agree except they have αὐτοῖς instead of αὐτούς; i.e., P74 02C 33) and 08 206 with twenty others,

including nine Westerns plus (Vg e p w l 189 bo) G. 05 is joined by d. The Byz/PWR was influential, having impacted sa IrLat. 05 built upon the PWR. It appears that a proto-Byz editor preferred the OT personal name for God, ὁ κύριος. The translations are divided.[170] The discourse structure points to Luke's intentional use of ὁ θεός. When the whole section of 16:7–10 is considered, NA28 preserves a Trinitarian lesson. First the Holy Spirit gave direction, then the Spirit of Jesus, and then finally God. Although the names "Holy Spirit" and "Spirit of Jesus" both refer to the Spirit of God, Luke still brings to mind the harmonious work of the Trinity. NA28 is probably the original as confirmed by the PWR.

87. (BTO) (β-NTR) (16:16/24) Byz/614 reads πύθωνος (vs. πύθωνα, NA28) and is found in 10/10 core PWR MSS and 4/10 best ECM MSS (i.e., 33 1175 1739 2200) and P45 P127C 04C3 05C1 08 etc., including 26/27 Westerns plus Chrys EustA e gig 189. MS 614 is the PWR. NA28 is joined by 6/10 best ECM MSS (i.e., P74 01 02 03 04* 81) and 05* 326 1837 plus Or Vg d p w l. The meaning of both readings appears to be almost identical. The complete coherence of the PWR with the Byz proves that the Byz/PWR is ancient. P45 offers more evidence for its antiquity. The correction of 04* and 05* shows that the Byz had authority. The alignment of 40 percent of the best ECM MSS enhances the argument. The presence of two Byz MSS (i.e., 326 1837) among its witnesses indicates that both they and NA28 could be a result of a scribal gloss. Finally, the domination of the Westerns is the most helpful. Since many of the "Westerns" are Alex in nature (e.g., 945 1891 2298), there needs to be a good reason for 26/27 Westerns to depart the original (e.g., "to clarify" as occurred at 21:25/16–20 or 24:6/20–8/14). Metzger asserts that the NA28 reading is harder and thus correct.[171] By implication, he is referring to πύθων being an accusative of apposition vs. a genitive.[172] But is this construction so hard as to cause all but nine MSS to defect? Consider the reading γῇ Αἰγύπτῳ vs. γῆ Αἰγύπτου at 7:36/18–20. There, almost every Byz MSS and 9/28 Westerns retain the apposition. In contrast, 50 percent of the best ECM MSS lost

---

170. See Metzger, *Textual Commentary*, 393, who asserts that internal evidence is also indecisive. The committee decided it was safest to follow the core Alex MSS. Soden, *Schriften des Neuen Testaments*, 2:556, agrees.

171. Metzger, *Textual Commentary*, 396; see Barrett, *Commentary on Acts*, 2:785.

172. See Wallace, *Greek Grammar*, 198–99.

it (i.e., P74 03 04 1739 2200). The accusative appears to be a local gloss made by a proto-Alex scribe. Therefore, the Byz/PWR is probably original.[173]

88. (BTO) (α-NTR) (16:18/16) Byz/614 has δὲ ὁ Παῦλος (vs. δὲ Παῦλος, NA28) and is found in 10/10 core PWR MSS, 6/10 best ECM MSS (i.e., 04 33 81 1175 1739 2200), and P127[vid] 05 08 etc., including 26/26 Westerns plus Chrys SevGab. 614 is the PWR. The ECM marks it as a SGL. NA28 is joined by just P45 P74 01 02 03 876 1704. The meaning seems unaffected either way. There is no obvious reason for almost the entire textual tradition to add the article. Consider the anarthrous Παῦλος καὶ Σιλᾶς at 16:25/9–14. The only ECM MSS to insert the article are P127 and 05 before Paul and 04 before Silas. No MSS insert the article before both. In summary, NA28 has resulted from an ancient oversight in the Alex tradition. Byz/PWR is original and the SGL can be removed.[174]

89. (BTO) (α-NTR) (16:24/28–30) Byz/614 reads αὐτῶν ἠσφαλίσατο (vs. ἠσφαλίσατο αὐτῶν, NA28) and is found in 10/10 core PWR MSS, 3/10 best ECM MSS (i.e., 1175 1739 2200), and P127 04C3 05C1 08 etc., including 24/27 Westerns plus Chrys Vg d e p w l 189. Of the three Westerns that disagree, two agree in word order but have a plural verb. The other probably started with NA28 and then dropped αὐτῶν to eliminate its awkward position. 614 is the PWR. NA28 is joined by 7/10 best ECM MSS (i.e., P74 01 02 03 04* 33 81) and 1735 L1188 plus no other evidence. It appears that an ancient proto-Alex scribe copied down ἠσφαλίσατο first, noticed the error, and then wrote αὐτῶν without fixing the word order. The Byz wording of τοὺς πόδας <u>αὐτῶν</u> ἠσφαλίσατο could still be translated, "he secured their feet," even without αὐτῶν, the article serving the role of the pronoun. This fact might have facilitated the temporary oversight of αὐτῶν. Byz/PWR is original.[175]

90. (BTO) (β-SI) (16:31/17) Byz/614 reads χριστόν (vs. omits, NA28) and is found in 10/10 core PWR MSS and 4/10 best ECM MSS

---

173. Soden, *Schriften des Neuen Testaments*, 2:557, agrees. Boismard and Lamouille, *Texte occidental reconstitution*, 2:113, find the Byz consistent with Lucan style as seen at Luke 4:33 and 13:11.

174. Wachtel, "Text-Critical Commentary," 25, favors the Byz reading as does Soden, *Schriften des Neuen Testaments*, 2:558.

175. Soden, *Schriften des Neuen Testaments*, 2:558, agrees.

(i.e., 04 1175 1739 2200) and 05 08 etc., including 26/28 Westerns plus Chrys ChrysH⁽ᵐˢ⁾ Euth d e sa sy^Aram sy^p sy^h Ä. 614 is the PWR. NA28 is joined by 6/10 best ECM MSS (i.e., P74 01 02 03 33 81) and P127 with eight others plus Chrys^mss Cyr Epiph Vg gig p w l 189 bo. Of the fifteen MSS upholding NA28, 5 are Byz (i.e., 103 1243 1563 1832 2243). This fact suggests that an eye skip caused the loss of χριστόν in these Byz MSS. The implication is that the scribe of an important proto-Alex archetype may have done the same thing to produce NA28. The sequence in uncial script without spacing would look something like TONK̲N̲I̲N̲X̲N̲KAI with lines over the three consecutive nomina sacra (ν has been underlined above to highlight the reason for an eye skip). The probability of an eye skip is enhanced when the character of 03, the best ECM MS, is evaluated in other NT books concerning this appellation. For example, at Rom 13:14 both NA28 and the Byz read τὸν κύριον Ἰησοῦν Χριστὸν while 03 alone has τὸν χριστὸν Ἰησοῦν. Once again, at 1 Cor 16:23 the Byz text reads τοῦ κυρίου Ἰησοῦ χριστοῦ while 03 as joined by 01* 33 sa and a few others lacks χριστοῦ.[176] The division of the core Alex MSS further weakens the evidence for NA28. Moreover, the Byz/PWR also has a greater versional variety. The sequence ἐπι τὸν κύριον Ἰησοῦν Χριστὸν only occurs otherwise at 11:17. Thus, while + χριστόν might be from assimilation to 11:17, it is not likely that the Byz/PWR would have added χριστόν merely to polish the text.[177] Only at 19:4 has the Byz added a form of χριστός to further identify Jesus.[178] Some agreements in phrasing are indeed intentional and original (see δέομαι + κύριος at 8:22, 24 in NA28, vs. disharmony in Byz/PWR; εἶναι τὸν χριστὸν Ἰησοῦν at 18:5, 28 in NA28, vs. omission of εἶναι at 18:5 in Byz/PWR). In the Byz, both 11:17 and 16:31 have the same structure, starting with a form of πιστεύω followed by the identical phrase. The agreement appears designed to emphasize that the leading apostle to the Jews and the chief apostle to

---

176. This is the NA28 reading. More support can be gained from CNTTS database (i.e., MSS 1243 1563). In addition, from von Soden may be gleaned: 2 226 823 1311 1611 1835. The list is short.

177. The Byz shows some propensity for other name glosses. For example, sometimes the Byz either adds or subtracts "Jesus" from the text (plus: see 3:26; 5:41; 9:28; 19:10; minus: see 9:17; 13:23; 16:7; 24:24). In one place the Byz has replaced Ἰησοῦ Χριστοῦ with κυρίου (see 10:48). However, in all these cases the Byz reading retains far less Western and/or translation support.

178. However, χριστόν does occur as part of a seven-word plus at 2:30/34.

the gentiles were unified in their message. Although the sa and Ä typically align with NA28, they join the Byz here. Finally, the almost complete unity of the Westerns provides further confirmation that the Byz/PWR is probably original.[179]

91. (BTO) (β-INS) (16:40/24–30) Byz/614 reads ἰδόντες τοὺς ἀδελφοὺς παρεκάλεσαν αὐτούς καὶ ἐξῆλθον (vs. ἰδόντες παρεκάλεσαν τοὺς ἀδελφοὺς ——— καὶ ἐξῆλθαν, NA28) and is found in 10/10 core PWR MSS, 2/9 best ECM MSS (i.e., 1739 2200), and (P45) 08 etc., including 24/27 Westerns etc. plus Chrys Vg e p w l 189 sy^h (sy^p) Ä A G. 614 is the PWR. NA28 is joined by 7/9 best ECM MSS (i.e., P74 01 02 03 33 81 1175) and six others. It lacks variety. Either reading may be supported by (sa bo). The isolated nature of NA28 suggests that a primitive Alex scribe mistakenly wrote παρεκάλεσαν in front of τοὺς ἀδελφούς instead of after it. A later scribe then deleted αὐτούς because it no longer fit following τοὺς ἀδελφούς. Such is probably the proto-Alex archetype underneath NA28. Of the five readings in the ECM, four have τοὺς ἀδελφούς first and include αὐτούς later. BL indicate that NA28 has used ἰδόντες absolutely.[180] They show Luke utilizing it in this manner at fourteen other places (see Luke 1:12; 2:17; 5:8; 7:39; 9:54; 10:32, 33; 11:38; 17:14; 18:15, 43; 19:7; Acts 3:12; 7:31). However, at every other location the antecedent is found in a prior position. Therefore if NA28 is chosen here, Luke's style implies the referent should be Lydia. However, that does not fit the context. Thus, even though Barrett follows NA28, he still understands brethren to be the referent.[181] Byz/PWR is probably original.

92. (BTO) (β-INS) (17:14/20) Byz/614 has ὡς (vs. ἕως, NA28, vs. omits, 05) and is found in 9/10 core PWR MSS and 206 2200 etc., including fifteen Westerns plus Chrys sy^h. 614 is the PWR. NA28 is joined by 8/9 best ECM MSS and 08 181 etc., including five Westerns plus Vg d e gig p w 189. MS 05 is joined by some Westerns (i.e., 431 915 1890) and six others plus sy^p Ä. 05 probably began with the NA28 and then removed ἕως to clarify. The use of ἕως would fit if Paul had directed the brethren to go with him "as far as to the sea." However, the subject of the sentence is not Paul but the brethren. The error

---

179. Soden, *Schriften des Neuen Testaments*, 2:559, agrees. Bengel, *Novum Testamentum*, 199, disagrees and marks the Byz with a rating of δ.

180. Boismard and Lamouille, *Texte occidental reconstitution*, 2:118, 258.

181. Barrett, *Commentary on Acts*, 2:775.

probably took place because the grammatical object τὸν Παῦλον was fronted in the verse to a location where the subject would be expected. The word choice ὡς is unusual but clear as Barrett shows below. It was corrupted by assimilation to 17:15/14 either on purpose or unconsciously. Metzger thinks that ὡς was a Byz gloss to mean something like "as if" to indicate that Paul's friends led him to the sea under the pretense of an impending sea voyage.[182] He cites Luke 24:50, Acts 21:5, and Acts 26:11 as proof that Luke utilized the style of ἕως plus a preposition.[183] That is true but those three verses are quite sensible. The first describes Jesus leading the disciples as far as Bethany. The second speaks of the believers from Tyre going with Paul as far as the beach beyond the city. Finally, Paul persecuted the Christians as far away as foreign places. But here, "The brethren sent Paul to go as far as the sea" is confused. Barrett seems right that Luke has used ὡς ἐπί as a known idiom that means "toward."[184] The brethren sent Paul toward the sea, and after that they brought him safely to Athens either by sea or land.[185] Byz/PWR is probably original.

93. (BTO) (α-NTR) (17:15/32) Byz/614 reads Τιμόθεον (vs. τὸν Τιμόθεον, NA28) and is found in 10/10 core PWR MSS, 5/9 best ECM MSS (i.e., P74 02 1175 1739 2200), and 05 044 etc., including twenty Westerns plus Chrys^pt. 614 is the PWR. NA28 is joined by 4/9 best ECM MSS (i.e., 01 03 33 81) and P45 08 etc., including four Westerns plus Chrys^pt. The inclusion of the article before Timothy is the smoother reading especially since Silas and Timothy were just mentioned in 17:14, both with the article.[186] It is hard to explain how the unusual single article with two names came to be so strongly attested in all three traditions if it were not original. Interestingly, there are twelve MSS that attempted to smooth the preceding verse by dropping the article that precedes "Timothy" in order to match the Byz/PWR reading here. These offer more evidence for the authenticity of the imbalance. The single article construction was

---

182. Metzger, *Textual Commentary*, 404.

183. Cf. Boismard and Lamouille, *Texte occidental reconstitution*, 2:121, 244.

184. Barrett, *Commentary on Acts*, 2:806, 819–20; see Haenchen, *Acts of the Apostles*, 509.

185. Bruce, *Book of the Acts*, 328.

186. See Wachtel, "Text-Critical Commentary," 26.

probably done to highlight the common role that Silas and Timothy possessed as assistants to Paul.[187] Byz/PWR is probably original.

94. (BTO) (α-INS) (17:21/28–34) Byz/614 reads τι <u>καὶ</u> ἀκούειν (vs. τι ἢ ἀκούειν <u>τι</u>, NA28, vs. ἢ ἀκούειν τι, Vg/WRR, vs. τι ἢ ἀκούειν, 05) and is found in 10/10 core PWR MSS, 5/9 best ECM MSS (i.e., 33 81 1175 1739 2200), and 08 181 etc., including 23/25 Westerns plus Bas Chrys GregNy SymS e (bo Ä). 614 is the PWR. ECM offers a SGL between Byz/PWR and NA28. NA28 is joined by 4/9 best ECM MSS (i.e., P74 01 02 03) and just 104 1838 plus (sa). The last two MSS are not Alex. Vg is joined by p w l 189 sy[h] (sa). MS 05 is joined by ThdtAnc d A G. It seems that the isolated NA28 reading resulted from the WRR as preserved by the Vg et al. The WR editor appears to have started with the Byz and reworded it. By utilizing ἢ vice καί and by placing τι at the end, the WRR created a much easier reading, i.e., the Athenians did not care whether they were speaking or hearing if it was something new. 05 tweaked the WRR by moving the τι to the start possibly by influence from the mainstream text. In the interest of clarity, a proto-Alex editor evidently began with the WRR and added τι at the start to balance the clause grammatically. Uncharacteristically, NA28 offers the most explicit reading. In contrast, Wachtel assesses the Byz as an unsuccessful effort at smoothing.[188] However, it is doubtful that 5/9 best ECM MSS and the bo Ä would depart NA28 for the rougher Byz/PWR if it were not original. Byz/PWR is original as confirmed by almost every Greek MS.

95. (BTO) (α-SI) (17:23/32–40) Byz/614 has <u>ὃν</u> οὖν ἀγνοοῦντες εὐσεβεῖτε <u>τοῦτον</u> (vs. <u>ὃ</u> οὖν ἀγνοοῦντες εὐσεβεῖτε <u>τοῦτο</u>, NA28) and is found in 9/9 core PWR MSS, 3/8 best ECM MSS (i.e., 33 1739 2200), and 01C2 02C 08 044 etc., including 22/24 Westerns plus Chrys Clem CosmIn Cyr FlavA Or[pt] Phot e sy[p] sy[h]. 614 is the PWR. NA28 is joined by 5/8 best ECM MSS (i.e., P74[vid] 01* 02* 03 1175) and just 05 plus Or[pt] Vg d gig p w l 189. Either reading might be supported by the Coptic sa and bo. First, it should be noted that two of the core ECM MSS were corrected to Byz. Second, when 05 Vg and the OL align with limited other support, they often preserve the WRR. In fact, the shift of the original text from masculine to neuter

---

187. See Wallace, *Greek Grammar*, 277–78.
188. Wachtel, "Text-Critical Commentary," 26.

can be seen in the WRR at 17:27/2-38. In that location, the WRR changes the idea from seeking God to the more abstract seeking of the divine nature. Here the neuter appears to be a gloss made to emphasize that the Greeks were merely worshiping inanimate things. Perhaps a primitive editor thought that Paul should not say, "Whom you worship," because idols are not personal beings. The Byz/PWR is more natural in the context. Paul had just spoken about the high place dedicated Ἀγνώστῳ θεῷ and then he makes that God known. In contrast, Barrett favors the neuter because the Byz was interested to show that the true God is personal and because ὃν better fits with the antecedent θεός.[189] Yet surely Paul wanted to do so as well, and his grammar ought to be excellent before such a distinguished audience. Origen offers ancient evidence for both readings. Clement gives slightly earlier testimony for only the Byz. The fathers are seven to one in favor of the masculine construction. Therefore, while the two neuter elements are surprising, they appear to come from the WR. Byz/PWR is original.[190]

96. (ATO) (β-SI) (17:26/2-8) Byz/614 reads ἐξ ἑνὸς αἵματος (vs. ἐξ ἑνὸς, NA28) and is found in 10/10 core PWR MSS and (05) (08), including 23/26 Westerns and Chrys NilAnc^vid Thdrt gig ar A G (sy^p sy^h). 614 is the PWR and probably also the WRR.[191] NA28 is joined by 9/9 best ECM MSS and 35* 181 323 629 630 1875 1891 2718 L1178 plus Clem Vg p w 189 (sa bo Ä). Its three Westerns are 181 1739 (also one of the best ECM MSS) and 1891. Impressively, core Byz MS 35* is also among the few supporters. NA28 might reflect the loss of αἵματος by eye skip. It is also hard to explain the source of the Byz/PWR if it was not original. Recognizing the problem, Metzger asserts that an eye skip is possible. He also remarks that it might have been deleted to avoid a perceived disharmony with Gen 2:7. Finally, he admits that αἵματος is not the word one would expect to be added as a gloss.[192] However, the committee decided to call "blood" a Western reading and lean on external evidence. Similarly, Wachtel finds the Byz/PWR as unusual but still secondary

---

189. Barrett, *Commentary on Acts*, 2:838-39.

190. Boismard and Lamouille, *Texte occidental reconstitution*, 1:187, favor the neuter, but Bengel, *Gnomon*, 2:665-66, assumes the masculine in his extended discussion.

191. Wachtel, "Against the Text-Type Concept," 145-46, also asserts that the Byz/PWR was the basis for the reading of 05 08 etc.

192. Metzger, *Textual Commentary*, 404-5.

as a result of the solid Alex core witnesses standing against it.[193] Barrett creatively suggests that "blood" might have been added as an attempt to declare the "unity of all races" in a way that Greeks could understand because they, unlike the Hebrews, lacked the foundational understanding that all humans came from one man created by God.[194] BL thinks that αἵματος is part of the Western and original reading and was lost by an eye skip.[195] Bengel prints αἵματος but in *Gnomon of the New Testament* speaks of it as having been added.[196] Haenchen and Bruce both choose the shorter text.[197] In conclusion, NA28 should be considered original with αἵματος being a very clever and primitive gloss.

97. (ATO) (α-SI) (#18:21/4–6, 9, 10, 24) Byz/614 has ἀπετάξατο αὐτοῖς (vs. ἀποταξάμενος καὶ, NA28, vs. ἀποταξάμενος αὐτοῖς καὶ, 1175) and is found in 10/10 core PWR MSS and many others plus Chrys gig 189 sy^h (see chapter 2). 614 is the PWR. NA28 is joined by 5/8 best ECM MSS (i.e., P74 01 02 03 33) and just 05 1409 L1188 plus Vg e p. MS 1175 is found in 3/8 best ECM MSS (i.e., 1175 1739 2200) and twenty-six others, including ten Westerns plus d w. The 1175 reading is important because its indirect testimony bolsters NA28. 1175 evidently began with NA28 and then added αὐτοῖς probably from the Byz/PWR. Either the Byz/PWR or NA28 may be joined by: sa bo sy^p. As will be shown, this variant is linked with those immediately following it (see 18:21/9, 10, 24). In fact, from the Coptic (i.e., sa bo) agreement with NA28 in the latter three variation units, it is safe to assume that the sa and bo also equal NA28 at 18:21/4–6. Concerning linking, the witnesses that have the ten-word plus at 18:21/9, usually agree at the other three variants. Those without it, normally agree at all four variants in an alternate manner. Consider the entire verse at 18:21. Byz/PWR reads: ἀλλ' ἀπετάξατο αὐτοῖς εἰπών, Δεῖ με πάντως τὴν ἑορτὴν τὴν ἐρχομένην ποιῆσαι εἰς Ἱεροσόλυμα. Πάλιν δὲ ἀνακάμψω πρὸς ὑμᾶς, τοῦ θεοῦ θέλοντος. Καὶ ἀνήχθη ἀπὸ τῆς Ἐφέσου.[198] The underlined words mark places of disagreement with

193. Wachtel, "Against the Text-Type Concept," 146.
194. Barrett, *Commentary on Acts*, 2:841–42.
195. Boismard and Lamouille, *Texte occidental reconstitution*, 2:123.
196. Bengel, *Novum Testamentum*, 201; Bengel, *Gnomon*, 2:665.
197. Haenchen, *Acts of the Apostles*, 515; Bruce, *Book of the Acts*, 332.
198. Byz is here represented by the readings marked as Byz both in the ECM and in HF1985. For some reason, RP05 lacks the καί (error?) in the last sentence against the

NA28. NA28 begins differently (as shown above), lacks the long portion, and does not include the two subsequent conjunctions. As a result, NA28 preserves three participles and two finite verbs. In contrast, the Byz/PWR has three participles, four finite verbs, and one infinite. Normally, the Byz reading with the mixed verbal forms would seem to be more Lucan. However, in this travel narrative, Luke has used participles abundantly. For example, all three traditions agree at 18:18, 18:22, and 18:23, in preserving three participles with just one or two finite verbs. Haenchen argues that the words about going to Jerusalem for the coming feast were not by Luke but were inserted later, being built from the ideas in 19:21 and 20:16.[199] Thus he judges them to be created by inference rather than from historical reports. Either could be true. As in the first variant, the Byz/PWR at 18:21/9 also has solid attestation. It is joined by 10/10 core PWR MSS and many others, including thirteen Western plus Chrys (sy[p.mss] sy[h] d gig w ar). NA28 is joined by 7/8 best ECM MSS and seventeen others, including eight Westerns plus Vg e p 189 sa bo Ä A G. If NA28 is the oldest form, the revision process involved several steps. After deciding to insert the words, the Byz/PWR editor was forced to change the grammatical structure. First, he had to adjust the initial participle into a finite verb and drop the conjunction. As a result, the added ten words required a period/colon after Ἱεροσόλυμα. The following sentence now called for a conjunction, and so he supplied δέ. Because the sentence now ended after θέλοντος, he supplied a period/colon. As a result, it was natural to add καί prior to ἀνήχθη. In this way, the reader was provided with a seamless gloss explaining why Paul did not stay longer in Ephesus. Alternatively, the Byz/PWR might be the oldest reading but still not original. Perhaps Luke removed the ten-word section from his working edition prior to publishing Acts, having found it unnecessary. After marking it for deletion, he rearranged the grammar himself. Later a successor of Luke, with access to Luke's working edition, may have reintroduced some of the omitted clauses into a popular edition of Acts. This hypothetical process seems to best explain a group of ten longer readings that appear to be Lucan

---

vast majority of MSS.

199. Haenchen, *Acts of the Apostles*, 543–44.

but still secondary (see 2:30/34; 10:32/37; 15:24/30–34; 20:24/27; 21:25/16–20; 23:30/45; 24:6/20–8/14; 28:16/12–16; 28:29/2–24).

98. (ATO) (α-NTR) (18:26/40–46) NA28/614 reads τὴν ὁδὸν τοῦ θεοῦ (vs. τὴν τοῦ θεοῦ ὁδόν, Byz, vs. τὴν ὁδὸν τοῦ κυρίου, 08) and is joined by 6/8 best ECM MSS, 8/10 core PWR MSS, and many others, including fourteen Westerns. 614 is the PWR. The Byz MSS are nearly unanimous. Beyond them, the only ECM MSS joining it are: 044 636 1827 2805. It has no Westerns. The Byz order is more unnatural (harder) and if found in core Alex MSS would generally be accepted (cf. 19:20/8–20). Most versions join either NA28/PWR or the Byz. MS 08 offers five more Westerns plus e p w 189 sa^{ms} sy^p in confirmation of NA28's word order. In summary, NA28/PWR is original as confirmed by the Westerns.

99. (ATO) (α-INS) (19:3/5) NA28/614 omits (vs. πρὸς αὐτούς, Byz) and is found in 8/8 best ECM MSS, 8/10 core PWR MSS, and P41 05 08 18 35 etc., including eighteen Westerns plus Ath Vg d e gig p w 189 bo^{mss} sy^h. The alignment of the PWR with NA28 in avoiding the gloss shows its primitive excellence and its resistance to correction from the Byz standard. NA28/PWR is original.

100. (ATO) (α-INS) (19:12/50) NA28/614 has ἐκπορεύεσθαι (vs. ἐξέρχεσθαι ἀπ' αὐτῶν, Byz) and is found in 8/8 best ECM MSS, 7/10 core PWR MSS, and (P38) 05 08 35^{*vid} etc., including twenty Westerns plus (Vg d e gig p r w 189 bo sy^p sy^h). Beyond its tradition, only twelve MSS (six are Western) plus Chrys (sa bo^{ms}) join the Byz. The Byz changed the verb and added ἀπ' αὐτῶν from its use earlier in the verse. NA28 is original as confirmed by the PWR and the Westerns overall.

101. (BTO) (α-NTR) (19:20/8–20) Byz/614 reads ὁ λόγος τοῦ κυρίου (vs. τοῦ κυρίου ὁ λόγος, NA28) and is found in 10/10 core PWR MSS, 5/8 best ECM MSS (i.e., P74 33 1175 1739 2200), and (01C2) 181 206 etc., including twenty-two Westerns plus (sa bo sy^h Ä). 614 is the PWR. ECM lists twelve readings. Of them, eight have the Byz word order and two were completely rewritten. NA28 is joined by just (01*) 02 03 plus no translations. While τοῦ κυρίου might have been fronted for emphasis, the word order brings more confusion than clarity. The positioning even encourages the reader to consider τοῦ κυρίου with the preceding οὕτως κατὰ κράτος and read it

as, "Thus according to the might of the Lord, the word grew and prevailed." Barrett asserts that this understanding of the syntax is unlikely, given that κράτος lacks the article.[200] The error was simple to make and likely occurred after the proto-Alex archetype was already established. As a result, it did not impact most Alex witnesses, including the important Coptic bo and sa translations. As stated above, the word order mistakes of Alex scribes are too often readily accepted (see 18:26/40–46).[201] There should be no doubt that Byz/PWR is original.[202]

102. (ATO) (α-NTR) (19:25/38) NA28/614 has ἡμῖν (vs. ἡμῶν, Byz) and is joined by 7/8 best ECM MSS, 8/10 core PWR MSS, and 05 08 044 35* etc., including nineteen Westerns. 614 is the PWR. Byz has its native support and sixteen others, including six Westerns plus Chrys sy^p sy^h. NA28 has the more precise dative of advantage.[203] Although the Byz has more translations, NA28 is original as confirmed by the PWR and Westerns overall.

103. (BTO) (β-SI) (19:27/54–58) NA28/614 reads <u>τῆς</u> μεγαλει<u>ότητος</u> αὐτῆς (vs. <u>τὴν</u> μεγαλει<u>ότητα</u> αὐτῆς, Byz) and is found in 7/10 core PWR MSS, 8/8 best ECM MSS, 5/72 listed ECM Byz MSS (i.e., 218 323 1359 1718 2374; a minority of the seventy-two are lacuna), and thirty-three others, including nineteen Westerns. 614 is the PWR. Byz is joined by 014 (020) 025 056 1 35 etc. plus Chrys. It appears that the genitive occurred by a primitive mistake and was popular in the proto-Alex and Western traditions. The genitive might have occurred by simple assimilation to the following αὐτῆς. Alternatively, it might stem from the larger grammatical structure. In NA28 (with the clauses separated by //), the complete verse reads,[204] (1) οὐ μόνον δὲ τοῦτο κινδυνεύει ἡμῖν τὸ μέρος εἰς ἀπελεγμὸν ἐλθεῖν // (2) ἀλλὰ καὶ <u>τὸ</u> τῆς μεγάλης θεᾶς Ἀρτέμιδος <u>ἱερὸν</u> εἰς οὐθὲν <u>λογισθῆναι</u>, // (3) μέλλειν τε καὶ καθαιρεῖσθαι <u>τῆς</u> μεγαλει<u>ότητος</u> αὐτῆς // (4) ἣν ὅλη ἡ Ἀσία καὶ ἡ οἰκουμένη σέβεται. Barrett seems to translate based

---

200. Barrett, *Commentary on Acts*, 2:914.
201. Metzger, *Textual Commentary*, 418–19.
202. Soden, *Schriften des Neuen Testaments*, 2:571, agrees.
203. See Wallace, *Greek Grammar*, 142–44.
204. There are also some minor variations in the three traditions. The Byz places ἱερόν before Ἀρτέμιδος. In addition, the Byz has δὲ καὶ, NA28 has τε καὶ, and the PWR has τε.

upon what the passage ought to mean in rendering it as, "Not only does this mean for us a risk that this line of business may come into disrepute but also that the temple of the great goddess Artemis may be reckoned as nothing, *and she* whom all Asia and the inhabited world worship will be cast down from her greatness."[205] In order to do so, he translates the fourth clause before the third, and inserts the italicized words. In contrast, NA28 would appear to mean, "But not only is this portion in danger for us of coming into dishonor but also the temple of the great goddess Artemis is *in danger of* being reckoned as nothing, and even *the temple* is about to be deposed of her majesty, which all Asia and the inhabited world worship." The second clause uses the infinitive λογισθῆναι in the passive following τὸ ἱερὸν, i.e., "The temple is *in danger of* being reckoned." As a result, there may have been a tendency to read the third clause in the same way with an assumed subject followed by a descriptive infinitive, i.e., And even *the temple* is about to be deposed of her majesty." The third clause in the Byz reads (though here δέ is corrected to τε), μέλλειν τε καὶ καθαιρεῖσθαι τὴν μεγαλειότητα αὐτῆς, i.e., "Her majesty is about to be destroyed," and displays an unexpected change in the sentence flow. In contrast to clause two, the subject of the infinitive comes after it. Apparently, this flexible style was corrupted early on. That the genitive was an error is revealed by the feminine relative pronoun, commencing clause four. The use of ἥν indicates that Luke was referring to the subject of the previous infinitive as found only in the Byz, τὴν μεγαλειότητα αὐτῆς. The whole clause reads, ἣν ὅλη ἡ Ἀσία καὶ ἡ οἰκουμένη σέβεται. Here is the next potential motivation for the Byz to be changed. The implication of the Byz is that the whole world was in the custom of worshiping the magnificence of Artemis. Per the Byz, Demetrius states plainly that if the temple were devalued and subsequently destroyed, the magnificence of Artemis would vanish. Western editors know that people rarely worship a temple as a god and thus assume the Byz cannot be right in asserting that the loss of the temple would mean loss of the greatness of Artemis herself.[206] So we tend to think

---

205. Barrett, *Commentary on Acts*, 2:915.

206. Rius-Camps and Read-Heimerdinger, *Message of Acts*, 4:64, who see fault in the Byz for this implication. They prefer to think of the goddess Artemis as separable from the temple and the true object of the Ephesians' worship. They decide for the reading of 05.

that if the temple was destroyed, Artemis could live on with less visible glory. Such is a reasonable inference. However, if Artemis herself is the subject of the fourth clause, where is her antecedent?[207] Having evaluated the NA28 reading, Ropes called it a "monstrous sentence," partially fixed by the Byz. Instead, he favors a reading near to that of 05.[208] Yet 05 is abbreviated and clearly a gloss. Here the profoundness of the original shines forth. One of Paul's major teaching points for Asia Minor was that anything made by hands is not a god (see 19:26). Demetrius was arguing the opposite. Because human hands can make gods, human hands can also destroy her majesty, and even Artemis herself. She is inextricably linked to the temple. Demetrius's admission proves Paul's precept. In summary, a primitive error of some sort brought the confusion. The Byz was spared the mistake and is probably original.[209]

104. (ATO) (α-SI) (20:1/24–26, 28) NA28/614 has μαθητὰς καὶ παρακαλέσας (vs. μαθητὰς, Byz) and is found in 7/7 best ECM MSS, 10/10 core PWR MSS, (05C2) 08 (1884) etc., including 24/26 Westerns and sixty-eight total MSS plus Vg (d) e gig (w ar) 189 sy^p sy^h A G (sa bo Ä). 614 is the PWR. While just 1/7 core Byz MSS joins NA28, 14/68 that join NA28 are Byz (per ECM assessment). The Byz has just two Westerns plus Chrys. It appears that the proto-Byz text once agreed with NA28/PWR. However, Byz scribes later preferred a smoother reading that had been corrupted by an eye skip from the –ας ending of the preceding μαθητάς to the same ending in παρακαλέσας. The short reading became part of the main Byz text. NA28 is original as confirmed by the translations, PWR, and Western MSS. A similar phenomenon occurs in the following variant at 20:1/28 where NA28/614 has ἀσπασάμενος (vs. καὶ ἀσπασάμενος, Byz). Here just 4/7 best ECM MSS, 7/68 Byz's from above (i.e., 104 326 398 459 1609 1735 1837), and 9/10 core PWR MSS preserve the original short reading. Therefore, the PWR tradition has preserved the original text most purely across both variants. Though the PWR archetype is closely related to the Byz tradition, variants such as this one offer proof that its primitive text form usually persisted unchanged.

207. Haenchen, *Acts of the Apostles*, 573, says that ἥν has its antecedent in αὐτῆς. It is a logical deduction. But if so, the grammar is quite strange.

208. Ropes, *Beginnings of Christianity*, 186.

209. Bengel, *Novum Testamentum*, 204, agrees and he marks the NA28 reading with a δ rating. See Bengel, *Gnomon*, 2:682.

105. (BTO) (β-SI) (20:4/7) Byz/614 has ἄχρι τῆς Ἀσίας (vs. omits, NA28) and is found in 4/8 best ECM MSS (i.e., 02 1175 1739 2200), 10/10 core PWR MSS, and (05) 08 etc., including 27/27 Westerns plus Chrys A G (d e gig w sy^p sy$^{h.txt}$/sy^{hmg}). 614 is the PWR. NA28 is joined by 4/8 best ECM MSS (i.e., P74 01 03 33) and just 629 plus Vg p* 189 sa bo sy^{Aram} Ä. The translations are divided. Even 50 percent of the best ECM MSS join the Byz/PWR. The exclusive Western support breaks the tie, implying that a primitive scribe of the Alex tradition removed the words. It should be remembered that seventeen of these twenty-seven Westerns are mixed MSS, and their general alignment is Alexandrian. In contrast, Metzger says, "It is difficult to understand how" the words would be deleted if they were in the autograph.[210] Yet the commentaries show that the presence of the words makes for a difficult reading, and such hardness might cause their omission. They do not make much sense if applied to all of Paul's companions that are mentioned in 20:4. Why would 20:4 assert that these seven men accompanied Paul as far as Asia and then 20:5 indicate they all journeyed separate from Paul to Troas (i.e., Asia)? Ropes attempts to solve the problem by interpreting συνείπετο as "associated" even though "accompanied" is more likely in light of *TLG's* glosses.[211] His solution is very complicated. Though he rightly recognizes the editors of 05 and sy^{hmg} were confused at 20:4/2–6, he attributes to them the creation of ἄχρι τῆς Ἀσίας. However, alignments like this between 05/sy^{hmg} and the Byz/PWR normally point to what 05/sy^{hmg} has inherited from them. This direction of influence is confirmed here because while 05 and sy^{hmg} have numerous changes in 20:3–4, the Byz/PWR does not. Significantly, it appears that the Byz and Western scribes understood the phrase differently than those of Alex, and thus they embraced ἄχρι τῆς Ἀσίας. The verse begins by stating, with the singular συνείπετο, that Sopater, the Berean, son of Pyrrhus, accompanied Paul and then lists the other six men. It may be that the unusual 3S was meant to refer only to Sopater and a 3P συνείποντο was meant to be assumed for the other men. Luke's editorial note would then mean that only Sopater remained back and traveled with Paul, and only as far as Asia. The others sailed ahead and waited for them at

---

210. Metzger, *Textual Commentary*, 421.
211. Ropes, *Beginnings of Christianity*, 190–91.

Troas.²¹² Once all arrived, Sopater departed the group, and the others accompanied Paul to Syria (see 21:3) and Jerusalem (see 21:17). In summary, the limited but high-quality Greek support for NA28 points to a local correction of what seemed nonsensical. The Coptic sa and bo favor the Alex reading as they normally do. The Vg Ä and sy^Aram likely adopted the Alex reading because of its clarity. Byz/PWR is probably original.

106. (ATO) (α-SI) (20:4/10) Byz/614 omits (vs. Πύρρου, NA28) and is found in 10/10 core PWR MSS, including twelve Westerns plus Chrys sy^p sy^h.txt (Ä). 614 is the PWR. NA28 is joined by 8/8 best ECM MSS and 05 08 etc., including fourteen Westerns plus OrLat Vg e gig p w 189 sa bo sy^Aram sy^hmg. NA28 has the unexpected mention of Sopater's father in contrast to Paul's other companions listed only by their hometowns. It has better translation support than the related NA28 reading at 20:4/7. More importantly, the Westerns are divided as compared to their perfect coherence against NA28 in 20:4/7. Likewise, instead of the best ECM MSS being divided in half, 8/8 support NA28. The Byz/PWR has probably removed the name because it seemed to clash. Perhaps Paul knew the father well, and so Luke listed his name. A solid number of 38 ECM MSS uphold the longer original reading both here and at 20:4/7, including the Alex core MSS 02 1175 1739 2200, and the Western friendly (05) 08. Likewise, von Soden prints both longer readings.²¹³ NA28 is original.

107. (PAO) (β-SI) (20:5/6) 614/NA28 reads προελθόντες (vs. προσελθόντες, Byz/ECM) and is found in 7/10 core PWR MSS, 2/6 best ECM MSS (i.e., P74 2200), and 03C2 05 1 18 35 330 etc., including fifteen Westerns plus Chrys Vg d e gig p w 189 sa bo sy^p sy^h (προέρχομαι is used two times in Luke, three times in Acts, and nine total times in the NT). 614 is the PWR. The italicized MSS are part of the Byz core. Byz/ECM is joined by 4/6 best ECM MSS (i.e., 01 03* 1175 1739) and 08 014 020 etc., including thirteen Westerns plus sy^Aram (προσέρχομαι is used ten times in Luke, ten times in Acts, and eighty-six times in the NT). PWR/NA28 offers the less common word, the one that best fits the context, and the one most distinctly

---

212. See Haenchen, *Acts of the Apostles*, 581–82, who says that only Tychicus and Trophimus, who were native to Asia, sailed first.

213. Soden, *Schriften des Neuen Testaments*, 2:575.

Lucan.²¹⁴ As stated above (see 20:4/7), six of the seven men listed at 20:4 (Sopater excepted) preceded Paul to Troas. Evidently the sigma was added accidentally, and it became the primary Byz reading and a common reading of Alexandria. Many of the MSS corrupted by the sigma were further maligned when they harmonized 20:13/6 away from προελθόντες (NA28) in order to agree with the error here. Although the ECM marks the latter variant as a SGL, NA28 is most likely authentic with its support of 6/9 best ECM MSS, 9/10 core PWR MSS, and 03C2 206 etc., including nineteen Westerns plus sa bo. Here PWR/NA28 is probably original, as confirmed by its dominant translation attestation.²¹⁵

108. (BTO) (β-INS) (20:24/6-8) Byz/614 has οὐδενὸς λόγ<u>ον</u> ποιοῦμαι <u>οὐδὲ ἔχω</u> (vs. οὐδενὸς λόγ<u>ου</u> <u>ἔχω οὐδὲ</u> ποιοῦμαι, P74, vs. οὐδενὸς λόγ<u>ου</u> ποιοῦμαι, NA28) and is found in 10/10 core PWR MSS and 08 014 020 025 35 etc., including twenty Westerns plus Bas Chrys PsIgn^vid e (sy^h Ä). 614 is the PWR. It also has the indirect support of P74 01C2 02 (05*) 33 plus eight others that switched the word order.²¹⁶ Including the following four words, the Byz/PWR means something like, "I take consideration of nothing nor do I esteem my life precious to myself." The nothing refers to the predicted persecutions he would face. This reading is not simple.²¹⁷ NA28 is joined by 4/8 best ECM MSS (i.e., 01* 03 04 1175) and just P41 05C2 431 plus gig sa bo A G. The isolated Alex reading possibly arose in two steps. First, οὐδὲ ἔχω was lost by accident. Next, a proto-Alex scribe corrected λόγον to λόγου to make sense of what remained. P74 01C2 and 02 reveal a divided Alex tradition. The Alex λόγου does not explain the dominance of λόγον in the ECM (found in all but thirteen MSS). If οὐδὲ ἔχω was inserted after NA28's οὐδενὸς λόγου ποιοῦμαι, what would explain the change to the accusative λόγον? The revision

---

214. See Ropes, *Beginnings of Christianity*, 190–92, who favors the ECM reading because of his understanding of 20:4.

215. Barrett, *Commentary on Acts*, 2:949, agrees, and Wachtel, "Text-Critical Commentary," 29–30, admits that προελθόντες is better contextually.

216. Bengel, *Novum Testamentum*, 206, preferred this reading to the Byz, rating it β.

217. Metzger, *Textual Commentary*, 424–25, prefers NA28, calling it "awkward" and "idiomatic." Wachtel, "Against the Text-Type Concept," 146, considers NA28 to be the harder and original wording. Barrett, *Commentary on Acts*, 2:971, notes the "obscure" nature of NA28 but still chooses it. Ropes, *Beginnings of Christianity*, 196, perceives that the Byz merged the Alex original with that of 05. His explanation is unlikely because here the Byz equals the PWR and the PWR is normally more primitive than 05.

apparently flowed in the other direction. Consider, e.g., five of the thirteen MSS that preserve λόγου. These MSS otherwise match the Byz precisely, suggesting that they derived from it. In addition, per the ECM supplement, the remaining Latin witnesses (Vg d p w 189) all support a longer form.[218] Moreover, the supplement states that the Greek *Vorlage* used by the sa and bo editors might have included + οὐδὲ ἔχω, but because of translation technique the editors dropped the words. Byz/PWR is probably original.

109. (ATO) (β-SI) (20:24/27) Byz/614 reads μετὰ χαρᾶς (vs. omits, NA28) and is found in 10/10 core PWR MSS, 3/7 best ECM MSS (i.e., 04 1175 1739), and 08 206 etc., including 23/24 Westerns plus e sy^h. 614 is the PWR. NA28 is joined by 4/7 best ECM MSS (i.e., 01 02 03 33) and P41 05 and eight others plus Vg d gig p w 189 sa bo sy^p Ä. Since 05 is the only Western to deviate, it was probably conformed here to the Alex, as it commonly was. Although the Byz/Western alignment demonstrates great antiquity, the words might be an insertion from Pauline language (see Phil 1:4; Col 1:11; 1 Thess 1:6; Heb 10:34; 13:17). Conversely, an ancient Alex scribe might have removed them because joy did not fit with the context of Paul's sober speech. Although Ropes called μετὰ χαρᾶς "doubtful" because it lacked Western authority, modern research has removed that objection.[219] Von Soden accepted the plus.[220] Bengel considered the longer reading original, having rated the Alex reading as ε.[221] It is difficult to comprehend how all Westerns could have been corrupted when many of them are mainly Alex in nature. Likewise, it difficult to conceive why NA28 should have so much translation support if it were not original. Some insight may be gained from a nearby variant (see 20:31/31). The PWR reads ἕκαστον ὑμῶν (vs. ἕκαστον, NA28/Byz). It is joined by 05 08 etc., including 22/27 Westerns plus Antioch Bas^{pt} Chrys^{pt} Vg e gig p w 189 sa bo sy^p sy^h. The NA28/Byz reading is joined by 7/8 best ECM MSS etc., including five Westerns plus Bas^{pt} Chrys^{pt} Ephr^G, and *no* translations. Even though the PWR has all the versions and great Western support, the alignment of the Alex and Byz traditions for a rougher reading is

---

218. See ECM 3:2, 281.
219. Ropes, *Beginnings of Christianity*, 197.
220. Soden, *Schriften des Neuen Testaments*, 2:578.
221. Bengel, *Novum Testamentum*, 206.

stronger evidence. If that is true, all the ancient versions have erred at 20:31. Yet the same is most likely not valid here because the Alex is aligned with the translations. Moreover, the shorter reading is particularly difficult because it remains doubtful that anyone would purposely delete μετὰ χαρᾶς. Likewise, the morphology of the surrounding words makes deletion by an eye skip also unlikely. The phenomenon found here can be observed at least nine other times in the book Acts (see 2:30/34; 10:32/37; 15:24/30-34; 18:21/4-6, 9, 10, 24; 21:25/16-20; 23:30/45; 24:6/20-8/14; 28:16/12-16; 28:29/2-24). The words seem to have been removed by Luke as unnecessary prior to his final edition. A later editor reinserted it. This hypothesis could explain its great support, Lucan nature, and secondary status. NA28 is probably original.

110. (ATO) (α-SI) (20:25/39) Byz/614 reads τὴν βασιλείαν <u>τοῦ θεοῦ</u> (vs. τὴν βασιλείαν, NA28, vs. τὴν βασιλείαν <u>τοῦ Ἰησοῦ</u>, 05) and is found in 8/10 core PWR MSS and 08 014 020 35 etc., including 21/25 Westerns plus Thdrt Vg e p w 189 sa[ms] bo[mss] sy[p.ms] Ä A. NA28 is joined by 6/8 best ECM MSS (i.e., P74 01 02 03 04 33) and just ten others, including three Westerns plus Chrys bo[mss] sy[p.mss] sy[h] A[ms] G. MS 05 is joined by d and sa and evidently spun off the Byz/PWR. The translation evidence is closely divided and indicates a primitive change. While the longer reading is dominant among Westerns, the popularity of the phrase (NT: twenty-six times; Acts: three times; see 14:22; 28:23, 31) suggests it was infused.[222] The translation variety of NA28 suggests that τοῦ θεοῦ was not lost by accident. NA28 is original.[223]

111. (SGLR) (γ-INS) (21:5/56-6/6) Byz/614 reads προσηυξάμεθα <u>Καὶ ἀσπασάμενοι</u> ἀλλήλους (vs. προσευξάμενοι <u>ἀπησπασάμεθα</u> ἀλλήλους, NA28) and is found in 10/10 core PWR MSS and 014 020 35 etc., including fifteen Westerns plus Chrys. 614 is the PWR. NA28 is found in 8/9 best ECM MSS and nine others and includes just two Westerns. Its compound verb <u>ἀπησπασάμεθα</u> delimits the dual possibilities of the simple form (i.e., to greet or say farewell, *TLG*) in favor of the explicit sense of goodbye (*TLG*). This word occurs only here in the NT and just six times in *TLG*. Notice that Luke already

---

222. Soden, *Schriften des Neuen Testaments*, 2:578, thought the addition came from 28:31.

223. See Barrett, *Commentary on Acts*, 2:973.

used the flexible simple form in 20:1 to communicate farewell. Why not use it again? NA28 gains secondary support from MS 1739 and nineteen others, including seven Westerns. It reads with the simple form ἠσπασάμεθα that lacks the prefix ἀπ-. The translations cannot clear up the problem. The choice is between the Byz/PWR with the sequence, from καὶ θέντες all the way to ἐνέβημεν/ἀνέβημεν εἰς τὸ πλοῖον, being participle-finite verb-participle-finite verb that includes a form of the simple ἀσπάζομαι, against NA28 with the order participle-participle-finite verb-finite verb that includes a form of the compound ἀπασπάζομαι. Both yield good style but the Byz/PWR better matches the sequence of 21:7–8. Also, within Acts, Luke always uses the nominative participle form of ἀσπάζομαι (see 18:22; 20:1; 21:7, 19; 25:13). BL shows that this form only otherwise occurs at Heb 11:13.[224] Did the Byz/PWR maintain Lucan style and the Alex polish the syntax or did the Byz/PWR harmonize to parallels? The reading should be a SGL.

112. (ATO) (α-SI) (21:22/10–14) NA28/614 reads ἀκούσονται ὅτι ἐλήλυθας (vs. <u>δεῖ πλῆθος συνελθεῖν</u> ἀκούσονται <u>γὰρ</u> ὅτι ελήλυθας, Byz, vs. same as Byz except word order, P74) and is found in 8/10 core PWR MSS, 4/9 best ECM MSS (i.e., *03f1 04* 1175f2 1739*), and *307f1* 431f1 *436 453f1 2818f3* plus sa bo sy[p] sy[h] Ä. Byz is supported by 05* 014 020 35 etc. plus Chrys (d sy[Aram]) and less closely by (Vg e gig p w 189). P74 is found in 5/9 best ECM MSS (i.e., P74 01* 02 33 2200; though 01* lacks γὰρ) and 01C2 08f1 1739A etc., including forty-four total MSS. There are twelve alternatives. It appears that the Byz and P74 represent attempts to fill out the meaning. The short text could be paraphrased, "We must do something since the zealous Jews will know that you are here." The longer text implies, "We must gather the zealous Jews together and do something for they will know that you are here." NA28/PWR avoids the gloss and preserves the original reading. It is important to notice that of the supporters for NA28 here, only the italicized ones can be considered Alexandrian, since only they stand closer to the ECM text than to the Byz.[225] Given that 8/10 core PWR MSS support the original text, the PWR tradition is the most stable tradition at this variant. The alignment of the PWR is often very significant.

---

224. Boismard and Lamouille, *Texte occidental reconstitution*, 2:147, 234.
225. See CBGM.

113. (ABI) (21:25/14) 614 has ἀπεστείλαμεν (vs. ἐπεστείλαμεν, NA28/Byz) and is found in 4/10 core PWR MSS (i.e., 614 1292 2412 2495), 03 04* 05 049, and nine others, including eight Westerns plus (bo). 614 is the PWR. It means to send or send away and in this context the object of "letter" is implied. It probably arose from an itacism. Alternatively, the change might have been from a mental assimilation to ἀποστέλλω due to its abundant use. While ἐπιστέλλω is rarely used in the NT (only Acts 15:20 and Heb 13:22), ἀποστέλλω is common (NT: 132 times; Luke: 26 times; Acts: 24 times). That fact that ἀπεστείλαμεν is less suitable could indicate its unedited nature. In contrast to the PWR, the standard reading refers explicitly to sending by a letter and is joined by 6/9 best ECM MSS (i.e., P74 01 33 1175 1739 2200), 6/10 core PWR MSS, 02C 04C2 08, and the Byz core of 014 020 025 0142 1 18 35 330 398 424 1241 etc., including nineteen Westerns plus Chrys Vg d gig p w 189 sa. Notice how most but not all PWR MSS were corrected to the Byz standard. Because core Alex MSS 03 04* and WR MS 05 err together with the primitive PWR against the mainstream reading, the PWR edition is probably the source of the mistake. NA28/Byz is original.

114. (ATO) (β-SI) (21:25/16–20) Byz/614 reads κρίναντες μηδὲν τοιοῦτον/τοιοῦτο τηρεῖν αὐτούς εἰ μὴ φυλάσσεσθαι αὐτοὺς (vs. κρίναντες φυλάσσεσθαι αὐτοὺς, NA28) and is found in 10/10 core PWR MSS and 04 (05*) 05C2 08 014 020 35 etc., including eighteen Westerns plus Chrys A G (d e sy[h]). 614 is the PWR. The great antiquity of the Byz reading is implied by its alignment with so many Westerns despite the existence of nineteen alternative readings. In all, 27/28 Westerns support a longer reading. NA28 is joined by 6/9 best ECM MSS (i.e., P74 01 02 03 33 1175) and just 1409 2344[vid] L1188. However, its strong translation support includes: sy[Aram] (Vg p w 189 sa bo sy[p] Ä). One must ask, if the Byz/PWR was original, why would there be so many readings? Its complexity probably caused most of the others. The short reading actually fits the context better. The leaders of the church in Jerusalem were not then concerned with easing the burden on the gentiles but rather with strengthening Paul's testimony among the believing Jews. Therefore, a terse statement, instructing the gentiles about what to observe, makes the most sense. On the other hand, the expanded reading has excellent grammar and is consistent with Lucan style. In summary, this variant is one

of about ten that appear to come from Luke himself (see 2:30/34; 10:32/37; 15:24/30–34; 18:21/4–6, 9, 10, 24; 20:24/27; 23:30/45; 24:6/20–8/14; 28:16/12–16; 28:29/2–24). Perhaps Luke shortened his working copy prior to the final edition by removing unnecessary details. Later an editor with access to Luke's working copy decided to reinsert the clauses because of their clarifying nature. NA28 is original as confirmed by the translations. Metzger, Barrett, and von Soden agree.[226] In contrast, Bengel judged the short reading as inferior, rating it δ.[227]

115. (ATO) (α-NTR) (21:27/48–54) NA28/614 has ἐπ᾽ αὐτὸν <u>τὰς χεῖρας</u> (vs. <u>τὰς χεῖρας</u> ἐπ᾽ αὐτόν, Byz) and is joined by 9/9 best ECM MSS, 10/10 core PWR MSS, and 05 08 18 35 etc., including twenty-two Westerns plus AlMon Chrys. 614 is the PWR. Byz is joined by 014 020 etc., including six Westerns. Although the Byz text seems to manifest a word order gloss, it is the Western MSS that make that conclusion certain. NA28/PWR is original.

116. (ATO) (α-INS) (21:29/6) NA28/614 reads <u>προ</u>εωρακότες (vs. ἑωρακότες, Byz) and is found in 9/10 core PWR MSS, 8/8 best ECM MSS, and 05 08 etc., including twenty-one Westerns plus d e gig 189 bo sy[Aram] sy[p] sy[h]. 614 is the PWR. Byz is joined by 025 049 35 etc., including four Westerns plus Chrys Vg p w. One might suspect that NA28 was polished by the addition of the prefix. However, the PWR, most Westerns, and most translations imply that it was the Byz that erred by dropping the prefix accidentally. NA28 is original.

117. (BTO) (α-INS) (21:31/24–26) Byz/614 has ὅτι ὅλη <u>συγκέχυται</u> (vs. ὅτι ὅλη <u>συγχύννεται</u>, NA28) and is found in 10/10 core PWR MSS, 4/8 best ECM MSS, and 044 206 etc., including 24/26 Westerns. 614 is the PWR. NA28 is joined by 4/8 best ECM MSS (i.e., 01* 02 03* 33) and just 03C2 05 (1501) L1188. NA28 follows the few MSS that attempt to use the present tense perhaps to make the discourse livelier: "All of Jerusalem is stirred up!" The problem is that of the three different spellings, only 03*'s is found in *TLG*. In fact, its reading is the only example in *TLG*. The corrector 03C2 then revised it to a spelling absent from *TLG*. The editor should probably have used the form συγχέεται to achieve a PMI-3S since this spelling was known

---

226. Metzger, *Textual Commentary*, 429; Barrett, *Commentary on Acts*, 2:1015; Soden, *Schriften des Neuen Testaments*, 2:583.

227. Bengel, *Novum Testamentum*, 208.

(seventeen times in *TLG*). For NA28 to be correct, Luke would be responsible for a word form that extremely few scribes considered valid. Wachtel favors it because it has four of the best ECM MSS and the geographically independent testimony of 05.[228] It seems rather that 03 generated the confusion seen in its relatives 01 02 33. Moreover, 05 is built upon an Alex text base and was drastically revised with Western readings.[229] Overall, 05 preserves a text significantly inferior to that of Irenaeus. Moreover, Irenaeus is already a potential descendant of a great multitude of Greek MSS.[230] After receiving its Western form, 05 was later repeatedly aligned to Alex readings.[231] It is by no means an independent witness. Byz/PWR uses the perfect: "All of Jerusalem has been stirred up!" Byz/PWR is original.

118. (BTO) (β-NTR) (21:34/18–24) Byz/614 reads μὴ δυνάμενος δὲ (vs. μὴ δυναμένου δὲ αὐτοῦ, NA28, καὶ μὴ δυναμένου αὐτοῦ, 05) and is found in 10/10 core PWR MSS, 2/8 best ECM MSS (i.e., 1739 2200), and 044 206 etc., including 21/25 Westerns plus Chrys. 614 is the PWR. NA28 is joined by 6/8 best ECM MSS and twenty-one others total but only four Westerns. NA28 has indirect support from 05, which is unique in the Greek. 05 is joined by Vg d gig p w 189 and is probably the WRR. Given the solid support for the Byz/PWR, the small chance that Luke used a genitive absolute in a nonstandard manner, and the limited support for NA28, Byz/PWR is probably original.[232] The genitive absolute was evidently a primitive gloss within the proto-Alex tradition. It led to the WRR, which changed the conjunction that caused the word order change. Perhaps because the text still makes sense, the Alex scribes never corrected it.

119. (BTO) (β-SI) (22:9/19) Byz/614 has ἐθεάσαντο καὶ ἔμφοβοι ἐγένοντο (vs. ἐθεάσαντο, NA28) and is found in 10/10 core PWR MSS, 2/8 best ECM MSS (i.e., 1739 2200), and 020 025 05 08 35 etc., including 24/26 Westerns plus (e gig sa sy^h Ä). 614 is the PWR. NA28 is joined by 6/8 best ECM MSS (i.e., P74 01 02 03 33 1175), eight Byz MSS (i.e., 014 049 326 808 1127 1241 1837 1852), and sixteen others, including just two Westerns plus Vg p w 189 bo sy^p. Notice the

---

228. Wachtel, "Text-Critical Commentary," 32.
229. Wachtel, "Against the Text-Type Concept," 142.
230. Strutwolf, "Text Apostelgeschichte bei Irenäus," 176–81.
231. Ropes, *Beginnings of Christianity*, lxxx–lxxxiii.
232. Barrett, *Commentary on Acts*, 2:1022, notices the strange usage but still accepts it.

Byz/PWR is joined by the earliest Coptic evidence in the sa and the normally conservative Ä. While fear is mentioned in the Western glosses at 9:6/2–4 (i.e., τρέμων τε θάμβων) and 26:14/10–14 (i.e., εἰς τὴν γῆν διὰ τὸν φόβον ἐγὼ μόνος), the wording is not close and the attestation is limited. The longer, well-attested reading here probably inspired those. Most likely NA28 has resulted from an eye skip from the preceding word ἐθεάσαντο to the end of ἐγένοντο. Metzger acknowledges this possibility, but the committee preferred to judge it a Western gloss.[233] BL assert that the words have forcibly introduced a new theme because of assimilation to the Lucan Western reading at 9:5 (9:6 in the ECM) and have disturbed the sentence flow.[234] Yet their selection for the expansion at 9:6 certainly has a greater impact on the context. It explicitly mentions fear, describes the vanity of fighting against God, and includes Paul's request for guidance. Moreover, all ECM MSS of Acts 9 testify unitedly that Paul's companions were speechless, suggesting they were amazed and afraid. Acts 26 explains that they fell to the ground, implying they were terrified. Therefore, it does not seem unnatural for the text to state here that his companions were afraid. Von Soden cites Luke 24:37 as the cause of an assimilation.[235] By doing so, he recognizes its Lucan nature. Similarly, Haenchen notes the wording is like parallels (see Luke 24:5, 37; Acts 10:4; 24:25).[236] The fact that 8/30 of NA28's supporters are Byz suggests the same parablepsis likely occurred more than once independently. Less likely, these MSS were revised to the Alex text. Byz/PWR is probably original. Bengel agrees and rates the omission as δ.[237]

120. (PAO) (β-INS) (22:12/26–28) 614/HF1985 reads ὑπὸ πάντων τῶν κατοικούντων ἐν Δαμασκῷ Ἰουδαίων (vs. ὑπὸ πάντων τῶν κατοικούντων Ἰουδαίων, NA28/RP05) and is found in 8/10 core PWR MSS, 4/8 best ECM MSS (33 1175 1739 2200), eight key Byz MSS (i.e., 014 020 049 0142 18 35* 424 1241) etc., including 20/27 Westerns plus (sa p w 189 Ä). In addition, four more Westerns are related to it because they all include ἐν/εἰς Δαμασκῷ. 614 is the

---

233. Metzger, *Textual Commentary*, 430.
234. Boismard and Lamouille, *Texte occidental reconstitution*, 2:62–63, 154.
235. Soden, *Schriften des Neuen Testaments*, 2:586.
236. Haenchen, *Acts of the Apostles*, 626.
237. Bengel, *Novum Testamentum*, 209.

PWR. NA28/RP05 is joined by 4/8 best ECM MSS (i.e., P74 01 02 03), 08 025 1 35C1, and sixteen others, including three Westerns plus Vg e (bo). Though this is the reading of RP05, it is not correct to call it an Alex/Byz aligned reading. The Byz support is mostly late. Hodges and Farstad 1985 (HF1985) show the Byz tradition as split.[238] Notice that only 11/52 Byz MSS within the ECM join RP05.[239] The other forty-one support a form of the long reading. NA28/RP05 is somewhat awkward. Barrett does well to translate it as "all the resident Jews."[240] It appears to derive from a proto-Alex scribe who expected a genitive after κατοικούντων and thus jumped over ἐν Δαμασκῷ to Ἰουδαίων. The earliest Byz tradition had the long reading but later removed it perhaps by reference to the Alex. The short form does not appear to be Lucan. There are thirteen other occasions in Acts and one in Luke where the author uses a participle form of κατοικέω. Each time he ties it to a place. Moreover, they are all named places except one (see Acts 1:20). The longer reading is evidently not a gloss because it preserves ἐν Δαμασκῷ prior to Ἰουδαίων. If the goal was to smooth the text, one might have expected, ὑπὸ πάντων τῶν Ἰουδαίων τῶν κατοικούντων ἐν Δαμασκῷ (cf. 9:22) or simply ὑπὸ πάντων Ἰουδαίων ἐν Δαμασκῷ. Similarly, it could have simplified to ὑπὸ πάντων τῶν ἐν Δαμασκῷ Ἰουδαίων, as is found in MSS 1505 and 2495. In summary, the PWR preserves the most Lucan reading. It has solid support from all three traditions and is found in the sa and Ä. 614/PWR is probably original.[241]

121. (BTO) (α-INS) (22:23/4) Byz/614 has δὲ (vs. τε, NA28) and is found 26/26 Westerns, all Byz MSS, and 6/9 best ECM MSS (i.e., P74 01 33 1175 1739 2200) etc. plus Chrys Vg e gig p w 189. MS 614 is the PWR. NA28 is joined by only 02 03 04 plus sy[h]. NA28 is also easier because τε explicitly links 22:23 with the preceding verse. Some time after the proto-Alex archetype was established, a trusted Alexandrian exemplar received a stylistic gloss. Byz/PWR is original.

---

238. Hodges and Farstad, *Greek New Testament*, 452.

239. Out of the MSS shown in the apparatus at 22:12/26–28, a total of fifty-two are categorized as Byz according to the supplementary volume (ECM 3:2, 8).

240. Barrett, *Commentary on Acts*, 2:1029.

241. See Metzger, *Textual Commentary*, 431, and Barrett, *Commentary on Acts*, 2:1040, who both call the long reading a gloss.

122. (ATO) (α-NTR) (23:8/16) NA28/614 reads μήτε ἄγγελον μήτε πνεῦμα (vs. μηδὲ ἄγγελον μήτε πνεῦμα, RP05) and is found in 9/10 core PWR MSS, 8/9 best ECM MSS, and 08 18 35 etc., including 25/27 Westerns plus Cyr. 614 is the PWR. RP05 is joined by P74 014 020 etc., including two Westerns plus Chrys. NA28 is smoother with μήτε twice. While the unified Alex core make NA28 probable, the unified Westerns make it almost certain. NA28/PWR is original.

123. (ATO) (α-INS) (23:9/14–26) NA28/614 has τινὲς τῶν γραμματέων τοῦ μέρους τῶν Φαρισαίων (vs. τινὲς τῶν Φαρισαίων, P74, vs. οἱ γραμματεῖς τοῦ μέρους τῶν Φαρισαίων, Byz) and is found in 8/10 core PWR MSS, 5/9 best ECM MSS (i.e., 01 03 1175 1739 2200), and 181 206 etc., including sixteen Westerns plus (gig sa sy^p). 614 is the PWR. P74 is found in 3/9 best ECM MSS (i.e., P74 02 33) and eight others plus Vg e p w 189 bo. P74 made an eye skip and is joined by the usually reliable bo and Vg. This unity in error among few witnesses may point to a shared ancestry between P74 02 Vg and bo. Byz is joined by just five Westerns and has smoothed the text. The PWR has stayed true despite fourteen alternative readings. NA28/PWR is both more complex and original.

124. (ATO) (α-SI) (23:9/59) Byz/614 reads μὴ θεομαχῶμεν (vs. omits, NA28) and is found in 10/10 core PWR MSS and 014 020 35 2200 etc., including nineteen Westerns plus Chrys sa (sy^p). 614 is the PWR. NA28 is joined by 9/10 best ECM MSS and eleven others plus AmAl Vg e gig p h w 189 bo sy^h Ä. Though limited, the evidence for NA28 is strong, especially considering its difficulty. Luke purposefully left the dialogue open ended. A primitive proto-Byz scribe evidently added the words by analogy to 5:39, in order to complete what the scribes might have been saying.[242] Barrett selects the shorter reading and helpfully suggests that "what" should go at the beginning of the previous clause.[243] It would thus say, "What if a spirit or angel has spoken to him?" Bengel long ago preferred the shorter reading and rated it β.[244] NA28 is original but the Byz/PWR is extremely old.

125. (ATO) (α-INS) (23:11/21) NA28/614 has θάρσει (vs. θάρσει Παῦλε, Byz) and is found in 9/10 best ECM MSS, 7/9 core PWR MSS, and

---

242. See Metzger, *Textual Commentary*, 432.
243. Barrett, *Commentary on Acts*, 2:1052, 1067.
244. Bengel, *Novum Testamentum*, 211.

08 35* etc., including fifteen Westerns plus Chrys^pt Vg e gig sa bo sy^p sy^h. 614 is the PWR. Byz is joined by 04C3 014 35C 81 etc., including eight Westerns plus Chrys^pt OrLat Thdrt p h w 189. NA28 is confirmed as original by the Westerns and translations.

126. (PAO) (a-SI) (#23:30/10-18) (3ways) NA28/614 reads εἰς τὸν ἄνδρα ἔσεσθαι ἐξαυτῆς (vs. εἰς τὸν ἄνδρα μέλλειν ἔσεσθαι ὑπὸ τῶν Ἰουδαίων ἐξαυτῆς, Byz, vs. εἰς τὸν ἄνδρα ἔσεσθαι ἐξ αὐτῶν, 01/1505) and is joined by P74 03 044 1292 2374 2412 2464 (bo). 614 is *not* the PWR. Byz is joined by 014 020 35 etc., including four Westerns plus Chrys (sa). 01/1505 is joined by 02 08(*f) (33) 81 1175 1739 1890* 2138 2200 2495 and fourteen others, including eleven Westerns plus e (sy^h, + μέλλειν). There are thirteen alternatives at this complex variant. Initially NA28/614 (reading a.) seems to best explain the others. It may have been corrupted very early to reading b. (see 01/1505) when ΕΞΑΥΤΗΣ was changed to ΕΞΑΥΤΩΝ. Presumably, the editor read the former sequence as two words, i.e., ἐξ αὐτῆς. Seeing a problem, he corrected it to ἐξ αὐτῶν in order to refer to the Jews. Wachtel asserts that the rarity of ἐξαυτῆς contributed to the mistake.[245] He also said that its presence in ten of thirteen readings and in the majority of MSS confirms its originality. However, even though it is rare, the use of ἐξαυτῆς as recent at 21:32 in a parallel context makes a misunderstanding of the term unlikely. Furthermore, the commander again acts with urgency at 23:23 by ordering 470 military troops to assist Paul in a safe transport to Caesarea. Moreover, the term is used at 10:33 in a similar context. Though Cornelius sends *for* Peter and the commander sends *to* the governor, both gave a command to send quickly. These parallel situations emphasize prompt action and probably contributed to "seeing" ἐξαυτῆς when it was not really there. Because its presence in one of the shortest readings is so smooth, there is no apparent motive for specifying who was guilty of the plot, as was done in most Greek MSS. The fact that ἐξαυτῆς occurs only in a minority of the best ECM MSS, speaks against it. It does receive support from some of the core PWR MSS (i.e., 614 1292 2412). While these MSS are seldom revised later by the Alex tradition, they do occasionally display changes isolated from their friends (see 13:33/20; 17:24/32-34; 18:2/60; 24:14/28-36; 26:30/2-4). In summary, instead of

---

245. Wachtel, "Text-Critical Commentary," 33.

ἐξαυτῆς, the original reading appears to end with ἐξ αὐτῶν as found in 01/1505. This reading is found in 7/9 best ECM MSS and 4/10 core PWR MSS (i.e., 1505 1890* 2138 2495) etc., including eleven Westerns plus e. 1505 is the PWR. The use of ἐξ αὐτῶν is Lucan, being found in his Gospel nine times and six other times in Acts (see 11:20, 28; 15:22; 17:4, 12; 23:21). The last reference has the same context. As to the Byz, it is convoluted here. It conflates reading a. (MS 614) and b. (MS 01), clarifies ἐξ αὐτῶν by expansion, and adds μέλλειν (see 23:15, 20, 27). The antiquity and contextual suitability of ἐξαυτῆς explains how it became part of most alternate readings. However, its absence from most of the best ECM MSS reveals its derived nature. Therefore, 01/PWR is original.[246]

127. (ATO) (β-INS) (23:30/45) Byz/614 reads ἔρρωσο (vs. omits, NA28) and is found in 10/10 core PWR MSS, 5/9 best ECM MSS (i.e., 01 81 1175 1739 2200), and 08 020 35 (915) etc., including 26/26 Westerns plus Chrys e w ar 189 sy^p sy^h. 614 is the PWR. NA28 is joined by 4/9 best ECM MSS (i.e., P74 02 03 33) and 228 629 996 2344 L1188, including 0 Westerns plus Vg gig p sa bo Ä. The ECM considers it a SGL reading. The fact that ἔρρωσο is an alternate spelling of the same word as found in the apostolic decree (see ἔρρωσθε at 15:29), makes it even more likely to be original. If the word was inserted from the parallel, there is no reason to change the spelling. Wachtel suggests that the omission might have been accidental due to the similar form of the preceding ἐπὶ σοῦ or even purposeful.[247] The perfect Western coherence, majority of best ECM MSS, unified Byz (only MS 228 deviates), and solid translations show that the Byz/PWR is extremely ancient. Still the motivation to delete ἔρρωσο appears to be lacking given that all the best ECM MSS include the closing at 15:29. As noted in other places, such readings appear to be Lucan but still secondary (see 2:30/34; 10:32/37; 15:24/30–34; 18:21/4–6, 9, 10, 24; 20:24/27; 21:25/16–20; 24:6/20–8/14; 28:16/12–16; 28:29/2–24).

128. (ABI) (24:6/20–8/14) RP05^mg/614 has + καὶ κατὰ τὸν ἡμέτερον νόμον ἠθελήσαμεν κρῖναι/κρίνειν παρελθὼν δὲ Λυσίας ὁ χιλίαρχος

---

246. Metzger, *Textual Commentary*, 433, asserts that 01 has a "serious claim to be original." Barrett, *Commentary on Acts*, 2:1085, suggests that 01 "could be right." Soden, *Schriften des Neuen Testaments*, 2:592, prints the 01 wording as original.

247. Wachtel, "Text-Critical Commentary," 34.

μετὰ πολλῆς βίας ἐκ τῶν χειρῶν ἡμῶν ἀπήγαγεν κελεύσας τοὺς κατηγόρους αὐτοῦ ἔρχεσθαι ἐπί σου/σε (vs. omits, NA28/RP05^txt) and is joined by 08 044 0142 35* 398 424C and fifty-eight others, including 26/26 Westerns plus e gig p/2 w ar sy^p sy^h A. 614 is the PWR. NA28/RP05^txt is joined by 6/10 best ECM MSS (i.e., P74 01 02 03 81 1175), 8 core Byz MSS (i.e., 014 020 025 049 18 35C 424* 1241), and ten others plus Vg p* 189 sa bo Ä G. The translation support is very evenly balanced. Significantly, the relatively pure Byz MS 35 commonly preserves very ancient readings. When it is corrected, it is generally revised to the Byz standard. Contrary to expectations, 35* had the long reading and then 35C removed it. This fact helps confirm that the long reading was part of the proto-Byz tradition. Byz editors later judged it to be a gloss (see 014 020 025; oldest extant Byz MSS). The revised Byz is aligned with the earliest core Alex MSS P74 01 02 03. In harmony with this fact, both Byz editions (i.e., RP05 and HF1985) place the longer reading of twenty-seven words in the margin. The grammar/syntax, suitable wording, divided Byz, and perfect coherence among Westerns unite to suggest that the reading was written by Luke but still secondary (see 2:30/34; 10:32/37; 15:24/30–34; 18:21/4–6, 9, 10, 24; 20:24/27; 21:25/16–20; 23:30/45; 28:16/12–16; 28:29/2–24).[248] Although an ancient scribe may have removed the words due to their biased reporting, more likely Luke himself deleted them as unnecessary, prior to publishing his one and only edition. NA28/RP05^txt is probably original.

129. (ATO) (α-INS) (24:10/40–46) NA28/614 reads εὐθύμως (vs. εὐθυμότερον, Byz) and is found in 9/9 best ECM MSS and 9/10 core PWR MSS etc., including seventeen Westerns plus (Vg e p w 189). 614 is the PWR. Instead of the simple adverb, the Byz has a comparative and is joined by six Westerns. The Byz is confirmed as a stylistic gloss by the Westerns. NA28/PWR is original.

130. (BTO) (β-INS) (24:12/24) Byz/614 has ἐπισύστασιν (vs. ἐπίστασιν, NA28, vs. ἀποστασίαν, 81C) and is found in 10/10 core PWR MSS and 014 020 025 35 206 2200 etc., including nineteen Westerns plus Chrys Epiph^ms. 614 is the PWR. NA28 is joined by 6/9 best ECM MSS (i.e., P74 01 02 03 33 1739) and nineteen others, including

---

248. Boismard and Lamouille, *Texte occidental reconstitution*, 1:8–9, 159, 190, 202, 224, 226, choose a modified form of the long reading here. In addition, they mark each of the italicized passages as being part of Luke's first edition.

five Westerns plus Epiph^T Ä. MSS 81*f1 and 1175f2 either attest to 81C or to NA28. The Byz/PWR word commonly refers to a "riotous gathering," while NA28 suggests a stoppage, a concern, or one's attention (see *TLG*). Barrett understands it as a "collecting" as in the "collecting of a crowd."[249] 81C uses ἀποστασία as its root and derives from the more ancient form ἀπόστασις (*TLG*). Both can mean a "defection, revolt" (*TLG*). The Byz word fits the context best. It seems doubtful that Paul would say that he did not form a crowd by stopping them. With another syllable, he could have argued that he did not form a riotous crowd. Moreover, if Paul had indeed spoken that opaquely, would not Luke have clarified the meaning? The reading of 2/9 best ECM MSS (i.e., 81 1175) appears to be an effort to fix the vague ἐπίστασιν. Because NA28 has solid Alex core MS support, its reading is ancient. It would appear to stem from a proto-Alexandrian scribe who accidentally lost the syllable -συ- from the word's middle. In fact, the best of the best ECM MSS, 03, is known for reducing compound words to simple forms.[250] Von Soden is probably right to attribute the variant to scribal harmonization with 2 Cor 11:28.[251] He thought it was the Byz that did it. Rather, it seems that NA28 harmonized this passage to match the NA28/original reading at 2 Cor 11:28 (i.e., "my concern/priority"). Meanwhile, the Byz has harmonized 2 Cor 11:28 to the Byz/original reading here (i.e., "a riot"). Therefore, each tradition uses its word twice and only twice in the NT. NA28 is best in 2 Corinthians and the Byz is best in Acts. Because the NA28 reading here is also found in 6 Byz MSS (i.e., 218 398 1359 1563 1718 1852), this group and the proto-Alex archetype might have both made the same oversight independently. Byz/PWR is probably original.

131. (BTO) (α-NTR) (24:13/2) Byz/614 reads οὔτε (vs. οὐδὲ, NA28) and is found in 6/9 best ECM MSS (i.e., P74 02 33 1175 1739 2200), 10/10 core PWR MSS, and 08 181 etc., including 25/25 Westerns plus Epiph. 614 is the PWR. NA28 is joined by just 01 03 81 Epiph. ECM records the variant as a SGL. The easier reading is NA28 because it seems to mark a slight change in content from 24:12 from 24:13 by using the conjunction οὐδέ instead of the adverb οὔτε, already found

---

249. Barrett, *Commentary on Acts*, 2:1103.
250. Fee, "P75, P66, and Origen," 261.
251. Soden, *Schriften des Neuen Testaments*, 2:594.

three times in 24:12. Barrett points to a superior sense in NA28.[252] However, that is not uncommon with a grammatical gloss. Its meager support exposes it as secondary. If οὐδέ was original, surely more of the early scribes would have maintained it even if they did not fully recognize its significance. Wachtel states that οὐδέ can be used to create climax when it precedes the last element of several "negative statements."[253] He speculates that the earliest scribes may have overlooked this feature. Byz/PWR is original.

132. (ATO) (β-INS) (24:14/46–56) NA28/614 reads τοῖς ἐν τοῖς προφήταις (vs. τοῖς προφήταις, Byz) and is found in 6/10 core PWR MSS, 5/8 best ECM MSS, and 08 044 etc., including 18 Westerns. 614 is the PWR. Byz is joined by 2/8 best ECM MSS (i.e., 02 33) and 01C2 014 020 025 383 2147 2495 etc., including 7 Westerns. The Byz reading is less balanced, making it possibly more primitive. On the other hand, the wording of NA28 is conducive for an eye skip. The only translations specific enough to be listed could support either reading. Most of the core Alex MSS favor NA28 but that only makes its wording probable. However, the bulk of the Westerns provide confirmation. NA28/PWR is probably original.

133. (ATO) (α-INS) (24:18/4) NA28/614 has αἷς (vs. οἷς, Byz) and is found in 8/10 core PWR MSS, 10/10 best ECM MSS, and 08 044 etc., including eighteen Westerns. 614 is the PWR. The Byz reading has a solid core of Byz ECM MSS (i.e., 014 020 025 049 0142 1 18 35 330 398 1241; but not 424), and is joined by eighteen Westerns. According to Barrett, if οἷς is read as a neuter, it gives an easier reading by referring to the entire previous verse.[254] On the other hand, the Byz is harder if οἷς is read as masculine (per RP05 digital parsing) because it lacks a grammatical antecedent. It appears to be a *constructio ad sensum* to the *people of* my nation in 24:17. If NA28 is original, it points back to the offerings and is medium in difficulty.[255] The translations do not help. In contrast, the PWR edition and Westerns offer independent testimony in favor of NA28. Moreover, NA28 is strengthened by the unusual placement of καὶ προσφοράς within the NA28 variant at 24:17/10–26. Unlike the Byz (reading

---

252. See Barrett, *Commentary on Acts*, 2:1103.
253. Wachtel, "Text-Critical Commentary," 34.
254. Barrett, *Commentary on Acts*, 2:1108.
255. See Barrett, *Commentary on Acts*, 2:1108.

d.) and the PWR (reading b.), which essentially place alms and offerings in order, NA28 has alms, a finite verb, and then offerings at the end. Upon first look, the structure seems to minimize the offerings. However, Luke apparently wanted to set apart προσφοράς so that it might be tightly joined with the immediately following ἐν αἷς in 24:18. By doing so, Luke highlighted a central point of actual disagreement between Paul and the zealous Jews. Paul understood the sacrificial system to be superseded while these Jews considered it unceasingly binding upon all Jews. NA28 is original as confirmed by the Westerns.

134. (BTO) (β-INS) (24:20/14–18) By/614 reads ἐν ἐμοὶ ἀδίκημα στάντος μου (vs. ἀδίκημα ἐν ἐμοὶ στάντος μου, 1739, vs. ἀδίκημα στάντος μου, NA28) and is found in 10/10 core PWR MSS and 04 08 014 020 35 etc., including 18/23 Westerns plus Chrys Vg e gig p w 189 (sa bo sy^p sy^h). 614 is the PWR. MS 1739 is joined by 630 945 1704 1751 1891 2200 2298 and includes four Westerns. Therefore, two of the best ECM MSS (i.e., 1739 2200) were evidently revised to the Byz/PWR. However, they inserted ἐν ἐμοί in a smoother location. Overall, 22/23 Westerns uphold the longer reading. NA28 is found in 7/10 best ECM MSS (i.e., P74 01 02 03 33 81 1175) and just 181 1718 1875 2344 L1188 plus Ä. Although the core Alex MSS are mostly united, the bo and sa retain the words. In other places, these Coptic translations prove to be extremely faithful. In respect to the long expansions found jointly in the Byz/PWR (see 2:30; 10:32; 15:24; 18:21; 21:25; 24:6–8; 28:16; 28:29), the bo avoids each one. The sa includes just two of them (see 10:32; 28:16). Interestingly, the Ä only has the expansion at 10:32. Does that mean Ä was the only faithful translation here? Von Soden suggests ἐν ἐμοί entered from the parallels (see Luke 23:4, 14, 22; John 18:38; 19:4, 6).[256] To these could be added a near parallel at Acts 28:18, also spoken by Paul. Overall, it seems more likely that a proto-Alex scribe removed the phrase to simplify the wording and that Ä inherited the mistake.[257] It was inevitable that the Alex scribes in guarding against corruption from expansion would at times overcorrect and lose an original reading. The words are Pauline (e.g., Rom 7:17–18) and

---

256. Soden, *Schriften des Neuen Testaments*, 2:596.

257. See Barrett, *Commentary on Acts*, 2:1110, who calls ἐν ἐμοί "superfluous and not easily combined with the genitive that follows." On the other hand, Metzger, *Textual Commentary*, 435, says the addition makes the text "more explicit."

Lucan, more difficult in the context, have the best Greek MS variety, and are overwhelmingly supported by the translations. Byz/PWR is probably original.

135. (ATO) (α-NTR) (24:21/16–20) NA28/614 has ἐν αὐτοῖς ἑστώς (vs. ἑστώς ἐν αὐτοῖς, Byz) and is found in 9/9 best ECM MSS and 8/10 core PWR MSS etc., including seventeen Westerns. 614 is the PWR. Byz word order is smoother, and it is joined by 014 020 025 35 etc., including six Westerns. Most Westerns were faithful here to avoid even a word order gloss. They should not be hastily judged as having revised the text in places like 24:20/14–18 above given their repeated ability to be conservative. NA28/PWR is original.

136. (ATO) (α-INS) (24:25/20–24) NA28/614 reads κρίματος τοῦ μέλλοντος (vs. κρίματος τοῦ μέλλοντος ἔσεσθαι, Byz) and is found in 9/10 core PWR MSS, 8/10 best ECM MSS, and 08 044 etc., including fifteen Westerns. 614 is the PWR. Byz provides a smoothing gloss and is joined by 014 020 35 etc., including nine Westerns plus Chrys. Once again, NA28 is original as confirmed by the Westerns.

137. (ATO) (α-SI) (24:26/21) Byz/614 has ὅπως λύσῃ αὐτόν (vs. omits, NA28) and is found in 6/10 core PWR MSS (i.e., 383 614 1292 1611 2147 2412; but 383 and 2147 have λύσει) and 307 431 1890C etc., including ten Westerns plus Chrys bo (sa). 614 is the PWR. NA28 is joined by 8/9 best ECM MSS, 4/10 core PWR MSS (i.e., 1505 1890* 2138 2495), and 08 181 etc., including eleven Westerns plus Vg e gig s p w 189 sy[Aram] sy[p] sy[h] Ä. The harder reading lacks the clarifying words. NA28 has better translation support. Half of the Westerns refrain from adding and are more conservative here than the bo and sa. NA28 is original as confirmed by the translations and the divided Westerns.

138. (ATO) (α-INS) (25:2/8–10) NA28/614 reads οἱ ἀρχιερεῖς καὶ οἱ πρῶτοι (vs. ὁ ἀρχιερεὺς καὶ οἱ πρῶτοι, Byz) and is joined by 10/10 best ECM MSS, 9/10 core PWR MSS, and 08 020 18 35 424C 1241 etc., including 21 Westerns plus Chrys[pt] Vg e gig p w 189 sa bo sy[p] sy[h] Ä. 614 is the PWR. The Byz is joined by 014 025 049 etc. incl. 4 Westerns plus sy[Aram] (Chrys[pt]). On internal evidence, the plural οἱ ἀρχιερεῖς appears to be a harmonization with 25:15. However, the external evidence is strongly against it, including the perfect coherence among the best ECM MSS, the unified PWR MSS, the overall

Western tradition, and nearly every translation. Even some of the core Byz MSS (italicized) join the chorus. The Byz reading evidently arose for a different reason. It may have become the singular, "chief priest," by influence from what came before (see 24:1). NA28 is original as confirmed by the Westerns and translations.

139. (ATO) (α-SI) (25:6/6–20) (3ways) 614 has ἐν αὐτοῖς ἡμέρας πλείους ὀκτὼ ἢ δέκα (vs. ἐν αὐτοῖς ἡμέρας πλείους ἢ δέκα, Byz, vs. ἐν αὐτοῖς ἡμέρας οὐ πλείους ὀκτὼ ἢ δέκα, NA28) and is found in 8/10 core PWR MSS plus 206* and fifteen others, including thirteen Westerns overall plus sy^h. 614 is the PWR. What a fascinating variant! ECM lists twelve alternate readings. Byz is joined by 014 020 025 35 383* 1890C etc., including six Westerns plus Chrys. NA28 is joined by 9/10 best ECM MSS (but 01 changed the word order) and twenty-nine others, including seven Westerns plus Vg e gig w^{vid} 189 (bo). The text was convoluted very early. First the negative οὐ was lost from the NA28 reading, and it became the PWR and that of 206*. The corrector 206C managed to fix the error. Many MSS "fixed" the PWR by removing the now unnecessary ὀκτώ and thus created the Byz reading (see 1890C above). The corrector 383C "fixed" the Byz by inserting the missing οὐ but not the absent ὀκτώ. NA28 has the reading that best explains the others and is original.

140. (ATO) (α-INS) (25:21/30–36) N28/614 has ἕως οὗ ἀναπέμψω αὐτὸν (vs. ἕως οὗ πέμψω αὐτὸν, Byz) and is found in 8/10 core PWR MSS, 10/10 best ECM MSS, and forty-four others, including seventeen Westerns plus e. 614 is the PWR. Byz is joined by 014 020 35 383 2147 etc., including seven Westerns plus Chrys^{vid} Vg p^{vid} w 189. The Byz has an edge in translation support, but most translations are not specific enough to reconstruct their Greek *Vorlage*. NA28/PWR is more precise because ἀναπέμπω can mean to "send up to a higher authority" (*TLG*). That would make the Byz a simplification or accidental loss. Conversely, the precision could have been a scribal gloss. NA28 is original as confirmed by the Westerns.

141. (BTO) (β-NTR) (25:22/11) Byz/614 reads Ἀγρίππας δὲ πρὸς τὸν Φῆστον ἔφη (vs. same except omits ἔφη, NA28, vs. replaces ἔφη with εἶπεν, 206) and is joined by 6/10 best ECM MSS (i.e., P74 04 81 1175 1739 2200), 10/10 core PWR MSS, and 08 181 307 etc., including 23/25 Westerns plus Chrys (e gig ar 189). MS 614 is the PWR. NA28 is joined by just 01* 01C2b 02 03 33 629 2344 L1188

plus Vg p w. MS 206 is joined by just 429 and 522 and includes 2/25 Western MSS. Thus, all Byz and Western MSS agree in giving ἔφη or εἶπεν. Even 60 percent of the best ECM MSS do the same. It is unrealistic here to argue that 01* 02 03 have nearly alone preserved the original. Although their reading is a bit harder, it was certainly not a given that scribes would have felt the need to insert a verb of speaking (see 26:28/13 where 9/9 best ECM MSS and 8/10 core PWR MSS etc. lack ἔφη; see 26:29/2–6 where 9/9 best ECM MSS and 5/10 core PWR MSS refrain from adding either εἶπεν or ἔφη). NA28 seems to be an error by assimilation to 26:28/2–12 where it reads similarly, ὁ δὲ Ἀγρίππας πρὸς τὸν Παῦλον, with no verb after it. But that harder reading is in parallel to 26:29/2–6, which also lacks a verb of speaking. If NA28 is received here, it does not agree with its parallel later in the verse where Luke uses φησίν for Festus's reply. Byz/PWR is probably original.[258] It seems that the proto-Alex archetype once matched the Byz but was revised, possibly in the archetype for 03.

142. (BTO) (β-INS) (25:22/23) Byz/614 has ὁ δέ, αὔριον, φησίν (vs. αὔριον, φησίν, NA28) and is joined by 5/10 best ECM MSS (i.e., 04 33 81 1739 2200) and 10/10 core PWR MSS etc., including 24/25 Westerns (MS 181, the final Western MS, adds πρὸς αὐτόν to the Byz/PWR) plus Chrys e sy^h. 614 is the PWR. The Byz is awkward. NA28 is joined by 5/10 best ECM MSS (i.e., P74 01 02 03 1175) and 1842 plus Vg gig p 189 sa bo. As in 25:22/11 above, NA28 appears to be an Alex gloss designed to remove what seemed superfluous. Its source could be the archetype of 03, given that MS 03 tends to have missing articles.[259] Byz/PWR is probably original.[260]

143. (BTO) (β-NTR) (25:24/58) 614 reads ἐπιβοῶν (vs. ἐπιβοῶντες, Byz/614f, vs. βοῶντες, NA28) and uses a verb that refers back to the grammatical antecedent, τὸ πλῆθος, while the other two readings refer to the semantic antecedent, i.e., the Jews. However, since 614 is joined by only the uncorrected 1890(*f, Cf2) and 2412, the ECM editors are right to attribute the deviation to a simple mistake. Instead, 614f is the PWR. The Byz/PWR is found in 5/10 best ECM MSS (i.e., 04 33 1175 1739 2200), 10/10 core PWR MSS, and

---

258. Soden, *Schriften des Neuen Testaments*, 2:600, agrees.
259. See Fee, "P75, P66, and Origen," 261.
260. Soden, *Schriften des Neuen Testaments*, 2:600, agrees.

08 181 etc., including 23/23 Westerns plus Chrys. NA28/ECM is joined by 5/10 best ECM MSS (i.e., P74 01 02 03 81) and just 93 665 L1188. Its sparse testimony suggests that NA28 arose from a primitive Alex scribe who dropped the ἐπί prefix. MS 03 is known for manifesting the simple in lieu of compound words.[261] Byz/PWR is probably original.[262]

144. (BTO) (β-INS) (26:4/34–36) Byz/614 has ἐν (vs. ἔν τε, NA28) and is found in 10/10 core PWR MSS, 5/10 best ECM MSS (i.e., 04 33 81 1739 2200), and 206 522 etc., including eighteen Westerns plus Chrys sy[h.ms] (Vg e p w 189). MS 614 is the PWR. NA28 is joined by 5/10 best ECM MSS (i.e., P74 01 02 03 1175) and twenty-one others, including five Westerns plus sy[h.ms]. NA28 is smoother and appears to clarify how all the Jews could know Paul's way of life. If he only served in Jerusalem, the reader might wonder how all Israel could know him. By introducing τε, the text indicates that Paul ministered outside of Jerusalem. Evidently, a primitive Alex scribe introduced the gloss after the other reading was well established, explaining the divided Alex core. The shorter reading has the best external evidence with nearly all Byz's, a perfectly coherent PWR, most Westerns, 50 percent of the best Alex's, and more translations.[263] Paul has made the general point that he learned and served in the chief city (see 22:3). It is silent about where else he might have served. Byz/PWR is probably original.[264]

145. (ATO) (α-INS) (26:6/18) NA28/614 reads + ἡμῶν (vs. omits, Byz) and is found in 10/10 best ECM MSS and 9/10 core PWR MSS etc., including twenty Westerns plus Chrys e gig p w 189 sy[p] sy[h]. Byz is joined by 014 020 35C, including six Westerns. Is ἡμῶν a stylistic gloss acquired from 26:7? If ἡμῶν was found in the Byz, that would be the common assumption. However, the external evidence shows the smoother reading is better here. The Byz lost the pronoun by accident. NA28 is original as confirmed by the PWR and Westerns overall.

---

261. Fee, "P75, P66, and Origen," 261.

262. Soden, *Schriften des Neuen Testaments*, 2:600, agrees.

263. Boismard and Lamouille, *Texte occidental reconstitution*, 2:175, add the following support to the Byz: sa bo Ä G A.

264. Barrett, *Commentary on Acts*, 2:1150–51, accepts NA28 and discusses in detail what it could mean.

146.(BTO) (β-INS) (26:10/12–16) Byz/614 has καὶ πολλοὺς (vs. καὶ πολλοὺς τε, NA28, καὶ πολλοὺς δὲ, 307) and is found in 10/10 core PWR MSS and 4/10 best ECM MSS (i.e., 03 1175 1739 2200) etc., including 22/24 Westerns plus Chrys. 614 is the PWR. NA28 is joined by 6/10 best ECM MSS (i.e., P74 01 02 04 33 81) and just 08 048 096 330 1501 L1188. The Latin may support either. 307 is apparently an attempt to improve NA28 and is joined by some MSS that lean to the Alex text overall (i.e., 453 610 1678 2818) and the mixed-text MS 180. It is hard to make sense of both καί and τε in this verse. If they are translated "and also," the "also" does not fit because Paul is illustrating how he opposed the name of Jesus rather than introducing a different point. Here he offers the first out of two specific ways in which he opposed Christianity. Some translations like the NASB attempt to understand τε as if it were part of a "not only . . . but also" statement, but the Greek must be stretched to achieve it. Barrett recognizes the problem and states, "It is impossible to see any purpose that might be served by τε in this sentence," and yet he ascribes it to Luke.[265] Most likely NA28 represents a mistake in the earliest stage of the proto-Alex tradition. Wachtel observed similar ancient mistakes in the Byz tradition of the Catholic Epistles and called them untypical Byz readings.[266] They are untypical because they provide no advantage over the original text. They were created by simple accidents or by failed attempts to improve the text. For example, consider the Byz reading at Jas 2:18.[267] NA28 reads, δεῖξόν μοι τὴν πίστιν σου χωρὶς τῶν ἔργων, κἀγώ σοι δείξω ἐκ τῶν ἔργων μου τὴν πίστιν. Instead of χωρίς, the Byz has ἐκ two times. It has evidently assimilated the ἐκ from the second clause into the first. Even the 1550 edition of Stephanus includes the error though he takes note of an alternate reading (the correct one) in the margin. For an untypical Byz reading in Acts, consider the text at 20:26/18–20 where it has καθαρός ἐγω instead of καθαρός εἰμι (see also 26:10/24–28; 26:15/16–18). Despite their inferiority, mistakes of this category persisted. Therefore, the reading of NA28 evidently arose in a proto-Alex archetype. Perhaps, the scribe wrote τε as the solitary conjunction after πολλούς without noticing that he already

---

265. Barrett, *Commentary on Acts*, 2:1155.
266. Wachtel, *Byzantinische Text*, 74.
267. Wachtel, *Byzantinische Text*, 224–26.

had copied down καί from his exemplar. Subsequent Alex MSS like 03 observed the error and corrected it to the standard. But most core Alex MSS were not fixed. Relatively pure Byz MS 330 matches NA28 and it evidently arrived at the same error independently. MS 1501 is a secondary Western MS, and it has the problem as well. In summary, the Byz/PWR is probably original.

147. (ATO) (β-NTR) (26:10/24–28) NA28/614 reads ἐν φυλακαῖς (vs. φυλακαῖς, Byz) and is found in 10/10 best ECM MSS and 4/10 core PWR MSS (i.e., 614 1292 2147 2412) etc., including seventeen Westerns. 614 is the PWR. Byz is joined by 014 025 35 etc., including eight Westerns plus Chrys. It is possible that ἐν was added to smooth the text. However, the Westerns suggest that the preposition was overlooked, making the fuller reading correct (see 26:10/12–16 regarding untypical Byz readings). NA28/PWR is probably original.

148. (ATO) (α-NTR) (26:12/24) NA28/614 has τῶν ἀρχιερέων (vs. παρὰ τῶν ἀρχιερέων, Byz) and is joined by 6/10 best ECM MSS (i.e., P74 01 02 03 81 1175) and 8/10 core PWR MSS etc., including twelve Westerns plus Vg e gig p w 189. Byz is joined by 04 014 020 35 etc., including twelve Westerns plus Chrys. The presence of παρά is likely the result of a scribal gloss. NA28 is confirmed by the PWR and the translations.[268]

149. (ATO) (α-SI) (26:15/16–18) NA28/614 reads ὁ δὲ κύριος (vs. ὁ δὲ, Byz) and is found in 9/9 best ECM MSS and 9/10 core PWR MSS etc., including twenty Westerns plus sy^h (Vg e p w 189 sa bo sy^p). 614 is the PWR. Byz is joined by 014 025 35 etc., including four Westerns plus Chrys. Though the Byz is the "unpolished" reading, it is still secondary due to the external evidence (see 26:10/12–16, regarding untypical Byz readings). NA28/PWR is original.

150. (BTO) (α-SI) (26:16/44) NA28/614 has εἶδές με (vs. εἶδες, Byz) and is joined by 3/9 best ECM MSS (i.e., 03 1175 1739; but 04* is possible), 8/10 core PWR MSS, and fourteen others, including thirteen Westerns overall plus sa sy^p sy^h. 614 is the PWR. Byz is joined by 5/9 best ECM MSS (i.e., P74 01 02 81 2200) and 04C2 08 014 020 35 etc., including nine Westerns plus Chrys Vg e gig p w 189 bo. MS 614 is the PWR. ECM lists it as a SGL reading. NA28 has the

---

268. Soden, *Schriften des Neuen Testaments*, 2:602, agrees and implies that the Byz was assimilated to 9:14.

marks of a Western gloss created and/or selected by the PWR editor, perpetuated in the Syriac, and received into the ancient Coptic sa. Its limited support in the best ECM MSS suggests that there was an early trend in Alex against it. Its absence from both the bo and the Vg give further evidence for this conclusion. Most likely it was a popular Western reading known in Alexandria in the first half of the second century. Though NA28 is the harder reading, it seems unlikely for either the Lord Jesus or Paul to have spoken in this way and for Luke to write in this manner. The wording is simply awkward. The Byz has the greatest variety in terms of Greek MSS, boasts of nearly equal versional testimony, and includes the normally reliable bo. Perhaps με was introduced to emphasize that Paul's most important vision was his sight of the glorified Christ.[269] I suggest the PWR should be punctuated as, εἰς τοῦτο γὰρ ὤφθην σοι, προχειρίσασθαί σε ὑπηρέτην καὶ μάρτυρα ὧν τε εἶδές, με, ὧν τε ὀφθήσομαί σοι, and translated as, "For this purpose I appeared to you, to appoint you a minister and witness both of what you saw, me, and of what I will show to you." The PWR editor and early Alex MSS like 03 valued the wording and sustained it. Such style is barely more feasible in Paul's own writings. If NA28 is original at Col 2:2, Paul's τοῦ μυστηρίου τοῦ θεοῦ, Χριστοῦ, is unusual but quite smooth in comparison. Wachtel complains about NA28 making no grammatical sense.[270] He suggests that scribes must have found something good in it for it to be retained in quality MSS.[271] Although NA28/PWR stirs up an interesting discussion, the Byz represents the pure original.[272]

151. (BTO) (α-INS) (26:20/12, 17) Byz/614 reads καὶ Ἱεροσολύμοις, εἰς πᾶσάν τε (vs. τε καὶ Ἱεροσολύμοις, πᾶσάν τε, NA28) and is joined by nearly all ECM MSS. Two variants will be reviewed together. At the first one, Byz/614 omits τε with the support of 4/9 best ECM MSS

---

269. See Barrett, *Commentary on Acts*, 2:1159.

270. See Wachtel, "Text-Critical Commentary," 35–36.

271. See Metzger, *Textual Commentary*, 438, who shows the committee's lack of confidence by putting με in brackets. Ropes, *Beginnings of Christianity*, 237, felt the difficulty of με combined with its attestation in key witnesses (i.e., MS 03 614-group sy[p] sy[h] Amb Aug) confirmed it. Boismard and Lamouille, *Texte occidental reconstitution*, 2:177, accept it and do well to point out that 04* probably once had με. They add A and G as further support for με.

272. Soden, *Schriften des Neuen Testaments*, 2:603, agrees as does Haenchen, *Acts of the Apostles*, 680.

(i.e., 33 1175 1739 2200) and 10/10 core PWR MSS etc., including 23/24 Westerns and Chrys. NA28 is joined by 5/9 best ECM MSS (i.e., P74 01 02 03 81) and just 048 93 104 459 665 1838. At the second variant, Byz/614 is found in 5/9 best ECM MSS (i.e., 33 81 1175 1739 2200) and 10/10 core PWR MSS etc., including 24/24 Westerns plus Chrys Vg e gig p 189 sy[h]. NA28 is joined by 4/9 best ECM MSS (i.e., P74 01 02 03) and just 048[vid] 436 plus w. NA28 utilizes the τε καί sequence that typically means "both . . . and" (see 4:27) or "and . . . and" (see 2:10), but its use here does not seem to fit. Luke does utilize τε καί (per NA28 but not Byz/PWR) in a manner where it could mean "and also" at 9:15 and 19:27. At 9:15, NA28 has solid support. At 19:27, it has limited evidence, but it seems to best explain the eighteen alternatives. Here NA28 has neither strong support nor does it explain the single alternative. The sense of "both . . . and" here is awkward because of the structure of the preceding words. Moreover, it might work better with the following word Ἱεροσολύμοις if it included τοῖς ἐν, as does the first entity. However, τοῖς ἐν is only found in the PWR MSS and a few others. Therefore, the NA28 reading appears to be an attempted scribal improvement that became part of the proto-Alex archetype. At 26:20/17, NA28 is joined by just four core Alex MSS (P74 01 02 03) and 048[vid] 436. MS 048 is also Alex and the 436 is a mixed text. At 26:20/12, the same four core Alex MSS and 048 are joined by one of the best ECM MSS (i.e., 81), Western MS 1838, and four Byz MSS (i.e., 93 104 459 665). The coherence among the core suggests that both edits were done purposely and simultaneously. Ropes asserts that the NA28 reading may preserve a "very ancient accidental error (-ΟΙΣΕΙΣ)."[273] If he is right, the loss of εἰς might have motivated the adding of τε to smooth the reading. Because four Byz MSS join NA28 at the first variant, it appears that a Byz editor independently attempted to insert the τε καί structure there. In summary, the proto-Alex text read with τε included and εἰς removed. Most likely these were secondary changes made at one time. The scribe evidently wanted to use the τε καί sequence and doing so removed the need for εἰς. The best ECM MSS became divided when some of their ancestors corrected to the mainstream. The Byz is elegant and appears to be unedited. It is also backed by the PWR, a near perfect Western coherence, almost half

---

273. Ropes, *Beginnings of Christianity*, 237.

of the best ECM MSS, and most of the translations. Therefore, the Byz/PWR is original.[274]

152. (ATO) (α-NTR) (26:21/12) NA28/614 has ὄντα (vs. omits, Byz) and is joined by 7/9 best ECM MSS, 9/10 core PWR MSS, and forty-one others, including eighteen Westerns and ten Byz MSS plus Vg e gig p h w 189 sy^h. 614 is the PWR. Byz is joined by 2/9 best ECM MSS (i.e., 02 03) and 014 020 35 etc., including six Westerns plus Chrys. The inclusion of the participle is more difficult. Most of the Byz tradition and two core Alex's have smoothed the text by dropping the participle. NA28/PWR is original as confirmed by the external evidence.

153. (ATO) (α-SI) (27:2/10) NA28/614 reads μέλλοντι (vs. μέλλοντες, Byz) and is found in 9/10 core PWR MSS, 8/8 best ECM MSS, and 044 35* 181 424C 1241 etc., including 23/25 Westerns plus Vg s p sa bo sy^Aram sy^p sy^h. 614 is the PWR. Byz is joined by 014 020 35C 383 1838 etc., including only two Westerns plus Chrys. NA28/PWR is favored already by its versions and its contextual suitability. It even has three core Byz MSS (italicized) that agree. Were all the travelers about to go to places in Asia (Byz) or was the ship destined for places in Asia? If there was any doubt, the Western tradition confirms NA28 is original.[275]

154. (BTO) (α-NTR) (27:11/27) Byz/614 has τοῦ Παύλου (vs. Παύλου, NA28) and is found in 10/10 core PWR MSS and includes all ECM MSS except P74 01 02 03 81 1241. MS 614 is the PWR. The ECM marks it with a SGL. Adding the article makes the reference to Paul anaphoric.[276] However, was the article inserted for that reason? More likely Luke simply included the article for stylistic purposes (see 27:1, 3, 9). While some scribes might have noticed a difference in this verse and added the article, it is highly doubtful that many ancient scribes would have done so. Even 4/9 best ECM MSS retain the article. Rather, it appears the proto-Alex archetype was missing the article and caused 5/9 best ECM MSS to inherit the error. In

---

274. Metzger, *Textual Commentary*, 438–39, admits that the NA28 wording is "hardly tolerable as Greek" but the committee judged the Byz to be an attempt to improve it. Barrett, *Commentary on Acts*, 2:1163, citing Dibelius, recognizes the quality of the Byz wording. Yet he does not choose it. Soden, *Schriften des Neuen Testaments*, 2:603, surprisingly accepts both the Alex τε and the Byz εἰς.

275. Bengel, *Novum Testamentum*, 217, already chose the Alex reading long ago and rated it as β.

276. Wachtel, "Text-Critical Commentary," 37.

fact, these are the top five ranked MSS out of the top ten listing.²⁷⁷ Wachtel thinks the article was more likely added than omitted. That is generally true. If the decision was between two first-century MSS, the anarthrous would be favored. However, 03 is the earliest MS of the group, dated to the fourth century. Moreover, variants involving the loss of an article are a common occurrence. In addition, as Wachtel mentions, 03 is not a trustworthy guide in terms of articles.²⁷⁸ In terms of transmission, it is improbable that just these six ECM MSS are correct. Byz/PWR is original.²⁷⁹

155. (ATO) (α-INS) (27:19/18) Byz/614 reads ἐρρίψαμεν (vs. ἔρριψαν, NA28) and is found in 10/10 core PWR MSS and 020 025 35 etc., including thirteen Westerns plus Chrys sy^p sy^h Ä. 614 is the PWR. NA28 is joined by 9/9 best ECM MSS etc., including eight Westerns plus Vg gig s p w 189 sa bo. The external evidence is relatively equal. Moreover, it is hard to decide the better reading from internal factors because the subject alternates between "they" and "we" (see 27:16–20) in the wider context. Nevertheless, given that the sailors (lit. "they") were called upon to cast out some things (see 27:18), and to throw out the grain (see 27:38), it is most probable that the sailors were the ones who tossed out the ship's tackle. NA28 is original as confirmed by its core, the best mix of translations, and the internal logic.²⁸⁰

156. (ATO) (α-SI) (27:23/14–28) ECM/614 has τοῦ θεοῦ—οὗ εἰμι ᾧ καὶ λατρεύω—ἄγγελος (vs. same except + ἐγὼ in brackets after εἰμι, NA28, vs. ἄγγελος τοῦ θεοῦ οὗ εἰμι ᾧ καὶ λατρεύω, Byz) and is found 7/10 core PWR MSS (i.e., 614 1292 1505 1611 2138 2412 2495; 2495 reverses ᾧ and καὶ) and 6/10 best ECM MSS (i.e., 03 04* 33 1175 1739 2200) etc., including eleven Westerns plus Chrys^pt. 614 is the PWR. The ECM lists seventeen alternatives. NA28 is joined by 3/10 best ECM MSS (i.e., P74^vid 01 02) and five others. It offers important indirect testimony for the ECM reading. Byz is joined by 020 025 35 etc., including five Westerns plus Chrys^pt (Vg s p w 189). If the Byz sequence were original, what would have emboldened an influential scribe to move ἄγγελος to the end? Emphasis could have been

---

277. Wachtel, "Text-Critical Commentary," 37.
278. Wachtel, "Text-Critical Commentary," 37; see Fee, "P75, P66, and Origen," 261.
279. Soden, *Schriften des Neuen Testaments*, 2:606, agrees.
280. Soden, *Schriften des Neuen Testaments*, 2:607, agrees.

achieved by simply moving ἄγγελος after τοῦ θεοῦ. Moreover, given the smoothing tendency of the PWR archetype, the highly unusual word order is barely something its editor would tolerate much less create. Perhaps Luke placed ἄγγελος at the end to emphasize God as the omnipotent ruler of life itself.[281] ECM/PWR is original. The best ECM MSS and the PWR edition both show great faithfulness here.[282]

157. (ATO) (α-INS) (28:1/6–8) NA28/614* reads τότε ἐπέγνωμεν (vs. τότε ἐπέγνωσαν, Byz, vs. οἱ περὶ τὸν Παῦλον ἐκ τοῦ πλοός τότε ἐπέγνωμεν, 614Cf) and is found in 8/10 best ECM MSS, 6/10 core PWR MSS, and twelve others plus (Vg gig p w 189 sa bo sy^p sy^h). 614 is the PWR. Byz is joined by 020 025 35 etc., including ten Westerns plus Chrys (Ä). 614Cf and 2774 have inserted a popular expansion no earlier than the thirteenth century. MS 020 and twenty-two others picked it up, too, but combined it with the Byz ἐπέγνωσαν instead. The Byz lost the personal touch of the 1P somewhere in its transmission. NA28 is original as confirmed by the PWR and dominant translation evidence.

158. (ATO) (α-NTR) (28:2/20) NA28/614 has ἄψαντες (vs. ἀνάψαντες, Byz) and is found in 8/10 core PWR MSS, 10/10 best ECM MSS, and twenty-four others, including fourteen Westerns. 614 is the PWR. Byz is joined by 020 025 35 383 2147 etc., including eight Westerns plus Chrys Dam. Since ἅπτω can mean "to touch" (NT: thirty-five times) or "to kindle" (NT: three times, Luke 8:16; 11:33; 15:8) while ἀνάπτω normally means "kindle" (NT: twice, Luke 12:49; Jas 3:5), the Byz has made the meaning explicit. NA28 is original as confirmed by the PWR and the Westerns overall.

159. (ATO) (α-NTR) (28:3/28) NA28/614 reads ἀπό (vs. ἐκ, Byz) and is found in 9/10 core PWR MSS, 9/9 best ECM MSS, core Byz MSS 020 025 0142 330 424, and 181 467 etc., including eighteen Westerns. 614 is the PWR. Byz is joined by 049 1 35 etc., including six Westerns. NA28 has the best variety. NA28 is original as confirmed by the PWR, most Westerns, and some core Byzantines.

160. (ATO) (α-NTR) (28:4/26–30) NA28/614 has πρὸς ἀλλήλους ἔλεγον (vs. ἔλεγον πρὸς ἀλλήλους, Byz) and is found in 9/10 core PWR MSS and 9/10 best ECM MSS etc., including sixteen Westerns plus Vg

---

281. See Barrett, *Commentary on Acts*, 2:1201.
282. See Wachtel, "Text-Critical Commentary," 37.

gig s p w 189 syʰ G. 614 is the PWR. Byz is joined by 020 025 35 etc., including six Westerns plus Chrys A. NA28 is original as confirmed by translations and Westerns.

161. (ATO) (α-INS) (28:10/24–26) NA28/614 reads πρὸς τὰς χρείας (vs. πρὸς τὴν χρείαν, Byz) and is found in 7/9 best ECM MSS (i.e., P74 01 02 03 33 1175 1739), 7/10 core PWR MSS, and nine others, including eleven total Westerns plus syʰ. 614 is the PWR. Byz is joined by 020 025 35 81 2200 etc., including ten Westerns plus Chrys. The accusative singular (AS) is more difficult because the preceding τά seems to prepare for the plural. However, the singular is ubiquitous in the NT in contrast to the accusative plural (only at Tit 3:14). The NT contains the AS χρείαν forty times, including eight within Luke-Acts (see Luke 5:31; 9:11; 15:7; 19:31; 19:34; 22:71; Acts 2:45; 4:35). While the singular is surprising, it appears to derive from familiar usage. It is appropriate in Acts 2:45 and 4:35 where each of the poor disciples was given as much money as he or she needed. But here the AS appears to be incongruous. In summary, the rarity of the plural, the likelihood of assimilation, the support of the PWR, and the suitability to the context all point in one direction, NA28 is original.[283]

162. (ATO) (α-INS) (28:11/10) NA28/614 has ἀνήχθημεν (vs. ἤχθημεν, Byz) and is found in 9/10 core PWR MSS, 8/9 best ECM MSS, and *020 025 1 18 35C* etc., including nineteen Westerns plus Chrys. 614 is the PWR. Byz is joined by 049 0142 35* etc., including five Westerns. NA28 has far greater variety and even includes some core Byz MSS (italicized). It means, "We were put to sea" (*TLG*). The ἀν- prefix was dropped by accident. Notice that scribal error has caused the Byz reading to be less refined (i.e., harder). It means, "We were brought." NA28 is original as confirmed the PWR and the Westerns overall.[284]

163. (ATO) (β-SI) (28:16/12–16) Byz/614 reads ὁ ἑκατόνταρχος παρέδωκεν τοὺς δεσμίους τῷ στρατοπεδάρχῃ τῷ δὲ Παύλῳ ἐπετράπη (vs. ἐπετράπη τῷ Παύλῳ, NA28) and is joined by 0142 1 18 35 and nearly all extant MSS to include nineteen Westerns plus (gig p syʰ** sa). 614 is the PWR. NA28 is joined by 6/7 best ECM MSS (i.e., 01 02 03 81 1175 1739), 4/10 core PWR MSS (i.e., 1505 1890* 2138 2495), and 23 total MSS,

---

283. Soden, *Schriften des Neuen Testaments*, 2:611, and Boismard and Lamouille, *Texte occidental reconstitution*, 1:224, agree.

284. Bengel, *Novum Testamentum*, 219, agrees and rates the Byz as ε. Soden, *Schriften des Neuen Testaments*, 2:611, also agrees.

including 6 Westerns plus Chrys Vg w 189 bo sy^p sy^h Ä. Though the MSS are limited, their authority is solid, and they are joined by many versions. If Luke created two editions, here is a good proof text. The longer reading fits seamlessly. Rather than two editions, this variation seems to reflect final editing by Luke that removed portions that were not necessary for his purposes (see 2:30/34; 10:32/37; 15:24/30–34; 18:21/4–6, 9, 10, 24; 20:24/27; 21:25/16–20; 23:30/45; 24:6/20–8/14; 28:29/2–24). Though he excised them, a successor of Luke appears to have reinserted them into a popular MS. NA28 is original.[285]

164. (ATO) (α-NTR) (28:17/38–42) NA28/614 has ἐγώ ἄνδρες ἀδελφοί (vs. ἄνδρες ἀδελφοί ἐγώ, Byz, vs. ἐγώ ἀδελφοί, 1505) and is found in 6/10 core PWR MSS, 6/9 best ECM MSS (i.e., 02 03 33 81 1175 1739), and thirty others, including twelve Westerns plus Vg p w 189 bo. MS 614 is the PWR. Byz is joined by 020 025 35 383 2147 2200 etc., including six Westerns plus Chrys sa sy^p. 1505 is joined by 2495 sy^h and began with the PWR but later dropped ἄνδρες. Therefore, these two core PWR MSS further strengthen the harder reading with ἐγώ at the start, perhaps for the strongest emphasis. NA28 is original as confirmed by the PWR.

165. (BTO) (α-NTR) (28:23/10) Byz/614 reads ἧκον (vs. ἦλθον/ἦλθαν, NA28) and is found in 10/10 core PWR MSS and 044 2200 etc., including fourteen Westerns plus Chrys. 614 is the PWR. NA28 is joined by 8/9 best ECM MSS and 181 307 330 etc., including eight Westerns. Per *BW* data, the NA28 lemma occurs 632 times in the NT (Luke: 101, Acts: 50). The Byz/PWR lemma occurs just 26 times in the NT (Luke: 5, Acts: 0). The form ἧκον is unique. The PAI-3P form of ἥκω can mean either "they are present" or "they have come" (*TLG*). The IAI-3P, as seen here, can mean, "they came" or "they had come" (*TLG*). This ambiguity may have motivated the change. Alternatively, a primitive scribe might have misread the unusual word as if it were the common one due to graphical similarity. Because ἥκω is rare but still Lucan, the common one is most likely due to

---

285. Soden, *Schriften des Neuen Testaments*, 2:611, retains the long reading. Boismard and Lamouille, *Texte occidental reconstitution*, 1:224, mark the long reading as Lucan by printing it as their Western text. Metzger, *Textual Commentary Greek New Testament*, 443, and Barrett, *Commentary on Acts*, 2:1232, attributes the addition to a Western gloss.

substitution. It was the reading of the proto-Alex archetype.[286] The Byz/PWR retains the harder word and is probably original.

166. (ATO) (α-SI) (28:29/2–24) Byz/614 has + καὶ ταῦτα αὐτοῦ εἰπόντος ἀπῆλθον οἱ Ἰουδαῖοι πολλὴν ἔχοντες ἐν ἑαυτοῖς συζήτησιν (vs. omits, NA28) and is joined by 10/10 core PWR MSS and 020 025 35 etc., including nineteen Westerns plus Chrys gig p w ar 189 sy^{h**}. 614 is the PWR. NA28 is joined by 8/9 best ECM MSS and fourteen others plus Vg e sa bo sy^p sy^h Ä A G. Both the Byz and PWR have adopted a "mainstream" reading.[287] Metzger suggests the verse was likely added to smooth the transition from 28:28 to 28:30.[288] Barrett thought the verse was inserted to emphasize that the Jews did not categorically reject the message.[289] Rather than a scribal creation, the verse might be from Luke himself and then removed by him prior to publishing his one and only edition. Perhaps he decided it was unnecessary (see 2:30/34; 10:32/37; 15:24/30–34; 18:21/4–6, 9, 10, 24; 20:24/27; 21:25/16–20; 23:30/45; 24:6/20–8/14; 28:16/12–16). NA28 is original.[290]

167. (ATO) (α-INS) (28:30/6–14) NA28/614 omits (vs. ὁ Παῦλος, Byz) and is found in 7/8 best ECM MSS, 8/10 core PWR MSS, and 08 044 etc., including twelve Westerns plus Chrys (Vg e w bo^{mss} sy^h). 614 is the PWR. Byz is joined by 020 025 35 383 2147 etc., including eleven Westerns plus gig s p 189 sy^{h**} (sa bo^{mss} sy^p). The Byz has more translation support. However, this mix of translations suggests that the Byz reading is probably a result of the WR. Because the Byz text and the WR have the insertion of 28:29, the gap since the last explicit mention of Paul at 28:25 is even greater. Therefore, ὁ Παῦλος was inserted by the WRR (see sy^{h**} gig p 189) to clarify. The WRR not only impacted the Byz tradition but also the Coptic sa and part of the bo. NA28 is original as confirmed by the PWR.

---

286. See Barrett, *Commentary on Acts*, 2:1243, who comments that the Byz might be correct. Soden, *Schriften des Neuen Testaments*, 2:612, chooses the Byz as original.

287. Wachtel, "Against the Text-Type Concept," 147.

288. Metzger, *Textual Commentary*, 444.

289. Barrett, *Commentary on Acts*, 2:1250.

290. Soden, *Schriften des Neuen Testaments*, 2:613, agrees. In contrast, Boismard and Lamouille, *Texte occidental reconstitution*, 1:226, mark the long reading as Lucan and Western.

RESULTS

Overall, there are 94 recommended new readings in the following categories: 85 BTO, 5 PAO, and 4 OTO. Most of the recommended changes were found in Acts 1–17 (i.e., 71/94). More specifically, minus the OTO readings, the Byz/PWR offered 90 improvements (i.e., 67 in Acts 1–17 and 23 in Acts 18–28). Therefore, in terms of corrections per chapter, the Byz/PWR scribes were more successful in preserving the original in the first portion (i.e., 4:1 in part one; 2:1 in part two). It was mentioned in chapter 1 that the total differences between NA28 and RP05 (minus the bracketed words and alternate spellings) was about 879. The ECM has moved toward the Byz text by a net change of 32, bringing the total down to 847.[291] In addition, the editors of the ECM sometimes chose different lengths (vs. the NA28 editors) for the variant units, increasing the total by 15 (see appendix). Thus, the ECM (mostly Alex in nature) and RP05 (Byz tradition) disagree about 862 times. Therefore, 85 BTO improvements equate to receiving about 10 percent of the formerly disapproved Byz readings. In addition, a SGL was recommended on two occasions (see 13:46/36; 21:5/56–6/6). Finally, 2 readings were marked as ABI (see 21:25/14; 24:6/20–8/14) for their insight into the textual landscape.

Although no readings of the category ATO had to be defended, given their prior acceptance into NA28, 69 were addressed. The results both manifest the quality of the core Alex MSS and repeatedly confirm their readings by means of one or more of the following groups of witnesses: the PWR, the Western MSS overall, the most ancient translations, and the fathers. For example, 40/69 ATO readings have the support of the PWR (i.e., those *without* asterisks below). Of the remaining 98 readings, only 8 more (*with* an asterisk below) demonstrate agreement between the PWR and NA28. However, for these the Byz text is evidently original (i.e., BTO). The specific variants include:

*2:7/5; *5:32/6–8; 5:38/42; *7:32/21, 25; 8:32/38–40; 9:19/14–22; 9:38/30–34; *11:26/16–24; 13:24/20–26; *13:26/26; *14:17/40; 15:29/8–12; 16:7/34; 18:26/40–46; 19:3/5; 19:12/50; 19:25/38; *19:27/54–58; 20:1/24–26, 28; 21:22/10–14; 21:27/48–54; 21:29/6; 23:8/16; 23:9/14–26; 23:11/21; 24:10/40–46; 24:14/46–56; 24:18/4; 24:21/16–20; 24:25/20–24; 25:2/8–10; 25:21/30–36; 26:6/18; 26:10/24–28; 26:12/24; 26:15/16–18; *26:16/44;

---

291. ECM 3:1:1, intro, 34–35.

26:21/12; 27:2/10; 27:23/14–28; 28:1/6–8; 28:2/20; 28:3/28; 28:4/26–30; 28:10/24–26; 28:11/10; 28:17/38–42; 28:30/6–14.

Only 11/48 agreements occur in Acts 1–14 with just 5/11 appearing to be original. In contrast, 37/48 occur in Acts 15–28 with 35/37 appearing to be the original. Therefore, the PWR preserves many more original readings in the second half of Acts.

In addition, an interesting group of 10 expanded readings was discussed in detail because they have great external support, display high linguistic quality, and seem to be written by Luke but then removed prior to his one and only published edition (see *2:30; 10:32; 15:24; 18:21; 20:24; 21:25; 23:30; 24:6–8; 28:16; 28:29*). The long additions are italicized and contain expansions of 4–27 words. These readings are the joint heritage of both the Byz and PWR traditions.[292] For more discussion, see comments at each of the ten entries above.

Some general observations follow. Of the 85 BTO variants, 13 are significant (SI), 36 insignificant (INS), and 36 are not translatable (NTR). From the 94 new readings, 20 are SI, 37 INS, and 37 NTR. Of the 20 SI readings, 18 are part of the 98 marked SI at the end of chapter 2.[293] Of the 20 corrections classified as SI, just 4 have an addition of two words (see 4:8/27; 4:24/28–30; 10:11/14–30; 10:30/25) and just 2 have an addition of three words (20:4/7–10; 22:9/19). Of the 38 readings listed as INS/NTR in chapter 2, where the Byz differs from NA28 by two or more words, just 9 are proposed as being original in the Byz tradition (see 4:5/22–34; 4:32/12–20; 7:18/12–14; 7:32/21–25; 8:18/31; 13:40/10–18; 20:24/6–8; 24:20/14–18; 25:22/23). All these readings are merely two words different except 7:32/21–25 where the Byz is four words longer. In summary, of the 83 cases listed in chapter 2 for all categories (i.e., SI, INS, and NTR) where the Byz text is two or more words different from NA28, 14 were assessed as BTO and 1 as OTO. Therefore, only a minority of the longer readings appear to be original. In fact, whenever the Byz/PWR witnesses agreed on a text that was four or more words longer than the Alex, the results were the worst. For example, 8 of the 10 readings considered as

---

292. Although the longest addition at 24:6–8 is found only in the RP05 margin, it would appear to be the primitive proto-Byz reading that was later corrected with reference to the Alex tradition. This conclusion is consistent with Wachtel, "Against the Text-Type Concept," 147.

293. Two were not listed because NA28 and RP05 were already essentially agreed. However, at 3:6/46–48, the SGL needs to be removed. At 22:12/26–28, the PWR is probably the original text.

possibly Lucan (see the ones italicized above) are in this category. All were judged to be secondary. The Byz and PWR do join the Alex in resisting the popular ancient insertion of 8:37. However, only the Byz joins the Alex in rejecting the expansion of 15:34.

The need for correction was found most often in places where three or more of the top ten ECM MSS depart from the group. That is the case in 80/94 recommended revisions. In 14/94 suggested corrections, the best ECM MSS are united with no more than two MSS defecting (see 1:16/13; 2:37/32; *4:17/20; *4:25/2-24; 7:56/14; 10:30/25; 13:20/2-16; 16:40/24-30; *17:14/20; *19:27/54-58; 20:5/6; 21:34/18-24; 22:9/19; *28:23/10). Moreover, in 5/94 occasions (i.e., those asterisked above), only 0-1 best ECM MS defects. Therefore, whenever the best ECM MSS approach perfect coherence, they were seldom wrong. It is important to recognize that in 35/94 places of proposed revision, at least 50 percent of the best ECM MSS stand behind the Byz:

> 1:5/16-22; 1:16/45; 1:25/4-12; 2:7/5; 3:26/6-10; 4:21/20; 4:24/28-30; 4:37/18-20; 5:16/18; 5:19/12; 7:46/22-24; 7:60/22-28; 8:5/10; 8:18/31; 8:33/19; 10:19/30; 11:11/24; 11:23/12-14; 12:15/34-36; 13:10/38; 13:40/10-18; 14:8/8-18; 15:20/11; 16:18/16; 17:15/32; 17:21/28-34; 19:20/8-20; 21:31/24-26; 22:23/4; 24:13/2; 25:22/11; 25:22/23; 25:24/58; 26:4/34-36; 26:16/44.

In summary, the Byz tradition has a significant contribution to make for improving the text of the GNT. In addition, the PWR, more narrowly, and the consensus of the Western MSS, more broadly, proved valuable in a supportive role for helping to confirm either the Alex or Byz readings as original. A new text-critical canon proved useful toward this end. The PWR also provided a few original readings of its own (see 5:34/30-40; 8:21/32-40; 20:5/6; 22:12/26-28; 23:30/10-18). Finally, there were 4 cases marked as OTO (see 3:6/46-48; 4:25/2-24; 9:25/6-22; 10:11/14-30).[294]

---

294. The first variant is marked as OTO vs. BTO to clarify that it is not just a Byz or a Byz/PWR reading. Rather, this wording was known everywhere and came to be approved also in Alexandria (see MSS P74 02 04 33 81 1739 2200 and the bo). The brackets in NA28 and the SGL in the ECM can be removed. The last three listed variants demonstrate how a reading not exactly matching any primary tradition can be the most likely candidate for the original. The proposed wording at 4:25 is technically a conjecture, but it is merely a word-order tweaking of the Alex reading that is currently printed in NA28.

5

Conclusion and Further Research

NOTEWORTHY TEXT-CRITICAL FINDINGS IN ACTS

THE PRESENT STUDY OF textual variants within the book of Acts has brought to light six important findings that will now be discussed.

(1) Recommended Revisions to NA28/ECM

As presented in chapter 4, the RP05 Byz text of Acts was evaluated and offers 85 readings that appear to be original against the text of NA28/ECM. Additionally, the PWR edition contributed 5 more recommended improvements. Lastly, "other text is original" (OTO) readings were judged to be original at four places. The new Acts-specific, text-critical canon proved to be very important for this assessment. In fact, 70 of the Byz's 85 recommended corrections agree with the PWR archetype.[1] The 85 revisions amount to about 10 percent of the estimated 862 differences between RP05 and the 2017 ECM of Acts.[2] The contribution

---

1. The disagreements include: 2:7/5; *2:41/18–28; *4:5/22–34; 5:32/6–8; *5:37/28, 7:32/21, 25; 11:26/16–24; *13:20/2–16; 13:26/26; *13:40/10–18; *14:8/8–18; 14:17/40; *15:23/4–8; 19:27/54–58; 26:16/44. The seven asterisked passages indicate a three-way division between the three principal traditions and thus manifest places of heightened textual instability. The eight others are evidently locations where the PWR editor wrongly revised to match a proto-Alex reading.

2. As discussed in chapter 2, RP05 ≠ NA28 about 1,060 times. However, 181 can be deleted since these are spelling differences or those enclosed by single brackets in

of the Byz text to the improvement of the standard editions is further magnified by considering the 155 split guiding line (SGL) readings that are part of the ECM.[3] According to its editors, the Byz already agrees with NA28 in 20 of the 155 locations. In 30 more places, the ECM's calculated Byz text (i.e., ByzECM) does not preserve an equally justified reading as compared to its reading a. (i.e., the NA28 printed text).[4] Therefore, the ByzECM wording was found to be equally justified as compared to the normally Alex-based NA28 reading at 105 of the 135 SGL readings or 77.8 percent of the time.[5] Similarly, if one considers the 155 SGL readings in comparison with RP05 (the Byz standard for this study), there are 27 that already agree with NA28 and just 10 where the Byz is not one of the competing readings.[6] As a result, RP05 competes with NA28/ECM in 118 of the 128 readings. Thus, in 92 percent of the SGL readings where RP05 is not already original, the Byz text provides one of the equivalent readings. Thus, if just half of the 118 RP05 variants could someday be confirmed as original, there would be 59 more Byz readings. Combining them with the 85 BTO readings implies that 144 Byz readings should displace the printed NA28 text, yielding a 17 percent change (i.e., 144/847). Clearly the Byz is very important if one of the aims of textual criticism is to provide the world with the best possible text of Acts.

(2) The PWR Archetype: The Best "Western" Text

If the foregoing analysis stands up to rigorous scrutiny, a more primitive, less edited, and more coherent "Western" text has indeed been found

---

NA28. Moreover, the ECM moves a net total of 32 corrections towards RP05, bringing the sum down to 847. See ECM 3:1:1, intro, 34. Finally, these 847 NA28 variants are equivalent to 862 variation units in the ECM apparatus (see end of ch. 4).

3. ECM 3:1:1, intro, 35–37.
4. Wachtel, "Notes on Acts," intro, 31.
5. The 105 readings are distinguished in ECM 3:2, 9–15.
6. The Byz of RP05 performs better than the ByzECM because the latter completely withholds the "Byz" symbol whenever its editors judged the Byz tradition to be divided (see ECM 3:2, 8). The twenty-seven places where the Byz equals NA28 (i.e., ECM reading a.) include: 3:6/46–48; 3:19/10; 4:28/18; 5:28/4; 6:4/20; 7:19/18; 7:30/30–32; 8:33/2–8; 9:2/28–32; 9:30/22; 10:19/18–22; 10:28/34–38; 12:3/26–28; 13:20/26; 13:38/28; 13:49/14; 14:17/18–20; 17:27/18; 18:23/26; 19:6/8–14; 19:21/26–30; *19:33/14; 20:22/28; 21:18/4; *24:27/22; *26:4/44; *28:15/22. In all but the four with asterisks, the PWR edition also agrees. The ten places with inferior RP05 readings include: 2:36/18–30; 4:12/22–40; 4:33/10–26; 8:21/32–40; 10:24/2–8; 11:3/6–18; 13:46/36; 21:13/2–8; 24:24/22–24; 26:17/26–28.

than all previous attempts to reconstruct its earliest form. Those efforts were typically based upon the unusual readings preserved in certain Greek MSS (e.g., Codex D plus P38 P48 P127 08), the mae translation, the Syriac Harklensis apparatus, OL MSS d e gig h, and ancient Latin fathers, including Cyprian. Those tireless labors have been foundational to this study. The PWR archetype has been reconstructed mainly from a group of ten minuscules, led by MSS 614 and 2412, and has superior text-critical value to the WR because it was most likely a principal source for the WR itself (see chapter 2). Barbara Aland's theory regarding the precedence of the 614-group was further confirmed in chapter 3.[7] In contrast, Tuckett dismissed Aland's assertion. He reasoned that the absence of the longer expansions and paraphrases, found in Codex D but not in MS 614, is not a convincing argument to show the chronological priority of the 614-group.[8] He suggested instead that those readings were gradually removed from the 614-group, earlier in their ancestry, by the powerful conforming influence of the Byzantine standard text. However, chapter 3 has shown that Tuckett's simpler approach does not match the overall data.[9] If his scenario was valid, the conforming Byz editors would *not* have been content to retain the approximate 201 obvious differences between the 614-group and the Byz text.[10] In particular, note the 75 PWR expansions absent from the Byz tradition as described below. Moreover, Delobel's study, addressing variants in Acts 15 and titled "The Nature of 'Western' Readings in Acts," affirmed Aland's assertion that the "Western" text arose in three steps with the first one being the formation of MSS like those of the 614-group.[11] In contrast, Thomas Geer has argued that a layer of ancient "Western" readings was placed upon Byz MSS of the ninth century or later in order to create the 614-group.[12] Chapter 3 assessed his viewpoint as being highly unlikely for at least three reasons: (1) numerous "late" Byz readings were shown in chapter 2 to form the basis of editing already seen in "early" readings

---

7. Aland, "Entstehung, Charakter und Herkunft," 26–28.

8. Tuckett, "How Early," 74–75.

9. Tuckett, "How Early," 75.

10. See "Chapter Summaries" at the end of chapter 3.

11. Delobel, "Nature of 'Western Readings,'" 69–70, joins with Barbara Aland in upholding the Alex tradition as the oldest and best text against the views of those who, since the 1980s, have promoted the "originality and/or Lucan origin of the 'Western' text" (e.g., Boismard-Lamouille, Strange, Rius-Camps, Delebecque, Amassari, and Tavardon). Delobel, "Nature of 'Western Readings,'" 70.

12. Geer, "Investigation of Western Cursives," 12.

of the 614-group; (2) revision towards the Byz would have been the norm rather than deviation from it; and (3) the more remarkable 614-group readings often have less group coherence than the subtle ones (see chapter 3). The final reason points to a long history of intermittent correction toward the Byz text rather than a late insertion of remarkable "Western" readings. Furthermore, if a late editor inserted "Western" readings, he needed an authoritative source. A MS preserving the ancient WR tradition might have sufficient authority. It is doubtful that a PWR MS would.

This study has estimated the origin of the PWR archetype to the period of AD 125–150 and the creation of the WR to AD 150–175. In contrast, Barbara Aland estimated the 614-group archetype to have sprouted somewhere in the second century or early third century, and the WR (Aland's "D-text") to have its birth in the "first half of the third century."[13] Specifically, she utilized the inconsistent agreement between the citations of Irenaeus (Ir) and a reconstructed text of the WR to show that Ir's Greek Acts was not derived from the WR. Instead, she considered the WR as having been created from MSS similar to Ir and MS 614.[14] However, she admitted that even if it is agreed that the Greek Acts MS used by Ir did not derive from the WR, that would not prove the WR did not exist in Ir's day. It could have been available already far away in Syria.[15] Her concession is significant because Ir's copy of Acts is safely dated to AD 150 or earlier. Aland also affirmed that the Greek of Ir was similar to that of the 614-group.[16] These statements cohere with the proposal that the PWR archetype was already extant before AD 150. Moreover, Aland reasoned that the original wording of the 614-group MSS (i.e., the PWR archetype) could only be approximated in a rough manner because of two reasons: (1) MSS of the same type as 614 sometimes manifest a large range of variation, and (2) the late date of the group's witnesses would surely have allowed some Byz readings to enter them.[17] On the contrary, this study has reconstructed the PWR archetype with a high degree of accuracy by use of "The Proto-Western Text Canon." The reference to ten primary witnesses enables many subsequent changes to be detected. Moreover, the leading MSS (e.g., 614 1292 1611 2412)[18] show

13. Aland, "Entstehung, Charakter und Herkunft," 27, 65.
14. Aland, "Entstehung, Charakter und Herkunft," 26–28, 55–56.
15. Aland, "Entstehung, Charakter und Herkunft," 64.
16. Aland, "Entstehung, Charakter und Herkunft," 49, 51.
17. Aland, "Entstehung, Charakter und Herkunft," 28.
18. In contrast to most PWR MSS, MS 1611 even refuses most Byz corrections in

minimal influence from Byz readings beyond Acts 5:32.[19] Finally, the determination of whether the WR was created in the second half of the second century or the first half of the third century remains uncertain. Tuckett argues for an early date based upon numerous agreements of Ir with the WR witnesses.[20] Meanwhile, Barbara Aland argues for a late date because of their disagreements. Indeed, many significant agreements and disagreements exist.[21] Nevertheless, it is difficult to defend a WR date beyond AD 200, given its abundant ancient evidence in the Egyptian (see mae), Syriac (see sy^{h**} sy^{hmg}), and OL translations.

Acts 1:1–5:32.

19. However, it is possible that the PWR archetype represented by 614 et al. might be a "second-generation" exemplar, i.e., the archetype of 614 et al. might be derived from the first-generation PWR archetype, the one used as a source for the WR. A "second-generation" might be dated 50, 100, or even 150 years later and be the cause of a second/final layer of changes, perhaps of many minor smoothing revisions. Alternatively, those changes may have been gradually acquired over one of those periods and then cemented in the second-generation. If there were two generations, a portion of the estimated 411 isolated PWR readings that stand against the united Byz/ECM and some of the estimated 105 isolated PWR readings that stand in a three-way division with the Byz and the ECM would be from the later date. If true, this alternate theory seems to have little impact on the results already obtained. Because the PWR archetype itself manifests no trend of conformity to the Byz text, that second layer would not have made the 614-group any more Byz. It would merely be a question of whether *all* these approximately 516 isolated PWR variants occurred prior to AD 150 or whether *most* occurred before AD 150 and the remaining were added sometime later. Thus, the restored PWR archetype is a mid-second-century text but there may be some exceptions, particularly in these independent revisions. A two-generation theory has the advantage that it might explain the few places where the WR seems to retain the more primitive reading (see, e.g., 5:39/19) and account for why the PWR and the WR are not agreed in many minor details. Either way, the PWR archetype, as reconstructed from the available evidence, suggests that this MS was a chosen exemplar from which many copies were made. The ten core PWR MSS are evidence to this end.

20. Tuckett, "How Early," 76–86.

21. At least twenty-one important agreements between Ir, Codex D (or sometimes E), and other key Western witnesses exist at 2:24/18, 2:33/38–40, 2:37/31, 3:13/42–44, 3:13/59, 3:14/14, 3:17/17, 4:9/9, 4:12/2–40, 4:31/49, 5:31/18, 8:37/2–44, 9:20/13, 14:15/22–38, 15:20/22–26, 15:20/37, 15:29/8–12, 15:29/17, 15:29/29, 17:27/2–38, and 17:31/8–12. In contrast, twelve key disagreements may be seen at 3:7/21, 3:8/2–32, 3:17/5, 3:17/6–8, 4:24/7, 5:32/9, 7:4/53, 10:28/11, 10:38/10–14, 10:41/36–42, 15:2/64–70, and 15:26/27. This list was gleaned from Aland, "Entstehung, Charakter und Herkunft," 43–56; Tuckett, "How Early," 76–81; and Strutwolf, "Text Apostelgeschichte bei Irenäus," 181–85.

(3) The Byz Is Better than the PWR Archetype

The Byz text is better than the PWR archetype for several reasons. First, the PWR archetype was founded primarily on a proto-Byz archetype and secondarily using a proto-Alex archetype (see chapter 2). More specifically, its editor may have commenced his work with reference to a proto-Byz MS, revised it using a proto-Alex MS, like P45 (Gospels-Acts), and then added his creative changes (see chapter 3 excursus on Acts 7).[22] The editor introduced many minor revisions to "improve" the style and clarify the meaning, similar to the editorial work found in P45.[23] This papyri MS also points to an archetype in the second century.

Secondly, the Byz editors refrained from adding many expansions seen in the PWR edition. These were interesting glosses that commonly clarify the meaning or offer additional detail.[24] The expansions come from parallel passages in Luke-Acts (e.g., 6:8/29; 14:10/9; 15:1/13; 15:4/45; 15:26/27; 19:5/19; 26:14/10–14; 27:2/34–38; 27:19/19; 28:30/29), from the LXX (e.g., 7:37/40; 7:43/49; 13:41/10), from marginal notes that are possibly from an eyewitness (e.g., 13:43/35; 17:12/13; 19:9/51; 19:28/13; 23:15/65; 23:29/12–16; 23:29/33; 24:27/19; 27:5/21; 27:15/23; 27:35/31; 28:19/9; 28:19/31), evidently from oral tradition (e.g., 5:39/19; 15:2/64–70; 15:29/17; 16:39/2–22; 23:25/2–12), from the mind of the editor (e.g., 13:28/11; 13:33/20; 13:39/13; 15:7/10–12), from the immediate context (e.g., 2:1/22; 12:25/8; 22:12/26–28), from marginal notes added for a liturgical setting (e.g., 18:8/38–40; 20:32/49), and from other

---

22. This hypothesis is warranted given the tight coherence between the PWR edition and the Byz tradition that manifests itself in at least three ways. First, both traditions include the ten additions that appear to be both Lucan and secondary to the "published" edition by Luke (see below). Second, in a great many places 9/10 or 10/10 core PWR MSS agree with the Byz text (against the ECM) in subtle/insignificant details (see notes at Acts 7 and 13 under "Chapter Summaries" at the end of chapter 3). Most of these places of minor agreement are pointers to a common source, dating back to the early second century. Third, the two traditions on several occasions have identical wording in places of manifold variation (see 4:25/2–24, sixteen readings; 5:24/14–28, fourteen readings; 10:11/14–30, eighteen readings; 10:12/8–28, twenty readings; 15:18/2–6, twenty-three readings; 18:21/9, thirteen readings; 21:25/16–20, twenty readings).

23. See Porter, "Developments in Acts," 47–57; Hurtado, *Texts and Artefacts*, 38–39.

24. Most of the following examples are discussed in chapter 2.

sources.[25] However, unlike the WR, the PWR archetype rarely manifests a paraphrastic rewording of the mainstream text.[26]

Although the Byz text refrains from many of the expanding glosses that are present in the PWR archetype, it does have a handful of its own additions. Both traditions likely began with a proto-Byz MS that was already influenced by the earliest "Western" clarifying tendencies. It was marked by smoothing, both semantically and grammatically, had obtained accidental corruptions, and had been lengthened in a few dozen places (see chapter 2 where two lists summed together offer eighty-three places where the Byz is two or more words different from NA28). Of the eighty-three variants, there are fifty-eight where the Byz and PWR are agreed. Moreover, of the twenty-five remaining differences, the Byz is shorter eight times and in five places both the Byz and PWR are longer, though not equal.[27] Therefore, the Byz text is two or more words longer than both the ECM and PWR editions at only twelve places. Moreover, the Byz variant at 7:32/21–25 appears to be original.[28] Evidently, beyond the middle of the second century only these eleven expansions entered the Byz text. The important observation is that the Byz text manifests very little evidence of large additions beyond those readings that it likely inherited from the proto-Byz archetype. In contrast, the PWR tradition was expanded by at least two words in a minimum of seventy-five cases. In fact, sixty-one have a significant impact (SI) to the understanding of the passage, while the remaining fourteen (asterisked) were found to be insignificant (INS):

*2:1/22; 2:43/22–28; *4:1/13; *4:9/9; *5:33/7; 5:39/19; 5:41/22–28; 6:8/29; 7:37/40; 7:43/49; 12:1/35; 12:20/14–22; 12:25/8;

---

25. See Schmid, "Conceptualizing 'Scribal' Performances," 50, 55–61, who explains how marginal notes entered Greek MSS. The variants categorized as "marginal notes possibly from an eyewitness" were either simple details or quotations that show little or no word variation in its witnesses. Those marked as "oral tradition" display significant variation and may have been inserted without reference to a written source.

26. Two prominent exceptions include 13:48/10–26 and 18:19/10–14 (linked with 18:22/1).

27. The Byz is shorter at *4:12/22–40, *4:27/6–26, 9:38/30–34, *17:13/50–56, *23:7/14–20, 25:6/6–20, 13:24/20–26, and *24:14/46–56. Those asterisked were probably caused by homoeoteleuton. The Byz text and PWR are both longer, though not equal, at these five locations: 3:22/4–6; 5:41/22–28; 13:40/10–18; 23:34/5; 24:22/2–10. Most likely 13:40/10–18 is original in the Byz.

28. The twelve variant readings include: 7:32/21–25; 7:37/26–28, 30–36; 9:19/14–22; 13:42/7; 13:42/8–16; 19:3/5; 19:12/50; 20:28/40; 21:8/10; 21:22/10–14; 23:30/10–18; 28:30/6–14.

*13:28/11; 13:33/20; 13:39/13; 13:41/10; 13:41/49; 13:43/35; 13:47/33; 14:10/9; 14:18/23; *14:25/13; 14:25/19; 15:1/13; 15:2/64–70; 15:4/45; 15:6/15; 15:7/10–12; *15:23/4–8; 15:26/27; 15:29/17; 15:34/2–12; 16:9/27; 16:11/2–4; 16:27/12–14; 16:35/26; 16:39/2–22; 17:5/2–22; 17:11/47; 17:12/13; 17:19/2–4; 18:8/38–40; 18:19/10–14 with 18:22/1[29]; *18:27/35; *18:28/13; 19:5/19; 19:9/8–24; 19:9/51; 19:28/13; 20:19/7; *20:23/35; 20:32/49; 21:36/19; *22:12/26–28; 22:29/47; 23:15/65; *23:24/17; 23:25/2–12; 23:29/12–16; 23:29/33; *24:9/2–6; 24:27/19; 26:14/10–14; 26:15/26; *26:20/15; 27:2/34–38; 27:5/21; 27:15/23; 27:19/19; 27:35/31; 28:16/20–22; 28:19/9; 28:19/31; 28:30/29.

Thirdly, the PWR edition is secondary to the Byz as evidenced by its many readings that stand against the united RP05/ECM wording. As compared to the RP05 Byz text that stands independent of an aligned ECM/PWR reading about 242 times, the PWR edition isolates itself from the other two traditions far more often, i.e., about 411 places. The implication is strong here that the PWR editor inadvertently moved his text away from the original.[30] Moreover, the revised nature of the PWR isolated variants can often be seen by their smoothing and clarifying character. For example, in chapter 3 its independent readings were shown to be probably inferior in all but 1 (see 8:21/32–40) of the 146 examples found across eight chapters of Acts (i.e., chapters 7–8, 13, 15, 17, 19, and 26–27). The same trend occurs for the rest of the book. In fact, when isolated, it offered just 5 original readings overall (see PAO readings in chapter 4). In contrast, the Byz performed a little better, offering 15 probably original isolated readings (see above).

(4) Important Contributions from All Three Core Traditions

For the book of Acts, the original text is best approximated with reference to the *ALEX* + BYZ + pwr, with the lowercase indicating lesser

---

29. This combined variant is not really an expansion. As described in chapter 2, the PWR editor had smoothed the passage, but confusion resulted when the standard reading was added to it later.

30. Although the ECM readings stand alone against the aligned Byz/PWR readings about 507 times, their demonstrable quality in Acts (e.g., their repeated confirmation from ancient translations and from text-critical rules) makes it nearly certain that most of them are original. See Zuntz, *Text of the Epistles*, 158. Some examples are provided in chapter 4 (the Alexandrian text is original (ATO) readings that lack Byz and PWR support).

importance and the italics pointing to the highest overall quality. The equation is somewhat reversed as compared to Zuntz's assessment of the value of the three traditions in the Pauline Epistles. His higher estimation of the "Western" over the Byz could be displayed as: Best Text = *ALEX* + byz + WESTERN. Two important points are emphasized by means of these equations. First, all three traditions have a significant contribution to make. Second, the Byz is more important than the "Western" text in Acts and has its own primitive history. Few textual critics since Westcott and Hort (WH) have even entertained this idea.[31] Although by 1854, Tregelles could describe Griesbach's theory of three ancient recensions as having "been thoroughly demolished," the influence of his theory continues to the present day.[32] A principle assumption for Griesbach was that the Byz text was completely derived from the earlier Alex and Western text traditions.[33] If correct, the Byz would have no primary role in textual criticism whatsoever. WH did not realize that this conception was an error and perpetuated it. Similarly, Gordon Fee has argued that the Byz text did not even exist in the second century because there is no proof for its pattern of readings until the fourth century.[34] He states that there are "no MSS even partly representing the Majority text until the fifth century."[35] He acknowledges the existence of a "Western" type of text in the second century in areas such as North Africa, Italy, and Southern France, but says that its witnesses do not cohere over "large portions of text."[36] In contrast to recognizing the existence of a rough "Western" text, he affirms, "In none of these areas does one find a single witness to the Majority text as a text form, but only sporadic attestation to the existence of some of the Byzantine readings."[37]

However, chapter 3 has identified about 507 Byz pattern readings aligned with the reconstructed, second-century PWR archetype. In addition, chapters 2–4 have shown that the Byz text is usually more primitive than the PWR and likely its basis. Therefore, an approximate Byz text does in fact exist for the book of Acts in the early second century. However,

---

31. Even Zuntz, *Text of the Epistles*, 280, 283, describes the Byz text as being a later but somewhat unfiltered version of the Alex text type.

32. See Tregelles, *Account*, 91.

33. Tregelles, *Account*, 84–85.

34. Fee, "Majority Text," 184.

35. Fee, "Majority Text," 184.

36. Fee, "Majority Text," 187.

37. Fee, "Majority Text," 187.

given its estimated 242 variant units, standing against the aligned Alex/PWR traditions, and the estimated 105 variant units divided in three ways, it would be more accurate to call it a second-century, proto-Byz text.[38] This state of affairs was partly anticipated by Zuntz (see above) and is consistent with the utilization of the CBGM in order to produce the ECM of Acts. Since readings from each tradition can be ancient and possibly original, all types of MSS are to be investigated rather than just those from one tradition. The CBGM recognizes that great mixture has occurred between the various textual traditions, making it necessary to use a representative sampling of all MSS when making textual decisions on a variant by variant basis, especially looking for the reading that can best explain the derivation of the others.[39] Though the Byz has suffered from a long history of secondary modifications, the CBGM has recognized it as having roots as old as the Alex text. As an example, the Byz reading was judged by the ECM editors to be superior to the Alex text in thirty-six places.[40] Wachtel's earlier 1995 study of the Catholic Epistles yielded a similar result.[41] Moreover, he stated that the oldest MSS also have an impressive amount of the same polishing characteristics as seen in the Byz text. The main difference was in the Byz's greater concentration of them.[42] These two factors merge to indicate the quality and antiquity of the Byz heritage. The viewpoint of Zuntz and Wachtel et al. has been confirmed in the present study of the book of Acts.

As stated above, the Alex text was found to remain closest to the original. This conclusion is in line with WH. It is also consistent with Tregelles who, three decades before WH's principal work, affirmed Griesbach's still earlier axiom that the most ancient witnesses are more likely to preserve the original.[43] Griesbach himself was following the lead of Johann Bengel from a generation prior.[44] Then, after all of them, Zuntz

---

38. The same could be said for the Alex text of the second century, i.e., it should technically be called proto-Alex. Yet in comparison with the Byz history, the proto-Alex text appears to have remained noticeably more stable as it developed into the Alex tradition.

39. Wachtel, "Notes on Acts," intro, 28–31.

40. Wachtel, "Notes on Acts," intro, 30–31.

41. Wachtel, *Byzantinische Text*, 87, 131.

42. Wachtel, *Byzantinische Text*, 76, 200.

43. Tregelles, *Account*, 84–85.

44. See Bengel, *Gnomon*, 1:14, 16, whose text-critical guideline numbers 8 and 12 weighed antiquity over all other characteristics in the NT witnesses, including variety and quantity.

preferred the oldest witnesses but did not favor them equally. In particular, he prized the Alex MSS because of their superior internal evidence, having found them to be significantly purer than the other traditions in the Pauline Epistles.[45] Similarly, this current study concludes that when either the Byz or PWR archetype reading stands isolated from the other two traditions, its wording is seldom original. In contrast, when most of the ten best ECM MSS agree (whose nature is primarily Alexandrian), they usually preserve the original reading. However, there is no simple formula for textual decisions. The fact that an original reading is occasionally isolated in the Byz or (less commonly) in the PWR edition, makes it essential to use a cross-section of all evidence. Much more importantly, the *greatest* text-critical value of the Byz and PWR traditions, in the book of Acts, lies in their ability to uncover original readings when they stand united. When they align against the Alex text (about 507 times), they repeatedly provide original readings. Though most of their unified readings appear to be secondary, an estimated 118 of the 507 (i.e., 23 percent) appear to be original.[46] They also provide strong confirmation for the Alex text and thereby rightfully increase confidence in the printed ECM wording. Namely, when either tradition aligns with the Alex, that reading has a very high probability of being original. If one were to equate Zuntz's "Western" text in the Pauline Epistles with the PWR edition in Acts, it is remarkable that nearly all his same conclusions are valid here.[47] Likewise, his assessment that "Western" readings shared by the Byz text anchor them far back into the second century seems to ring true for PWR edition readings that are shared by the Byz tradition.[48]

The value of the joint witness between the Byz text and the PWR edition can be practically observed from their agreement at 70 of the 85 readings that were judged to be original in the Byz (see chapter 4, "BTO" readings). These readings were preferred based upon their superior combined external and internal evidence. Similarly, of the 118 SGL readings (see above) that have RP05 support for a variant that opposes NA28, it

---

45. Zuntz, *Text of the Epistles*, 156, 214, 269, 283.

46. The total of 118 comes from the earlier discussion. Above it was found that 70 BTO readings are aligned with the PWR edition. Also, if merely half of the 97 Byz/PWR aligned SGL readings are assumed to be original, about 48 more must be added to the 70.

47. Zuntz, *Text of the Epistles*, 158–59.

48. Zuntz, *Text of the Epistles.*, 142, 150–51.

turns out that 97 are also aligned with the PWR edition.⁴⁹ This high correlation demonstrates that one is right to expect high quality when the Byz and PWR traditions agree. If just the aligned readings were accepted from both groups, the revisions to NA28 would be a not insignificant group of 167 (i.e., 70 + 97). That is not to say that all the aligned variants should be accepted, and the others rejected. Rather it is being argued that the 85 revisions should be embraced, if justified, and that the SGL readings should presently remain as they are due to their uncertain nature. The two groups were combined merely to highlight the quality of these Byz/PWR readings. It should also be noticed that the other 36 (i.e., 15 + 21) are isolated Byz readings with a solid claim for originality as well.

(5) One Lucan Edition and yet Ten Divided Readings

No evidence was found to support the long-standing theory of two different Lucan editions that differ greatly in length and details.⁵⁰ On the other hand, evidence was acquired that suggests Luke may have removed the following ten expanded readings just prior to publishing his solitary edition: 2:30/34; 10:32/37; 15:24/30–34; 18:21/4–6, 9, 10, 24; 20:24/27; 21:25/16–20; 23:30/45; 24:6/20–8/14; 28:16/12–16; 28:29/2–24.⁵¹ These

---

49. Observe that 37 of the 155 SGL readings (i.e., the 27 already equal to the Byz and the 10 that lack a competing Byz variant) are listed above in footnotes. The remaining 118 SGL readings offer a viable alternative to NA28 (i.e., ECM reading a.). It is interesting that all but the following 21 variants are aligned with the PWR edition: 2:7/5; 3:9/6–12; 4:7/8–12; 4:33/4–6; 5:32/6–8; 7:35/32; 8:32/38–40; 9:34/18–20; 10:42/20; 10:48/2–6; 11:18/12; 11:18/28–40; 13:26/26; 13:45/25; 15:29/8–12; 17:3/34–40; 20:13/6; 21:3/36–40; 25:20/8; 26:16/44; 26:21/12. These are part of the list in ECM 3:1:1, intro, 35–37.

50. Metzger, *Textual Commentary*, 222–36.

51. However, the variants at 18:21 and 28:16 have features that suggest these may come from a first-century editor. Unlike the other eight examples, it would not have sufficed for Luke to just place text-critical symbols before and after the section of the words to be deleted. At 18:21, for example, about three other changes were required for the remaining words to be fluid Greek (see chapter 4). At 28:16, a move from the longer Byz/PWR reading to the ECM wording would require not only the deletion of the descriptive words but also the removal of the particle δέ from the sequence that follows: τῷ δὲ Παύλῳ ἐπετράπη. Observe also that the ECM word order is different, showing ἐπετράπη τῷ Παύλῳ. The more likely scenario here is that a non-Lucan editor inserted the words ὁ ἑκατόνταρχος παρέδωκεν τοὺς δεσμίους τῷ στρατοπεδάρχῃ in front of the ECM reading without any other changes, as seen in PWR MSS 1292 1611 and the sy^{h**} (see reading k.). Then the proto-Byz editor (see Byz/PWR reading b.) cleaned it up by adding the conjunction and smoothing the word order. Others "corrected" it differently, leading to eleven readings. Thus, if Luke himself made the shortening changes at

longer readings are usually distinguished by their combination of dominant external support, high linguistic quality, and natural Lucan style. Other than the two minor changes at 20:24 and 23:30, the rest are four to twenty-seven words longer. These readings apparently point to a most primitive common ancestor of both the Byz text and the PWR archetype.[52] The Greek MS support for the long readings typically includes almost every "Western" leaning MS listed within the new text-critical canon (see chapter 4).

In terms of translations, the longer readings have the best support from sy^h and the OL gig. The Byz/PWR agrees with sy^h in 8/10 locations (exceptions: 28:16, 29; joined by sy^{h**} instead) and gig in 7/10 locations (exceptions: 2:30; 20:24; 23:30). Thus, together they join the long reading only 50 percent of the time (i.e., 10:32; 15:24; 18:21; 21:25; 24:6–8). Therefore, the longer readings lack consistent widespread translation support. In contrast, the bo and Vg join the core Alex MSS in preserving the shorter reading every time. In addition, the Ä and sa join it 8/10 times and 7/10 times respectfully. In fact, all four translations jointly support the shorter reading 70 percent of the time (exceptions: 10:32; 18:21; 28:16). None of the readings supply anything essential to the context.

All the long readings seem to be clarifying remarks. Their disharmonious qualities (i.e., excellence in the context and yet absent from several of the best authorities), suggest both Lucan authorship and Lucan final editing. In 8/10 occasions, Luke could have trimmed his working edition simply by inserting two text-critical symbols into the MS itself. Therefore, the longer text would most likely not have been erased. Perhaps someone in Luke's circle had access to it and, acting in good faith, reintroduced the excised words into a popular copy of Acts. They were helpful to him, and he thought they would benefit others. Alternatively, it could be argued that Luke created two almost identical editions, except for the ten readings shown here.[53] The first edition included the ten readings and was a private copy for Theophilus. The second was trimmed of

---

18:21 and 28:16, a successor of Luke would have had to reverse several editorial notes from Luke's working edition in order to reintroduce them.

52. Although the addition at 24:6–8 is printed only in the margin of RP05, the quality and quantity of the Byz MSS that support it combined with its alignment with the PWR edition both imply that it is from the proto-Byz archetype. Wachtel, "Against the Text-Type Concept," 147, agrees and suggests that the words were removed from the Byz standard during the late K^r recension.

53. See Holmes, "From 'Original Text,'" 657–58, who explains that in the first-century context the author might have two or three copies at the point of initial publication.

these unnecessary details and was a public copy for a particular church and intended to be copied for other churches. This proposal is inviting because it better explains the reintroduction of phrases previously removed by Luke. The divided tradition would have been a natural result if Theophilus had decided to have his private copy reproduced for another church. However, given that scribal oversight appears to have impacted every extant MS at 4:25/2–24 and 8:7/2–20 (MS 614 excepted), as described below, it is more likely that just one copy was produced and given to Theophilus. It was then subsequently copied for the churches. Nevertheless, Luke's source (i.e., original edition) was pure of the two scribal mistakes that entered when it was copied for Theophilus.

(6) Two Probable Conjectures

Given Luke's demonstrable expert linguistic ability, two variant readings at 4:25/2–24 (see chapter 4) and 8:7/2–20 (see chapter 3) strongly oppose his style. These are the only locations in Acts that suggest to this author that a primitive oversight may have occurred that infiltrated the entire extant Greek MS record. Although the printed text of the ECM could be regarded as original and both readings described as momentary Lucan lapses into awkward grammar, the skill and carefulness of Luke combined with the simplicity of the proposed solutions suggest that the conjectured readings are more likely original. The first case is apparently a word order mistake within a complex sentence that yielded much variation. The second is not a pure conjecture since it has solitary support in the first hand of the scribe who copied MS 614. However, unless a significant amount of ancient evidence turns up to support the inclusion of the prefix συν-, it appears that somewhere in the transmission history between the PWR archetype and the copyist of MS 614, a clever scribe fixed the problem by conjecture. The dropping of the prefix on a compound word was a common scribal error and can be found in some of the very best MSS.[54] If these are the only locations that warrant the consideration of conjecture, the text of Acts has indeed been wonderfully preserved across two millennia.

---

54. See Fee, "P75, P66, and Origen," 261.

CONCLUSION AND FURTHER RESEARCH

TEXT-CRITICAL IMPLICATIONS OF THE FINDINGS

The findings above enable a revised sketch of the primitive textual history of Acts. The most important conclusion is that the Byz text has a high probability of being important for improving the accuracy of other NT books as well.

(1) Clarifying the Textual History of Acts

As discussed above, an estimated ten variant units, separating Luke's working edition from his final published edition, evidently generated an anomaly in the textual transmission of the book of Acts. As depicted below in figure 5.1, following that initial stage, the textual history proceeded down two principal paths, i.e., one leading to the proto-Alex archetype and one guiding to the proto-Byz archetype (with "Western" editing tendencies). The Alex road was straighter (i.e., purer) possibly because its editors placed a high value upon the precise wording of the biblical text.[55] According to Zuntz, this small group of scholars was highly skilled in the principles of "philological criticism."[56] Therefore, when they needed to stabilize the biblical tradition, they had superior methods for doing so.[57]

---

55. See Zuntz, *Text of the Epistles*, 279–80.
56. Zuntz, *Text of the Epistles*, 251–52, 269–73, 275, 279–81.
57. See Zuntz, *Text of the Epistles.*, 267, 279–80. For the Pauline Epistles, Zuntz inferred that a minority of the editors in Alexandria began to apply rigorous philological criticism to the NT at about AD 150, leading to a remarkably pure proto-Alex text by AD 200. For him, P46 and in the later Codex B (p. 56) are proof of such work. One could also note P75 in the Gospels. On the other hand, he regarded the Byz text as having resulted from a multi-century mixing of the purer Alex MSS with that of popular and less guarded MSS (p. 280). Given my estimated early period (i.e., AD 125–150) for the creation of the PWR edition and its apparent relationship to the Byz and Alex traditions, this study asserts that the process described by Zuntz began even earlier for Acts, near AD 125. Moreover, it infers the existence of *both* a proto-Alex and proto-Byz archetype at that time. If correct, the proto-Byz archetype, *just like* the proto-Alex archetype, also had its own independent pathway back to the original by Luke. The shared readings found in the principle extant MSS of the Byz Acts (e.g., 014 020 025 049 18 35, etc.) and those found in the principle MSS of the Alex Acts (e.g., 03 P74, etc.) separately point back to common ancestors underlying each tradition, archetypes existing in the early second century. It appears that both traditions stabilized their text then. In contrast, Zuntz proposed that the Byz work began about AD 200 (p. 56). Evidently, two factors hindered the Byz editors. First, their archetype was not nearly as pristine as that of the Alex editors. Second, their guiding principle for correcting the MSS was not as conducive to precision (see below). The proto-Byz, text-critical labors were a factor in the solidification of the Byz text of Acts.

CONCLUSION AND FURTHER RESEARCH

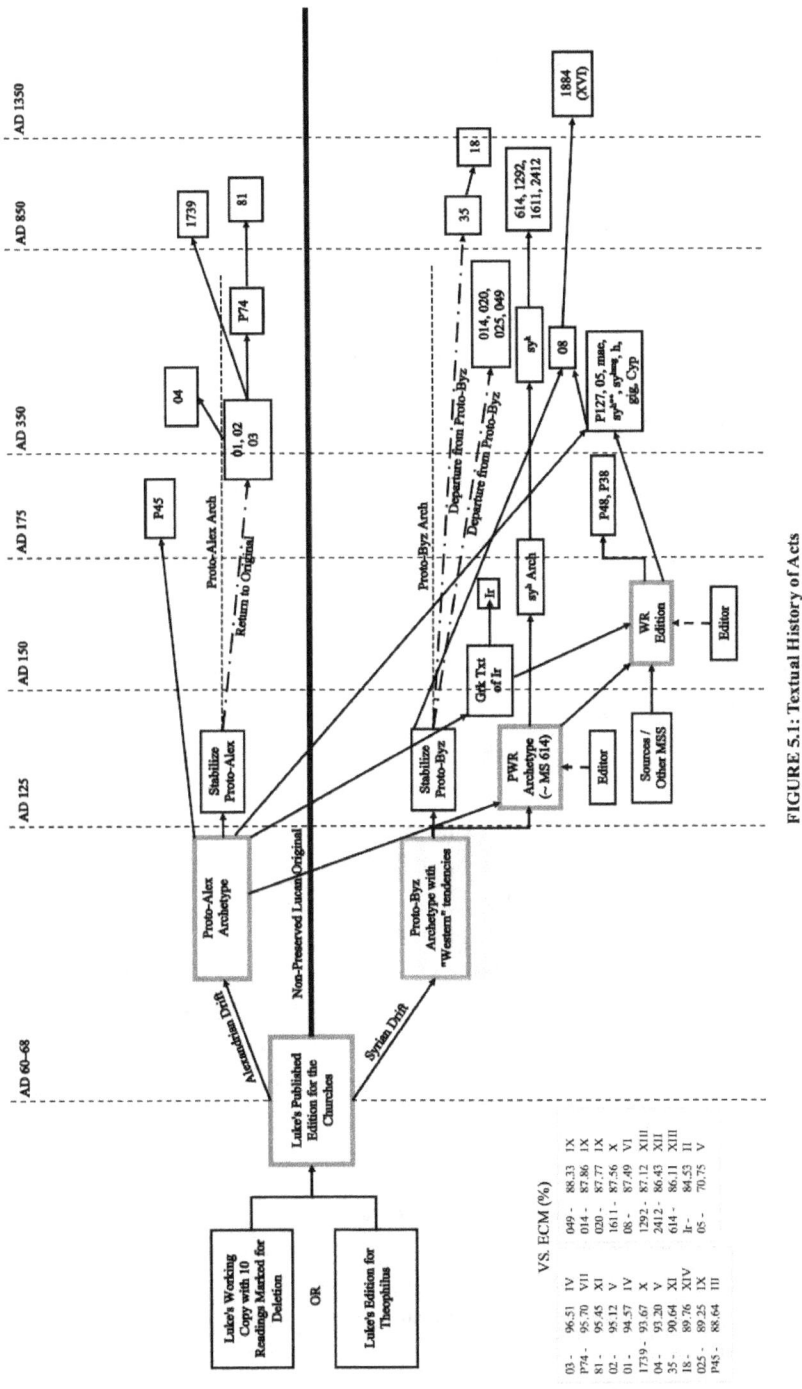

FIGURE 5.1: Textual History of Acts

Zuntz asserted that they were guided by the contemporary practices previously learned from Alexandrian text-critical work upon the Greek classics. As an important initial step, the earliest and best MSS available were acquired.[58] In contrast, the earliest Syrian editors apparently valued the meaning conveyed by the text most of all. Thus, in the most primitive period leading up to the proto-Byz archetype, the scribes allowed for more freedom in the wording and permitted some clarifying remarks to enter. Their more libertarian attitude was apparently for the most part intolerant of major changes. Once copies of the proto-Byz archetype or MSS similar to it became established as exemplars, the previous freedom was dampened. However, since its editors lacked the Alex critical knowledge, they apparently chose to improve their exemplars by choosing that reading, from among alternatives, which fits the context in the clearest manner.[59] Not surprisingly, their changes normally moved their text away from the original.

In a new and revised compilation of his own writings, Larry Hurtado describes the former approach as being exemplified in P75 (Luke-John) and the latter in P45 (Gospels-Acts).[60] Additionally, he draws an analogy from the work of expert palaeographer Eric Turner who found "two broad tendencies in ancient papyri of classical literary texts."[61] Turner had described the first as being more accurate and tied to Aristotle's "attitude toward books" and the second as more fluid and tied to Plato's.[62] Significantly, Hurtado summarizes that the earliest extant papyri do not preserve the "larger variants that reflect a major change in the text" or the "major additions in the Codex Bezae text of Acts."[63] He thus implies that the most primitive editors and copyists usually resisted this kind of liberty in the transmission process.[64]

The relative purity in both streams suggests that both traditions attempted to stabilize their NT MSS. Perhaps it was concern for the danger of widespread corruption that motivated them to act. The later problems caused by Marcion would have likely increased the motivation toward this end. Their initial efforts seem to have born fruit by around AD 125

58. Zuntz, *Text of the Epistles*, 274–75.
59. See Zuntz, *Text of the Epistles*, 55; Wachtel, *Byzantinische Text Briefe*, 73.
60. Hurtado, *Texts and Artefacts*, 38.
61. Hurtado, *Texts and Artefacts*, 38–39.
62. Hurtado, *Texts and Artefacts*, 38–39.
63. Hurtado, *Texts and Artefacts*, 42.
64. Hurtado, *Texts and Artefacts*, 42.

and to have resulted in a few exemplars receiving preference in each region from which copies should be made. Some proof of a common archetype behind these two traditions can be found in their binding errors, i.e., mistakes that are common to the core members of each tradition.⁶⁵ The most influential exemplar in Alexandria will be identified here as the proto-Alex archetype and likewise the most revered one in Syria referred to as the proto-Byz archetype. An example of their editorial caution can be seen in that they both reject the major insertions at 8:37, 15:29, and 15:34 that were most likely already popular by that time.

However, a conservative approach to textual transmission was not universal. With an openness to more freedom, the PWR editor apparently built upon a proto-Byz archetype and introduced occasional corrections from a respected proto-Alex MS akin to P45. He then brought in many minor smoothing changes of his own. They are revisions of the same nature as those seen in P45.⁶⁶ In addition, the editor welcomed marginal readings (but not 8:37 and 15:20) and other additions. For example, the PWR archetype manifests about seventy-five additions that are at least two words longer than what is seen in either the Byz or Alex traditions. These are expansive glosses beyond those already established in the proto-Byz archetype. In contrast, the later Byz text has only inserted about eleven glosses of similar length subsequent to the proto-Byz archetype. The PWR editor likely completed his work sometime between AD 125 and 150. Next, possibly in the period of AD 150–175, the Western Redaction (WR) editor created a much-expanded edition of Acts by using various sources, including a copy of the PWR archetype, a Greek MS similar to that used by Ir, other Acts MSS with marginal readings, possibly oral tradition, and his own paraphrasing/smoothing of the Greek text before him. His rewording of the text demonstrates a significantly more fluid approach to textual transmission. This WR editor revised Acts comprehensively, and his work was appreciated in many ancient communities. It was translated into the OL near AD 200, into Syriac around AD 200–250, and into Coptic possibly around AD 250. Because the Latin father Cyprian quotes the book of Acts ca. AD 250 in a manner very close to OL MS h, and with words near to a reconstructed WR text, an estimated date for the WR's existence in OL is easy to prove.⁶⁷ Although the best extant evidence for the WR in the Syrian language is

65. See Wachtel, *Byzantinische Text*, 82; Zuntz, *Text of the Epistles*, 56, 62.
66. Porter, "Developments in Acts," 47–57.
67. See Metzger and Ehrman, *New Testament*, 102; ECM 3:2, 138.

the Syriac Harklensis (sy^h) translation, dated AD 616, with its apparatus offering sy^{h**} and sy^{hmg} readings, it reflects the earlier Syriac Philoxeniana (sy^{ph}), dated AD 507/508. More importantly, the Western text of sy^{ph} can already be partly confirmed from the earlier Syriac Peshitta (sy^p), dated early fifth century, and the still earlier Old Syriac of the Acts, preserved only among "Eastern fathers."[68] The continuity of the WR in Syriac points back to an Old Syriac translation of Acts probably around AD 200 with a "Western" character.[69] As for the ancient Coptic evidence for the WR, the best representative is the Middle Egyptian (mae). However, its date of creation is unknown. Despite this limitation, Metzger has affirmed that "Western" readings can already be seen in the Sahidic (sa) translation that he dates to the first half of the third century.[70] This latter assertion is important because Metzger describes the sa as a text characterized as having numerous minor "Western" readings but lacking the long ones. Consequently, he judges that it must have been "Western" originally and then later purged of its long readings.[71] The above combined translation testimony implies that the WR was formed no later than AD 200 and possibly many years before then.

Overall, each of the four traditions (having here delineated the PWR edition from the WR) experienced a significantly different transmission history. The proto-Alex archetype appears to have been improved as it matured into the proto-Alex tradition. Following that, it changed little qualitatively as it matured into the Alex text. While its editors purged away deviations, they also introduced some secondary readings by their textual choices.[72] In contrast, the proto-Byz archetype experienced a greater number of secondary changes on the way to becoming the Byz text of today. It appears that few of its "corrections" were made back to the original. Most of its editing is of the smoothing and clarifying nature, typical of this textual tradition.[73] In order to approximate the proto-Byz text, several important steps are necessary. First, remove from RP05 the estimated 242 readings where the PWR edition and the ECM align. The assumption is that the Byz's uniqueness in these places is probably

68. Metzger and Ehrman, *New Testament*, 97–98.

69. Metzger and Ehrman, *New Testament*, 98.

70. Metzger, *Early Versions of NT*, 127, 133; Metzger and Ehrman, *New Testament*, 110.

71. Metzger, *Early Versions of NT*, 127.

72. Zuntz, *Text of the Epistles*, 272.

73. Wachtel, *Byzantinische Text*, 73.

a result of a later change by a Byz editor or scribe. The second step is to restore those 15 readings where the Byz text appears to be original and yet independent of both the ECM and the PWR edition (see the 15 BTO readings in chapter 4). The third step involves judging the 105 readings that are divided in three ways to see if it was the Byz text or the PWR edition that moved away from the proto-Byz archetype. The clearly more primitive readings should be assigned to the proto-Byz archetype. These steps go a long way toward uncovering more precisely what the proto-Byz text read in the early second century.

Like the proto-Alex archetype, the PWR edition is easier to reconstruct than the proto-Byz text. Its advantage is partly because its leading representatives such as MSS 614 and 2412 manifest a tradition that has seldom been conformed to either the Byz or Alex texts. Both MSS 1292 and 1611 are also relatively free of revision. Most of the remaining six core PWR MSS were thoroughly but inconsistently revised to the Byz text. Some of them also show an occasional tendency toward conformity to the Alex text. Despite its overall steadiness, when the PWR archetype originally deviated from the proto-Byz archetype, it produced about 411 readings that stand against a united Alex/Byz text. This fact, combined with the clarifying nature of 75 of its expansions, suggests that nearly all its isolated readings are inferior (see chapter 3). As a result, the PWR edition is a great deal further away from the autograph than is the modern Byz text. Nevertheless, it is superior to the WR. Having evidently utilized a copy of the PWR edition, a Greek MS like that of Ir, other sources, and his own style, the WR editor created an interesting edition. Given its derived and expansive nature, the WR does not usually stand in competition with the other traditions for original readings. Though the "Western" text of Acts has impressive quality, as many scholars have observed, the textual evidence suggests that the best of the "Western" is rather to be found in the earlier PWR edition. The irony of history is that once the inferior WR was created, it experienced a period of widespread popularity. Moreover, copies of the WR in Greek continued to be further revised in the same vein. These changes upon changes can be observed in several of the primary representatives such as Codex D, P38, P48, P127, the mae, and the sy^{hmg} / sy^{h**}. The complex textual history of Codex D also reveals that, between itself and the WR, its intermediate ancestors were repeatedly revised by MSS of the Alex tradition.[74]

74. See Ropes, *Beginnings of Christianity*, lxxx–lxxxiv; Boismard and Lamouille, *Texte occidental reconstitution*, 1:111–18.

(2) Byz Is Most Likely Important for Other NT Books

Three conclusions from this study of Acts make it highly probable that the Byz tradition has a similar important role to play in other NT books: (1) the roots of the Byz text are as old as any other ancient tradition; (2) Byz readings aligned with a primitive "Western" text (i.e., the PWR edition) were often found to be better than those of the Alex tradition and to be original; and (3) some of the isolated Byz readings were also found to be original. Ultimately, the accuracy and value of any text tradition needs to be evaluated separately within each NT book. In Acts it was shown that while the Byz has a greater smoothing tendency than the Alex tradition, that fact should not prejudice the Byz text in places where there is no apparent smoothing. Nor should a presumption of smoothing be accepted, as if it were a proof, when the ancient translations and/or fathers positively support the "easier" text. In fact, some readings are clearly smoother in the Alex tradition and yet were still judged as original in the ECM of Acts (e.g., 5:38/42; 23:8/16; 26:6/18). Moreover, it is a known fact that clarifying and simplifying changes were never systematically accomplished on the Byz text.[75] Therefore, the Byz tendency should not be overdrawn. In fact, overall, the Byz tradition retains the second-best text of Acts. It has a quality superior to both the PWR edition and the WR of Acts. One of WH's major criticisms of the Byz text proves to be almost nonexistent in Acts.[76] A clear case of Byz conflation occurs at 20:28 and a conflation/expansion happens at 23:30/10–18. Beyond these, it is difficult to find them. Similarly, scribal conformity of a passage to a parallel occurs repeatedly in both the PWR edition and the WR. For example, beyond those isolated PWR assimilations listed above, the PWR did so also at these eighteen places: *3:22/4–6 (see 3:25); 5:36/50 (see 5:37); *10:12/8–28 (see 11:6); 10:31/24 (see 10:4); 13:23/18–26 (ἤγειρεν, see 13:22); 13:41/49 (see 15:13); 13:47/33 (see 15:12 et al.); 15:1/13 (see 15:5); 15:6/15 (idea from 15:22); 15:14/8–14 (ἐξελέξατο, see 15:7); 15:37/16 (see 12:12); 15:39/10 (see 13:13); 16:35/8 (see 16:36); 17:26/10–14 (see 17:28); 19:35/2 (see 19:33); 22:5/10–12 (see 23:2); 26:15/26 (see 22:8); 27:36/14 (see 27:33–34). Most are from nearby locations. The WR also assimilates repeatedly (see chapter 2). The Byz avoided all but the two marked with asterisks. For an isolated Byz assimilation, see 7:37/26–28

---

75. See Scrivener, *Plain Introduction*, 2:293; Zuntz, *Text of the Epistles*, 55; Wachtel, *Byzantinische Text*, 80–81, 89.

76. Westcott and Hort, *Introduction*, 93–107.

(see 3:22). Once again, the Byz was careful. Although the Byz can be exposed as making passages less difficult (see 4:25/2–24), the RP05 Byz text also maintains other hard readings such as three negatives within four words (see 26:26/28–40). The only one of the ten best ECM MSS to maintain the original here was MS 01* and it was then "corrected." Therefore, the Byz text should be perpetually utilized to improve the standard editions in other NT books. Much detailed work, as expertly done in the ECM of Acts, will be necessary to obtain optimal results.

SUGGESTIONS FOR FUTURE RESEARCH

The present study brought to light six related avenues for future research. Each will be described briefly in the following paragraphs.

(1) Research the Gospel of Luke to determine if a similar textual history exists as that discovered here. The evaluation could take advantage of the scholarly work already completed by the editors of the International Greek New Testament Project (IGNTP) who published two volumes on Luke in 1984 and 1987 respectively. If a similar history is found, a Proto-Western Reading (PWR) archetype could once again be reconstructed and used alongside the Byz tradition to increase the accuracy of the standard editions. Luke is the most natural Gospel to begin with due to its common author, allowing lessons learned in Acts to be more readily applied therein. Even if no such PWR archetype exists for Luke, if the ancient roots of the Byz text can once again be confirmed, a noticeable improvement to the text of Luke should result. The ancient papyri of Luke such as P45 and P75 will help with identifying the most primitive readings. Lessons learned from both Acts and Luke could then be used to evaluate the other Gospels. Similarly, the ongoing work on the IGNTP for John could be harnessed for evaluating that book.

(2) Conduct a full assessment of the estimated 411 isolated PWR archetype readings in Acts that are opposed by the joint testimony of the Alex and Byz traditions. Chapter 3 already evaluated 146 variant units across eight chapters of Acts. The remaining ones should be considered and the results for the entire book summarized. Since these readings (except two that are probably original, i.e., 20:5/6 and 22:12/26–28) were either created or selected by the PWR archetype editor, much can be learned about his early second-century approach toward transmitting the NT text. In addition, the estimated 105 readings divided between

the three traditions should be evaluated because they evidently were secondary revisions from the same editor (except three that are probably original, i.e., 5:34/30–40; 8:21/32–40; 23:30/10–18).

(3) Similar to number two, conduct a full assessment of the estimated 242 isolated Byz readings in Acts that are opposed by the joint testimony of the Alex and PWR traditions. Their independence implies that most of these probably entered the standard Byz text subsequent to existence of a popular proto-Byz archetype near AD 125. In chapter 4, just eight of these possessed sufficient comprehensive evidence to suggest their probable originality in Acts (see 2:7/5; 5:32/6–8; 7:32/21, 25; 11:26/16–24; 13:26/26; 14:17/40; 19:27/54–58; 26:16/44). At the same time, further evaluate the estimated 105 readings divided between the three traditions to see if any more of them are original. In chapter 4, just seven of these were assessed as probably original (see 2:41/18–28; 4:5/22–34; 5:37/28; 13:20/2–16; 13:40/10–18; 14:8/8–18; 15:23/4–8). By evaluating these variants, much can be learned potentially about how and why the proto-Byz text changed as it matured into the modern Byz text.

(4) Conduct a study of the ten primitive expansive readings jointly testified by the Byz/PWR traditions. These variant units are here described as written by Luke and yet secondary to his published edition of Acts. The research would endeavor to determine if such classification is appropriate. If so, it would validate whether either more or less readings belong to this group. Finally, it would present the best possible explanations for their existence and offer to the broader theological community the most likely cause, given what is known of editing and copying NT Greek MSS in the early period. The results have the potential of resolving whether there is any tangible evidence for Luke creating more than one edition. If the answer is yes, it would help constrain what is meant by two Lucan editions.

(5) Based upon the data presented in this work, it is possible to reconstruct a basic critical edition of the PWR archetype, estimated to have originated in the period of AD 125–150. That reconstruction would be based upon MS 614 except in those places where another leading core PWR MS is identified as best preserving the archetypical PWR (see appendix). The MSS listed within "The Proto-Western Text Canon" (see chapter 4) that uphold each particular PWR reading could be listed, with the core PWR MSS set apart. For quick comparison, the apparatus could display the competing readings in the ECM and RP05 Byz texts. In order to assist with a ready appreciation of the differences in the PWR

edition as compared to the other traditions, an English translation could be supplied. Such an edition could be an important tool for future studies regarding the textual transmission of Acts and the "Western" text overall.

(6) Minus the "other text is original" (OTO) readings, there were ninety recommended improvements to the ECM based upon the Byz and PWR traditions (see chapter 4). Research to find out why so many (sixty-seven, i.e., 74.4 percent) occurred in Acts 1–17. Assuming the general accuracy of the recommendations, seek to determine if the inherent Jewishness of Acts 1–15 assisted the proto-Byz editors. In other words, were the proto-Byz text editors better at preserving Greek that was more Semitic? If so, one could expect the same kind of improved accuracy in the Byz text of the Gospels.

Appendix:
Three Traditions and PWR Reconstruction

DESCRIPTION FOR THE READER

THE END OF CHAPTER 3 provided alignment summaries of the Alex (as approximated by the ECM text), the Byz (i.e., per the RP05 edition), and PWR traditions listed out for each chapter of Acts. This appendix provides the specific variant units that undergird those summaries, utilizing the ECM format for identifying unique variants. Therefore, each variant will be listed by its chapter, verse, and word number(s), i.e., PWR = Byz (30): 7:1/12; 7:3/36; etc. For clarification, "PWR = Byz" indicates places where these two agree but are opposed by the ECM. Likewise, "PWR = ECM" means that these two agree and are opposed by the Byz. These notes will enable a quick comparison of the three traditions for any chapter of Acts. The number in the parentheses always gives the total quantity of variant units for that category.

In addition, as stable as MS 614 and its companion MS 2412 are in retaining the PWR archetype's wording, they manifest some errors. Moreover, in a few places they were likely revised by another tradition.[1] Therefore, whenever MS 614 *does not* preserve the PWR, a leading MS of the core PWR MSS that *does* retain it will be listed in parentheses, i.e., 1:13/51(1611). Although 614 and 2412 were copies made from the same *Vorlage*, their differences are sometimes interesting.[2] This summary will

---

1. The section 1:1—5:32 is an example. As noted in chapter 2, MSS 614 and 2412 were repeatedly revised to agree with the Byz text in this portion. Therefore, MS 1611 et al. must be relied upon instead.

2. See 8:7/2–20 where 614* disagrees with 614C and 2412. Their common *Vorlage* is evident by their closeness of text and binding errors, i.e., isolated agreement in error.

enable the reader to duplicate the results of this study if desired. If it looks like MS 614 has suffered from an accidental change, the letter E (i.e., error) will precede it. Lacking any marking below, it can be assumed that MS 614 equals the wording of the PWR archetype. From this data, the (approximated) PWR archetype can be reproduced for the book of Acts. Such a tool could be useful for study and future research. The end of the appendix will also have a few other notes regarding variant calculations under the subtitle "Calculations."

ALIGNMENTS

Acts 1:

- a. PWR = Byz (16): 1:5/16–22; 1:6/10; 1:8/24–26; 1:13/8–14; 1:13/30–38; 1:14/15; 1:14/33; 1:15/22; 1:16/13; 1:16/45; 1:17/8; 1:20/44; 1:21/20; 1:22/34–38; 1:25/4–12; 1:25/18

- b. PWR = ECM (0): N/A

- c. PWR ≠ ECM/Byz (7): 1:4/4; 1:11/44; 1:13/51(1611); 1:14/17(1611); 1:15/28(1611); 1:21/37(1611); 1:23/8(1611)

- d. 3 Ways (0): N/A

- e. MS 614 suffers from an accidental or purposeful scribal change subsequent to the PWR edition at the following (5) locations: E1:10/24–26(1611); E1:10/28(1611); E1:14/30(1611); E1:20/44(1611); E1:22/26(1611/2412)

- f. Note(s): MS 1611 is the best representative of the PWR from 1:1—5:32

Acts 2:

- a. PWR = Byz (30): 2:1/20; 2:4/6–10; 2:4/30–32; 2:7/8–10; 2:7/16–26; 2:12/22–24; 2:13/6–8; 2:14/42; 2:17/74; 2:22/22–28; 2:22/63; 2:23/19; 2:23/22; 2:27/16; 2:30/34; 2:30/38–40; 2:31/22–24; 2:31/26; 2:33/20–26; 2:33/38–40; 2:36/18–30; 2:37/8–10; 2:38/2–12; 2:38/36–40; 2:40/10; 2:40/12–18; 2:41/6–8; 2:42/21; 2:43/2; 2:47/38–3:1/4

- b. PWR = ECM (3): 2:7/5; 2:14/4–6; 2:37/32

According to CBGM, they disagree only 90 times out of 7,395 variant units. MS 2412 will often be noted when it differs from 614.

APPENDIX: THREE TRADITIONS AND PWR RECONSTRUCTION

   c. PWR ≠ ECM/Byz (10): 2:6/29(1611); 2:28/14; 2:30/16–18(1611); 2:33/42–48(1611); 2:37/12–14; 2:38/28–30; 2:40/28–32; 2:42/7; 2:43/22–28; 2:45/24

   d. 3Ways (3): 2:1/22; 2:31/18–20; 2:41/18–28(1611)

   e. MS 614 suffers from an accidental or purposeful scribal change subsequent to the PWR edition at the following (3) locations: E2:17/50(1611/2412); E2:23/26(1611/2412); E2:28/10(1611/2412)

   f. Note(s): at 2:28/14, MS 614 is probably the PWR but it manifests a spelling error

Acts 3:

   a. PWR = Byz (13): 3:7/14–16; 3:7/24–28; 3:10/2–4; 3:10/10; 3:11/14; 3:11/20–28; 3:12/6; 3:13/47; 3:22/22; 3:25/6–8; 3:25/34; 3:26/6–10; 3:26/17

   b. PWR = ECM (4): 3:3/24–26; 3:9/6–12(1611); 3:11/6(1611); 3:18/22–28(1611)

   c. PWR ≠ ECM/Byz (6): 3:8/20–32(1611); 3:11/8(1611); 3:20/16; 3:20/30–32; 3:23/31; 3:26/20(1611)

   d. 3Ways (2): 3:21/34–42(1611); 3:22/4–6(1611)

   e. MS 614 suffers from an accidental or purposeful scribal change subsequent to the PWR edition at the following (4) locations: E3:5/12–18(1611); E3:12/36(1611/2412); E3:18/30–32(1611); E3:25/28(1611/2412)

   f. Note(s): n/a

Acts 4:

   a. PWR = Byz (14): 4:2/20–34; 4:6/4–20; 4:8/27; 4:12/18; 4:16/6; 4:17/20; 4:21/20; 4:24/28–30; 4:25/2–24; 4:31/26–32; 4:32/12–20; 4:34/6–12; 4:36/2; 4:37/18–20

   b. PWR = ECM (9): 4:7/8–12(1611); 4:11/20(1611); 4:14/4(1611); 4:16/46(1611); 4:18/9(1611); 4:19/14–18(1611); 4:27/6–26(1611); 4:32/34; 4:33/4–6(1611)

   c. PWR ≠ ECM/Byz (12): 4:1/13(1611); 4:3/15; 4:9/9(1611); 4:10/60(1611); 4:11/14–16; 4:15/6–12(1611); 4:15/16(1611);

APPENDIX: THREE TRADITIONS AND PWR RECONSTRUCTION

    4:18/28;   4:22/4–14(1611);   4:24/8–22(1611);   4:32/10(1611); 4:35/22–26

d. 3 Ways (2): 4:5/22–34(1611); 4:12/22–40(1611)

e. MS 614 suffers from an accidental or purposeful scribal change subsequent to the PWR edition at the following (7) locations: E4:9/14(1611/2412); E4:13/28(1611/2412); E4:14/24(1611); E4:17/28–38(1611); E4:28/20(1611); E4:29/32–34(1611); E4:30/39(1611)

f. Note(s): it is interesting to note that MS 1611 preserves the PWR in every place but three (i.e., 4:3/15; 4:11/14–16; 4:18/28), and that MS 614 has retained just these three

Acts 5:

a. PWR = Byz (19): 5:5/35; 5:9/2–10; 5:10/8; 5:12/18–28; 5:15/4–10; 5:15/24; 5:16/18; 5:18/9; 5:19/8; 5:19/12; 5:22/2–8; 5:23/7; 5:23/28; 5:24/14–28; 5:26/34; 5:32/21; 5:36/28–30; 5:38/24; 5:40/31

b. PWR = ECM (8): 5:3/43; 5:32/6–8; 5:33/2–6; 5:36/32; 5:38/42; 5:39/14; 5:39/18; 5:42/30–34

c. PWR ≠ ECM/Byz (16): 5:1/8–10(1611); 5:4/14(1611); 5:5/6; 5:10/14(1611); 5:12/14; 5:15/42; 5:16/2–10; 5:24/30(1611); 5:33/7; 5:33/12; 5:35/4; 5:36/16–22; 5:36/50; 5:39/11; 5:39/19(1611); 5:41/7

d. 3 Ways (6): 5:3/6–10(1611); 5:8/6–10; 5:34/30–40; 5:36/26; 5:37/28; 5:41/22–38

e. MS 614 suffers from an accidental or purposeful scribal change subsequent to the PWR edition at the following (9) locations: E5:2/2–10(1611/2412); E5:7/28(1611/2412); E5:8/18–22(1611/2412); E5:19/22–24(1611); E5:23/2(1611/2412); E5:23/28–32(1611); E5:35/30(1611/2412); E5:37/46(1611/2412); E5:39/6–10(1611)

f. Note(s): n/a

Acts 6:

a. PWR = Byz (3): 6:3/4; 6:13/22–24; 6:13/32–36

b. PWR = ECM (4): 6:3/21; 6:3/28; 6:8/8–12; 6:15/10

c. PWR ≠ ECM/Byz (7): 6:2/24–28; 6:7/10; 6:7/42; 6:8/29; 6:9/2–4; 6:11/18–20; 6:15/14

APPENDIX: THREE TRADITIONS AND PWR RECONSTRUCTION

   d. 3Ways (0): n/a

   e. MS 614 suffers from an accidental or purposeful scribal change subsequent to the PWR edition at the following (2) locations: E6:1/34(1611/2412); E6:13/11(1611)

   f. Note(s): n/a

Acts 7:

   a. PWR = Byz (30): 7:1/12; 7:3/36; 7:7/18–22; 7:8/37; 7:8/45; 7:10/52; 7:11/10–14; 7:12/10; 7:12/12–14; 7:14/10–16; 7:15/2–4; 7:16/38; 7:17/18; 7:18/12–14; 7:19/24–30; 7:22/28; 7:25/28–30; 7:26/18; 7:26/33; 7:27/32; 7:30/27; 7:31/24–28; 7:33/30–32; 7:39/26–36; 7:40/46; 7:46/22–24; 7:48/2–14; 7:51/8; 7:56/14; 7:60/22–28

   b. PWR = ECM (10): 7:16/20–22; 7:32/21, 25; 7:34/46; 7:35/30–32; 7:35/40; 7:35/42–44; 7:37/30–36; 7:38/54; 7:52/48; 7:58/26

   c. PWR ≠ ECM/Byz (18): 7:4/32–34; 7:5/28–34; 7:9/15; 7:10/32; 7:14/26–32; 7:20/39; 7:21/22; 7:22/22–26(1611/2412); 7:28/8–10; 7:28/18–22; 7:36/18–20; 7:37/6; 7:37/40; 7:41/16; 7:43/49; 7:44/10; 7:52/28–34; 7:55/2–4

   d. 3Ways (2): 7:21/2–10; 7:37/26–28

   e. MS 614 suffers from an accidental or purposeful scribal change subsequent to the PWR edition at the following (16) locations: E7:2/50(1611); 7:10/30(1611); E7:14/2–6(1611); E7:16/4–40(1611/2412); E7:20/24(1611); E7:22/22–26(1611/2412); 7:25/16–24(1611); E7:29/22–24(1611/2412); E7:35/10(1611); E7:40/16–18(1611); E7:42/35(614C fixed it); 7:44/28(1611); 7:56/20–24(1611/2412); E7:57/6–8(1611/2412); 7:59/19(1611/2412); E7:60/30–36(1611)

   f. Note(s): at 7:56/20–24, MS 614 aligns with P74 in reading "Son of God"

Acts 8:

   a. PWR = Byz (13): 8:2/16; 8:5/10; 8:6/2–8; 8:8/2–8; 8:12/13; 8:13/30–38; 8:14/34; 8:18/31; 8:25/22; 8:25/38; 8:27/22; 8:30/16–20; 8:33/19

   b. PWR = ECM (6): 8:10/2–6; 8:16/2; 8:16/32–34; 8:18/2–4; 8:22/16–22; 8:32/38–40

APPENDIX: THREE TRADITIONS AND PWR RECONSTRUCTION

c. PWR ≠ ECM/Byz (14): 8:7/24; 8:9/36–40; 8:10/15; 8:14/18(1611); 8:19/26; 18:20/18–22; 8:24/11; 8:24/16–24; 8:25/18–20; 8:26/22; 8:29/16–24; 8:35/28; 8:38/16–22; 8:39/8

d. 3 Ways (3): 8:7/2–20(614C/2412); 8:10/30–32; 8:21/32–40

e. MS 614 suffers from an accidental or purposeful scribal change subsequent to the PWR edition at the following (8) locations: E8:9/26–28(1611/2412); E8:14/18(1611); E8:19/16–18(1611); E8:23/18(1611); E8:26/11(1611/2412); E8:31/22–24(1611); E8:32/50(1611); 8:39/6(1611)

f. Note(s): at 8:7/2–20, MS 614* uniquely offers a reading that makes excellent sense

Acts 9:

a. PWR = Byz (28): 9:3/24–28; 9:5/15; 9:6/22; 9:8/4; 9:10/26–32; 9:12/6–10; 9:12/20; 9:13/10; 9:13/28–38; 9:15/42; 9:18/8–14; 9:18/16; 9:21/48; 9:25/6–22; 9:26/4–8; 9:26/10; 9:28/10–14; 9:28/20; 9:28/28–30; 9:29/22–24; 9:31/2–56; 9:33/12–14; 9:33/26; 9:36/32–34; 9:37/24–26; 9:40/14; 9:42/18–20; 9:43/6–10

b. PWR = ECM (6): 9:8/14–16; 9:15/22–24; 9:17/40–44; 9:19/14–22; 9:20/16; 9:38/30–34

c. PWR ≠ ECM/Byz (10): 9:3/10–12; 9:6/16; 9:17/2–6; 9:18/20–28; 9:30/18; 9:31/40; 9:34/2–10; 9:36/27; 9:40/60; 9:41/14–16

d. 3 Ways (3): 9:24/16–20; 9:34/18–20; 9:38/44–50

e. MS 614 suffers from an accidental or purposeful scribal change subsequent to the PWR edition at the following (7) locations: E9:5/15(1611); 9:7/18(1611/2412); 9:7/20–28(1611); 9:15/48–50(1611); E9:27/32(1611); 9:32/16(1611/2412); E9:36/4(1611/2412)

f. Note(s): n/a

Acts 10:

a. PWR = Byz (24): 10:1/7; 10:2/23; 10:4/50; 10:5/8–12; 10:5/20–26; 10:7/16; 10:7/20–24; 10:8/6–8; 10:10/18; 10:10/20; 10:11/14–30; 10:12/8–28; 10:14/20–26; 10:16/14–16; 10:17/29; 10:19/28; 10:19/30; 10:20/20–22; 10:30/25; 10:30/26–38; 10:32/37; 10:37/20; 10:46/23; 10:47/8–12

APPENDIX: THREE TRADITIONS AND PWR RECONSTRUCTION

b. PWR = ECM (9): 10:3/12–20; 10:9/10; 10:17/40–44; 10:17/52; 10:26/8; 10:33/52; 10:42/20; 10:47/34; 10:48/4

c. PWR ≠ ECM/Byz (13): 10:5/16; 10:6/2–4; 10:6/6–12; 10:9/18; 10:22/26; 10:24/12; 10:26/16–20; 10:30/15; 10:31/24; 10:36/2; 10:36/6; 10:37/6–10; 10:39/16

d. 3Ways (4): 10:23/2–16; 10:24/2–8; 10:39/4–6; 10:48/8–18

e. MS 614 suffers from an accidental or purposeful scribal change subsequent to the PWR edition at the following (9) locations: E10:14/26(614C); E10:24/32(1611/2412); E10:25/22(1611/2412); E10:29/20(1611); 10:30/28(1611); E10:32/8(1611/2412); 10:36/24(1611/2412); E10:39/42(1611/2412); E10:40/22(1611)

f. Note(s): n/a

Acts 11:

a. PWR = Byz (21): 11:2/2–6; 11:4/4; 11:7/2–6; 11:9/6–16; 11:10/14–18; 11:11/24; 11:12/16–18; 11:13/29; 11:13/35; 11:17/38–42(1611); 11:18/21; 11:20/22; 11:20/28–30; 11:21/20; 11:22/38–40; 11:23/12–14; 11:25/6–8; 11:26/2–6; 11:26/44; 11:28/26–40; 11:28/47

b. PWR = ECM (7): 11:13/4; 11:16/10; 11:18/12; 11:18/28–40; 11:22/20–26; 11:26/16–24; 11:26/26–30

c. PWR ≠ ECM/Byz (5): 11:5/40; 11:19/50; 11:25/12; 11:27/4–10; 11:28/28–30

d. 3Ways (3): 11:3/6–18; 11:8/12–18; 11:12/4–12

e. MS 614 suffers from an accidental or purposeful scribal change subsequent to the PWR edition at the following (4) locations: 11:16/17(1611); E11:17/30(1611/2412); E11:30/8(1611); 11:30/24(1611/2412)

f. Note(s): at 11:17/38–42, MSS 614 and 2412 were revised to the Alex reading; given the many agreements of the PWR with the ECM from 11:16–26, it would appear that the PWR editor utilized a proto-Alex MSS to revise this portion away from the proto-Byz; the PWR at 11:27/4–10 is likely the result of an accident, and MS 03 agrees with it

APPENDIX: THREE TRADITIONS AND PWR RECONSTRUCTION

Acts 12:

a. PWR = Byz (12): 12:3/2–4; 12:5/22–24; 12:5/28–42; 12:8/14(1611); 12:9/7; 12:12/14; 12:13/4–6; 12:15/34–36; 12:17/34–36; 12:19/37(1611); 12:23/22–24; 12:25/23

b. PWR = ECM (3): 12:8/4; 12:11/8–12; 12:22/10–18

c. PWR ≠ ECM/Byz (12): 12:1/14–22; 12:1/35; 12:4/26–36; 12:5/26; 12:11/26–32; 12:12/36; 12:14/23; 12:17/20–32; 12:20/14–22; 12:23/6–12; 12:25/8; 12:25/10–14

d. 3Ways (2): 12:6/8–14; 12:20/5

e. MS 614 suffers from an accidental or purposeful scribal change subsequent to the PWR edition at the following (4) locations: E12:8/18(1611); 12:14/40–44(1611); E12:15/2–10(1611); 12:17/2–10(1611).

f. Note(s): n/a

Acts 13:

a. PWR = Byz (30): 13:1/5; 13:4/2; 13:4/12–16; 13:4/21; 13:4/31; 13:9/2–18; 13:10/38; 13:11/34–36; 13:14/16–22; 13:15/38–40; 13:17/12; 13:19/18–22; 13:22/10–14; 13:25/8–12; 13:25/16–18; 13:26/36–38; 13:33/16; 13:33/28–36; 13:35/2; 13:38/41; 13:41/18–22; 13:41/32; 13:43/40; 13:44/22–28; 13:45/28; 13:45/29; 13:46/4–6; 13:46/36; 13:50/15; 13:52/4

b. PWR = ECM (14): 13:2/37; 13:6/18–20; 13:13/12–16; 13:15/42–48; 13:17/38–40; 13:24/20–26; 13:26/26; 13:42/7; 13:42/8–16; 13:42/20–26: 13:43/44–46; 13:44/2–6; 13:45/25; 13:50/43

c. PWR ≠ ECM/Byz (17): 13:5/38; 13:7/24–28; 13:8/28–32; 13:10/30; 13:17/22–26; 13:27/8; 13:28/11; 13:33/20; 13:34/2; 13:39/5; 13:39/13; 13:41/10; 13:41/34; 13:49; 13:43/35; 13:47/6–8; 13:47/33

d. 3Ways (8): 13:4/24–26; 13:6/6–10; 13:20/2–16(1611); 13:23/18–26; 13:31/29, 30–32; 13:40/10–18; 13:48/10–26; 13:51/12–14

e. MS 614 suffers from an accidental or purposeful scribal change subsequent to the PWR edition at the following (4) locations: E13:21/4(1611/2412); E13:41/40(1611); E13:43/38(1611); 13:51/23(1611/2412).

APPENDIX: THREE TRADITIONS AND PWR RECONSTRUCTION

f. Note(s): at E13:43/38, MSS 614, 1292, and 2412 all swapped a letter and thus are bound by a common mistake; across 13:42–45, it appears that the PWR was corrected by a proto-Alex MSS because of its six agreements in a short range

Acts 14:

a. PWR = Byz (17): 14:8/34(1611/2412); 14:9/24–26; 14:10/24; 14:11/2–4; 14:12/2–6(1611); 14:13/2–4; 14:13/21; 14:15/42–44; 14:17/2; 14:17/12; 14:19/40; 14:21/28; 14:21/34–36; 14:23/8–12; 14:24/14; 14:27/14; 14:28/5

b. PWR = ECM (7): 14:7/4–6; 14:8/30; 14:10/20; 14:11/13; 14:14/24–30; 14:17/40; 14:20/6–10

c. PWR ≠ ECM/Byz (16): 14:8/21; 14:10/9(383); 14:13/8–14; 14:13/24–26; 14:15/20–24; 14:15/28–38; 14:18/6; 14:18/23; 14:20/16–20; 14:22/12; 14:23/14; 14:23/31; 14:23/32; 14:25/13; 14:25/19; 14:27/18–26

d. 3Ways (2): 14:2/6–10; 14:8/8–18(1292)

e. MS 614 suffers from an accidental or purposeful scribal change subsequent to the PWR edition at the following (6) locations: E14:8/8–18(1292); E14:8/34(1611/2412); 14:10/9(383); E14:12/22–24(1611/2412); E14:18/20–22(1611/2412); E14:23/20(1611)

f. Note(s): at 14:12/2–6, MSS 614 and 2412 were revised to the Alex; at 14:18/20–22, both MSS 614 and 1292 make an itacism that appears to be a binding error

Acts 15:

a. PWR = Byz (21): 15:1/26; 15:1/32–34; 15:2/4; 15:3/18–20; 15:4/10; 15:6/4; 15:7/6; 15:8/12–22; 15:17/52; 15:18/2–6; 15:20/11; 15:22/52; 15:23/16–20; 15:24/30–34; 15:28/8–12; 15:30/10; 15:33/24–26; 15:36/12–16; 15:36/30–32; 15:39/4–6; 15:40/20

b. PWR = ECM (5): 15:14/23; 15:25/10; 15:28/30–34; 15:29/8–12; 15:38/34–38

c. PWR ≠ ECM/Byz (22): 15:1/13; 15:2/64–70; 15:4/11; 15:4/30–32; 15:4/36–44; 15:4/45; 15:6/15; 15:6/20–24; 15:7/10–12; 15:10/32–40; 15:11/2; 15:14/8–14; 15:19/22; 15:22/24; 15:23/24–28; 15:25/29; 15:26/27; 15:27/16–24(1611); 15:29/17; 15:34/2–12; 15:37/16; 15:39/10

APPENDIX: THREE TRADITIONS AND PWR RECONSTRUCTION

d. 3Ways (6): 15:7/36–44(1611); 15:22/40–46; 15:23/4–8; 15:36/27; 15:37/6–8; 15:37/10

e. MS 614 suffers from an accidental or purposeful scribal change subsequent to the PWR edition at the following (7) locations: 15:7/34(1611); 15:7/36–44(1611); E15:15/4–6(1611); E15:17/6(1611); E15:20/14(1611); E15:20/18(1611/2412); 15:31/8–12(1611)

f. Note(s): n/a

Acts 16:

a. PWR = Byz (20): 16:4/33; 16:6/11; 16:7/20; 16:9/20–26; 16:10/30–36; 16:12/30–34; 16:13/18; 16:15/44; 16:16/10–12; 16:16/24; 16:16/26–28; 16:17/40; 16:18/16; 16:24/4–8; 16:24/28–30; 16:31/17; 16:32/16–28; 16:38/20–30; 16:40/6–10; 16:40/24–30

b. PWR = ECM (16): 16:1/4–6; 16:1/8–16; 16:1/36–38; 16:6/2–4; 16:7/2–4; 16:7/14; 16:7/34(1611/2412); 16:9/28; 16:11/7; 16:11/16–18; 16:18/35; 16:26/24–28; 16:34/13; 16:34/20–24; 16:37/44–56; 16:38/2

c. PWR ≠ ECM/Byz (12): 16:3/18; 16:9/27; 16:11/2–4; 16:13/4; 16:14/24; 16:14/28–32; 16:21/6–20; 16:25/24–26; 16:27/12–14; 16:29/14–16; 16:35/8; 16:35/26

d. 3Ways (6): 16:3/26–46; 16:9/12–16; 16:10/16–20; 16:12/2; 16:12/12–16; 16:39/2–22

e. MS 614 suffers from an accidental or purposeful scribal change subsequent to the PWR edition at the following (7) locations: E16:7/12–8/8(1611/2412); E16:26/6(1611/2412); E16:26/22(1611); E16:28/18(1611); E16:32/26(1611/2412); 16:35/14–16(1611); E16:38/6–18(1611/2412)

f. Note(s): the scribe of MS 614 made an eye skip, deleting 16:7/12–8/8; the scribe of MS 2412 corrected to the standard at 16:27/12–14

Acts 17:

a. PWR = Byz (18): 17:1/6–16; 17:1/26–28; 17:5/34–36; 17:10/8–14; 17:10/40–46; 17:14/20; 17:15/6; 17:15/32; 17:16/24–30(1611); 17:21/28–34; 17:23/32–40; 17:24/32–34(1611); 17:25/6–8; 17:25/28–32; 17:26/2–8; 17:26/18–24; 17:30/26–30; 17:32/26–33/8

APPENDIX: THREE TRADITIONS AND PWR RECONSTRUCTION

b. PWR = ECM (11): 17:4/32–36; 17:5/48(1611); 17:6/12; 17:7/26–30; 17:11/29; 17:13/50–56; 17:14/30; 17:15/13; 17:18/13(1611); 17:27/4–6; 17:31/2

c. PWR ≠ ECM/Byz (15): 17:2/28–30; 17:4/10; 17:6/30; 17:11/47; 17:12/4–6(1611); 17:12/13; 17:13/12; 17:14/2–8; 17:17/24–36; 17:18/6; 17:18/18; 17:18/68; 17:19/2–4; 17:25/20–26; 17:26/10–14

d. 3 Ways (4): 17:3/34–40; 17:5/2–22; 17:14/28; 17:20/24–30(1611)

e. MS 614 suffers from an accidental or purposeful scribal change subsequent to the PWR edition at the following (4) locations: E17:17/4–6(1611); E17:20/24–30(1611); E17:24/32–34(1611); E17:28/34(1611/2412)

f. Note(s): MS 614 is the PWR at 17:2/28–30 but it is misspelled (i.e., it is shown as 614f1 in the ECM to indicate the spelling error); MSS 614, 1292, and 2412 unite in a mistake at 17:17/4–6 and again at 17:24/32–34, and thus show a binding error; at the latter occasion, MS 1718 joins them

Acts 18:

a. PWR = Byz (19): 18:1/2–6(1611); 18:2/24; 18:3/28–30; 18:5/44; 18:7/8; 18:7/16–20; 18:9/10–10; 18:12/6–8; 18:13/12–14; 18:15/34–36; 18:17/6; 18:18/44–50; 18:19/2; 18:19/28(1611); 18:20/14; 18:21/4–6; 18:21/9; 18:21/10; 18:26/22–26

b. PWR = ECM (7): 18:2/42; 18:5/28–30; 18:11/2–4; 18:14/31; 18:15/6–8; 18:25/36–38; 18:26/40–46

c. PWR ≠ ECM/Byz (9): 18:7/6; 18:8/36; 18:8/38–40; 18:19/10–14(1292/2412f); 18:22/1(syp syhmg); 18:27/8–14; 18:27/35; 18:27/44–48; 18:28/13

d. 3 Ways (0): n/a

e. MS 614 suffers from an accidental or purposeful scribal change subsequent to the PWR edition at the following (12) locations: 18:1/2–6(1611); E18:2/60(1611); 18:5/46–48(1611/2412); E18:14/20; E18:14/20(1611/2412); E18:18/22(1611/2412); E18:18/46(1611/2412); E18:19/28(1611); E18:20/6(1611); E18:20/18(1611/2412); E18:25/12(1611/2412); E18:27/2(1611/2412)

APPENDIX: THREE TRADITIONS AND PWR RECONSTRUCTION

  f. Note(s): MSS 614, 1292, and 2412 show a binding error at 18:2/60; at 18:22/1, the PWR is best preserved in the back translations from the sy^p and sy^{hmg}

Acts 19:

  a. PWR = Byz (14): 19:1/30; 19:1/36–2/8; 19:4/9; 19:11/12–24; 19:12/12; 19:14/6–20; 19:16/4; 19:20/8–20; 19:24/26–30; 19:29/6–8; 19:30/2–6; 19:33/10; 19:37/24; 19:39/8

  b. PWR = ECM (19): 19:2/24–26; 19:3/5; 19:4/44; 19:10/35; 19:12/50; 19:13/6–8; 19:13/9; 19:13/56–58(1611); 19:15/14–16; 19:16/6–26; 19:16/27; 19:16/28–30; 19:25/38; 19:27/34–38; 19:27/54–58; 19:35/26; 19:35/47; 19:40/32–34; 19:40/36

  c. PWR ≠ ECM/Byz (20): 19:3/2–4, 6–10(1611); 19:5/19; 19:9/8–24(876); 19:9/37; 19:15/6–8; 19:15/19; 19:17/24; 19:18/8; 19:19/4; 19:21/48; 19:25/2; 19:26/57; 19:27/8–16; 19:28/13; 19:33/14; 19:34/16; 19:35/2; 19:37/11; 19:37/20–22; 19:38/2–6

  d. 3 Ways (3): 19:9/51; 19:13/46; 19:27/46–52

  e. MS 614 suffers from an accidental or purposeful scribal change subsequent to the PWR edition at the following (11) locations: E19:3/2–4, 6–10(1611); E19:8/16(1611/2412); 19:9/8–24(876); 19:13/50–52(1611); E19:16/40, 44(1611); E19:19/6(1611); E19:20/4–6(1611/2412); E19:27/20(1611/2412); E19:33/16(1611); E19:35/10(1611/2412); E19:40/30(1611/2412)

  f. Note(s): the PWR at 19:9/8–24 was greatly corrupted and it appears it was only retained by the Western friendly MS 876, though it is not one of the 10 core PWR MSS; at 19:13/56–58, MSS 614 and 2412 were conformed to the Byz, which is rare for them

Acts 20:

  a. PWR = Byz (30): 20:1/14; 20:3/12–14; 20:3/34; 20:4/7; 20:4/10; 20:9/2; 20:11/10; 20:13/16; 20:13/36–38; 20:14/6; 20:15/28–30; 20:16/2; 20:16/36–42; 20:19/16; 20:21/15; 20:21/23; 20:21/34; 20:22/8–10; 20:23/20; 20:24/6–8; 20:24/27; 20:25/39; 20:27/14–24; 20:28/3; 20:28/50–54; 20:29/2; 20:29/5; 20:32/32; 20:32/37; 20:32/38

  b. PWR = ECM (9): 20:1/24–26; 20:1/28; 20:5/4; 20:7/16; 20:13/6; 20:23/28–34; 20:24/13; 20:26/18–20; 20:28/40

APPENDIX: THREE TRADITIONS AND PWR RECONSTRUCTION

c. PWR ≠ ECM/Byz (22): 20:4/34; 20:5/6; 20:6/43; 20:9/8–12; 20:12/4; 20:13/20; 20:14/14; 20:15/2; 20:15/32; 20:18/21; 20:19/7; 20:23/6–12; 20:23/18; 20:23/35; 20:24/18–20; 20:24/36; 20:26/2–4; 20:31/31; 20:32/4; 20:32/49; 20:35/12–14; 20:37/22–24

d. 3 Ways (3): 20:1/32–36; 20:32/12–14; 20:37/2–8

e. MS 614 suffers from an accidental or purposeful scribal change subsequent to the PWR edition at the following (5) locations: E20:4/8(1611); E20:4/12(1611); E20:18/34(1611/2412); E20:20/6(1611/2412); E20:32/8(1611/2412)

f. Note(s): the PWRs at 20:13/20 and 20:14/14 are marked as a spelling error by the ECM; however, given its widespread support, it might be an alternate spelling

Acts 21:

a. PWR = Byz (20): 21:3/26; 21:4/2–4; 21:4/6; 21:4/34; 21:5/56–6/6; 21:9/8–12; 21:10/5; 21:14/14–22; 21:17/14; 21:20/12; 21:20/14–18; 21:20/30–34; 21:24/30; 21:25/16–20; 21:25/30–38; 21:31/2–4; 21:31/24–26; 21:33/28–30; 21:34/18–24; 21:36/14

b. PWR = ECM (13): 21:3/36–40; 21:6/8; 21:8/10; 21:11/22–24; 21:22/10–14; 21:24/22; 21:24/54–60; 21:27/48–54; 21:28/42; 21:29/6; 21:33/2–4; 21:37/32–36; 21:40/38

c. PWR ≠ ECM/Byz (18): 21:2/8; 21:6/16–18(1292/2412); 21:11/26–34; 21:13/42–60; 21:14/6; 21:21/48; 21:24/16–18; 21:25/14; 21:25/24; 21:27/14; 21:27/16–34; 21:27/42; 21:28/64–66; 21:36/10–12; 21:36/19; 21:37/2–4; 21:37/6–22; 21:39/4

d. 3 Ways (2): 21:13/2–8; 21:34/10(1292)

e. MS 614 suffers from an accidental or purposeful scribal change subsequent to the PWR edition at the following (6) locations: E21:3/16(1611/2412); 21:6/16–18(1292/2412); E21:8/22–24(1611); E21:9/8(1611/2412); 21:31/28(1611); E21:32/10–12(1611)

f. Note(s): at 21:21/48, the PWR edition apparently had a spelling error; at 21:34/10, MSS 614, 1611, and 2412 all appear to be revised by the Alex reading

APPENDIX: THREE TRADITIONS AND PWR RECONSTRUCTION

Acts 22:

a. PWR = Byz (8): 22:3/3; 22:9/19; 22:18/34–38; 22:20/31; 22:23/2; 22:23/4; 22:29/42–46; 22:30/31

b. PWR = ECM (8): 22:12/8–10; 22:16/30; 22:26/19; 22:27/17; 22:28/4; 22:30/22; 22:30/44; 22:30/50–62

c. PWR ≠ ECM/Byz (18): 22:2/14; 22:3/56–58; 22:4/18; 22:5/10–12; 22:6/30(614f); 22:7/14; 22:11/32; 22:12/26–28; 22:15/8; 22:20/12–18; 22:22/10–14; 22:24/36–40; 22:25/8–12; 22:25/24–42; 22:29/47; 22:30/4–6(1890); 22:30/20; 22:30/27

d. 3Ways (5): 22:20/32–34; 22:24/4–10; 22:25/2–6; 22:26/10–18(1611); 22:30/36–40

e. MS 614 suffers from an accidental or purposeful scribal change subsequent to the PWR edition at the following (6) locations: E22:6/2(1611); E22:13/22(1611); E22:17/28(1611); E22:23/10(1611/2412); E22:26/22(1611); E22:30/4–6(1890)

f. Note(s): at 22:25/2–6, the PWR does not make much sense and appears to be an error from the accidentally insertion of a sigma

Acts 23:

a. PWR = Byz (16): 23:6/30; 23:6/48–50; 23:7/8; 23:9/59; 23:10/34; 23:13/12–18; 23:15/22–24; 23:15/26; 23:17/36–40; 23:21/52–56; 23:22/14; 23:27/36–42; 23:28/4; 23:29/30–32; 23:30/45; 23:32/14–18

b. PWR = ECM (8): 23:8/16; 23:9/14–26; 23:10/10; 23:11/21; 23:28/20–28; 23:29/20(1611); 23:31/24–34; 23:35/20

c. PWR ≠ ECM/Byz (22): 23:1/36–40; 23:2/10–16; 23:5/2–8; 23:5/25; 23:9/38; 23:12/4; 23:15/6–18; 23:15/32–36; 23:15/38–42; 23:15/65; 23:23/26–28; 23:23/34; 23:24/15; 23:24/17; 23:26/6–12; 23:29/12–16; 23:29/33; 23:30/34–44; 23:33/4; 23:34/6–26; 23:35/2–6; 23:35/8–10

d. 3Ways (11): 23:1/2–12; 23:7/14–20; 23:12/8–14; 23:18/36–40; 23:20/24–34; 23:20/38; 23:25/2–12; 23:28/6–18; 23:30/10–18(1505/1890*); 23:34/5; 23:35/22–34(1611)

e. MS 614 suffers from an accidental or purposeful scribal change subsequent to the PWR edition at the following (1) location: E23:29/4(1611)

APPENDIX: THREE TRADITIONS AND PWR RECONSTRUCTION

f. Note(s): at 23:29/20, MSS 614 and 2412 were revised by the Byz text, which does not happen often with these MSS; at 23:30/10–18, it appears MSS 614, 1292, and 2412 each deviated from the PWR and joined an ancient secondary Alex reading (see MS 03)

Acts 24:

a. PWR = Byz (10): 24:5/16–20; 24:12/24; 24:13/2; 24:15/24–26; 24:16/14–16; 24:20/14–18; 24:23/30–32; 24:24/22–24; 24:24/44–52; 24:26/21

b. PWR = ECM (14): 24:1/20–22; 24:2/30; 24:10/4; 24:10/40–46; 24:11/6; 24:14/46–56; 24:16/6–8; 24:18/4; 24:19/16; 24:21/16–20; 24:23/3; 24:23/10; 24:25/20–24; 24:27/24–26

c. PWR ≠ ECM/Byz (18): 24:1/26–30; 24:1/34; 24:2/32; 24:6/20–8/14; 24:9/2–6; 24:10/18; 24:10/31; 24:12/22; 24:15/2; 24:15/20; 24:16/18–32; 24:20/10; 24:22/25; 24:24/6–8; 24:24/40; 24:25/50; 24:26/2–14; 24:27/19 (instead of 24:27/20–42)[3]

d. 3Ways (7): 24:11/28–32; 24:13/6–14; 24:17/10–26; 24:19/4–12; 24:21/8–14; 24:21/32–38(1611); 24:22/2–10

e. MS 614 suffers from an accidental or purposeful scribal change subsequent to the PWR edition at the following (4) locations: E24:10/6–12(1611); 24:14/28–36(1611); E24:19/28–32(1611); E24:21/32–38(1611)

f. Note(s): at 24:21/32–38, MSS 614 and 2412 have an itacism in their *Vorlage* and thus read ἡμῶν instead of ὑμῶν (not noted in the ECM)

Acts 25:

a. PWR = Byz (17): 25:2/4; 25:4/18–20; 25:5/6–12; 25:7/10–14; 25:7/30; 25:9/40; 25:11/6; 25:15/36; 25:16/23; 25:22/11; 25:22/23; 25:23/52–54; 25:24/58(614f/1611); 25:24/64–66; 25:25/6; 25:25/18–20; 25:25/33

b. PWR = ECM (10): 25:2/8–10; 25:8/2–6; 25:9/8–12; 25:14/10; 25:18/16; 25:20/12; 25:21/30–36; 25:23/39; 25:24/34; 25:26/54

---

3. Both Ropes and Heike Omerzu (also Clark's reconstruction) seem correct in suggesting that this "Western" insertion, as confirmed also in sy^{hmg}, had completely replaced the standard wording of 24:27/20–42. Therefore, the PWR and WRR reconstructions should lack the standard wording here. See Ropes, *Beginnings of Christianity*, ccxvii; Omerzu, "Darstellung der Römer," 173–74; Clark, *Acts of the Apostles*, 155.

319

c. PWR ≠ ECM/Byz (13): 25:2/2; 25:6/28; 25:10/32; 25:10/44; 25:13/2–10; 25:16/42–44; 25:17/6–8; 25:19/34; 25:20/8–10; 25:21/26–28; 25:24/32; 25:26/50; 25:27/6–8

d. 3 Ways (4): 25:5/22–28; 25:6/6–20; 25:18/20–24; 25:25/8–16

e. MS 614 suffers from an accidental or purposeful scribal change subsequent to the PWR edition at the following (5) locations: 25:8/36(1611/2412); E25:16/36(1611); E25:17/28(1611); E25:24/58(614f/1611); E25:24/66(1611/2412)

f. Note(s): N/A

Acts 26:

a. PWR = Byz (15): 26:2/30–32; 26:3/29; 26:4/34–36; 26:6/10–12; 26:7/36–40; 26:10/12–16; 26:14/18–24; 26:17/12–14; 26:20/12; 26:20/17; 26:23/26–28; 26:25/2–6; 26:28/22–24; 26:29/20–26; 26:30/2–4

b. PWR = ECM (12): 26:6/18; 26:10/24–28; 26:12/6; 26:12/24; 26:14/4; 26:15/16–18; 26:16/44; 26:20/36; 26:21/12; 26:26/44–52; 26:28/13; 26:29/2–6

c. PWR ≠ ECM/Byz (11): 26:1/14; 26:5/4; 26:6/20–22; 26:10/44; 26:14/10–14; 26:15/26; 26:18/20; 26:20/15; 26:22/50; 26:25/28; 26:26/28–40

d. 3 Ways (9): 26:1/18–22; 26:1/30–36; 26:3/4–24; 26:17/26–28; 26:18/10; 26:21/6–10(1611); 26:22/10; 26:24/14–20; 26:31/18–28

e. MS 614 suffers from an accidental or purposeful scribal change subsequent to the PWR edition at the following (6) locations: E26:2/4–3/10(1611); E26:16/52(1611); E26:21/6–10(1611); E26:23/16(1611/2412); E26:23/24(1611/2412); E26:31/28(1611)

f. Note(s): at 26:2/4–3/10, both MSS 614 and 2412 manifest an eye skip and therefore the problem was in their *Vorlage*; the fact that the Alex, Byz, and PWR readings have the most support at 26:3/4–24, among twenty-two alternatives, points to their common antiquity; at 26:18/10, the PWR may preserve the original text because it uses the word that in the NT normally means "to turn away" and it fits well in the context

APPENDIX: THREE TRADITIONS AND PWR RECONSTRUCTION

Acts 27:

a. PWR = Byz (13): 27:3/36; 27:11/10–20; 27:11/27; 27:12/26; 27:16/14–16; 27:19/18; 27:20/34–36; 27:30/40–44; 27:33/8–12; 27:34/40; 27:37/2; 27:37/6–16; 27:39/34

b. PWR = ECM (7): 27:2/10; 27:21/4; 27:23/14–28; 27:32/4–18; 27:34/8; 27:38/4; 27:39/36–38

c. PWR ≠ ECM/Byz (29): 27:1/30–34; 27:2/5; 27:2/34–38; 27:5/21; 27:6/22; 27:7/40–42; 27:9/12–20; 27:15/23; 27:17/21; 27:19/19; 27:20/12–18; 27:21/22; 27:21/40; 27:27/36; 27:29/4; 27:30/10; 27:30/26–38; 27:31/22–30; 27:33/16–22; 27:34/9; 27:34/18–22; 27:35/31; 27:36/14; 27:39/16; 27:40/38; 27:41/28–30; 27:41/38; 27:43/26; 27:44/8

d. 3 Ways (3): 27:2/14; 27:29/6–8, 10–12(1611/2412); 27:34/30–38

e. MS 614 suffers from an accidental or purposeful scribal change subsequent to the PWR edition at the following (11) locations: E27:3/28(1611); E27:5/12(1611); E27:6/24–28(1611); E27:7/34(1292); E27:16/20–24(1611); E27:17/6(1611); E27:28/8(1611/2412); E27:28/26(1611/2412); E27:30/30(1611/2412); E27:41/10(1611/2412); E27:44/38–46(1611)

f. Note(s): at 27:7/34, only MSS 614, 1611, and 2412 make an itacism and thereby manifest a binding error; at 27:7/40–42, the PWR edition shows the result of an eye skip; at 27:30/26–38, the PWR edition accidentally dropped off προφάσει; at 27:44/8, the PWR accidentally acquired an extra tau; the PWR produced a great many independent minor changes and thus felt liberty to improve the account of Paul's shipwreck

Acts 28:

a. PWR = Byz (16): 28:3/12; 28:3/34; 28:6/46; 28:6/50–54; 28:9/16–24; 28:13/4; 28:15/16; 28:16/6; 28:16/12–16; 28:19/30; 28:22/28–32; 28:23/10; 28:25/52; 28:26/2; 28:28/18; 28:29/2–24

b. PWR = ECM (13): 28:1/6–8; 28:2/4; 28:2/20; 28:3/28; 28:4/26–30; 28:5/8; 28:9/4; 28:10/24–26; 28:11/10; 28:17/14; 28:17/38–42; 28:23/43; 28:30/6–14

c. PWR ≠ ECM/Byz (19): 28:2/26; 28:3/36; 28:7/36–42; 28:10/20; 28:14/24–30; 28:15/22; 28:16/9; 28:16/20–22; 28:17/66–68(1611);

APPENDIX: THREE TRADITIONS AND PWR RECONSTRUCTION

28:18/3; 28:19/6–8; 28:19/9; 28:19/31; 28:23/52; 28:30/4; 28:30/29; 28:31/26; 28:31/30–32(1611); 28:31/35

d. 3Ways (2): 28:14/10–14; 28:30/2

e. MS 614 suffers from an accidental or purposeful scribal change subsequent to the PWR edition at the following (8) locations: E28:4/34(1611/2412); E28:6/14(1611); 28:6/44(1611/2412); E28:11/16(1611/2412); 28:12/12–14(1611); E28:17/70(1611); 28:27/58(1611); E28:31/20–22(1611/2412)

f. Note(s): at 28:10/20, the PWR edition apparently read τὰς πρὸς τᾶς χρείας, showing an accidental sigma on the first word because of the sequence; most PWR MSS corrected the error; in fact, MS 1890* retains the evidence as seen in its corrector (see 1890C); because six of the thirteen PWR/ECM agreements occur in the first five verses, it may be that a proto-Alex archetype was used to correct the PWR here

CALCULATIONS

NA28 vs. RP05 Equivalent Variants (181):

a. (43) The variant has the same word but NA28 encloses it with a single bracket (listed according to the ECM apparatus): 1:8/36; 1:11/16; 2:34/24; 3:6/46–48; 3:25/52; 4:4/18–26; 4:28/18; 4:30/6–14; 5:28/4; 7:3/22; 7:13/34–36; 7:19/18; 7:25/12; 8:33/2–8; 9:22/14–16; 10:19/18–22; 10:36/6; 10:39/26–30; 11:13/12; 11:22/38–40; 12:3/26–28; 12:17/16; 12:21/18; 13:14/26; 13:20/26; 13:33/16; 13:38/28; 15:24/14; 16:9/6–8; 16:29/24; 16:36/10–14; 17:22/6; 19:6/8–14; 19:8/26; 19:40/26–28; 23:6/62–64; 23:23/2–14; 23:30/34–44; 25:17/6–8; 26:4/12–22; 26:4/44; 26:26/28–40; 27:41/42–48

b. (138) The variant has the same meaning but a different spelling (listed according to the ECM apparatus): 1:2/24; 1:3/26–30; 1:8/4; 1:11/6; 1:11/32; 1:13/48–50; 1:14/22; 1:19/34; 1:22/20; 1:23/14; 1:23/24; 1:24/6; 1:26/20; 2:7/12–14; 2:23/28; 2:25/12; 2:26/6; 2:38/44; 3:7/34; 3:22/2; 3:23/24; 4:9/24; 4:20/12; 4:22/4–14; 4:22/18–20; 4:23/34; 4:24/22; 4:25/26; 4:35/16–18; 5:1/14; 5:29/14; 6:2/18; 6:11/24; 6:14/42; 7:10/4; 7:11/30; 7:20/10; 7:23/10; 7:26/34; 7:28/18–22; 7:29/6; 7:30/8; 7:31/6; 7:32/34; 7:35/6; 7:36/40; 7:37/8,

APPENDIX: THREE TRADITIONS AND PWR RECONSTRUCTION

12; 7:39/18; 7:40/24; 7:42/50–62; 7:43/24, 26; 7:44/34; 8:9/24; 9:32/28; 9:35/4; 9:35/14, 20; 9:36/16; 9:38/8; 9:40/36; 10:22/6; 10:26/16–20; 10:28/32; 10:34/26; 10:38/8; 10:39/36; 10:45/16; 11:2/12; 12:2/14; 12:6/6; 12:7/50–62; 12:10/14; 12:10/40; 12:11/34–38; 12:15/2–10; 12:16/16–20; 13:1/56; 13:6/32; 13:18/6–8; 13:21/36; 13:46/16; 14:19/2–4; 15:9/4; 16:4/12–16; 16:11/24–26; 16:12/20–22; 16:20/12; 16:22/20; 16:31/6; 16:36/24; 16:37/22–32; 16:40/32; 17:21/22; 17:27/10–12; 17:32/20; 18:3/20; 18:14/54; 18:19/10–14; 18:21/2; 19:2/30–32; 19:3/18; 19:6/38; 19:7/14; 19:21/36; 19:32/36; 20:15/12; 21:15/18; 21:32/10–12; 22:20/6–8; 22:24/18; 22:26/8; 23:4/8; 23:13/8; 23:14/16; 23:21/26; 23:27/8; 23:34/14; 24:11/18–20; 24:19/36; 24:22/24; 25:1/8–10; 25:20/26; 26:15/6; 26:29/54–58; 27:6/8; 27:12/18; 27:14/20–15/2; 27:16/12; 27:17/26; 27:30/26–38; 27:33/36–42; 27:35/2; 27:40/36; 27:41/12; 27:43/6; 27:43/34; 28:8/18; 28:14/24–30; 28:21/10

Why Does the ECM Have More Variant Units Than NA28?

a. NA28 differs from RP05 a grand total of about 1,060 times per the RP05 apparatus. When the above 181 benign variants are removed, the total reduces to 879. The ECM revised NA28 so that it moved a net total of 32 variant units closer to RP05 and thus preserves 847 meaningful differences from RP05 (see ECM 3.1.1, Intro, 34–35). These same 847 variation units appear as 862 in the ECM apparatus. The calculations below show why. The delta of +15 variant units occurs because the editors sometimes turned one NA28 variation into two/three ECM variant units and vice versa. The breakdown is as follows below:

b. (43) ECM adjusted single NA28 variant (as listed per RP05 apparatus) into two variation units: 2:1/20, 22; 2:20/24, 28; 2:33/38–40, 43; 2:40/10, 12–18; 3:13/8, 12; 5:19/8, 12; 7:12/10, 12–14; 7:35/40, 42–44; 7:37/26–28, 30–36; 9:18/8–14, 16; 9:26/4–8, 10; 10:10/18, 20; 10:19/28, 30; 13:11/34–36, 38–46; 13:15/38–40, 42–48; 15:1/26, 32–34; 15:4/10, 12–28; 15:17/48–50, 52; 15:37/6–8, 10; 16:7/14, 20; 16:11/2–4, 7; 16:16/24, 26–28; 17:14/28, 30; 19:13/6–8, 9; 19:16/4, 6–26; 19:16/27, 28–30; 20:1/24–26, 28; 20:4/7, 10; 20:29/2, 5; 20:32/37, 38; 21:4/2–4, 6; 21:20/12, 14–18; 22:20/31, 32–34; 22:23/2, 4; 23:15/22–24, 26; 23:28/4, 6–18; 24:21/8–14, 16–20; 25:2/4, 8–10;

323

APPENDIX: THREE TRADITIONS AND PWR RECONSTRUCTION

26:20/12, 17; 27:2/10, 14; 27:16/12, 14–16; 27:30/26–38, 40–44; 27:39/34, 36–38. As a result, the ECM changed by +43 variants.

c. (1) ECM adjusted single NA28 variant into three variation units: 5:36/26, 28–30, 32. As a result, the ECM changed by +2 variants.

d. (24) ECM reduced two NA28 variants into a single variation unit: 2:38/2–12; 2:47/38–3:1/4; 3:21/34–42; 4:32/12–20; 8:7/2–20; 9:25/6–22; 9:38/44–50; 10:11/14–30; 11:3/6–18; 11:28/26–40; 13:20/2–16; 17:23/32–40; 17:32/26–33/8; 18:1/2–6; 19:1/36–2/8; 19:14/6–20; 20:1/32–36; 20:15/28–30; 20:24/6–8; 20:27/14–24; 21:22/10–14; 24:13/6–14; 24:17/10–26; 28:16/12–16. As a result, the ECM changed by -24 variants.

e. (3) ECM reduced three NA28 variants into a single variation unit: 9:31/2–56; 17:5/2–22; 27:23/14–18. As a result, the ECM changed by -6 variants.

f. The combined result of these editorial decisions makes the ECM display 15 variation units more than the NA28 text.

Bibliography

Aland, Barbara. "Entstehung, Charakter und Herkunft des Sog. Westlichen Textes Untersucht an der Apostelgeschichte." *Ephemerides Theologicae Lovanienses* 62 (1986) 5–65.
Aland, Barbara, et al., eds. *The Greek New Testament*. 5th ed. Stuttgart: Deutsche Bibelgesellschaft, 2014.
Aland, Kurt, and Barbara Aland. *The Text of the New Testament: An Introduction to the Critical Editions and to the Theory and Practice of Modern Textual Criticism*. Translated by Erroll F. Rhodes. 2nd ed. Grand Rapids: Eerdmans, 1995.
Anderson, Hugh, et al., eds. *The New Testament in Historical and Contemporary Perspective*. Oxford: Basil Blackwell, 1965.
Anderson, Sir Robert. *The Coming Prince*. 10th ed. Grand Rapids: Kregel, 1984.
Arcieri, Mike. "The Text of Didymus the Blind in the Book of Acts, the Catholic Epistles, and the Apocalypse." PhD diss., McGill University, 2008.
Askeland, Christian. "The Coptic Versions of the New Testament." In *The Text of the New Testament in Contemporary Research: Essays on the Status Quaestionis*, edited by Bart D. Ehrman and Michael W. Holmes, 201–29. 2nd ed. NTTSD 42. Leiden: Brill, 2013.
Baker, Daniel J. "Acts 2:17–21: A Programmatic Text in Luke-Acts and in the New Testament." ThM thesis, Southeastern Baptist Theological Seminary, 2018.
Baldwin, Clinton. "The So-Called Mixed Text: An Examination of the Non-Alexandrian and Non-Byzantine Text-Type in the Catholic Epistles." PhD diss., Andrews University, 2007.
Barrett, Charles K. *A Critical and Exegetical Commentary on the Acts of the Apostles*. Vol. 1 of *International Critical Commentary*. Edinburgh: T&T Clark, 1994.
———. *A Critical and Exegetical Commentary on the Acts of the Apostles*. Rev. ed. International Critical Commentary 2. London: T&T Clark, 2010.
Bell, Lonnie David. "Textual Stability and Fluidity Exhibited in the Earliest Greek Manuscripts of John: An Analysis of the Second/Third-Century Fragments with Attention Also to the More Extensive Papyri (P45, P66, P75)." PhD diss., Edinburgh University, 2015.
Bengel, J. A. *Gnomon of the New Testament*. Translated by James Bandinel and Andrew R. Fausset. Vol. 1. Edinburgh: T&T Clark, 1858.
———. *Gnomon of the New Testament*. Translated by Andrew R. Fausset. 3rd ed. Vol. 2. Philadelphia: Smith, English, and Co., 1860.
———. Η Καινη Διαθηκη *Novum Testamentum Graecum ita adornatum ut textus probatarum editionum medullam margo variantium lectionum in suas classes*

distributarum locorumque parallelorum delectum apparatus subiunctus criseos sacrae millianae praesertim compendium, limam, supplementum ac fructum exhibeat inserviente Jo. Alberto Bengelio. Tübingen: Georgii Cottae, 1734.

Bentley, Richard. *Remarks Upon a Late Discourse of Free-Thinking in a Letter to F. H. D. D. by Phileleutherus Lipsiensis*. 2nd ed. London: John Morphew, 1713.

Bergh, Ronald Henry van der. "The Textual Tradition of Explicit Quotations in Codex Bezae Cantabrigiensis of the Acts of the Apostles." PhD diss., University of Pretoria, 2013.

Birdsall, J. N. "After Three Centuries of the Study of Codex Bezae: The Status Quaestionis." In *Codex Bezae: Studies from the Lunel Colloquium, June 1994*, edited by D. C. Parker and C.-B. Amphoux, xix–xxx. New Testament Tools and Studies 22. Leiden: Brill, 1996.

Black, David Alan. *Learn to Read New Testament Greek*. 3rd ed. Nashville: B&H, 2009.

———. *Rethinking New Testament Textual Criticism*. Grand Rapids: Baker Academic, 2002.

Black, Matthew. "The Holy Spirit in the Western Text of Acts." In *New Testament Textual Criticism: Its Significance for Exegesis: Essays in Honour of Bruce M. Metzger*, edited by Eldon Jay Epp and Gordon D. Fee, 159–70. Oxford: Clarendon, 1981.

Boismard, M.-É. "Le codex de Bèze et le texte occidental des Actes." In *Codex Bezae: Studies from the Lunel Colloquium, June 1994*, edited by D. C. Parker and C.-B. Amphoux, 257–70. New Testament Tools and Studies 22. Leiden: Brill, 1996.

———. "The Text of Acts: A Problem of Literary Criticism?" In *New Testament Textual Criticism: Its Significance for Exegesis: Essays in Honour of Bruce M. Metzger*, edited by Eldon Jay Epp and Gordon D. Fee, 147–58. Oxford: Clarendon, 1981.

———. *Le texte occidental des Actes des Apotres*. Ed. nouvelle. Etudes bibliques 40. Paris: Gabalda, 2000.

Boismard, M.-É., and A. Lamouille. *Le texte occidental des Actes des Apotres: Reconstitution et rehabilitation*. 2 vols. Éditions recherche sur les civilisations 17. Paris: École Biblique de Jerusalem, 1984.

Brock, Sebastian. "The Resolution of the Philoxenian/Harclean Problem." In *New Testament Textual Criticism: Its Significance for Exegesis: Essays in Honour of Bruce M. Metzger*, edited by Eldon Jay Epp and Gordon D. Fee, 325–44. Oxford: Clarendon, 1981.

———. "The Use of the Syriac Fathers for New Testament Textual Criticism." In *The Text of the New Testament in Contemporary Research: Essays on the Status Quaestionis*, edited by Bart D. Ehrman and Michael W. Holmes, 407–28. 2nd ed. NTTSD 42. Leiden: Brill, 2013.

Bruce, F. F. *The Book of the Acts*. Rev. ed. NICNT. Grand Rapids: Eerdmans, 1988.

———. *The Canon of Scripture*. Downers Grove, IL: InterVarsity, 1988.

Bruggen, Jakob van. "The Majority Text: Why Not Consider Its Exile?" In *The Bible as Book: The Transmission of the Greek Text*, edited by Scot McKendrick and Orlaith A. O'Sullivan, 147–53. London: British Library, 2003.

Burgon, John William. *The Revision Revised*. Collingswood, NJ: Dean Burgon Society, 2000.

Burk, John Christian F. *A Memoir of the Life and Writings of John Albert Bengel*. Translated by R. F. Walker. London: William Ball, 1837.

Burleson, Doug. "Case Studies in Closely Related Manuscripts for Determining Scribal Traits." PhD diss., New Orleans Baptist Theological Seminary, 2012.

Büsch, Gunnar. "The 'Western' Text of Acts Evidenced by Chrysostom?" In *Novum Testamentum Graecum: Editio Critica Maior. 3 Die Apostelgeschichte Teil 3 Studien*, edited by Holger Strutwolf et al., 186–220. Stuttgart: Deutsche Bibelgesellschaft, 2017.

Callahan, A. D. "Again: The Origin of the Codex Bezae." In *Codex Bezae: Studies from the Lunel Colloquium, June 1994*, edited by D. C. Parker and C.-B. Amphoux, 56–64. New Testament Tools and Studies 22. Leiden: Brill, 1996.

Campbell, William Sanger. "Who Are We in Acts? The First-Person Plural Character in the Acts of the Apostles." PhD diss., Princeton Theological Seminary, 2000.

Carter, T. "Marcion's Christology and Its Possible Influence on Codex Bezae." *Journal of Theological Studies* 61 (2010) 550–82.

Clark, Albert C. *The Acts of the Apostles: A Critical Edition with Introduction and Notes on Selected Passages*. Oxford: Clarendon, 1933.

Collins, Anthony. *A Discourse of Free-Thinking, Occasion'd by the Rise and Growth of a Sect Call'd Free-Thinkers*. London: University of Oxford Press, 1713.

Colwell, Ernest Cadman. "The Complex Character of the Late Byzantine Text of the Gospels." *Journal of Biblical Literature* 54 (1935) 211.

———. "Genealogical Method: Its Achievements and Its Limitations." *Journal of Biblical Literature* 66 (1947) 109–33.

———. "The Origin of Text-Types of New Testament Manuscripts." In *Early Christian Origins*, 128–38. Chicago: Quadrangle, 1961.

Delebecque, É. "L'art du conte et la faute du tribun Lysias selon les deux versions des Actes (22, 22–30)." *Laval Théologique et Philosophique* 40 (1984) 217–25.

———. "Les deux versions du discours de saint Paul a l'Areopage (Actes des Apotres, 17, 22–31)." *Les Études Classiques* 52 (1984) 233–50.

———. "La mesadventure des fils de Scevas selon ses deux versions (Actes 19:13–20)." *Revue des sciences philosophiques et theologiques* 66 (1982) 225–32.

Delobel, Joël. "The Nature of 'Western Readings' in Acts: Test-Cases." In *Recent Developments in Textual Criticism: New Testament, Other Early Christian and Jewish Literature: Papers Read at a Noster Conference in Münster, January 4–6, 2001*, edited by Wim Weren and Dietrich-Alex Koch, 69–94. Studies in Theology and Religion 8. Assen: Van Gorcum, 2003.

Dent, John Earle. "An Investigation of Text-Typing as a Textual Critical Methodology." ThM thesis, New Orleans Baptist Theological Seminary, 1985.

Doble, Peter, and Jeffrey Kloha, eds. *Texts and Traditions: Essays in Honour of J. Keith Elliott*. NTTSD 47. Brill, 2014.

Donaldson, Amy M. "Explicit References to New Testament Variant Readings Among Greek and Latin Church Fathers." PhD diss., University of Notre Dame, 2009.

Ehrman, Bart D. "Heracleon and the 'Western' Textual Tradition." *New Testament Studies* 40 (1994) 161–79.

Ehrman, Bart D., and Michael W. Holmes, eds. *The Text of the New Testament in Contemporary Research: Essays on the Status Quaestionis*. 2nd ed. NTTSD 42. Leiden: Brill, 2013.

Elliott, J. Keith. "An Eclectic Textual Study of the Book of Acts." In *The Book of Acts as Church History: Text, Textual Traditions, and Ancient Interpretations/Apostelgeschichte als Kirchengeschichte: Text, Texttraditionen, und Antike Auslegungen*, edited by Tobias Nicklas and Michael Tilly, 9–30. Beihefte zur Zeitschrift für die Neutestamentliche Wissenschaft 120. Berlin: De Gruyter, 2003.

———. Review of *The Byzantine Text-Type and New Testament Textual Criticism*, by H. A. Sturz. *Novum Testamentum* 28 (1986) 282.

———. "The Text of Acts in the Light of Two Recent Studies." *New Testament Studies* 34 (1988) 250–58.

———. "Thoroughgoing Eclecticism in New Testament Textual Criticism." In *The Text of the New Testament in Contemporary Research: Essays on the Status Quaestionis*, edited by Bart D. Ehrman and Michael W. Holmes, 745–70. 2nd ed. NTTSD 42. Leiden: Brill, 2013.

Epp, Eldon Jay. "Anti-Judaic Tendencies in the D-Text of Acts: Forty Years of Conversation." In *The Book of Acts as Church History: Text, Textual Traditions, and Ancient Interpretations/Apostelgeschichte als Kirchengeschichte: Text, Texttraditionen, und Antike Auslegungen*, edited by Tobias Nicklas and Michael Tilly, 111–46. Beihefte zur Zeitschrift für die Neutestamentliche Wissenschaft 120. Berlin: de Gruyter, 2003.

———. "The Claremont Profile Method for Grouping New Testament Miniscule Manuscripts." In *Studies in the Theory and Method of New Testament Textual Criticism*, edited by Eldon Jay Epp and Gordon D. Fee, 211–20. Studies and Documents 45. Grand Rapids: Eerdmans, 1993.

———. *Perspectives on New Testament Textual Criticism: Collected Essays, 1962–2004*. Edited by Eldon Jay Epp. Supplements to Novum Testamentum 116. Leiden: Brill, 2005.

———. "Text-Critical Witnesses and Methodology for Isolating a Distinctive D-Text in Acts." *Novum Testamentum* 59 (2017) 225–96.

———. "Textual Clusters: Their Past and Future in New Testament Textual Criticism." In *The Text of the New Testament in Contemporary Research: Essays on the Status Quaestionis*, edited by Bart D. Ehrman and Michael W. Holmes, 519–77. 2nd ed. NTTSD 42. Leiden: Brill, 2013.

———. *The Theological Tendency of Codex Bezae Cantabrigiensis*. Cambridge: Cambridge University Press, 1966.

———. "Traditional 'Canons' of New Testament Textual Criticism: Their Value, Validity, and Viability-or Lack Thereof." In *The Textual History of the Greek New Testament: Changing Views in Contemporary Research*, edited by Klaus Wachtel and Michael W. Holmes, 79–127. SBL 8. Atlanta: SBL Press, 2011.

Epp, Eldon Jay, and Gordon D. Fee, eds. *New Testament Textual Criticism: Its Significance for Exegesis: Essays in Honour of Bruce M. Metzger*. Oxford: Clarendon, 1981.

———. *Studies in the Theory and Method of New Testament Textual Criticism*. Studies and Documents 45. Grand Rapids: Eerdmans, 1993.

Ericsson, Dwight Elwood. "The Book of Acts in the Greek New Testament." PhD diss., The University of Chicago, 1961.

Fee, Gordon D. "The Majority Text and the Original Text of the New Testament." In *Studies in the Theory and Method of New Testament Textual Criticism*, edited by Eldon Jay Epp and Gordon D. Fee, 183–208. Studies and Documents 45. Grand Rapids: Eerdmans, 1993.

———. "Modern Textual Criticism and the Revival of the Textus Receptus." *JETS* 21 (1978) 19–33.

———. "P75, P66, and Origen: The Myth of Early Textual Recension in Alexandria." In *Studies in the Theory and Method of New Testament Textual Criticism*, edited by Eldon Jay Epp and Gordon D. Fee, 247–73. Studies and Documents 45. Grand Rapids: Eerdmans, 1993.

———. Review of *The Byzantine Text-Type and New Testament Textual Criticism*, by H. A. Sturz. *JETS* 28 (1985) 239–42.

———. "The Significance of Papyrus Bodmer II and Papyrus Bodmer XIV–XV for Methodology in New Testament Textual Criticism." PhD diss., University of Southern California, 1966.

———. "The Use of the Greek Fathers for New Testament Textual Criticism." In *The Text of the New Testament in Contemporary Research: Essays on the Status Quaestionis*, edited by Bart D. Ehrman and Michael W. Holmes, 351–73. 2nd ed. NTTSD 42. Leiden: Brill, 2013.

Feiler, Paul Frederick. "Jesus the Prophet: The Lucan Portrayal of Jesus as the Prophet Like Moses." PhD diss., Princeton Theological Seminary, 1986.

Foster, Barry Michael. "The Contribution of the Conclusion of Acts to the Understanding of Lucan Theology and the Determination of Lucan Purpose." PhD diss., Trinity Evangelical Divinity School, 1997.

Friedeman, Caleb T. "The Revelation of the Messiah: The Christological Mystery of Luke 1–2 and Its Unveiling in Luke-Acts." PhD diss., Wheaton College, 2018.

Gäbel, Georg. "The Text of P127 (P.Oxy. 4968) and Its Relationship with the Text of Codex Bezae." *Novum Testamentum* 53 (2011) 107–52.

———. "'Western Text,' 'D-Text Cluster,' 'Bezan Trajectory,' or What Else?—A Preliminary Study." In *Novum Testamentum Graecum: Editio Critica Maior. 3 Die Apostelgeschichte Teil 3 Studien*, edited by Holger Strutwolf et al., 83–136. Stuttgart: Deutsche Bibelgesellschaft, 2017.

Geer, Thomas C. *Family 1739 in Acts*. Society of Biblical Literature Monograph Series 48. Atlanta: Scholars Press, 1994.

———. "An Investigation of a Select Group of So-Called Western Cursives in Acts." PhD diss., Boston University, 1985.

Gibson, Samuel James. "The Liturgical and Textual Tradition of Acts and Paul in the Byzantine Apostolos Lectionary." PhD diss., University of Birmingham, 2016.

Greer, Joseph P. "The Primary Source for the Explicit Old Testament Quotations in the Greek Text of Luke's Gospel in Codex Bezae." ThM thesis, New Orleans Baptist Theological Seminary, 2017.

Gurry, Peter J. "The Harklean Syriac and the Development of the Byzantine Text: A Historical Test for the Coherence-Based Genealogical Method (CBGM)." *Novum Testamentum* 60 (2018) 183–200.

———. "The Number of Variants in the Greek New Testament: A Proposed Estimate." *New Testament Studies* 62 (2016) 97–121.

Güting, E. "The Methodological Contribution of Günther Zuntz to the Text of Hebrews." *Novum Testamentum* 48 (2006) 359–78.

Haenchen, Ernst. *The Acts of the Apostles: A Commentary*. Translated by Bernard Noble et al. Philadelphia: Westminster, 1971.

Haupt, Benjamin Douglas. "Tertullian's Text of the New Testament Outside the Gospels." PhD diss., University of Birmingham, 2019.

Heimerdinger, Jenny. "The Contribution of Discourse Analysis to Textual Criticism: A Study of the Bezan Text of Acts." PhD diss., University of Wales, Bangor, 1994.

———. "The Seven Steps of Codex Bezae: A Prophetic Interpretation of Acts 12." In *Codex Bezae: Studies from the Lunel Colloquium, June 1994*, edited by D. C. Parker and C.-B. Amphoux, 303–10. New Testament Tools and Studies 22. Leiden: Brill, 1996.

Helton, Stanley N. "The Text of Acts of the Apostles in the Writings of Origen." PhD diss., New Orleans Baptist Theological Seminary, 2014.

Hendriks, Wim. "The Case for the Primacy of the Western Text." *Estudios bíblicos* 72 (2014) 411–36.

Herbison, David Richard. "Reconstructing the Text of the Church: The 'Canonical Text' and the Goal of New Testament Textual Criticism." ThM thesis, Trinity Western University, 2015.

Hernández, Juan, Jr. "The Relevance of Andrew of Caesarea for New Testament Textual Criticism." *Journal of Biblical Literature* 130 (2011) 183–96.

Heuer, M. H. "An Evaluation of John W. Burgon's Use of Patristic Evidence." *JETS* 38 (1995) 519–30.

Hill, C. E. *Who Chose the Gospels? Probing the Great Gospel Conspiracy*. Oxford: Oxford University Press, 2012.

Hodges, Zane Clark, and Arthur L. Farstad, eds. *The Greek New Testament According to the Majority Text*. 2nd ed. Nashville: Thomas Nelson, 1985.

Holmes, Michael W. "Early Editorial Activity and the Text of Codex Bezae in Matthew (Textual, Criticism)." PhD diss., Princeton Theological Seminary, 1984.

———. "From 'Original Text' to 'Initial Text': The Traditional Goal of New Testament Textual Criticism in Contemporary Discussion." In *The Text of the New Testament in Contemporary Research: Essays on the Status Quaestionis*, edited by Bart D. Ehrman and Michael W. Holmes, 711–44. 2nd ed. NTTSD 42. Leiden: Brill, 2013.

———. "The 'Majority Text Debate': New Form of an Old Issue." *Themelios* 8 (1983) 13–19.

———. "Reasoned Eclecticism in New Testament Textual Criticism." In *The Text of the New Testament in Contemporary Research: Essays on the Status Quaestionis*, edited by Bart D. Ehrman and Michael W. Holmes, 771–802. 2nd ed. NTTSD 42. Leiden: Brill, 2013.

———. Review of *The Byzantine Text-Type and New Testament Textual Criticism*, by H. A. Sturz. *Trinity Journal* 6 (1985) 225–28.

———. "When Criteria Conflict." In *Texts and Traditions: Essays in Honour of J. Keith Elliott*, edited by Peter Doble and Jeffrey Kloha, 11–24. NTTSD 47. Leiden: Brill, 2014.

Horton, Charles, ed. *The Earliest Gospels: The Origins and Transmission of the Earliest Christian Gospels—The Contribution of the Chester Beatty Gospel Codex P45*. Journal for the Study of the New Testament Supplement Series 258. London: T&T Clark International, 2004.

Houghton, H. A. G. "The Use of the Latin Fathers for New Testament Textual Criticism." In *The Text of the New Testament in Contemporary Research: Essays on the Status Quaestionis*, edited by Bart D. Ehrman and Michael W. Holmes, 375–405. 2nd ed. NTTSD 42. Leiden: Brill, 2013.

Hull, Robert Fulton. "The Effect of Textual Criticism on Some Recent English Translations of the New Testament." PhD diss., Princeton Theological Seminary, 1977.

Hurtado, Larry W. Review of *The Byzantine Text-Type and New Testament Textual Criticism*, by H. A. Sturz. *Catholic Biblical Quarterly* 48 (1986) 149.

---. *Texts and Artefacts: Selected Essays on Textual Criticism and Early Christian Manuscripts*. The Library of New Testament Studies 584. London: Bloomsbury T&T Clark, 2018.

Janeway, John Raymond. "An Investigation of the Textual Criticism of the New Testament Done by Spanish Scholars with Special Relation to the Theories and Text of Westcott and Hort." PhD diss., University of Southern California, 1958.

Juckel, Andreas. "Der 'harklensische Apparat' der Acta Apostolorum." In *Novum Testamentum Graecum: Editio Critica Maior. 3 Die Apostelgeschichte Teil 3 Studien*, edited by Holger Strutwolf et al., 228–45. Stuttgart: Deutsche Bibelgesellschaft, 2017.

Kenyon, Frederic G. *The Text of the Greek Bible*. 3rd ed. London: Duckworth, 1975.

---. *The Western Text in the Gospels and Acts*. Vol. 24 of *From the Proceedings of the British Academy*. London: Oxford University Press, 1938.

Kilpatrick, G. D. "The Greek New Testament Text of Today and the Textus Receptus." In *The New Testament in Historical and Contemporary Perspective*, edited by Hugh Anderson et al., 189–206. Oxford: Basil Blackwell, 1965.

Klijn, A. F. J. *A Survey of the Researches into the Western Text of the Gospels and Acts: Part Two: 1949–1969*. Supplements to Novum Testamentum 21. Leiden: Brill, 1969.

Ko, Young Real. "Augmenting Hoskier's and Schmid's Works: A Textual Analysis of Revelation." PhD diss., New Orleans Baptist Theological Seminary, 2009.

Köstenberger, Andreas J., et al. *The Cradle, the Cross, and the Crown: An Introduction to the New Testament*. Nashville: Broadman & Holman, 2009.

Lake, Kirsopp, and Silva Lake. "The Acts of the Apostles." *Journal of Biblical Literature* 53 (1934) 34–45.

Lanier, Gregory R. "Quantifying New Testament Textual Variants: Key Witnesses in Acts and the Catholic Letters." *New Testament Studies* 64 (2018) 551–72.

---. "Taking Inventory on the 'Age of the Minuscules': Later Manuscripts and the Byzantine Tradition within the Field of Textual Criticism." *Currents in Biblical Research* 16 (2018) 263–308.

McConaughy, Daniel Leigh. "Research on the Early History of the Syriac Text of Acts Chapters One and Two." PhD diss., The University of Chicago, 1985.

McKendrick, Scot, and Orlaith A. O'Sullivan, eds. *The Bible as Book: The Transmission of the Greek Text*. London: British Library, 2003.

Metzger, Bruce M. *The Early Versions of the New Testament: Their Origin, Transmission, and Limitations*. Oxford: Clarendon, 1977.

---. "Lucian and the Lucianic Recension of the Greek Bible." *New Testament Studies* 8 (1962) 189–203.

---. *A Textual Commentary on the Greek New Testament: A Companion Volume to the United Bible Societies' Greek New Testament*. 4th ed. Stuttgart: Deutsche Bibelgesellschaft, 1994.

Metzger, Bruce M., and Bart D. Ehrman. *The Text of the New Testament: Its Transmission, Corruption, and Restoration*. 4th ed. New York: Oxford University Press, 2005.

Mullen, Roderic Lynn. "Cyril of Jerusalem and the Text of the New Testament in Fourth-Century Palestine." PhD diss., The University of North Carolina at Chapel Hill, 1994.

Murphy, S. Jonathan. "In the Shadow of Giants: The Narrative Function of Stephen, Philip, and Barnabas in the Book of Acts." PhD diss., Dallas Theological Seminary, 2009.

Nestle, Eberhard, and Erwin Nestle. *Novum Testamentum Graece*. Edited by Barbara Aland et al. 28th ed. Stuttgart: Deutsche Bibelgesellschaft, 2012.

Niccum, Larry Curt. "The Book of Acts in Ethiopic (with Critical Text and Apparatus) and Its Relation to the Greek Textual Tradition." PhD diss., University of Notre Dame, 2000.

Nicklas, Tobias, and Michael Tilly, eds. *The Book of Acts as Church History: Text, Textual Traditions, and Ancient Interpretations/Apostelgeschichte als Kirchengeschichte: Text, Texttraditionen, und Antike Auslegungen*. Beihefte zur Zeitschrift für die Neutestamentliche Wissenschaft 120. Berlin: De Gruyter, 2003.

Omerzu, Heike. "Die Darstellung der Römer in der Textüberlieferung der Apostelgeschichte." In *The Book of Acts as Church History: Text, Textual Traditions, and Ancient Interpretations/Apostelgeschichte als Kirchengeschichte: Text, Texttraditionen, und Antike Auslegungen*, edited by Tobias Nicklas and Michael Tilly, 147–81. Beihefte zur Zeitschrift für die Neutestamentliche Wissenschaft 120. Berlin: De Gruyter, 2003.

Pack, Frank. "The Methodology of Origen as a Textual Critic in Arriving at the Text of the New Testament." PhD diss., University of Southern California, 1948.

Panten, Kenneth E. "A History of Research on Codex Bezae, with Special Reference to the Acts of the Apostles: Evaluation and Future Directions." PhD diss., Murdoch University, 1995.

Pardee, Cambry G. "Scribal Harmonization in Greek Manuscripts of the Synoptic Gospels from the Second to the Fifth Century." PhD diss., Loyola University Chicago, 2016.

Park, Chang Shik. "An Analysis of the Textual Relationships and Characteristics of Selected Manuscripts of the K(x) Group in John." PhD diss., New Orleans Baptist Theological Seminary, 2001.

Parker, D. C. *Codex Bezae: An Early Christian Manuscript and Its Text*. Cambridge: Cambridge University Press, 1992.

———. "Codex Bezae: The Manuscript as Past, Present, and Future." In *The Bible as Book: The Transmission of the Greek Text*, edited by Scot McKendrick and Orlaith A. O'Sullivan, 43–50. London: British Library, 2003.

Parker, D. C., and C.-B. Amphoux, eds. *Codex Bezae: Studies from the Lunel Colloquium, June 1994*. New Testament Tools and Studies 22. Leiden: Brill, 1996.

Parsons, Mikeal Carl. "The Ascension Narratives in Luke-Acts." PhD diss., The Southern Baptist Theological Seminary, 1985.

Pelt, Michael Riley. "Textual Variation in Relation to Theological Interpretation in the New Testament." PhD diss., Duke University, 1966.

Pervo, Richard I. *Acts: A Commentary*. Edited by Harold W. Attridge. Hermeneia. Minneapolis: Fortress, 2009.

Pinchard, Laurent. "The Greek Text of the Gospel of Matthew: A Renewed Text-Critical Approach with a Focus on the Issue of Harmonizations in Codex Bezae." PhD diss., University of Wales, Trinity Saint David, 2015.

Porter, Stanley E. "Developments in the Text of Acts Before the Major Codices." In *The Book of Acts as Church History: Text, Textual Traditions, and Ancient Interpretations/Apostelgeschichte als Kirchengeschichte: Text, Texttraditionen, und*

Antike Auslegungen, edited by Tobias Nicklas and Michael Tilly, 31–67. Beihefte zur Zeitschrift für die Neutestamentliche Wissenschaft 120. Berlin: de Gruyter, 2003.

Praeder, Susan Marie. "The Narrative Voyage: An Analysis and Interpretation of Acts 27-28." PhD diss., Graduate Theological Union, 1980.

Quarles, Charles L. *Matthew. Exegetical Guide to the Greek New Testament.* Nashville: B&H Academic, 2017.

Rahlfs, Alfred. *Septuaginta.* Stuttgart: Deutsche Bibelgesellschaft, 1979.

Ralston, Timothy J. "The 'Majority Text' and Byzantine Origins." *New Testament Studies* 38 (1992) 122–37.

———. "The Majority Text and Byzantine Texttype Development: The Significance of a Non-Parametric Method of Data Analysis for the Exploration of Manuscript Traditions." PhD diss., Dallas Theological Seminary, 1994.

Read-Heimerdinger, J. "The Apostles in the Bezan Text of Acts." In *The Book of Acts as Church History: Text, Textual Traditions, and Ancient Interpretations/ Apostelgeschichte als Kirchengeschichte: Text, Texttraditionen, und Antike Auslegungen,* edited by Tobias Nicklas and Michael Tilly, 263–80. Beihefte zur Zeitschrift für die Neutestamentliche Wissenschaft 120. Berlin: De Gruyter, 2003.

———. *The Bezan Text of Acts: A Contribution of Discourse Analysis to Textual Criticism.* Journal for the Study of the New Testament Supplement Series. London: Sheffield Academic, 2002.

Reeves, Rodney Richard. "Methodology for Determining Text-Types of New Testament Manuscripts (Textual Criticism)." PhD diss., Southwestern Baptist Theological Seminary, 1986.

Richter, Siegfried G. "Der Wegweiser zum Mittelägyptischen in der ECM." In *Novum Testamentum Graecum: Editio Critica Maior. 3 Die Apostelgeschichte Teil 3 Studien,* edited by Holger Strutwolf et al., 221–27. Stuttgart: Deutsche Bibelgesellschaft, 2017.

Rius-Camps, J., and J. Read-Heimerdinger. *Acts 1:1—5:42: Jerusalem.* Vol. 1 of *The Message of Acts in Codex Bezae: A Comparison with the Alexandrian Tradition.* JSNT 257. London: T&T Clark, 2004.

———. *Acts 6.1-12.25: From Judaea and Samaria to the Church in Antioch.* Vol. 2 of *The Message of Acts in Codex Bezae: A Comparison with the Alexandrian Tradition.* Library of New Testament Studies 302. New York: T&T Clark, 2006.

———. *Acts 13.1-18.23: The Ends of the Earth, First and Second Phases of the Mission of the Gentiles.* Vol. 3 of *The Message of Acts in Codex Bezae: A Comparison with the Alexandrian Tradition.* Library of New Testament Studies 365. London: T&T Clark, 2007.

———. *Acts 18.24—28.31: Rome Via Ephesus and Jerusalem.* Vol. 4 of *The Message of Acts in Codex Bezae: A Comparison with the Alexandrian Tradition.* Library of New Testament Studies 415. London: T&T Clark, 2009.

———. "The Variant Readings of the Western Text of the Acts of the Apostles (XIV) (Acts 8:1b–40)." *Filología Neotestamentaria* 15 (2002) 111–30.

———. "The Variant Readings of the Western Text of the Acts of the Apostles (XV) (Acts 9:1–30)." *Filología Neotestamentaria* 16 (2003) 133–45.

———. "The Variant Readings of the Western Text of the Acts of the Apostles (XVI) (Acts 9:31–11:18)." *Filología Neotestamentaria* 17 (2004) 45–88.

———. "The Variant Readings of the Western Text of the Acts of the Apostles (XVII) (Acts 11:19–12:25)." *Filología Neotestamentaria* 18 (2005) 135–65.

———. "The Variant Readings of the Western Text of the Acts of the Apostles (XVIII)." *Filología Neotestamentaria* 19 (2006) 99–112.

———. "The Variant Readings of the Western Text of the Acts of the Apostles (XIX) (Acts 13:13–43)." *Filología Neotestamentaria* 20 (2007) 127–40.

Robinson, Maurice A. "Appendix: The Case for Byzantine Priority." In *The New Testament in the Original Greek: Byzantine Textform 2005*, edited by Maurice A. Robinson and William G. Pierpont, 533–86. Southborough, MA: Chilton, 2005.

———. "Crossing Boundaries in New Testament Textual Criticism: Historical Revisionism and the Case of Frederick Henry Ambrose Scrivener." Edited by Daniel B. Wallace. *TC: A Journal of Biblical Textual Criticism* 7 (2002) paragraphs 1–77. https://jbtc.org/v07/Robinson2002.html.

———. "Investigating Text-Critical Dichotomy: A Critique of Modern Eclectic Praxis from a Byzantine-Priority Perspective." *Faith and Mission* 16 (1999) 16–31.

———. "The Recensional Nature of the Alexandrian Text-Type: A Response to Selected Criticisms of the Byzantine-Priority Theory." *Faith and Mission* 11 (1993) 46–74.

———. "Rule 9, Isolated Variants, and the 'Test-Tube' Nature of the NA27 / UBS4 Text: A Byzantine-Priority Perspective." In *Translating the New Testament: Text, Translation, Theology*, edited by Stanley E. Porter and Mark J. Boda, 27–61. Grand Rapids: Eerdmans, 2009.

———. "Textual Interrelationships Among Selected Ancient Witnesses to the Book of Acts." ThM thesis, Southeastern Baptist Theological Seminary, 1975.

Robinson, Maurice A., and William G. Pierpont, eds. *The New Testament in the Original Greek: Byzantine Textform 2005*. Southborough, MA: Chilton, 2005.

Ropes, James Hardy. *The Text of Acts*. Vol. 3 of *The Beginnings of Christianity. Part 1: The Acts of the Apostles*. Edited by F. J. Foakes Jackson and Kirsopp Lake. London: Macmillan, 1926.

Ross, Allen P. *Introducing Biblical Hebrew*. Grand Rapids: Baker Academic, 2001.

Royse, James R. "Scribal Habits in Early Greek New Testament Papyri." ThM thesis, Graduate Theological Union, 1981.

———. "Scribal Tendencies in the Transmission of the Text of the New Testament." In *The Text of the New Testament in Contemporary Research: Essays on the Status Quaestionis*, edited by Bart D. Ehrman and Michael W. Holmes, 461–78. 2nd ed. NTTSD 42. Leiden: Brill, 2013.

Runge, Steven E. *Discourse Grammar of the Greek New Testament: A Practical Introduction for Teaching and Exegesis*. Lexham Bible Reference Series. Peabody, MA: Hendrickson, 2010.

Savelle, Charles H. "The Jerusalem Council and the Lukan Perspective of the Law in Acts." PhD diss., Dallas Theological Seminary, 2013.

Scanlin, H. P. "The Majority Text Debate: Recent Developments." *The Bible Translator* 36 (1985) 136–40.

Schmid, Ulrich. "Conceptualizing 'Scribal' Performances: Reader's Notes." *The Textual History of the Greek New Testament: Changing Views in Contemporary Research*. Edited by Klaus Wachtel and Michael W. Holmes. SBL 8. Atlanta: SBL Press, 2011.

Scrivener, Frederick H. A. *Contributions to the Criticism of the Greek New Testament: Being the Introduction to an Edition of the Codex Augiensis and Fifty Other Manuscripts*. Cambridge: Deighton and Bell, 1859.

———. *A Plain Introduction to the Criticism of the New Testament: For the Use of Biblical Students.* Vol. 1. London: Forgotten, 2018.

———. *A Plain Introduction to the Criticism of the New Testament: For the Use of Biblical Students.* Vol. 2. Eugene, OR: Wipf & Stock, 1997.

Shields, David Dwayne. "Recent Attempts to Defend the Byzantine Text of the Greek New Testament." PhD diss., Southwestern Baptist Theological Seminary, 1985.

Silva, Moisés. Review of *The Byzantine Text-Type and New Testament Textual Criticism*, by H. A. Sturz. *Westminster Theological Journal* 48 (1986) 187–90.

Soden, Hermann von. *Die Schriften des Neuen Testaments in Ihrer Ältesten Erreichbaren Textgestalt Hergestellt auf Grund Ihrer Textgeschichte.* 2 vols. Göttingen: Vandenhoeck und Ruprecht, 1911–1913.

Spottorno, Ma Victoria. "Le codex de Beze et le texte Antiochien dans les Actes des Apôtres." In *Codex Bezae: Studies from the Lunel Colloquium, June 1994*, edited by D. C. Parker and C.-B. Amphoux, 311–16. New Testament Tools and Studies 22. Leiden: Brill, 1996.

Strange, W. A. *The Problem of the Text of Acts.* Society for New Testament Studies Monograph Series 71. Cambridge: Cambridge University Press, 1992.

Streeter, Burnett Hillman. *The Four Gospels.* London: Macmillan, 1951.

Stroup, Christopher Robert. "Jewish Acts in the Polis: Ethnic Reasoning and the Jewishness of Christians in Acts of the Apostles." PhD diss., Boston University, 2016.

Strutwolf, Holger. "Der Text der Apostelgeschichte bei Irenäus von Lyon und der Sogenannte 'Westliche Text.'" In *Novum Testamentum Graecum: Editio Critica Maior. 3 Die Apostelgeschichte Teil 3 Studien*, edited by Holger Strutwolf et al., 149–85. Stuttgart: Deutsche Bibelgesellschaft, 2017.

Strutwolf, Holger, et al., eds. *Novum Testamentum Graecum: Editio Critica Maior. 3 Die Apostelgeschichte Teil 1, 1 Text: Kapitel 1–14.* Stuttgart: Deutsche Bibelgesellschaft, 2017.

———. *Novum Testamentum Graecum: Editio Critica Maior. 3 Die Apostelgeschichte Teil 1, 2 Text: Kapitel 15–28.* Stuttgart: Deutsche Bibelgesellschaft, 2017.

———. *Novum Testamentum Graecum: Editio Critica Maior. 3 Die Apostelgeschichte Teil 2 Begleitende Materialien.* Stuttgart: Deutsche Bibelgesellschaft, 2017.

———. *Novum Testamentum Graecum: Editio Critica Maior. 3 Die Apostelgeschichte Teil 3 Studien.* Stuttgart: Deutsche Bibelgesellschaft, 2017.

Sturz, Harry A. *The Byzantine Text-Type and New Testament Textual Criticism.* Nashville: Nelson, 1984.

Taylor, D. G. K. *Studies in the Early Text of the Gospels and Acts: The Papers of the First Birmingham Colloquium on the Textual Criticism of the New Testament.* Text-Critical Studies 1. Atlanta: SBL Press, 1999.

Tregelles, Samuel Prideaux. *An Account of the Printed Text of the Greek New Testament.* London: Bagster and Sons, 1854.

Trobisch, David. "The Need to Discern Distinctive Editions of the New Testament in the Manuscript Tradition." In *The Textual History of the Greek New Testament: Changing Views in Contemporary Research*, edited by Klaus Wachtel and Michael W. Holmes, 43–48. SBL 8. Atlanta: SBL Press, 2011.

Tuckett, Christopher. "How Early Is the 'Western' Text of Acts?" In *The Book of Acts as Church History: Text, Textual Traditions, and Ancient Interpretations/ Apostelgeschichte als Kirchengeschichte: Text, Texttraditionen, und Antike*

Auslegungen, edited by Tobias Nicklas and Michael Tilly, 69–86. Beihefte zur Zeitschrift für die Neutestamentliche Wissenschaft 120. Berlin: De Gruyter, 2003.

Tyndale, William. *Tyndale's New Testament*. Edited by David Daniell. New Haven: Yale University Press, 1995.

Um, Hyo-Sook. "Messianic Psalms in Luke-Acts." PhD diss., The University of Manchester, 2001.

Wachtel, Klaus. *Der Byzantinische Text der Katholischen Briefe: Eine Untersuchung zur Entstehung der Koine des Neuen Testaments*. Arbeiten zur Neutestamentlichen Textforschung 24. Berlin: de Gruyter, 1995.

———. "Conclusions." In *The Textual History of the Greek New Testament: Changing Views in Contemporary Research*, edited by Klaus Wachtel and Michael W. Holmes, 217–26. SBL 8. Atlanta: SBL Press, 2011.

———. "Notes on the Text of the Acts of the Apostles." In *Novum Testamentum Graecum: Editio Critica Maior. 3 Die Apostelgeschichte Teil 1, 1 Text: Kapitel 1–14*, edited by Holger Strutwolf et al., 28–33. Stuttgart: Deutsche Bibelgesellschaft, 2017.

———. "On the Relationship of the 'Western Text' and the Byzantine Tradition of Acts—A Plea Against the Text-Type Concept." In *Novum Testamentum Graecum: Editio Critica Maior. 3 Die Apostelgeschichte Teil 3 Studien*, edited by Holger Strutwolf et al., 137–48. Stuttgart: Deutsche Bibelgesellschaft, 2017.

———. "Text-Critical Commentary." In *Novum Testamentum Graecum: Editio Critica Maior. 3 Die Apostelgeschichte Teil 3 Studien*, edited by Holger Strutwolf et al., 1–38. Stuttgart: Deutsche Bibelgesellschaft, 2017.

Wachtel, Klaus, and Michael W. Holmes, eds. *The Textual History of the Greek New Testament: Changing Views in Contemporary Research*. SBL 8. Atlanta: SBL Press, 2011.

Wallace, Daniel B. *Greek Grammar Beyond the Basics: An Exegetical Syntax of the New Testament*. Grand Rapids: Zondervan, 1996.

———. "Historical Revisionism and the Majority Text Theory: The Cases of F. H. A. Scrivener and Herman C. Hoskier." *New Testament Studies* 41 (1995) 280–85.

———. "The Majority Text: A New Collating Base?" *New Testament Studies* 35 (1989) 609–18.

———. "The Majority Text Theory: History, Methods, and Critique." In *The Text of the New Testament in Contemporary Research: Essays on the Status Quaestionis*, edited by Bart D. Ehrman and Michael W. Holmes, 711–44. 2nd ed. NTTSD 42. Leiden: Brill, 2013.

———. "Some Second Thoughts on the Majority Text." *Bibliotheca Sacra* 146 (1989) 270–90.

Wasserman, Tommy, and Peter J. Gurry. *A New Approach to Textual Criticism: An Introduction to the Coherence-Based Genealogical Method*. Resources for Biblical Study 80. Atlanta: SBL Press, 2017.

Weber, Robert, and Roger Gryson, eds. *Biblia sacra iuxta Vulgatam versionem*. Quintam. Stuttgart: Deutsche Bibelgesellschaft, 2007.

Weber, Ryan W. "Unforgiven: The Textual Problem and Interpretation of Luke 23:34a and Anti-Judaism in the Early Church." ThM thesis, Wake Forest University, 2012.

Westcott, B. F., and F. J. A. Hort. *Introduction to the New Testament in the Original Greek with Notes on Selected Readings*. Peabody, MA: Hendrickson, 1988.

———. *The New Testament in the Original Greek*. New York: Cosimo, 2007.

White, John Paul. "Lucan Composition of Acts 7:2–53 in Light of the Author's Use of Old Testament Texts." PhD diss., Southwestern Baptist Theological Seminary, 1992.

Whitlock, Matthew G. "Unity in Conflict: A Study of Acts 4:23–31." PhD diss., The Catholic University of America, 2008.

Williams, Peter J. "The Syriac Versions of the New Testament." In *The Text of the New Testament in Contemporary Research: Essays on the Status Quaestionis*, edited by Bart D. Ehrman and Michael W. Holmes, 143–66. 2nd ed. NTTSD 42. Leiden: Brill, 2013.

Wilson, Andrew. "Scribal Habits in the Greek New Testament Manuscripts." *Filología Neotestamentaria* 24 (2011) 95–126.

Wilson, J. M. *The Acts of the Apostles: Translated from the Codex Bezae with an Introduction on Its Lucan Origin and Importance*. London: SPCK, 1923.

Wisse, Frederik. "The Claremont Profile Method for the Classification of Byzantine New Testament Manuscripts: A Study in Method." PhD diss., The Claremont Graduate University, 1968.

Wu, Wei-Ho John. "A Systematic Analysis of the Shorter Readings in the Byzantine Text of the Synoptic Gospels." PhD diss., Dallas Theological Seminary, 2002.

Zhang, Wenxi. "Paul Among Jews: A Study of the Meaning and Significance of Paul's Inaugural Sermon in the Synagogue of Antioch in Pisidia (Acts 13:16–41) for His Missionary Work Among the Jews." PhD diss., The Catholic University of America, 2010.

Zuntz, Günther. *The Text of the Epistles: A Disquisition Upon the Corpus Paulinum, the Schweich Lectures of the British Academy, 1946*. London: Oxford University Press, 1953.

General Index

accuracy of texts, xxiv, 2, 3, 19, 24, 33, 35, 37–38, 74, 110, 116, 133, 171, 201, 283, 289, 294–96, 300–301, 303. *See also* divine preservation; scribal faithfulness
Aland, B., xx, 29–31, 32n195, 35–36, 107, 111, 113, 143, 282n7, 282n11, 283–84
Aland, K., 21
Aland, K. and B., 31n191, 107n2, 112n13
Alexandria, 14, 21–22, 24–25, 33n203, 34, 113, 126, 171, 197, 203, 206, 209, 213, 220, 223–24, 247, 269, 279n, 294n57, 297
Anderson, R., 222
Antioch of Syria, 6, 14, 18, 19, 24–25, 32, 91, 113, 134, 138
antiquity: as observed in Alexandrian manuscripts, 13, 27–28, 82–83, 88, 97, 104, 114, 171–72, 182, 190, 218, 220, 230, 235, 238, 242, 244–45, 251, 253, 256, 258, 266, 275, 282n11, 289, 320; as observed in all manuscripts, xxii–xxiv, 28, 104, 183, 294–300; as observed in Byzantine manuscripts, xxv, 13–16, 19, 21, 25–26, 28, 38, 78, 82, 85, 88, 93, 104, 110n3, 114, 171–72, 182, 186–87, 194–95, 201, 219, 228, 231–32, 239, 248–49, 251, 256, 261, 278n292, 288–89, 292, 300, 302, 320; as observed in Western manuscripts, 14, 23, 27, 32, 59, 63, 67–68, 71, 74, 77–78, 85, 88, 93, 104, 114, 118, 130, 137, 142, 146, 164, 171–72, 182, 194, 197, 201, 208, 210–11, 213, 218, 227, 230, 232, 239, 241–42, 244, 248–49, 251, 256, 258, 281, 284n19, 292, 302, 320
archetype(s): Codex D, 29, 42–43, 47, 50, 146; Other, 14, 23, 25, 52, 85, 87, 104, 126, 185, 265, 285; proto-Alexandrian, 13, 97–98, 190, 192, 195, 198, 200–201, 208, 211, 214, 217, 223–24, 227–28, 234–35, 242, 265, 267, 270–71, 276, 285, 294, 294n57, 297–99, 322; proto-Byzantine, 116, 208, 285–86, 292n52, 294, 294n57, 296–99, 302; PWR (Proto-Western Reading), xxii–xxiii, xxv, 28–29, 29n181, 30–32, 34–38, 58–59, 69, 71, 77–78, 103–5, 107, 110–11, 113–14, 116–17, 122, 130, 143, 157–58, 170–74, 200, 216, 221, 224, 244, 255, 260, 273, 280–83, 284n19, 285–86, 288, 290, 292–93, 297, 299, 301, 306; WR (Western Redaction), 29–30, 32, 35, 38, 58

Barrett, C. K., 57, 80, 100n52, 118, 126, 135–37, 148, 152, 154, 177–78, 180, 186, 189, 197, 201n86, 204, 205n95, 210, 211n108, 213, 215, 218, 220–21, 223, 235–36,

GENERAL INDEX

Barrett, C. K. (continued), 238–39, 242, 247n217, 252, 253n232, 255–56, 258n246, 260–61, 262n257, 266n264, 267, 271n274, 275n, 276
Bengel, J. A., xxi, 5–6, 173, 185, 215n118, 217, 222, 229n166, 235n179, 238n190, 239, 244n209, 247n216, 248, 252, 254, 256, 271n275, 274n284, 289
Bentley, R., 3–5, 7, 10
Black, D. A., 213, 229
Black, M., 51
Boismard, M.-É., xxiii, 12, 29n182, 34n206, 40, 42n9, 52, 53n, 56–59, 62, 69–71, 76–77, 100, 112n14, 125, 172n3, 190n57, 192, 194n, 195, 204, 215, 218, 233n173, 235, 238n190, 239, 250, 254, 259n, 266n263, 269n271, 275n, 276n290
Bruce, F. F., 19n103, 182n31, 188n48, 226n157, 236n185, 239
Burgon, J. W., 10, 23
Burk, J. C., 5n24
Büsch, G., 21n129

canons, text-critical, xxi–xxii, xxiv–xxv, 5–6, 9, 16n91, 26–28, 171–73, 211n106, 279–80, 283, 292, 302
Clark, A. C., 12
Collins, A., 3
Colwell, E. C., 32n193

Delebecque, E., 12, 282n11
Delobel, J., 36, 282n11
differences, significance of. *See* variants, significance of
divine inspiration, 10–11. *See also* original text
divine preservation, 4, 10–11. *See also* accuracy of texts; original text

Ehrman, B. D., 1n1, 1n2, 2n6, 3n10, 6n28, 7n34, 7n38, 26n162, 187, 297n67, 298n68
Elliott, J. K., 13
Epp, E. J., 26–27, 29n179, 34n207, 35–36

eye skip. *See* homoeoteleuton

Farstad, A. L., 10n54, 255
Father, God the, xi, 89, 231
Fee, G. D., 19–20, 21n129, 23, 28, 37, 110n3, 174, 175n9, 260n250, 265n259, 266n261, 288, 293n

Gäbel, G., 29n179, 34n208, 35–36
Geer, T. C., 29n180, 31, 37n223, 111–13, 175n11, 282
Gryson, R., 17n95
Gurry, P. J., 27n173

Haenchen, E., 36, 125, 202, 209, 239–40, 244n207, 246n212, 254, 269n272
harmonization, 25, 86–88, 96, 112, 114, 118, 123, 136, 142, 150, 176, 182, 193, 201n83, 201n84, 212, 260, 263
Hodges, Z. C., 10n54, 255
Holmes, M. W., 292n53
Holy Spirit, 50, 51n, 57, 190, 206, 214, 231–32
homoeoteleuton, 9, 43, 47, 49–50, 53, 58, 78, 80–81, 85, 94, 119, 127–28, 130, 143, 153, 176–77, 183, 187–88, 194–195, 198, 208, 212, 214, 225–27, 231, 234, 238–39, 244, 249, 254, 256, 261, 286n27, 314, 320–21
Hort, F. J. A., xxv, 2, 9n49, 9n50, 202n87, 225n154, 288, 300n76
Hurtado, L. W., 89n, 285n23, 296

Jerusalem, 55, 57–58, 91, 101, 134, 191, 240, 246, 251–52, 266
Jesus: as fully God, 57, 89, 196, 232; as Israel's promised deliverer, 131, 224; as Lord, 89; as Messiah/Christ, 139–40, 233–34; as Nazarene, 76, 149; as person of the Trinity, 89, 232; as Redeemer, 89; as Savior, xi, 131; as Yahweh, 57, 196; baptism in the name of, 182; death of, 54; deity of, 57, 196, 232; disciples

of, 209; faith in, xi, 182, 224; forgiveness in, 182; identity of, 77, 149, 223–24; name of, 57, 62, 70, 98, 145, 182, 196, 267; personal knowledge of, 128; post-resurrection appearances of, 50, 236, 269; sufferings of, 53–54, 207; teaching of, 10
Juckel, A., 33n202, 39n4, 63n24

Kenyon, F. G., 12, 13n67
Kilpatrick, G. D., 26
Klijn, A. F. J., 32n194, 32n195
Köstenberger, A. J., 127n

Lamouille, A., xxiii, 12, 29n182, 34n206, 40, 42n9, 52, 56–59, 62, 69–71, 76–77, 100, 112n14, 125, 172n3, 190n57, 192, 194n, 195, 204, 215, 218, 233n173, 235, 238n190, 239, 250, 254, 259n, 266n263, 269n271, 275n, 276n290
Lucan style, 48, 53n16, 69, 76–77, 94, 100, 126, 137, 194–95, 204, 206–7, 214, 224, 231, 233n173, 247, 250, 254–55, 258, 263, 275, 293, 302
Lucan yet secondary, xxiv, 180, 215–16, 229, 239–41, 248–49, 251–52, 258–59, 274–76, 278–79, 285n22, 291–93
Luke's: circle, 229, 292; editing, xxiv, 12, 29n182, 56, 127, 181, 216, 229, 240, 245, 252, 259n, 292n51, 293–94; precision and style, 146, 176, 196, 201, 206, 208, 212–13, 216, 218, 223, 228, 232, 235, 293

McConaughy, D. L., 49n
Metzger, B. M., xxiii-n3, 1n1, 1n2, 2n6, 3n10, 6n28, 7n34, 7n38, 12n59, 12n60, 12n61, 12n64, 14n75, 26n162, 33, 38n, 49n, 58n, 83n, 94, 96, 126, 147n, 176n13, 178n19, 179n21, 180–81, 182n28, 183, 184n36, 185n37, 186–87, 188n52, 189, 191, 193n68, 194n, 195, 197–98, 199n80, 201n84, 206n, 209–211, 213, 215, 217n129, 220, 223, 225, 227n161, 229n165, 232, 236, 238, 242n201, 245, 247n217, 252, 254, 255n241, 256n242, 258n246, 262n257, 269n271, 271n274, 275n, 276, 291n50, 297n67, 298, 298n68

Nestle, E. and E., 9n51

old. *See* antiquity
Omerzu, H., 319n
original text, xxi–xxv, 1, 3–4, 7–8, 10–16, 18–19, 21–25, 27, 29n182, 31, 31n187, 32n193, 37, 277–81, 282n11, 286–87, 287n30, 289–90, 290n46, 291, 292n53, 293, 294n57, 296, 298–303, 320. *See also* divine inspiration

Pervo, R. I., 183, 187, 225n156
Pierpont, W. G., xxii-n, 10, 16n88
Porter, S. E., 59n22, 205n93, 285n23, 297n66
primitive. *See* antiquity

Quarles, C. L., 174n8, 182n30

Rahlfs, A., 207n99
Ralston, T. J., 26
Read-Heimerdinger, J., 12, 42, 44, 243n206, 282n11
Richter, S. G., 33n200, 39n3
Rius-Camps, J., 12, 42, 44, 243n206, 282n11
Robinson, M. A., xxii-n, 10, 16n88, 26n164, 32n193, 126n29
Rome, 12, 25, 32, 33n199
Ropes, J. H., 13–15, 31, 34n205, 36, 39n5, 42n9, 42n10, 49n, 70, 132, 136, 179n21, 191n62, 192, 193n66, 203n, 209, 210n103, 222, 244–45, 247n214, 247n217, 248, 253n231, 269n271, 270, 299n, 319n
Ross, A. P., 188n47

Royse, J. R., 16, 26–27
Runge, S. E., 135n35, 145, 149n

salvation, gospel of, 133–34, 140, 144, 182, 204
Schmid, U., 286n25
scribal faithfulness: against conflation and glosses, 89–90; against harmonization, 86–89; against intrusion of readings, 84–86; among translations, 121, 262; as demonstrated in Alexandrian tradition, 113, 189, 210, 273; as demonstrated in Byzantine tradition, xxiii, 85–86, 90–92, 94–98; as demonstrated in PWR tradition, xxiii, 28, 55, 59, 104, 263, 273; for upholding difficult readings, 90–92; quantified, 101–4. *See also* accuracy of texts
Scrivener, F. H. A., 4, 7–8, 9n47, 11n56, 14, 17, 25, 26n163, 300n75
second-century, xxii–xxiii, 1, 13, 15–16, 19, 22–23, 25, 28, 31–32, 36–37, 39, 73, 110, 110n3, 171, 269, 283–84, 284n19, 285, 285n22, 286, 288–90, 294n57, 299, 301
Soden, Hermann von, 13–14, 15n81, 15n82, 29, 30n186, 36–37, 175, 176n12, 178n18, 181n25, 181n26, 182–83, 187n44, 188n50, 191n60, 191n61, 196n, 199n79, 200n81, 202, 205n94, 207n98, 207n100, 210n105, 212n, 214n117, 225n154, 226, 227n162, 228n, 229, 232n170, 233n173, 233n174, 233n175, 234n176, 235n179, 242n202, 246, 248, 249n222, 252, 254, 258n246, 260, 262, 265n258, 265n260, 266n262, 268n, 269n272, 271n274, 272n279, 272n280, 274n283, 274n284, 275n, 276n286, 276n290
Strange, W. A., 12, 32n194, 282n11
Streeter, B. H., 24–25, 32n196, 113n16, 117n

Strutwolf, H., 30, 47n, 253n230, 284n21
Sturz, H. A., 11, 15, 22n139, 28, 37n224, 110n3, 110n4

Tregelles, S. P., 4–5, 7–9, 14, 17–18, 288–89
Trinity, The, 232
Tuckett, C., 30n184, 282, 284
Tyndale, W., 2

variants, significance of, xxi–xxii, 3, 5, 101–4, 173, 277–79, 285–91

Wachtel, K., 15n87, 16n91, 18–21, 27n173, 27n174, 29n179, 35–36, 79n, 80, 91n, 94, 97, 100n52, 102n54, 115, 131, 136, 139n41, 152, 175n10, 177n15, 178n19, 179, 180n23, 183, 184n35, 187n44, 187n45, 188–90, 192n65, 193, 195, 198n176, 201n83, 201n84, 205n96, 207, 208n, 216–17, 219n138, 221, 224n152, 225–26, 227n163, 228n, 230, 233n174, 236n186, 237–38, 239n193, 247n215, 247n217, 253, 257–58, 261, 267, 269, 271n276, 272, 273n282, 276n287, 278n292, 281n4, 289, 292n52, 296n59, 297n65, 298n73, 300n75
Wallace, D. B., 10n54, 10n55, 181n27, 186n40, 213n111, 214, 229n167, 232n172, 237n187, 242n203
Wasserman, T., 27n173
Weber, R., 17n95
Westcott, B. F., xxv, 2, 9n49, 9n50, 202n87, 225n154, 288, 300n76
Western Redaction, xxii, 29–37, 39, 40–41, 54, 105, 114, 170, 297
Wilson, A., 27, 191
Wilson, J. M., 147n

Zuntz, G., 21–22, 23n145, 34, 113, 287n30, 288n31, 289, 290n45, 290n47, 290n48, 294, 294n57, 296, 297n65, 298n72, 300n75

Scripture Index

OLD TESTAMENT/ HEBREW BIBLE

Genesis
2:7	142, 238
3:5	204
3:7	204
15:13–14	197
31:33	202
46:27	202

Exodus
1:5	118
1:8	198
2:12	50
2:14	119
3:1–6	200
3:2	199
3:6	95, 201
3:10	123
3:12	198
3:13–16	196
3:13–15	123
3:14–15	198
3:14	57
3:15–16	201
3:16	188
4:2	124
4:4	124
4:10	xi
4:17	124
6:2–3	196
19:3	202
20:22	202

Leviticus
1:1	121
1:3	121
1:5	121
1:13	121
1:14	121
2:16	121
3:5	121
3:11	121
11:3	121
11:4	121
11:5	121
11:6	121
11:7	121
11:45	121
26:41	202–3

Deuteronomy
10:22	118
18:15	63, 86, 120, 227

2 Samuel
7:1–5	201
7:12	180

1 Kings
6:1	222

2 Kings
6:17	204
6:20	204

1 Chronicles
28:3	198

2 Chronicles
35:21	198

Psalms
16:10	86, 181
41:9	177
69:25	177
109:8	177
113:1	202
132:5	201n84
132:11	180
136:1	xi

Isaiah
8:14	202
8:17	202
14:1	202
29:22	202
45:20–23	196
48:1	202
49:6	133
53:7	46, 207
58:1	202

Jeremiah
2:4	202
5:20	202
9:25	202–3
15:10	223

Ezekiel
20:5	202
44:7	203
44:9	203

Joel
2:28–32	43

Amos
3:13	202
5:25 LXX	121
5:27b	63, 121
7:6	202
9:8	202

Obadiah
17	202
18	202

Micah
2:7	202
3:1	202
3:9	202

Habakkuk
1:5	132

NEW TESTAMENT

Matthew
1:20	174
3:12	124
4:4	10
5:18	11
7:11	225n154
9:5	183
10:14	133
10:20	231
16:13	223
16:15	223
19:16–17	7
19:17	223
24:36	11

Mark
2:9	183
2:23	218n134
7:34	204

8:27	223	12:49	273
8:29	223	12:50	126
9:49	9	12:51	136
10:18	223	13:11	213, 233n173
12:15	223	13:12	196
		14:4	196

Luke

		15:7	274
		15:8	273
1:6	207	16:22	218n134
1:12	235	17:14	235
1:33	202	18:10	176
1:68	94	18:15	235
2:4	176	18:19	223
2:10	206	18:31	176
2:17	235	18:43	235
2:23	204	19:2	213
2:25	94, 174	19:4	176
2:37	215n119	19:7	235
3:15–16	224	19:28	176
4:33	233n173	19:31	274
4:38	126	19:34	274
5:8	235	19:43	126
5:18	213	20:26	207
5:19	176	21:35	226
5:23	183	22:28	67, 137
5:31	274	22:30	94
5:33	215n119	22:43–44	24
6:1	218n134	22:58	194
6:6	218n134	22:63	126
6:12	218n134	22:71	274
6:37	196	23:4	262
7:39	235	23:14	262
8:16	273	23:16	196
8:37	126	23:22	196, 262
8:45	126	23:34a	336
9:5	133	23:51	47
9:11	274	24:5	254
9:18	223	24:19	207
9:20	223	24:31	204
9:28	176	24:32	204
9:54	235	24:33	150
10:17	150	24:37	254
10:32	235	24:38	176
10:33	235	24:45	204
11:13	225n154	24:50	236
11:33	273	24:52	206
11:38	235	24:53	9
12:18	9		

SCRIPTURE INDEX

John

5:8	183
6:7	194
7:19	223
7:53	48, 67
8:58	57, 196
12:20	176
18:38	262
19:4	262
19:6	262

Acts

1–17	277, 303
1–15	303
1:1–15:3	39
1–14	278
1–7	116
1:1–5:42	333
1:1–5:32	59, 112n14, 116, 284n18, 305n1, 306
1–4	110, 112n14
1–2	331
1	158, 306
1:2	40
1:3	40
1:8	226
1:11	178
1:20	255
2	131, 159, 182, 306
2:1	32n192
2:4	50
2:17–21	325
2:27	86, 181
2:30	278, 292
2:34	176
2:38	71, 144
2:39	225n154
2:45	274
3	159, 307
3:1	176
3:2–4:18	36n216
3:12	235
3:13	122–23, 201
3:19–20	102n53
3:19	150
3:20	102n53
3:22	301
3:25	300
3:26	150
4	159, 307
4:5	218n134
4:8	xxi
4:8b–12	47
4:23–31	337
4:23	196
4:25	xxiv, 279
4:35	191, 274
5	160, 308
5:2	191
5:23	61
5:31	182, 193
5:32	61, 112, 160, 185, 193, 284
5:36	48
5:37	300
5:38	62
5:39	xxiii, 32n192
6:1–12:25	333
6	107, 116, 160, 308
6:8	32n192
7–8	287
7	107, 116–17, 122, 125, 130, 160, 285, 285n22, 309
7:2–53	337
7:10	207
7:18	xxi
7:21	119
7:23	176
7:30	xxi
7:31	235
7:32	123
7:37	32n192
7:42	121
7:43	xxiii
7:46	xxi
7:57	126
7:58	85
8–14	116
8	116, 125, 161, 309
8:1–12	206
8:1b–40	333
8:1	85, 206
8:2	206
8:7	xxiv, 206

8:8	206	13:1–18:23	333
8:9	206	13	116, 129, 162, 285n22, 287, 312
8:10	206		
8:13	206	13:1	91
8:18	51	13:3	215n119
8:24	226	13:13–43	334
8:25	150	13:13	88, 300
8:26	50	13:16–41	337
8:29–10:14	39	13:17	xxi
8:32	206	13:20	xxi
8:37	279, 297	13:22	83, 300
8:39	50, 176	13:26	83
9	161, 254, 310	13:30	83
9:1–30	333	13:33	32n192
9:3	218n134	13:37	83
9:4	51, 223	13:39	32n192
9:6	51	14	163, 313
9:31–11:18	333	14:1	218n134
9:32	218n134	14:15	150
9:35	150	14:18–20	36n216
9:37	218n134	14:22	249
9:39	215	14:23	215n119
9:43	218n134	15–28	278
10	161, 310	15–21	116
10:4	176, 254, 300	15	107, 116, 134, 164, 282, 287, 313
10:9	176		
10:14	87	15:2	176
10:25	218n134	15:3	55, 206
10:30	xxi	15:5	300
10:32	278, 292	15:7	300
10:33	257	15:12–13	132
10:44	51	15:12	133, 300
11	162, 311	15:13	300
11:1–2	36n216	15:17	114
11:2	176	15:19	150
11:6	300	15:20	251
11:8	87	15:22	258, 300
11:19–12:25	334	15:24	278, 292
11:20	258	15:29	xxiii, 32n192, 55, 228, 258, 297
11:21	150		
11:23	215	15:30	196
11:26	218n134	15:33	196
11:28	258	15:34	52, 91, 100, 279, 297
11:29–30	91	15:37	87
12	162, 312, 329	15:40	91
12:10	76	16	164, 314
12:12	300	16:14	204
12:25	32n192	16:16	218n134

Acts (continued)

Reference	Pages
16:30	223
16:36	196, 300
16:39	xxiii, 32n192
17	116, 139, 164, 287, 314
17:3	204
17:4	258
17:10	215
17:12	258
17:23	xxi
17:28	300
17:31	77
18–28	277
18	165, 315
18:5	126
18:21	278, 291n51, 292
18:22	57, 101, 250
18:24–28:31	333
18:27–19:6, 12–16	143
18:27	215
19–24	107
19	107, 116, 143, 165, 287, 316
19:1	101, 218n134
19:6	51
19:9	xxiii, 32n192
19:10	77
19:27	87
19:33	300
20	165, 316
20:1	250
20:12	82
20:24	278, 292
20:28	300
21	166, 317
21:1	218n134
21:2–10	39
21:5	218n134, 236
21:6	176
21:7	250
21:12	176
21:15	176
21:16–18	39
21:19	133, 250
21:25	278, 292
21:32	257
21:40	72
22–28	116
22	107, 167, 318
22:1	84
22:6	218n134
22:7	223
22:8	76, 300
22:9	xxi
22:10–20	39
22:14	197
22:17	150, 218n134
22:29–28:31	39
23	107, 143, 167, 318
23:2	300
23:8	81
23:11–17, 25–29	143
23:15	32n192, 90, 258
23:20	90, 258
23:21	258
23:23	257
23:25	xxiii, 32n192
23:27	90, 258
23:29	32n192, 74
23:30	278, 292
24	107, 116, 167, 319
24:6–8	278, 292, 292n52
24:11	176
24:25	254
25	168, 319
25:1	176
25:2	88
25:4	88
25:6	88
25:7	88
25:9–10	88
25:9	176
25:13	250
26–27	287
26	107, 116, 148, 168, 254, 320
26:11	236
26:14–15	32n192
26:14	223
26:16	xxi
26:20	133, 150
26:23	133
26:32	196

27–28	107, 333	11:28	260
27	107, 116, 152, 168, 321	12:14	225n154
27:15	32n192	**Galatians**	
27:28	194	2:4–5	134
27:30	85	2:21	217
27:33–34	300	3:19	124
27:35	32n192		
27:38	85	**Ephesians**	
27:40	85	1:13	174
27:44	218n134	6:18	176n13
28	169, 321		
28:8	126, 218n134	**Philippians**	
28:15	82	1:4	248
28:16	32n192, 278, 291n51, 292	2:10–11	196
28:17	218n134	4:6	176
28:18	196, 262	**Colossians**	
28:19	32n192	1:4	217
28:20	94	1:11	248
28:23	249	2:2	196
28:25	196		
28:27	150	**1 Thessalonians**	
28:28	133	1:6	248
28:29	102, 278, 292	4:8	174
28:30	32n192		
28:31	40, 249	**2 Thessalonians**	
Romans		1:12	217
7:17–18	262	**1 Timothy**	
9:20	223	2:1	176n13
11:26	150	5:5	176n13
13:14	234		
1 Corinthians		**2 Timothy**	
2:9	176	3:15–16	10
3:10	217	**Titus**	
11:1	137	3:14	274
14:26	197		
15:33	149	**Hebrews**	
16:23	234	2:7	194
2 Corinthians		2:9	194
6:1	217		
6:16	197		
8:1	217		

Hebrews (continued)

10:34	248
11:13	250
13:17	248
13:22	251

James

2:18	267
3:5	273

2 Peter

1:21	10

2 John

1:1	225n154

Revelation

13:1	176
14:11	176

Acts Textual Variant Index

1:2/2–24	40		252, 258–59, 275–76, 291
1:3/38	40		
1:5/16–22	174, 279	2:31/22–24	86, 102, 181
1:5/33	40	2:32/4	44
1:6/10	174	2:33/38–42	44
1:8/24–26	175	2:33/38–40	284n21
1:13/8–14	175	2:34/16–22	44
1:14/15	102, 176	2:36/18–30	281n6
1:14/19	41	2:37/31	284n21
1:15/22	103, 176	2:37/32	30n184, 90, 181, 279
1:16/13	30n184, 177, 279	2:37/37	44
1:16/45	177, 279	2:38/28–30	60
1:21/37	59	2:38/36–40	103, 181
1:25/4–12	103, 178, 279	2:40/28–32	60
1:26/30	42–43	2:41/6–8, 6–14	92
		2:41/6–8	92, 103
2:1/2–22	42	2:41/18–28	182, 280n1, 302
2:1/22	59, 78, 285–86	2:43/22–28	60, 286
2:7/5	179, 277, 279, 280n1, 291n49, 302	2:43/29, 22–29	93
		2:45/2–12	44
2:7/8–10	103, 180	2:45/22–46/26	44
2:12/17	42	2:47/38–3:1/4	102
2:14/14	42		
2:14/18–22	43	3:3/2	45
2:16/18	43	3:6/32–40	99
2:17/16–18	43	3:6/46–48	93, 183, 278n293, 279, 281n6
2:18/42–44	43		
2:19/28–38	43	3:7/14–16	183
2:20/24–28	103	3:7/21	284n21
2:24/18	43, 284n21	3:8/2–32	45, 284n21
2:30/16–18	60	3:9/6–12	291n49
2:30/30	30n184	3:11/2–28	45, 47, 56
2:30/34	102, 180, 216, 229, 234n178, 241, 249,	3:11/6	103
		3:13/2–28	45

3:13/8, 12	30n184, 102, 122–23	4:37/18–20	191, 279
3:13/42–44	30n184, 45, 284n21		
3:13/59	30n184, 284n21	5:12/37	48
3:14/14	46, 284n21	5:15/4–10	95
3:17/5	46, 284n21	5:15/47	48
3:17/6–8	284n21	5:16/18	191, 279
3:17/17	30n184, 46, 284n21	5:18/27	48, 67
3:19/10	281n6	5:19/12	192, 279
3:19/16–20	46	5:21/40	48
3:21/34–42	184	5:22/10–20	61
3:22/4–6	102, 184, 286n27, 300	5:24/14–28	102, 285n22
		5:28/4	281n6
3:22/16–22	120, 125	5:31/18	48, 284n21
3:23/31	60	5:32/6–8	192, 277, 280n1, 291n49, 302
3:26/6–10	30n184, 185, 279		
3:26/17	103, 120, 125, 185	5:32/9	284n21
3:26/20	60	5:33/7	61, 286
		5:34/30–40	193, 279, 302
4:1/13	61, 286	5:35/8	48
4:5/22–34	103, 186, 278, 280n1, 302	5:36/16–22	61
		5:36/50	300
4:7/8–12	291n49	5:37/28	194, 280n1, 302
4:8/27	30n184, 94, 102, 186, 278	5:37/40	48
		5:38/12–20	62
4:9/9	30n184, 61, 284n21, 286	5:38/27	49
		5:38/42	195, 277, 300
4:10/67	46	5:39/19	62, 285–86
4:12/2–40	30n184, 46, 284n21	5:40/22–28	57
4:12/8–12	46	5:40/31	195
4:12/22–40	102, 281n6, 286n27	5:41/22–28	62, 196, 286, 286n27
4:16/6	90, 187	5:42/30–34	49
4:17/19	47		
4:17/20	94, 187, 279	6:3/4	197
4:18/2	45, 47, 56	6:4/20	281n6
4:21/20	90, 188, 279	6:5/9	49
4:22/22–26	30n184	6:7/10	62
4:24/7	47, 284n21	6:8/29	62, 99, 285–86
4:24/28–30	94, 188, 278–79	6:10/10–22	49
4:25/2–24	102, 189, 279, 285n22, 293, 301	6:10/23	49
		6:13/9	49
4:27/6–26	102, 286n27	6:13/22–24	103
4:28/18	281n6	6:15/35	49
4:31/49	30n184, 47, 284n21		
4:32/12–20	103, 190, 278	7:1/9	49
4:32/23	47	7:4/32–34	117
4:33/4–6	291n49	7:4/53	50, 284n21
4:33/10–26	281n6	7:5/28–34	117
4:36/2	103	7:7/18–22	197

ACTS TEXTUAL VARIANT INDEX

7:9/15	118	7:58/26	124
7:10/32	118	7:60/22–28	95, 204, 279
7:14/26–32	118		
7:16/20–22	122	8:5/10	205, 279
7:17/18–22	30n184	8:7/2–20	125, 293, 305n2, 310
7:17/18	103	8:7/24	127
7:18/12–14	103, 198, 278	8:8/2–8	205
7:19/18	281n6	8:9/36–40	127
7:19/24–30	199	8:10/15	127
7:20/39	63, 118	8:10/30–32	103, 127
7:21/2–10	114n, 118–19, 125	8:13/30–38	103
7:21/22	114n, 118–19	8:14/18	127
7:22/22–26	119	8:16/32–34	103
7:24/9	50	8:18/31	96, 103, 206, 278–79
7:24/22–26	50	8:19/26	127
7:28/8–10	119	8:20/18–22	128
7:28/18–22	119	8:21/32–40	97, 128, 207, 279,
7:30/27	103, 199		281n6, 287, 302
7:30/30–32	281n6	8:22/16–22	96, 103
7:31/24–28	103	8:24/11	128
7:32/3	95	8:24/16–24	96–97, 128
7:32/21, 25	95, 103, 122, 160,	8:25/18–20	129
	199–200, 277–78,	8:26/22	129
	280n1, 286, 302, 309	8:29/6–8	96
7:34/46	123	8:29/16–24	129
7:35/25	86	8:32/38–40	207, 277, 291n49
7:35/32	123, 291n49	8:33/2–8	281n6
7:35/40	123	8:33/19	207, 279
7:35/42–44	124	8:35/28	129
7:36/18–20	119	8:37/2–44	50, 85, 284n21
7:37/6	120	8:37/32–44	30n184
7:37/26–28	102, 120, 125,	8:38/16–22	129
	286n28, 300	8:39/8	129
7:37/30–36	124, 286n28	8:39/14–16	50
7:37/40	63, 86, 120, 285–86		
7:38/54	103, 124	9:2/28–32	281n6
7:41/16	121	9:4/29	51
7:43/49	63, 121, 285–86	9:5/15	103
7:44/10	121	9:5/20	51
7:46/22–24	95, 103, 201, 279	9:6/2–4	51
7:47/10	95	9:17/40–44	103
7:51/8	202	9:19/14–22	103, 208, 277, 286n28
7:52/28–34	122	9:20/13	30n184, 284n21
7:52/48	124	9:20/16	103
7:55/2–4	122	9:25/6–22	103, 209, 279
7:55/26–38	50	9:26/4–8	103
7:56/14	203, 279	9:28/10–14	78, 102
7:56/26–30	95	9:28/28–30	103

9:30/18	63	11:28/28–30	64
9:30/22	281n6		
9:34/18–20	64, 291n49	12:1/35	64, 286
9:38/30–34	102, 211, 277, 286n27	12:3/26–28	281n6
9:38/44–50	78, 103	12:14/23	64
		12:15/34–36	219, 279
10:11/14–30	102, 211, 278–79, 285n22	12:20/5	103
		12:20/14–22	40, 64, 286
10:12/8–28	87, 102, 212, 285n22, 300	12:25/8	65, 285–86
		12:25/10–14	90
10:14/20–26	83, 87		
10:16/14–16	212	13:4/24–26	129
10:19/18–22	281n6	13:5/38	65, 130
10:19/30	213, 279	13:6/6–10	83, 130
10:24/2–8	281n6	13:7/24–28	65, 130
10:25/2–32	51	13:8/28–32	130
10:28/11	284n21	13:10/30	130
10:28/34–38	281n6	13:10/38	219, 279
10:30/25, 26–38	214	13:14/2–4	53
10:30/25	102, 279	13:17/22–26	130
10:31/24	300	13:20/2–16	103, 130, 220, 279, 280n1, 302
10:32/37	102, 180, 215, 229, 241, 249, 252, 258–59, 275–76, 291	13:20/26	281n6
		13:23/18–26	83, 103, 131, 300
10:33/40–46	51	13:24/20–26	103, 222, 277, 286n27
10:33/48	52	13:25/16–18	223
10:33/52	103	13:26/26	97, 224, 277, 280n1, 291n49, 302
10:34/2–10	52		
10:38/10–14	284n21	13:27/8	131
10:38/28	52	13:28/11	65, 131, 285, 287
10:41/36–42	284n21	13:28/12–29/16	53
10:42/20	291n49	13:28/12–18	53
10:48/2–6	291n49	13:29/2–16	53
10:48/8–18	103	13:29/18–30	53
		13:31/29	65, 131
11:2/2–12	52–53, 56	13:31/30–32	131
11:2/14–24	53	13:33/16	97, 224
11:3/6–18	78, 281n6	13:33/20	65, 69, 131, 285, 287
11:6/14–42	87	13:33/28–36	54
11:8/12–18	83, 87	13:34/2	131
11:11/24	217	13:38/28	281n6
11:12/4–12	79	13:39/5	132
11:18/12	291n49	13:39/13	xiii, 66, 132, 285, 287
11:18/28–40	291n49	13:40/10–18	79, 98, 103, 132, 225, 278–79, 280n1, 286n27, 302
11:23/12–14	217, 279		
11:25/6–8	103		
11:26/2–54	53	13:41/10	66, 132, 285, 287
11:26/16–24	218, 277, 280n1, 302	13:41/34	132

13:41/49	66, 132, 287, 300	15:11/4–8	71
13:42/7	89, 103, 286n28	15:11/14	30n184
13:42/8–16	89, 102, 286n28	15:14/8–14	136, 300
13:43/35	66, 133, 285, 287	15:15/4–6	30n184
13:44/22–28	103	15:17/48–52	103
13:45/25	291n49	15:18/2–6	102, 114–15, 285n22
13:45/29	103	15:19/22	136
13:46/36	281n6	15:20/11, 12–14	227, 279
13:47/6–8	133	15:20/20–26	284n21
13:47/33	66, 133, 287, 300	15:20/37	30n184, 55, 68, 284n21
13:48/10–26	66, 133, 286n26		
13:49/14	281n6	15:22/24	136
13:51/12–14	133	15:22/40–46	137
		15:23/4–8	137, 228, 280n1, 287, 302
14:2/6–10	79		
14:2/29	54	15:23/16–20	102
14:7/7	54	15:23/24–28	137
14:8/8–18	98, 226, 279, 280n1, 302	15:24/30–34	102, 180, 216, 229, 241, 249, 252, 258–59, 275–76, 291
14:10/9	98, 285, 287		
14:13/24–26	67	15:25/10	30n184
14:14/24–30	103	15:25/29	137
14:15/28–38	54, 284n21	15:26/27	67, 137, 284n21, 285, 287
14:15/42–44	102		
14:17/16	91	15:27/16–24	137
14:17/18–20	281n6	15:28/8–12	30n184, 229
14:17/40	91, 227, 277, 280n1	15:29/8–12	230, 277, 284n21, 291n49
14:18/6	67		
14:18/23	48, 67, 287	15:29/17	30n184, 67, 138, 284n21, 285, 287
14:19/2–4	99		
14:19/16–22	54, 99	15:29/29	284n21
14:25/13	100, 287	15:34/2–12	85, 138, 287
14:25/19	67, 287	15:36/30–32	230
		15:37/16	300
15:1/13	67, 134, 285, 287, 300	15:38/34–38	87
15:2/30–48	55	15:39/10	300
15:2/64–70	67, 134, 284n21, 285, 287	15:40/20	103
15:4/11	67, 134	16:7/34	103, 231, 277
15:4/30–32	135	16:9/12–16	80
15:4/36–44	135	16:9/27	68, 287
15:4/45	135, 285, 287	16:10/30–36	103, 231
15:6/15	135, 287, 300	16:11/2–4	68, 287
15:6/20–24	135	16:12/12–16	80
15:7/10–12	67, 135, 285, 287	16:16/24	232
15:7/36–44	135	16:18/16	233, 279
15:10/32–40	67, 136	16:24/28–30	233
15:11/2	136	16:27/12–14	164, 287

16:31/17	103, 233	18:8/38–40	70, 285, 287
16:34/24–28	70	18:12/26–36	45, 47, 56
16:35/8–12	55, 69, 300	18:17/6	102
16:35/26	68, 287	18:17/24–32	101
16:39/2–22	68, 70, 285, 287	18:19/10–14	70, 286n26, 287
16:40/24–30	235, 279	18:20/14	103
		18:21/4–6, 9, 10, 24	
17:2/28–30	139		239, 249, 252, 258–
17:3/34–40	103, 139, 291n49		59, 275–76, 291
17:4/10	69, 140	18:21/4–6	100, 239, 249, 252,
17:5/2–22	103, 140, 287		258–59, 275–76, 291
17:6/30	140	18:21/9	57, 100, 102, 285n22
17:11/47	69, 140, 287	18:21/24–18:22/8	70
17:12/4–6	140	18:22/1	70, 286n26, 287
17:12/13	69, 141, 285, 287	18:23/26	281n6
17:13/12	141	18:25/36–38	103
17:13/50–56	102, 286n27	18:26/40–46	241, 277
17:14/2–8	141	18:27/2–30	56
17:14/20	235, 279	18:27/35	71, 143, 287
17:14/28	141	18:27/36–42	143
17:15/32	236, 279	18:27/44–48	71, 143
17:17/24–36	69, 141	18:28/13	71, 143, 287
17:18/6	141		
17:18/18	141	19:1/2–30	56, 101, 143
17:18/68	141	19:2/34–40	57, 143
17:19/2–4	142, 287	19:3/2–4, 6–10	143
17:20/24–30	142	19:3/5	103, 241, 277, 286n28
17:21/28–34	237, 279	19:4/44	103
17:23/32–40	103, 237	19:5/19	71, 143–44, 285, 287
17:24/32–34	30n184, 65, 69	19:6/8–14	281n6
17:25/20–26	141	19:9/8–24	71, 144, 287
17:26/2–8	30n184, 103, 238	19:9/37	144
17:26/10–14	69, 142, 300	19:9/51	71, 112, 144, 285, 287
17:27/2–38	284n21	19:10/35	103
17:27/4–6	103	19:12/30	48
17:27/18	281n6	19:12/50	103, 241, 277, 286n28
17:28/22–30	30n184	19:13/46	72, 81, 143–44
17:28/40	69	19:14/2–20, 21	57, 143
17:30/26–30	103	19:14/6–20	92
17:31/8–12	284n21	19:15/6–8	145
17:32/26–33	101	19:15/19	145
		19:17/24	145
18:1/2–6	103	19:18/8	145
18:2/60	65, 69	19:19/4	145
18:4/18–20	55	19:20/8–20	241, 279
18:5/28–30	103	19:21/26–30	281n6
18:6/1	56	19:21/48	145
18:7/16–20	103	19:24/22–24	146

ACTS TEXTUAL VARIANT INDEX

19:25/2	145	21:25/16–20	102, 180, 216, 229,
19:25/12–16	146		232, 241, 249, 251,
19:25/21	146		258–59, 275–76,
19:25/38	242, 277		285n22, 291
19:26/57	146	21:27/48–54	252, 277
19:27/8–16	146	21:29/6	252, 277
19:27/46–52	146	21:31/24–26	252, 279
19:27/54–58	103, 280n1	21:34/18–24	253, 279
19:28/13	72, 112, 147, 285, 287	21:36/19	166, 287
19:33/14	147, 281n6	21:40/38	88, 112
19:34/16	147		
19:35/2	72, 147, 300	22:2/14	88, 112
19:35/47	87	22:5/10–12	300
19:37/11	72, 147	22:6/30	73
19:37/20–22	147	22:7/31	58
19:38/2–6	147	22:8/28–30	51
		22:9/19	76, 102, 253, 278–79
20:1/24–26, 28	244, 277	22:10/6–10	51
20:1/24–26	103, 244, 277	22:12/26–28	254, 278n293, 279,
20:4/7–10	278		285, 287, 301
20:4/7	102, 245	22:15/8	112
20:4/10	246	22:16/30	103
20:5/6	103, 246, 279, 301	22:20/12–18	73
20:13/6	291n49	22:20/31	85
20:15/28–30	85, 102	22:23/4	255, 279
20:19/7	166, 287	22:25/8–12	112
20:22/28	281n6	22:25/24–42	73
20:23/35	72, 287	22:26/19	103
20:24/6–8	103, 247, 278	22:29/47	112, 287
20:24/27	102, 166, 180, 216,	22:30/31	103
	229, 241, 248, 252,		
	258–59, 275–76, 291	23:7/14–20	81, 102, 286n27
20:24/36	72	23:8/16	256, 277, 300
20:25/39	102, 249	23:9/14–26	256, 277
20:28/40	89, 286n28	23:9/59	103, 256
20:32/49	166, 285, 287	23:11/21	256, 277
		23:15/6–18	73, 143
21:1/45	57	23:15/65	143, 285, 287
21:3/36–40	291n49	23:16/19	143
21:5/56–6/6	249, 277	23:20/38	103
21:8/10	87, 102, 286n28	23:24/17	167, 287
21:13/2–8	281n6	23:25/2–12	73, 143, 285, 287
21:18/4	281n6	23:27/36–42	143
21:20/12–18	103	23:29/2	143
21:20/30–34	103	23:29/12–16	74, 285, 287
21:21/48	73	23:29/33	75, 285, 287
21:22/10–14	102, 250, 277, 286n28	23:30/10–18	90, 103, 257, 279,
21:25/14	251, 277		286n28, 300, 302

Reference	Pages
23:30/45	180, 216, 229, 241, 249, 252, 258–59, 275–76, 291
23:34/5	75, 103, 286n27
23:34/6–26	75
23:35/2–6	75
24:2/30	103
24:6/20–8/14	180, 216, 229, 232, 241, 249, 252, 258, 275–77, 291
24:9/2–6	167, 287
24:10/40–46	259, 277
24:12/24	259
24:13/2	260, 279
24:13/6–14	83
24:14/46–56	103, 261, 277, 286n27
24:18/4	261, 277
24:20/14–18	103, 262, 278
24:21/16–20	263, 277
24:21/32–38	81
24:22/2–10	81, 103, 286n27
24:23/30–32	103
24:24/22–24	281n6
24:24/44–52	103
24:25/20–24	263, 277
24:26/21	103, 263
24:27/19	75, 285, 287
24:27/22	281n6
25:2/8–10	263, 277
25:6/6–20	103, 264, 286n27
25:7/30	103
25:8/2–6	88
25:10/32	75
25:16/23	103
25:20/8	291n49
25:21/30–36	264, 277
25:22/11	264, 279
25:22/23	103, 265, 278–79
25:24/58–68	58
25:24/58	265, 279
25:25/2–32	58
25:26/54	88
26:1/14	148
26:1/18–22	148
26:1/30–36	82, 148
26:3/4–24	148
26:4/34–36	266, 279
26:4/44	281n6
26:5/4	149
26:6/18	266, 277, 300
26:6/20–22	149
26:10/12–16	267
26:10/24–28	268, 277
26:10/44	149
26:12/24	268, 277
26:14/10–14	76, 149, 285, 287
26:14/18–24	103
26:14/42–50	51, 58
26:15/16–18	268, 277
26:15/26	76, 149, 287, 300
26:16/44	103, 268, 277, 279, 280n1, 291n49
26:17/26–28	149, 281n6
26:18/10	150
26:18/20	150
26:20/12, 17	269
26:20/15	150, 287
26:21/6–10	150
26:21/12	271, 278, 291n49
26:22/10	151
26:22/50	151
26:24/14–18	151
26:25/28	151
26:26/28–40	92, 151, 301
26:30/2–4	103
26:31/18–28	152
27:1/30–34	152
27:2/5	152
27:2/10	103, 271, 278
27:2/14	152
27:2/34–38	152, 285, 287
27:5/21	76, 153, 285, 287
27:6/22	153
27:7/40–42	153
27:9/12–20	153
27:11/27	271
27:15/16	49
27:15/23	76, 153, 285, 287
27:17/21	153
27:19/18	272
27:19/19	85, 154, 285, 287
27:20/12–18	154

27:21/22	154	28:4/26–30	273, 278
27:21/40	154	28:10/24–26	274, 278
27:23/14–28	272, 278	28:11/10	274, 278
27:27/36	154	28:13/4	103
27:29/4	154	28:14/10–14	82
27:29/6–8, 10–12	155	28:15/22	281n6
27:30/10	155	28:16/12–16	103, 180, 216, 229, 241, 249, 252, 258–59, 274, 276, 291
27:30/26–38	155		
27:31/22–30	155		
27:33/16–22	156	28:16/20–22	76, 287
27:34/9	156	28:17/38–42	275, 278
27:34/18–22	156	28:18/3	77
27:34/30–38	156	28:19/9	77, 285, 287
27:35/31	76, 156, 285, 287	28:19/31	82, 285, 287
27:36/14	156, 300	28:23/10	275, 279
27:39/16	156	28:23/43	89
27:40/38	156	28:26/2	103
27:41/28–30	157	28:29/2–24	103, 180, 216, 229, 241, 249, 252, 258–59, 275–76, 291
27:41/38	157		
27:43/26	157		
27:44/8	157	28:30/2	84
		28:30/6–14	103, 276, 278, 286n28
28:1/6–8	273, 278	28:30/29	77, 285, 287
28:2/20	273, 278	28:31/16	89
28:3/28	273, 278	28:31/35	77

www.ingramcontent.com/pod-product-compliance
Lightning Source LLC
Chambersburg PA
CBHW071144300426
44113CB00009B/1080